Time Out

Venice

timeout.com/venice

Penguin Books

PENGUIN BOOKS

Published by the Penguin Group
Penguin Books Ltd, 27 Wrights Lane, London W8 5TZ, England
Penguin Books USA Inc., 375 Hudson Street, New York, New York 10014, USA
Penguin Books Australia Ltd, Ringwood, Victoria, Australia
Penguin Books Canada Ltd, 10 Alcorn Avenue, Toronto, Ontario, Canada M4V 3B2
Penguin Books (NZ) Ltd, 182-190 Wairau Road, Auckland 10, New Zealand

Penguin Books Ltd, Registered Offices: Harmondsworth, Middlesex, England

First published 1999
Second edition 2001
10 9 8 7 6 5 4 3 2 1

Copyright © Time Out Group Ltd, 1999, 2001
All rights reserved

Colour reprographics by Icon, Crown House, 56-58 Southwark Street, London SE1
and Precise Litho, 34-35 Great Sutton Street, London EC1.
Printed and bound by Cayfosa-Quebecor, Ctra. de Caldes, Km 3 08 130 Sta, Perpètua de Mogoda, Barcelona, Spain.

Edited and designed by
Time Out Guides Limited
Universal House
251 Tottenham Court Road
London W1T 7AB
Tel + 44 (0) 20 813 3000
Fax + 44 (0) 20 813 6001
Email guides@timeout.com
www.timeout.com

Editorial

Editor Anne Hanley
Deputy Editor Nicholas Royle
Listings Researchers Chiara Barbieri, Patrizia Lerco
Proofreader Marion Moisy
Indexer Selena Cox

Editorial Director Peter Fiennes
Series Editor Ruth Jarvis
Deputy Series Editor Jonathan Cox
Editorial Assistant Jenny Noden

Design

Art Director John Oakey
Art Editor Mandy Martin
Senior Designer Scott Moore
Designers Benjamin de Lotz, Lucy Grant
Picture Editor Kerri Miles
Deputy Picture Editor Olivia Duncan-Jones
Scanning & Imaging Dan Conway
Ad make-up Glen Impey

Advertising

Group Commercial Director Lesley Gill
Sales Director Mark Phillips
International Sales Co-ordinator Ross Canadé
Advertisement Sales (Venice) Venezia News
Advertising Assistant Catherine Shepherd

Administration

Publisher Tony Elliott
Managing Director Mike Hardwick
Financial Director Kevin Ellis
Marketing Director Christine Cort
Marketing Manager Mandy Martinez
Group General Manager Nichola Coulthard
Production Manager Mark Lamond
Production Controller Samantha Furniss
Accountant Sarah Bostock

Features in this guide were written and researched by:
Introduction Anne Hanley. **History** Anne Hanley, Dalbert Hallenstein. **Venice Today** Anne Hanley. **Waterland** Anne Hanley.
Architecture Lee Marshall. **Painting** Frederick Ilchman. **Literary Venice** Gregory Dowling. **Accommodation** Chiara Barbieri,
Ann Witheridge. **Sightseeing** Gregory Dowling, John Brunton, Lee Marshall. **Restaurants** Michela Scibilia, Lee Marshall,
John Brunton. **Bacari & Snacks** Lee Marshall, Michela Scibilia, John Brunton. **Cafés & Bars** Jill Weinstein, John Brunton.
Shops & Services Pamela Santini. **Glass** Louise Berndt. **By Season** Anne Hanley, Lee Marshall. **Children** Gregory Dowling,
Patrizia Lerco, Anne Hanley. **Contemporary Art** Chiara Barbieri, Anne Witheridge. **Film** Lee Marshall, Nicholas Royle. **Gay
& Lesbian** Thom Price, Gus Barker. **Music & Nightlife** Jasper Sharp, Andrew Williams, Massimo Ongaro. **Performing Arts**
Marco Bellussi, Chiara Barbieri, David Newbold, Valentina Bezzi. **Sport & Fitness** Lee Marshall, Sebastiano Giorgi.
Palladian Villas Frederick Ilchman, Lee Marshall. **Padua** JoAnn Titmarsh, Gus Barker. **Verona** Rita Baldassarre, Dalbert
Hallenstein. **Vicenza** Lee Marshall, Dalbert Hallenstein. **North from Venice** JoAnn Titmarsh, John Brunton. **Directory**
Pamela Santini, Chiara Barbieri, Anne Hanley.

The editor would like to thank the following: Chiara Barbieri, Gregory Dowling & Patrizia Lerco, Michela Scibilia &
Francesco Il Gigante. Special thanks to Lee & Clara Marshall.

Maps by LS International, via Sanremo 17, 20133 Milano, Italy.

Photography by Adam Eastland except: pages 6, 15, 16, 34, 36, 38, 75, 89, 110,126 AKG London; page 9 Ronald
Sheridan/Ancient Art & Architecture Collection; page 22 Press Association; page 39 The Bridgeman Art Library; page 131
Yann Arthus-Bertrand/Corbis; page 132 Fulvio Roiter/Corbis; page 134 Charles Philip Canagialosi/Corbis; page 189
Massimo Micheluzzi; page 202 Yasmin Brandolini d'Adda (Senaz Titolo 2000); page 219 Corbis; page 227, 265 Francesco
Venturi/Kea Publishing Services Ltd/Corbis; page 266 Elio Ciol/Corbis; page 269 Nik Wheeler/Corbis; page 271 Vanni
Archive/Corbis; page 205, 206 and 209 The Ronald Grant Archive; page 231 Archivo Iconografico, SA/Corbis; page 228
Colorific; page 233 Araldo de Luca/Corbis; page 234, 237, 238, 240, 242, 244, 245, 246, 247, 249, 250 and 254 Neil
Setchfield; page 197 Anne Hanley; pages 257, 258 and 262 World Pictures.

The following images were provided by the featured establishments/artists: 201,202, 207

Contents

Introduction

In 1999, more than 3.4 million visitors spent a night or more in the hotels of this improbable little city perched on sandbanks in a tidal lagoon. They floated along its canals accompanied by crooners who made the *palazzi* ring to the sound of old Neapolitan ditties, and packed themselves in piazza San Marco to feed pricey contraceptive-laced corn to swarms of invasive pigeons. By the Rialto and by the station they elbowed through crowds to buy revolving light-up *gondole* or Gabriel Batistuta shirts from tack-packed souvenir stalls. They ate mediocre pan-Italian food in neon-lit restaurants into which they had been ushered by persistent maîtres d'hôtel, and paid through the nose for the obligatory sit-down coffee at one of the famous cafés with wobbly tables gracing 'the drawing room of Europe'.

And they loved it; in their setting against the glory of this uniquely watery, uniquely beautiful city, factors that elsewhere might mar an Italian holiday are willingly accepted as part of the Venetian experience. Divorced in the visitor's mind from the rest of Italy – divorced, in fact, from reality – La Serenissima is an over-crowded, over-priced rule unto itself, which even the discerning traveller will accept with all its superficial faults, so overwhelming an experience is it.

But the city doesn't end there, and a holiday spent exclusvely pushing a path through the tourist tide between piazza San Marco and the Rialto is a holiday wasted. For beyond tourist Venice lies a quiet, echoing, doubly magical city: under-visited, yet packed with innumerable gems; filled with the colours, sounds and smells of everyday Venetian life.

Yes, there is everyday life in Venice, and therein lies the city's greatest charm. Naturally, it is everyday life with a twist: finding someone else's boat occupying your bit of *fondamenta*, for example, or your entrance hall flooded by an extra-high *acqua alta*; your long slog to work is generally over water rather than by commuter train, and your fitness routine is more likely to consist of rowing than working out in a gym.

Venetians, however, are partial to the same things as Italians across the water, and their city has – if you know where to look for them – all the usual trappings. There are good restaurants (and they're getting better, *see p144*) and there are neighbourhood bars where you won't need to consider a second mortgage in order to sip a *caffè* at a pavement table. There's a drinking (and snacking) culture second to none in Italy, revolving around that quintessentially Venetian institution, the *bacaro* (*see p159*).

And there are the Venetians themselves: slightly dour, tending towards the abrupt, but always ready to share the city's secrets with any visitor who shows more than the usual bridge-clogging, calle-blocking superficial interest in their stunning home.

ABOUT THE TIME OUT CITY GUIDES

The *Time Out Venice Guide* is one of an expanding series of *Time Out* City Guides, now numbering over 30, produced by the people behind London and New York's successful listings magazines. Our guides are all written and updated by resident experts who have striven to provide you with all the most up-to-date information you'll need to explore the city or read up on its background, whether you're a local or a first-time visitor.

THE LOWDOWN ON THE LISTINGS

Above all, we've tried to make this book as useful as possible. Addresses, telephone numbers, websites, transport information, opening times, admission prices and credit card details are all included in our listings, which were all checked and correct as we went to press. However, in Venice, small shops and bars often do not keep precise opening hours, and may close earlier or later than stated according to the level of trade. Similarly, arts programmes can change at the last moment. Before you go out of your way, we'd advise you to phone ahead and check opening times and other details. Bear in mind, too, that Venetians have a very flexible attitude to spelling, and will swing back and forth between Italian and dialect names for streets, *piazze* and districts; sometimes locals have no idea of what the 'official' name of their own street is, preferring, confusingly, quite different traditional names. We have given the most commonly used names; be prepared, however, to have to do some guesswork. While every effort has been made to ensure the accuracy of the information in this guide, the publishers cannot accept responsibility for any errors it may contain.

PRICES AND PAYMENT

We have noted where venues such as shops, hotels and restaurants accept the following credit cards: American Express (**AmEx**), Diners Club (**DC**), MasterCard (**MC**) and Visa (**V**). Many businesses also accept other cards, including Switch, Delta and JCB. In addition, some shops, restaurants and attractions take travellers' cheques issued by major financial institutions.

THE LIE OF THE LAND AND MAPS

We have divided the city by *sestieri*, the six 'quarters' of Venice. Note that house numbers in Venice don't begin and end in each street. They start in one arbitrary spot in any given sestiere and continue, apparently at random, to the last house in that district. Venetian addresses are, therefore, almost useless for the purposes of locating your goal. To make your task easier, our listings include the official address (sestiere and number), plus the name of the street in which each hotel, restaurant or bar is located. There's also a map reference, indicating the page and square on which an address will be found on our maps at the back of the book.

TELEPHONE NUMBERS

You must dial area codes with all numbers in Italy, even for local calls. Hence all Venice numbers begin with 041, whether or not you're calling from outside the city. From abroad, you must dial 39 (the international dialling code for Italy) followed by the number given in this book – including the initial 0.

There is an online version of this guide, as well as weekly events listings for over 30 international cities, at www.timeout.com.

ESSENTIAL INFORMATION

For all the practical information you might need for visiting the city, including emergency phone numbers and details of local transport, turn to the **Directory** chapter at the back of the guide. It starts on page 274.

LET US KNOW WHAT YOU THINK

We hope you enjoy the *Time Out Venice Guide*, and we'd like to know what you think of it. We welcome tips for any places that you consider we should include in future editions and take note of your criticism of our choices. There's a reader's reply card at the back of this book, or email us on veniceguide@timeout.com.

The Euro

As of 28 February 2002, the lira will cease to be legal tender, its place taken by the Euro (*see also p286* **The Euro cometh**). As this guide went to press, one Euro was worth around 60 British pence and 92 US cents, though these rates fluctuate. Currencies of Euro zone countries are pegged to the Euro.

L1,000	= €0.52
L5,000	= €2.58
L10,000	= €5.16
L25,000	= €12.91
L50,000	= €25.82
L100,000	= €51.64
L250,000	= €129.11
L500,000	= €258.23
€1	= L1,936
€2	= L3,872
€5	= L9,681
€10	= L19,363
€25	= L48,407
€50	= L96,813
€100	= L193,627
€250	= L484,067

Advertisers

We would like to stress that no establishment has been included in this guide because it has advertised in any of our publications and no payment of any kind has influenced any review. The opinions given in this book are those of *Time Out* writers and editors and are entirely independent.

VENICE'S LIVING GUIDE, DAY BY DAY

Venezia news

- exhibitions
- shows
- pubs, live-clubs
- maps
- movies
- services
- concerts
- restaurants

in the news stands!

In Context

Feature boxes

History

Through the centuries, in times of peace and war, Venice's watery setting has been both its magnificent strength and its fatal weakness.

In the fifth century AD, when Rome was making good its decline from world domination to provincial obscurity, Venice had not yet been born. For a city-state that would last for more than 1,000 years – half of those in a position of more or less total dominion over shipping routes and large swathes of territory in the eastern Mediterranean – its origins were decidedly unheroic.

Venice was born out of terror: terror of the barbarians who invaded the collapsing Roman Empire in the fifth century, and terror of the unpredictable, ugly moods of the Adriatic. The brutality of the Visigoths of Alaric, of the Huns of Attila, of the Ostrogoths and Lombards, drove thousands of sophisticated town-dwellers out onto the muddy, flood-prone islets and sand banks of the lagoon.

Enormous public works were necessary almost from the beginning to shore up and consolidate the islands. Huge amounts of timber had to be cut down and transported from nearby coastal pine forests to the islands. Here the trunks were sunk deep into the mud as foundations for the buildings – mainly wooden – of the villages scattered on islands all over the lagoon. But above all, the rivers, including the fast-flowing Brenta and Piave, which drain the eastern Dolomites and which threatened to silt up the lagoon, had to be tamed and diverted.

And yet this battle against nature helped to unite the lagoon-dwellers into a close-knit community and eventually into a republic that was to become one of the strongest and most stable nation states in European history. The battle never ended. Even in the 18th century, when the French were advancing on the lagoon and the Venetian Republic was near the end of its own decline and fall, the government invested its last resources into the construction of the *murazzi*, the massive sea walls that run between the Lido, Pellestrina and Chioggia.

THE ORIGINS: SALT AND FISH

Until the collapse of the Roman Empire, the islands of the lagoon hosted only tiny and transient fishing hamlets. The surrounding mainland, however, was one of the richest areas of the empire. Cities such as Padua, Verona, Aquileia and Altino were among the most prosperous in Roman Italy, and a myriad of smaller towns – among them Vicenza, Concordia and Belluno – were of almost equal importance. With the final disintegration of any semblance of public order and security in the latter part of the sixth century, their inhabitants finally fled for their lives. Those from Aquileia and Concordia gravitated towards the islands of the Grado lagoon, between Venice and Trieste. The inhabitants of Altino and Treviso made for the islands of Murano, Burano, Mazzorbo and Torcello in the northern section of the lagoon. Paduans pitched up on the central island of Rivo Alto ('high banks'), soon abbreviated to Rialto – the first nucleus of historical Venice. The island of Chioggia and the sandbanks to the north drew fugitives from Este and Monselice.

These influxes were meant to be temporary. But as economic life on the mainland collapsed, the lagoon islands came to be thought of as permanent homes. They offered enormous potential in the form of fish and salt, commodities that even in times of chaos were basic necessities. Once settled in the lagoon, the fugitives could also enjoy the relative peace and tranquillity that would be denied to the peoples of mainland Europe for centuries to come.

STUDIED NEUTRALITY

In 552 Justinian I, the emperor of Byzantium, was determined to reconquer Italy from the Barbarians. His first object was the city of Ravenna. But his troops were confronted with an almost insuperable problem: they had made their way overland, via the Dalmatian coast on the eastern side of the Adriatic, but were blocked by the Barbarian Goths who controlled the mainland to the north of Venice. The only way they could attack and take Ravenna was to be transported by ship from Grado to the northeast of Venice. The Byzantine commander Narsete requested the help of the lagoon confederation to ship his men across.

Already by this time, the lagoon communities had adopted a practice that was to mark Venetian diplomacy through its 1,250-year history: staying as far as possible from – and, where possible, profiting by – other people's quarrels. Justinian's request presented a dilemma: helping would be seen as a declaration of war by the Ostrogoths in Ravenna, with whom the lagoon communities

had reached a comfortable *modus vivendi* assuring safety on the mainland for their traders. Yet the Eastern emperor was offering vast monetary and political rewards for transporting his troops.

The communities eventually threw in their lot with Byzantium. Justinian conquered Ravenna, and went on to reconquer Rome itself. From this time on the communities of the lagoon became vassals of the Eastern Empire, with its capital in Constantinople. Venice would remain technically subject to the Byzantine emperors until well after the Sack of Constantinople – an attack led by Venetians – during the Fourth Crusade in 1204.

THE FIRST DOGES

It was not until AD 697, under the growing threat of the Barbarian Lombards who controlled the mainland, that the communities scattered around the lagoon, now officially recognised by Byzantium as a duchy, decided to convert their fragile confederation into a stronger, much more centralised state. In this year (or maybe not: some historians have dismissed the story as a Venetian myth) they elected one Paoluccio Anafesto to be their first doge, as the dukes of Venice became known. Yet right from the beginning *il Doge* was very different from the other feudal strongmen of Europe.

'Democracy of a kind ensured that no one had absolute power.'

In the first application of a system that would be honed into shape over the centuries (*see p11* **Venetian government**), the doge was elected for life by a council chosen by an assembly that represented all the various social groups and trades of the island communities. Technically, therefore, the leadership was elected democratically, although the strongest groups soon formed themselves into a dominant oligarchy. Yet democracy of a kind survived in the system of checks and balances employed to ensure that no one section of the ruling elite got its hands on absolute power. Venetians, fearing the creation of an immovable hereditary monarchy, hedged the office of doge about with all kinds of limitations.

The first ducal power struggle took place in 729. The doge in question, Ipato Orso, achieved the duchy's first outstanding victory as a military power when he dislodged the Lombards from Ravenna. Success, though, went to Orso's head, and he attempted to transform the doge's office into a hereditary monarchy.

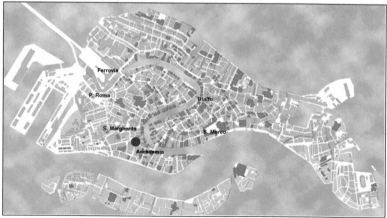

Virtual civil war wracked the lagoon for two years, ending only when a furious mob forced its way into Orso's house and cut his throat. Troubles continued with the two succeeding doges: both were accused of tyranny, and were not only deposed and exiled but also ceremonially blinded.

Despite moments of near-anarchy, the lagoon-dwellers were already becoming a major economic power in the upper Adriatic, the eastern Mediterranean, the Black Sea and North Africa. Craftsmen were sent abroad to Dalmatia and Istria to study the art of ship-building; they learnt so swiftly that by the seventh century the construction and fitting-out of sea-going vessels had become a thriving industry. Mercantile expansion and technical advances went hand in hand, as tradesmen brought back materials and techniques from far-flung places – especially from the Middle and Far East, where technical and scientific culture was far in advance of the West.

Thinking big: the *Apotheosis of Venice*.

THE WAR WITH PEPIN

In 781 Pepin, son of Charlemagne, invaded Italy and attacked the Lombards. Wariness of involving the lagoon in mainland struggles still dominated the duchy's policy and it played for time, unsure whether to sacrifice the alliance with Byzantium to this new and powerful player on the European scene. In the end, however, Pepin's designs on Istria and Dalmatia – part of the Venetian sphere of influence – caused relations to turn frosty. Exasperated by the duchy's fence-sitting, Pepin attacked its ally Grado on the mainland, executing its cardinal by hurling him from the town's highest tower. He then proceeded to take all the mainland positions around Venice, and besieged the lagoon communities from the sea.

In the mid-eighth century the confederation had moved its capital from Heraclea in the northern lagoon to Malamocco on the Adriatic coast, where it was now at the mercy of Pepin's naval forces. At this crucial juncture, in 810, a strong, effective leader suddenly emerged in the form of an admiral, Angelo Partecipazio. He immediately abandoned the besieged capital of Malamocco; almost overnight, the capital was moved to the island archipelago of Rialto in the centre of the lagoon.

Partecipazio's next move was a stroke of military genius. He ordered his fleet to head out of the lagoon through the strait of Malamocco to attack Pepin's ships, then to feign terror and head back into the lagoon. In hot pursuit, the deep-keeled Frankish ships ran aground on the sandbanks of the lagoon, allowing the locals, with their intimate knowledge of deep-water channels, to pick off the crews with ease until thousands had been massacred.

THE BIRTH OF 'VENETIA'

After his great victory against the Franks, Partecipazio was elected doge. During his reign, work began on a ducal palace on the site of the current one, and the confederation of islands that made up the lagoon duchy was given the name 'Venetia'. Around the same time Torcello, once a flourishing city, began to decline, as the surrounding lagoon waters silted up and malarial mosquitoes took over.

These were also the years when Venice set about embroidering a mythology worthy of its ambitions. After two local merchants stole the body of Saint Mark from Alexandria and brought it to Venice – traditionally in the year 829 – the city's previous Byzantine patron, Saint Theodore, was unceremoniously deposed and the Evangelist – symbolised by a winged lion – set up in his place. A shrine to the saint was erected in the place where St Mark's Basilica would later rise.

Crusader booty: the four
bronze horses were a potent
symbol of Venice's might.
See p13.

Angelo Partecipazio's overwhelming success in both military and civic government led to another tussle for power.

Before he died in 827, he made certain that his son Giustiniano would succeed him. When Giustiniano died two years later, his younger brother Giovanni was elected doge, despite mounting dissent and jealousy from rival families. It was a measure of Partecipazio's importance that his surname was to feature repeatedly in the ducal roll of honour over the next century, but the family was never allowed to achieve the hegemony that the Medici dynasty enjoyed in Renaissance Florence. In Venice, any sign of arrogance or dynastic ambition was greeted either with banishment or worse; one doge with aspirations beyond the role assigned to him, Pietro Candiano, was thrown to the dogs at the end of the tenth century.

BEGINNINGS OF EMPIRE

The development of the vast Venetian empire grew out of the mercantile pragmatism that dominated Venetian political thinking. Expansion was embarked upon for two main reasons: to secure safe shipping routes, and to create permanent trading bases. Harassed by Slav pirates in the upper Adriatic, the Venetians set up bases around the area from which to attack the pirate ships: gradually they took over the ports of Grado and Trieste, then expanded along the coastlines of Istria and Dalmatia. In some cases, Venetian protection against pirates was requested; in others, 'help' arrived unbidden.

With the coast well defended, the Venetians rarely bothered to expand their territories into the hinterland. There was, for many centuries, a certain mistrust of *terra firma*; Venetian citizens were not even allowed to own land outside of the lagoon until 1345.

Venetian government

From the earliest days of their confederation, the strong-willed inhabitants of the lagoon were determined to prevent power from coming to rest in the hands of one too-powerful individual or dynasty. The complex machinery of Venetian government, which evolved over the centuries, with layer upon layer of checks and balances, reflected this aim.

Maggior consiglio (great council) – the republic's parliament, with around 500 elected members, which in turn elected (and provided the candidates for) most other state offices, including that of doge.

Minor consiglio (lesser council) – elected by and from the *maggior consiglio*, this six-man team advised – or kept tabs on – the doge.

Senato (senate) – known until the late 14th century as the *pregadi*, the *senato* was the influential upper house of the Venetian parliament, which, by the early 16th century, had expanded to some 300 members.

Collegio dei savi (college of wise men) – a group of experts, elected by the *senato*, who staffed special committees to oversee all aspects of internal, marine and war policy.

Quarantie – the republic's three supreme courts; their 40 members were chosen by the *senato*.

Consiglio dei dieci (council of ten) – founded after Tiepolo's uprising in 1310 (*see p13*), the all-powerful council of ten was appointed by the *senato*; its extensive network of spies brought any would-be subversives to a closed-door trial in which defence lawyers were strictly forbidden. In time, the increasingly powerful *consiglio dei dieci* would have the Venetian Inquisition to assist it in its task.

Pien collegio (full college) – made up of the *minor consiglio* and the *collegio dei savi*, this became Venice's real government, eventually supplanting the *senato*.

Serenissima signoria (most serene lordships) – made up of the *minor consiglio*, the heads of the three *quarantie* courts and the doge, this body was vested with ultimate executive power.

Il doge (the duke) – elected for life in an infinitely complicated, cheat-proof system of multiple ballots, the sumptuously robed duke of Venice was glorious to behold. He could not, however, indulge in business of his own, could not receive foreign ambassadors alone, could not leave Venice without permission, could not accept personal gifts and could, if his republic tired of him, be thrown out of office. With all his family banned from high office for the term of his reign, many doges hailed from the less ambitious, less politically adept of Venice's clans. Most, moreover, were old and tired (the average age of doges between 1400 and 1570 was 72) by the time they donned the *biretta*, the distinctive horned hat. But the doge was the only official privy to all state secrets and eligible to attend meetings of all state organs; he could, if he played his cards right, have a determining effect on Venetian policy.

CARRY ON UP THE BOSPHORUS

The Crusades presented Venice with its greatest opportunity yet for expanding trade routes while reaping a profit. Transporting crusaders to the Holy Land became big business for the city. More importantly, the naïve crusaders were easy prey for the professional generals – the *condottieri* – who commanded Venice's army of highly trained mercenaries: far from helping to win back the Holy Land for Christendom, the eager crusaders were, as often as not, used to extend and consolidate the Venetian empire.

Never was this truer than in the case of the Fourth Crusade, which set off proudly from Venice in 1202 to reconquer Jerusalem. The Venetian war fleet was under the command of Doge Enrico Dandolo, who though 80 years old and completely blind retained his capacities as a supremely cunning leader, an outstanding tactician and an accomplished diplomat. Other European crusader leaders were persuaded to take time out to conquer the strategic Adriatic port of Zara, thus assuring Venice's control of much of the Dalmatian coastline. Even more surprisingly, they allowed themselves to be talked into attacking Constantinople.

Venice's special relationship with the Eastern empire had always had its ups and downs. In 1081 and 1082, Venice had done the Byzantine emperor a favour when it trounced the menacing Normans in the southern Adriatic – in return, it was granted duty-free trading rights throughout the empire. But in 1149 those trading privileges were withdrawn in disgust at the go-it-alone arrogance of the Venetians during the siege of Corfu.

Tension was running high as the Fourth Crusade set out. Dandolo saw that this was an ideal opportunity to remove the Byzantine challenge to Venetian trade hegemony once and for all. He pulled the wool over his fellow crusaders' eyes, with the noble argument that the eastern emperor must be ousted and replaced by someone willing to reunite the eastern Orthodox and western Roman churches.

They acquiesced, but there was little noble about the brutal, bloody, Venetian-led sacking of the city on 13 April 1204, nor about the horrendous pillaging that ensued. Far outstripping all their colleagues in greed and callousness, the Venetians looted all the city's greatest treasures, including the celebrated

Modern history starts here

At the end of the 19th century, travel writer Augustus Hare informed readers of his *Venice*: 'The monastery of Santa Maria Gloriosa dei Frari contains enormous collections of the Public Archives. Above three hundred chambers are filled with these treasures, which include the interesting correspondence of the Republic with foreign States.'

It was a curious understatement, given the furore that had surrounded this 'interesting correspondence' for several decades: until the 1830s, historians had relied on the anecdotal work of their predecessors for information on the past.

Then Europe's most illustrious historian – a German named Leopold Ranke – had happened across the Venetian state archive, an unequalled mass of material: the records of the Venetian republic, minutes of *scuole* and corporations, and – most importantly of all – *dispacci* (regular reports) and *relazioni* (end-of-term round-ups) penned over the centuries by zealous Venetian ambassadors to all the known world filled six kilometres of shelving in 298 rooms in the monastery of the Frari (*see p112*). With such sources, Ranke proclaimed, historians were

finally in a position to write 'a universal history of objective value'.

Historians flocked in droves to La Serenissima from all over Europe. Among them was a young Harold Acton – later to be Regius professor of History at Cambridge – who enthused, 'In proceeding from library to archive [...] we exchange doubt for certainty.'

Archive fever radiated from Venice to the rest of the Continent; long-neglected state papers were ransacked by serious young men in musty coats, sure that eternal truth was to be found amongst the dusty, crumbling papers of drear records offices. Letters and diaries – up to then disregarded as insignificant personal scribblings – were scoured for historical gems. And as the interminable seam of international archive ore was mined, Venice's contribution to it paled into relative insignificance. Ranke was denounced as superficial for having gone no further than the Venetian papers. And, ironically, the truth that archives were still believed to contain became ever more elusive.

Because the serious historian knew that there must be one more archive, one more diary, one more letter that held the key. And that had yet to be dusted off.

quartet of antique Greek horses that was transported back to Venice and placed above the main entrance of St Mark's Basilica (*see p75* **Horse Power**). Innumerable other artefacts – jewellery, enamels, golden chalices, statuary, columns and precious marbles – were plundered: they are now an inseparable part of the fabric of the *palazzi* and churches of Venice.

But the booty was only a minor consideration for the Venetians and their pragmatic doge: the real prize was the one handed out when the routed Byzantine empire was carved up. The Venetians were not interested in grabbing huge swathes of territory that they knew they couldn't hold. This was left to the French and German knights, who proceeded to lose most of their territories within a few decades.

Putting their intimate knowledge of eastern trade routes to excellent use, the Venetians selected for conquest those islands and ports that could guarantee their merchant ships a safe passage from Venice to the Black Sea and back. These included almost all the main ports on the Dalmatian coast, the more strategic of the Greek islands, the sea of Marmora and a number of strategic Black Sea ports.

For many years after the conquest of Constantinople, Venetian ships could sail from Venice to Byzantium without ever leaving waters controlled by the city. The Serene Republic, La Serenissima, had finally become a major imperial power. The city marked the turn of events by conferring a new title upon its doge: *Quartae Partis et Dimidiae Totius Imperii Romaniae Dominator* – Lord of a Quarter and Half a Quarter of the Roman Empire.

PLOTS AND LOCK-OUTS
In 1297, in what came to be known as the *Serrata del Maggior Consiglio*, the leaders of the Venetian merchant aristocracy decided to limit entry to the Grand Council to those families already in the club. Membership of the *maggior consiglio* was restricted to those who had held a seat there in the previous four years, or to descendants of those who had belonged at any point since 1172. Under these rules, only around 150 extended families were eligible for a place, but the number of council members leapt to some 1,200.

Up-and-coming clans were understandably indignant at the thought of being forever excluded from power and from a coveted place in the *Libro D'Oro* – the Golden Book – of the Venetian aristocracy. In 1310 a prosperous merchant, Baiamonte Tiepolo, harnessed the growing discontent by leading a popular rebellion against the aristocratic oligarchy. Had Tiepolo's standard-bearer not been felled by a loose brick knocked carelessly out of its place

by an old lady watching the shenanigans from her window in the Merceria, the uprising may have succeeded. But his troops fled in panic, the uprising was savagely crushed, and the much-feared Council of Ten was granted draconian police and judicial powers. An extensive network of spies and informers was set up to suppress any future plots.

'With Venice's mercantile power at its zenith, fortunes were lavished on building.'

In 1354 Doge Marino Faliero made a bid to undermine the powers of the Venetian oligarchy while increasing and consolidating his own powers as a permanent hereditary leader. This plot, too, was mercilessly suppressed and Faliero was beheaded.

The Council of Ten – along with the Venetian Inquisition that was also set up after the Tiepolo plot of 1310 – wielded its special powers most effectively after the Faliero incident, ensuring that this was the last serious attempt to attack the principle of rule by elite. It was at this time that lion's-head postboxes first appeared at strategic points around the city: Venetians were encouraged to drop written reports of any questionable activity through their marble mouths.

IMPERIAL GLORY
While Venice's mercantile power was at its zenith from the 13th to the 15th centuries, vast fortunes were built up and lavished on building, furnishing and decorating great *palazzi* and churches. It was at this time that the city took on the architectural form still visible today. For sheer luxury, Venice's lifestyle was unequalled anywhere else in Europe.

In the 14th and 15th centuries, Venice was one of the largest cities in Europe, with an estimated population of between 150,000 and 200,000, many connected with the city's booming mercantile activities. International visitors were astounded by its opulence and economic dynamism.

Salt had long ceased to be Venice's main trading commodity. When ships set sail from Venice for the Middle East, their holds were crammed with Istrian pine wood, iron ore, cereals, wool and salted and preserved meats. These were traded for finely woven textiles, exotic carpets, perfumes, gold and silverware, spices, precious stones of all kinds, ivory, wax and slaves: with a virtual monopoly on all these sought-after commodities, Venice was able to sell them on to the rest of Europe at enormous profit.

LIFESTYLES OF THE RICH AND FAMOUS

The Venetian aristocracy liked to live in some comfort. 'The luxury of any ordinary Venetian house,' wrote one traveller in 1492, 'is so extraordinary that in any other city or country it would be sufficient to decorate a royal palace.' Domestic luxury was not confined to the city. In this period the Venetian nobility was investing huge amounts of money in their summer villas on the mainland, which often surpassed their city establishments in magnificence, designed and decorated as they were by the leading Veneto architects and painters.

Venetians lavished the same kind of attention on their appearance. Fortunes were spent on the richest and most gorgeous textiles and jewellery. Venetian women were famous for the unbridled luxury of their clothing, of their furs and of their fabrics woven with gold and silver thread. Their perfumes and cosmetics were the envy of all Europe, as were the beauty and fascination of the estimated 12,000 courtesans (*see p106* **Quivers open to every arrow**) who dominated much of the social and cultural life of the city in the 15th century.

So dedicated were Venetians to the cult of love and earthly pleasures, that the Patriarch, Venice's cardinal, had to issue orders forbidding the city's nuns from going out on the town at night in ordinary clothes.

Sumptuous festivals of music, theatre and dance were almost daily occurrences. The visit of a foreign ruler, a wedding or funeral of a member of the nobility, a religious festival, a naval or military victory, or delivery from an epidemic were all excuses for public celebrations involving days of festivities and huge sums of money. The city's foreign communities – Jews, Armenians, Turks, Germans, French and Mongols, many of them permanent residents (*see p91* **Multi-cultural Venice**) – would celebrate their national or religious feast days with enormous pomp.

Despite the wealth of the city, and the full employment created by its trades and industries (at full stretch, the shipyard was capable of launching one fully equipped ship every day), life was not easy for the city's poor, who often lived in damp, filthy conditions.

Epidemics were frequent, sometimes killing as many as tens of thousands of people: more than half the city's population is estimated to have died in the Black Death of 1348-9. Social tension and discontent were also rife and sometimes led to rioting.

THE WAR WITH GENOA

The enormous wealth of the Venetian Republic and of its rapidly expanding empire inevitably provoked jealousy among the other trading nations of the Mediterranean – above all with the powerful maritime city-state of Genoa, Venice's main rival in its trade with the East.

Already in 1261 the Genoese had clashed with the Venetians when the former obliged the Byzantine emperor by helping to evict Venice's high-handed merchants from Constantinople. Skirmishes between the two Italian powers continued throughout most of the 14th century, regularly flaring up into major battles or periods of open warfare, and often resulting in disastrous defeats for Venice.

By 1379 the situation had become desperate for La Serenissima. The Genoese fleet and army had moved into the Gulf of Venice in the upper Adriatic and, after a long siege, had taken Chioggia, at the southern end of the lagoon. From here the Genoese attacked and occupied much of the lagoon, including Malamocco and the passage to the open sea. Venice was under siege and began to starve.

Then, in 1380, the city worked another of its miracles of level-headed cunning. Almost the whole of the Genoese fleet was anchored inside the fortified harbour of Chioggia. Vittor Pisani, the admiral of the Venetian fleet, ordered hundreds of small boats to be filled with rocks and building materials. Panicked by a surprise Venetian attack on the mouth of the port, the Genoese failed to notice that the small boats were being sunk in the shallow port entrance, preventing any escape. The tables had been turned, and Venice besieged the trapped Genoese fleet until it surrendered unconditionally. Genoa's days as a great naval power were over, and Venice exulted.

Ironically, however, this victory was to spell the beginning of the end for La Serenissima. For though the republic had reached the climax of its prosperity and had re-acquired its supremacy in the East, concentrating its energies on fighting Genoa was to prove a fatal foreign policy mistake. Venice's leaders badly underestimated the threat posed by the emergence of the Turks as a military power in Asia Minor and the Black Sea area. Convinced – wrongly and ultimately fatally – that diplomacy was the way to deal with the threat from the East, Venice turned its attention to conquering other powers on the Italian mainland.

ON TO DRY LAND

For centuries Venice had followed a conscious policy of neutrality towards the various powers that had carved up the Italian mainland. The European political upheavals resulting from the turmoil of the Crusades from the end of the 12th century to the end of the 14th century put paid to that neutrality. The bitter rivalry between Venice and the

The mercantile city created a mythology worthy of its ambitions: Venice receives the riches of the sea from Neptune.

other Italian maritime states, especially Pisa and Genoa, inevitably brought it into conflict with their powerful mainland allies: the pope, the Scaligera dukes of Verona and a succession of Holy Roman emperors.

The defeat of the vast Scaligera empire (which included much of the Venetian hinterland) by Count Gian Galeazzo Visconti of Milan in 1387 brought Milanese much power too close to the lagoon for comfort: it was not only Venetian security which was under threat, but access to all-important trade routes through north-eastern Italy and across the Alps into northern Europe beyond as well. Venice began a series of wars that led to the conquest in 1405 of Verona and its enormous territories, of Padua, Vicenza, and a number of other significant towns, too.

By 1420 Venice had annexed Friuli and Udine; by 1441 La Serenissima controlled Brescia, Bergamo, Cremona and Ravenna as well. The land campaign continued until 1454, when Venice signed a peace treaty with Milanese ruler Francesco Sforza. Though Ravenna soon slipped from Venice's grasp, the rest of the republic's immense mainland territories were to remain more or less intact for almost 300 years.

BYE BYE BYZANTIUM
Even as Venice expanded on the mainland, events were conspiring to bring La Serenissima's reign as a political power and trading giant to a close. In 1453 the Ottoman Turks swept into Constantinople, and Venice's crucial trading privileges in what had been the Byzantine empire were almost totally lost. In 1487 Vasco da Gama rounded the Cape of Good Hope, and in 1489 he became the first European to reach Calcutta by sea, shattering Venice's monopoly on the riches of the East. The arrival of Portuguese ships laden with spices and textiles in Portuguese ports caused a sensation in Europe and despair in Venice. The Venetians hastily drew up plans to open a canal at Suez to beat the Portuguese at their own game, but the project came to nothing. Instead, cushioned by the spoil of centuries and exhausted by 100 years of almost constant military campaigns, the city sank slowly over the next two centuries into dissipation and decline.

But, as was only to be expected from a city as lavish as Venice, the decline was glorious. For most of the 16th century few Venetians behaved as if the writing was on the wall. Such was the enormous wealth of the city that the economic fall-out from the Turks' inexorable progress through the Middle East went almost unnoticed at first. Profits were not as massive as before, but the rich remained very rich and the setbacks in the East were partly counter-balanced by exploitation of the newly acquired *terra firma* territories.

As revenue gradually declined throughout the 16th century, spending on life's little pleasures increased, producing an explosion of art, architecture and music. Titian, Tintoretto, Veronese and Giorgione were hard at work in the city (*see chapter* **Venetian Painting**). Palladio, Sanmicheli and Scamozzi were

The great escape

Giacomo Casanova and Franz Kafka are not the most likely of literary companions. But there are clear similarities between the imprisonment of the Venetian adventurer in the prisons of the Doge's Palace in 1755, and the plot of *The Trial* – whose author is known to have read Casanova's account of the episode. Like most of the prisoners sentenced by the three *Inquisitori* of the Serene Republic, Casanova was not present at the trial itself, and was neither told why he had been sentenced, nor for how many years. Only the endings are different: Josef K is taken away to be executed, while Casanova manages to escape after 15 months behind bars.

Officially, the charge against the 30-year-old gambler, scholar and womaniser was that of 'public contempt for Holy Religion'. An informer, stonemason Giovanni Manuzzi, had been tailing him for months, sending regular reports to the *Inquisitori*. The arrest order, signed on 24 July 1755, was sparked by Manuzzi's discovery in Casanova's house of books dealing with black magic. But this may have been no more than a pretext for the detainment of a man who was disliked by the Venetian oligarchy not only for his loose morals, but also for keeping company (and sharing lovers) with foreign ambassadors. Though mid 18th-century Venice had few state secrets worth selling, this didn't stop its rulers from reading espionage into every exchange between influential foreigners and Venetian citizens.

Casanova was detained in the Leads, the attic space under the lead-lined roof of the Doge's Palace, which became an oven in summer and a fridge in winter. Nevertheless, these cells, which lay immediately above the meeting hall of the *Consiglio dei Dieci* (*see page 11* **Venetian government**), were considered the most comfortable in the building, and were reserved for gentlemen of some consequence, who could afford to pay for their food and other little extras. Casanova languished in this cramped cell – where he was unable to stand upright – for months, while fellow prisoners came and went (some to freedom, some to less salubrious lodgings on the other side of the Bridge of Sighs). His companions offer a good social cross-section of Venetian crimes and misdemeanours: a valet who had got his master's daughter pregnant, a Jewish moneylender who had made illegal loans to desperate aristocrats, a count sentenced to a week in the cooler for acting as interpreter in a gallant exchange between the Austrian ambassador and the wife of a Venetian diplomat.

After a plan to escape through a hole in the floor of his cell was foiled when he was transferred to more spacious quarters, Casanova finally managed his spectacular escape over the roof of the Palace on 31 October 1756. His account of this *fuga dai piombi* in the 12-volume *Histoire de ma vie* makes for exciting, action-hero reading; but it is difficult to know how much is embroidery. The fact of Casanova's escape is confirmed by a reference in the state records; but whether it was, as he claimed, the fruit of his own courage and cleverness, or the gift of a well-bribed prison guard, is less clear. The two cells Casanova was confined in can be visited as part of the special *Itinerari segreti* tour of Palazzo Ducale (*see p80*).

changing the face of architecture (*see chapters* **Architecture** and **Palladian Villas**). The city rang out to the music of the Gabriellis.

LEAGUE OF CAMBRAI

Meanwhile, on the mainland, Venice's arrogant annexation of territory had not been forgotten by the powers that had suffered at her hands. When Venice took advantage of the French invasion of Italy in the final years of the 15th century to extend its territories still further, the Habsburgs, France, Spain and the papacy were so incensed that they clubbed together to form the League of Cambrai, with the sole aim of annihilating Venice.

They came very close to doing so. One Venetian rout followed another, some Venetian-controlled cities defected to the enemy and others that did not were laid waste. Only squabbling within the League of Cambrai stopped Venice itself from being besieged. By 1516 the alliance had fallen to pieces and Venice had regained almost all its territories.

THE TURKS CLOSE IN

Its coffers almost empty, its mainland dominions in tatters, Venice was now forced to take stock of the damage that was being done by the Turks. A short-sighted policy of trying to keep the Ottoman empire at bay by diplomacy had already had devastating effects on Venice's position in the eastern Mediterranean.

In 1497, as the Ottomans stormed through the Balkans, coming almost within sight of the belltowers of Venice, La Serenissima had been obliged to give up several Aegean islands and the port of Negroponte; two years later it lost its forts in the Peloponnese, giving the Turks virtual control of the southern end of the Adriatic. And if Venice felt jubilant about securing Cyprus in 1489 by pressuring the king's Venetian widow Caterina Cornaro into bequeathing control of the island, the legacy involved the republic in almost constant warfare to keep the Turks off this strategically vital strip of land.

In 1517 Syria and Egypt fell to the Turks; Rhodes followed in 1522; and by 1529 the Ottoman empire reached across the southern Mediterranean as far as Morocco. The frightened European powers turned to Venice to help repulse the common foe. But mistrust of the lagoon republic was deep, and, in their determination to keep Venice from deriving too much profit from the war against the Turks, the campaign itself was botched.

In 1538 a Christian fleet was trounced at Preveza in western Greece; in 1571 Venice led a huge European fleet to victory against

hundreds of Turkish warships in the Battle of Lepanto, in what is now the Gulf of Corinth. But despite the massive propaganda campaign of self-congratulation and self-glorification that followed, it became apparent that the victory was hollow and that the Turks were as strong as ever. In a treaty signed after the battle in 1573, Venice was forced ignominiously to hand over Cyprus, its second-last major possession in the eastern Mediterranean (Crete, the final one, fell in 1669.)

SEVENTEENTH-CENTURY DROOP

By the 17th century the Venetian government was no longer under any illusion about the gravity of its economic and commercial crisis. In a report issued by the *Savi alla Mercanzia*, the state trading commission, dated 5 July 1610, it was noted that 'our commerce and shipping in the West are completely destroyed. In the East only a few businesses are still functioning and they are riddled with debt, without ships and getting weaker by the day. Moreover, and this must be emphasised, only a small quantity of goods are arriving in our city, and it is becoming increasingly difficult to find buyers for them. The nations which used to buy from us now have established their businesses elsewhere. We are facing the almost total annihilation of our commerce.'

'Down but not out, heroic attempts were made to regain the mauled empire.'

Venice was down but not quite out, however, and some heroic attempts were made to regain the empire that had been so disastrously mauled in the 16th century by the Turks. In 1617 a successful campaign was fought against the Uskoks, pirates financed by the Austrian Habsburgs, who had territorial ambitions in Istria and along the Dalmatian coast; in the process, some resounding blows were struck against the Turks of the region too. Between 1681 and 1687 Francesco Morosini, the brilliant commander of the Venetian fleet, succeeded in reconquering much of the territory that had been taken by the Turks in the preceding century, including the strategically vital island of Crete, and the Peloponnese. But these moments of victory and glory, celebrated with colossal pomp and ceremony in Venice itself, were almost invariably short-lived.

FINAL YEARS OF THE REPUBLIC

Exhausted by debts and the sheer effort of its naval campaigns, the Venetian republic lacked the resources needed to consolidate its victories and newly re-conquered territories. In 1699 the Treaty of Carlowitz had rewarded Francesco Morosini's naval and military victories, restoring much of Venice's eastern possessions and many of its trading privileges. But by 1718 the Venetian republic was struggling to keep its head above water as the Austrians and Turks forced it to cede most of these same territories in the humiliating Treaty of Passarowitz.

By the time the 'Venezia Trionfante' café (later Caffè Florian, *see p165* **Cafés & Bars**) opened for business in piazza San Marco in 1720, the republic was virtually bankrupt; its governing nobility had grown decadent and politically inert. But decadence was good for the city's growing status as the party capital of Europe.

Aristocratic women of all ages and marital states were accompanied in their gadding by handsome young *cisibei* (male escorts), whose professions of chastity fooled nobody. Masked nuns from fashionable convents were a common sight at the city's gambling houses and theatres; party-pooping church officials who tried to confine nuns to barracks at the convent by the church of San Zaccaria were met with a barrage of bricks on at least one occasion.

Priests, too, were not slow to join in the fun: composer-prelate Antonio Vivaldi had well-publicised affairs with members of his famous female choir. Father Lorenzo Da Ponte, Mozart's great Venetian librettist, was better known for his amorous conquests than for his sanctity. And though Giacomo Casanova, the embodiment of sexual excess (*see p16* **The great escape**), never actually donned a cassock, he had been a promising student of theology before he realised where his true vocation lay.

Bankrupt, politically and ideologically stagnant and no longer a threat to any of its former enemies, Venice directed its final heroic effort to survive not against those erstwhile foes but against the forces of nature. Even as Napoleon prepared to invade Venice itself in 1797, the city was spending the meagre funds left in its coffers on building the vast *murazzi*, the long stone and marble dyke designed to protect the city from the worst ravages of unpredictable Adriatic tides (*see chapters* **Waterland** and **Sightseeing: The Lido to Chioggia**).

On 12 May 1797 the last doge, Lodovico Manin, was deposed by the French who, even before the republic bowed to the inevitable and voted itself out of existence, had handed control of the lagoon city over to Austria under the terms of the Treaty of Loeben.

Key events

Mid-fifth century Roman Empire declines and falls.
c.450 First settlers arrive in lagoon, fleeing invading forces of Attila the Hun.
520 Lagoon communities recognised by Ostrogoth Emperor Theodoric as having best merchant fleet in the Adriatic.
552 Lagoon communities allow troops of Eastern Emperor Justinian I to pass through the lagoon to attack Ravenna, sparing them a long journey around by land, and placing the communities in the Byzantine sphere of influence.
697 First doge (duke) elected as Lombard barbarians rampage through mainland and threaten communities' capital at Heraclea.
729 Doge Ipato Orso seeks to make dukedom hereditary, sparking two-year civil strife.
c742 Capital moved to Malamocco; lagoon communities have virtual monopoly on eastern Adriatic trade.
810 Frankish King Pepin besieges lagoon communities from the sea after a long land campaign against mainland allies; Admiral Angelo Partecipazio moves capital to Rialto, lures deep-keeled Frankish boats into shallow lagoon and massacres Franks; Partecipazio elected doge; lagoon duchy named Venetia; economic and building boom begins; work starts on ducal palace.
829 Two Venetian merchants bring stolen body of St Mark from Alexandria; St Mark becomes Venice's patron saint, deposing the Byzantine St Theodore in an act of defiance towards the eastern empire.
1000 Venetian fleet destroys troublesome Dalmatian pirates, securing trading bases and taking absolute control of Adriatic sea routes.

(Manin consigned his doge's cap to the victors, saying, 'Take this, I don't think I'll be needing it any more.')

In 1805 Napoleon reversed this state of affairs, absorbing Venice back into his Kingdom of Italy. Until 1815, when the French emperor's star waned and Venice once again found itself back under Austrian control, Napoleon's Venetian plenipotentiaries were given free rein

1063 Construction work begins on St Mark's Basilica.

1081-2 Venice beats Normans in southern Adriatic, earning gratitude of Byzantine empire, which grants Venice the right to unrestricted trade throughout the Empire and waives customs tariffs.

1147-9 Venice helps Byzantium drive Normans from Corfu but is so arrogant and aggressive that a period of enmity follows, with Venetian traders being ejected from Constantinople.

1202-4 Doge Enrico Dandolo heads Fourth Crusade which sacks Constantinople; Venice acquires many Aegean islands, including Crete, Euboea; substantial Venetian colony remains in Constantinople.

1261 Byzantine emperor, aided by Genoese, evicts Venetians from Constantinople; grants Genoa trading privileges formerly held by Venice; Venice and Genoa periodically at war for 20 years.

1297 Electoral laws tightened to keep power in patrician hands, limit effective power of doges, in Serrata del Maggior Consiglio.

1310 Disgruntled merchant Baiamonte Tiepolo leads unsuccessful uprising to overthrow doge; Venetian Inquisition founded.

1348 Black Death leaves two thirds of Venice's population dead.

1381 Venice ends long-running skirmishes with Genoa in decisive battle at Chioggia; Peace of Turin ends Genoese influence in eastern Mediterranean.

14th-15th centuries Venice expands inland, annexing modern Veneto and Venezia-Friuli-Giulia regions, fighting series of wars – with Milan and Ferrara in particular – which reshapes political power balance on mainland and stokes antagonism of other Italian powers against Venice.

1453 Turks take Constantinople, ending Venice's trading privileges.

1479 Venice loses Negroponte and some Aegean islands to Turks.

1489 Caterina Cornaro, Venetian widow of Cypriot king, hands island over to Venice.

1499 Turks seize Venetian forts in Peloponnese, control entrance to Adriatic.

1508 League of Cambrai defeats Venice at Agnadello.

1527 City hit by plague; building work begins on Santa Maria della Salute.

1571 Venice and forces of Habsburg ally Charles V beat Turks at Lepanto; Venice loses Cyprus.

1606 Centuries-old antagonism between Venice and Vatican culminates when whole city is excommunicated in argument over temporal powers of the pope; interdict lifted one year later.

1669 Crete, Venice's last possession in eastern Mediterranean, falls to Turks.

1699 Venice takes control of Morea (Peloponnese) after brilliant campaign to expel Turks.

1718 Venice returns costly, unprofitable Morea to the Turks.

1797 Last doge, Lodovico Manin, deposed by Napoleonic French troops on 12 May; Venice handed over to Austria.

1805 Napoleon annexes Venice to his Kingdom of Italy.

1815 Venice returns to Austrian control.

1846 Railway bridge built linking Venice to mainland.

1848-9 Venetian patriot Daniele Manin sets up provisional republican government.

1866 Austrians, after defeat by Prussia, hand Venice over to newly united Italy.

1932 First road bridge built.

1966 Venice badly damaged by flooding.

1992 Venice granted metropolitan status.

1996 La Fenice opera house gutted by fire.

1997 Venetian 'freedom fighters' occupy the campanile in St Mark's Square.

to dismantle churches, dissolve monasteries and redesign bits of the city, including the wide thoroughfare now known as via Garibaldi and its adjoining public gardens.

The last, ill-fated spark of Venice's ancient independent spirit flared up in 1848, when lawyer Daniele Manin (no relation of the last doge) led a popular revolt against the Austrians. An independent republican government was set up, holding out valiantly against siege and bombardment for five heroic months. It was doomed to failure from the outset, however, and the Austrians were soon firmly back in the saddle, keeping their grip on this insignificant backwater until 1866, when a weakened Austria, badly beaten on other fronts by the Prussians, handed the city over to the newly united Italian state.

Venice Today

Spared from fanciful 'development' projects, Venice remains an anachronistic mirage languishing on the fringes of a thriving industrial hub.

Immersed in the shimmering mirage which is Venice, only the most jaundiced visitor is likely to perceive anything but the overwhelming (if occasionally somewhat odorous) beauty of the lagoon city. Yet for the inhabitants of Venice and the surrounding Veneto region, this idyll is just that: a mirage. What was once a wealthy, thriving, productive city is now under-populated, over-visited, chronically polluted and increasingly depleted of any vestiges of ordinary, workaday life.

On the *terra firma* side of the lagoon, however, it's a very different story. The little-visited Veneto region – its historic towns and Palladian villas sadly overshadowed by La Serenissima – is one of Europe's most prosperous hubs of thriving high-tech industry. Sidelined by the north-eastern economic miracle, and locked in a seemingly inexorable slide towards theme park status, Venice has never been more glaringly at odds with its dominions across the water.

In fact, politically speaking, Venice's star had ceased to shine even before the city capitulated to Napoleon's troops in 1797. Under Austrian rule between 1815 and 1866, it was relegated to the status of a picturesque, inconsequential backwater. But if the city suffered, the fate of its former mainland territories was even worse: with no industry to speak of, agriculturally behind the times, and – after centuries of rule from the Doge's palace – with a massive inferiority complex to boot, the Veneto ran the semi-feudal south a close race for the title of Italy's own Third World.

Between 1876 and 1901, almost 35 per cent of the 5.2 million desperate Italians who sought a better life abroad were fleeing from the crushing poverty of the Veneto and the neighbouring Friuli region. Massive industrialisation in Venice's mainland Porto Marghera area after World War I and – more extensively – World War II served to shift the more impoverished sectors of the population from agricultural to urban areas. As recently as 1961, 48 per cent of homes in the north-east had no running water, 72 per cent had no bathroom and 86 per cent had no heating.

What the people of the Veneto did have, however, was a deep-rooted attachment to their traditional crafts, and a cussedness of character unmatched anywhere else in Italy. In the past, both proved detrimental: in the age of heavy industry, small-scale manufacturing was a sure-fire loser; and when captains of heavy industry sought meek vassals to man the furnaces, many of the natives of the Veneto who protested were forcibly deported to populate Fascist new towns in the malarial swamps south of Rome.

It was not, in fact, until the 1970s that north-eastern determination came into its own. With a growing trend towards industrial downscaling, those family-run workshops that had tightened their belts and ridden out the bad times gradually became viable business concerns. So Giuliana Benetton's humble knitting machine gave birth to a global clothing empire based in Treviso, and the metal-working lessons imparted to Leonardo del Vecchio in his orphanage spawned Luxottica, the world's biggest producer of spectacle frames, in Belluno. The Zamperla brothers, fairground tinkers and creators of merry-go-rounds in Altavilla, expanded to produce 70 per cent of all the rides for Paris' Eurodisney, and Ivano Beggio progressed from tinkering with bikes in his father's cycle shop in Noale to running Aprilia, where 60 per cent of Europe's 250cc motorbikes are churned out.

The explosion of family-run industry was immense, rapid and disastrously unchecked, turning what had been a pleasant if unvaried agricultural landscape harbouring the occasional Palladian villa into a nightmare scenario of ribbon development: expanding towns gobbled up the green belt and the stately homes, while remaining arable land soon came to look like so many back lots for the aircraft-hangar-style premises housing the machinery of the economic miracle. Today, even the smallest towns here boast anything up to one manufacturing concern per seven inhabitants.

Theories explaining the north-eastern miracle are as numerous as they are unconvincing. Most sociologists and economists agree, however, that the region's historical links across the Alps to Austria, Germany and Eastern Europe and its family ties to successful emigrants further afield gave it a vocation for exportation unmatched anywhere else in Italy. The devaluation of the lira in 1992 gave what was already a healthy local economy a big boost. Through the mid-to-late 1990s, one-third of the country's huge

balance of trade surplus was generated in the north-east, and per capita exports from here stood at twice the national average.

But back in Venice, the city that had once held the whole of the eastern Mediterranean in its hands, the situation was not looking so rosy. The odd boat was still being constructed in small shipyards, a few glass-blowing workshops were still active on the island of Murano and a small fishing fleet was still operative. But as the *terra firma* became more and more industrialised, blue-collar workers looked across the water for employment. Then, realising that housing there was cheaper, dryer and easier to park in front of, they moved out in an exodus that has brought the population of island Venice plunging from around 170,000 in 1946 to not much more than 50,000 today.

'With depopulation, the things that made Venice a real city vanished.'

As Venetians vanished from this unique gem set in a murky sea, so did the things that had made it a real – if special – city rather than a museum exhibit. In the city centre, registered plumbers have all but disappeared, and finding a litre of milk or a loaf of bread can be an arduous task. With the result, naturally, that the city that has always been a tourist trap has fallen back almost exclusively on its easiest option: fleecing foreigners.

For generations, city authorities did nothing to remedy this situation. Ignoring the sizeable and authoritative school of thought that argued that Venice would lose much of its charm if it ceased to be a working city, they concentrated on courting the visitor. Successive councils came up with such visionary ideas as facilitating transport by building a monorail above the Gothic and Renaissance *palazzi* (on pylons which, so as not to be too obtrusive, would be 'lagoon-coloured', one councillor announced), constructing a motorway with immense car parks beneath the lagoon, and whizzing tourists between the many islands that make up the old city via a hydraulic passenger transport system reminiscent of the message tubes that once buzzed overhead in department stores.

But the most outlandish scheme of all came within a hair's breadth of being realised as recently as 1992 – the year in which municipal status was conferred on Venice, giving it easier access to vast quantities of central funding for totally unsuitable projects – when city luminaries offered to drain large stretches of the lagoon for the noble purpose of staging the

Real-life issues come to the fairy-tale lagoon.

Expo to beat all Expos in the year 2000. Only a desperate, last-ditch plea to the Bureau Internationale des Expositions from environmentalists and conservationists from all over the globe stopped this catastrophe.

The driving force behind the Expo dream was Venetian *per eccellenza* Gianni de Michelis, Italy's greasy-locked disco-dancing former foreign minister. De Michelis had lofty ambitions for his beloved native city: with the fall of communism in central and eastern Europe, he had visions of Venice taking up its rightful place at the hub of a huge trade and transport network that would turn the Balkans and Mitteleuropa into the economic powerhouse of a newly-vital Old World.

Stopped in his tracks by the bloody break-up of Yugoslavia, and by interfering public prosecutors who started asking embarrassing questions about rake-offs from public works contracts, De Michelis made a hurried and ignominious exit from the Venetian and national political scene, and none too soon. In environmental terms alone, Venice will be paying the price of political cronyism for generations to come (*see chapter* **Waterland**).

In the wake of the 1993 *Tangentopoli* bribes-for-contracts scandal, which did its best to unseat a whole political class, Venetians decided to try something new. Massimo Cacciari, a university philosophy professor with a bushy black beard and a sharp tongue, was elected mayor in November 1993 – and re-elected in 1997 – at the head of a left-leaning 'civic' alliance. Cacciari began to achieve results: he kick-started long-overdue maintenance work – though with so much in need of attention, what has been done is a drop in the ocean – and started looking seriously into ways of re-injecting life into the veins of what looked increasingly like a terminally ill city.

Cacciari's administration opened up space and infrastructure at the city's mainland industrial zone in Porto Marghera to small-scale high-tech industry, in an effort to lure some of the region's booming economy lagoon-wards. The project was not a great success: the links between regional producers and their home towns are so strong that most would rather curb growth than up sticks and shift operations to devastatingly ugly Marghera.

And it initiated projects aimed at encouraging traditional Venetian crafts in the city itself, though ex-islander artisans now used to damp-free facilities on the mainland have shown a marked reluctance to relocate back to the soggy lagoon.

'The region was fast becoming Italy's biggest economic success story.'

On the mainland, on the other hand, the anti-politics backlash of the early 1990s favoured the Northern League, then a relatively new formation which, depending on the mood swings of its irascible leader Umberto Bossi, favours fiscal autonomy, federation or complete independence for the regions of the north.

That the booming north-east loathed the central powers in Rome had become evident even before *Tangentopoli*. It was easy to see their point. Though the region was fast becoming the country's biggest economic success story, it was doing it alone: public spending on roads, transport and other essential infrastructure was lower here than almost anywhere else in the country.

When, on top of this, *Tangentopoli* revelations showed how much of the north-east's hard-earned income was percolating into the pockets of politicians in Rome, it was altogether too much. For a brief period, there were many – including Cacciari – who felt moved to issue dire warnings of imminent revolution in the disgruntled north-east.

Small industrialists caused distress in Rome by threatening tax boycotts throughout the mid-1990s. In autumn 1996 Bossi led his merry men on a symbolic gambol along the River Po, declaring the 'independence' of northern Italy at a rally on the riva degli Schiavoni in Venice on 15 September. And on 9 May 1997, a commando of eight self-styled guerrillas seeking to reinstate the Repubblica Serenissima grabbed headlines when, with a home-made tank and a small collection of antique weapons, they occupied the campanile in piazza San Marco, only to be flushed out by assault troops hours later amid a barrage of press attention.

If displays of secessionist fervour have died down since this slapstick climax, the desire for greater freedom from Rome remains, and has been espoused even by those further removed from the extremes of the Northern League (which in 1998 broke off diplomatic relations with its *Liga Veneta* ally) and its crazier offshoots.

Moreover, the dawn of the 21st century has done nothing to improve the prickly relationship between declining Venice and its former *terra firma* dominions. In 2000 Cacciari stepped down as mayor to stand for election as president of the Veneto regional council, (leaving the running of the city in the lower-profile but reportedly capable hands of Paolo Costa). Cacciari's bid for the regional job was resoundingly unsuccessful, confirming widespread fears across the north-east that the involvement of Venice or its leaders in any project – be it industrial or political – is the kiss of death.

Waterland

Singin' in the Rain antics are frowned on in the watery city: locals observe high-water etiquette and always have a pair of rubber boots handy.

To say that Venetian life revolves around water is to state the glaringly obvious. The extent to which it is true, and the truly unique problems it creates are not, however, immediately evident to the visitor, bewitched by the splendour of the place and by the fun-packed novelty of canals where roads should be.

Just imagine living here. Absolutely nothing is plain sailing.

If owning a boat for puttering around the canals seems enticingly romantic, the expense of renting boat-house space, or the bureaucratic hassles of procuring a permit to moor in the waterways (places are extremely difficult to get hold of and often stay in the same family for generations) soon reduce it all to painful mundanity. Without a means of transport of your own, however, you are dependent on *vaporetti*, on hideously expensive taxis, or on the complicated business of hiring transport contractors.

Moreover, unless you're lucky enough to have a canal-side residence, there is plenty of scope for pulled muscles in those last few metres between *fondamenta* and front door. Carrying a large load of shopping back from a mainland supermarket (plus junior in a push-chair) is bad enough. But a new sofa? Or a new kitchen? Or how about if you take it into your head to completely revamp your damp and flaking apartment? The complications of any construction job are magnified ten-fold in this uniquely problematic city.

But the ancestors of today's Venetians faced even greater brain-teasers when they decided to make their homes out in the lagoon: building Venice was no easy feat. The 100 or so marshy islands on which the city stands provided no firm foundations. To get around this problem, closely packed pinewood piles measuring 7.6 metres (25 feet) were driven through the mud down to the layer of compressed clay below the lagoon to make a firm basis for the houses and *palazzi* above. Deprived of the oxygen that wood-gobbling microbes need to destroy them, the piles can last for centuries. But with subsidence, and gradual accretion of weight up top, they all need to be adjusted, added to, or eventually replaced. It's no joke having a muddy pinewood forest hauled up through the floor of your front hall.

WATER CONSERVATION

Having chosen such an unlikely place to build a city, Venice's inhabitants were faced immediately with the problem of how to keep it from sinking, silting up or going up in smoke. Their descendants are dogged by the same conundrums today.

In such a water-logged city, fire would not seem, at first glance, to be a big problem. Yet, as the sad fate of La Fenice opera house shows (it was gutted by flames in January 1996), it certainly is. To keep buildings light on their mud-and-pine foundations, interiors were built exclusively of wood (as were the exteriors of Venice's earliest dwellings).

When a lighted candle toppled over in one house, it was only a matter of minutes before flames leapt out the windows and into the palazzo across the narrow calle. Gathering

Messing about in *gondole*

Made of more than 280 pieces of oak, larch, fir, elm, walnut, cherry, lime and cedar, each shaped over a fire of marsh canes from the lagoon, the gondola has been compared to almost everything, from the inevitable coffins to butterflies, serpents and violins. In the early 20th century, Venetian industrialist Count Volpi described it simply as 'the most beautiful thing God has made'.

This archetypal Venetian craft attained its present preening shape around the 18th century. It has no keel and is slender enough to slip round even the narrowest corners of Venice's waterways (not having horns, *gondolieri* yell 'oh-eh' to signify they are about to round a blind bend). Its rakish list to starboard is designed to make it rowable by a single gondolier. It owes its funereal colour to one of Venice's many sumptuary laws, designed to crack down on potentially destabilising displays of personal wealth. These laws, passed in 1630, established not only its colour, but the material of all the furnishings. Even the gondoliers' livery was stipulated as 'cloth garments with a single row of buttons down the trousers'.

Various explanations are given for the shape of the *ferro* (bow-prong): the six

teeth are said to represent the *sestieri* (districts) of the city, with the Giudecca sticking out the other side. There is, however, a faint possibility that the *ferro* is a rare example of something Venetian that is purely ornamental and serves no practical purpose whatsoever.

Like the city it symbolises, the gondola has now given itself up almost exclusively to tourism. It is expensive, anachronistic and clichéd… which doesn't stop starry-eyed visitors in droves spending the most romantic hour of their Venetian holiday afloat.

Gondola hire

There are official gondola stops on the **fondamenta Orseolo** (map II 4A), in front of the Hotel Danieli on the **riva degli Schiavoni** (map III 1B), by the **Vallaresso** vaporetto stop (map II 4B), by the railway station (map I 1B), by the **piazzale Roma** bus terminus (map I 1C), by the **Santa Maria del Giglio** vaporetto stop (map II 3B), at the jetty at the end of the **piazzetta San Marco** (map II 4B), at the end of **calle Santa Sofia** (map I 3C) near the **Ca' D'Oro** vaporetto stop, by the **San Tomà** vaporetto stop (map II 2A), by the Bauer Grundwald hotel in **campo San Moisè** (map II 4B), and on the **riva del Carbon** at the southern end of the Rialto bridge (map I 3C).

Fares are set by the *Ente gondola* (Gondola Board; 041 528 5075); in the unlikely event that a gondolier tries to overcharge you, address complaints to the *Ente*. Prices below are for the hire of the gondola, regardless of the number of passengers (up to six).
8am-8pm: L120,000 for 50 minutes; L60,000 for each additional 25 minutes.
8pm-8am: L150,000 for 50 minutes; L75,000 for each additional 25 minutes.
24hrs - 'processions': L100,000-L120,000 for 45 minutes.

Water-borne deliveries are no easy task in this uniquely problematic city.

speed and force as more and more dry old wood went up, conflagrations could be so immense that the flames leaped from one side of the Grand Canal to the other.

Venice's fire-fighters extinguish around 300 small to medium fires each year. When the big ones happen, the real difficulties begin: on dry land, large blazes are fought from above, but there's no way a long ladder can be run up from a boat, so comparatively ineffectual jets have to be aimed from low down; then there's the challenge of getting fire-fighting boats down narrow canals; and lastly, to make life really difficult, there's always a chance that, as happened at La Fenice, canals around the fire will have been drained to dig out centuries of accumulated detritus.

In a city whose power was based on maritime communications, silt was always public enemy number one. The Venetian Republic waged a constant and remarkably successful battle against it; as early as the 14th century, the many rivers that flowed into the lagoon from the mainland were canalised, and much of their mud-bearing water was diverted away from the lagoon directly out to sea. This also kept salt levels high in the lagoon, driving away malarial mosquitoes, which flourish in fresher water.

At the seaward end of the lagoon, *La Serenissima*'s engineers scored some notable victories against another major foe: the sea. Two of the original five openings to the sea were closed off, and long sea-walls – *i murazzi* – parallel to the lagoon entrances were built as a bulwark against the unpredictable, wind-enhanced Adriatic tides. Under French (1805-14) and Austrian (1815-61) rule, the parallel sea-walls were replaced by others at right angles that naturally deepened the entrances to the lagoon, allowing new generations of larger ships (and more sea water) to enter the lagoon. Deep channels were dredged to give these ships

an easy passage through the lagoon, and – after World War II – to the mushrooming petro-chemical industrial zone on the mainland at Porto Marghera (*see chapter* **Venice Today**).

By 1980, an estimated 55 million cubic metres of mud had been dredged from the lagoon, and a third of the original wetlands had been filled in with new man-made islands such as Tronchetto and Sant'Elena (a 19th-century expansion of what was previously a tiny islet).

Nowadays, the lagoon is a patchwork of channels up to 18m (59 feet) in depth, between shallow areas which, at low tide, are knee-deep. To get a clearer picture of lagoon topography, survey it from the campanile of the church of San Giorgio Maggiore. It is easy to make out the deeper shipping lanes, which are marked by rows of *bricole*, the characteristic three- or four-pile wooden markers driven into the lagoon bed and held together at the top by an iron hoop.

The disastrous effects of all this tinkering with a delicate natural ecosystem were seen most clearly in the great flood of November 1966, when a freak tide rolled unimpeded into the lagoon, pushing water levels to almost two metres (six feet) above normal, and doing inestimable damage to the city.

Less catastrophic examples of *acqua alta* (high water, *see p28* **Acqua alta**) are a regular feature of Venetian life in winter. 'Exceptional' high tides – more than one metre (three feet) above normal lagoon level – were registered on 132 occasions between 1988 and 1997. In the two months to Christmas 2000, *acqua alta* was an almost daily occurrence; on 11 November it reached 144cm (57 inches), flooding even the city's highest areas. As the water ebbs and flows – and as Venice settles a negligible 1mm each year – the powers that be have spent decades kicking around innumerable proposals for preventing Venice from succumbing to the tides.

Acqua alta

If you're in Venice between September and April, there's a fair-to-middling chance that you're going to get your feet wet: a high tide, coupled with a wind driving against the tidal outflow from the lagoon, and the city's lowest points will disappear for a couple of hours under several inches of water.

The first you'll know about it is two or three hours before an exceptionally high tide, when sirens around the city sound five ten-second blasts. As the *acqua alta* (high water) makes its slow but inexorable way into city streets, you might like to head for the nearest shop selling rubber boots (*see chapter* **Shopping**).

How far you are inconvenienced will depend on how far the lagoon rises above its normal level. During the *acqua alta* season, trestles and wooden planks are stacked up along flood-prone thoroughfares, ready to be hurriedly transformed into raised walkways by the city rubbish department as the water level rises. If the tide rises more than 120cm above its average level, even the walkways begin to float, and you'd do well to find a nice, dry and preferably high place to sit it out until the tide ebbs.

Acqua alta has an etiquette all of its own. It is most evident on the raised walkways

where Venetians wait their turn patiently, without the pushing and jostling that mark queues for *vaporetti* or market stalls; they proceed along the narrow planks slowly and with consideration for other users; and they expect tourists to do the same or risk an angry telling-off for their lack of manners.

The etiquette extends beyond the walkways, as anyone splashing, *Singin' in the Rain* style, through the high water will find out: the *calli* and *campi* may be waterlogged, but they continue to function as a municipal road network, and local road-users are understandably peeved if thoughtless tourists prevent them from reaching their destination in as dry a state as possible. Remember, too, that during *acqua alta* you can't see where the pavement stops and the canal begins.

A map posted at each vaporetto stop – copies of which are available at APT offices (*see pxx*)– shows flood-prone areas, and routes covered by raised walkways. If you want to avoid *acqua alta* water altogether, study this map and stick to higher ground. The tide office (*Centro maree*) provides *acqua alta* forecasts in Italian only (recorded message 041 520 6344).

In 2000 a controversial and very costly project to construct mobile pontoons across the Adriatic lagoon entrances was approved (the pontoons will lie on the seabed, rising into position to block the entrances only when water levels in the lagoon rise more than one metre), but, at the time of going to press, work had not begun. Environmentalists, who have roundly condemned the pontoon plan, have long been advocating a return of the lagoon to nearer its pre-dredging state, with deep-water channels filled in, and a ban on shipping into Porto Marghera, not to mention stiffer controls on motor-powered boats in and near the city canals. The *moto ondoso* (vibrations) caused by engines is, in fact, the biggest single cause of damage to the wooden piles upon which the whole of Venice rests.

WATER POLLUTION

The particular Venetian odour that rises from the canals on a sweltering July day (or, indeed, on any kind of day in any month) is the result of an unappealing cocktail of decaying rubbish and sewage pumped straight into the water from houses built long before hygienic methods

of waste disposal were given much thought. The mixture is given extra flavour by a selection of noxious chemicals from the industrial zone on the mainland at Porto Marghera – chemicals that, environmentalists claim, are responsible for the high incidence of respiratory disorders and tumours in Venice.

After many decades during which the petrol and solvents industries across in ugly Porto Marghera were left to pollute with impunity (emissions into the air went virtually unchecked; flushing out of storage tanks and waste water directly into the lagoon was common practice), more vigilant local administrators and a new generation of determined magistrates have curtailed the worst of the excesses, to the point where even the most critical environmentalists have been forced to admit that the water quality in the lagoon is improving.

The problem of heavy metals and other health-threatening non-degradable substances lurking in the mud will remain for years to come, however; in the meantime, check that the cockles and mussels adorning the spaghetti on your plate come from well outside the lagoon area.

Architecture

Borrowings, assimilations and daylight robberies shaped architectural styles that force you to take a stand.

Venice's architecture, like much else in the maritime republic, is based on borrowings, assimilations and daylight robberies. Not content with drawing architectural inspiration from Constantinople and Rome, and decorating its *palazzi* with looted treasures, it also looked beyond the lagoon for its architects. Of the four architects who can claim to having altered the fabric of the city, two are out-of-towners: Tuscan-born Jacopo Sansovino, and Andrea Palladio, from Padua. The native talents – early Renaissance master Mauro Codussi and baroque wonderboy Baldassare Longhena – usually get second billing. Codussi was unknown until his name was unearthed from archives towards the end of the 19th century.

RUSKIN'S RUSE

In his opinionated, overlong but immensely enjoyable work *The Stones of Venice*, John Ruskin set out to discredit 'the pestilent art of the Renaissance' in favour of 'healthy and beautiful' Gothic.

Architecture in Venice forces one to take a stand. Fans of the huge scroll brackets that

pretend to support the dome of La Salute may not appreciate the Gothic rigour of the Frari or Santi Giovanni e Paolo. The hair-shirt types who get their kicks from the latter probably consider the elaborate tracery of the Ca' D'Oro way too decadent. And while few will agree with Ruskin that the polychrome exterior of Santa Maria dei Miracoli is, however pretty, 'debased in style', others will rate the vernacular architecture of the city – its worn brick wall textures, marble well-heads and randomly inlaid bits of statuary – above such chocolate-box perfection.

Medieval & Byzantine

It all started in **Torcello**, where the **Cathedral** (*see p140*), founded in 639, is the oldest surviving building on the lagoon. It has been remodelled since then – notably in the ninth and 11th centuries – but still retains the simple form of an early Christian basilica. Next door, the 11th-century church of **Santa Fosca** (*see p140*) has a Greek cross plan – also found in **San**

Giacomo al Rialto (*see p107*), traditionally supposed to be the earliest church in Venice (though the present structure dates mainly from 1071). The portico of Santa Fosca exhibits a feature that recurs in the first-floor windows of 12th-century townhouses such as Ca' Loredan or Ca' Dona della Madonetta, both on the Grand Canal – stilted arches, where horseshoe-shaped arches are supported on slender columns.

The history of Venetian domestic architecture in this early period can be charted by following the development of the arch, which is the most typically Venetian of all structural devices. This is understandable in a city built on mud, where load-bearing capabilities were a prime consideration. In the latter part of the 13th century the pure, curved Byzantine arch began to sport a point at the top, under the influence of Islamic models – early examples of this can be seen in the heavily restored Albergo del Selvadego in calle dell'Ascensione, San Marco, and Palazzo Vitturi in campo Santa Maria Formosa. Soon this point developed into a fully fledged ogee arch – a northern Gothic trait, but one that has also been found in southern Indian cave art from as early as the third century BC.

SAN MARCO

Meanwhile, the **Basilica di San Marco** (*see p76*) was into its sixth century of growth. Founded in 829-32 by the Partecipazio family, the original church was modelled on the Church of the Apostles in Constantinople. This first church burnt down, but had been rebuilt by 1075. The main body of the church – and its Greek cross plan surmounted by five domes – dates from the 11th century; but it was embellished extensively over the next four centuries, sometimes with curious results (note the curved Byzantine arches on the façade surmounted by hopeful Gothic ogees). Two humbler 12th-century churches, **San Giacomo dell'Orio** (*see p110*) and **San Nicolò dei Mendicoli** (*see p116*), both feature squat belltowers apart from the church – a key feature of the Veneto-Byzantine style.

Gothic & Late Gothic

In the 14th and 15th centuries Venetian architecture developed an individual character unmatched before or since. It was at this time – when Venice had beaten Genoa for control of eastern Mediterranean sea routes, and when the Republic was engaged in large-scale *terra firma* expansion – that the city's own Arab-tinged version of Gothic came into its own.

By the mid-14th century the ogee arch (two concave-convex curves meeting at the top)

Sansovino's **Loggetta**. *See p32*.

had sprouted a point on its concave edge – producing the cusped arch, which distributes the forces pressing down on it so efficiently that Ruskin decreed that 'all are imperfect except these'. By the beginning of the 15th century, this basic shape had been hedged around with elaborate tracery and trefoils (clover-shaped openings) and topped with Moorish-looking pinnacles in a peculiarly Venetian take on the flamboyant Gothic style, which reached its apotheosis in the façades of the **Palazzo Ducale** (*see p80*) and the **Ca' D'Oro** (*see p98*) – both completed by 1440. The Palazzo Ducale was a prime example of the Venetian faith in tradition: a design first initiated in the 1340s – possibly by stonemason Filippo Calendario – was duplicated faithfully over the following century – a meeting marked by the florid **Porta della Carta** (1438; *see p81*).

CHURCHES & SCUOLE

Outside of Saint Mark's, church architecture mainly reflected the traditional building styles of the orders who commissioned the work: the cavernous brick piles of **Santi Giovanni e Paolo** (completed in 1430; *see p92*) and the **Frari** (1433; *see p112*) are classic examples of, respectively, the Dominican and Franciscan approaches. Both have a Latin cross plan, a façade pierced by a large rose window and a generous sprinkling of pinnacles. More individual are some smaller churches such as **Santo Stefano** (*see p86*) – with its wooden ship's keel roof – and the first *scuole* (*see p63*), such as the **Scuola Vecchia della Misericordia** (*see p100*), with its ogee windows and oddly Flemish-style roof gable. Both saw the involvement of Giovanni and Bartolomeo Bon, who also worked on the Ca' D'Oro. These talented mid-15th century sculptors and masons are among the first named 'architects' that have come down to us – though the work of planning and building was still overwhelmingly collaborative at this time.

THE VENETIAN PALAZZO

Majestic Grand Canal palaces such as **Ca' Foscari** (begun in 1452) and **Palazzo Pisani Moretta** continued to indulge the need for elaborate tracery windows, but behind the façade the structure went back centuries. The Venetian palazzo was not only a place of residence; in this mercantile city, it was also the family business headquarters, and the internal division of space reflects this.

The standard layout consisted of a ground floor with storerooms surrounding a long, open *androne* – used as an entrance to the rooms above, and for loading, unloading and storing commodities; a first-floor *piano nobile* – with high ceilings – where the family had its living quarters, bisected by a huge *salone* running the whole length of the building. Above this was a floor of servants' quarters, offices and more storerooms. In the grandest *palazzi*, the *piano nobile* was sometimes spread over two floors, with the lower one reserved for receiving guests and business visitors. On the roof, between those funnel-shaped chimneys, there may have been a raised wooden balcony or *altana*, where clothes were dried and Titianesque beauties came to bleach their hair in the sun. In a city where space was at a premium, courtyards were almost unheard of; at most, the *androne* itself might become a sort of roofed-in courtyard, as at the Ca' D'Oro or Ca' Rezzonico.

Early Renaissance

Venetians were so fond of their own gracefully oriental version of Gothic that they held on to it long after the New Classicist orthodoxy had taken over central Italy. For the second half of the 15th century, emergent Renaissance forms existed alongside the Gothic swansong. Sometimes they merged or clashed in the same building, as in the church of **San Zaccaria** (*see p92*), which was begun by Antonio Gambello in 1458 in the purest of northern Gothic styles but completed by Mauro Codussi in the local Renaissance idiom he was then elaborating; the transition is embodied in the façade, which is Gothic below, Renaissance above.

Next to nothing is known about Codussi's background, save that he may have trained under Giovanni Bon. What is certain is that in 1469 he was appointed *protomagister* (works manager) for the church of **San Michele in Isola** (*see p136*), the Franciscan monastery that is now the city's island cemetery. Within ten years he had completed the first truly Renaissance building in the city. The austere Istrian marble façade with its classical elements has something pre-Palladian about it, though the curves of the pediment and buttresses are pure Codussi, adapted from a late Gothic model (cf **San Giovanni in Bragora**, completed a year after San Michele). Flexibility was the

keyword for Codussi; **Santa Maria Formosa** (*see p91*) is the most Tuscan of his churches, but in **San Giovanni Crisostomo** (built by 1504) he adopted a Greek cross plan common to the earliest Venetian churches. His *palazzi*, such as **Palazzo Corner Spinelli** or **Palazzo Vendramin Calergi** on the Grand Canal, were equally influential but equally adapted to local traditions, grafting Albertian details on to a late-Gothic layout.

LOMBARDESQUE STYLE

Codussi took over a number of projects begun by Pietro Lombardo, who represents the other strand of early Renaissance architecture in Italy. This was based on the extensive use of inlaid polychrome marble, Corinthian columns and decorated friezes, in a style that owes much to Lombardo's training as a sculptor of funerary monuments. Lombardo's masterpiece is the jewel-like church of **Santa Maria dei Miracoli** (*see p102*), but he also designed – with the help of his sons Tullio and Antonio – the lower part of the façade of the **Scuola Grande di San Marco** (*see p93*), with its delightful *trompe l'oeil* relief work. The Lombardesque style, as it was known, was all the rage for a while, producing such photogenic charmers as tiny, lopsided **Ca' Dario** on the Grand Canal (1487-92).

High Renaissance

Codussi's influence lingered well into the 16th century in the work of architects such as Guglielemo dei Grigi and Scarpagnino, both of whom have been credited with the design of the **Palazzo dei Camerlenghi** (1525-8) next to the Rialto bridge. It was around this time that piazza San Marco took on the shape we see today, with the construction of the **Procuratie Vecchie** (*see p71*) and the **Torre dell'Orologio** (*see p84*), both to designs by Codussi and both demonstrating that in the centre of civic power, loyalty to the myth of Venice tended to override architectural fashions and impose a faintly antiquarian style that looked back to the city's Veneto-Byzantine origins.

SANSOVINO & SAN MARCO

It was not until the late 1520s that something really new turned up, in the form of Jacopo Sansovino, a Tuscan sculptor and would-be architect fleeing the Sack of Rome. Perhaps it was the influence of his new-found friends Pietro Aretino and Titian that secured him the prestigious position of *proto* of Saint Mark's only two years after his arrival, despite his lack of experience; certainly the gamble paid off, as

Sansovino went on to create a series of buildings that changed the face of the city. He began to refine his rational, harmonious Renaissance style in designs for the church of **San Francesco della Vigna** (begun in 1532; *see p90*) and **Palazzo Corner della Ca' Grande** on the Grand Canal, Venice's first Roman-style palazzo, which owes a heavy debt to Bramante. But it was in piazza San Marco that Sansovino excelled himself, in three buildings all planned in the course of two years, 1536 and 1537. **La Zecca** (*see p84*) – the state mint – with its heavy rustication and four-square solidity, is a perfect financial fortress. The **Biblioteca Marciana** (*see p72*) next door (completed in 1554, also known as the Libreria Sansoviniana), which faces the **Doge's Palace**, is his masterpiece, disguising its classical regularity beneath a typically Venetian wealth of surface detail. Finally, the little **Loggetta** (*see p77*) at the base of the Campanile showed that Sansovino was also capable of a lightness of touch that derived from his sculptural training.

PALLADIAN PRE-EMINENCE

Michele Sanmicheli, primarily a military architect, built the imposing sea defences on the island of Le Vignole, and two hefty Venetian *palazzi*, the **Palazzo Corner Mocenigo** (1559-64) in campo San Polo and the **Palazzo Grimani** (1556-75) on the Grand Canal. But it was another out-of-towner, Andrea Palladio, who would set the agenda for what was left of the 16th century (*see chapter* **Palladian Villas**). A star in his adopted town of Vicenza, the man who invented the post-Renaissance found it difficult to get a foothold in a city that valued flexibility above critical rigour. But he did design two influential churches: **San Giorgio Maggiore** (begun in 1562; *see p129*), and the **Redentore** (1577-92; *see p128*), the architect's most satisfying Venetian commission. Anyone who considers Palladio's designs to be over-simplistic should observe the subtle play of levels and orders on the exterior; this is one of the few churches in Venice that manages to re-create – on a much smaller scale and in an entirely different idiom – the multi-layered feel of the Basilica di San Marco. The church of the **Zitelle** (*see p127*), also on the Giudecca, was built to Palladio plans after the architect's death.

Palladio's pupil and follower Vincenzo Scamozzi designed the **Procuratie Nuove** (*see p71*) to complete the north side of piazza San Marco, which he helped to finish. At the same time, Antonio Da Ponte was commissioned to design a stone bridge at the **Rialto** (*see p68*) in 1588 after designs by Michelangelo and Palladio had been turned down.

La Salute: twirly bits in abundance.

Baroque

The examples of Sansovino and Palladio continued to be felt well into the 17th century, though buildings such as **Palazzo Balbi** (1582-90) on the Grand Canal, by Alessandro Vittoria, showed the first signs of a transition to baroque opulence. But it wasn't until the arrival on the scene of Baldassare Longhena in the 1620s that Venice got twirly bits in any abundance. Longhena was a local boy who first made his mark with the **Duomo** (*see p134*) in Chioggia. But it was with the church of **Santa Maria della Salute** (*see p123*) that he pulled out all the stops, creating perhaps the greatest baroque edifice outside of Rome. Commissioned in 1632, and 50 years in the making, this huge church dominates the southern reaches of the Grand Canal. Longhena's circular structure updates the Palaeochristian church plan so as to give it a theatrical vocation.

While La Salute was going up, Longhena was also busy designing a series of impressive *palazzi* for rich clients, including the Palazzo Belloni Battagia at San Stae and the huge Grand Canal hulk of **Ca' Pesaro** (begun in 1652; *see 109*). He also designed the façade of the **Ospedaletto** (1667-74; *see p89*), with its grotesque telamons.

This was a taste of things to come: the overwrought façade developed in the 1670s through the exuberance of the **Scalzi** (*see p98*) and **Santa Maria Del Giglio** (*see p87*) churches – both the work of Longhena's follower Giuseppe Scalzi – to the bombastic absurdity of **San Moisè** (*see p87*), a kitsch collaboration between Alessandro Tremignon and sculptor Heinrich Meyring.

Neoclassicism

During the 18th-century decline, tired variations on Palladio and Longhena dominated the scene. Domenico Rossi adorned Palladian orders with swags and statuary in the façades he designed for the churches of **San Stae** (1709-10; *see p111*) and the **Gesuiti** (1715-28; *see p101*). Sumptuous palaces continued to go up along the Grand Canal; one of the last was the solid **Palazzo Grassi** (*see p86*), built between 1748 and 1772. It was designed by Giorgio Massari, the most successful of the city's 18th-century architects. Massari also designed the church of **La Pietà** (*see p95*) – the Vivaldi church – the oval floorplan of which strikes a rare note of originality (though it may have been copied from a church by Sansovino that was swept away by Napoleon). The **Palazzo Venier dei Leoni** – now home to the Peggy Guggenheim Collection (*see p122*) – also dates from the mid-18th century. If it had ever been finished, this huge palazzo would have been as boring as Palazzo Grassi, but funds ran out after the first storey, giving Venice one of its most bizarrely endearing landmarks.

Giannantonio Selva's **La Fenice** opera house (1790-2; *see p87*) – reduced to a burnt-out shell on the night of 29 January 1996 – was one of the Serene Republic's last building projects. The arrival of Napoleon in 1797 was marked as much by destruction – of churches and convents – as by architectural progress, though a result of the clearances was the creation of the city's first public gardens, the **Giardini Pubblici** (*see p94*), and the nearby via Garibaldi. Piazza San Marco took on its present-day appearance at this time, too, when the Procuratie Vecchie and Nuove were united by the neoclassical **Ala Napoleonica** (*see p71, p79*). Restoration rather than building dominated the Austrian

occupation of Venice (1815-66). One project, though, put an end to the city's long history of isolation: the construction of the railway bridge linking Venice to Mestre, from 1841 to 1842.

SINCE THE RISORGIMENTO

Curiously, the years when Venice became a part of modern Italy were also the years when it began to rediscover its Gothic and Byzantine past. An example is the **Palazzo Franchetti** next to the Ponte dell'Accademia, a 15th-century edifice redesigned in neo-medieval style (1878-82) by opera composer and librettist Camillo Boito. One of the city's most elegant neo-Gothic constructions is the cemetery of **San Michele** (1872-81; *see p135*), whose pinnacle-and-arch brick facing dominates the northern lagoon view. Another landmark from the same period is the **Molino Stucky** (1897-1920; *see p127*), a huge pasta mill and grain silo at the western end of the Giudecca designed in turreted Hanseatic Gothic style by Ernest Wullekopf. The turn of the century was also a boom time for hotels, with the **Excelsior** on the Lido (1898-1908; *see p47*) setting the eclectic, Moorish-Byzantine agenda.

Shortage of space has meant that modern architecture has made a minimal impact. Only locally born modernist Carlo Scarpa (*see p267*) – a master of multi-faceted interiors – had a chance to build up a body of work, with the Olivetti showroom (1957-8) in piazza San Marco, the ground-floor reorganisation of the **Museo Querini Stampalia** (1961-3; *see p90*), and the atrium of the University Institute of Architecture (1985). There are also one or two adventurous public housing projects around outlying areas of the city or lagoon, such as Giancarlo De Carlo's low-income housing on the island of Mazzorbo (1979-86), an asymmetrical arrangement inspired by the colourful domestic architecture of Burano.

Don't miss **Ruskin recommends**

Palazzo Ducale
'It is the central building of the world.' *See p80.*

St Mark's Basilica
'A treasure-heap, it seems, partly of gold, and partly of mother-of-pearl... a confusion of delight.' *See p76.*

Santa Maria Assunta
'Nothing is more remarkable than the finish and beauty of all the portions of the building.' *See p140.*

Palazzo Grimani
'There is not an erring line, nor a mistaken proportion, throughout its noble front.' *See p67.*

Santa Maria dei Miracoli, Scuola Grande di San Marco
'The two most refined buildings in this style [Renaissance grafted on Byzantine] in Venice are the small Church of the Miracoli and the Scuola di San Marco.' *See p100, p93.*

Venetian Painting

If you thought workshop assistants and clever marketing were an invention of the Young British Artists, think again. What's more, the Venetians knew how to paint.

That foreign collectors – and in particular the greatest and most peremptory collector of all, Napoleon Bonaparte – deprived Venice of many of its masterpieces is hard to believe as you enter one more marvel-packed church, or experience yet another major museum. The acres of painted canvas and wood panel that remain in the lagoon city may be a fraction of what existed in former times, but it's a glorious fraction, displayed against a peerless backdrop, and often – uniquely – in the very settings for which the works were created.

One of the pleasures of the backstreets of Venice is discovering pictures in obscure churches. Seeing these paintings in their original sites reveals how aware painters were of the relation of their works to the surrounding architecture, light and existing pictures. Yet, exceptionally, the paintings also relate to the physical context of Venice itself. What makes

Venetian painting distinctive – the decorated surfaces, asymmetry, shimmering light effects and, above all, warm tonalities – can also be found in the lagoon environment. Venetian visual culture in the Renaissance encompassed the richness of Byzantine mosaics and Islamic art; the haphazard arrangement of streets and canals with strong shadows; and light experienced through haze or reflected off moving water.

Venetian painting began with mosaics. The glittering 12th- and 13th-century mosaics of San Marco or Torcello provided a visual model of shimmering splendour and a repertory of stories that later painters drew upon for narrative paintings. Although the execution of mosaics was entrusted to specialists, important painters contributed designs.

Venetian church interiors were once covered with frescos; the damp Venetian climate has meant that very few survive. The official history of Venetian painting begins in the 1320s with the first painter to emerge from medieval anonymity, **Paolo Veneziano** (c1290-1362), who worked in egg tempera on wood panel. He championed the composite altarpiece, which would become one of the key formats of Venetian painting. His polyptychs, such as *The Coronation of the Virgin* in the Accademia, were ornately framed, compartmentalised works featuring sumptuous fabrics, a preference for surface decoration and pattern over depth, and a seriousness – or stiffness – derived from Byzantine icons. A love of drapery and textile patterns proved to be a Venetian constant, still visible in Veronese's paintings in the 16th century and in Tiepolo's in the 18th.

Although many painters worked in Venice in the century after Paolo, the next major legacy was that of a team, **Giovanni d'Alemagna** (John of Germany) and his brother-in-law **Antonio Vivarini**, who were active in the mid-15th century. Their three altarpieces in San Zaccaria (dated 1443), one in San Pantalon, and a large canvas in the Accademia demonstrate the transition from Gothic to Renaissance. All have benefited from recent restorations that recapture the original courtly elegance and three-dimensional details in *pastiglia* (raised ornament). Although Italian art historians give precedence to Antonio, the sudden decline in the quality of his works after Giovanni's death in 1450 indicates that his partner was the brains behind the operation. Antonio's younger brother **Bartolomeo Vivarini**, who ran the family workshop from the 1470s until about 1491, learned Renaissance style from both painting and sculpture, as seen in the lapidary figures in the altarpiece (1474) in the Cappella Corner of the Frari.

By the next generation, the main players become more clearly defined. From about 1480 **Giovanni Bellini** directed the dominant workshop in Venice. Most of Bellini's sizeable output, stretching from the late 1450s until his death in 1516, was painted on wood panel rather than the newer canvas. He cornered the market in small devotional panels commissioned by cultivated private clients. The important group of early Bellini pictures in the Museo Correr and the many variations on the Madonna and Child theme in the Accademia show how varied and moving these subjects could be. Equally impressive is Bellini's stunning series of altarpieces. In these he perfected the subject of the *Sacra Conversazione* (Sacred Conversation), where standing saints flank a seated figure, usually the Virgin Mary, within a setting that evokes the gold mosaics and costly marbles of the basilica di San Marco. The inner glow afforded

by the new medium of oil paint allowed Bellini to model his figures with an astonishing delicacy of light and shadow. One can follow his progress through a series of altarpieces that remain *in situ*: in Santi Giovanni e Paolo, the Frari, San Zaccaria and San Giovanni Crisostomo. A letter home by German painter Albrecht Dürer in 1506 shows that Bellini's fame was great in his own lifetime: 'Giovanni Bellini is very old but he is still the best painter of all.' (And if you like the paintings, you'll love the cocktail.)

Giovanni's elder brother, **Gentile Bellini**, enjoyed even greater official success: from 1474 until his death in 1507 he directed the decoration of the Palazzo Ducale, replacing crumbling frescos with huge canvases. He also performed a diplomatic role for the Venetian government by travelling to Constantinople in 1479 to paint for the Ottoman sultan. Although his Palazzo Ducale canvases were destroyed by fire in 1577, his *Procession in Piazza San Marco* (1496), now in the Accademia, shows his ability to depict sumptuous public spectacle with choreographed verve.

Three painters born in the second half of the 15th century and active in the 16th are worth seeking out. **Cima da Conegliano** (c1459-1517) offers a stiffer style than Bellini, with figures standing in dignified repose against crisp landscapes. Cima's best altarpieces, in the Accademia, and at San Giovanni in Bragora, the Madonna dell'Orto, and the Carmini, all demonstrate a mastery of light.

Vittore Carpaccio (c1465-1525) specialised in narrative works for the *scuole*. These canvases tell a story from left to right, and offer enough miscellaneous detail to immerse the viewer in the daily life of Renaissance Venice. Two intact cycles from around 1500 are among the treasures of Venetian painting: the St Ursula cycle in the Accademia, and that of St George and St Jerome in the Scuola di San Giorgio degli Schiavoni. A striking *Supper at Emmaus* (1513) in the church of San Salvador, recently restored and now attributed to Carpaccio, continues the anecdotal detail in a surprisingly monumental vein.

Lorenzo Lotto (c1480-1556), active throughout the first half of the 16th century, spent much of his career outside Venice: he was an entrepreneur who knew how to create markets in provincial centres. His best altarpieces in Venice, in the Carmini and Santi Giovanni e Paolo, combine an uncanny accuracy in rendering landscape or cloth with a deeply felt spirituality. His impressive portraits – like the *Portrait of a Youth* in the Accademia – employ an unusual horizontal format and convey a seemingly modern melancholy.

At the beginning of the 16th century, Venetian painting took a dramatic turn. Three of Bellini's pupils – Giorgione, Sebastiano del Piombo and Titian – experimented with new secular subject matter and new ways of handling paint. **Giorgione** (c1477-1510) remains one of the great enigmas of art. No other reputation rests on so few surviving pictures. The hard contours and emphasis on surface pattern seen in earlier Venetian painting here soften, and for the first time the atmosphere becomes palpable, like damp lagoon air. Two haunting pictures in the Accademia, *The Tempest* and *La Vecchia*, may be deliberately enigmatic, more concerned with mood than story. It can be argued that the modern concept of the painting was born in Venice around 1500. For the first time, three conditions that we now take for granted were met: these works were all oil on canvas, painted at the artist's initiative, and not for a specific location.

Sebastiano del Piombo (c1485-1547) left his mark with a similar emphasis on softened contour and tangible atmosphere. His major altarpiece, painted some time around 1507 and still in San Giovanni Crisostomo, shows a *Sacra Conversazione* in which some of the figures are seen in profile, rather than head on, and hidden in shadow. Even more exciting is a set of standing saints painted as organ shutters, now in the Accademia, which show an unprecedented application of thick paint (*impasto*).

Events conspired to boost the early career of **Titian** (Tiziano Vecellio, c1488-1576; *see also* **Don't miss: Titian's best** *p125*) when, in the space of only six years (1510-16), Giorgione fell victim to the plague, Sebastiano del Piombo moved to Rome and Giovanni Bellini died. Titian soon staked his claim with a

dynamic *Assumption of the Virgin* for the high altar of the Frari (1518). There he dominated the enormous space by creating the largest panel painting in the world. Although Titian gained fame throughout Europe for his portraits and mythological paintings, no examples of these survive in Venice. The lagoon city is, however, the place to appreciate *in situ* the 70-year span of his religious work. These include a second altarpiece in the Frari (the *Madonna di Ca'Pesaro*, which is a *Sacra Conversazione* rotated on its axis), the virile *St Christopher* fresco in the Palazzo Ducale and the ceiling paintings in the sacristy of the Salute.

By the 1560s, in works such as the extraordinary *Annunciation* in San Salvador, Titian's handling of paint had become so loose that forms were not so much defined by contours as caressed into being. Line was replaced by quivering patches of warm colouring. Canvas, which had originally been seen as a cheap and durable substitute for fresco or wood, was now a textured surface to exploit. Contemporaries swore that the old artist painted as often with his fingers as with the brush. Nowhere is this tactile quality more apparent than in Titian's final painting, a *Pietà*, originally intended for his tomb, and now in the Accademia. Left unfinished at his death during the plague of 1576, this picture summarises the Venetian artistic tradition, with its glittering mosaic dome and forms so dissolved as to challenge the very conventions of painting.

Instead of mourning Titian's death, Jacopo Robusti (c1518-94) – better known as **Tintoretto** – probably breathed a sigh of relief. Though he rose to fame in the late 1540s, he had to wait until he was 58 years old before he could claim the title of Venice's greatest living painter. Yet Tintoretto was canny

Paolo Veneziano: *Coronation of the Virgin.*

enough to learn from his rival. He supposedly inscribed the motto 'The drawing of Michelangelo and the colouring of Titian' on the wall of his studio. Tintoretto's breakthrough work, *The Miracle of the Slave* (1548), in the Accademia, offered a brash attempt at this synthesis, combining Michelangelo's confident muscular anatomies with Titian's shimmering paint surface. Tintoretto's huge figures engaged in violent action also marked the end of the decorative narrative painting tradition perfected by Carpaccio.

Unlike Titian, Tintoretto is an artist who can only be appreciated in Venice. Among the dozens of works in his home town, the soaring choir paintings in the Madonna dell'Orto (c1560) or the many canvases at the Scuola Grande di San Rocco (1564-87) amaze in their scale and complexity. Tintoretto offered his clients free pictures or steep discounts, revealing a knack for marketing. His many workshop assistants, including two sons and a daughter, allowed Tintoretto to increase production to unprecedented quantities. Like his contemporaries Bassano and Veronese, Tintoretto went even further than Titian in the liberation of the brush stroke. Rough brushwork and *impasto* served as a sort of signature for these artists. The tradition of bravura handling that goes from Rubens to Delacroix to De Kooning begins with the action painters of 16th-century Venice. (*See also* **Top five Tintorettos** *p82*.)

Paolo Veronese (1528-88) made his impact in Venice with a love of rich fabrics and elegant poses that contrasts with Tintoretto's agitated

Buyer's market

In art-filled Renaissance Europe, no city could compete with Venice as a market for art. Government and institutions, which awarded commissions by committee, preferred consensus among artists and tended to perpetuate conservative taste.

Private patrons, on the other hand, were less constrained. Without a ruling family to set an aesthetic standard, dozens of noble families and a vast middle class assured a diverse market for pictures. Paintings could be found at prices so low that 90 per cent of artisan households owned one (usually a Madonna), while nobles decorated their *palazzi* with upmarket pictures, and fretted over attributions.

In the early 16th century, discriminating Venetians began to value the artist's name more than the subject matter; the pleasure derived from owning a 'Bellini' or a 'Giorgione' established modern art collecting.

This market attracted talented artists from out of town, fostering ruthless competition. The painters' guild repeatedly protested against outside competition, and newcomers felt the squeeze, as a 1506 letter by Dürer indicates: 'The painters here, let me tell you, are very unfriendly to me. They have summoned me three times before the magistrates, and I have had to pay four florins to their *scuola*.'

Disagreement over prices sometimes led painters and patrons to resort to impartial arbiters. That painters like Lotto often accepted lower valuations suggests that buyers had the upper hand.

A painter's fame naturally affected his ability to negotiate prices. A marvellous early work by newcomer Tintoretto, the *Presentation of the Virgin* (c1552) in the Madonna dell'Orto, was one of the great bargains of the Renaissance. For the large, two-sided work (now displayed in the church as three separate pictures), Tintoretto received only 35 ducats, a cask of wine and two bushels of flour. (In the same years, the foreman of the Arsenale received an annual salary of 100 ducats, plus a residence and perks.) A decade later Veronese was able to conclude a much more lucrative deal. According to the 1562 contract for a huge *Marriage at Cana* for the monastery refectory at San Giorgio Maggiore, the monks agreed to give the painter 324 ducats, a cask of wine and his meals, even supplying him with canvas and stretcher.

Veronese's vast picture (6.6 x 9.9 m) aroused much admiration (Napoleon was so impressed, he later stole it for the Louvre), but for hundreds of years, painting was considered a poor cousin to sculpture. The five under-life-size bronze figures by Girolamo Campagna for the high altar of San Giorgio Maggiore offer a revealing example. Although Campagna had to supply the materials, the 1592 contract assigned the sculptor 1650 ducats – more than five times the price of the giant Veronese canvas in the monastery next door. The high cost of marble and bronze meant that buying pictures, even immense ones, was a relative bargain.

figures. Veronese's *savoir-faire* is best seen in the overpopulated feasts he painted for monastery refectories. The example in the Accademia got its painter into hot water. When confronted by the Inquisition in 1573 over a *Last Supper* in which figures of 'buffoons, drunkards, Germans, dwarfs' apparently insulted church decorum, Veronese pleaded artistic licence. He cleverly got around the Inquisition's command to alter the picture by changing the title to *The Feast in the House of Levi*. Veronese's wit can also be seen in one of the few great 16th-century mythological paintings remaining in Venice: *The Rape of Europa* in the Palazzo Ducale, with its leering, slightly comical bull. His supreme ensemble piece is in San Sebastiano, a church that features altars, ceilings, frescos and organ shutters all painted by Veronese, as well as the artist's tomb.

Venetian painting was also practised outside of Venice: **Jacopo Bassano** (c1510-92) was an artist based in a provincial centre who kept pace with the latest innovations. Although his work is best seen in his hometown of Bassano del Grappa (*see p264*), canvases in the Accademia and an altarpiece in San Giorgio Maggiore display characteristic Venetian flickering brushwork and dramatic chiaroscuro.

With the following generation, the golden age of Venetian painting drew to a close. The super-prolific **Palma il Giovane** (c1548-1628), who completed Titian's *Pietà*, now in the Accademia, created works loosely in the style of Tintoretto. His finest pictures, such as the *Crucifixion* in the Madonna dell'Orto or those in San Giacomo dell'Orio or the Oratorio dei Crociferi, all date from the 1580s. After the deaths of Veronese and Tintoretto it seems that the pressure was gone and the quality of Palma's work took a nose-dive.

In the years that followed, the baroque in Venice was represented largely by out-of-towners (**Luca Giordano**, whose recently restored altarpieces adorn the Salute) or by

Titian's *Annunciation* in San Rocco.

bizarre posturing (Gian Antonio Fumiani's stupefying canvas ceiling in San Pantalon). Exaggerated light effects ruled the day. It was only at the beginning of the 18th century, as Venetian political and economic power slipped away, that Venetian painting experienced a resurgence. In the first half of the century, **Giambattista Piazzetta** (1683-1754) produced a ceiling painting in Santi Giovanni e Paolo and a sequence of altarpieces (particularly those in Santa Maria della Fava, the Gesuati, and San Salvador), all demonstrating restrained elegance and a muted palette of gold, black and brown. He enlivened otherwise static compositions by placing the figures in a zigzag arrangement.

Giambattista Tiepolo (1696-1770), the greatest painter of the Venetian rococo, adapted Piazzetta's zigzag scheme for use with warm pastel colours. In his monumental ceilings in the Gesuati, the Pietà and Ca' Rezzonico, Tiepolo reintroduced fresco on a large scale after more than two centuries of canvas ceilings. Perhaps the most satisfying place to view Tiepolo is the upper room of the Scuola Grande dei Carmini (1744), where the disproportionately low ceiling provides a close-up view of his technique. The essence of the Venetian rococo is to be found in the sites where architecture, sculpture and painting were employed to form a unified whole: the Gesuati, Santa Maria della Fava, San Stae and Ca' Rezzonico.

In the 18th century, both local and foreign collectors provided a constant demand for portraits and city views. A woman artist, **Rosalba Carriera** (1675-1757), developed a refined style of portrait using pastels. **Canaletto** (1697-1768; *see picture p34*) and **Guardi** (1712-93) offered views of Venice, respectively in sharp focus and softly blurred. The popularity of these landscape paintings as Grand Tour souvenirs means that although examples exist in the Accademia and Ca'Rezzonico, both artists are seen at their best in Britain. A different aspect of 18th-century painting, and perhaps Guardi's masterpiece, can be seen in the astonishingly delicate *Stories of Tobias* (1750-3) decorating the organ loft in the church of Angelo Raffaele. **Pietro Longhi** (1702-85) was a sort of Venetian Hogarth, painting amusing, naïve genre scenes in which the social life of his day was gently satirised.

By the time of Napoleon's conquest in 1797, Venetian painting, like Venetian military power, was a spent force. The capital of the art world in the 19th century was Paris. Over the following 200 years, Venice's unique setting and collections have proved a magnet for foreign artists; Venice now exhibits painters, rather than producing them.

Literary Venice

It may have produced few literary stars of its own, but the lagoon city has attracted an entire firmament.

Most people would be hard put to it to name three famous Venetian writers. A little brain-racking might eventually bring up the names of **Marco Polo**, **Casanova** (pictured above) and **Goldoni** – but only one of these is primarily known for his literary works. Literature was perhaps too private an art for this most public and vaunting of cities. If other writers cared to come here, that was fine by Venice – particularly if their presence enhanced the city's image.

Venetian literary sensibility can perhaps be judged by the fact that when the poet Petrarch left his library to the city in gratitude for its hospitality, the city subsequently appears to have mislaid it. It was not, in fact, till the advent of printing, and its lucre-generating potential, that Venice really awoke to the

virtues of books. In the 15th and 16th centuries, partly thanks to the relative laxity of its censorship, Venice was one of the most important centres of the European printing trade, with over 100 active presses producing books in dozens of different languages. Apart from anything else, printed books were then objects of great beauty – and catching the eye was (and still is) Venice's speciality.

But if Venice hasn't bred many writers, it has attracted them. And often enough disgusted them (*see p40* **Love it or hate it**). This is particularly true of English writers, who have been swaying between love and loathing, romantic admiration and puritan disapproval, for centuries now.

Venice really enters English literature with Shakespeare. He never actually set foot here, but nonetheless the city of *The Merchant of Venice* and *Othello* is a more fully realised place than, say, the Sicily of *Much Ado About Nothing*. Clearly Venice was already as powerful an image abroad as New York is today; the Rialto bridge and gondolas could be mentioned as casually as Brooklyn Bridge and yellow cabs. Shakespeare's Venice is very much a mercantile city, as well as an imperial one, defending Christianity against the Turks. There are no sunsets over the lagoon, no gondola serenades. Venice is the city of deals, of exchanges, of bonds – and of law, which cannot in any circumstances be impeached, 'Since that the trade and profit of the city/Consisteth of all nations.' But it is also a place of licentiousness and scheming, where people are not necessarily what they seem. To use Iago's definition of Desdemona, the typical citizen is a 'super-subtle Venetian'.

The first detailed description by an English visitor was that of the insatiable literary traveller **Thomas Coryat**, who set out on foot from Odcombe in Devon in 1608. Coryat furnishes one of the first of many gobsmacked-tourist descriptions of Venice (*see below* **Love it or hate it**). He dazedly records the precious stones and marbles, assesses the bell-tower, counts the churches. Everything is tested and measured (he flings his arms round pillars), including the famous courtesans: 'As for herself, she comes to thee decked like the queen and goddess of love… Also the ornaments of her body are so rich, that except thou dost even geld thy affections… she will very near benumb and captivate thy senses. For thou shalt see her decked with many chains of gold and oriental pearl like a second Cleopatra.'

It's difficult not to see an association with the city here – enchantingly bedecked in riches. But Coryat gives fair warning: 'If thou shouldest wantonly converse with her, and not give her that *salarium iniquitatis*, which thou hast promised her… she will either cause thy throat to be cut, or procure thee to be arrested…' Just in case we were getting the wrong idea, he adds hastily: 'Because I have related so many particulars of them, as few Englishmen that have lived many years in Venice can do the like… I believe thou wilt cast an aspersion of wantonness upon me and say that I could not know all these matters without mine own experience. I answer thee that although I might have known them without my experience, yet for my better satisfaction, I went to one of their noble houses (I will

Love it or hate it

Abhorrent, green slippery city or Paradise? The jury's out…

FOR

Thomas Coryat *Coryat's Crudities* (1611)
Such is the rarenesse of the situation of Venice, that it doth even amaze and drive into admiration all strangers that upon their first arrival behold the same.

Lord Byron
Venice & I agree very well – in the mornings I study Armenian – & in the evenings I go out sometimes – & indulge in coition always.

IN UN MAI SPENTO AMORE PER VENEZIA
EZRA POUND
TITANO DELLA POESIA
QUESTA CASA ABITÓ PER MEZZO SECOLO
COMUNE DI VENEZIA

Charles Dickens
The gorgeous and wonderful reality of Venice is beyond the fancy of the wildest dreamer. Opium couldn't build such a place…

John Ruskin
Thank God I am here; it is the Paradise of cities.

Ezra Pound
Venice is an excellent place to come to from Crawfordsville, Indiana (270).

William Sansom
The centre that glitters like a diamond – austerely hard, but gleaming sensuous – a radiant terraqueous jewel.

AGAINST

William Shakespeare *Othello*
In Venice they do let God see the pranks They dare not show their husbands; their best conscience Is not to leave undone, but keep unknown.

Edward Gibbon *Memoirs of My Life*
The spectacle of Venice afforded some hours of astonishment and some days of disgust….

confess) to see the manner of their life, and observe their behaviour.' The eternal tourist, watching the glass-blowing but never buying.

In the more cynical 18th century, wariness predominated over bedazzlement. Venice was viewed less as a real place and more as a metaphor – usually a negative one. English travellers set their burgeoning sense of national self-importance against Venice's decline. This admonitory use of the city was to culminate in the works of **John Ruskin**, whose whole theory of architecture – elaborated at enormous length in *The Stones of Venice* – sprang out of his need to demonstrate that the Venetian Gothic architecture of the 13th and 14th centuries was a sign of moral and intellectual health, while the classicism of the Renaissance and its elaboration in the baroque was the objective correlative of the city's slide into decadence.

During the period of the Grand Tour the English came to Italy as to a great museum, picking up fragments of culture, works of art and Italian vices. Venice gets one contemptuous mention in **Alexander Pope**'s *Dunciad*, as a place of languorous dissoluteness, while **Edward Gibbon** was even more dismissive (*see p40* **Love it or hate it**).

And even those who came specifically in search of its dissolute pleasures were soon fed up. **James Boswell** wrote: 'For the first week I was charmed by the novelty and beauty of so singular a city, but I soon wearied of travelling continually by water, shut up in those lugubrious gondolas.' It was already a cliché to compare gondolas with coffins.

Enthusiasm returned with the Romantics. Suddenly, decadence was the whole point. Where Gibbon had snorted, writers such as **William Beckford**, **Lord Byron** and **Percy Shelley** thrilled. They went in search of shudders by visiting the prisons of the Palazzo Ducale; they saw romance in the double aspect of decay and splendour, in the mix of nature and art.

Byron is the most interesting expatriate writer of the period – mainly because he had a twofold reaction to Venice's twofold aspects. In his immensely fashionable and immensely successful poem *Childe Harold's Pilgrimage* – a sort of cross between *A Year in Provence* and *Fear and Loathing in Las Vegas* – he draws Venice as a dream; the city is depopulated, seen at 'airy distance' as if conjured up by an enchanter's wand. Its past is the melodramatic one of the 'anti-myth': the dungeons, the Council

---

stinking ditches dignified with the pompous denomination of Canals; a fine bridge spoilt by two Rows of houses upon it, and a large square decorated with the worst Architecture I ever yet saw...

Lord Byron
Marino Faliero
Thou den of drunkards with the blood of princes! Gehenna of the waters! Thou sea-Sodom!

Percy Bysshe Shelley
I had no conception of the excess to which avarice, cowardice, superstition, ignorance, passionless lust, & all the inexpressible brutalities which degrade human nature could be carried, until I had lived a few days among the Venetians.

Robert Browning
As for Venice and its people, merely born to bloom and drop,
Here on earth they bore their fruitage, mirth and folly were the crop,
What of soul was left, I wonder, when the kissing had to stop.

Ralph Waldo Emerson
It is a great oddity – a city for beavers – but to my thought a most disagreeable residence... there is always a slight smell of bilgewater about the thing.

Mark Twain *A Tramp Abroad*
She... is become... a peddler of glass beads for women and trifling toys and trinkets for school-girls and children.

Henry James
The Venice of to-day is a vast museum where the little wicket that admits you is perpetually turning and creaking, and you march through the institution with a herd of fellow-gazers.

DH Lawrence
Lady Chatterley's Lover
Abhorrent green, slippery city, Whose Doges were old and had ancient eyes.

Thomas Mann
This was Venice, this the fair frailty that fawned and that betrayed, half fairy-tale, half snare...

of Ten, vendettas, stilettos, anonymous denunciations. It is a purely literary creation, based more on a self-propagating writerly tradition than on observation.

But in *Beppo*, also written in 1818 – Byron draws a very different picture, describing Venice at Carnival time: in this version, a menacing Turk turns out to be a lost husband; and when this husband finds his wife has taken a lover, no stilettos are pulled; instead they discuss the situation over coffee and all three then settle down to live together happily ever after (a more or less realistic picture of the ménage that the poet enjoyed in Venice with his landlord's wife Marianna Segati and her condescending husband). This is the realistically low-key, chatty Venice to be found in **Goldoni**'s comedies (which Byron enjoyed).

Byron enjoyed the contrast with England, the 'tight little island' he had left – and appreciated the tolerance of Venetian society, where 'a woman is virtuous (according to the code) who limits herself to her husband and one lover – those who have two, three or more are a little wild.' He continued to mine the Venetian seam in his lugubrious historical verse dramas *The Two Foscari* and *Marino Faliero* (both 1821).

Byron became one of the legends of Venice – and he ably fed the myth with his feats of strength and cultivated eccentricities, which included swimming from the Lido all the way down the Grand Canal, keeping a menagerie of monkeys, dogs and foxes, and swimming home from amorous *conversazioni*, pushing a candle in front of him on a little board. In the end, of course, he became weary and was ready to find consolation in his last and faithful attachment to Teresa Guiccioli, with whom he left the city.

Throughout the 19th century travellers drifted through Venice in their closed gondolas, apparently having no contact with the inhabitants. In their accounts of their visits, they fall into swoons or trances; the city casts its spell, enchants them or mesmerises them. 'Je végète, je me repose, j'oublie,' murmurs **George Sand** tipsily. It is Turner's Venice they describe: a dreamscape where the buildings seem less substantial than the dazzling light and shimmering water, where the *palazzi* and churches merge mirage-like into their reflections.

In **Dickens**' *Pictures From Italy* the chapter devoted to Venice is entitled 'An Italian dream'. Dickens recounts the experience of floating through the city, even through St Mark's, which loses its solidity, and is described in terms of colour, perfumes, obscurity; in the end, he gives up trying to describe and merely babbles: 'unreal, fantastic, solemn, inconceivable throughout…'

The strongest reaction to all this came from **Ruskin**. He can be prejudiced, inconsistent and

sometimes plain barmy, but his great virtue is his determination to tell the truth – to be honest about his own feelings. Perhaps the greatest contribution he made to Venetian studies was his continual emphasis on the physical reality of the place. In an age when most visitors were continuing to see it through a golden haze of romantic enchantment, Ruskin focused his attention on the stones of Venice – the crumbling, corroded stones, bricks and marble. It didn't do much for his marriage, but it revolutionised Venetian studies.

Every major writer on Venice after Ruskin – **Proust**, **WD Howells**, **Henry James** – had to struggle to break free from Ruskin. It took some courage to like the baroque with Ruskin's fulminations ringing in one's ears. But gradually a new taste arose, one in which the famous ambivalence of Venice played a key role, attracting sexually ambivalent writers such as **John Addington Symonds** and **Frederick Rolfe** – the self-styled 'Baron Corvo' – who, in between liaisons with gondoliers, described an intriguing and androgynous city. At the same time the mysterious secrecy of the city was perfect for a novelist such as James, who wrote: 'Venice is the refuge of endless strange secrets, broken fortunes and wounded hearts.' He was perhaps also attracted by a city whose topography was almost as labyrinthine as his own syntax.

After World War I it was time for a fresh onset of disgust, with **TS Eliot** and **DH Lawrence** seeing the city as irredeemably commercial and sordid. Eliot describes a city where 'the rats are underneath the piles'. Both Eliot and **Ezra Pound** reworked, in a different light, Ruskin's moral disapprobation of Venice; in both poets, the city unlocked their not-so-latent anti-Semitism (see, for example, Pound's dismissal of post-Quattrocento Venetian painting: 'with usura the line grows thick'). But after he was released from a US hospital for the criminally insane, where he had been confined for his active wartime support for Mussolini's Fascist regime, Pound chose to divide most of his last years (1958-72) between Venice and Rapallo. He lies buried in the cemetery island of San Michele (*see p135*).

But like the sluggish, steady tide of the Lido, the old, sinister fascination has since returned. Sex, lies and dirty canals remain the staple elements of most contemporary literature set in Venice, and have crossed over into cinema – most notably in Nicolas Roeg's *Don't Look Now* (based on a short story by **Daphne du Maurier**). The city is also murky, treacherous and damp in works by **Ian McEwan**, **Barry Unsworth** and **Lisa St Aubin de Téran**. Childe Harold still rules, it seems.

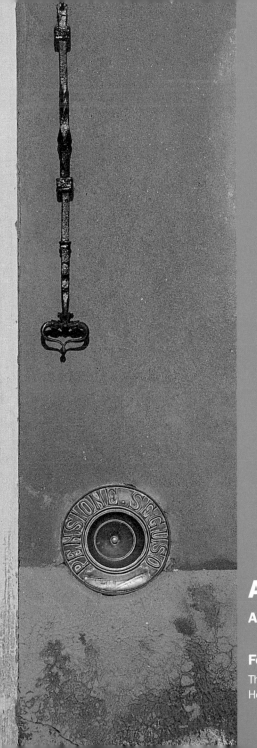

Accommodation

Accommodation

Hotel-packed it may be, but Venice is a seller's market: it pays to choose carefully and book early.

Don't let the huge selection of hotels in Venice fool you into thinking it must be a buyer's market: good accommodation deals are thin on the ground. Once you have resigned yourself to the idea that value for money is a relative concept, you may, however, find 'bargains'.

Cramped conditions and old buildings mean there can be huge variations within the same establishment; a luxury hotel that charges upwards of L600,000 for a double room with canal view may also have a decent single overlooking an alley for L200,000 or less. Some high-charging hotels offer low-season midweek deals at a fraction of their usual prices: it pays to check hotel websites.

Selecting your area carefully will enhance your enjoyment: the residential Dorsoduro contains generally calmer, more classically charming hotels; nearer piazza San Marco you'll find the plush, the brash and the cramped, depending on your taste and budget.

Genre has a bearing, too: the modern annexe or extreme refurbishment will provide more mod cons than the old palazzo with bouncy floors and cranky plumbing, but it may be a little short on Venetian magic.

Finally, when booking, think carefully about which bit of the hotel you want to be in: upper storeys have more light and less noise (but check there's a lift); rooms giving on to a courtyard may be quiet but you won't have views over canals or the lagoon. If you go for the 'canal view', ascertain beforehand how much of a view it is: you may end up paying a huge extra for a small sliver of Grand Canal only visible out of the bathroom window.

By and large, most hotels will exchange currency. They'll organise babysitting at an extra charge; laundry, dry cleaning and sometimes air-conditioning are also considered extras. Baby cots or supplementary beds can often be squeezed into bedrooms; expect to pay an extra 20-40 per cent on top of the room price. Where breakfast is not included in the price of the room, this is specified in the listings below.

NO ROOM AT THE INN

Pitching up in Venice with no hotel room booked is a very risky business, even in what elsewhere would count as the low season. If you have no place to lay your head, go straight to an

The **Bauer Grunwald** has deluxe rooms in its 13th-century wing. *See p45.*

AVA (Venetian Hoteliers Association) bureau at the station, piazzale Roma or the airport. They will help you track down a room, charging a small commission that you can claim back on your first night. If you're not fussy about the state of your room or don't mind a bathroom located in the corridor, try the cheaper hotels around the station. Or in real desperation, try the many hotels on the mainland in Mestre and around the airport: they are mainly cheaper, plentiful and only ten minutes away by train or bus, but despite what the tourist office may tell you, they definitely aren't Venice.

FINDING THE HOTEL

Finding your way around Venice is not easy and finding your hotel can be devilishly hard when you've just blown in. You are best advised to obtain detailed directions before you arrive, and make sure you know where the closest vaporetto stop, campo (square) or landmark is (often Venetian directions relate to the nearest church).

Hotels listed below are marked with numbered blue dots on the maps at the back of this guide.

Deluxe

Bauer Grunwald & Grand Hotel 1

San Marco 1459, campo San Moisè (041 520 7022/ fax 041 520 7557/www.bauervenezia.com/ info@bauervenezia.com). Vaporetto Vallaresso. **Rates** L290,000-L820,000 single; L320,000-L1,900,000 double; L990,000-L6,600,000 suite; breakfast L44,000-L55,000 extra. **Credit** AmEx, DC, MC, V. **Map** II 4B. With a few deluxe rooms in its 13th-century Gothic section and many more in its ghastly 1960s annexe, the Bauer offers extremely comfortable accommodation fitted out with all the necessary mod cons but rather too much in the plush-but-characterless luxury hotel mould. A great variety of reception rooms and an enormous terrace on the Grand Canal. **Hotel services** *Air-conditioning. Babysitting. Bar. Car park. Conference facilities (at the Zitelle on the Giudecca). Currency exchange. Dry cleaning. Fax. Garden. Laundry. Lift. Multi-lingual staff. Non-smoking rooms. Restaurant. Safe. Theatre reservations. Tours arranged.* **Room services** *Air-conditioning. Fax and PC point (in suites). Jacuzzi (not in all). Hairdryer. Minibar. Room service (24-hour). Safe. Telephone. TV (satellite).*

Cipriani 2

Giudecca 10, fondamenta San Giovanni (041 520 7744/fax 041 520 3930/www.orient-expresshotels.com/www.cipriani.orient-express.com/ info@hotelcipriani.it). Vaporetto hotel boat from Vallaresso stop. **Closed** mid Nov-late Mar. **Rates** L600,000-L1,200,000 single; L950,000-L1,900,000 double; L2,250,000-L4,700,000 suite. **Credit** AmEx, DC, MC, V. **Map** II 4C. Set in three acres of verdant paradise on the eastern tip of the Giudecca island, this offers tennis courts, an Olympic-sized pool, a private harbour for your yacht and a higher-than-average chance of rubbing shoulders with your favourite film star. The rooms are exquisitely decorated, many with marble bathrooms. If this seems too humdrum, take an apartment in the neighbouring 15th-century Palazzo Vendramin, complete with butler service and a private garden. Despite the possibility of unlimited use of the motorboat to San Marco, many guests choose not to leave the premises, begging the question: do they come here for Venice or for the Cipriani itself? **Hotel services** *Air-conditioning. Babysitting. Bar. Car park. Conference facilities (for 100+). Courtesy*

boat. Currency exchange. Dry cleaning. Fax. Garden. Gym. Laundry. Lift. Marina. Multi-lingual staff. Non-smoking rooms. Restaurant. Safe. Sauna. Solarium. Swimming pool. Tennis courts. Theatre reservations. Tours arranged. **Room services** *Air-conditioning. Fax and PC point. Jacuzzi. Hairdryer. Minibar. Radio. Room service (24-hour). Safe. Telephone. TV (satellite).*

Danieli 3

Castello 4196, riva degli Schiavoni (041 522 6480/fax 041 520 0208/www.sheraton.com/ danieli@sheraton.com). Vaporetto San Zaccaria. **Rates** L400,000-L750,000 single; L600,000-L1,450,000 double; L1,111,000-4,510,000 suite; breakfast L41,800-L71,500 extra. **Credit** AmEx, DC, MC, V. **Map** III 1B. Just round the corner from piazza San Marco, the Danieli is split between an unprepossessing 1940s building and the 14th-century Palazzo Dandolo: a room in the latter is definitely preferable if it's atmosphere you're after. The rooms are sumptuously decorated with Rubelli and Fortuny fabrics, antique furnishings and marble bathrooms. There are spectacular views across the lagoon from the stunning roof terrace. The Sheraton group's tennis courts, golf course, swimming pool, riding facilities and beach on the Lido are open to guests of the Danieli. Balzac, Dickens, Proust and Wagner all stayed here. **Hotel services** *Air-conditioning. Babysitting. Bar. Car park. Conference facilities (for up to 120). Courtesy boat. Currency exchange. Dry cleaning. Fax. Garden. Laundry. Lift. Multi-lingual staff. Non-smoking rooms. PC rental. Restaurant. Safe. Theatre reservations. Tours arranged.* **Room services** *Air-conditioning. Fax point. Hairdryer. Minibar. Radio. Room service (24-hour). Safe (in most rooms). Telephone. TV (satellite).*

The best Hotels

For splashing out

The **Cipriani**, Venice's priciest and the only one in the islands with a pool. *See p45.*

For avoiding Murano glass

The **Ca' Pisani**, Venice's only 'design' hotel, with a 1930s feel. *See p48.*

For expiring in a boater

The **Des Bains**, where *Death in Venice* was written and filmed. *See p47.*

For Rialto action

The **Locanda Sturion**, where rooms overlook the world's best-known bridge. *See p55.*

For feeling Gothic

La Calcina, where Ruskin was moved to write *The Stones of Venice*. *See p55.*

Time is what you make of it.

Des Bains 4

Lungomare Marconi 17, Lido (041 526 5921/
fax 041 526 0113/www.sheraton.com/
desbains@sheraton.com). Vaporetto Lido. **Closed**
mid Nov-mid March. **Rates** L370,000-L740,000
single; L550,000-L1,000,000 double; L1,500,000 suite.
Credit AmEx, DC, MC, V. **Map** Lido.

Thomas Mann wrote, and Luchino Visconti filmed,
Death in Venice in this glorious art deco hotel set in
its own park. Des Bains has a private beach just
across the street and access to tennis courts, a golf
course and riding facilities. A water taxi ferries
guests to San Marco every half hour.
Hotel services *Air-conditioning. Babysitting.*
Bar. Conference facilities (for up to 350). Car park.
Courtesy boat. Currency exchange. Dry cleaning.
Fax. Garden with pool. Gym. Laundry. Lift.
Massage parlour. Multi-lingual staff. Non-smoking
rooms. Restaurant. Safe. Tennis courts. Theatre
reservations. Tours arranged. **Room services**
Air-conditioning. Fax and PC point. Hairdryer.
Minibar. Radio. Room service (18-hour). Telephone.
TV (satellite).

Europa & Regina 5

San Marco 2159, corte Barozzi (041 240 0001/fax
041 523 3043/www.westin.com/www.sheraton.com/
europaregina@sheraton.com). Vaporetto Vallaresso.
Rates L300,000-L700,000 single; L600,000-
L1,500,000 double; L1,749,000-3,000,000 suite;
breakfast L42,350-L71,500 extra. **Credit** AmEx, DC,
MC, V. **Map** II 4B.

Situated off calle larga XXII Marzo, the recently
refurbished Europa oozes opulence. The spacious
rooms have ornate Venetian-style decor. Guests
have access to the Sheraton group's sports facilities
at the Lido. The restaurant, La Cusina, on a terrace
with a wonderful view over the Grand Canal, is a cut
above the average hotel restaurant.
Hotel services *Air-conditioning. Babysitting. Bar.*
Car park. Cell phone rental. Conference facilities (for
up to 120). Courtesy boat. Currency exchange. Dry
cleaning. Fax. Garden. Laundry. Lift. Multi-lingual
staff. Non-smoking rooms. Restaurant. Safe. Theatre
reservations. Tours arranged. **Room services** *Air-*
conditioning. Fax and PC point. Hairdryer. Minibar.
Radio. Room service (24-hour). Safe (in some rooms).
Telephone. TV (satellite).

Excelsior 6

Lungomare Marconi 41, Lido (041 526 0201/
fax 041 526 7276/www.westin.com/
excelsior@sheraton.com). Vaporetto Lido. **Rates**
L700,000-L1,000,000 single; L650,000-L1,250,000
double; L2,000,000-L2,800,000 suite. **Credit** AmEx,
DC, MC, V. **Map** Lido.

The early-1900s pseudo-Moorish Excelsior hosts
hordes of celebrities when the Venice Film Festival
(*see p204* **The Film Festival**) swings into action
each September (the festival headquarters is situated just over the road). Demand a sea-facing room
for a view of beach happenings and the Adriatic
beyond. The Excelsior's beach huts are the last
word in luxury. There are tennis courts and a water
taxi to San Marco.

Hotel services *Air-conditioning. Babysitting. Bar.*
Car park. Cell phone rental. Conference facilities (for
up to 100). Courtesy boat. Currency exchange. Dry
cleaning. Fax. Garden. Laundry. Lift. Multi-lingual
staff. Non-smoking rooms. Restaurant. Safe. Theatre
reservations. Tours arranged. **Room services** *Air-*
conditioning. Hairdryer. Minibar. Radio. Room
service (24-hour). Safe. Telephone. TV (satellite).

Gritti Palace 7

San Marco 2467, campo Santa Maria del Giglio (041
794 611/fax 041 520 0942/www.sheraton.com).
Vaporetto Santa Maria del Giglio. **Rates** L400,000-
L900,000 single; L600,000-L1,700,000 double;
L2,475,000-L4,829,000 suite. **Credit** AmEx, DC, MC,
V. **Map** II 3B.

Queen Elizabeth (the current one) opted to stay here,
which says it all really. Expect no postmodern frills,
just a studied air of old-world charm and nobility.
Refined and opulent, adorned with antiques and
fresh flowers, each room is uniquely decorated. The
reception desk is one of the finest. A courtesy boat
ferries guests to the Sheraton group's swimming and
sports facilities on the Lido. An aperitif on the vast
canal terrace is an experience in itself.
Hotel services *Air-conditioning. Babysitting. Bar.*
Conference facilities. Currency exchange. Dry
cleaning. Fax. Garden. Laundry. Lift. Multi-lingual
staff. Non-smoking rooms. Restaurant. Safe. Theatre
reservations. Tours arranged. **Room services** *Air-*
conditioning. Fax point (in the suites). Hairdryer.
Minibar. Radio. Room service (24-hour). Telephone.
TV (satellite).

Londra Palace 8

Castello 4171, riva degli Schiavoni (041 520
0533/fax 041 522 5032/www.hotelondra.it/
info@hotelondra.it). Vaporetto San Zaccaria. **Rates**
L452,000-L665,000 single; L375,000-L1,100,000
double; L726,000-L1,150,000 suite. **Credit** AmEx,
DC, MC, V. **Map** III 1B.

Elegant but restrained, the Londra Palace offers
traditional rooms with antiques, paintings and the
occasional piece of 19th-century Biedermeier furniture. If you can't do without a phone by your Jacuzzi,
this is the place to come. Tchaikovsky composed his
fourth symphony during a stay here in 1877. You
can compose your masterpiece while sunbathing on
the roof terrace.
Hotel services *Air-conditioning. Babysitting.*
Bar. Currency exchange. Dry cleaning. Fax. Laundry.
Lift. Multi-lingual staff. Restaurant. Safe. Theatre
reservations. Terrace. Tours arranged. **Room**
services *Air-conditioning. Hairdryer. Jacuzzi.*
Minibar. Radio. Room service (24-hour). Safe.
Telephone. TV (satellite).

Luna Hotel Baglioni 9

San Marco 1243, calle Larga dell'Ascensione
(041 528 9840/fax 041 528 7160/
www.baglionihotels.com/luna.venezia@baglionihotels.
com). Vaporetto Vallaresso. **Rates** L390,000-
L550,000 single; L610,000-L950,000 double;
L1,200,000-L1,800,000 suite. **Credit** AmEx, DC, MC,
V. **Map** II 4B.

Conveniently situated for *aperitivi* in Harry's Bar (*see p166*), this is the oldest hotel in Venice, dating back to the late 15th century. But after a modern make-over with rather too much shiny marble and heavy chandeliers, this fact is not immediately obvious, except in the conference room, which still has its original fresco and stuccoed decoration. A quarter of the rooms have beautiful views of the Giardinetti Reali, the lagoon and across the Bacino di San Marco to Palladio's church of San Giorgio Maggiore beyond.

Hotel services *Air-conditioning. Bar. Conference facilities (for up to 100). Currency exchange. Dry cleaning. Fax. Laundry. Lift. Multilingual staff. Non-smoking rooms. Restaurant. Safe. Theatre reservations. Tours arranged.* **Room services** *Air-conditioning. Fax point (in the suites). Hairdryer. Jacuzzi (in the suites). Minibar. Radio. Room service (18-hour). Safe. Telephone. TV (satellite).*

Monaco & Grand Canal   10

San Marco 1325, calle Vallaresso (041 520 0211/fax 041 520 0501/mailbox@hotelmonaco.it). Vaporetto Vallaresso. **Rates** L230,000-L500,000 single; L350,000-L900,000 double; L950,000-L1,150,000 suite. **Credit** AmEx, DC, MC, V. **Map** II 4B.

In an 18th-century palazzo overlooking the Grand Canal, the Monaco has friendly, efficient staff, elegant decor, and a good restaurant, with a large canal terrace used in the summer that allows you to eat while keeping an eye on Grand Canal traffic. Its small scale makes it one of the most enjoyable of the deluxe hotels in Venice. A fire is lit in the cosy bar in winter.

Hotel services *Air-conditioning. Babysitting. Bar. Conference facilities (for up to 40). Currency exchange. Dry cleaning. Fax. Garden. Laundry. Lift. Multi-lingual staff. Restaurant. Safe. Theatre reservations. Tours arranged.* **Room services** *Air-conditioning. Hairdryer. Minibar. Radio. Room service (24-hour). Safe. Telephone. TV (satellite).*

Upper range

Accademia – Villa Maravege   11

Dorsoduro 1058, fondamenta Bollani (041 521 0188/fax 041 523 9152/ pensione.accademia@flashnet.it). Vaporetto Accademia. **Rates** L140,000-L200,000 single; L220,000-L400,000 double. **Credit** AmEx, DC, MC, V **Map** II 2B.

This wonderful 17th-century villa, which used to be the Russian embassy, has two shady, leafy gardens, one of which surrounds a Palladian-style annexe. Breakfast is served in one of the gardens or in the wood-panelled breakfast area. The rooms are stylishly done out with marble floors.

Hotel services *Air-conditioning. Babysitting. Bar. Currency exchange. Dry cleaning. Fax. Garden. Laundry. Multi-lingual staff. Safe. Tours arranged.* **Room services** *Air-conditioning. Hairdryer. Room service (14-hour). Telephone. TV (satellite).*

Bellini   12

Cannaregio 116, lista di Spagna (041 524 2488/ fax 041 715 193/www.boscolohotels.com/ reception@bellini.boscolo.com). Vaporetto Ferrovia. **Rates** L180,000-L370,000 single; L250,000-L530,000 double; L600,000 suite. **Credit** AmEx, DC, MC, V. **Map** I 1B.

Glitzy, glam and very imposing, with its silk damask wallpaper with matching curtains, inlaid marbles and Murano chandeliers. It's the only deluxe conveniently situated a stone's throw from the station, though this means it's slap bang in the centre of an area that is noisy, thronged with tourists, distant from the main cultural sights and better restaurants.

Hotel services *Air-conditioning. Babysitting. Bar. Conference facilities (for up to 20). Courtesy boat. Currency exchange. Dry cleaning. Fax. Laundry. Lift. Multi-lingual staff. Non-smoking rooms. Restaurant. Safe. Theatre reservations. Tours arranged.* **Room services** *Air-conditioning. Hairdryer. Minibar. Radio. Room service (24-hour). Safe. Telephone. TV (satellite).*

Ca' Pisani   13

Dorsoduro 979/A, rio Terà Foscarini (041 277 1478/fax 041 277 1061/www.capisanihotel.it/ info@capisanihotel.it). Vaporetto Accademia. **Rates** L320,000-L400,000 single; L360,000-L480,000 double; L440,000-L550,000 suite. **Credit** AmEx, DC, MC, V **Map** II 2B.

Opened in November 2000 to much fanfare and frantic booking, the Ca' Pisani's luxurious, understated designer-chic rooms in retro 1930s and '40s style are a refreshing change from the usual fare of glitz, gilt and Murano glass. Conveniently located, with friendly staff and large rooms. There's a sauna, and a discount at the gym round the corner.

Hotel services *Air-conditioning. Babysitting. Bar. Currency exchange. Dry cleaning. Fax. Laundry. Lift. Multi-lingual staff. Restaurant. Safe. Sauna. Solarium. Spa. Theatre reservations. Tours arranged.* **Room services** *Air-conditioning. Fax line. PC connection. Room service. Safe. Telephone. TV (satellite).*

Continental   14

Cannaregio 166, lista di Spagna (041 715 122/fax 041 524 2432/continental@ve.nettuno.it). Vaporetto Ferrovia. **Rates** L180,000-L280,000 single; L200,000-L420,000 double. **Credit** AmEx, DC, MC, V. **Map** I 1B.

The off-putting padded-wall effect does not extend beyond the corridors in the Continental, where the rooms are pleasantly decorated. Some have high ceilings and some have views over the Grand Canal. The reception rooms are rather oppressive but there is a lovely little terrace on the Grand Canal. If the gushing service is not too much for you, this is definitely a step up from most three-stars near the station.

Hotel service *Air-conditioning. Babysitting. Bar. Currency exchange. Dry cleaning. Fax. Laundry. Lift. Multi-lingual staff. Restaurant. Safe. Terrace on Grand Canal. Theatre reservations. Tours arranged.* **Room services** *Air-conditioning. Hairdryer. Room service (15-hour). Safe. Telephone. TV (satellite).*

Giorgione 15

*Cannaregio 4587, campo dei Santi Apostoli (041
522 5810/fax 041 523 9092/ www.hotelgiorgione.it/
giorgione@hotelgiorgione.com). Vaporetto Ca' d'Oro.*
Rates L154,000-L260,000 single; L232,000-L484,000
double; L330,000-L580,000 suite. **Credit** AmEx, DC,
MC, V. **Map** I 4B.

Set in the tranquil residential area of Cannaregio, the
Giorgione exudes warmth and comfort, rather than
glitz. The older 15th-century palazzo joins the newer
part around a flower-filled courtyard with a central
lily pond. Some split-level rooms have verandas
overlooking the rooftops and the courtyard below.
Hotel services *Air-conditioning. Babysitting. Bar.
Currency exchange. Dry cleaning. Fax. Garden.
Laundry. Lift. Multi-lingual staff. Non-smoking
rooms. Safe. Theatre reservations.* **Room services**
*Air-conditioning. Hairdryer. Minibar. Radio. Room
service (24-hour). Safe. Telephone. TV (satellite).*

La Colombina 16

*Castello 4416, calle del Remedio (041 277
0525/fax 041 277 6044/www.hotelcolombina.com/
info@hotelcolombina.com). Vaporetto San Zaccaria.*
Rates L220,000-L430,000 single; L320,000-L690,000
double. **Credit** AmEx, DC, MC, V. **Map** III 1A.

Close to San Marco but far away from the crowds,
the Colombina has decor that is a modern take on
the usual Venetian: the Murano chandeliers are
there, but the overall effect is understated. The
baths are marble, and some rooms have balconies
with views over the canal beneath the Bridge of
Sighs. Very friendly staff.

Hotel services *Air-conditioning. Babysitting.
Bar. Conference room. Currency exchange. Dry
cleaning. Laundry. Lift. Multi-lingual staff. Theatre
reservations. Tours arranged.* **Room services** *Air-
conditioning. Minibar. Hairdryer. Room service. Safe.
TV (cable and satellite).*

La Fenice et des Artistes 17

*San Marco 1936, campiello della Fenice (041 523
2333/fax 041 520 3721/fenice@fenicehotels.it).
Vaporetto Santa Maria del Giglio.* **Rates** L90,000-
L220,000 single; L150,000-L420,000 double. **Credit**
AmEx, DC, MC, V. **Map** II 3A.

A favourite haunt of musicians, and of opera
groupies who flock here to be close to La Fenice. The
rooms are classical in style, some with paintings that
leave a little to be desired on the taste front. There
is also a small outdoor courtyard.
Hotel services *Air-conditioning. Bar. Dry
cleaning. Fax. Garden. Laundry. Lift. Multi-lingual
staff.* **Room services** *Air-conditioning (70%).
Minibar in 10%. Room service (14-hour). Safe.
Telephone. TV (satellite).*

Locanda ai Santi Apostoli 18

*Cannaregio 4391/A, campo Santi Apostoli (041 521
2612/fax 041 521 2611/aisantia@tin.it). Vaporetto
Ca' d'Oro.* **Closed** mid Dec-mid Feb. **Rates**
L230,000-L330,000 single; L280,000-L460,000 double.
Credit AmEx, DC, MC, V. **Map** I 3C.

A big entrance door from the busy strada Nuova
leads you into the wonderful courtyard of this
Venetian palazzo. The *locanda* (inn) is on the third
floor and can be reached via a lift or, by the energetic,

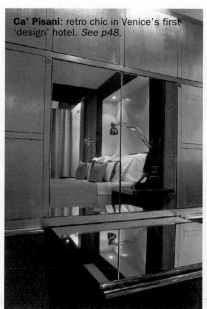

Ca' Pisani: retro chic in Venice's first
'design' hotel. *See p48.*

The **Locanda ai Santi Apostoli** has individually decorated rooms. *See p49.*

via a wonderful wide flight of stone stairs. There are only 12 rooms but all are spacious and individually decorated; a couple have views over the Grand Canal to the Rialto Market, others over the rooftops.
Hotel services *Air-conditioning. Babysitting. Bar. Currency exchange. Dry cleaning. Fax. Laundry. Lift. Multi-lingual staff. Non-smoking rooms. Safe. Theatre reservations. Tours arranged.* **Room services** *Air-conditioning. Hairdryer. Minibar. Radio. Room service (24-hour). Telephone. TV (satellite).*

Marconi & Milano 19

San Polo 729, riva del Vin (041 522 2068/ fax 041 522 9700/www.hotelmarconi.it/ info@hotelmarconi.it). Vaporetto Rialto. **Rates** L80,000-L350,000 single; L120,000-L450,000 double. **Credit** AmEx, DC, MC, V. **Map** I 3C.
A stone's thrown from the Rialto bridge, and well placed for a morning stroll through the fish market,

the reception rooms in this former tavern are done out in a wonderful old-world bachelor style; the rooms are simpler. Two of them look out on to the Grand Canal; the others have the advantage of being much quieter.
Hotel services *Air-conditioning. Babysitting. Bar. Currency exchange. Dry cleaning. Fax. Garden. Laundry. Multi-lingual staff. Non-smoking rooms. Safe. Theatre reservations. Tours arranged.* **Room services** *Air-conditioning. Hairdryer. Minibar. Radio. Room service (24-hour). Safe. Telephone. TV (satellite).*

Metropole 20

Castello 4149, riva degli Schiavoni (041 520 5044/ fax 041 522 3679/hotel.metropole@venezia.it). Vaporetto San Zaccaria. **Closed** mid Jan-Feb. **Rates** L230,000-L490,000 single; L350,000-L760,000 double. **Credit** AmEx, DC, MC, V. **Map** III 2B.
The hotel's gorgeous garden offers a refuge from the tourist trudge: the only sounds are the occasional bells od neighbouring churches and water trickling in the fountain. The elegant rooms have many antiques from the owner's own collection. They also have views over the lagoon, the canal at the back or on to the garden.
Hotel services *Air-conditioning. Babysitting. Bar. Car park. Conference facilities (for up to 100). Currency exchange. Dry cleaning. Fax. Garden. Laundry. Lift. Multi-lingual staff. Non-smoking rooms. Restaurant. Safe. Theatre reservations. Tours arranged.* **Room services** *Air-conditioning. Hairdryer. Minibar. Room service (24-hour). Safe. Telephone. TV (satellite).*

San Cassiano – Ca' Favretto 21

Santa Croce 2232, calle de la Rosa (041 524 1768/fax 041 721 033/www.sancassiano.it/ cassiano@sancassiano.it). Vaporetto San Stae. **Rates** L80,000-L350,000 single; L120,000-L450,000 double. **Credit** AmEx, MC, V. **Map** I 3C.
The rooms of this 14th-century Gothic building are elegant and some of the reception rooms look out over the Grand Canal to the Ca' D'Oro: there is also a lovely veranda on the Canal. It's difficult to find, but worth the search.
Hotel services *Air-conditioning. Babysitting. Bar. Fax. Courtyard. Multi-lingual staff. Non-smoking rooms. Safe.* **Room services** *Air-conditioning. Hairdryer. Minibar. Radio. Room service (24-hour). Safe. Telephone. TV (satellite).*

San Moisè 22

San Marco 2058, Piscina San Moisè (041 520 3755/fax 041 521 0670/www.sanmoise.it/ info@sanmoise.it). Vaporetto Vallaresso. **Rates** L121,000-L350,000 single; L173,000-L450,000 double. **Credit** AmEx, DC, MC, V. **Map** II 4B.
The slightly grotty reception does not bode well, but the bedrooms are quite spacious, some with wonderfully high ceilings and some with views on to a tranquil canal, where the calm is punctuated only by shouts from passing gondoliers.
Hotel services *Air-conditioning. Babysitting. Bar. Currency exchange. Dry cleaning. Fax.*

Laundry. Multi-lingual staff. Non-smoking rooms. Safe. Theatre reservations. Tours arranged. **Room services** Air-conditioning. Hairdryer. Minibar. Radio. Room service (24-hour). Safe. Telephone. TV (satellite).

Santo Stefano   23
San Marco 2957, campo Santo Stefano (041 520 0166/fax 041 522 4460). Vaporetto Accademia/San Samuele. **Rates** L190,000-L320,000 single; L220,000-L420,000 double. **Credit** AmEx, MC, V. **Map** II 3A.
This hotel, in a 15th-century guard tower, has 11 tasteful rooms. The top-floor rooms have amazing vistas across surrounding rooftops. Staff can be brusque. **Hotel services** Air-conditioning. Babysitting. Bar. Dry cleaning. Fax. Laundry. Lift. Multi-lingual staff. Safe. Theatre reservations. Tours arranged. **Room services** Air-conditioning. Hairdryer. Minibar. Radio. Room service (24-hour). Safe. Telephone. TV (satellite).

Saturnia & International   24
San Marco 2398, via XXII Marzo (041 520 8377/fax 041 520 7131/www.hotelsaturnia.it/ info@hotelsaturnia.it). Vaporetto Vallaresso. **Rates** L230,000-L460,000 single; L360,000-L720,000 double. **Credit** AmEx, DC, MC, V. **Map** II 3B.
A friendly atmosphere pervades this hotel in a 14th-century palazzo, the interior of which has been done up in a neo-Byzantine style. The rooms veer between faux-Renaissance (beamed ceilings, damask-covered walls) and faux-Charles Rennie Mackintosh. **Hotel services** Air-conditioning. Babysitting. Bar. Conference facilities (for up to 60). Currency exchange. Dry cleaning. Fax. Garden. Laundry. Lift. Multi-lingual staff. Non-smoking rooms. Restaurant. Safe. Solarium. Theatre reservations. Tours arranged. **Room services** Air-conditioning. Hairdryer. Minibar. Radio. Room service (18-hour). Safe. Telephone. TV (satellite).

Savoia & Jolanda   25
Castello 4187, riva degli Schiavoni (041 520 6644/ 522 4130/fax 041 520 7494/www.el.moro.com/ savoia&jolanda/savoia.ve.san@iol.it). Vaporetto San Zaccaria. **Rates** L240,000-L270,000 single; L350,000-L450,000 double. **Credit** AmEx, DC, MC, V. **Map** III 1B.
A hotel of two halves, the Savoia offers rooms with balconies and views across the Bacino di San Marco to Palladio's church of San Giorgio Maggiore in one direction, and others facing back towards the glorious façade of San Zaccaria on the landward side. The decor manages to be luxurious without going over the top.
Hotel services Air-conditioning. Babysitting. Bar. Currency exchange. Dry cleaning. Fax. Garden. Laundry. Lift. Multi-lingual staff. Non-smoking

Hotels by area

San Marco
Deluxe Bauer Grunwald & Grand Hotel (*p45*); Europa & Regina (*p47*); Gritti Palace (*p47*); Luna Hotel Baglioni (*p47*); Monaco & Grand Canal (*p48*).
Upper range La Fenice et des Artistes (*p49*); San Moisè (*p22*); Santo Stefano (*p52*); Saturnia & International (*p52*).
Moderate Ala (*p53*); Bel Sito & Berlino (*p53*); De l'Alboro (*p53*); Do Pozzi (*p55*); Flora (*p55*); Locanda Fiorita (*p55*); San Fantin (*p56*).
Budget Gallini (*p59*); San Samuele (*p60*).

Castello
Deluxe Danieli (*p45*); Londra Palace (*p47*).
Upper range La Colombina (*p49*); Metropole (*p51*); Savoia & Jolanda (*p52*).
Moderate Casa Fontana (*p53*); Bucintoro (*p53*); Locanda La Corte (*p55*); Scandinavia (*p56*).
Budget Caneva (*p57*); Casa Linger (*p53*); Locanda Canal (*p59*); Locanda Silva (*p60*).
Hostels Foresteria Valdese (*p60*).

Cannaregio
Upper range Bellini (*p48*); Continental (*p48*); Giorgione (*p49*); Locanda ai Santi Apostoli (*p49*).

Moderate Tintoretto (*p57*); Zecchini (*p57*).
Budget Adriatico (*p57*); Al Vagon (*p57*); Guerrini (*p59*); Rossi (*p60*).
Hostels Archie's House (*p60*); Foresteria Santa Fosca (*p60*).

San Polo & Santa Croce
Upper range Marconi & Milano (*p51*); San Cassiano – Ca' Favretto (*p51*).
Moderate Locanda Sturion (*p55*).
Budget Iris (*p59*).

Dorsoduro
Upper range Accademia – Villa Maravege (*p48*); Ca' Pisani (*p48*).
Moderate Agli Alboretti (*p53*); Alla Salute da Cici (*p53*); American (*p53*); La Calcina (*p55*); Locanda San Barnaba (*p55*); Messner (*p56*); Pantalon (*p56*); Seguso (*p57*); Tivoli (*p57*).
Budget Antica Locanda Montin (*p57*); Locanda San Trovaso (*p59*).

Giudecca & San Giorgio
Deluxe Cipriani (*p45*).
Hostels Istituto Canossiano (*p60*); Ostello di Venezia (Youth Hostel) (*p60*).

Lido
Deluxe Des Bains (*p47*); Excelsior (*p47*).

rooms. Restaurant. Safe. Theatre reservations. Tours arranged. **Room services** *Air-conditioning. Hairdryer. Minibar (in 70% of rooms). Room service (24-hour). Safe. Telephone. TV (satellite).*

Moderate

Agli Alboretti   26
Dorsoduro 884, rio Terà Foscarini (041 523 0058/ fax 041 521 0158/alboretti@gpnet.it). Vaporetto Accademia. **Closed** Jan. **Rates** L155,000-170,000 single; L220,000-L260,000 double. **Credit** AmEx, DC, MC, V. **Map** II 2B.
This hotel with a vaguely nautical air also has its own restaurant and pretty outdoor eating area, where breakfast is served in summer. The simply-decorated rooms are comfortable, if rather small.
Hotel services *Air-conditioning. Bar. Fax. Garden. Laundry. Multi-lingual staff. Restaurant. Safe.* **Room services** *Air-conditioning. Hairdryer. Room service (24-hour). Telephone. TV (satellite).*

Ala   27
San Marco 2494, campo Santa Maria del Giglio (041 520 8333/fax 041 520 6390/ www.hotelala.it/alahtlve@gpnet.it). Vaporetto Santa Maria del Giglio. **Rates** L160,000-L240,000 single; L230,000-L360,000 double. **Credit** AmEx, DC, MC, V. **Map** II 3B.
The Ala's classically decorated rooms have a variety of views, on to campo Santa Maria del Giglio, a little side canal and the Grand Canal itself. Check out the armour collection in the entrance hall.
Hotel services *Air-conditioning. Babysitting. Bar. Currency exchange. Dry cleaning. Fax. Garden. Laundry. Lift. Multi-lingual staff. Non-smoking rooms. Safe. Theatre reservations. Tours arranged.* **Room services** *Air-conditioning. Hairdryer. Minibar. Safe. Telephone. TV (satellite).*

Alla Salute da Cici   28
Dorsoduro 222, fondamenta Ca' Balà (041 523 5404/fax 041 522 2271/hotel.salute.dacici@iol.it). Vaporetto Salute. **Closed** Dec. **Rates** L100,000-L190,000 single; L130,000-L250,000 double. **No credit cards. Map** II 3B.
This pleasant hotel with simple modern rooms is a stone's throw from the major sites, but well away from the hubbub. Perfectly situated for summer strolls along the Zattere.
Hotel services *Babysitting. Bar. Currency exchange. Fax. Garden. Multi-lingual staff. Non-smoking rooms. Safe. Theatre reservations.* **Room services** *Hairdryer. Telephone.*

American   29
Dorsoduro 628, fondamenta Bragadin (041 520 4733/fax 041 520 4080/www.hotelamerican.com/ hotameri@tin.it). Vaporetto Accademia. **Closed** late Nov-mid Dec. **Rates** L200,000-L300,000 single; L250,000-L410,000 double. **Credit** AmEx, MC, V **Map** II 3B.
In the peaceful residential area of the Dorsoduro, the American has generally spacious rooms decorated in antique-generic 'Venetian style'. Some rooms have

verandas adorned with fresh flowers facing on to the delightful rio di San Vio.
Hotel services *Air-conditioning. Babysitting. Bar. Fax. Garden. Laundry. Multi-lingual staff. Safe. Theatre reservations. Tours arranged.* **Room services** *Hairdryer. Minibar. Room service (24-hour). Safe. Telephone. TV (satellite).*

Bel Sito & Berlino   30
San Marco 2517, campo Santa Maria del Giglio (041 522 3365/fax 041 520 4083/belsito@iol.it). Vaporetto Santa Maria del Giglio. **Closed** late Nov-mid Dec. **Rates** L140,000-L227,000 single; L215,000-L345,000 double. **Credit** AmEx, MC, V. **Map** II 3B.
Equidistant from the Accademia and piazza San Marco, with what remains of La Fenice nearby. The rooms are decorated in cod 18th/19th-century style, half of them looking out on to the church of Santa Maria del Giglio.
Hotel services *Air-conditioning. Bar. Currency exchange. Fax. Laundry. Multi-lingual staff. Safe. Theatre reservations. Tours arranged.* **Room services** *Air-conditioning. Hairdryer. Minibar (in 70% of rooms). Room service (18-hour). Telephone. TV (satellite).*

Bucintoro   31
Castello 2135, riva San Biagio (041 522 3240/fax 041 523 5224). Vaporetto Arsenale. **Closed** Jan, Dec. **Rates** L100,000-L150,000 single; L200,000-L270,000 double. **No credit cards. Map** III 2B.
All the rooms in this friendly family-run hotel have stunning views across the lagoon to the island of San Giorgio Maggiore with its Palladian church. Whistler once stayed here, and it continues to be a favourite place for visiting artists. For such a setting, it is amazingly good value.
Hotel services *Bar. Fax. Garden. Multi-lingual staff. Non-smoking rooms. Restaurant. Safe. Theatre reservations.* **Room services** *Hairdryer. Room service (15-hour). Telephone.*

Casa Fontana   32
Castello 4701, campo San Provolo (041 522 0579/fax 041 523 1040/www.hotelfontana.it/ htlcasa@gpnet.it). Vaporetto San Zaccaria. **Rates** L100,000-L170,000 single; L150,000-L270,000 double. **Credit** AmEx, DC, MC, V. **Map** III 1B.
There is a wonderfully warming contrast as you exit the tack-packed campo San Provolo and enter this family-run hotel. The decor is rather olde worlde; some of the rooms have balconies and some at the top have a view over the spire of San Zaccaria.
Hotel services *Bar. Fax. Safe.* **Room services** *Fan. Telephone. TV (satellite).*

De l'Alboro   33
San Marco 3894B, corte dell'Alboro (041 522 9454/ fax 041 5228404). Vaporetto Sant'Angelo. **Closed** mid Jan-early Feb. **Rates** L150,000-L300,000 single; L150,000-L380,000 double. **Credit** AmEx, DC, MC, V. **Map** II 3A.
In a peaceful spot sandwiched between Palazzo Grassi and Palazzo Fortuny, the De l'Alboro is off the main tourist route but within easy reach of the

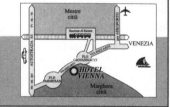

Rialto bridge and campo Santo Stefano. The bedrooms are clean though rather ordinary.
Hotel services *Air-conditioning. Babysitting. Bar. Currency exchange. Dry cleaning. Fax. Laundry. Lift. Multi-lingual staff. Safe. Theatre reservations. Tours arranged.* **Room services** *Air-conditioning. Hairdryer. Minibar. Safe. Telephone. TV (satellite).*

Do Pozzi   34

San Marco 2373, via XXII Marzo (041 520 7855/fax 041 522 94137/hotel.dopozzi@flashnet.it). Vaporetto Santa Maria del Giglio. **Closed** mid Jan-early Feb. **Rates** L110,000-L220,000 single; L160,000-L330,000 double. **Credit** AmEx, DC, MC, V. **Map** II 3B.
This hotel has a homely, friendly feeling. Some of the rooms are a bit cramped, but there is an enchanting attention to detail. It's situated very near to piazza San Marco, but off the main tourist street, down a little alley to a lovely outdoor courtyard where guests can have their meals, with an ancient well (*pozzo*) in the middle.
Hotel services *Air-conditioning. Babysitting. Bar. Courtyard. Dry cleaning. Fax. Laundry. Lift. Multi-lingual staff. Restaurant. Safe. Tours arranged.* **Room services** *Air-conditioning. Fax point. Hairdryer. Minibar. Room service (24-hour). Telephone. TV (satellite).*

Flora   35

San Marco 2283A, calle XXII Marzo (041 520 5844/fax 041 522 8217/www.hotelflora.it/ info@hotelflora.it). Vaporetto Vallaresso. **Rates** L170,000-L300,000 single; L215,000-L400,000 double. **Credit** AmEx, DC, MC, V. **Map** II 3B.
This small hotel near piazza San Marco offers a dreamy, tranquil stay in the palazzo adjacent to the one that Venetians call – quite inexplicably – Desdemona's house. The decor veers somewhat towards the twee. There is a warm cosy bar and a tiny garden with small wrought-iron tables and a fountain in the middle.
Hotel services *Air-conditioning. Babysitting. Bar. Currency exchange. Dry cleaning. Fax. Garden. Laundry. Lift. Multi-lingual staff. Safe. Theatre reservations. Tours arranged.* **Room services** *Air-conditioning. Hairdryer. Safe. Telephone. TV (satellite).*

La Calcina   36

Dorsoduro 780, fondamenta delle Zattere (041 520 6466/fax 041 522 7045/lacalcina@iol.it). Vaporetto Zattere or Accademia. **Rates** L80,000-L160,000 single; L180,000-L280,000 double. **Credit** AmEx, DC, MC, V **Map** II 2B.
Ruskin stayed here in 1876 while writing his masterwork *The Stones of Venice*. The interior decor is classic and cool; the rooms have parquet floors, and have recently been refurbished but without being over-modernised in the process. Andrea Palladio's Redentore church across the water can be admired while sipping cocktails at the Calcina's floating bar-terrace on the Giudecca canal. The hotel also has a roof terrace.

Hotel services *Air-conditioning. Bar. Fax. Laundry. Multi-lingual staff.* **Room services** *Air-conditioning. Hairdryer. Room service (24-hour). Safe. Telephone.*

Locanda Fiorita   37

San Marco 3457, campiello Nuovo (041 523 4754/ fax 041 522 0843/locafior@tin.it). Vaporetto Sant'Angelo. **Rates** L100,000-L190,000 single; L160,000-L220,000 double. **Credit** AmEx, DC, MC, V. **Map** II 3A.
This small family-run hotel, just off campo Santo Stefano, has refurbished rooms with beamed ceilings; two rooms have wonderful views through the vine-covered entrance to the airy *campiello*.
Hotel services *Currency exchange. Fax. Garden-courtyard. Multi-lingual staff. Safe. Theatre reservations.* **Room services** *Hairdryer. Air-conditioning (in some rooms). Room service (24-hour). Telephone. TV (satellite).*

Locanda La Corte   38

Castello 6317, calle Bressana (041 241 1300/ fax 041 241 5982/www.locandalacorte.it/ booking@locandalacorte.it). Vaporetto Fondamente Nove. **Closed** early Jan. **Rates** L150,000-L240,000 single; L190,000-L340,000 double; L260,000-L340,000 suite. **Credit** AmEx, DC, MC, V. **Map** III 1A.
In a 16th-century palazzo, the La Corte is a recent addition to Venice's hotels. The 14 rooms and two suites are pleasant, and the little courtyard, where breakfast is served in summer, is a delight.
Hotel services *Air-conditioning. Babysitting. Courtyard/garden. Fax. Laundry. Lift. Multi-lingual staff. Theatre reservations. Tours arranged.* **Room services** *Air-conditioning. E-mail connection. Minibar. Telephone. TV (satellite).*

Locanda San Barnaba   39

Dorsoduro 2486, calle del Traghetto (tel/fax 041 241 1233/www.locanda-sanbarnaba.com/info@locanda-sanbarnaba.com). Vaporetto Ca' Rezzonico. **Rates** L130,00-L200,000 single; L210,000-L320,000 double; L300,000-L400,000 suite. **Credit** AmEx, DC, MC, V. **Map** II 2B.
Arguably the best hotel in this area, the San Barnaba is spanking new, right by the vaporetto stop, and has welcoming family-hotel-style staff. Fourteen large rooms, some with frescos, and all with a successful mix of antique furniture and modern textiles. There's a small courtyard and roof terrace, too.
Hotel services *Air-conditioning. Babysitting. Bar. Currency exchange. Fax. Garden. Laundry. Multi-lingual staff. Non-smoking rooms. Safe. Theatre reservations.* **Room services** *Air-conditioning. Hairdryer. Minibar. Telephone. TV (satellite).*

Locanda Sturion   40

San Polo 679, calle dello Sturion (041 523 6243/fax 041 522 8378/sturion@tin.it). Vaporetto Rialto. **Rates** L150,000-L210,000 single; L250,000-L360,000 double. **Credit** AmEx, V. **Map** I 3C.
The sign of the 'sturgeon' (*sturion* in Venetian dialect) can be seen in Carpaccio's *Miracle of the Cross* (1494) in the Accademia. By then, the hotel had already been

Away from the hubbub: the **Messner** (*see p56*) and **Alla Salute da Cici** (*see p53*).

open for business for 200 years, its position by the Rialto bridge making it a favourite with visiting merchants. Today it is one of the best-value Grand Canal locations – though only two rooms and the breakfast room look out over the big water; others give on to a quiet calle. Service is friendly, and there is a library of books on Venice. A drawback is the lack of a lift. **Hotel services** *Air-conditioning. Concert reservations. Currency exchange. Fax. Multi-lingual staff.* **Room services** *Air-conditioning. Hairdryer. Kettle. Minibar. Radio. Room service (24-hour). Safe. Telephone. TV (satellite).*

Messner   41
Dorsoduro 216, fondamenta Ca' Balà (041 522 7443/fax 041 522 7266/messner@doge.it). Vaporetto Salute. **Closed** two weeks in Dec. **Rates** L140,000-L155,000 single; L140,000-L230,000 double. **Credit** AmEx, DC, MC, V. **Map** II 3B.
A recent refurbishment was rather over-zealous, and the Messner's immaculately clean rooms may be too uncompromisingly modern for many tastes. The hotel has a charming shady courtyard, however, and there is a warm, helpful and welcoming atmosphere. **Hotel services** *Air-conditioning. Bar. Currency exchange. Fax. Garden. Multi-lingual staff. Non-smoking rooms. Restaurant. Safe.* **Room services** *Air-conditioning. Hairdryer. Safe. Telephone. TV (satellite) in 50% of rooms.*

Pantalon   42
Dorsoduro 3942, crosera San Pantalon (041 710 896/ fax 041 718 683/hotelpantalon@iol.it). Vaporetto San Tomà. **Rates** L90,000-L280,000 single; L150,000-L360,000 double. **Credit** AmEx, DC, MC, V. **Map** II 2A.

Located deep in university territory, in Dorsoduro, the Pantalon hotel has recently been refurbished and modernised in Barbie-doll style. The roof terrace is pleasant, though. **Hotel services** *Air-conditioning. Currency exchange. Dry cleaning. Fax. Laundry. Multi-lingual staff. Safe. Solarium. Theatre reservations. Tours arranged.* **Room services** *Air-conditioning. Hairdryer. Minibar. Radio. Room service (24-hour). Safe. Telephone. TV (satellite).*

San Fantin   43
San Marco 1930/A, campiello della Fenice (tel/fax 041 523 1401). Vaporetto Santa Maria del Giglio. **Closed** mid Nov-mid Feb. **Rates** L75,000-L200,000 single; L120,000-L270,000 double. **Credit** MC, V. **Map** II 3A.
A charming hotel centrally located by the La Fenice opera house and not far from San Marco. The rooms are simple and pleasant. **Hotel services** *Bar. Currency exchange. Fax. Multi-lingual staff. Safe.* **Room services** *Telephone.*

Scandinavia   44
Castello 5240, campo Santa Maria Formosa (041 522 3507/fax 041 523 5232/www.scandinavia. hotelinvenice.com/scandinavia@hotelinvenice.com). Vaporetto San Zaccaria. **Closed** mid Jan-early Feb. **Rates** L150,000-L300,000 single; L200,000-L400,000 double. **Credit** AmEx, MC, V. **Map** I 4C.
Situated on the wonderfully lively and quintessentially Venetian square of Santa Maria Formosa, this hotel is done up in pseudo 18th-century style with lashings of Murano glass. The hotel's rooms are all cosy and some even have balconies with

views over the campo and on to Mauro Codussi's wonderfully curvaceous church (*see p91*).
Hotel services *Air-conditioning. Bar. Currency exchange. Fax. Multi-lingual staff. Non-smoking rooms. Safe. Theatre reservations.* **Room services** *Air-conditioning. Hairdryer. Minibar. Room service (24-hour). Safe. Telephone. TV (satellite).*

Seguso   45

Dorsoduro 779, Zattere (041 528 6858/fax 041 522 2340). Vaporetto Zattere or Accademia. **Closed** Dec-mid Feb. **Rates** L80,000-L230,000 single; L130,000-L290,000 double. **Credit** AmEx, MC, V. **Map** II 2B.
You'll need to book ahead to secure a room in this popular hotel with its cosy dark reception rooms cluttered with books and antiques. Obligatory half board, which makes staying at the pensione dearer than it might at first appear, does not seem to put off the many regulars.
Hotel services *Babysitting. Bar. Fax. Garden. Lift. Multi-lingual staff. Restaurant. Safe.* **Room services** *Room service (24-hour). Telephone.*

Tintoretto   46

Cannaregio 2316, campiello della Chiesa di Santa Fosca (041 721 522/fax 041 721 791/ tintoretto@doge.it). Vaporetto San Marcuola. **Closed** Jan. **Rates** L80,000-L195,000 single; L120,000-L295,000 double. **Credit** AmEx, DC, MC, V. **Map** I 3B.
This is pastel-galore decor at its best. Some of the rooms have views on to the calm Santa Fosca canal. Near the fondamenta Nuove, it is in a handy spot for getting boats to the outer islands.
Hotel services *Air-conditioning. Babysitting. Bar. Currency exchange. Fax. Multi-lingual staff. Non-smoking rooms. Safe. Theatre reservations. Tours arranged.* **Room services** *Air-conditioning. Hairdryer. Room service (24-hour). Safe. Telephone. TV (satellite).*

Tivoli   47

Dorsoduro 3838, crosera San Pantalon (041 524 2460/fax 041 522 2656). Vaporetto San Tomà. **Closed** mid Dec-mid Jan. **Rates** L60,000-L200,000 single; L130,000-L250,000 double. **No credit cards.** **Map** II 2A.
This relatively large, if somewhat unatmospheric hotel is a good place to seek out when all the other places you wanted to stay in are full. It has a small but wonderful courtyard, which some of the rather dark rooms look on to.
Hotel services *Fax. Garden. Safe.* **Room services** *Hairdryer. Room service (24-hour). Telephone. TV (satellite).*

Zecchini   48

Cannaregio 152, lista di Spagna (041 715 611/fax 041 715 066). Vaporetto Ferrovia. **Rates** L60,000-L240,000 single; L60,000-L330,000 double. **Credit** MC, V. **Map** I 1B.
Located on a bustling street rather too close to the railway station, the Zecchini provides rooms of varying sizes for groups. The decor is rather grim, but the staff are friendly and helpful.

Hotel services *Air conditioning. Bar. Currency exchange. Fax. Safe.* **Room services** *Hairdryer. Telephone. TV (satellite).*

Budget

Adriatico   49

Cannaregio 224, lista di Spagna (041 715 176/fax 041 717 275). Vaporetto Ferrovia. **Closed** early Nov-early Dec. **Rates** L100,000-L150,000 single; L150,000-L210,000 double. **Credit** AmEx, DC, MC, V. **Map** I 2B.
Extremely basic it may be, but the Adriatico is clean. There's a tiny breakfast room.
Hotel services *Bar. Fax.* **Room services** *Hairdryer. Telephone.*

Al Vagon   50

Cannaregio 5619, campiello Riccardo Selvatico (tel/fax 041 528 5626). **Vaporetto** *Ca' d'Oro.* **Closed** Jan. **Rates** L90,000-L190,000 single; L100,000-L210,000 double; breakfast L10,000 extra. **Credit** MC, V. **Map** I 4C.
Just off campo Santi Apostoli and a minute's walk from Rialto, this hotel is cheap and cheerful with basic but not overly cramped rooms, all which have their own bathrooms.
Hotel services *Fax. Restaurant. Safe. Theatre reservations.* **Room services** *Telephone.*

Antica Locanda Montin   51

Dorsoduro 1147, fondamenta delle Eremite (041 522 7151/fax 041 520 0255). Vaporetto Accademia or Zattere. **Rates** L100,000-L250,000 double. **Credit** AmEx, MC, V. **Map** II 2B.
It tends to be difficult to get a booking in this delightful seven-bedroom locanda. It owes its immense popularity to the fact that it is also home to one of Venice's most famous and (currently) most overrated restaurants.
Hotel services *Bar. Garden. Restaurant. Safe.* **Room services** *Telephone.*

Caneva   52

Castello 5515, ramo dietro la Fava (041 522 8118/ fax 041 520 8676). Vaporetto Rialto. **Closed** mid Dec-mid Feb. **Rates** L70,000-L130,000 single; L140,000-L180,000 double. **Credit** AmEx, MC, V. **Map** I 4C.
This hotel is in a central spot between the Rialto and San Marco. The canal out back is a high-density gondola route. Basic, but efficiently run.
Hotel services *Fax. Multi-lingual staff. Safe.*

Casa Linger   53

Castello 3541, salizada Sant'Antonin (041 528 5920/fax 041 528 4851). Vaporetto Arsenale. **Rates** L70,000-L140,000 single; L130,000-L180,000 double. **Credit** MC, V. **Map** III 2B.
A long, narrow flight of stairs leads to this unassuming little hotel, in which most of the rooms are airy and spacious. Breakfast is served in the bedrooms. It's situated on a busy street with a true down-home Venetian atmosphere: local housewives congregate at the greengrocer's in the

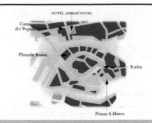

Cluttered with books and antiques, the ever-popular **Seguso**. *See p57.*

street below, a rare commodity in Venice. The downside is that it's quite a hike from the nearest vaporetto stop.
Hotel services *Fax. Safe.* **Room services** *Telephone. TV (on request).*

Gallini   54
San Marco 3673, calle della Verona (041 520 4515/fax 041 520 9103/www.veniceinfo.it/ hgallini@tin.it). Vaporetto Sant'Angelo. **Closed** mid Nov-mid Feb. **Rates** L70,000-L190,000 single; L100,000-L260,000 double. **Credit** AmEx, MC, V. **Map** II 3A.
The Gallini has a great variety of rooms, ranging from expensive for this category to a few which are very cheap if you have no objection to hiking along the corridor for a bath. Some of the bedrooms on the top floor have a wonderful view over the rooftops; one even has a private (though not particularly glamorous) little roof terrace.
Hotel services *Air-conditioning. Babysitting. Currency exchange. Fax. Multi-lingual staff. Safe. Theatre reservations. Tours arranged.* **Room services** *Air-conditioning (in 20% of rooms) Hairdryer. Room service (14-hour). Telephone. TV (in some).*

Guerrini   55
Cannaregio 265, calle delle Procuratie (041 715 333/fax 041 715 114). Vaporetto Ferrovia. **Closed** Jan-carnevale. **Rates** L90,000-L230,000 single; L140,000-L240,000 double. **Credit** AmEx, DC, MC, V. **Map** I 2B.

Set in a quiet alley, this hotel is handy for the station without being too close to the noisy, crowded lista di Spagna. The decor is classically simple.
Hotel services *Bar. Fax. Multi-lingual staff. Safe. Theatre reservations.* **Room services** *Room service (24-hour). Telephone.*

Iris   56
San Polo 2910, calle del Cristo (tel/fax 041 522 2882/htiris@tin.it). Vaporetto San Tomà. **Rates** L125,000-L170,000 single; L170,000-L240,000 double. **Credit** AmEx, DC, MC, V. **Map** II 2A.
In a quiet area between the Frari and San Tomà, the Iris has a pleasant courtyard and simple bedrooms.
Hotel services *Bar. Fax. Theatre reservations.* **Room services** *Hairdryer. Telephone.*

Locanda Canal   57
Castello 4422/C, fondamenta del Remedio (041 523 4538/fax 041 241 9138/www.italyhotels.it). Vaporetto San Zaccaria. **Rates** L100,000-L180,000 double. **No credit cards.** **Map** III 1A.
This small, tidy family-run hotel has a rather extraordinary eating area behind plastic folding doors.
Hotel services *Fax. Safe.*

Locanda San Trovaso   58
Dorsoduro 1350/51, fondamenta delle Eremite (041 277 1146/fax 041 277 7190/ www.locandasantrovaso.com/info@locandasantrovaso .com). Vaporetto San Basilio or Zattere. **Rates** L150,000 single; L220,000 double. **Credit** AmEx, MC, V. **Map** II 2B.

Small (there are just seven large rooms), sweet (18th-century Venetian style without too many chintzy frills), and recently opened, the San Trovaso has a friendly, family feel. It's located on a quiet *fondamenta* behind a gondola-maker's workshop (*see picture p119*). Some may consider the lack of phones and televisions in the bedrooms a disadvantage.
Hotel services *Multilingual staff. Roof terrace. Theatre reservations.* **Room services** *Fan.*

Locanda Silva   59
Castello 4423, fondamenta Remedio (041 522 7643/ fax 041 528 6817). Vaporetto San Zaccaria. **Closed** Jan, Dec. **Rates** L65,000-L80,000 single; L100,000-L180,000 double. **No credit cards. Map** III 1A.
A large hotel with spacious rooms, the Silva is situated in a quiet canal-side street just off the buzzing square of Santa Maria Formosa.
Hotel services *Fax. Multi-lingual staff. Safe.* **Room services** *Telephone.*

Rossi   60
Cannaregio 262, calle delle Procuratie (041 715 164/ fax 041 717 784). Vaporetto Ferrovia. **Closed** Jan-mid Feb. **Rates** L50,000-L140,000 single; L50,000-L160,000 double. **Credit** AmEx, MC, V. **Map** I 2B.
For a one-star near the busy, noisy and generally to be avoided area around the station, this is quite a find. Large and relatively clean, it is at the end of a cosy alleyway just off the lista di Spagna.
Hotel services *Currency exchange. Fax. Multi-lingual staff. Safe. Theatre reservations.* **Room services** *Fan. Telephone.*

San Samuele   61
San Marco 3358, salizzada San Samuele (tel/fax 041 522 8045). Vaporetto San Samuele or Sant'Angelo. **Rates** L50,000-L80,000 single; L70,000-L190,000 double. **No credit cards. Map** II 3A.
Most of the rooms in this lovely hotel have window boxes full of cascading geraniums overlooking the art gallery-lined salizzada San Samuele. This is a clean and friendly establishment that is a notch above most of its fellow one-stars.
Hotel services *Fax. Multi-lingual staff. Safe. Theatre reservations.*

Hostels

Archie's House   62
Cannaregio 1814/B, rio Terrà San Leonardo (041 720 884). Vaporetto San Marcuola. **Rates** L30,000-L40,000 a bed. **No credit cards. Map** I 2B.
This is grottsville extraordinaire, but seems to be popular all the same, especially with gap-year students. You enter through a dirty courtyard bearing a disturbing resemblance to the inside of a rubbish skip. The rooms are relatively clean, however, and it's handy for the bars in fondamenta della Misericordia. Sheets cost L2,000 extra. Hot showers cost L1,500 (five minutes). No alcohol is allowed on the premises.

Foresteria Santa Fosca   63
Cannaregio 2372, fondamenta Daniele Canal (tel/fax 041 715 775). Vaporetto San Marcuola. **Closed** Oct-June. **Rates** L35,000-L45,000 double. **No credit cards. Map** I 3B.
This student-run hostel is not best-known for its efficiency, so make sure you have double confirmation of your booking.

Foresteria Valdese   64
Castello 5170, calle della Madonetta (tel/fax 041 528 6797). Vaporetto San Zaccaria. **Rates** L31,000 a bed; L90,000-L120,000 double. **No credit cards. Map** III 1A.
Just off the lively campo Santa Maria Formosa, in a wonderful palazzo with high ceilings and flaking frescos, this is a really beautiful spot. An impressive flight of stone stairs leads up to dormitories, doubles and self-catering flats. The hostel is run by Waldensian Evangelicals and generally attracts slightly older guests.

Istituto Canossiano   65
Giudecca 428, fondamenta del Ponte Piccolo (tel/fax 041 522 2157). Vaporetto Palanca. **Rates** L30,000 a bed. **No credit cards. Map** II 2C.
This is a women-only hostel run by lovely, friendly nuns. It is simple and clean, and one of the cheapest places to sleep in Venice. The price includes sheets and blankets. One major disadvantage is that guests must be in by 10.30pm (10pm in the winter). The hostel is situated on the Giudecca.

Ostello di Venezia (Youth Hostel)   66
Giudecca 86, fondamenta delle Zitelle (041 523 8211/fax 041 523 5689). Vaporetto Zitelle. **Rates** L27,000 bed & breakfast; L14,000 lunch or dinner. **No credit cards. Map** II 4C.
A vaporetto ride away from the main island, this youth hostel offers stunning and unique views across the lagoon towards the church of Santa Maria Della Salute and San Marco. Written reservations are needed, especially during the summer months. Unadventurous but very cheap meals are served.

Campsites

In summer, the coastal strip of the **Litorale del Cavallino** – the fatter northward continuation of the Lido, on the other side of the Porto del Lido shipping lane – is one huge wall-to-wall campsite. Some sites are so luxurious that, once transport costs are added, they can turn out to be more pricey than a budget hotel for those who plan to make the trip across to Venice each day. But if you want to combine a beach holiday with a couple of day trips to Venice, they are ideal. For further information, ring the seasonal (*May-Sept*) information line run by Assocamping: 041 968 071 (English spoken). There are a couple of sites in Mestre (*see p138*), too.

Sightseeing

Feature boxes

Introduction

After you've seen some of the most amazing sights Europe has to offer, leave the main routes and get well and truly lost – if you can.

You don't 'go sightseeing' in Venice. The whole city is special, even the council flats: however far you wander, you never drift into a belt of suburban villas; even what passes for urban squalor here is crying out to be admired. There are highlights, of course. The **Basilica di San Marco** (*see p76*) is one of Christendom's greatest churches; the **Gallerie dell'Accademia** (*see p122*) contain an unparalleled selection of Renaissance art; and the **Rialto** is a potent symbol of mercantile energy as well as a fine bridge. But one of the joys of Venice consists in leaving the main routes – and getting lost.

When you do get lost, don't be alarmed: as the *calli* close in around you, and visions of red-hooded dwarves flash before your eyes, take comfort in the knowledge that the city is small and you'll soon hit a busy thoroughfare. Until that happens, enjoy the feel of village Venice – or, more appropriately, island Venice. The city is made up of over 100 islands, and every one has something to offer, even if it is only a carved well-head or a cat gnawing a fish bone. The real knack to enjoying Venice is to take your time.

Venice is divided into six *sestieri*, which on the map look like fairly random divisions. But they are worth getting to grips with, first because all addresses include the sestiere name, and second because each district has a different flavour. Cradled by the great lower bend of the Grand Canal is the sestiere of **San Marco**, the heart of the city; east of here is **Castello**, one of the most lived-in areas; stretching to the west and north between Santi Giovanni e Paolo and the railway station is **Cannaregio**, whose western stretches are among the most peaceful parts of Venice. South of the Grand Canal is **San Polo**, bristling with churches; to the west is **Santa Croce**, short on sights but not atmosphere; while to the south is **Dorsoduro**, one of the city's most elegant and artsy districts, with its wide Zattere promenade looking across to the long residential island of the **Giudecca** – the honorary seventh sestiere.

Churches

Napoleon, like more than a few modern tourists, clearly thought there were too many of these and he had 49 ecclesiastical institutions destroyed or converted to other uses. However,

there are still well over 100, at least half of them in regular use. It is worth remembering that Venice grew up originally as a host of separate island-communities, each clustered around its own parish church and saint. The bridges were an afterthought.

Despite Napoleon, the churches contain an inestimable heritage of artistic treasures. Most of the major churches have reliable opening-times; hours in minor churches are more idiosyncratic, depending on the good will or whim of the priest or sacristan. It's well worth exploring these, too, since there is not a single one that does not contain some item of interest, whether it be a shrivelled relic or a glowing Madonna with *bambino*. In general, early morning and late afternoon are the best times for church-crawling. But it's best never to pass an opportunity by: if you see one open without a service under way, go in and poke around. No Sunday opening times are given in listings for churches that open only for Sunday mass.

Museums & galleries

There is nothing state-of-the-art about the city's museums and galleries; they all adhere to the basic pre-modern requirement that a museum should be a passive container for beautiful or instructive things. But some of those things are very beautiful indeed, especially in treasure troves such as the **Gallerie dell'Accademia** (*see p122*), which rivals the Uffizi as Italy's richest collection of paintings. Instruction can be fun, too. The **Museo Storico Navale** (*see p94*) provides a colourful introduction to Venice's maritime past; a grasp of the elaborate mechanism of Venetian government (*see p11* **Venetian government**) and the history of its doges will turn the slog around the **Palazzo Ducale** into a voyage of discovery.

Then there are the curiosities – **Ca' d'Oro** (*see p98*), where a patchy gallery with the occasional gem is housed inside one of the city's most extraordinary architectural frames; the unloved **Museo Archeologico** (*see p77*) in piazza San Marco, which is of interest as a document in the history of connoisseurship; and the eclectic **Museo della Fondazione Scientifica Querini Stampalia** (*see p90*), a private foundation with a fascinating collection of scenes of 18th-century Venetian life, a glorious Bellini (the painter, not the cocktail), and a late-opening library that is one of Venice's more unusual nightlife attractions.

Scuole

A unique blend of art treasure house and social institution, Venice's *scuole* (schools) were devotional lay brotherhoods. Unlike similar institutions elsewhere in medieval Europe, they were subject to the State rather than the Church. The earliest were founded in the 13th century; by the 15th century there were six *scuole grandi* and as many as 400 minor *scuole*. The *scuole grandi* had annually elected officers drawn from the 'citizen' class (those sandwiched between the governing patriciate and the unenfranchised *popolani*), who had the chance to play Doge and Grand Council, thus damping down any discontent that might have shaken one of Europe's longest-lasting oligarchies. While members of the *scuole grandi* (*see* **Scuola di San Rocco** *p114*, **Scuola di San Giovanni Evangelista** *p105*) were mainly drawn from the wealthier professional classes, the humbler *scuole piccole* were either exclusively devotional groups, trade guilds or confraternities of foreign communities (*see* **Scuola di San Giorgio degli Schiavoni** *p96*). When done with providing funds for dowries, scholarships and emergency relief, the wealthier confraternities would turn to building and beautifying their own meeting houses (the *scuole* themselves) in a less-than-humble spirit of self-promotion.

The *scuole* were dissolved by Napoleon in 1806, and most of the buildings were put to new uses. Only three survived or were refounded in the mid-19th century, with their artistic treasures intact. *Oratori* were an earlier and more mystic product of the religious enthusiasms that affected Venice between the 11th and the 13th centuries, when a host of religious orders sprang up in the city.

Admission & tickets

In summer, expect to queue to enter the **Accademia** and the **Palazzo Ducale**. Other museums rarely present any overcrowding problems except during special exhibitions. April and May are traditional months for Italian school trips: this can mean sharing your Tintorettos with gangs of bored teenagers.

Entry to all state-owned museums is free for EU citizens under 18 and over 65. Charges and concessions at city-run and privately owned museums vary; it pays to carry a selection of ID (student card, press card and so on).

For one week each spring – designated the *Settimana dei Beni Culturali* (Cultural Heritage week) – all state-owned galleries and museums are free. See www.beniculturali.it for details.

Cumulative tickets

Many of Venice's landmarks offer **cumulative tickets**, which cut costs if you are planning to visit all the sights covered by any given ticket. These schemes include:

MUSEI DI PIAZZA SAN MARCO/MUSEI CIVICI VENEZIANI

The museums around piazza San Marco (but not the paying sections of the Basilica) can only be entered on a cumulative ticket (L18,000; L10,000 concessions; L6,000 6-14s; no credit cards), valid for three months. The ticket covers Palazzo Ducale, Museo Correr, Museo Archeologico Nazionale, and the museum section of the Biblioteca Marciana (Libreria Sansoviniana). The cumulative ticket can be bought at the museums. Outside San Marco, it also allows access to Palazzo Mocenigo, the Museo del Vetro and the Museo del Merletto.

Information on sights covered by the scheme can be found on www.museiciviciveneziani.it.

ACCADEMIA

The Gallerie dell'Accademia (*see p122*), Ca' d'Oro (*see p98*), and Ca' Pesaro-Museo Orientale (*see p109*) can be visited on a cumulative ticket costing L18,000 (L9,000 concessions) from participating sights. No credit cards are accepted.

CHORUS

The following churches belong to the Chorus scheme (www.chorus-ve.org), which funds upkeep and restoration by charging for entry:
San Marco: Santa Maria del Giglio (*see p87*), Santo Stefano (*see p86*).
Castello: Santa Maria Formosa (*see p91*), San Pietro in Castello (*see p96*).
Cannaregio: Santa Maria dei Miracoli (*see p102*), Sant'Alvise (*see p101*), Madonna dell'Orto (*see p100*).
San Polo & Santa Croce: San Polo (*see p108*), San Stae (*see p111*), I Frari (*see p112*), San Giacomo dell'Orio (*see p110*).
Dorsoduro: San Sebastiano (*see p117*).
Giudecca: Santissimo Redentore (*see p128*).

There's an admission fee of L3000 for each; alternatively, invest in a cumulative ticket (L15,000; L10,000 students). Individual and cumulative tickets can be bought in the participating churches and at ACTV-Vela shops (*see p275*). Participating churches are equipped with audioguides (L3,000 per church; L6,000 for all Chorus churches) in English. No credit cards are accepted.

Sightseeing

The Grand Canal

Whether favouring the left bank or the right, there can be few more imposing waterways in the world.

The *Canal Grande* (Grand Canal), about three and a half kilometres (two and a half miles) in length, snakes through Venice, its great double backwards-S curve giving the city's *sestieri* their shape. The most interesting stretch is between Vallaresso vaporetta stop, near Piazza San Marco, in the south-east and the station *(ferrovia)* in the north-west. The trip takes about half an hour and is worth repeating at different times of day (and night).

The Canal is still the main thoroughfare of Venice; in the great days of the city's trading empire it would have been alive with cargo boats from all over the Mediterranean. A Grand Canal address was not only socially but commercially desirable; and the architecture of the *palazzi* that line it is as practical as it is impressive. Most of the notable buildings were built between the 12th and 18th centuries. When a family decided to rebuild a palazzo, they usually maintained the same basic structure – for the good reason that they could build on the same foundations, resulting in some interesting style hybrids. The Grand Canal offers many

examples of *palazzi* in which Veneto-Byzantine or Gothic features are incorporated into Renaissance or baroque styles.

For centuries the *palazzi* generally followed the same plan: a main water-entrance opening on to a large hall with storage space on either side; a *mezzanino* with offices; a *piano nobile* (main floor – sometimes two in grander buildings) consisting of a spacious reception hall lit by large central windows and flanked on both sides by residential rooms; and a land-entrance at the back. Over the centuries all kinds of architectural frills and trimmings were added, but the underlying form was stable – and, as always in Venice, it is form that follows function.

In the following description of the most notable *palazzi*, many names recur, for the simple reason that families expanded, younger sons inheriting as well as older ones. Compound names indicate that the palazzo passed through various hands. Originally the term 'palazzo' was reserved for the Doge's Palace. Other *palazzi* were known as Casa or Ca' for short: this is still true of some of the older ones, such as Ca' d'Oro.

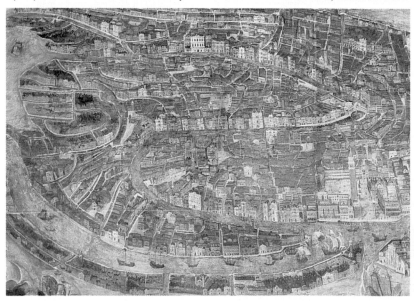

The Salute shore

The view of the left bank begins with the **Dogana di Mare** (Customs House, 1677), with its tower, gilded ball and weather vane figure of Fortune. All ships wanting to enter Venice could have their cargoes examined by customs officials, who were based here. The warehouses beyond are 19th century.

After the Patriarchal Seminary, by Longhena (1671), is the church of **Santa Maria della Salute** (*see p123*). Baldassare Longhena's audacious baroque creation took 50 years to build. On 21 November a procession from San Marco makes its way across a bridge of boats to the church (*see p196*).

Vaporetto stop Salute

The former abbey of **San Gregorio** is the first building beyond this stop, with a fine 14th-century relief of St Gregory over a Gothic doorway. (Beyond can be seen the apse of the former church of the same name.)

Palazzo Salviati is a 19th-century building with gaudy mosaics advertising the products of the Salviati glassworks.

Next comes the pure, lopsided charm of the Renaissance **Ca' Dario**, built in the 1470s, perhaps by Pietro Lombardo, with decorative use of coloured marbles and chimney pots. Venetians say the palazzo is cursed; certainly the list of former owners who have met sticky ends is impressive. Woody Allen was once rumoured to have been on the point of buying it.

Next but one is the single-storey **Palazzo Venier dei Leoni**. Work ground to a halt in 1749 when the family opposite objected to their light being blocked by such a huge pile. Art collector Peggy Guggenheim lived here from 1949-79; she was the last person in Venice to have her own private gondola. The building now contains the **Peggy Guggenheim Collection** (*see p122*). Check out the brass horse and rider (1948) by Marino Marini overlooking the canal. In his autobiography, English art

---

South-east

The San Marco shore

Vaporetto stop Vallaresso

At the corner of Calle Vallaresso is the self-effacing **Harry's Bar**, the near-legendary Venetian watering-hole, founded by Arrigo Cipriani senior in the 1930s (*see p166*).

The first notable building is **Ca' Giustinian**, in the late Gothic style of the 1470s. Once a hotel where Verdi, Gautier, Ruskin and Proust stayed; George Eliot's honeymoon here was ruined when her husband fell off the balcony into the Grand Canal and nearly died. It is now the headquarters of the Biennale.

The **Europa & Regina hotel** was once the home of Kay Bronson, an American society hostess whose hospitality was much appreciated by Henry James. A little further on is the narrow Gothic **Palazzo Contarini Fasan**, traditionally, but quite arbitrarily, known as Desdemona's house. Recently restored, it has beautiful balconies with wheel-tracery.

Vaporetto stop Santa Maria del Giglio

The massive rusticated ground floor of the **Palazzo Corner della Ca' Grande** (now the Prefecture) influenced Longhena's baroque *palazzi*. The highest of High Renaissance, the imposing pile was commissioned in 1537 from Sansovino for Giacomo Cornaro, and built after 1545. Ruskin called it 'one of the worst and coldest buildings of the central Renaissance'.

After one of the few Grand Canal gardens comes the bashful **Casetta delle Rose**, set back behind its own small trellised garden. Canova had a studio here, and Gabriele D'Annunzio, who set one of his most sensuous novels, *Il Fuoco* (*Fire*), in Venice stayed in the house.

There are more literary associations in the two **Palazzi Barbaro**, the penultimate buildings before the Accademia Bridge. The second one – 15th-century Gothic, with a fine but battered Renaissance water entrance – still partly belongs to the Curtis family, who played host to Henry James at intervals between 1870 and 1875. The building was the model for Milly Theale's palazzo in *The Wings of the Dove*. At the foot of the bridge is **Palazzo Franchetti**, built in the 15th century but much restored and altered in the 19th; recently acquired by the Istituto Veneto, it is now used as a conference centre.

Ponte dell'Accademia

In 1932 the iron Ponte dell'Accademia built by the Austrians was replaced by a 'temporary' wooden one. When this was discovered to be on the point of collapse in 1984, the Venetians had grown too fond of it to imagine anything else spanning the Canal, so it was rebuilt in 1984 exactly as before.

The **Ca' del Duca** incorporates in one corner a part of the rusticated base and columns of a palace that Bartolomeo Bon was going to build for the Cornaro family. In 1461 it was bought by Francesco Sforza, Duke of Milan, but fortunately the bombastic plan for the site was abandoned.

Vaporetto stop San Samuele

Beyond this stop is **Palazzo Grassi** (*see p86*), built 1748-72 by Giorgio Massari. This was the last of the great patrician *palazzi*, built in grand style in 1748-72 when the city was in terminal decline. It was bought by Fiat in the 1980s and restored at the speed and expense that only huge PR-conscious corporations can allow themselves. Mammoth history-of-world-civilisation exhibitions are held here regularly.

A little further on are the four **Palazzi Mocenigo**, with blue and white poles in the water. The central double palazzo (16th century) was where Byron and his menagerie of foxes, monkeys and dogs lived from 1818-19; he wrote to a friend: 'Venice is not an expensive residence... I have my gondola and about 14 servants... and I reside in one of the Mocenigo palaces on the Grand Canal; the rent... is two hundred a year (and I gave more than I need have done).'

forger Eric Hebborn describes being chatted up by Peggy next to this sculpture, with its immodest protrusion: 'Peggy put her hand on the bronze erection and said in a sultry sexy kind of voice... "Eric, the whole heat of Venice seems to concentrate itself in this spot." With which she unscrewed the object, and to my horror, thrust it into my hand and invited me to kiss her. Thinking it impolite to refuse a lady, I gave her a gallant peck on the cheek and returned the metal penis with: "I'm sorry, Peggy, but this is a lot harder than mine is".'

After pretty Gothic **Palazzo da' Mula** comes 16th-century **Palazzo Barbarigo**, disfigured by some tacky 19th-century mosaics. The building gives on to **campo San Vio**, one of the few *campi* on the Grand Canal. In the corner is the Anglican church of **St George**.

Accademia bridge

Vaporetto stop Accademia

Once the church and monastery of Santa Maria della Carità, the **Galleria dell'Accademia** now boasts an unrivalled collection of Venetian paintings (*see p122*).

The first palazzo after the Accademia Bridge houses the British Vice-Consulate. Just before the Ca' Rezzonico stop is the 15th-century **Palazzo Loredan**.

Vaporetto stop Ca' Rezzonico

Ca' Rezzonico (*see p119*) is a baroque masterpiece by Longhena. It was begun in 1667 for the Bon family, then sold to the Rezzonico family. Robert Browning died here, while staying with his profitably married but otherwise talentless son Pen, who bought the palazzo with his wife's money. Later guests included Whistler and Cole Porter. The building now contains the Museum of 18th-Century Venice.

After two smaller buildings come three magnificent mid-15th century Gothic palazzi. The first two are the **Palazzi Giustinian**; the last and largest is **Ca' Foscari** (being restored as this guide went to press). Wagner stayed in Palazzo

Giustinian in the winter of 1858-9, composing part of *Tristan und Isolde*. He declared that the horn prelude to the third act was inspired by the mournful cries of the gondoliers. It was at Ca' Foscari that Henry III of France was lavishly entertained in 1574 – so lavishly that his reason seems to have been knocked permanently askew. Doge Francesco Foscari died here of a broken heart after being ousted from office. The palazzo is now the headquarters of Venice's Università Ca' Foscari.

The **rio Ca' Foscari**, on which the palazzo stands, becomes the **rio Novo**, a canal dug in the 1930s to provide a short-cut to the car park and station. Traffic seriously undermined the foundations of the buildings along the canal. Public transport stopped using the rio Novo in the 1980s.

Looking down the rio, you can see the archways of the city's fire station. Between it and **Palazzo Balbi** is a minor building, on a site once scheduled to hold Frank Lloyd Wright's Centre for Foreign Architectural Students. In the end his designs were judged too radical for so conspicuous a spot.

Palazzo Balbi (1582-90), with obelisks (an indication that an admiral lived here), is the seat of the Veneto Regional Council.

Vaporetto stop San Tomà

A little way beyond the stop is the **Palazzo Pisani Moretta**, a large Gothic palazzo of the 15th century.

Just beyond the rio San Polo is the 16th-century **Palazzo Cappello Layard**. In the last century Sir Henry Austen Layard, archaeologist and British ambassador to Constantinople, lived here.

Vaporetto stop San Silvestro

Before the Rialto bridge are a few houses with Veneto-Byzantine windows and decorations.

Vaporetto stop Sant'Angelo

Next is the small-scale **Palazzo Corner Spinelli**, built in the last decade of the 15th century by Mauro Codussi. It is one of the most beautiful early Renaissance buildings in Venice, with a rusticated ground floor, elegant balconies and Codussi's characteristic round arches incorporating twin smaller arches.

Three *palazzi* further on stands the pink **Palazzo Benzon**, home of Countess Marina Querini-Benzon, a great society figure at the end of the 18th century. Byron was charmed by her when she was already in her sixties. She inspired a popular song, which the gondoliers apparently sang before international tourism imposed '*O Sole Mio*': '*La biondina in gondoleta*'.

After several more *palazzi* comes another High Renaissance building of similar dimensions to Sansovino's Ca' Corner: **Palazzo Grimani**, by Sanmicheli. From Verona, he was famous as a military architect, and this building is characteristically massive and assertive. The Grimani family were nouveaux riches, and the story goes that they wanted each one of their windows to be larger than the front door of the palazzo that used to stand opposite.

Palazzo Farsetti and **Palazzo Loredan** are Veneto-Byzantine buildings that now house the Town Hall and various municipal offices. Though heavily restored, these two adjoining palazzi are among the few surviving examples of the 12th-century Venetian house, with its first-floor polyforate window. **Palazzetto Dandolo** is a Gothic building that appears to have been squeezed tight by its neighbours. Enrico Dandolo, the blind Doge who led the assault on Constantinople in 1204, was born in an earlier palazzo on this site.

Vaporetto stop Rialto

Just after the Rialto stop is **Palazzo Manin Dolfin**, with a portico straddling the fondamenta. The façade is by Sansovino (late 1530s); the rest was rebuilt by Ludovico Manin, the forlorn last Doge of Venice. It now belongs to the Bank of Italy.

Ponte del Rialto

At the foot of the bridge is the **Fondaco dei Tedeschi**, a huge residence-cum-warehouse leased to the German community from the 13th century on. The present building was built by Spavento and Scarpagnino in 1505-8 after a fire. The façade once had glorious frescoes by Titian and Giorgione – now in a sad state of repair in the Ca' d'Oro gallery. The Fondaco is now the main post office.

The **Ca' da Mosto**, once the site of the Leon Bianco (white lion) hotel, is one of the earliest Veneto-Byzantine palazzi on the Grand Canal. Just beyond the rio dei Santi Apostoli is **Palazzo Mangilli Valmarana**, built in 1751 for Joseph Smith, the British consul, who amassed the huge collection of Canaletto paintings that now belongs to the Queen. The building is now the Argentinian Consulate.

Vaporetto stop Ca' d'Oro

Beyond the vaporetto stop is the **Ca' d'Oro** (see p98) itself, the most gorgeously ornate Gothic building on the Canal. Restoration work on it was finished in 1984, after 20 years of labour. However, for all its ornaments, it is sober in comparison with its original appearance, when its decorative features were gilded or painted in ultramarine blue and cinnabar red. It has an

Rialto bridge

The Ponte di Rialto was built in 1588-92 by the aptly named Antonio Da Ponte. Until the 19th century it was the only bridge over the Grand Canal. It replaced a wooden one, which can be seen in Carpaccio's painting of *The Miracle of the True Cross* in the Accademia (*see p122*). After the decision was taken to build it, 60 years passed, during which designs by Michelangelo, Vignola, Sansovino and Palladio were rejected. Da Ponte's simple but effective project eventually got the green light, probably because it maintained the utilitarian features of the previous wooden structure, with its double row of shops. The bridge thus acts as a logical continuation of the market at its foot. Palladio's design was far more beautiful, but made no provision for the sale of Nike shoes and plastic gondolas.

Beyond the Rialto bridge, the **Palazzo dei Camerlenghi** (1523-5) is built around the curve of the canal; the walls lean noticeably. It was the headquarters of the Venetian Exchequer, with a debtors' prison on the ground floor.

The **Fabbriche Vecchie** by Scarpagnino was built after a fire in the early 16th century. Just beyond them, the longer **Fabbriche Nuove**, by Sansovino, is now the Court of Assizes.

The covered fish market or **Pescaria** has occupied a site here since the 14th century. The current neo-Gothic construction, however, was only built in 1907, replacing an iron one.

Further on is the large **Palazzo Corner della Regina**, with a rusticated ground floor featuring grotesque masks, some just above water level. It was built for a branch of the Corner family, who were descended from Caterina Cornaro, Queen of open loggia on the *piano nobile*, like the Doge's Palace, but unlike any other palazzo after the Byzantine period.

The next building of note, after a fairly dull stretch, is **Palazzo Vendramin Calergi**, an impressive Renaissance palazzo built by Codussi in the first decade of the 16th century. The double-arched windows seen in Palazzo Corner Spinelli are used here on a larger scale. Porphyry insets decorate the façade. Wagner died here in 1883. It is the winter home of the Casinò.

Vaporetto stop San Marcuola

Beyond the wide Cannaregio Canal is **Palazzo Labia**, the 18th-century home of the seriously rich Labia family. The story goes that parties ended with the host throwing his gold dinner plates into the canal to demonstrate his wealth; the servants would then be ordered to fish them out again. A famous fancy-dress ball thrown here in 1951 by a Mexican millionaire continued this tradition of conspicuous consumption. The building is now the regional headquarters of the RAI (the Italian state broadcaster). It contains suitably sumptuous frescoes by Tiepolo.

Next door is the church of **San Geremia**; from the Canal, the apse of the chapel of Santa Lucia is visible.

Unusually narrow **Palazzo Flangini** is a 17th-century building by Sardi. Despite all the picturesque stories of quarrelling brothers, it owes its shape to the simple fact that the family's money ran out.

Ponte degli Scalzi

At the foot of the Ponte degli Scalzi is the fine baroque façade of the **Scalzi** church, recently restored (*see p98*).

Cyprus; Catherine was born in an earlier house on the site. The present palazzo dates from the 1720s.

On the rio di Ca' Pesaro, and with a magnificent side wall curving along the canal in gleaming marble, is **Ca' Pesaro** (*see p109*), a splendid example of Venetian baroque by Longhena.

Vaporetto stop San Stae

The church of **San Stae** has a baroque façade by Domenico Rossi, with exuberant sculpture (*see p111*).

The **Depositi del Megio** (state granaries) have a battlemented plain brick façade. The sculpted lion is a modern replacement of the original, destroyed at the fall of the Republic.

On the other side of the Rio del Megio stands the **Fontego dei Turchi**, a 19th-century reconstruction of the original Veneto-Byzantine building, which was leased to Turkish traders in the 17th century as a residence and warehouse. Some of the original material was used but the effect as a whole is one of pastiche. Once lived in by the poet Torquato Tasso, it's now the Natural History Museum (due to reopen in 2003).

Vaporetto stop Riva di Biasio

Scalzi bridge

The Ponte degli Scalzi which leads across to the station was built in stone by Eugenio Miozzi in 1934.

Just beyond the **Ponte degli Scalzi** is the church of San Simeone Piccolo, with its high green dome and Corinthian portico. For those arriving in Venice it acts as a picturesque introduction to the city.

North-west

Vaporetto stop Ferrovia

San Marco

Explore beyond the basilica and *palazzi* edging 'the drawing room of Europe': this sestiere offers a surfeit of riches indeed.

This sestiere is the heart of the city. But its sights are not confined to **piazza San Marco** itself. Three main thoroughfares link the key points of San Marco, forming a rough triangle: one from piazza San Marco to the Rialto bridge (*see p68*), one from the Rialto to the Accademia bridge (*see p66*), and one from the Accademia to piazza San Marco. Even in this busiest of *sestieri*, it is possible to stray into the centre of the triangle and feel as if you are off the beaten track.

Piazza San Marco

Napoleon famously referred to the square as the 'drawing-room of Europe'. His description catches some of the quality of the place: it may not be homely, but it is a supremely civilised meeting place, with architecture that is impressive but not intimidating. Byzantine rubs shoulders with Gothic, Roman Classical, late Renaissance… it covers 1,000 years of Venetian history. The vertically challenged emperor intended to add to the furnishings of this open-air drawing-room with a statue of himself in the centre of the western wing. It was never erected: the Venetians have always kept the square clear of public monuments and statues (sometimes stooping to mendacity to do so – *see p89* **Monument to Bartolomeo Colleoni**). This is typical of Venice, where history is always communal rather than personal.

The north side of the square dates from the early 16th century. Its 'troops of ordered arches' (to quote Ruskin) take up a motif suggested by an earlier Byzantine building that can still be seen in Gentile Bellini's painting *Translation of the Relics of the Cross* in the **Gallerie dell'Accademia** (*see p122*). Here resided the Procurators of St Mark's, who were in charge of the maintenance of the basilica – hence the name of this whole wing, the **Procuratie Vecchie**.

Construction of the **Procuratie Nuove** on the other side of the square went on for most of the first half of the 17th century; it was built to designs by Vincenzo Scamozzi on the model of the **Biblioteca Marciana** (*see p72*) around the corner. Napoleon, of course, had to join the two wings at the far end – not for the sake of symmetry but in order to create the ballroom that was lacking in the Procuratie Nuove, which had become the imperial residence. So, in 1807,

down came Sansovino's church of San Geminiano (one of around 40 tidied away by the emperor), and up went the **Ala Napoleonica**, which now houses the **Museo Correr** (*see p77*). The cafés under the arches have their history, too; but the most important thing to know about them these days is that a cup of coffee at an outside table will double your day's expenses.

PIAZZETTA DEI LEONCINI
On the north side of the basilica is this small square, named after two small marble lions that have been rubbed smooth by generations of children's bottoms. The large palazzo at the far end of the square is the 19th-century residence of the patriarch (cardinal) of Venice.

LA PIAZZETTA
Between the basilica and the lagoon, the Piazzetta, as it is so economically known, is the real entrance to Venice, defined by two free-standing columns of granite (from Syria or

Piazza San Marco: drawing room of Europe.

Sightseeing

Constantinople). Generations of foreign visitors disembarked here, to be immediately struck by all that pomp and magnificence. The area directly in front of the **Palazzo Ducale** corresponded to the modern-day parliamentary lobby. Known as the *broglio*, it was the place where councillors conferred and connived – hence the term 'imbroglio'.

The man who erected the two columns in the 12th century supposedly asked for the right to set up gambling tables between them. The authorities agreed, but soon put a damper on the jollity by using the pillars to string 'em up (criminals, that is) for public edification – which is why superstitious locals avoid walking between them. The winged lion on top of the easternmost column is in fact a chimera from Persia, Syria or maybe China; the wings and book are Venetian additions. St Theodore, who tops the other one, was Venice's first patron saint.

La Piazzetta: the real entrance to Venice. *See p71.*

BY THE LAGOON

West of the Piazzetta are the **Giardinetti Reali** (Royal Gardens), created by the French, who had the old granaries pulled down to provide a view for the Royal Residence they had set up in the Procuratie Nuove. The dainty neo-classical coffeehouse by Gustavo Selva is now the city's main tourist office.

By the Vallaresso vaporetto stop is **Harry's Bar** *(see p166)*, the most famous watering hold in the city, founded in the 1920s. Ernest Hemingway, Orson Welles and many other famous drinkers have contributed to the legend of the place, and the price of the food.

Going the opposite way from the Piazzetta, you cross the **Ponte della Paglia** (Bridge of Straw). If you can elbow your way to the side of the bridge, there is a photo-op view of the **Bridge of Sighs**, famous in legend and poetry (Byron's *Childe Harold*, for example) as linking the Palazzo Ducale to the prisons and thus, supposedly, offering a last glimpse of the outside to the condemned wretches. From the Bridge of Straw there is also a superb view of the Renaissance façade of the Palazzo Ducale, by Antonio Rizzo, which even Ruskin– a fan of the Byzantine and Gothic – was forced to admire against his will.

TICKETS

The museums around piazza San Marco (but not the paying parts of the basilica) must be visited on a cumulative ticket. *See* Musei di piazza San Marco/Musei Civici Veneziani, *p63*. Information on the sights covered can be found on the website www.museiciviciveneziani.it.

Biblioteca Marciana/Libreria Sansovino

San Marco 13A, piazzetta San Marco (041 522 4951/http://marciana.venezia.sbn.it). Vaporetto Vallaresso. **Open** *Apr-Oct* 9am-7pm daily (last entry 5.30pm). *Nov-Mar* 9am-5pm daily (last entry 3.30pm). **Admission** with cumulative ticket *(see p63* **Musei di Piazza San Marco**). **Map II 4B**.

Opposite the seat of government stands the universal symbol of learning and culture, the city's library *(marciana* translates as 'of Mark'). In 1468 the great humanist scholar Cardinal Bessarion of Trebizond left his collection of Greek and Latin manuscripts to the State. This time the Venetians didn't lose them, as they had done with Petrarch's library *(see p39)*, although they didn't get round to constructing a proper home for them until 1537. Jacopo Sansovino, a Florentine architect who had settled in Venice after fleeing from the Sack of Rome in 1527, was appointed to create the library. Palladio described it as the 'richest and most ornate building since antiquity'.

With this building, Sansovino brought the ideas of the Roman Renaissance of Bramante and Michelangelo into Venice, although, with its

From the **Campanile**: the tallest
landmark, the most spectacular
view. *See p76.*

Horse power

When Venice led the Sack of Constantinople in 1204 (*see chapter* **History**) she did so with a precise shopping list. The list was partly political (remove the Byzantine emperor), partly strategic (secure control over vital ports in the eastern Mediterranean) and partly religio-cultural. Saintly relics were crucial, as were enamel cameos to be incorporated into the Pala d'Oro (*see p80*) and the miracle-working Nicopoeia icon.

But biggest and best and unquestionably most significant were the four bronze horses that now grace the Basilica di San Marco. Unleashed from their pedestals atop the emperor's box in the Hippodrome, they were to become as much a symbol of Venice as the winged lion of St Mark: when the Genoese Admiral Pietro Doria set out to conquer Venice in 1379, he talked of curbing the city's 'unbridled horses', not clipping the lion's wings.

The horses' origins are uncertain. For many years they were attributed to a Greek sculptor of the fourth century BC, but the idea that they may be an original Roman work of the second century AD has recently come into favour: the half-moon shape of their eyes is said to have been a Roman characteristic.

They were at first placed in front of the Arsenal, but around 1250 they found their place of honour on the terrace of the Basilica, supreme expressions of Venetian pride. Local painters – who often had little acquaintance with real horses – frequently included them in their works: a centurion is mounted on one of the horses in Tintoretto's *Crucifixion* in San Rocco (*see p114*); one appears in miniature on the mantelpiece in Carpaccio's *St Augustine in his Study* (*see p96*). Canaletto, in a caprice, restored them to their Byzantine pedestals, set up in the Piazzetta.

In 1797 it was Napoleon's turn to play looter, and the horses did not return to Venice until after his defeat at Waterloo. Apart from the parentheses of the World Wars, during which they were put in safe storage, they remained on the terrace until 1974, when they were removed for restoration. Since 1982 they have been on display in a room inside the basilica, with perfect but soulless copies replacing them on the terrace.

abundance of statuary, he also appealed to the Venetian love of surface decoration. His original plan included a barrel-vault ceiling. This collapsed shortly after construction, however, and the architect was immediately clapped into prison. His friends Titian and Aretino had to lobby hard to have him released.

The working part of the library is now housed in **La Zecca** (*see p84*) and contains 750,000 volumes and around 13,500 manuscripts, mainly Greek. The Old Library, the **Libreria Sansoviniana** – now a museum – is entered from the Piazzetta, at no.13A. Vittoria's monumental staircase with stucco decoration leads up to the anteroom, in which a partial reconstruction has been made of Cardinal Grimani's collection of classical statues, as arranged by Scamozzi (1596). On the ceiling is *Wisdom*, a late work by Titian.

The main room has a magnificent ceiling, with seven rows of allegorical medallion-paintings, produced by a number of Venetian Mannerist artists as part of a competition. Veronese's *Music* (sixth row from entrance), perhaps the least Mannerist in style, was awarded the gold chain by Titian. In a room off the staircase landing is Fra Mauro's Map of the World (1459), a fascinating testimony to the precision of Venice's geographical knowledge, with extraordinarily accurate depictions of China and India.

Not courtesans but noblewomen. *See p77.*

Palazzo Ducale. *See p80.*

Campanile

Open *Apr-Sept* 9.30am-30 mins before sunset daily. *Nov-Mar* 9.30am-3.30pm daily. **Admission** L10,000. **No credit cards**. **Map** II 4A.

Venice's most famous landmark – and at almost 99m (325ft) the tallest building in the city – was first built between 888 and 912. Its present appearance, with the stone spire and the gilded angel on top, dates from 1514. The Campanile served both as a watch-tower and a bell-tower. It provided a site for public humiliations: people of 'scandalous behaviour' were hung in a cage from the top. More wholesome fun was provided by the *volo dell'anzolo*, when an intrepid *arsenalotto* (Arsenale shipwright) would slide down a rope strung between the Campanile and the **Palazzo Ducale** to mark the end of Carnival.

In July 1902 the whole thing fell down. Some blamed old age, weak foundations and lightning damage; others, such as arch old Augustus Hare, put it down to 'gross neglect and criminal misusage'. The Campanile was tidy in its collapse, imploding in a neat pyramid of rubble; the only victim was the custodian's cat.

It was rebuilt exactly 'as it was, where it was', to use the formula of the town council (recently exhumed for the rebuilding of the **La Fenice** opera

Basilica di San Marco

Throughout history, the Basilica di San Marco has provoked extreme reactions. Some, like Ruskin, pitch head first into purple prose: 'The crests of the arches break into a marble foam, and toss themselves far into the blue sky in flashes and wreaths of sculpted spray.' Others, resentful of its opulence, take the dissenting view. Mark Twain described it as 'a vast and warty bug taking a meditative walk'.

The church is often seen as the living testimony of Venice's links with Byzantium. But it is also an expression of the city's independence. In the Middle Ages any self-respecting city-state had to have a truly important holy relic. So when two Venetian merchants swiped the body of St Mark from Alexandria in 828, concealed from prying Moslem eyes under a protective layer of pork, they were going for the very best – an Evangelist, and an entire body at that. Fortunately there was a legend (or one was quickly cooked up) that the saint had once been caught in the lagoon in a storm, and so it was fitting that this should be his final resting-place.

It is perhaps equally fitting that this most sacred monument, symbol of the city, is built around a piece of plunder, however divinely

sanctioned. The Venetians, who had started out with nothing but salt and fish, had by necessity become traders but they never looked askance at a bit of straightforward looting as well. The basilica – like the city as a whole – is encrusted with trophies brought back from Venice's greatest spoilatory exploit, the Sack of Constantinople in 1204, during the free-for-all that went under the name of the Fourth Crusade.

The present basilica is the third on the site. It was built mainly between 1063-94, although the work of decoration continued all the way through to the 16th century. The church only became the Cathedral of Venice in 1807, ten years after the fall of the Republic; until then the bishop exerted his authority from San Pietro in Castello (*see p96*), on the eastern outskirts of the city.

Next door to the **Palazzo Ducale**, Venice's most important church was associated with political as much as spiritual power. Venetians who came to worship here were very much aware that they were guests of the Doge, not the Pope, and the basilica was an integral part of the city's self-glorifying mythology.

The great triumphal arches of the façade are an expression of civic pride; and even the house, *see p87*). Holy Roman Emperor Frederick III rode a horse to the top of the old version in 1451; these days, visitors take the lift. The view through the anti-suicide grate is superb, taking in the Lido, the Dolomites and the whole lagoon.

Sansovino's little **Loggetta** at the foot of the tower, which echoes the shape of a Roman triumphal arch, was also rebuilt, jigsaw-fashion, using bits found in the rubble. During sessions of the Grand Council, guards recruited from the Arsenale used to keep watch here. In the 18th century the Loggetta took on a more popular function as the place where the state lottery was drawn.

Museo Archeologico

San Marco, piazzetta San Marco (041 522 4951). Vaporetto San Zaccaria or Vallaresso. **Open** *Apr-Oct* 9am-7pm daily (last entry 5.30pm). *Nov-Mar* 9am-5pm daily (last entry 3.30pm). **Admission** with cumulative ticket (*see p63* **Musei di Piazza San Marco**). **Map** II 4B.

This seldom-visited collection of Greek and Roman art and artefacts is interesting not so much for the quality of the individual pieces as for the light they cast on the history of collecting. Assembled mainly by Cardinal Domenico Grimani and his nephew Giovanni, mainly from Roman finds, the collection is a discerning 16th-century humanist's attempt to surround himself with the classical ideal of beauty; as such these statues were much copied by Venetian artists. Among the highlights are the original fifth-century BC Greek statues of goddesses in Room 4, which are among the few such works known to the Italian Renaissance, the Grimani Altar in Room 6, and the intricate cameos and intaglios in Room 7 or Room 12 (depending on temporary exhibitions).

Museo Correr

San Marco, piazza San Marco/sottoportego San Geminian (041 522 5625/fax 041 520 0935). Vaporetto San Zaccaria/Vallaresso. **Open** *Apr-Oct* 9am-7pm daily (last entry 5.30pm). *Nov-Mar* 9am-5pm daily (last entry 3.30pm). **Admission** with cumulative ticket (*see p63* **Musei di Piazza San Marco**). **Map** II 4A.

The Museo Correr is Venice's civic museum, dedicated to the history of the Republic – which means that it acts as a storeroom for all the bits and pieces that didn't fit in elsewhere. Based on the private collection of Venetian nobleman Teodoro Correr (1750-1830), it is elevated beyond mere curiosity value by the second-floor gallery, which is a must for anyone interested in Venetian early Renaissance painting. The museum is housed in the **Ala Napoleonica**,

Venetians' sincere devotion to their patron saint, which supported the costly decoration lovingly bestowed on the building over the centuries, had a strong nationalist element.

EXTERIOR

The first view of the basilica from the western end of the square is an unforgettable experience. It's particularly impressive in the evening, when the mosaics on the façade glow in the light of the setting sun (as they are mostly 17th- and 18th-century replacements, the distance improves them). The façade consists of two orders of five arches, with clusters of columns in the lower order; the upper arches are surmounted by the fantastic Gothic tracery that inspired Ruskin to reach for those metaphors.

The only original mosaic is the one over the north door. This shows *The Translation of the Body of St Mark to the Basilica*, and contains the earliest known representation of the church, dating from around 1260. Of curiosity value is the 17th-century mosaic over the south door, which shows the body of St Mark being filched from Alexandria and the Moslems reeling back in disgust from its crafty pork wrapping.

The real treasures, though, are the sculptures, particularly the recently restored group of three carved arches around the central portal, a masterpiece of Romanesque work. The inner curve of the outer arch is the liveliest, with its detailed portrayals of Venetian trades and crafts such as shipbuilding, hunting and fishing. The upper order, with its fine 14th-century Gothic

Palazzo Ducale: the symbol and hub of political power. *See p80.*

▶ Basilica di San Marco (continued)

sculpture by the Dalle Masegne brothers and later Tuscan and Lombard sculptors, can be seen from the **Loggia** (*see p81*).

The south façade, towards the Palazzo Ducale, was the first side seen by visitors from the sea and is thus richly encrusted with trophies from Constantinople and the wars against Genoa, all proclaiming Venice's might. There was a ceremonial entrance to the basilica here as well, but this was blocked by the construction of the **Zen Chapel** (*see p80*) in the 16th century. At the corner stand the **Tetrarchs**, a fourth-century porphyry group of four conspiratorial-looking kings. These come from Constantinople, and are usually accepted as representing Diocletian and his Imperial colleagues. However, popular lore has it that they are four Saracens turned to stone after an attempt to burgle the Treasury.

The two free-standing pillars in front of the Baptistry door, with Syrian carvings from the fifth century, come from Acre, as does the stumpy porphyry column on the corner, known as the **Pietra del Bando**, where decrees of the Signoria were read. It bore the brunt of the fall of the Campanile in 1902 (*see p75*); hence its rather battered appearance.

The north façade, facing Piazzetta dei Leoncini, is also studded with loot. One example is the carving of 12 sheep on either side of a throne bearing a cross, a Byzantine work of the seventh century. Note the beautiful 13th-century Moorish arches of the **Porta dei Fiori**, which enclose a Nativity scene.

The narthex (entrance porch) has an opus sectile marble floor; a small lozenge of porphyry by the central door is said to mark the spot where the Emperor Barbarossa paid homage to Pope Alexander III in 1177. The influence of Islamic art comes through in the few remaining grilles that cover the wall niches where early doges were buried. Above, a series of fine 13th-century mosaics by Venetian craftsmen in the Byzantine style show scenes from the Old Testament.

INTERIOR

Come every day for the rest of your life with a small portable helicopter and you might begin to feel that you have seen everything contained in this cave of wonders. Failing that, make more than one visit, preferably at different times of day, to appreciate the varying effects of light on the mosaics. The lambent interior exudes splendour and mystery, even when bursting with tourists. It is in many ways an exercise in obsession: for centuries the Venetians continued to add to the wing that closes off the narrow western end of the piazza. Napoleon demolished the church of San Geminiano to make way for this exercise in neo-classical regularity, complete with that essential imperial accessory, a ballroom. The spirit of these years is conserved in the first part of the collection, dedicated to the beautifully soulless sculpture of Antonio Canova, who was born in Possagno (*see p269*) and whose first Venetian commission – the statue of *Daedalus and Icarus*, displayed here – brought him immediate acclaim. Some of the works on display are plaster models rather than finished marble statues. The historical collection beyond here, which occupies most of the first floor of the **Procuratie Vecchie** (*see p71*), documents Venetian history and social life in the 16th and 17th centuries. Among the globes, lutes, coins and robes some interesting sidelights are thrown on the life of the Republic. Room 6 features Lazzaro Bastiani's famous portrait of Doge Francesco Foscari (c1460). The next room is dedicated to Ducal elections, with a collection of gilded wooden hands that look like props from a De Chirico painting. These were used to count votes. Room 11 has a collection of Venetian coins, plus Tintoretto's fine painting of *St Justine and the Treasurers*. Beyond are rooms dedicated to the

Arsenale (*see p95*): a display of weaponry and some occasionally charming miniature bronzes – a favourite and much-collected art form of the Venetian Renaissance.

The bulk of one's critical energy should be saved, however, for the **Quadreria** picture gallery upstairs – perhaps the best place in the city to get a grip on the development of Venetian painting between the Byzantine stirrings of Paolo Veneziano and the full-blown Renaissance storytelling of Carpaccio. Rooms 24 to 29 are dedicated to Byzantine and Gothic painters – note Paolo Veneziano's fine *St John the Baptist* and the rare allegorical fresco fragments from a 14th-century private house in Room 27. Room 30 fast-forwards abruptly with the macabre, proto-Mannerist *Pietà* of Cosme Turà; beyond here, the Renaissance gets into full swing, with Antonello da Messina's *Pietà with Three Angels*, haunting despite the fact that the faces have nearly been erased by cack-handed restoration. The Bellinis get Room 36 to themselves – note the rubicund portrait of Doge Giovanni Mocenigo, painted by Gentile Bellini just before his departure for Constantinople in 1475. The gallery's most fascinating work, though, must be Vittorio Carpaccio's *Two Venetian Noblewomen* – long known erroneously as *The Courtesans* – in

its treasures, leaving not an inch uncovered.

The form is that of a Greek Cross, surmounted by five great 11th-century domes. The surfaces – all the surfaces – are covered by more than 4,000 square metres of mosaics, the result of 600 years of labour. The finest pieces, dating from the 12th and 13th centuries, are the work of Venetian craftsmen influenced by Byzantine art but developing their own independent style. The chapels and Baptistry were decorated in the 14th and 15th centuries; a century later, replacements of earlier mosaics were made using cartoons by such artists as Titian and Tintoretto. However, most of these later mosaics are fundamentally flawed by the attempt to achieve the three-dimensional effects of Renaissance painting.

In the apse, *Christ Pantocrator* is a faithful 16th-century reproduction of a Byzantine original. Beneath, in what may be the oldest mosaics in the church, are four protectors of Venice: St Nicholas, St Peter, St Mark and St Hermagoras. The central dome of the *Ascension*, with its splendidly poised angels and apostles, dates from the early 13th century. It is said to have influenced fresco painting in the area as well as the sculptures on the façade. The Passion scenes on the west vault (12th century) are a striking blend of Romanesque and Byzantine styles. The

Pentecost dome (towards the entrance) was probably the first to be decorated; it shows the *Descent of the Holy Spirit*. Four magnificent angels hover in the pendentives.

Worth seeking out is the scene of the *Miraculous Rediscovery of the Body of St Mark* in the right transept. This refers to an episode that occurred after the second basilica was destroyed by fire, when the secret of the whereabouts of the body was lost. The Evangelist obligingly opened up the pillar where his sarcophagus had been hidden (it's just opposite and is marked by an inlaid marble panel).

Notice, too, the magnificent 12th-century marble, porphyry and glass mosaics of the floor, which has been much restored.

Basilica di San Marco

Piazza San Marco (041 522 5205). **Open** *Apr-Oct* 9.45am-5pm Mon-Sat; 2-5pm Sun. *Nov-Mar* 9.45am-4.30pm Mon-Sat; 2-4.30pm Sun. Before 9.45am private prayer and Mass only, from the piazzetta dei Leoncini door. **Admission** *basilica* free; for areas where admission is charged, see individual listings. **No credit cards. Map** II/4A.

Treasury

Open *Apr-Oct* 9.45am-5pm Mon-Sat; 2-5pm Sun. *Nov-Mar* 9.45am-4.30pm Mon-Sat; 2-4.30pm Sun. **Admission** L4,000. ▶

Sightseeing

The Drunkenness of Noah. *See p81.*

Room 38. These two bored women are not angling for trade: they're waiting for their husbands to return from a hunting expedition. This was confirmed when *A Hunt in the Valley* from the Getty Museum in Los Angeles was revealed to be this painting's companion panel. Back downstairs, past the frankly missable **Museo del Risorgimento** (of interest only to students of 19th-century freemasonry), the civic collection continues with rooms dedicated to the state barge, the *Bucintoro*, to Venetian festivities, and to the city's trade guilds. The last two rooms show how Venetians enjoyed themselves, with paintings of fairground trials of strength and some portable gambling accessories.

Palazzo Ducale (Doge's Palace)

San Marco, piazzetta San Marco (041 522 4951/ fax 041 528 5028). Vaporetto San Zaccaria. **Open** *Apr-Oct* 9am-7pm daily (last entry 5.30pm). *Nov-Mar* 9am-5pm daily (last entry 3.30pm). **Admission** with cumulative ticket (*see p63* **Musei di Piazza San Marco**). **Map** II 4A.

An unobtrusive side door halfway down the right wall of the nave in San Marco leads straight into the courtyard of the Palazzo Ducale (Doge's Palace). Today's visitors take a more roundabout route, but that door is a potent symbol of the entwinement

▶ Basilica di San Marco (continued)

A hoard of exquisite Byzantine gold and silver work – reliquaries, chalices, candelabras – most of it Crusade plunder. If you can stand the glitter, the highlights are a silver perfume censer in the form of a church and two 11th-century icons of the Archangel Michael.

Baptistry & Zen Chapel

The Baptistry contains the Gothic tomb of Doge Andrea Dandolo and some interesting mosaics such as the famous image of Salome dancing, but has long been closed. Special permission (041 522 5202) is needed to visit it and the adjoining Zen Chapel, with its bronze tomb of Cardinal Zen.

Chancel & Pala d'Oro

Open *Apr-Oct* 9.45am-5pm Mon-Sat; 2-5pm Sun. *Nov-Mar* 9.45am-4.30pm Mon-Sat; 2-4.30pm Sun. **Admission** L3,000.
The Chancel is separated from the body of the church by the iconostasis – a red marble rood screen by the Gothic sculptors Jacobello and Pier Paolo Dalle Masegne, with fine naturalistic statues of the Madonna, the apostles and St George. Access to the Chancel is via the San Clemente chapel to the right, with its mosaic showing merchants

Rustico di Torcello and Buono di Malamocco, apparently about to FedEx the body of St Mark to Venice.

St Mark's sarcophagus is visible through the grate underneath the altar. It was moved here from the 11th-century crypt in 1835; the crypt remains a popular venue for society weddings, though it's closed to the rest of us.

The indigestibly opulent *Pala d'Oro* (Gold Altar-Piece) is a Byzantine work and, just for a change, was acquired honestly. It was made in Constantinople in 976 on the orders of Doge Pietro Orseolo I and further enriched in later years with amethysts, emeralds, pearls, rubies, sapphires and topaz, topped off with a Gothic frame and resetting in 1345.

It's a worldly corner of the church, this. Set in the frame of the curving sacristy door are bronze busts of its maker, Sansovino, and his friends, Titian and Aretino, who helped to get him out of prison in 1545 (*see p72* **Biblioteca Marciana**). Aretino was a poet and playwright who moved to Venice in 1527 after scandalising Rome with his 'Lewd Sonnets'. A great satirist and hedonist, he is said to have died laughing at a filthy joke about his sister.

The left transept contains the chapel of the Madonna Nicopeia (the Victory-Bringer), named after the tenth-century icon on the altar – another Fourth Crusade acquisition that Byzantine emperors used to carry into of Church and State in the glory days of La Serenissima. If the basilica was the Republic's spiritual nerve centre, the Doge's Palace was its political and judicial hub. The present site was the seat of ducal power from the ninth century onwards, though most of what we see today dates from the mid-15th century. Devastating fires in 1574 and 1577 took their toll, but after much debate it was decided to restore rather than replace – an enlightened policy for the time.

The architectural form of the building testifies to Venetian confidence in the impossibility of invasion or attack: whereas Renaissance seats of government in other Italian towns look like castles, this is very definitely a palace. It is the great Gothic building of the city, but is also curiously Eastern in style, achieving a marvellous combination of lightness and strength. The ground floor was open to the public; the work of government went on in the more closed part above. This arrangement resulted in a curious reversal of the natural order. The building gets heavier as it rises: the first level has an open arcade of simple Gothic arches, the second a closed loggia of rich, ornate arcading. The top floor is a solid wall broken by a sequence of Gothic windows. And yet somehow it doesn't seem awkward.

The piazzetta façade was built in the 15th century as a continuation of the 14th-century waterfront façade. On the corner by the **Ponte di Paglia** (Bridge of Straw) is an exquisite marble relief carving of the *Drunkenness of Noah* from the early 15th century, while on the piazzetta corner is a statue of Adam and Eve from the late 14th century.

The capitals of the pillars below date from the 14th to the 15th centuries, although more than a dozen of them are 19th-century copies (some of the originals are on display inside). On the waterfront side (ninth pillar from the left) is what appears to be a boy eating an ice-cream cone; don't disappoint your kids by telling them it's really a chicken leg.

The **Porta della Carta** (or 'paper gate' – so called because it was where permits were checked), between the palace and the basilica, is a grand piece of florid Gothic architecture and sculpture (1438-42) by Bartolomeo and Giovanni Bon. The statue of Doge Francesco Foscari and the lion are copies dating from 1885, the originals having been smashed by the French in 1797.

Behind the palace's fairy-tale exterior the machinery of empire whirred away with the same assembly-line efficiency that went into the building of ships over at the Arsenale.

battle. She is still much revered: early in the morning, praying Venetians can often be seen here confiding in her. The St Isidore chapel beyond, with its 14th-century mosaics, is reserved for private prayer and confessions. The same goes for the Mascoli chapel. The altarpiece, with a swaying Virgin between St Mark and St James, is a striking piece of Gothic statuary. The chapel's mosaics, thought to be mostly by Michele Giambono and dating from 1430-50, have a definite Renaissance look to them, with backgrounds of classical architecture.

Loggia & Museo Marciano

Open *Apr-Oct* 9.45am-5pm daily. *Nov-Mar* 9.45am-4.30pm daily. **Admission** L3,000.
Of all the pay-to-enter sections of the basilica, this is definitely the most worthwhile – and it's the only part of the church that can be visited on a Sunday morning. Up a narrow stairway from the narthex are the bronze horses that vie with the book-bearing lion of St Mark as the city's symbol; here, too, is Paolo Veneziano's exquisite *Pala Feriale*, a painted panel that was used to cover the *Pala d'Oro* on weekdays. The loggia also provides a marvellous view over the square. The original bronze horses are now kept indoors. They are the greatest piece of loot – apart from the body of St Mark himself – in the

whole city. They come from Constantinople, where they stood above the Hippodrome, advertising a great day out at the races.

Anyone really interested in the inner workings of the Venetian state should take the 75-minute *Itinerari Segreti* tour (L24,000; L14,000 students; L8,000 6-14s; tours 10am-noon in Italian, English and French; book at least one day in advance). This takes you into those parts of the palace that the official route does not touch: cramped wooden administrative offices; the chambers of the *Cancelleria segreta*, where all documents were written up in triplicate by a team of 24 clerks; the chamber of the three heads of the Council of Ten, connected by a secret door in the wooden panelling to the *Sala del Consiglio dei Dieci*, and the torture chambers beyond. The tour ends up in the leads – the cells underneath the roof from which Casanova staged his famous escape (probably by bribing the guard, though his own account is far more Action Hero, *see p16* **The Great Escape**).

Following reorganisation, the main visit – for which an audioguide is recommended – now begins at the **Porta del Frumento** on the lagoon side of the palace, rather than at the main Piazzetta entrance via the Porta della Carta. The **Museo dell'Opera**, just to the left of the ticket barrier, has the best of the 14th-century capitals from the external loggia; the ones you see outside are copies.

In the main courtyard stands the **Arco dei Foscari** – another fine late Gothic work, commissioned by Doge Francesco Foscari in 1438, when Venice was at the height of its territorial influence. It was built by Antonio Bregno and Antonio Rizzo; Rizzo also sculpted the figures of Adam and Eve (these, too, are copies; you will come across the originals inside the palace), which earned him gushing accolades and led to his appointment as official architect in 1483, after one of those disastrous fires. Rizzo had time to oversee the building of the overblown **Scala dei Giganti** (where Doges were crowned) and some of the interior before he was found to have embezzled 12,000 ducats; he promptly fled, and died soon after.

The official route now leads up the ornate **Scala d'Oro** staircase by Jacopo Sansovino, with stuccoes by Vittoria outlined in 24-carat gold leaf.

First floor: Doge's apartments

And to think this is supposed to be the domestic side of the operation. In reality, the Doge's private life was entirely at the service of La Serenissima, and even his bedroom had to keep up the PR effort. These rooms are sometimes closed or used for temporary exhibitions; when open, the **Sala delle Mappe** (also known as the Sala dello Scudo) merits scrutiny.

Here, in a series of 16th-century maps, is the known world as it radiated from Venice. Note the New World map to the right of the entrance door, with Bofton (Boston) and Isola Longa (Long Island) clearly marked. Further on, it's worth seeking out Titian's well-hidden fresco of *St Christopher*, which, astonishingly, took the artist a mere three days to complete.

Second floor: State rooms

This grandiose series of halls provided steady work for all the great 16th-century Venetian artists. Titian, Tintoretto, Veronese, Palma il Vecchio and Jacopo Bassano all left their mark, though the sheer acreage that had to be covered, and the subjects of the canvases – either allegories or documentary records of the city's pomp and glory – did not always spur them to the heights.

The **Sala delle Quattro Porte** was where the *Collegio* – the inner cabinet of the Republic – met before the 1574 fire. After substantial renovation it became an ambassadorial waiting room, where humble envoys could gaze enviously at Andrea Vicentino's portrayal of the magnificent reception given to the young King Henry III of France in 1574 (the triumphal arch that you can see in the picture was put up overnight). The **Anticollegio**, restored in part by Palladio, has a

Top five Tintorettos

The Miracle of the Slave
Accademia *see p122*.
Tintoretto's dynamic painting (1548) of muscular figures and super-hero intervention shook up both Venetian tradition and Titian's supremacy.

The Crucifixion
Scuola di San Rocco *see p114*.
El Greco thought this giant canvas (1565) the greatest painting in the world, while the normally loquacious Ruskin was rendered nearly speechless: 'It is beyond all analysis and above all praise.' Enough said.

The Israelites at Mt Sinai
Madonna dell'Orto *see p100*.
One of the tallest paintings of the Renaissance, this awesome picture (1560) depicts Moses receiving the Ten Commandments on Mt Sinai, with the impatient Israelites below preparing to cast the golden calf.

Mythologies
Palazzo Ducale *see p80*.
Four mythological paintings in the Anticollegio display Tintoretto's strong draughtsmanship along with an unexpected elegance and tenderness.

The Last Supper
San Polo *see p108*.
An athletic Christ administers the sacrament with outstretched arms replicating the pose of the Crucifixion.

spectacular gilded stucco ceiling, four Tintorettos and Veronese's blowsy, Mannerist *Rape of Europa*. Beyond here is the **Sala del Collegio**, where the inner cabinet convened.

The propaganda paintings on the ceiling are by Veronese; note the equal scale of the civic and divine players, and the way that both Justice and Peace are mere handmaidens to Venice herself. But for real hubris you have to stroll into the next room, the **Sala del Senato**, where Tintoretto's ceiling centrepiece shows *The Triumph of Venice*. Here the Senate, which by 1450 had grown from 60 to 300 members, met to debate questions of foreign policy, war and commerce, and to hear the reports of returning Venetian ambassadors.

Beyond are the **Sala del Consiglio dei Dieci** and the **Sala della Bussola**, where the arcane body set up specifically to act as a check on the Doge considered matters of national security. In the former, note Veronese's ceiling panel of *Juno Offering Gifts to Venice*. By the time this was painted in 1553, the classical gods had started to replace St Mark in Venice's self-aggrandising pantheon.

Here the itinerary (which is liable to change) heads through a bristling **Armoury**, whose ingenious instruments of war impressed early visitors. But, as one 17th-century tourist pointed out, the collection was established so that 'if the People should conspire against the Nobles, and make any Attempt against them while they are sitting, they might be furnished with Arms upon the Spot to defend themselves.'

First floor: State rooms

The **Sala dei Censori** now leads down to a *liagò* (covered, L-shaped loggia), which gives onto the **Sala della Quarantia Civil Vecchia** (the civil court) and the **Sala del Guariento**. The latter's faded 14th-century fresco of *The Coronation of the Virgin* by Guariento (for centuries hidden behind Tintoretto's *Paradiso* in the Sala del Maggior Consiglio) looks strangely innocent amid all this worldly propaganda. The shorter arm of the liagò has the originals of Antonio Rizzo's stylised marble sculptures of Adam and Eve from the Arco del Foscari. Next comes the **Sala del Maggior Consiglio** – the largest room in the palace. It had to be big, as by 1512, according to historian Marin Sanudo, 2,622 patrician men were entitled to sit on the greater council. This was in effect the Republic's lower house – though with the top-heavy Venetian system of government, this council of noblemen had fairly limited powers. Before the fire of 1577, the hall had been decorated with paintings by Bellini, Titian, Carpaccio and Veronese – a choice collection that was so costly to commission that in 1515 a group of patricians complained about the expense. When these works went up in smoke, they were replaced by less exalted works – with one or two exceptions. Tintoretto's *Paradise* on the far wall, sketched out by the 70-year-old artist but completed after his death in 1594 by his son Domenico, is liable to induce vertigo, as much for its theological complexity as its

huge scale. But this huge choral composition – which members would have had plenty of time to contemplate during the Council's protracted voting sessions – drew a deliberate comparison between the celestial hierarchy (as featured in Dante) and Venice's equally complex but equally inviolate power structure. In the ceiling panels are works by Veronese and Palma il Giovane; note, too, the frieze of ducal portraits carried out by Domenico Tintoretto and assistants, with the black veil marking the place where Marin Falier's face would have appeared had he not conspired against the state in 1356. On the left side of the hall, a balcony gives a fine view over the southern side of the lagoon. A door leads from the back of the hall into the **Sala della Quarantia Civil Nuova** – the Republic's second civil court – where a small bookshop has been set up, while the **Sala dello Scrutinio** beyond, where the votes of the *Maggior Consiglio* were counted, is not accessible.

Criminal courts and prigioni

Backtracking through the **Sala del Maggior Consiglio**, a small door on the left leads past the **Scala dei Censori** to the **Sala della Quarantia Criminale** – the criminal court. The next room retains some original red and gold leather wall coverings. Beyond is a small room that has been arranged as a gallery, with Flemish paintings from Cardinal Grimani's collection, originally hidden

Prison gate: the **Bridge of Sighs**. *See p84.*

from public view. The hysterical religious mysticism of Bosch's *Inferno* strikes an odd note here: though rational, Venice was not immune to religious fanaticism. The route now leads over the **Bridge of Sighs** to the **Prigioni Nuove**, where petty criminals were kept. Lifers were sent down to the waterlogged *pozzi* (wells) in the basement of the palazzo itself. By the 19th century most visitors were falling for the tour guide legend that, once over the Bridge of Sighs, prisoners would 'descend into the dungeon which none entered and hoped to see the sun again', as Mark Twain put it. But when this new prison wing was built in 1589, it was acclaimed as a paragon of comfort; in 1608 English traveller Thomas Coryat remarked, 'I think there is not a fairer prison in all Christendom.'

Some of the cells have their number and capacity painted over the door; one has a *trompe l'œil* window, drawn in charcoal by a bored inmate. On the lowest level is a small exercise yard, where an unofficial tavern used to operate. Up the stairs beyond is a display of Venetian ceramics found during excavations, and more cells, one with a fascinating display of cartoons and caricatures left by 19th-century internees.

Back across the Bridge of Sighs, the tour ends on the lower floor in the **Avogaria** – the offices of the clerks of court. Next to this a bookshop has been set up (open 9am-4pm). On the ground-floor is a welcome (though not particularly cheap) cafeteria; beyond the cafeteria are the old kitchens, where the restored mechanism from the Torre dell'Orologio (Clock Tower, *see below*) can be seen, together with the statues of the Magi and the Angel (usually only seen during Ascension week), all waiting to be replaced in the restored tower; it is likely to be a long wait.

Torre dell'Orologio

San Marco 147, piazza San Marco (041 522 4951/ www.museiciviciveneziani.it). Vaporetto San Zaccaria. **Map** II 4A.

The clock tower, designed by Maurizio Codussi, was built between 1496 and 1506; the wings were an addition, perhaps by Pietro Lombardo. Above the clock face is the Madonna. During Ascension Week and at Epiphany, the Magi come out and bow to her every hour, in an angel-led procession. At other times of year, the burly Moors on the roof, made of gun-metal and cast in 1497, strike the hour. Another Moore, Roger – who has been cast plenty of times since 1497 – sent a villain flying through the clock face in the film *Moonraker*.

In 1999 the clock was restored. However, the building as a whole has been hidden since 1998 behind a lifesize photograph of itself and, owing to legal wrangling with the proprietors of the adjoining buildings, restoration work seems to be at a standstill. The official re-opening date is 2002, but don't hold your breath; in the meantime the original mechanism and statues can be seen in the Palazzo Ducale (*see p80*).

La Zecca

San Marco 7, piazzetta San Marco (041 520 8788). Vaporetto Vallaresso. **Open** 9am-7pm Mon-Fri; 9am-1.30pm Sat. **Admission** free. **Map** II 4B.

The Mint, designed by Sansovino, was completed by 1547. It coined Venice's famous gold ducats – later referred to as *zecchini*, precursor of the English 'sequins'. It is more impregnable in appearance than the neighbouring Biblioteca Marciana (*see p72*), though the façade had to accommodate large windows on the *piano nobile* (for relief from heat) and open arches on the ground floor, where the Procurators of St Mark's owned a number of cheese shops. The architect's son, author of the first famous guidebook to the city, described the building as 'a worthy prison for all that precious gold'. It now houses most of the contents of the civic library.

Piazza San Marco to the Rialto

Piazza San Marco is linked to the Rialto by the busiest, richest and narrowest of shopping streets: the **Mercerie**. The name is plural, since it is divided into five parts: the Merceria dell'Orologio, di San Zulian, del Capitello, di San Salvador and del 2 Aprile. The name means 'haberdashers', but we know from John Evelyn's 1645 account of 'one of the most delicious streets in the world' that the luxury textile emporia were flanked by shops selling perfumes and medicines too. Most of the big-name designers are to be found here now, and most of Venice's short-stay tourists too. The **Ponte dei Baretteri** (the Hatmakers' Bridge), in the middle of the Mercerie, is, by the way, a minor record-holder in Venice: there are six different roads and alleys leading directly off the bridge.

The Mercerie emerge near **campo San Bartolomeo**, the square at the foot of the Rialto, with the statue of playwright Carlo Goldoni looking amusedly down on the milling crowds. This square, together with the nearby **campo San Luca**, is where young Venetians come to hang out and meet up of an evening. Most Italian towns have their *corso* where the citizens parade at *passeggiata* time; Venetians, perhaps because they are always walking, are a little more static in their evening encounters. **Calle dei Stagneri** leads out of the *campo* to the 18th-century church of **Santa Maria della Fava**.

San Salvador

Campo San Salvador (041 523 6717). Vaporetto Rialto. **Open** *May-Sept* 9am-noon, 4-6.30pm Mon-Sat; 4-6.30pm Sun. *Oct-Apr* 9am-noon, 3-6pm Mon-Sat; 3-6pm Sun. **Map** II 4A.

If you can't make it to Florence on this trip, come to San Salvador instead, which has one of Venice's most

Santo Stefano: a multi-coloured treat. *See p86.*

Brunelleschi-esque interiors: a pass-the-baton effort begun by Giorgio Spavento in 1506, continued by Tullio Lombardo and completed by Sansovino in 1534. But even though the geometrical sense of space and the use of soft-toned greys and whites exudes Tuscan elegance, the key to the structure is in fact a combination of three domed Greek Crosses, which look back to the Byzantine tradition of St Mark's. The church contains two great Titians, the *Annunciation* at the end of the right-hand aisle (with the signature 'Tizianus fecit, fecit', the repetition was intended either to emphasise the wonder of his unflagging creativity, or is a simple typo – take your pick) and the *Transfiguration*, on the high altar (which conceals a silver reredos, revealed on request).

There's also some splendid Veneto-Tuscan sculpture, including Sansovino's monument to Doge Francesco Venier, between the second and third altar on the right. Here, too, at the end of the right transept, is the tomb of Cristina Cornaro, Queen of Cyprus (died 1510), a pawn in a game of Mediterranean strategy which ended with her being forced into abdicating the island to Venetian rule. By way of compensation she was palmed off with the town of Asolo (*see p269*) and the title 'Daughter of the Republic'.

Santa Maria della Fava

Campo della Fava (041 522 4601). Vaporetto Rialto.
Open 8.30am-noon, 4.30-6.20pm Mon-Sat. **Map** II 4A.
Saint Mary of the Bean – the name refers to a popular bean-cake that was turned out by a bakery that used to stand nearby – is on one of the quieter routes between the Rialto and San Marco. This 18th-century church is worth visiting for two paintings by the city's greatest 18th-century artists, which

neatly illustrate their contrasting temperaments. Tiepolo's *Education of the Virgin* (first altar on the right) is an early work, painted when he was still under the influence of Giovanni Battista Piazzetta; but the bright colours and touchingly human relationships of the figures are nonetheless in great contrast with the sombre browns and reds of the latter's *Virgin and Child with St Philip Neri* (second altar on the left). In Piazzetta's more earnest painting, which still bears traces of Counter-Reformation gravity, the lily, bishop's mitre and cardinals' hats show the worldly honours rejected by the saint.

San Zulian

Mercerie San Zulian (041 523 5383). Vaporetto Vallaresso or San Zaccaria. **Open** 8.30am-2pm Mon-Sat. **Map** II 4A.
The classical simplicity of Sansovino's façade (1553-5) is offset by a grand monument to Tommaso Rangone, a wealthy and far-from-self-effacing showman-scholar from Ravenna, whose fortune was made by a treatment for syphilis, and who wrote a book on how to live to 120 (he only made it to 80 himself). He unilaterally declared his library to be one of the seven wonders of the world, and had himself prominently portrayed in all three of Tintoretto's paintings for the Scuola di San Marco (now in the Accademia). The interior has a ceiling painting of *The Apotheosis of St Julian* by Palma il Giovane, here in Tintoretto-mode, and a more Titianesque *Assumption* by the same painter on the second altar on the right, which also has good statues of St Catherine of Alexandria and Daniel by Alessandro Vittoria. The first altar on the right has a *Pietà* by Veronese. San Giuliano (Zulian to Venetians), curi-

Nicolò Tommaseo, with books.

ously, is one of only two churches in Venice that you can walk all the way around. (The other is the Angelo Raffaele in Dorsoduro, *see p116*.)

The Rialto to the Accademia Bridge

The route from the Rialto to the Accademia passes through a series of ever-larger squares. From cosily cramped campo San Bartolomeo, the well-marked path leads to campo San Luca with its bars and cakeshops. Beyond this is campo Manin with its 19th-century statue of Daniele Manin, leader of the 1848 uprising against the Austrians (*see chapter* **History**). An alley to the left of this campo will lead you to the **Scala del Bovolo**, a striking Renaissance spiral staircase. Back on the main drag, the busy calle della Mandola takes you into broad **campo Sant'Angelo** with its dramatic view of **Santo Stefano**'s leaning tower; off calle della Mandola to the right is the gothic **Palazzo Fortuny**, once home to the fashion designer Mariano Fortuny.

Just before the Accademia bridge, **campo Santo Stefano** is second only to piazza San Marco in the sestiere in size. Until 1802, when part of the stand collapsed, this was where *corse al toro* (bullfights) took place. Nowadays, the tables of three bars scarcely encroach on the space where small children play on their bikes

(officially banned in the city, but a blind eye is turned) or kick balls around the statue of Risorgimento ideologue Nicolò Tommaseo, known locally as *Cagalibri* (bookshitter) for reasons that are obvious when the monument is viewed from the rear. On the Grand Canal to the north-west of campo Santo Stefano is **campo San Samuele**, with a deconsecrated 11th-century church and the vast **Palazzo Grassi**, now an exhibition centre.

Palazzo Fortuny

San Marco 3780, campo San Benedetto (041 520 0995/ fax 041 522 3088). Vaporetto Sant'Angelo. **Open** *during exhibitions* 10am-6pm Tue-Sun (hours subject to change). **Admission** varies. **No credit cards. Map** II 3A.
With the museum closed for long-term reorganisation (due to reopen in 2004), the only way to see the charming 15th-century palazzo that belonged to Spanish fashion designer Mariano Fortuny (1871-1949) is to catch an exhibition. These are usually photographic, photography being one of Fortuny's interests, alongside theatrical set design, cloth dyes, and silk dresses.

Palazzo Grassi

San Marco 3231, campo San Samuele (041 523 1680/www.palazzograssi.it). Vaporetto San Samuele. **Open** during exhibitions 10am-7pm Tue-Sun (hours subject to change). **Admission** varies. **No credit cards. Map** II 2A.
This superbly regular 18th-century palazzo on the Grand Canal was bought by Fiat in 1984 and converted by architect Gae Aulenti into a high-profile exhibition space. Since then it has unleashed one blockbuster show after another, doing for civilisations such as the Celts, Mayans and Etruscans what Fiat does for cars. It is a light and well-organised space with a good shop, bookshop and café, and the quality of the exhibits is often so high that one forgets the over-the-top packaging.

Santo Stefano

Campo Santo Stefano (041 522 5061/www.chorus-ve.org). Vaporetto San Samuele/Accademia. **Open** 10am-5pm Mon; 8am-5pm Tue-Sat; 1-5pm Sun. **Admission** L3,000 (*see also p63* **Chorus**). **No credit cards. Map** II 3A.
Santo Stefano is an Augustinian church, built in the 14th century and altered in the 15th. The façade has a magnificent portal in the florid Gothic style. The large interior, with its splendid ship's keel roof, is a multicoloured treat, with different marbles used for the columns, capitals, altars and intarsia, and diamond-patterned walls, as on the Palazzo Ducale. On the floor is a huge plaque to Doge Morosini (best known for blowing up the Parthenon) and a more modest one to composer Giovanni Gabrielli. On the interior façade to the left of the door is a Renaissance monument to Giacomo Surian by Pietro Lombardo and his sons, decorated with skulls and festoons. In the sacristy are two tenebrous late works by

Tintoretto: *The Washing of the Feet* and *The Agony in the Garden* (*The Last Supper* is by the great man's assistants) and three fanciful works by Gaspare Diziani (*Adoration of the Magi, Flight into Egypt, Massacre of the Innocents*). From the first bridge on the *calle* that leads from the campo towards piazza San Marco, there's a good view of the apse of Santo Stefano with a canal passing underneath it.

Scala Contarini del Bovolo

San Marco 4299, corte dei Risi (041 270 2464/fax 041 270 2458/catalogo@patriarcatovenezia.it). Vaporetto Rialto. **Open** *Apr-Oct* 10am-6pm daily. *Nov-Dec* 10am-4pm Sat, Sun. **Admission** L4,000. **No credit cards. Map** II 3A.
Follow the signs for the Scala del Bòvolo from campo Manin and you will emerge in a courtyard dominated by this elegant Renaissance spiral staircase, built c1499 by Giovanni Candi. Such staircases are called *scale a chiocciola* (snail staircases); *bòvolo* is Venetian dialect for snail. It was restored in 1986 and has recently been opened to the public; the view from the top makes the climb worthwhile.

From the Accademia to piazza San Marco

The route from Santo Stefano back to piazza San Marco zigzags at first, passing through small squares, including **campo Santa Maria del Giglio** (aka Santa Maria Zobenigo) with the most boastful church-façade in Venice. It winds past banks and hotels, along with a few top-dollar antique shops, to end in wide **via XXII Marzo**, with an intimidating view of the freshly restored baroque statuary of **San Moisè**. To the left from here are the gutted remains of Venice's once-glorious opera-house, **La Fenice**. Press on and you are ready for the greatest view in the world: piazza San Marco from the west side.

San Moisè

Campo San Moisè (041 528 5840). Vaporetto Vallaresso. **Open** 3.30-6.30pm Mon-Sat; 9.30-11am Sun. **Map** II 4B.
The baroque façade of San Moisè has been lambasted by Ruskin ('one of the basest examples of the basest school of the Renaissance') and just about everybody else as one of Venice's truly ugly pieces of architecture. Inside, an extravagant piece of baroque sculpture occupies the high altar, representing not only Moses receiving the stone tablets but Mount Sinai itself. Near the entrance is the grave of John Law, author of the Mississippi Bubble scheme that almost sunk the French central bank in 1720.

Santa Maria del Giglio

Campo Santa Maria Zobenigo (041 275 0462/ www.chorus-ve.org). Vaporetto Santa Maria del Giglio. **Open** 10am-5pm Mon-Sat; 1-5pm Sun. **Admission** L3,000 (*see also p63* **Chorus**). **No credit cards. Map** II 3B.

This church's façade drew the censure of Ruskin for its total lack of any Christian symbols (give or take a token angel or two). Built between 1678 and 1683, it's really a huge exercise in defiant self-glorification by Admiral Antonio Barbaro, who was dismissed by Doge Francesco Morosini for incompetence in the War of Candia (Crete). On the plinths of the columns are relief plans of towns where he served, including Candia; his own statue (in the centre) is flanked by representations of Honour, Virtue, Fame and Wisdom. The interior is more devotional. You may not have heard of the painter Antonio Zanchi (1631-1722), but this is definitely his church. Particularly interesting is *Abraham Teaching the Egyptians Astrology* in the sacristy, while the Cappella Molin has *Ulysses Recognised by His Dog* (an odd subject for a church). The chapel also contains a *Madonna and Child* proudly but probably erroneously attributed to Rubens. Behind the altar are two paintings of the Evangelists by Tintoretto, formerly organ-doors.

Teatro La Fenice

San Marco 1983, campo San Fantin. Vaporetto Santa Maria del Giglio. **Map** II 3A.
All that remains of Venice's great opera house, where operas by Rossini, Verdi, Stravinsky and Britten opened, is the façade on to the square, by Gianantonio Selva. The rest went up in flames on the night of 29 January 1996, and it wasn't an accident. The theatre – named 'The Phoenix' – is at last showing some signs of rising from the ashes. The official re-opening date is February 2002, but it would be unwise to do any breath-holding.

San Moisè: truly ugly.

Sightseeing

ARTE COMMUNICATIONS
Exhibition projects
Since 1984

Paolo De Grandis & Paivi Tirkkonen

2001

Events
49. Biennale di Venezia
4th Participation of Taiwan
1st Participation of Singapore
1st Participation of Hong Kong
1st Participation of Jamaica
2nd Participation of Latvia

OPEN 2001
4th International Exhibition
of Sculptures and Installations
Venice Lido Italy

Via P. Orseolo II, 16 - 30126 Venezia Lido Italy
Tel. +39 041 5264546 Fax +39 041 2769056
artgrand@iol.it - artecommunications.com

Castello

A sestiere of two halves, Castello has fabulous churches and sumptuous *palazzi*, as well as old shipyards and a football stadium.

Castello is Venice's largest sestiere, extending from the Rialto to Sant'Elena at the eastern tip of the city. Its name is believed to derive from a fortress on the island of San Pietro, one of the earliest inhabited sites in the lagoon. A sestiere of two very different halves, Castello's grander northern and western area, around **Santi Giovanni e Paolo** and **San Zaccaria**, was closely linked with the centres of power, while the districts around the **Arsenale** to the east were home to Venice's most important industries.

Northern & western Castello

The Bridge of Sighs marks the border between the *sestieri* of San Marco and Castello, so the quaint **Museo Diocesano di Arte Sacra** (*see p90*) and the stately **San Zaccaria** (*see p92*), although closely associated with San Marco, actually belong to Castello. But the true heart of northern and western Castello lies inward from here: campo **Santa Maria Formosa** (literally 'Shapely St Mary'), a large, bustling, irregular-shaped square on the road to just about everywhere. It has a fine church (*see p91*), a small market, a couple of bars and an undertaker's. Nearby is the quintessentially Venetian museum-cum-library of the **Querini-Stampalia** (*see p90*). Constantly buzzing with both Venetians and tourists, the square is surrounded by *palazzi* that range in style from the very grand to the very homely. It is, in fact, Castello in miniature.

For grandeur, head north-east from here towards campo **Santi Giovanni e Paolo**. This square is second only to piazza San Marco in monumental magnificence. The Gothic red brick of the Dominican church is beautifully set off by the glistening marble on the *trompe l'œil* façade of the **Scuola di San Marco** and the bronze of the equestrian **Monument to Bartolomeo Colleoni** (*see below*) gazing contemptuously down.

It's a short walk through narrow *calli* from Santi Giovanni e Paolo to the Fondamenta Nuove, where the northern lagoon comes into view. Murano and further-flung Burano and Torcello are visible on clear days, as are the foothills of the Dolomites. The cemetery island San Michele is always in sight, acting as a grim *memento mori* for patients in the hospital.

Negroponte's **Madonna Enthroned**. *See p90.*

Eastwards from Santi Giovanni e Paolo, a road called Barbaria delle Tole passes the extraordinary baroque church of the **Ospedaletto** by Baldassare Longhena, with its alarmingly teetering façade adorned by leering faces. This long road will take you into one of the least touristy areas of the city. Here, beyond the old gasworks, is the imposing church of **San Francesco della Vigna** (*see p90*), an austere construction the remoteness of which is part of its charm.

Monument to Bartolomeo Colleoni

Campo Santi Giovanni e Paolo. Vaporetto Fondamente Nove. **Map III** 1A.
Colleoni was a famous *condottiere* (mercenary soldier), who left a legacy to the Republic on condition that a statue be erected to him in front of St Mark's. Not wishing to clutter up St Mark's Square with the statue, but loath to miss out on the money, Venice's wily rulers found a solution to their conundrum in 1479 when they hit upon the idea of relegating him to a space in front of the Scuola di San Marco. Geddit? In order, perhaps, to make up for this flagrant deception, the Republic did Colleoni

Monument to Colleoni. *See p89.*

proud, commissioning the Florentine artist Andrea Verrocchio to create an equestrian statue that is widely agreed to be one of the world's finest. On Verrocchio's death it was completed, together with the pedestal, by Alessandro Leopardi (1488-96). It is not a portrait, since Verrocchio never saw Colleoni, but a stylised representation of military pride and might. Colleoni's coat of arms (on the pedestal) includes three fig-like objects, a reference to his name, which in Italian sounds very similar to *coglioni* – testicles.

Museo della Fondazione Scientifica Querini Stampalia

Castello 5252, campo Santa Maria Formosa (041 271 1411/querini.stampalia@provincia.venezia.it/ www.provincia.venezia.it/querini). Vaporetto San Zaccaria/Rialto. **Open** *Museum* 10am-1pm, 3-6pm Tue-Thur, Sun; 10am-1pm, 3-10pm Fri, Sat. *Library* 4pm-midnight Mon-Fri; 2.30pm-midnight Sat; 3-7pm Sun. **Admission** *museum* L12,000; L8,000 students, over 60s; *library* free. **Credit** MC, V. **Map** III 1A.

This Renaissance palazzo and its art collection were bequeathed to Venice by Giovanni Querini, a 19th-century scientist, man of letters and successful silk producer. He came from one of the city's most ancient families, which was permanently excluded from running for the dogeship after Marco Querini's involvement in the 1310 Bajamonte Tiepolo plot. Giovanni Querini specified in his will that a library and reading room should also be created here which would open 'particularly in the evenings for the convenience of scholars', and that the foundation should promote 'evening assemblies of scholars and scientists'. The Querini Stampalia still exudes something of its founder's cultural generosity and ecumenicism: the first-floor library is a great place to study on misty autumn evenings, and the Foundation organises conferences, debates and concerts (5pm, 8.30pm Fri,

Sat; included in admission price). The ground floor and gardens, redesigned in the 1960s by Carlo Scarpa (*see p267* **Carlo Scarpa**), offer one of Venice's few successful examples of modern architecture. On the second floor, the gallery contains some important paintings, including Palma il Vecchio's portraits of Francesco and Paola Querini, for whom the palace was built in the 16th century, and a marvellous *Presentation in the Temple* by Giovanni Bellini. It also has a fascinating series of minor works, such as Gabriele Bella's 67 paintings of Venetian festivals, ceremonies and customs, and a selection of Pietro Longhi's winning scenes of bourgeois life in 18th-century Venice.

Museo Diocesano di Arte Sacra

Castello 4312, ponte della Canonica (041 522 9166). Vaporetto San Zaccaria. **Open** 10.30am-12.30pm Mon-Sat. **Admission** free. **Map** III 1B.

An odd hotchpotch of a collection, which can seem haphazard until you realise its purpose: to act as a storeroom and restoration clinic for works of art from local churches and monasteries. Given the nature of the collection, it's difficult to say what will be on view at any one time, but items that have nowhere else to go include the 15th-century Cross of the Patriarch from San Pietro in Castello. There is also a series of stolen and recovered marble sculptures from the former convent of San Clemente, one of the abandoned islands of the lagoon. The thieves shoved rubber tyres over Faith and Charity and used a motorboat to drag them along the bottom of the lagoon; you can still see the tyre marks at the back. There's a pretty Romanesque cloister, too.

San Francesco della Vigna

Campo San Francesco della Vigna (041 520 6102). Vaporetto Celestia. **Open** *Apr-Oct* 9am-12.30pm, 3-6.30pm Mon-Sat; 3-6.30pm Sun. *Nov-Mar* 8am-12.30pm, 3-7pm Mon-Sat; 3-6.30pm Sun. **Map** III 2A.

San Francesco may be off the beaten track, but the long trek over to the down-at-heel area beyond the gasworks, where the church's Palladian façade is half-concealed by the surrounding buildings, is well worth it.

In 1534 Jacopo Sansovino was asked by his friend Doge Andrea Gritti to design this church for the Observant Franciscan order. The Tuscan architect opted for a deliberately simple style of building, to match the monastic rule adopted by its inhabitants. The façade (1568-72) was a later addition by Andrea Palladio; it is the first example of his system of superimposed temple fronts.

The dignified, solemn interior consists of a single broad nave with side chapels, which are named after the families who paid for them – and who held no truck with Franciscan notions of modesty and self-effacement. The Cappella Giustiniani on the left of the chancel is not one of them: its marvellous cycle of sculptures by Pietro Lombardo and school were moved here from an earlier church on the same site. In the nave, the fourth chapel on the right has a

Resurrection attributed to Paolo Veronese. In the right transept is a fruity, flowery *Madonna and Child Enthroned*, a signed work by the Greek artist Antonio da Negroponte (c1450). From the left transept a door leads into the Cappella Santa, which contains a *Madonna and Saints* by Giovanni Bellini (1507, perhaps assisted by Girolamo da Santacroce), while the fifth chapel on the left is home to Paolo Veronese's first Venetian commission, the stunning *Holy Family with Sts John the Baptist, Anthony the Abbot and Catherine* (c1551).

Santa Maria Formosa
Campo Santa Maria Formosa (041 523 4645).
Vaporetto San Zaccaria/Rialto. **Open** 10am-5pm
Mon-Sat; 1-5pm Sun. **Admission** L3,000 (*see also*
p63 **Chorus**). **No credit cards. Map** III 1A.
In the pre-Freudian seventh century, St Magnus, Bishop of Oderzo, had a rather pleasant vision in which the Virgin appeared as a buxom ('formosa') matron, and a church was built in this busy, bustling square to commemorate the fact. The present church was designed by Mauro Codussi in 1492 and has something fittingly buxom about it. It has two façades, one on the canal (1542), the other on the campo (1604). The baroque campanile has a grotesque mask, memorably reviled by Ruskin but

now recognised as a portrait of a victim of von Recklinghausen's disease – the condition that affected the Elephant Man. Codussi retained the Greek cross plan of the original church in his own Renaissance design; the spatial effects reveal how strong the Byzantine tradition remained in Venice. The first chapel in the right aisle has a triptych by Bartolomeo Vivarini of *The Madonna of the Misericordia* (1473), including a realistic *Birth of the Virgin.*

The altar in the right transept was the chapel of the Scuola dei Bombardieri, with an altarpiece of St Barbara, patron saint of gunners (because her father was struck by lightning when preparing to kill her), by Palma il Vecchio. The model was apparently the artist's daughter. George Eliot described it as 'an almost unique presentation of a hero-woman'. Half-hidden by the elaborate high altar is one of the few works on show in Venice by a woman artist: an 18th-century *Allegory of the Foundation of the Church, with Venice, St Magnus and Santa Maria Formosa* by Giulia Lama. She has been described as a pupil of Giovani Battista Piazzetta, but Piazzetta's only known portrait from life (in the Thyssen-Bornemisza collection in Madrid) is of Giulia Lama: its tenderness suggests she was more than a mere pupil.

Multi-cultural Venice

While droves of multi-cultural tourists may be a comparative novelty, the babble of foreign tongues in piazza San Marco is nothing new. As Antonio observes in Shakespeare's *The Merchant of Venice*, 'the trade and profit of the city consisteth of all nations'. The kind of trade (plastic gondolas, moonlight serenades) may have changed, but the city has always been ready to welcome any spending-bent visitor, whatever their colour, creed or (within reason) credit-balance.

The city was host to a great many foreign communities, many of which had their own places of worship, shops, warehouses and *scuole* (*see p63*). The Jewish Ghetto (*see p103*) is only the most obvious – and, with its repressive restrictions, probably the least representative – example.

In general foreigners, while undoubtedly watched over, enjoyed freedom of movement. ('However suspicious Venetians are said to be, I found it much easier for an Englishman to look over *their* docks, than for a foreigner to find his way into ours,' wrote one English traveller of a visit to the Arsenale in 1789).

In many cases, foreign communities made lavish use of the services of Venice's finest

artists and architects. The *fondaco dei tedeschi* (*see p68*; though *tedeschi* means 'Germans', it was used as a blanket term for northern Europeans) was one of the finest palaces on the Grand Canal, frescoed outside by Titian and Giorgione. The *scuola* of the Slavs still preserves its splendid cycle of Carpaccio paintings (*see p96* **Scuola di San Giorgio degli Schiavoni**).

Venetian tolerance was not always approved of; many of the stricter Christian nations regarded with suspicion Venice's hospitality towards the Turks, who had their own *fondaco* on the Grand Canal, complete with 24 shops, 52 bedrooms, a mosque and a haman. But practical Venice knew that while wars may flare up and fizzle out, business goes on for ever.

In several instances historical institutions survive, serving the needs of foreign residents or visitors: the old *scuole* still function as community centres for Jews, Greeks and Slavs. And the Armenians not only have a church near piazza San Marco and a college in Dorsoduro, but have had an entire island in the lagoon to themselves since the 18th century (*see p141*).

Santi Giovanni e Paolo (San Zanipolo)

Campo Santi Giovanni e Paolo (041 523 5913). Vaporetto Fondamente Nove. **Open** 9am-12.30pm, 3.30-7pm Mon-Fri; 9am-12.30pm, 3.30-6pm Sat; 3-6pm Sun. **Map** III 1A.

Santi Giovanni e Paolo was founded by the Dominican order in 1246 but only finished in 1430. Twenty-five doges were buried here between 1248 and 1778; from the 15th century onwards all ducal funerals were held here. The vast interior – 101m (331ft) long – is a single spatial unit; the simple columns serve to enhance the unity of the whole, rather than dividing the body of the church into separate aisles. The monks' choir was removed in the 17th century, leaving nothing to impede our view. Santi Giovanni e Paolo is an historical document, packed with monuments not only to doges but also to Venetian heroes. The entrance wall is entirely dedicated to a series of funerary tributes to the Mocenigo family. The grandest – the masterpiece of Pietro, Tullio and Antonio Lombardo – belongs to Pietro Mocenigo, who died in 1476: the doge stands on his own sarcophagus, supported by three warriors representing the three ages of man. The religious reference above – the three Maries at the sepulchre – seems almost an afterthought.

Renaissance elegance continues in the second altar on the right, which features an early polyptych by Giovanni Bellini (1465) in its original frame.

Hard-working eastern Castello.

Continuing down the right side of the church, the huge baroque mausoleum by Andrea Tirali (1708) has two Valier doges and a *dogaressa* taking a bow before a marble curtain. Tirali also designed the Chapel of St Dominic, notable for its splendid ceiling painting by Giovani Battista Piazzetta of *St Dominic in Glory* (c1727). The right transept has a painting of *St Antonine Distributing Alms* (1542) by the mystically minded Lorenzo Lotto, who asked only for a decent funeral as payment – but then died in Loreto. On the right of the chancel, with its baroque high altar, is the Gothic tomb of Michele Morosini, which Ruskin, predictably, loved. Opposite is the tomb of Doge Andrea Vendramin, by the Lombardo family, which the architectural arbiter just as predictably hated. Just to confirm his prejudice, he climbed a ladder and was shocked to discover that the sculptor had not bothered to carve the unseen side of the face.

The rosary chapel, off the left transept, was gutted by fire in 1867, just after two masterpieces by Titian and Bellini had been placed there for safe keeping. It now contains paintings and furnishings from suppressed churches. The ceiling paintings, *The Annunciation*, *Assumption* and *Adoration of the Shepherds*, are by Paolo Veronese, as is another *Adoration* to the left of the door.

San Zaccaria

Campo San Zaccaria (041 522 1257). Vaporetto San Zaccaria. **Open** 10am-noon, 4-6pm Mon-Sat; 4-6pm, Sun. **Map** III 1B.

Founded in the ninth century, this church has always had close ties with the Palazzo Ducale. Eight Venetian rulers were buried in the first church on the site, one was killed outside, and another died while seeking sanctuary inside. This is another holy booty church: the body of St Zacharias, the father of John the Baptist, was brought to Venice in the ninth century, at the same time as that of St Mark; it still lies under the second altar on the right. The current church was begun in 1444 but took decades to complete, making it a curious combination of Gothic and Renaissance. The interior is built on a Gothic plan – the apse, with its ambulatory and radiating cluster of tall-windowed chapels, is unique in Venice – but the architectural decoration is predominantly Renaissance. Similarly, the façade is a happy mixture of the two styles. Inside, every inch is covered with paintings, of varying quality. Giovanni Bellini's magnificently calm *Madonna and Four Saints* (1505), on the second altar on the left, leaps out of the confusion. The Chapel of St Athanasius in the right aisle contains carved 15th-century wooden stalls and *The Birth of St John the Baptist*, an early work by Tintoretto. The adjoining Chapel of St Tarasius (open, together with the sacristy, same hours as the church; admission L2,000) was the apse of an earlier church on the site; it has three altarpieces by Antonio Vivarini and Giovanni d'Alemagna (1443) – stiff, iconic works in elaborate Gothic frames that are in keeping with the architecture of the chapel. Definitely not in keeping are the frescoed saints in the fan vault by the Florentine artist Andrea del Castagno. Although painted a year before the altarpieces, they have a realistic vitality that is wholly Renaissance in spirit.

Attached to the church was a convent (now a Carabinieri barracks), where aristocrats with more titles than cash dumped female offspring to avoid having to rake together a dowry. The nuns were not best known for their piety. While tales of rampant licentiousness may have been exaggerated, a painting in Ca' Rezzonico (*see p119*) shows that such convents were considered sophisticated *salons* rather than places of contemplation.

Scuola Grande di San Marco (Ospedale Civile)

Campo Santi Giovanni e Paolo (041 529 4111).
Vaporetto Fondamente Nove. **Open** 24 hrs daily.
Map III 1A.

This is one of the six *scuole grandi*, the philanthropic confraternities of Venice (*see p63*). It's now occupied by the civic hospital, which extends all the way back to the lagoon. The façade by Pietro Lombardo and Giovanni Buora (1487-90) was completed by Mauro Codussi (1495). It has magnificent *trompe l'œil* panels by Tullio and Antonio Lombardo (protected from stray footballs by perspex panels), representing two episodes from the life of St Mark and his faithful lion. Over the doorway is a lunette of *St Mark with the Brethren of the School* attributed to Bartolomeo Bon.

Southern & eastern Castello

If Venice's fairy-tale charm is getting too much, head for eastern Castello. The low-rise, close-clustered buildings of this working-class area housed the employees of the **Arsenale** (*see p95* **Arsenale**) – Venice's Docklands – most of which now lies poignantly derelict.

Like the East End or Brooklyn, eastern Castello had its foreign communities, as local churches testify. There's **San Giorgio dei Greci** (Greeks; *see p95*), with its adjoining museum of icons, and the **Scuola di San Giorgio degli Schiavoni** (Slavs; *see p96*), with its captivating cycle of paintings by Vittorio Carpaccio. Indeed, the great promenade along the lagoon – the **riva degli Schiavoni** – was named after the same community.

Inland from the Riva is the quaint Gothic church of **San Giovanni in Bragora** (*see p95*) and, further back in the warren of streets, the church of **Sant'Antonin**, probably the only church in Venice in which an elephant has been shot. The unfortunate animal escaped from a circus on the Riva in 1819 and took refuge in the church, only to be finished off by gunners summoned from the Arsenale. A lively dialect poem, *Elefanteide* by Pietro Buratti, was written to commemorate the event.

Back on the riva degli Schiavoni is the church of **La Pietà** (*see p94*), where Vivaldi was choir master; it is now frequently used for concerts. Head on eastwards past the **Ca' di Dio**, once a hostel for pilgrims setting out for the Holy Land and now an old people's home, and the **Forni Pubblici** (public bakeries), where the biscuit (*bis-cotto*, literally 'twice-cooked') – that favourite, scurvy-encouraging staple of ancient mariners – was reputedly invented.

Crossing the bridge over the rio dell'Arsenale, you can see the grand Renaissance entrance to the huge shipyard, once a hive of empire-dominating industry and closely guarded secrets, now a desolate expanse of crumbling warehouses and empty docks.

Beyond the rio dell'Arsenale, the wide **via Garibaldi** forks off to the left. This road and the nearby public gardens (*see below*) are a legacy of the years of French occupation in the early 19th century. In the few years that they ruled the city, the French imposed some sound examples of modern town planning as well as some mean-spirited priest-bashing that put paid to 49 churches and convents.

For proof that Venice is not a dead city, head here in the morning to catch the bustle at the market close to the monument to Garibaldi, a dignified statue perched on a rocky island in the middle of a turtle-filled pond. Otherwise, take an evening stroll and join Venetians *en masse*, from kiddies on tricycles to old men propping up the bars.

Via Garibaldi leads eventually to the island of **San Pietro**, where the former cathedral stands forlornly among modest, washing-garlanded houses. For centuries before relocating to St Mark's, the bishop (later patriarch) of Venice was relegated here, at a safe distance from the decision-making centre. Nowadays the island has a pleasant backwoods feel to it; on the feast of Sts Peter and Paul (June 29), locals spill on to the patchy grass in front of the church for the nearest thing Venice offers to a village fête, complete with *al fresco* dining, dancing, music and gallons of wine. Bring your boots.

Back on the lagoon, the riva degli Schiavoni changes its name after the rio dell'Arsenale to become the **riva dei Sette Martiri**, named after seven partisans executed here in 1944. Created in 1936, this long, wide section is often dwarfed by moored cruise ships. By the vaporetto stop of the same name, you'll find the shady **Giardini pubblici**, public gardens that took the place of four suppressed convents. A Renaissance archway from one has been reconstructed in a corner. In another corner lies the entrance to the **Biennale**, where a collection of seedy pavilions remains locked up except for those few weeks every two years

Sightseeing

The French destroyed four monasteries to create the **Giardini pubblici**. *See p93*

when a major contemporary art bonanza (*see chapter* **Contemporary Art**) attracts an ever-dwindling number of devotees.

The Riva ends in the sedately residential district of **Sant'Elena**. This, in Venetian terms, is a 'modern' district. In 1872, work began to fill in the *barene* (marshes) that lay between the edge of the city and the ancient island of Sant' Elena, with its charming Gothic church (*see p96*), which now stands just the other side of the football stadium.

Sant'Elena has a distinctly suburban feel to it: children play and dogs are walked in grassy expanses dotted with ilex and pine trees. It's the ideal spot for an evening drink as the sun sets dramatically over the lagoon.

Museo dell'Istituto Ellenico

Castello 3412, ponte dei Greci (041 522 6581). Vaporetto San Zaccaria. **Open** 9am-12.30pm, 1.30-4.30pm Mon-Sat; 10am-5pm Sun. **Admission** L7,000; L4,000 students under 25. **No credit cards.** **Map** III 1B.
The Byzantine side of Venice is played up in this temple of icons. The adjacent church of San Giorgio dei Greci was a focal point for the Greek community, which was swollen by refugees after the Turkish capture of Constantinople in 1453. There has been a Greek church, college and school on this site since the end of the 15th century, and the museum is an essential adjunct to the centre for Byzantine studies next door. The oldest piece in the collection is the 14th-century altar cross behind the ticket desk. The icons on display mainly follow the dictates of the Cretan school, with no descent into naturalism, though some of the 17th- and 18th-century pieces make jarring and often kitsch compromises with Western art. The best pieces are those that take no quarter in their hieratic flatness, such as *Christ in Glory Among the Apostles* and the *Great Deesis* from the first half of the 14th century. Also on display are priestly robes and other Greek rites paraphernalia.

Museo Storico Navale

Castello 2148, campo San Biagio (041 520 0276). Vaporetto Arsenale. **Open** 8.45am-1.30pm Mon-Fri; 8.45am-1pm Sat. **Admission** L3,000. **No credit cards.** **Map** III 2B.
Housed in an old granary, this museum dedicated to ships and shipbuilding is a treasure trove. It continues an old tradition: under the Republic, the models made for shipbuilders in the final design stages were kept in a special building inside the Arsenale. Some of the models on display here are survivors from that original collection. The ground floor has warships, cannons, explosive speedboats and dodgy-looking manned torpedoes, plus a display of ships through the ages. On the first floor are ornamental trimmings and naval instruments, plus a series of impressive models of Venetian ships, including a huge 16th-century galleass. Here, too, is a richly gilded model of the Bucintoro, the Doges' state barge. The second floor has uniforms, more up-to-date sextants and astrolabes, and models of modern Italian navy vessels. On the third floor there are models of Chinese and Korean junks, cruise ships and liners, and a series of fascinating naïf votive paintings, giving thanks for shipwrecks averted. A room at the back has a display of gondolas, including a 19th-century example with a fixed cabin, and the last privately owned gondola in Venice, which belonged to Peggy Guggenheim (*see p122*).

La Pietà (Santa Maria della Visitazione)

Riva degli Schiavoni (041 523 1096). Vaporetto San Zaccaria. **Open** for concerts only. **Map** III 1B.
Attached to the girls' orphanage of the same name, the church of La Pietà was most famous for its music. Antonio Vivaldi, violin master and choir master here in the first half of the 18th century, wrote some of his finest music for his young charges. The present building by Giorgio Massari was begun in 1745, four years after Vivaldi's death. Music inspired its architecture: the interior, which is reached by

A galley in just a few hours

The word 'Arsenale' derives from the Arabic 'Dar Sina'a', meaning 'place of industry': the industry, not to mention the efficiency, of Venice's Arsenale was legendary. When the need arose, the *arsenalotti* could assemble a galley in just a few hours.

Shipbuilding activities began here in the 12th century; before long all Venice's galleys were constructed within its confines. At the height of the city's power, 16,000 men were employed. Production continued to expand until the 16th century, when Venice entered its slow but inexorable economic decline.

The imposing land gateway by Antonio Gambello (1460) in campo dell'Arsenale is the first example of Renaissance classical architecture in Venice, although the capitals of the columns are 11th-century Veneto-Byzantine. The gateway was modelled on

a Roman arch in the Istrian city of Pola. The winged lion gazing down from above holds a book without the traditional words *Pax tibi Marce* (Peace to you, Mark), perhaps a sign that it was installed when Venice was at war.

Outside the gate, four Greek lions keep guard. Those immediately flanking the terrace were looted from Athens by Doge Francesco Morosini in 1687; the larger one stood at the entrance to the port of Piraeus and bears runic inscriptions on its side, hacked there in the 11th century by Norse mercenary soldiers in Byzantine service. The lion whose head is clearly less ancient than its body came from Delos and was placed here to commemorate the recapture of Corfu in 1716.

In campo della Tana, on the other side of the Rio dell'Arsenale, is the entrance to the **Corderia**, or rope factory, an extraordinary building 316 metres (1,038 feet) long. Closed and forlorn-looking most of the time, the Corderia's doors open when it houses the overflow from the Biennale (*see p203*).

Since shipbuilding ceased in 1917, the Arsenale has remained navy property. Officers in smart uniforms cut fine figures against the brickwork but appear to put the decaying facilities to no practical use.

Arsenale
Campo dell'Arsenale. Vaporetto Arsenale.
Map III 2-3B.

Sightseeing

crossing a vestibule distinctly resembling a theatre foyer, has the oval shape of a concert hall. It is still used as such. The ceiling has a *Coronation of the Virgin* by Giambattista Tiepolo (1755).

San Giorgio dei Greci
Fondamenta dei Greci (041 523 9569). Vaporetto San Zaccaria. **Open** 9am-12.30pm, 3-4.30pm Mon, Wed-Sat; Sun only for 10.30am service. **Map** III 1B.
By the time the church of San Giorgio was begun in 1539, the Greeks were well established in Venice and held a major stake in the city's numerous scholarly printing presses. Designed by Sante Lombardo, the church's interior is fully Orthodox in layout, with its women's gallery, and high altare behind the iconostasis. A heady smell of incense lends the church an Eastern mystique, enhanced by dark-bearded priests in flowing robes. The distinctive campanile is decidedly lopsided. Next to the church are the Scuola di San Nicolò (now the Museo dell'Istituto Ellenico; *see above*) and the Collegio Flangini (now seat of the Istituto Ellenico di Studi Bizantini e post-Bizantini), both by Baldassare Longhena.

San Giovanni in Bragora
Campo Bandiera e Moro (041 520 5906). Vaporetto Arsenale. **Open** 9.30-11am, 3-6pm Mon-Fri; 8.30-11am Sat. **Map** III 2B.
San Giovanni in Bragora (the meaning of *bragora* is as obscure as the date of the foundation of the first church on this site) is an intimate Gothic structure.

Insular **San Pietro in Castello**. *See p96.*

The church where composer Antonio Vivaldi was baptised (the entry in the register is on show), San Giovanni also contains some very fine paintings. Above the high altar is the *Baptism of Christ* (1492-5) by Cima da Conegliano (which could 'only properly be seen by standing on the altar', wrote Victorian traveller Augustus Hare), with a charming landscape recalling the countryside around the painter's home town of Conegliano, on the Veneto mainland. A smaller Cima, on the right of the door to the sacristy, shows *Constantine Holding the Cross and St Helen* (1502). To the left of the door is a splendidly heroic *Resurrection* (1498) by Alvise Vivarini, in which the figure of Christ is based on a statue of Apollo, now in the Museo Archeologico.

San Pietro in Castello

Campo San Pietro (041 523 8950). Vaporetto Giardini. **Open** 10am-5pm Mon-Sat; 1-5pm Sun. **Admission** L3,000 *(see also p63* **Chorus**). **No credit cards. Map** III 4B.

Until 1807, San Pietro in Castello was the cathedral of Venice, and its remote position testifies to the determination of the Venetian government to keep the clerical authorities well away from the centres of temporal power. The island of San Pietro may be connected to the rest of Venice by two long bridges, but even today it has a distinctly insular feel to it. There has probably been a church here since the seventh century, but the present building was constructed in 1557 to a design by Andrea Palladio. San Pietro's lofty interior looks as if it has seen better days, but it contains some minor gems. The body of the first patriarch of Venice, San Lorenzo Giustiniani, is preserved in an urn elaborately supported by angels above the high altar: a magnificent piece of baroque theatricality designed by Baldassare Longhena (1649). In the right-hand aisle is perhaps the church's most interesting artefact, the so-called 'St Peter's Throne', a delicately carved marble work from Antioch containing a Moslem funerary stele and verses from the Koran. The baroque Vendramin Chapel in the left transept was again designed by Longhena, and contains a *Virgin and Child* by the prolific Neapolitan Luca Giordano. Outside the entrance to the chapel is a late work by Paolo Veronese, *Sts John the Evangelist, Peter and Paul*. San Pietro's canalside 'church green' of scrappy grass under towering trees and a punch-drunk campanile in white marble is a charming place to relax and have a picnic.

Sant'Elena

Servi di Maria 3, campo Chiesa Sant'Elena (041 520 5144). Vaporetto Sant'Elena. **Open** *Apr-Oct* 4-7pm Mon-Sat; 5-7pm Sun. *Nov-Mar* 5-6.30pm Mon-Sat; 5-6pm Sun. **Map** off II4C.

The red-brick Gothic church of Sant'Elena is reached by a long avenue alongside the precarious-looking mesh of scaffolding that constitutes Venice's football ground. Though it contains no great works of art (the church was deconsecrated in 1807, turned into an iron foundry, and not opened again until

The residential **Sant'Elena** district, a welcome bit of green. *See p94.*

1928), its austere Gothic nakedness is a relief after all that Venetian ornament. In a chapel to the right of the entrance lies the body of St Helena, the irascible mother of the Emperor Constantine and finder of the True Cross. Curiously enough, her body is also to be found in the Aracoeli church in Rome.

Scuola di San Giorgio degli Schiavoni

Castello 3259A, calle dei Furlani (041 522 8828). Vaporetto San Zaccaria. **Open** *Apr-Oct* 9.30am-12.30pm, 3.30-6.30pm Tue-Sat; 9.30am-12.30pm Sun. *Nov-Mar* 10am-12.30pm, 3-6pm Tue-Sat; 10am-12.30pm Sun. **Admission** L5,000; L3,000 5-18s, groups of over 20. **No credit cards. Map** III 2A.

This unassuming *scuola* (*see p63*) was the only such institution whose members were united by ethnic origin. The Schiavoni were Venice's Slav inhabitants, who had become so numerous and influential by the end of the 15th century that they could afford to build this meeting house by the side of their church, San Giovanni di Malta. The *scuola* houses one of Vittore Carpaccio's two great Venetian picture cycles. In 1502, eight years after completing his St Ursula cycle (now in the Accademia, *see p122*), Carpaccio was commissioned to paint a series of canvases illustrating the lives of the Dalmatian saints George, Tryphone and Jerome. In the tradition of the early Renaissance *istoria* (narrative painting cycle), there is a wealth of incidental detail, such as the decomposing virgins in *St George and the Dragon*, or the little dog in the painting of *St Augustine in His Study* (receiving the news of the death of St Jerome in a vision) – with its paraphernalia of humanism (astrolabe, shells, sheet music, archaeological fragments). It's worth venturing upstairs to see what the meeting hall of a working *scuola* looks like. San Giorgio degli Schiavoni still provides scholarships, distributes charity and acts as a focal point for the local Slav community.

Cannaregio

Venice's narrowest calle, Europe's original Ghetto and the most ornate palazzo on the Grand Canal grace this northernmost sestiere.

Cannaregio is Venice's second-largest sestiere, stretching across the north-west of the city from the station almost to the Rialto bridge. Its name derives either from *Canal Regio* (regal canal) or from the *canne* (reeds) that grew there in profusion. Cannaregio was settled well before AD 1000, when the first dwellings were built on the islands of San Giovanni Crisostomo and Santi Apostoli, close to the Rialto. The areas adjacent to the Grand Canal were built up next. The urban sprawl proceeded northwards, engulfing the convents and monasteries – the **Misericordia**, the **Madonna dell'Orto** (*see p100*), the **Servi**, **Sant'Alvise** (*see p101*) – on what were, until then, remote islands.

With the construction of the railway and road bridges to the mainland in the 19th century, the mainly residential and religious nature of the sestiere changed. A large slaughterhouse (now converted into university facilities) was built at the northern end of the Cannaregio Canal. Abandoned churches and convents were taken over by industry. A wide pedestrian route, the **Strada Nuova**, was built roughly parallel to the Grand Canal to funnel travellers swiftly through to the city centre. But the sestiere contains treasures in its own right.

La Maddalena: inspired by the Pantheon.

From the station to the Rialto

For centuries, Cannaregio has been the first bit of Venice most travellers see. Before the bridges to the mainland were built, the **Cannaregio Canal** (*see p102*) was the stately point of entry for boats bearing visitors from across the lagoon. Nowadays, tourists spill from the station and, after passing the magnificent baroque façade of the **Scalzi** church, find themselves in a quivering hive of tacky souvenir stalls, grotty bars and downmarket hotels on and around the **Lista di Spagna**.

The squalor is, mercifully, circumscribed. Heading away from the station towards the Rialto, the Lista leads to the large **Campo San Geremia**, overlooked by the church of the same name (containing the shrivelled body of St Lucy), and **Palazzo Labia**, now occupied by the RAI (Italian state television). The palazzo contains frescos by Tiepolo, visible by

appointment (041 781 277). Once you're over the Cannaregio Canal, by way of a grandiose bridge with obelisks, the station seems aeons away. Off to the right, in a square giving on to the Grand Canal, is the church of **San Marcuola** (*see p99*), with an unfinished façade. Just a little further on, the more picturesque 18th-century church of **La Maddalena**, inspired by the Pantheon in Rome, stands in a small square with an assortment of fantastic chimney-pots.

Beyond this, the wide **Strada Nuova** begins. Off to the left is the church of **San Marziale** (*see p99*), with whimsical ceiling paintings, while, on the Strada Nuova itself, stands the church of **Santa Fosca**, another mainly 18th-century creation. Down a calle to the right is the entrance to the **Ca' d'Oro** (*see p98*), Venice's most splendid Gothic palazzo.

The Strada Nuova ends by the church of **Santi Apostoli** (*see p99*), and the route to the Rialto soon becomes reassuringly narrow and crooked, passing the church of **San Giovanni Crisostomo** (*see p99*) and the adjacent courtyard of the **Corte Seconda del Milion**, where Marco Polo was born. There's a plaque commemorating him on the rear of the **Teatro Malibran** (formerly the Teatro di San Giovanni Crisostomo, one of Venice's earliest theatres and opera houses). Some of the Veneto-Byzantine-style houses in the courtyard would have been there when he was born in 1256. There's a splendidly carved horseshoe arch, much admired by Ruskin.

Ca' d'Oro (Galleria Franchetti)

Cannaregio 3932, calle Ca' d'Oro (041 523 8790/ guided tours in Italian 041 520 0345). Vaporetto Ca' d'Oro. **Open** 8.15am-7pm Tue-Sun. *Courtyard Apr-Oct* 8.15am-6pm Tue-Sun. **Admission** L6,000 (*see also p63* **Accademia**). **No credit cards.** Map I 3B.

In its 15th-century heyday, the façade of this pretty townhouse on the Grand Canal must have looked a psychedelic treat: the colour scheme was light blue and burgundy, with 24-carat gold highlights. Though the colour has worn off, the Grand Canal frontage of Ca' d'Oro – built for merchant Marin Contarini between 1421 and 1431 – is still the most elaborate example of the florid Venetian Gothic style outside of the Doge's Palace. Inside, little of the original structure and decor has survived the depredations of successive owners. The pretty courtyard was reconstructed with its original 15th-century staircase and well-head a century ago by Baron Franchetti, who assembled the collection of paintings, sculptures and coins that is exhibited on the first and second floors. The highlight of the collection is Mantegna's St Sebastian, one of the painter's most powerful late works; the Palladian frame contrasts oddly with the saint's existential anguish. The rest is good in parts, though not necessarily the parts you would expect. A small medal of Sultan Mohammed II by Gentile Bellini (a souvenir of his years in Constantinople) is more impressive than the worse-than-faded frescos by Titian and Giorgione from the Fondaco dei Tedeschi.

Gli Scalzi

Fondamenta degli Scalzi (041 715 115). Vaporetto Ferrovia. **Open** 9am-noon, 3.30-5.30pm Mon-Sat; 3.30-5.30pm Sun. **Map** I 1B.

Officially Santa Maria di Nazareth, this church is universally known as Gli Scalzi after the order of *Carmelitani Scalzi* (Barefoot Carmelites) to whom it belongs.They bought the plot in 1645 and commissioned Baldassare Longhena to design the church. The fine façade (1672-80) is the work of Giuseppe Sardi; it was paid for by a newcomer to Venice's ruling patricians, Gerolamo Cavazza, determined to make his marble mark on the landscape. The interior is striking for its coloured marble ('a perfect type of the vulgar abuse of marble in every possible way,' wrote Ruskin), and massively elaborate

Venetian green

At first glance, Venice is the most urban of cities: a desultory attempt at a public park in Castello, a formal plot round the corner from St Mark's. But aerial photographs of Venice show a surprising number of clumps of green punctuating the red tiles of the city's roofs. Granted, most of these are private spaces, jealously held secret gardens. Tourists are lucky if they get a passing glimpse over a high wall. Some of the finest of these privileged retreats are on the Giudecca; together with extensive market-gardens, they are reminders of the island's former Arcadian charms.

The public gardens that do exist are relatively recent additions; for some, we have to thank Napoleon. He had the state granaries pulled down to create the **Giardinetti Reali** (*see p72*) around the corner from St Mark's, and numerous churches and convents destroyed to make way for the **Giardini pubblici** (*p93*) in Castello.

The **Giardini Papadopoli** (*see p112*), near piazzale Roma, were created in 1810 over the Convent of Santa Croce, which gave that

sestiere its name; they were lopped to their present forlorn dimensions when the rio Novo was cut through in the 1930s to provide swift access from the carpark to St Mark's.

Gardens not being Venice's main attraction, little attention has traditionally been paid to restful green and flowerbeds. In recent years, however, the town council has spruced up its green areas; the city no longer has to rely exclusively on window-boxes for its floral colour.

For a sylvan retreat, try the **Parco Savorgnan** (*see p103*), formerly a private garden, off the Cannaregio Canal or, at the other end of the city, the *pineta* (pine forest) of **Sant'Elena** (*see p96*); both have children's play-areas.

There's a small stretch of green, complete with picturesque classical 'ruins', by the church **Sant'Alvise** (*see p101*), and – most romantic of all – public gardens behind the **Redentore** (*see p128*) on the Giudecca, with a view over the lonely southern lagoon. (*See also* **Lagoon Picnics** *p162*.)

North-western Cannaregio: lagoon views.

baldachin over the high altar. There are many fine baroque statues, including the *St John of the Cross* by Giovanni Marchiori in the first chapel on the right and the anonymous marble crucifix and wax effigy of Christ in the chapel opposite. An Austrian shell that plummeted through the roof in 1915 destroyed the church's greatest work of art, Tiepolo's fresco of *The Transport of the House of Loreto*, but spared some of the artist's lesser works – frescos of the *Angels of the Passion* and *Agony in the Garden* in the first chapel on the left and *St Theresa in Glory*, which hovers gracefully above a hamfisted imitation of Bernini's sculpture *Ecstasy of St Theresa*, in the second on the right. In the second chapel on the left lie the mortal remains of the last Doge of Venice, Lodovico Manin.

San Giovanni Crisostomo
Campo San Giovanni Crisostomo (041 522 7155).
Vaporetto Rialto. **Open** 8.30am-noon, 3.30-7pm Mon-Sat; 3.30-7pm Sun. **Map** I 4C.
This small church by Mauro Codussi is dedicated to St John Chrysostomos, archbishop of Constantinople, and shows a fittingly marked Byzantine influence in its Greek-cross form. It contains two great paintings. On the right-hand altar is *Saints Jerome, Christopher and Louis of Toulouse*, signed by Giovanni Bellini and dated 1513. This late work is one of his few Madonna-less altarpieces and shows the old Master ready to experiment with the atmospheric colouring techniques of such younger artists as Giorgione. On the high altar hangs *Saints John the Baptist, Liberale, Mary Magdalene and Catherine* by Sebastiano del Piombo (c. 1509), who trained under Bellini but was also influenced by Giorgione. Henry James was deeply impressed by the figure of Mary Magdalene: she looked, he said, like a 'dangerous, but most valuable acquaintance'. On the left-hand altar is *Coronation of the Virgin*, a fine relief (1500-02) by Tullio Lombardo.

San Marcuola
Campo San Marcuola (041 713 872). Vaporetto San Marcuola. **Open** 10am-noon, 5-6pm Mon-Sat.
Map I 2B.

There was no such person as St Marcuola; the name is a Venetian mangling of the over-complicated Santi Ermagora e Fortunato, two early martyrs. The church, designed by 18th-century architect Giorgio Massari, is enlivened by an unfinished façade and contains some vigorous statues by Gianmaria Morleiter. In the chancel is a *Last Supper* by Tintoretto (1547), his first treatment of what was to become a favourite subject. Opposite is a 17th-century copy of another Tintoretto (*The Washing of the Feet*); the original is in Newcastle, Tyne and Wear.

San Marziale
Campo San Marziale (041 719 933). Vaporetto San Marcuola or Ca' d'Oro. **Open** 4-6pm Mon-Sat.
Map I 3B.
The real joy of this church is its ceiling, with its four luminous paintings by the vivacious Bellunese colourist Sebastiano Ricci (1700-05). Two of them depict *God the Father with Angels* and *St Martial in Glory*; the other two recount the miraculous story of the wooden statue of the Madonna and Child to be found on the second altar on the left, which apparently made its own way here by boat from Rimini. The high altar has an equally fantastic baroque extravaganza: a massive marble group of Christ, the world and some angels looms over the altar while St Jerome and companions crouch awkwardly beneath.

Santi Apostoli
Campo SS Apostoli (041 523 8297). Vaporetto Ca' d'Oro. **Open** 7.30-11.30am, 5-6pm Mon-Sat.
Map I 4C.
According to tradition, the 12 apostles appeared to the seventh-century Bishop of Oderzo, St Magnus, telling him to build a church where he saw 12 cranes together – a not uncommon sight when Venice was little more than a series of uninhabited islands poking out of marshes. The ancient church was rebuilt in the 17th century. Its campanile (1672), crowned by an onion dome added 50 years later, is a Venetian landmark. The Cappella Corner, off the right side of the nave, is a century older than the rest of the structure. It was built by Mauro Codussi for the deposed and depossessed Queen Caterina Cornaro of Cyprus (*see chapter* **History**); she was buried here in 1510 alongside her father and brother but subsequently removed to San Salvador (*see p84*). On the altar is a splendidly theatrical *Communion of St Lucy* by Giambattista Tiepolo; the young saint, whose gouged-out eyes are in a dish on the floor, is bathed in a heavenly light. The chapel to the right of the high altar has remnants of 14th-century frescos.

North-western Cannaregio

The north-western areas of Cannaregio are quieter and more laid-back. Built around three long parallel canals, it has no large bustling squares and (with the exception of the Ghetto, *see p103*) no sudden surprises – just the occasional view over the northern lagoon.

Sightseeing

The area contains its landmarks, including the old (14th-century) and new (16th-century) **Scuole della Misericordia**, the 'new' one being a huge building by Sansovino, its façade never completed; long used as a gym, it now awaits conversion into an auditorium and multimedia music archive.

Behind the scuole, the picturesque **Campo dell'Abbazia**, overlooked by the baroque façade of the **Abbazia della Misericordia** and the Gothic façade of the **Scuola Vecchia**, is one of the most peaceful retreats in Venice; on the façade of the latter it is still possible to see the outlines of sculptures by Gothic master Bartolomeo Bon, which were removed in 1612 and are now in London's Victoria and Albert Museum.

On the northernmost canal are the churches of the **Madonna dell'Orto** (*see p100*) and **Sant'Alvise** (*see p101*), as well as many fine *palazzi*. The palazzo at the beginning of the *fondamenta* along this canal, **Palazzo Contarini dal Zaffo**, was built for Gaspare Contarini, a 16th-century scholar, diplomat and cardinal. Behind, a large garden stretches down to the lagoon; in its far corner stands the **Casinò degli Spiriti** (best seen from fondamente Nuove). Designed as a meeting place for the 'spirits' (wits) of the day, the name and the lonely position of the construction have given rise to numerous ghost stories.

The **Madonna dell'Orto** area may have been the home of an Islamic merchant community in the 12th and 13th centuries, centring on a since-destroyed Fondaco (meeting-place and storehouse) degli Arabi. Opposite the church is the 15th-century **Palazzo Mastelli**, also known as *del Camello* because of its relief of a turbaned figure with a camel. The Arabic theme continues in the **Campo dei Mori** across the bridge, named after the three stone figures set into the façade of a building, all wearing turbans. The one with the comically prominent iron nose – dubbed 'Sior Antonio Rioba' – was the Venetian equivalent of Rome's Pasquino: disgruntled citizens or local wits would hang their rhyming complaints on him overnight, or use him as a pseudonym for published satires. The three figures are believed to be the Mastelli brothers, owners of the adjacent palazzo, who came to Venice as merchants from the Greek Peloponnese (then known as Morea – which offers another explanation of the campo's name).

Madonna dell'Orto

Campo Madonna dell'Orto (041 719 933). Vaporetto Madonna dell'Orto. **Open** 10am-5pm Mon-Sat; 1-5pm Sun. **Admission** L3,000 (*see also p63* **Chorus**). **No credit cards. Map** I 3A.

The 'Tintoretto church' was originally dedicated to St Christopher (a magnificent statue of whom stands over the main door), the patron saint of the gondoliers who ran the ferry service to the islands from a nearby jetty. However, a cult developed around a large unfinished and supposedly miraculous statue of the Madonna and Child that stood in the nearby garden of sculptor Giovanni de Santi; in 1377 the sculpture was solemnly transferred into the church (it's now in the chapel of San Mauro), and its name was changed to the Madonna of the Garden. The church was rebuilt between 1399 and 1473, and a monastery was constructed alongside. The beautiful Gothic façade is similar to those of the Frari and SS Giovanni e Paolo, although the false gallery at the top is unique. The sculptures are all fine 15th-century works. But it is the numerous works by Tintoretto that have made the Madonna dell'Orto famous. Tradition has it that the artist began decorating the church as penance for insulting a doge: in fact, it took very little to persuade Tintoretto to get his palette out, and the urgent sincerity of his work here speaks for itself.

Two colossal paintings dominate the side walls of the chancel. On the left is *The Making of the Golden Calf*: the bearded figure helping to carry the calf is said to be the artist himself, while the lady in blue may be Mrs Tintoretto. Opposite is a gruesome *Last Judgment*. Like Dante and Michelangelo, Tintoretto had no qualms about mixing religion and myth: note the classical figure of Charon ferrying the souls of the dead. Tintoretto's paintings in the apse include

Awaiting conversion: **La Misericordia**.

I Gesuiti: indescribably table-clothy.

St Peter's Vision of the Cross and *The Beheading of St Christopher*, both maelstroms of swirling angelic movement. On the wall of the right aisle is the *Presentation of the Virgin in the Temple*, a calmer, more reverential work. It was painted as a deliberate response to Titian's masterpiece of the same theme in the Accademia, and is more characteristically mystical in tone.

The Contarini Chapel, off the left aisle, contains the artist's beautiful *St Agnes Reviving the Son of a Roman Prefect*. Once again, it is the swooping angels that steal the show in their dazzling blue vestments. Tintoretto, his son Domenico and his artistically gifted daughter Marietta are buried in a chapel off the right aisle. When the Tintorettos get too much for you, take a look at Cima da Conegliano's masterpiece *Saints John the Baptist, Mark, Jerome and Paul* (1494-5) over the first altar on the right. The saints stand under a ruined portico against a sharp wintry light. There used to be a small *Madonna and Child* by Giovanni Bellini in the chapel opposite but it was stolen one day in 1993 when the priest forgot to turn the alarm on.

Sant'Alvise

Campo Sant'Alvise (041 524 4664). Vaporetto Sant'Alvise. **Open** 10am-5pm Mon-Sat; 1-5pm Sun. **Admission** L3,000 (*see also p63* **Chorus**). **No credit cards. Map** I 2A.
A pleasingly simple Gothic building of the 14th century, Sant'Alvise's interior was remodelled in the 17th century with extravagant, if not wholly convincing, *trompe l'oeil* effects on the ceiling. On the inner façade is a *barco*, a hanging choir of the 15th century with elegant wrought-iron gratings, formerly used by the nuns of the adjacent convent. Tiepolo's huge *Road to Calvary* on the right wall of

the chancel is a vivid work, with ill-suited circus-pageantry, complete with trumpets and prancing horses. In the sacristy are eight charmingly naïve biblical paintings in tempera, fancifully attributed by Ruskin to the ten-year-old Carpaccio.

North-eastern Cannaregio

North-eastern Cannaregio is more intriguingly closed in, with many narrow alleys (including the Venetian record-holder, **calle Varisco**, 52cm wide at its narrowest point), charming courtyards and well-heads, but no major sights, with the exception of the spectacularly ornate church of **I Gesuiti** (*see below*), the **Oratorio dei Crociferi** (*see p102*) and, further east, the miniature marvel of **Santa Maria dei Miracoli** (*see p102*). Titian had a house here, with a garden extending to the lagoon.

I Gesuiti

Campo dei Gesuiti (041 528 6579). Vaporetto Fondamente Nove. **Open** *Apr-Oct* 10am-noon, 5-7pm daily. *Nov-Mar* 10am-noon, 4-6pm daily. **Map** I 4B.
The Jesuits were never very popular in Venice, and it wasn't until 1715 that they felt secure enough to build a church here. Even then they chose a comparatively remote plot on the edge of town. But once they made up their mind to go ahead, they went all out: local architect Domenico Rossi was given explicit instructions to dazzle the Venetians. The result leaves no room for half-measures: you love it or you hate it, and for the past couple of centuries, most people have done the latter, considering the result the ultimate in church kitsch. The exterior, with a façade by Gian Battista Fattoretto, is conventional enough;

Turbaned figure and camel lend an Arabic air to **Palazzo Mastelli**. *See p100.*

the interior is anything but. All that tassled, bunched, overpowering drapery is not the work of a rococo set-designer gone berserk with brocades: it's plain old green and white marble. Bernini's altar in St Peter's in Rome was the model for the baldachin over the altar, by Fra Giuseppe Pozzo. The statues above the baldachin are by Giuseppe Torretti, as are the rococo archangels at the corners of the crossing. Titian's **Martyrdom of St Lawrence** (1558-9), over the first altar on the left side, came from an earlier church on this site, and was one of the first successful night-scenes ever painted. According to writer WD Howells – who labelled the church 'indescribably table-clothy' – the saint is the only person in the building not to suffer from the cold.

Oratorio dei Crociferi

Cannaregio 4905, Campo dei Gesuiti (041 270 2464/fax 041 270 2458/ catalogo@patriarcatovenezia.it). Vaporetto Fondamente Nove. **Open** *Apr-Oct* 10am-1pm Fri-Sun. *Nov-Mar* by appointment. **Admission** L3,000. **No credit cards. Map** I 4B.
Founded in the 13th century by Doge Renier Zeno, the oratory is a sort of primitive *scuola* (*see p63*), with the familiar four-square central meeting hall but without the quasi-masonic ceremonial trappings. Palma il Giovane's colourful cycle of paintings shows Pope Anacletus instituting the order of the Crociferi (cross-bearers), and dwells on the pious life of Doge Pasquale Cicogna, who was a fervent supporter of the order.

Santa Maria dei Miracoli

Campo Santa Maria Nova (041 275 0462). Vaporetto Rialto or Fondamente Nove. **Open** 10am-5pm Mon-Sat; 1-5pm Sun. **Admission** L3,000 (*see also p63* **Chorus**). **No credit cards. Map** I 4C.
Arguably one of the world's most exquisite churches, Santa Maria dei Miracoli was built in the 1480s to house a miraculous image of the Madonna, reputed to have revived a man who had spent half an hour underwater in the Giudecca Canal, and to have cancelled all traces of a knife attack on a woman. The building is the work of the Lombardo family, early Renaissance masons who fused architecture, surface detail and sculpture into a unique whole. Pietro Lombardo may have been a Lombard by birth but he soon got into the Venetian way of

doing things, employing Byzantine spoils left over from work on St Mark's to create a work of art displaying an entirely Venetian sensitivity to texture and colour. There is an almost painterly approach to the use of multicoloured marble in the four sides of the church, each of which is of a slightly different shade. The sides have more pilasters than are strictly necessary, making the church appear longer than it really is. Inside, 50 painted ceiling panels by Pier Maria Pennacchi (1528) are almost impossible to distinguish without binoculars – so you can turn your attention to the church's true treasures: the delicate carvings by the Lombardi on the columns, steps and balustrade. Look out for the child's head that so distressed Ruskin, who wondered how any sculptor, after creating something this lifelike, could be so 'wanting in all human feeling, as to cut it off, and tie it by the hair to a vine leaf'.

Cannaregio Canal

For Venetians, only the grandest of their waterways are canals; the others are *rii* (*rio* in the singular). For centuries the main route into Venice from the mainland, the Cannaregio Canal is fitted out in suitably impressive fashion with wide *fondamente* on each side and several imposing *palazzi*. It's spanned by two stately bridges, the **Ponte delle Guglie** (Bridge of the Obelisks, 1823), and the **Ponte dei Tre Archi**, the only three-arch stone

Santa Maria dei Miracoli: exquisite.

bridge in Venice, built by Andrea Tirali in 1688. Heading towards the lagoon from the Ponte delle Guglie on the right-hand *fondamenta*, you pass the *sottoportico* leading to the Jewish Ghetto (*see p103*).

Beyond this stands the **Palazzo Nani** (no.1105), a fine Renaissance palazzo of the 16th century. Two hundred metres further on is the **Palazzo Surian-Bellotto** (no.968): in the 18th century this was the French embassy, where Jean Jacques Rousseau worked – reluctantly – as a secretary. Beyond, **Santa Maria delle Penitenti**, with its unfinished façade, was formerly a home for the city's fallen women.

On the left bank is the **Palazzo Priuli-Manfrin** (nos.342-3), another Tirali creation from 1735, in a neoclassical style of such severe plainness that it prefigures 20th-century purist art.

The imposing 17th-century **Palazzo Savorgan** (no.349) – now a school – has huge coats of arms and reliefs of helmets; the owners were descended from Federigo Savorgnan who, in 1385, became the first non-Venetian to be admitted to Venice's patrician ruling clique.

Behind it is the **Parco Savorgnan**, a charming public garden that is one of Venice's better-kept secrets (*see p98* **Venetian Green**). A little further on, the **Ponte della Crea** spans a canal that was covered over for centuries, only to be re-excavated in 1997.

After passing the Ponte dei Tre Archi (with the Renaissance church of **San Giobbe** off to the left) the *fondamenta* continues to the ex-slaughterhouse, built in the 19th century by the Austrians. Long used by a rowing club, it has recently been taken over and revamped by Venice University's economics faculty.

San Giobbe

Campo San Giobbe (041 524 1889). Vaporetto Ponte Tre Archi. **Open** 10am-noon, 3-6pm Mon-Sat; 3.30-6pm Sun. **Map** I 1A.

Job (Giobbe) – like Moses and Jeremiah – has been raised by Venice to the status of saint, despite his Old Testament pedigree. The church named after him was built to celebrate the visit in 1463 of St Bernardino of Siena, a Franciscan friar and high-profile evangelist. The first Venetian creation of Pietro Lombardo, it introduced a new classical style, immediately visible in the superb doorway (three statues by Pietro Lombardo that once adorned it are now in the sacristy). The interior of what was probably the first single-naved church in Venice is unashamedly Renaissance. The Lombardo family are responsible for the beautiful carvings in the domed sanctuary, all around the triumphal arch separating the sanctuary from the nave, and on the tombstone of San Giobbe's founder Cristoforo Moro, in the centre of the sanctuary floor. The name of this doge has given rise to associations with Othello, the Moor of Venice;

some imaginative souls have even seen the mulberry symbol in his tombstone (a *moro* is a mulberry tree as well as a Moor) as the origin of Desdemona's unfortunate handkerchief, which was 'spotted with strawberries'. The church's artistic treasures – altarpieces by Giovanni Bellini and Vittore Carpaccio – are now in the Accademia (*see p122*). An atmospheric *Nativity* by Gerolamo Savoldo remains, as does an *Annunciation with Saints Michael and Anthony* triptych by Antonio Vivarini. The Martini Chapel, the second on the left, is a little corner of Tuscany in Venice. Built for a family of silk-weavers from Lucca, it is attributed to the Florentine Bernardo Rossellino. The glazed terracotta medallions of Christ and the Four Evangelists are by the Della Robbia studio – the only examples of their work in Venice.

The Ghetto

The word ghetto (like arsenal and ciao) is one that Venice has given to the world. It meant an iron-foundry, a place where iron was *gettato* (cast). Until 1390, when the foundry was transferred to the Arsenale, casting was done on a small island in Cannaregio. In 1516 it was decided to confine the city's Jewish population to this island; there they remained until 1797.

Venetian treatment of the Jews was by no means as harsh as in many European countries, but neither was it a model of open-minded benevolence. The Republic's attitude was governed by practical considerations. Business was done with Jewish merchants at least as early as the tenth century. It was not until 1385, however, that Jewish money-lenders were given permission to reside in the city itself. Twelve years later, permission was revoked amid allegations of irregularities in their banking practices. For a century after that, residence in Venice was limited to two-week stretches.

In 1509, when the Venetian mainland territories were overrun by foreign troops, great numbers of Jews took refuge in the city. The clergy seized the opportunity to stir up anti-Jewish feeling and demanded their expulsion. Venice's rulers, however, had begun to see the economic advantages of letting them stay, and in 1516 a compromise was reached. In a decision that was to mark the course of Jewish history in Europe, the refugees were given residence permits but confined to the Ghetto.

Restrictions were many and tough. Gates across the bridges to the island were closed an hour after sunset in summer and two hours after in winter, not reopening until dawn. During the day, Jews had to wear distinctive badges. Most trades other than money-lending were barred to them. One exception was medicine, for which they were justly famous:

Sightseeing

Disgruntled citizens pinned pasquinades to metal-nosed **Sior Antonio Rioba**. *See p100.*

Venetian practicality allowed Jewish doctors the privilege of leaving the Ghetto at night for professional calls. Another was music: Jewish singers and fiddlers were hired to entertain guests at private parties.

The Ghetto became a stop on the tourist trail. In 1608 traveller Thomas Coryat came to gaze at the Jews – never having seen any in England – and marvelled at the 'sweet-featured persons' and the 'apparel, jewels, chains of gold' of the women.

The original inhabitants were mostly Ashkenazim from Germany; they were joined by Sephardim escaping from persecution in Spain and Portugal and then, increasingly, by Levantine Jews from the Ottoman Empire. These latter proved key figures in trade between Venice and the East, particularly after Venice lost so many of her trading posts in the eastern Mediterranean. By the mid-16th century the Levantine Jews, by far the richest community, were given permission to move from the *Ghetto Nuovo* to the confusingly named *Ghetto Vecchio* (the old Ghetto, the site of an earlier foundry); in 1633 they expanded into the *Ghetto Nuovissimo*.

Nonetheless, conditions remained cramped, and the height of the buildings in the **campo del Ghetto Nuovo** shows how the inhabitants, denied the possibility of expanding in a horizontal direction, did so vertically, creating the first high-rise blocks in Europe. A recent study has calculated that at certain periods overcrowding was such that the inhabitants must have had to take it in turns to sleep. Room was found for five magnificent synagogues, each new influx of immigrants wanting its own place of worship. The **German**, **Levantine** and **Spanish synagogues** can be visited as part of the **Museo della Comunità Ebraica** tour (*see below*).

With the arrival of Napoleon in 1797, Jews gained full rights of citizenship; many chose to remain in the Ghetto. In the deportations during the Nazi occupation of Italy in 1943, 202 Venetian Jews were sent to the death camps, including the chief rabbi and 20 inmates of an old people's home. The Jewish population of Venice and Mestre now stands at about 500, though only around a dozen Jewish families still live in the Ghetto. The Ghetto remains, however, the centre of spiritual, cultural and social life for the Jewish community: there's a museum, a library, a kosher restaurant (*see p157* **Gam-Gam**), a bakery and a nursery school. Orthodox religious services are held in the Scuola Spagnola in the summer and in the Scuola Levantina in winter.

Museo della Comunità Ebraica

Cannaregio 2902B, campo del Ghetto Nuovo (041 715 359). Vaporetto Ponte delle Guglie or San Marcuola. **Open** *June-Sept* 10am-7pm Mon-Fri, Sun; guided tours hourly 10.30am-5.30pm. *Oct-May* 10am-5pm Mon-Thur, Sun; 10am-half hour before sunset Fri; guided tours hourly 10.30am-4.30pm. **Admission** *Museum only* L5,000; L3,000 students. *Museum & synagogue tour* L12,000; L9,000 students. **No credit cards. Map** I 2A.

Venice's Jewish community has been enjoying a renaissance recently, and this well-run museum and cultural centre – founded in 1953 – has been spruced up accordingly, with the addition of a bookshop and kosher café. In the small museum itself there are ritual objects in silver – Trah finials, Purim and Pesach cases, menorahs – sacred vestments and hangings, and a series of marriage contracts. To get the most out of the experience, the museum should be visited as part of the guided tours in English and Italian. These take in three synagogues – the **Scola Canton** (Ashkenazi rite), the **Scola Italiana** (Italian rite) and the **Scola Levantina** (Sephardic rite).

San Polo & Santa Croce

Bustling markets and a host of Titians and Tintorettos pack these two *sestieri* in the upper loop of the Grand Canal.

These two *sestieri* nestle within the upper loop of the Grand Canal, San Polo constituting roughly the southern half, around the Rialto and campo San Polo, and Santa Croce the northern and western half, between campo San Giacomo dell'Orio and piazzale Roma. Local postmen are probably the only ones who can say precisely where one sestiere ends and the other begins.

If a real division can be pointed to in this area, it is in fact between east and west, with the rio di San Polo (which changes its name three times on its way north) as boundary-line. To the east of this canal lies the most ancient and densely built-up area of Venice, around the **Rialto market**. To the west is a once-rural district whose fulcrum is the monumental religious complex of **I Frari** (*see p112*) and the *scuole* of **San Rocco** (*see p114*) and **San Giovanni Evangelista**.

The Rialto markets

Tradition has it that one of the earliest settlements in the lagoon was on this point of higher ground – 'Rivoaltus' – at the very centre of the Grand Canal. The district has been the commercial heart of the city since the market was moved here from campo San Bartolomeo in 1097. The present layout of the market and adjacent buildings is the result of an overall reconstruction project by Scarpagnino after a fire in 1514, which destroyed the whole area. As usual in Venice, the project made use of the previous foundations, so the present street-plan probably reflects quite faithfully the earliest urban arrangement, with long, narrow parallel blocks running behind the grand *palazzi* along the riva del Vin, and smaller, squarer blocks further inland for the market-workers.

The socially important **scuola di San Giovanni Evangelista**. *See p111.*

San Giacomo di Rialto. *See p107.*

At the foot of the **Rialto bridge** (*see p68*), where the tourist stalls are thick on the ground, stands – to the left – the **Palazzo dei Dieci Savi**, which housed the city's tax-inspectors

(it is now used by the ancient but extant lagoon water authority, *Il Magistrato alle Acque*), and – to the right – the **Palazzo dei Camerlenghi**, which housed the finance department.

Beyond, the small church of **San Giacomo di Rialto** (known affectionately as San Giacometto; *see p107*) is generally agreed to be the first of the city's churches (tradition has it that it was founded in AD 421). All around it stretch the markets, around which commercial and administrative buildings and areas of low-cost housing for the traders mushroomed after trade was shifted from the other side of the canal. Despite the overabundance of souvenir stalls, the Rialto market remains the best place to buy your fruit, veg and – for those who can take the sight of fish and crustaceans in their squirming death-throes – seafood.

The larger streets and squares are named after the merchandise that is still sold there (Naranzeria – oranges; Casaria – cheese; Speziali – spices; Erberia – vegetables), while the narrower alleys mostly bear the names of ancient inns and taverns (some still in operation), such as 'The Monkey', 'The Two Swords', 'The Two Moors', 'The Ox', 'The Bell'; then as now, market-traders hated to be too far from liquid refreshment.

Quivers open to every arrow

If Venice has always had amorous associations, its top slot in the honeymoon-destination charts is a relatively recent one. In Elizabethan England, 'Venice' was considered a fitting name for a brothel. Elizabethan traveller Thomas Coryat reported that Venice's 20,000 courtesans – his probably over-enthusiastic estimate – were one of the city's principal and least resistible attractions: 'Many are esteemed so loose that they are said to open their quivers to every arrow,' he wrote.

Venice's rulers knew better than to try to stamp out the activity; instead, they regulated it. An ordinance of 1562 stipulated what clothes and furnishings prostitutes could and could not adopt (no gold, silver or silk; no tapestries or fancy materials on the walls of their houses).

In keeping with the city's zoning policy, they also tried to confine the areas of activity. One of these early red-light districts was Ca' Rampana near the Rialto, which has given Italian the word *carampana* (slut). There are also five *calli de le Stue*, *stue* being the

ovens used to heat public baths, which were steamy in all senses of the word.

But such regulations were aimed not only at confining prostitutes' activities, but also at curbing other less 'acceptable' vices. On designated *ponti delle Tette* (tit bridges), prostitutes were encouraged to display their wares to attract young men, thus saving them from same-sex perdition.

Thoughts of perdition were brushed under the carpet by the nuns of Venice who were, according to Casanova (*see p16 **The great escape***), excellent lovers. He reports that there was not one who could not be had for money. Although undoubtably tainted by his usual wishful thinking, Casanova's claims had some grain of truth; the fact that many convents were dumping grounds for patricians' undowried daughters probably did not encourage piety. In the 14th century the *Maggior Consiglio* intervened to save nuns from their own sinful inclinations, passing a law prohibiting monks from entering Venetian convents; only one confessor – strictly over the age of 60 – was to be admitted.

On the other side of campo San Giacomo, behind the fruit stalls, is a 16th-century statue of a kneeling figure supporting a staircase leading up to a small column of Egyptian granite, from which laws and sentences were pronounced. It was to this figure – the *Gobbo di Rialto* (the Hunchback of the Rialto, although he is in fact merely crouching) – that naked malefactors clung in desperate and bloody relief, since the statue marked the end of the gauntlet they were condemned to run from piazza San Marco as an alternative to gaol.

The ruga degli Speziali leads to the **Pescaria** (fishmarket; Tue-Sat morning). The present neo-Gothic arcade (1907) replaced the iron structure of the previous century. Beyond the market extends a warren-like zone of medieval low-rent housing interspersed with proud *palazzi*; this area is traversed by two main pedestrian routes from the Rialto bridge, one running westward, more or less parallel to the Grand Canal, towards campo San Polo, and the other zigzagging north-westwards via a series of small squares towards campo San Giacomo dell'Orio and the station.

San Giacomo di Rialto

Campo San Giacomo (041 522 4745). Vaporetto Rialto. **Open** 10.30am-noon, 4-5.30pm Mon-Sat. **Map** I 3C.

The traditional foundation date for this church is that of the city itself: 25 March 421 AD (which, Jan Morris informs us, was a Friday). It has undergone several radical reconstructions since its foundation, the last in 1601. Nonetheless, out of respect for the history of the building, the original Greek Cross plan was always preserved, as were its minuscule dimensions. The interior has columns of ancient marble with 11th-century Corinthian capitals. According to Francesco Sansovino (son of the architect and author of the first guide to the city in 1581), the brick dome may have been a model for the domes of St Mark's. In 1177 Pope Alexander III granted plenary indulgence to all those who visited the church on Maundy Thursday, and among the eager visitors every year was the Doge. The special role of this church in Venetian history was given official recognition after 1532, when Pope Clement VII bestowed the patronage of the church on the Doge, basically annexing it to the Ducal Chapel of St Mark's.

West from the Rialto

The route to campo San Polo traverses a series of straight, busy shopping streets, passing the permanently closed church of **San Giovanni Elemosinario** and the deconsecrated church of **Sant'Aponal**, which has fine Gothic sculpture on its façade. To the south of this route, towards the Grand Canal, stands the church of **San Silvestro** (*see p108*), with a

good Tintoretto, while to the north is a fascinating network of quiet, little-visited alleys and courtyards.

Curiosities worth seeking out include **Palazzo Molin-Cappello**, birthplace of Bianca Cappello, who in 1563 was sentenced to death *in absentia* for eloping with a bank clerk but who managed to right things between herself and the Most Serene Republic by subsequently marrying Francesco de' Medici, Grand Duke of Tuscany. Nearby is Campiello Albrizzi, overlooked by **Palazzo Albrizzi**, which contains one of the most sumptuous baroque interiors (closed to the public) in Venice. And just round the corner is the **Ponte delle Tette**, or the Tit Bridge – named after the prostitutes who plied their trade here (*see p106* **Quivers open to every arrow**).

After the shadowy closeness of these *calli*, the open expanse of **campo San Polo** comes as a sudden sunlit surprise. This is the largest square on this side of the Grand Canal and in the past was used for popular festivals such as bull-baiting, religious ceremonies, parades and theatrical

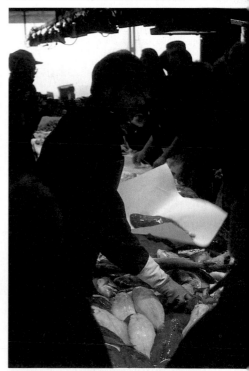

The **Pescaria**: squirming death-throes.

Sightseeing

Campo San Polo (*see p107*): the biggest square on this side of the Grand Canal...

spectacles as well as weekly markets. Venue of an open-air film season in the summer (*see p207*), it functions mainly as a vast children's playground.

The curving line of *palazzi* on the east side of the square is explained by the fact that these buildings once gave on to a canal, which was subsequently filled in. They still have a water-entrance, on the other side, which means that when they were first built access was by boat or bridge only. The two **Palazzi Soranzo** (nos.2169 and 2170-1) are particularly attractive Gothic buildings, especially the former, with marble facing and good capitals. In the 18th century this house had three bridges leading to it.

In the north-west corner is a view of **Palazzo Corner** (the main façade is on the rio di San Polo), a 16th-century design by Sanmicheli. Novelist Frederick Rolfe stayed here – until his English hosts read the manuscript of his work, *The Desire and Pursuit of the Whole*, which contained vitriolic portraits of their friends. They turned him out of the house, thus earning a place for themselves in this ultimate grudge novel.

Casanova was another habitué of one of the splendid Gothic *palazzi* on this campo, managing to get himself adopted as a son by the old senator who lived there.

San Polo

Campo San Polo (041 275 0462). Vaporetto San Silvestro/San Tomà. **Open** 10am-5pm Mon-Sat; 1-5pm Sun. **Admission** L3,000 (*see also p63* **Chorus**). **No credit cards. Map** I 2C.
The church of San Polo faces away from the square,

towards the canal, although later buildings have deprived it of its façade and water-entrance. The campanile (1362) has two 12th-century lions at the base, one brooding over a snake and the other toying with a human head, which Venetians like to think of as that of Count Carmagnola, who was beheaded for treachery in 1402. This basically Gothic church was extensively altered in the 19th century, when a neo-classical look was imposed on it. Some of this was removed in 1930, but the interior remains an awkward hybrid. Paintings include a *Last Supper* by Tintoretto, to the left of the entrance, and another of those snappily named Tiepolos: *The Virgin Appearing to St John of Nepomuk.* Giambattista Tiepolo's son, Giandomenico, is the author of a brilliant cycle of *The Stations of the Cross* in the Oratory of the Crucifix (entrance under the organ). He painted these – and the ceiling paintings – at the age of 20.

San Silvestro

Campo San Silvestro (041 523 8090). Vaporetto San Silvestro. **Open** 7.30-11.30am, 4-6pm Mon-Sat. **Map** I 3C.
This church was rebuilt in the neo-classical style between 1837 and 1843. It contains a *Baptism of Christ* by Tintoretto over the first altar on the right (c1580), with the River Jordan represented as a mountain brook. Off the right aisle (ask the sacristan to let you in) is the former School of the Wine-Merchants; on the upper floor there's a chapel with 18th-century frescos by Gaspare Diziani. Opposite the chuch is the house (No.1022) where Giorgione died in 1510.

North-west from the Rialto

The north-western route from the Rialto (follow the yellow signs to Ferrovia) takes you zigzagging past the fishmarket, through campo San Cassiano, then over a bridge into campo Santa Maria Mater Domini. Before entering the campo, it is worth admiring the view from the bridge of the curving marble flank of **Ca' Pesaro** (*see below*), seat of the Oriental Museum and Museum of Modern Art, on the Grand Canal. On the far side of this square, which contains a number of fine Byzantine and Gothic buildings, the yellow roadsign, in true Venetian fashion, indicates that the way to the station is to the left and to the right.

The quieter route to the right curls parallel to the Grand Canal. The road towards Ca' Pesaro passes **Palazzo Agnusdio**, a small 14th-century house with an ogival five-light window decorated with bas-reliefs of the Annunciation and symbols of the Evangelists; the house used to belong to a family of sausage-makers who were given patrician status in the 17th century.

Many of the most important sights face on to the Grand Canal, including the 18th-century church of **San Stae** (*see p111*) and the **Fondaco dei Turchi** (the Warehouse of the Turks, which houses the city's long-closed Natural History Museum, due to re-open in 2003). On the wide road leading towards San Stae is **Palazzo Mocenigo** (*see p110*), with the Museum of Textiles and Costumes. A short distance away is the quiet square of **San Zan Degolà** (San Giovanni Decollato, *see p111*), with its well-preserved 11th-century church. From here, a series of narrow roads leads past the church of **San Simeone Profeta** (*see p111*) to the foot of the Scalzi Bridge across the Grand Canal.

Leave campo Santa Maria Mater Domini by the route to the left, on the other hand, and you'll make your way past the near-legendary **Da Fiore** (*see p155*) to the house (no.2311) where Aldo Manuzio (Aldus Manutius) set up the Aldine Press in 1490, and where the humanist Erasmus came to stay in 1508. To the right by a building with a 14th-century relief of Faith and Justice above its doorway, the rio Terà del Parrucchetta (apparently named after a seller of animal-fodder who used to wear a ridiculous wig, or *parrucca*) leads to the large leafy campo **San Giacomo dell'Orio**. The church has its back and sides to the square; when the church was built, the main entrance was from the water.

Ca' Pesaro (Museo Orientale)

Santa Croce 2076, fondamenta Ca' Pesaro (041 524 1173). Vaporetto San Stae. **Open** 8.15am-2pm Tue-Sun. **Admission** L4,000 (*see also p63* **Accademia**). **No credit cards. Map** I 3B.

Of the two museums housed in this robust baroque palazzo, only the Museo Orientale is currently visitable; the other – the patchy Museo di Arte Moderna – is *in restauro* and due to reopen by the end of 2001. If Japanese art and weaponry of the Edo period (1600-1868) is your thing, you'll love this eclectic collection, put together by Count Enrico di Borbone – a nephew of Louis XVIII – in the course of a round-the-world voyage between 1887 and 1890. After the count's death the collection was sold off to an Austrian antique merchant; it bounced back to Venice after World War I as reparations. The Museo Orientale might seem an odd museum for such a monocultural city as Venice, but if you come here after the Palazzo Ducale and the Museo Correr, all this ceremonial paraphernalia will seem oddly familiar. The collection features parade armour, dolls, decorative saddles and case upon case of curved samurai swords forged by smiths who had to perform a ritual act of purification before putting their irons in the fire. There is a lady's gilded litter that looks as if it was made for a dwarf, and lacquered picnic cases that prove that the Japanese obsession with compactness predates Sony. The final rooms have some good examples of musical instruments, and an Eastern miscellanea, including Chinese crockery and Indonesian shadow puppets.

... a sudden sunlit surprise.

Sightseeing

Titian's **Madonna di Ca' Pesaro**. *See p113.*

Palazzo Mocenigo

Santa Croce 1992, salizzada San Stae (041 721 798). Vaporetto San Stae. **Open** *Apr-Oct* 10am-5pm Tue-Sun. *Nov-Mar* 10am-4pm Tue-Sun. **Admission** L8,000; L5,000 concessions (*see also p63* **Musei Civici Veneziani**). **No credit cards. Map** I 2-3B.
Small but perfectly formed, the Palazzo Mocenigo will not come top of anyone's museum list, but it is a good place to while away half an hour. The museum serves a double purpose. The interior gives a fine illustration of the sort of furniture and fittings an 18th-century Venetian noble family liked to surround itself with. The Mocenigo family (which also owned a complex of *palazzi* on the Grand Canal) provided the Republic with seven doges, and the paintings, friezes and frescos by late 18th-century artists such as Jacopo Guarana and Gian Battista Canal glorify their achievements. In the rooms off the main Salone, which in typical Venetian fashion runs the length of the building, the neo-classical influence already makes itself felt. Here, too, are the dusty display cases that serve the museum's other function: to act as a chronicle of Venetian 18th-century dress. An *andrienne* dress with bustles so horizontal you could rest a cup and saucer on them, antique lace and silk stockings, a whalebone corset – it's a patchy but charming collection, complemented by a library devoted to Venetian fashions.

San Cassiano

Campo San Cassiano (041 721 408). Vaporetto San Stae. **Open** 9am-noon, 5-6pm Tue-Sat. **Map** I 3C.
This church has a singularly dull exterior and a heavily decorated interior, with a striking ceiling by the Tiepolesque painter Constantino Cedini. It

contains three major Tintorettos in the Chancel: *Crucifixion, Resurrection* and *Descent into Limbo*. The Crucifixion is particularly interesting for its viewpoint; as Ruskin puts it, 'the horizon is so low, that the spectator must fancy himself lying full length on the grass, or rather among the brambles and luxuriant weeds, of which the foreground is entirely composed'. In the background the soldiers' spears make a menacing forest against a stormy sky. Off the left aisle is a small chapel with coloured marbles and inlays of semi-precious stones. On the wall opposite the altar is a painting by Antonio Balestra, which at first glance looks like a dying saint surrounded by *putti*. On closer inspection it transpires that the chubby children are in fact hacking the man to death: the painting represents *The Martyrdom of St Cassian*, a teacher who was murdered by his pupils with their pens. This, of course, makes him the patron saint of schoolteachers.

San Giacomo dell'Orio

Campo San Giacomo dell'Orio (041 524 0672). Vaporetto Riva di Biasio. **Open** 10am-5pm Mon-Sat; 1-5pm Sun. **Admission** L3,000 (*see also p63* **Chorus**). **No credit cards. Map** I 2C.
Campo San Giacomo dell'Orio (St James of the wolf, the laurel-tree, the rio or the Orio family – take your pick) has a pleasantly downbeat feel, with its plane trees, bars and children. Architecturally it is dominated by the church, which has plump, rounded apses and a stocky 13th-century campanile. As with most older Venetian churches, the main entrance faces the canal rather than the campo. The interior is a fascinating mix of architectural and decorative styles. The columns have Veneto-Byzantine capitals of the 12th or 13th century; one has a sixth-century flowered capital and one is a solid piece of smooth verde antico marble, perhaps from a Roman temple sacked for souvenirs during the Fourth Crusade. Note, too, the fine 14th-century ship's keel roof. The Sacrestia Nuova, in the right transept, was built in 1903 on the site of the Scuola del Sacramento. This was the original home of the five gilded compartments on the ceiling with paintings by Veronese: an *Allegory of the Faith* surrounded by four *Doctors of the Church*. Among the numerous other paintings in the room is *St John the Baptist Preaching* by Francesco Bassano, which includes portraits of Bassano's family and Titian (in the red hat).
Behind the High Altar is *The Madonna and Four Saints* by Lorenzo Lotto, one of his last Venetian paintings. There is a good work by Giovanni Bonconsiglio at the end of the left aisle, *St Lawrence, St Sebastian and St Roch*; St Sebastian is conventionally untroubled by his arrow, but St Roch's plague-sore has an anatomical precision that is quite unsettling; the saint is without his usual sore-licking dog. The third of these saints, St Lawrence, also has a chapel all to himself in the left transept, with a central altarpiece by Veronese and two fine early works by Palma il Giovane. As you leave, have a look at the curious painting to the left of the

main door, a naïve 18th-century work by Gaetano Zompini, showing a propaganda miracle involving a Jewish scribe who attempted to profane the body of the Virgin on its way to the sepulchre. His hands were promptly lopped off by divine intervention; they can be seen sticking to the coffin.

San Simeone Profeta

Campo San Simeone Profeta (041 718 921). Vaporetto Ferrovia. **Open** 8am-noon, 5-6pm Mon-Sat; 5-6pm Sun. **Map** I 1-2B.

More commonly known as San Simeone Grande, this small church of ancient, possibly tenth-century, foundation underwent numerous alterations in the 18th century. The interior preserves its ancient columns with Byzantine capitals. Immediately to the left of the entrance is Tintoretto's *Last Supper*, with the priest who commissioned the painting standing to one side, a curiously spectral figure in glowing white robes. The other major work is the stark, powerful statue of a recumbent *St Simeon*, with an inscription dated 1317 attributing it to an otherwise unknown Marco Romano.

San Stae

Campo San Stae (041 275 0462). Vaporetto San Stae. **Open** 10am-5pm Mon-Sat; 1-5pm Sun. **Admission** L3,000 (*see also p63* **Chorus**). **No credit cards. Map** I 3B.

Stae is the Venetian version of Eustachio or Eustace, a martyr saint who was converted to Christianity by the vision of a stag with a crucifix between his antlers (St Hubert had a similar experience). This church on the Grand Canal has a dramatic late baroque façade (1709) by Swiss-born architect Domenico Rossi. The form is essentially Palladian but enlivened by a number of vibrant sculptures, some apparently on the point of leaping straight out of the façade. Venice's last great blaze of artistic glory came in the 18th century, and the interior is a temple to this swansong. On the side walls of the Chancel, all the leading painters operating in Venice in 1722 were asked to pick an apostle, any apostle. The finest of these are: left wall, lower row: Tiepolo's *Martyrdom of St Bartholomew* and Sebastiano Ricci's *Liberation of St Peter*, perhaps his best work; right wall, lower row: Pellegrini's *Martyrdom of St Andrew* and Piazzetta's *Martyrdom of St James*, a disturbingly realistic work showing the saint as a confused old man in the hands of a loutish youth.

Santa Maria Mater Domini

Campo Santa Maria Mater Domini (041 721 408). Vaporetto San Stae. **Open** 10am-noon Mon-Fri. **Map** I 2C.

This church, recently restored by the Venice in Peril fund, is set just off the campo of the same name, which has a number of fine *palazzi*. It was built in the first half of the 16th century to a project by either Giovanni Buora or Codussi. The façade is attributed to Jacopo Sansovino; the harmonious Renaissance interior alternates grey stone with white marble. The *Vision of St Christine* on the second altar on the right is by Vincenzo Catena, a spice-merchant who seems to have painted in his spare time. St Christine was rescued by angels after being thrown into Lake Bolsena with a millstone tied round her neck; in the painting she adores the Risen Christ, while angels hold up the millstone for her.

San Zan Degolà (San Giovanni Decollato)

Campo San Giovanni Decollato (041 524 0672). Vaporetto Riva di Biasio. **Open** 10am-noon Mon-Sat. **Map** I 2B.

The church of Headless Saint John, or San Zan Degolà in Venetian dialect, stands in a quiet campo near the Fondaco dei Turchi; it's a good building to visit if you want a relief from baroque excesses and ecclesiastic clutter. It was restored and reopened in 1994 after being closed for nearly 20 years, and preserves much of its original 11th-century appearance. The interior has Greek columns with Byzantine capitals supporting ogival arches, and an attractive ship's keel roof. During the restoration a splendidly heroic 14th-century fresco of St Michael the Archangel came to light in the right apse. The left apse has some of the earliest frescos in Venice, Veneto-Byzantine works of the early 13th century.

From the Frari to Piazzale Roma

At the heart of the western side of the two *sestieri* lies the great Gothic bulk of **Santa Maria Gloriosa dei Frari** (*see p112* **I Frari**), with its 70-metre-high (230ft) campanile, matched by the Renaissance magnificence of the **church** and **Scuola of San Rocco** and the **Scuola of San Giovanni Evangelista**. These buildings contain perhaps the greatest concentration of innovative and influential works of art in the city outside piazza San Marco.

And it ain't just art: the monastery buildings of the Frari contain the State Archives (*see p12* **Modern history starts here**), a monument to the Venetian reluctance ever to throw anything away. In 300 rooms, about 15 million volumes and files are conserved, relating to all aspects of Venetian history, starting from the year 883. It is said that only the Spanish archives at Simancas approach them in scope and detail. Faced with this daunting wealth of information, ranging from ambassadors' dispatches on foreign courts to spies' reports on noblemen's non-regulation cloaks, grown historians have been reduced to quivering wrecks.

Beyond the archives is the **Scuola di San Giovanni Evangelista**, one of the six *scuole grandi* (*see p63*) that played such an important part in the complex Venetian system of social checks and balances. The courtyard is protected by a screen with a magnificent eagle pediment and a frieze of leaf-sprays by Pietro Lombardo, while the building itself contains a double-staircase by Maurizio Codussi.

North of here runs rio Marin, a canal with *fondamente* on both sides, lined by some fine buildings; these include the late-16th century **Palazzo Soranzo Capello**, with a small garden (to the rear) that figures in D'Annunzio's torrid novel *Il Fuoco* and Henry James' more restrained *The Aspern Papers*, and the 17th-century **Palazzo Gradenigo**, the garden of which was once large enough to host bullfights.

South-west of the Frari is the quiet square of **San Tomà**, with a church on one side and the Scuola dei Calegheri (Cobblers) opposite; the scuola (now a library) has a protective mantle-spreading Madonna over the door and above it a relief by Pietro Lombardo of *St Mark Healing the Cobbler Annanius*, who became Bishop of Alexandria and subsequently the patron saint of shoemakers. Directly south of here is campo **San Pantalon**; its church (*see p114*) has an extraordinary Hollywood-rococo interior.

Heading west from the Frari, the route leads past the church and *scuola* of **San Rocco** (*see p114*), treasure-houses for Tintoretto-lovers, and ends up in a fairly dull area of 19th-century housing, which replaced medieval gardens and orchards. At the edge of this stands the baroque church of **San Nicolò dei Tolentini** (*see p113*); the adjoining monastery houses part of the Venice University Architecture Institute.

If you're looking for a picnic spot, you could do better than the rather forlorn **Giardino Papadopoli**, a small park with Grand Canal views that stands on the site of the church and convent of Santa Croce. The name survives as that of the sestiere, but the church is one of many suppressed by the French at the beginning of the 19th century.

All that remains of Santa Croce is a crenellated wall next to a hotel on the Grand Canal. The garden was much larger until the rio Novo was cut in 1932 and 1933 to provide faster access from the new car park to the St Mark's area. The decision was much contested at the time, and as the canal had to be closed to regular waterborne traffic in the early 1990s owing to subsidence in the adjacent buildings, it would seem that the protesters had a point.

Beyond the garden there is little but the carbon-monoxide kingdom of **piazzale Roma** and the multi-storey car parks.

One last curiosity is the complex of bridges across the rio Novo known as **Tre Ponti**; the interlocking bridges are in fact five, and from them there is a view of 12 other bridges: a record in Venice.

I Frari

Campo dei Frari (041 522 2637). Vaporetto San Tomà. **Open** 9am-6pm Mon-Sat; 1-6pm Sun. **Admission** L3,000 (*see also p63* **Chorus**). **No credit cards. Map** I 2C.

A gloomy Gothic barn, the brick house of God known officially as Santa Maria Gloriosa dei Frari may not be the most elegant church in Venice, but it is certainly one of the city's most significant artistic storehouses after the Accademia and the Scuola di San Rocco. The Franciscans were granted the land in about 1250 and they completed a first church in 1338. At this point they changed their minds and started work on a larger building, facing the opposite way, which was finally completed just over a century later. The church is 98m (320ft) long, 48m (158ft) wide at the transept and 28m (92ft) high – just slightly smaller than Santi Giovanni e Paolo (*see p92*) – and has the second-highest campanile in the city. And while the Frari may not have as many dead Doges as its Dominican rival, it undoubtedly has the artistic edge.

This is one church where the entrance fee is not a recent imposition; tourists have been paying to get into the Frari for over a century. Entrance is via the left transept, but it's best to begin your visit from the back, where you can enjoy the long view of the building, with Titian's *Assumption* above the High Altar acting as a focus.

Right aisle

In the second bay, on the spot where Titian is believed to be buried (the only victim of the 1575-6 plague who was allowed a city burial) is a loud *Monument to Titian*, commissioned nearly 300 years after his death by the Emperor of Austria. On the third altar is a finer memorial, Alessandro Vittoria's statue of *St Jerome*, generally believed to be a portrait of his painter friend.

Right transept

To the right of the sacristy door is the *Tomb of the Blessed Pacifico* (a companion of St Francis) attributed to Nanni di Bartolo and Michele da Firenze (1437); the sarcophagus is surrounded by a splendidly carved canopy in the florid Gothic style. The door itself is framed by Lorenzo Bregno's tomb of Benedetto Pesaro, a Venetian general who died in Corfu. To the left of the door is the first equestrian statue in Venice, the *Monument to Paolo Savelli* (died 1405). The third chapel on the right side of this transept has an altarpiece by Bartolomeo Vivarini, in its original frame, while the Florentine Chapel, next to the Chancel, contains the only work by Donatello in the city: a striking wooden statue of a stark, emaciated *St John the Baptist*.

Sacristy

Commissioned by the Pesaro family, this contains one of Bellini's greatest paintings: the *Madonna and Child with Sts Nicholas, Peter, Benedict and Mark*, still in its original frame. 'It seems painted with molten gems, which have been clarified by time,' wrote Henry James, his eye, as ever, firmly on the prose structure, 'and it is as solemn as it is gorgeous

Roundel in **campiello d'Angaran**. *See p114.*

and as simple as it is deep.' Also in the sacristy is a fine Renaissance tabernacle, possibly by Tullio Lombardo, for a Reliquary of Christ's blood.

Chancel

The High Altar is dominated by Titian's painting of the *Assumption*, a visionary work that seems to open the church up to the heavens. In the golden haze encircling God the Father, there may be a reminiscence of the mosaic tradition of Venice, as found in Bellini's altarpieces. The upward soaring movement of the painting may owe something to the Gothic architecture of the building, but the drama and grandeur of the work essentially herald the baroque.

On the right wall of the Chancel is the *Monument to Francesco Foscari*, the saddest Doge of all. The story of his forced resignation and death from heartbreak (1547) after the exile of his son Jacopo is recounted in Byron's *The Two Foscari*, which was turned into a particularly gloomy opera by Verdi. The left wall boasts one of the finest Renaissance tombs in Venice, the *Monument to Doge Niccolò Tron*, by Antonio Rizzo (1473). This is the first ducal tomb in which the subject is upright; he sports a magnificent bushy beard grown as a sign of perpetual mourning after the death of a favourite son.

Monks' Choir

In the centre of the nave (an unusual position in Italy) stands the Choir, with stalls carved by Marco Cozzi (1468), inlaid with superb intarsia decoration. The choir screen is a mixture of Gothic work by Bartolomeo Bon and Renaissance elements by the Lombardi.

Left Transept

In the third chapel, with an altarpiece by Bartolomeo Vivarini and Marco Basaiti, a slab on the floor marks the grave of composer Claudio Monteverdi. The Corner Chapel, at the end, contains a mannered statue of *St John the Baptist* by Sansovino; this sensitively wistful figure could hardly be more different from Donatello's work of a century earlier.

Left aisle

Another magnificent Titian hangs to the left of the side-door: the *Madonna di Ca' Pesaro*. This work was commissioned by Bishop Jacopo Pesaro in 1519 and celebrates victory in a naval expedition against the Turks led by the bellicose cleric in 1502. The Bishop is kneeling and waiting for St Peter to introduce him and his family to the Madonna. Behind, an armoured warrior bearing a banner has Turkish prisoners in tow.

This work revolutionised altar-paintings in Venice. It wasn't just that Titian dared to move the Virgin from the centre of the composition to one side, using the splendid banner as a counterbalance; the real innovation was the rich humanity of the whole work, from the beautifully portrayed family (with the boy turning to stare straight at us) to the Christ child, so naturally active and alive, twisting away from his mother (apparently a portrait of Titian's own wife) to gaze at the clustered saints around him. The timeless 'sacred conversation' of Bellini's paintings here becomes animated, losing some of its sacredness but gaining in drama and realism.

The whole of the next bay, around the side door, is occupied by another piece of Pesaro propaganda – the mastodontic *Mausoleum of Doge Pesaro* (died 1659), attributed to Longhena, with recently restored sculptures by Melchior Barthel of Dresden. Even the most ardent fans of the baroque have trouble defending this one, with its 'blackamoor' caryatides, bronze skeletons and posturing allegories; political incorrectness is the least of its faults. 'It seems impossible for false taste and base feeling to sink lower,' wrote Ruskin, and you can see his point.

The penultimate bay harbours a *Monument to Canova*, carried out by his pupils in 1827, five years after his death, using a design of his own, intended for the tomb of Titian. His body is buried in his native town of Possagno (*see p269*), but his heart is conserved in an urn inside the monument. The despondent winged lion has a distinct resemblance to the one in *The Wizard of Oz*.

San Nicolò da Tolentino

Campo dei Tolentini (041 710 806). Vaporetto Piazzale Roma. **Open** 9.30-11.15am, 5-6.30pm Mon-Sat. **Map** I 1C.

This church, usually known as I Tolentini, was planned by Scamozzi (1591-5). Its unfinished façade has a massive Corinthian portico added by Andrea Tirali (1706-14). The interior is a riot of baroque decoration, with lavish use of stucco and sprawling frescos. The most interesting paintings – as so often in the 17th century – are by out-of-towners. On the wall outside the chancel to the left is *St Jerome Succoured by an Angel*, by the Flemish artist Johann Liss, a work that anticipates the rococo exuberance of the Venetian 18th century. Outside the chapel in the left transept is *The Charity of St Lawrence* by the Genoese Bernardo Strozzi, in which the magnificently hoary old beggar in the foreground easily upstages the rather wimpish figure of the saint. In the chancel hangs an *Annunciation* by the prolific Neapolitan Luca Giordano and opposite is a splendidly theatrical *monument to Francesco Morosini* (a 17th-century patriarch of that name, not the Doge) by Filippo Parodi (1678), with swirling angels drawing aside a marble curtain to reveal the Patriarch lounging at ease on his tomb. In 1780 the priests of this church handed over all their silverware to a certain 'Romano', who claimed to have a secret new method for cleaning silver and jewellery. Guess what? He was never seen again.

San Pantalon

Campo San Pantalon (041 523 5893). Vaporetto San Tomà. **Open** 4-6pm Mon-Sat; 5-6pm Sun. **Map** II 2A.
The dedicatee of this church is St Pantaleon, court physician to Emperor Galerius, who was arrested, tortured and finally beheaded during Diocletian's persecution of the Christians. The saint's story is depicted inside the church in one of the most extraordinary ceiling-paintings in Italy – a huge illusionist work, painted on 40 canvases, by a Cecil B De Mille of the 17th century, Gian Antonio Fumiani. It took him 24 years to complete the task (1680-1704) and at the end of it all he fell with choreographic grace from the scaffolding to his death.

Veronese depicts the saint in less melodramatic fashion in the second chapel on the right, in what is possibly his last work, *St Pantaleon Healing a Child*. To the left of the Chancel is the Chapel of the Holy Nail. The nail in question, supposedly from the Crucifixion, is preserved in a small but richly decorated Gothic altar. On the right wall is a fine *Coronation of the Virgin* by Antonio Vivarini and Giovanni d'Alemagna.

Walking out of the church towards the canal, an archway on the left will take you into little **campiello d'Angaran**, where there is a carved roundel of a Byzantine Emperor, which experts believe possibly dates from the tenth century. Returning to the campo, a slab in the wall by the canal indicates the minimum length allowed for the sale of various types of fish.

San Rocco

Campo San Rocco (041 523 4864). Vaporetto San Tomà. **Open** *Apr-Oct* 8am-12.30pm, 3-5pm daily. *Nov-Mar* 8am-12.30pm Mon-Fri; 8am-12.30pm, 2-4pm Sat, Sun. **Map** I 2C.
If you have toured the school of San Rocco and are in the mood for more Tintorettos (perhaps after a shot of whisky or a lie-down), look no further. Built in Venetian Renaissance style by Bartolomeo Bon from 1489 to 1508 but radically altered by Giovanni Scalfarotto in 1725, the church has paintings by Tintoretto, or his school, on either side of the entrance door, between the first and second altar on the right, and on either side of the Chancel. Nearly all are connected with the life of St Roch; the best is probably *St Roch Cures the Plague Victims* (Chancel, lower right). The altar-paintings are all difficult to see: even Ruskin, Tintoretto's greatest fan, was completely baffled as to their subject matter.

Scuola Grande di San Rocco

San Polo 3054, campo San Rocco (041 523 4864/ sanrocco@libero.it/www.sanrocco.it). Vaporetto San Tomà. **Open** *Apr-Feb* 9am-5.30pm daily. *Nov, Mar* 10am-4pm daily. *Dec-Feb* 10am-1pm Mon-Fri; 10am-4pm Sat, Sun. **Admission** L9,000; L6,000 students under 26. **No credit cards. Map** I 2C.
The Archbrotherhood of St Roch was the richest of the six *scuole grandi* (*see p63*) in 15th-century Venice. Its members came from the top end of mercantile and professional classes. It was dedicated to Venice's other patron saint, the French plague-protector and dog-lover St Roch (San Rocco), whose body was brought here in 1485. The *scuola* operated out of rented accommodation for a number of years, but by the beginning of the 16th century, donations from the city's army of St Roch devotees allowed a permanent base to be commissioned. The architecture, by Bartolomeo Bon and Scarpagnino, is far less impressive than the interior decoration, which was entrusted to Tintoretto in 1564 after a competition in which he stole a march on rivals Salviati, Zuccari and Veronese by presenting a finished painting rather than the required sketch. In three intensive sessions over the following 23 years, Tintoretto went on to make San Rocco his *Divina Commedia*. Fans and doubters alike should start here; the former will no doubt agree with John Ruskin that paintings such as the *Crucifixion* are 'beyond all analysis and above all praise', while the latter may find their prejudices crumbling. True, the devotional intensity of his works can shade too much into kitsch for the postmodern soul; but his feel for narrative structure is timeless. To follow the development of Tintoretto's style, pick up the free explanatory leaflet and begin in the smaller upstairs hall – the Albergo. Here, filling up the whole of the far wall, is the *Crucifixion* (1565), of which Henry James commented: 'It is one of the greatest things of art… there is everything in it.' More than anything it is the perfect integration of main plot and subplots that strikes the viewer; whereas most paintings are short stories, this is a novel. Tintoretto began work on the larger upstairs room in 1575, with Old Testament stories on the ceiling and a Life of Christ cycle around the walls, in which the man who possessed what Vasari referred to as 'the most extraordinary mind that the art of painting has produced' experimented relentlessly with form, lighting and colour. Below the canvases is a characterful series of late 17th-century wooden carvings, including a caricature of Tintoretto himself, just below and to the left of *The Agony in the Garden*. Finally, on the ground-floor hall – which the artist decorated between 1583 and 1587, when he was in his sixties – the paintings reach a visionary pitch that has to do with Tintoretto's audacious handling of light and the impressionistic economy of his brushstrokes. The *Annunciation*, with its domestic Mary surprised while sewing, and *Flight into Egypt*, with its verdant landscape, are among the painter's masterpieces. Admission is free on August 16, the feast of St Roch.

Dorsoduro

From the classy, upmarket Salute area to plain, proletarian Santa Marta, Dorsoduro is a sestiere of extremes.

Dorsoduro (literally 'hard back') gives Venice its firm, smooth southern edge. It stretches all the way from the **Salute** to the dockland area of **Santa Marta** and **San Nicolò**. These two districts are as distant socially as they are geographically. The Salute area is cool and classy, with some of the highest property prices in the city, while Santa Marta is as plain and proletarian as they come. More or less midway between these extremes is the large square of **campo Santa Margherita** – a social and commercial hub of activity that is a magnet for Venice's shifting student population.

Western Dorsoduro

Eastern Dorsoduro is traditionally considered one of the earliest settlements, after the Rialto area. The evidence is there in the church of San Nicolò, founded as early as the seventh century. The full name of the church is **San Nicolò dei Mendicoli** (*see p116*) – 'of the beggars'. The locals have never been in the top income bracket, and in the past were mostly

fishermen or salt-pan workers. The area gave its name to one of two factions into which the Venetian proletariat was once divided: the Nicolotti. The Nicolotti were proud enough to maintain a certain form of local autonomy under a figure known as the Gastaldo, who, after his election, would be received with honours by the doge.

The area is still noticeably less sleek than central Venice, although fishing was superseded as a source of employment by the port long ago and subsequently by the Santa Marta cotton mill now converted for use by the Istituto Universitario di Architettura di Venezia. At the time of going to press, the downbeat district that grew up around here through the 20th century was slated for massive redevelopment to a design by the late Catalan architect Enric Miralles Moya: authorities hoped to reinject life into the area in a vast University-meets-London-style-Docklands project. If you venture this far you will find yourself having to cross a road with real live cars to get to the vaporetto stop.

The grand Palazzo Ariani with its Gothic tracery. *See p116.*

You can walk all around the **Angelo Raffaele**.

Moving eastwards, the atmosphere remains unpretentious around the church of **Angelo Raffaele** (*see p116*) and the church of **San Sebastiano** (*see p117*), with its splendid decoration by Paolo Veronese. Northwards from here, on the rio di Santa Margherita, are some rather grander *palazzi*, including Palazzo Ariani, with its magnificent Gothic tracery, almost oriental in its intricacy, and, further up, the grand Palazzo Zenobio, now an Armenian school and institute, containing early Tiepolo frescos (not accessible to the public) and giving on to an elaborate garden where plays are sometimes performed in the summer.

Angelo Raffaele

Campo Angelo Raffaele (041 522 8548). Vaporetto San Basilio. **Open** 8am-noon, 4-6pm Mon-Fri; 8am-noon, 4-6.30pm Sat; 8.30-noon Sun. **Map** II 1B.
This is one of the eight churches in Venice traditionally founded by St Magnus in the eighth century, although the present free-standing building – one of only two churches in the city that you can walk all the way around – dates from the 17th century. The unusually high ceiling has a lively fresco by Gaspare Diziani of *St Michael Driving out Lucifer*, with Lucifer apparently tumbling out of the heavy stucco frame into the church. There are matching *Last Suppers* on either side of the organ (by Bonifacio de' Pitati on the left and a follower of Titian on the right). But the real jewels of the church are on the organ loft, whose five compartments, painted by Giovanni Antonio Guardi (or perhaps his brother Francesco), recount the story of *Tobias and the Angel* (1750-3). They are works of dazzling luminosity, quite unlike anything else done in Venice at the time and with something pre-Impressionist about them.

San Nicolò dei Mendicoli

Campo San Nicolò (041 275 0382). Vaporetto San Basilio/Santa Marta. **Open** 10am-noon, 4-6pm Mon-Sat; 9.30-11am, 4-6pm Sun. **Map** off II 1B.
San Nicolò is one of the few Venetian churches to have maintained its 13th-century Veneto-Byzantine structure, despite numerous rearrangements and refurbishings. Between 1971 and 1977 the church underwent a thorough restoration by the Venice in Peril Fund, and traces of the original foundations were uncovered, confirming the tradition that dates the church's origins to the seventh century. Film buffs will recognise this as the church from Nicolas Roeg's dwarf-in-Venice movie *Don't Look Now*. The 15th-century loggia at the front is one of only two extant examples (the other is on the equally ancient San Giacomo di Rialto) of a once-common architectural feature, which served as a shelter for the homeless. The interior contains no major works of art, but a marvellous mishmash of architectural and decorative styles combines to create an effect of cluttered charm. The structure is that of a 12th-century basilica, with two colonnades of stocky columns topped by 14th-century capitals. Above are gilded 16th-century statues of the apostles. The paintings are mainly 17th century. There are some fine wooden sculptures, including a large statue of San Nicolò by the Bon studio. In the small campo outside the church is a column with a diminutive winged lion. Across the canal is the former convent of the Terese, in the process of being converted to an extension of the Architecture University. Just round the corner from the church there was, until a few years ago, a house full of monkeys. To the dismay of his neighbours, the retired docker who lived here decided to turn his house and narrow garden into a private zoo. On his death this mini-Longleat was closed, and new homes were found for the monkeys.

Bustling **campo Santa Margherita**.

San Sebastiano

Fondamenta di San Sebastiano (041 275 0462).
Vaporetto San Basilio. **Open** 10am-5pm Mon-Sat; 1-
5pm Sun. **Admission** L3,000 (*see also p63* **Chorus**).
No credit cards. Map II 1B.

This contains perhaps the most brilliantly colourful church interior in Venice – all the work of one
man, Paolo Veronese. One of Veronese's earliest
commissions in Venice (in 1555) was *The*
Coronation of the Virgin and the four panels of the
Evangelists in the Sacristy (under restoration).
From then on there was just no stopping him:
between 1556 and 1565 he painted three large ceiling paintings for the nave of the church, frescos
along the upper parts of the walls, organ shutters,
huge narrative canvases for the the chancel and the
painting on the high altar. The ceiling paintings
depict scenes from the life of Esther (*Esther Taken*
to Ahasuerus, Esther Crowned Queen by
Ahasuerus and *The Triumph of Mordecai*). Esther
was considered a forerunner of the Virgin, interceding for the Jews, just as the Virgin interceded
for mankind – or (more pertinently) for Venice.
These works are full of sumptuous pageantry: no
painter gets more splendidly shimmering effects
out of clothing, which is probably why Veronese's
nude Saint Sebastians are the least striking figures
in the compositions. These huge canvases, on the
side walls of the chancel, depict, on the right, *The*
Martyrdom of St Sebastian (who was in fact cud-
gelled to death – the arrows were just a first
attempt), and, on the left, *St Sebastian Encouraging*
St Mark and St Marcellan – two other Roman martyrs. Other paintings in the church include *St*
Nicholas, a late painting by Titian, in the first altar
on the right. Paolo Veronese and his brother
Benedetto are buried here.

Campo Santa Margherita to the Accademia

The heart of Dorsoduro is campo Santa
Margherita, an elongated square with a church
at either end. During the morning a market is in
operation here and there is a continual bustle of
shopping housewives, hurrying students and
dawdling pigeons; in the evening Venice's
under-30s come here to hang out at the various
bars and cafés, to the continual irritation of the
local residents. If Venice can be said to have
any nightlife, this is the place in which to
sample it (*see chapter* **Nightlife**).

There are several ancient *palazzi* around the
square, with Byzantine and Gothic features.
In the middle is the isolated **Scuola dei**
Varoteri, the School of the Tanners. At the
north end is the former church of **Santa**
Margherita, long used as a cinema and now
beautifully restored as a conference hall for the
university; the interior (if it is being used for a
conference, it is usually possible to sneak in at
the back for a quick gawp) is so unashamedly
theatrical it's difficult to imagine how it was
ever used for religious purposes. St Margaret's
dragon features on the campanile, and the saint
also stands triumphant on the beast between
the windows of a house at the north end of the

St Margaret triumphs over her beast.

Penniless patricians ended up in **campo San Barnaba**.

square; a miraculous escape from the dragon's guts for some reason makes her the patron saint of pregnant women. At the other end of the square is the **Scuola dei Carmini** (*see p121*) and the church of the **Carmini** (*see p119*).

Leaving the campo by the southern end you reach the picturesque rio di San Barnaba. At the eastern end of the fondamenta is the entrance to the swaggering Longhena palazzo of **Ca' Rezzonico** (*see p119*), home to the museum of 18th-century Venice.

The middle of the three bridges across the canal is Ponte dei Pugni, with white marble footprints indicating that this was one of the bridges where punch-ups were held between the rival factions of the Nicolotti, from the eastern quarters of the city, and the Castellani, from the west. These brawls, often extremely violent, were tolerated by the authorities, who saw them as a chance for the working classes to let off potentially disruptive steam. However, after a particularly bloody fray, in 1705 the Council of Ten banned them.

Past the most photographed greengrocer's in the world (a barge moored in the canal), is campo San Barnaba. The church of **San Barnaba** has nothing special about it except a picturesque 14th-century campanile and a *Holy Family* boldly attributed to Veronese, but the campo is a good place in which to sit outside a bar and watch the world go by. San Barnaba has never been grand. In the final years of the Republic it was where penniless patricians

used to end up, since apartments were provided here by the state for their use. The Barnabotti, as they were known, could make a few *zecchini* by peddling their votes in the Maggior Consiglio (*see p11* **Venetian government**); otherwise they hung around in their tattered silk, muttering (after 1789) subversive comments about Liberty, Fraternity and Equality.

It was this very canal that Katharine Hepburn fell into in the film *Midsummer Madness*, causing permanent damage to her eyesight. In *Indiana Jones and the Last Crusade*, on the other hand, Harrison Ford entered the church (which became a library in the film) and after contending with most of Venice's rat population, emerged from the pavement near one of the bars.

From the campo the busy route towards the Accademia crosses rio San Trovaso, a canal with twin *fondamente* lined by fine Gothic and Renaissance palaces, used either as secondary schools or university buildings. Off to the right is the church of **San Trovaso**, with two identical façades, one on to the canal and one on to its own campo. Beyond this, towards the Zattere, is a picturesque *squero*, one of the few remaining yards where gondolas are made.

The **Accademia**, Venice's art school and most important picture gallery, is just a short walk from here, situated at the foot of the reconstructed wooden bridge of the same name over the Grand Canal (*see p122* **Accademia**).

Ca' Rezzonico (Museo del Settecento Veneziano)

Dorsoduro 3136, fondamenta Rezzonico (041 241 8506). Vaporetto Ca' Rezzonico. **Open** *May-Oct* 9am-7pm Mon-Thur, Sat, Sun. *Nov-Apr* 9am-5pm Mon-Thur, Sat, Sun. **Admission** L12,000; L8,000 students 15-29; L6,000 6-14s. **No credit cards**. Closed for restoration until June 2001. **Map** II 2A.

The Museum of 18th-Century Venice is dedicated to the art of the twilight years of the Republic. But for most visitors the paintings on display here will appear less impressive than the fixed decoration that is the palazzo itself, an imposing Grand Canal affair designed by Baldassare Longhena for the Bon family in 1667. Their ambitions, however, exceeded their means, and the Bons were forced to sell the unfinished palace to the Rezzonico family – a dynasty of rich Genoese bankers who had bought their way into Venice's register of nobility, the *Libro d'Oro*. The Rezzonicos' bid for stardom was crowned in 1758 by two events: the election of Carlo Rezzonico as Pope Clement XIII, and the marriage of Ludovico Rezzonico into one of Venice's most ancient noble families, the Savorgnan. Tiepolo was called upon to celebrate the marriage on the ceiling of the *Sala del Trono*, and he replied with a composition so tumbling and playful that we forget this is all about money. Giovanni Battista Crosato's over-the-top ceiling frescos in the ballroom have aged less well but,

together with the Murano chandeliers and the intricately carved furniture by Andrea Brustolon, they provide an accurate record of the lifestyles of the rich and famous at the time. There are historical canvases by Piazzetta and Diziani, plus a few other gems: a series of detached frescos of pulcinellas, recently restored, from the Tiepolo family villa in Zianigo by Giambattista's son Giandomenico, capture the leisured melancholy of the monied classes at the end of the century, as the Serenissima went into terminal decline. There are some good genre paintings by Pietro Longhi, whom Michael Levey calls 'the Jane Austen of Venetian art', and a series of smooth pastel portraits by Rosalba Carriera, a female 'prodigy' who was kept busy by young French and English aristocrats eager to bring back a souvenir of their Grand Tour.

Santa Maria dei Carmini

Campo dei Carmini (041 522 6553). Vaporetto Ca' Rezzonico or San Basilio. **Open** 7.30am-noon, 2.30-6.30pm Mon-Sat; 4.30-6.30pm Sun. **Map** II 1A.

The church officially called Santa Maria del Carmelo has a tall campanile topped by a statue of the Virgin, a frequent target for lightning. It is richly decorated inside, with 17th-century gilt wooden statues over the arcades of the nave and, above, a series of baroque paintings illustrating the history of the Carmelite order. However, the best paintings in the church are a *Nativity* by Cima da Conegliano on the

A dying art: gondolas are made at the *squero* in **San Trovaso**. *See p118.*

Ca' Dario: pretty, lop-sided and cursed. *See p121*.

second altar on the right and *St Nicholas of Bari* by Lorenzo Lotto opposite; the latter has a dreamy landscape – one of the most beautiful in Italian art, according to art historian Bernard Berenson – containing tiny figures of St George and the dragon. In the chapel to the right of the high altar is a graceful bronze relief of *The Lamentation Over the Dead Christ* by the Sienese sculptor, painter, inventor, military architect and all-round Renaissance man Francesco di Giorgio.

San Trovaso

Campo San Trovaso (041 522 2133). Vaporetto Zattere. **Open** 8-11am, 3-6pm Mon-Sat. **Map** II 2B.
This church, which looks on to its quiet raised campo, has two almost identical façades, one at each end, both based on the sub-Palladian church of Le Zitelle (*see p127*) on the Giudecca. The story goes that San Trovaso was built on the very border of the two areas of the city belonging to the rival factions of the Nicolotti and Castellani, so that in the event of a wedding between members of the two factions, each party could make its own sweeping entrance and exit. There was no saint called Trovaso: the name is a Venetian telescoping of two other names: San Protasio and San Gervasio, two popular but historically obscure martyrs. There are five works by the Tintoretto family in the church; three are probably by the son, Domenico, including the two on either side of the high altar, which are rich in detail but poor in focus. In the left transept is a smaller-than-usual version of one of Tintoretto's favourite subjects, *The Last Supper*, and in the chapel to the left of the high altar is *The Temptations of St Anthony the Abbot*, with enough vices to tempt a saint (note the harlot with 'flames playing around her loins', as Ruskin so coyly put it).

On the side wall of this latter chapel is a charming painting in the international Gothic style by Michele Giambono, *St Chrisogonus on Horseback* (c1450); the saint is a boyish figure on a gold ground, with a shyly hesitant expression and a gorgeously fluttering cloak and banner. In the right transept, in the Clary Chapel, is a set of Renaissance marble reliefs showing angels playing musical instruments or holding instruments of the Passion. The only attribution scholars seem prepared to risk is to the conveniently named 'Master of San Trovaso' (c1470).

Scuola dei Carmini

Dorsoduro 2617, campo dei Carmini (041 528 9420). Vaporetto Ca' Rezzonico or San Basilio. **Open** *Apr-Oct* 9am-6pm Mon-Sat; 9am-1pm Sun. *Nov-Mar* 9am-4pm daily. **Admission** L8,000; L6,000 13-26s, over 65s; L3,000 6-12s. **No credit cards**. **Map** II 1A.
On the upper floor of this *scuola* maintained by the Carmelite order is one of the most impressive of Tiepolo's Venetian ceilingscapes. Begun in 1670 to plans by Baldassare Longhena, the building was spared the Napoleonic lootings that dispersed the furniture and fittings of most of the other Scuole. As a result, we have a fairly good idea of what an early-

to mid-18th century Venetian confraternity HQ must have looked like, from the elaborate Sante Piatti altarpiece downstairs to the staircase with its excrescence of gilded *putti* (cherubs).

Tiepolo's airy ceiling panels in the main first-floor hall, painted from 1740 to 1743, are best viewed with one of the mirrors provided. Don't even try to unravel the story – a celestial donation that supposedly took place in Cambridge, when Simon Stock received the scapular (the badge of the Carmelite order) from the Virgin herself. What counts, as always with Tiepolo, is the tumbling audacity of his off-centre composition. If the atmosphere were not so ultra-refined, there would be something disturbing in the Virgin's sneer of cold contempt and those swirling Turneresque clouds. In the two adjoining rooms are some Piazzettas and Padovaninos.

At the time of going to press, the central painting of the Virgin was under restoration, having plummeted from the woodworm-ridden ceiling in August 2000. It is scheduled to return in spring 2001.

Eastern Dorsoduro

The social tone rises as you go east. The area between the Accademia and the Salute is Venice's most elegant and artsy quarter, home to many real and would-be artists, writers and wealthy foreigners. Ezra Pound lived out his last years in a small house near the Zattere, Peggy Guggenheim patronised and hosted her collection of modern artists in her truncated palazzo on the Grand Canal (now the **Peggy Guggenheim Collection** – *see p122*), and artists now use the vast spaces of the old warehouses on the Zattere as studios. On a Sunday morning, **campo San Vio** becomes some corner of a foreign land, as British expatriates home in on the Anglican church of St George.

Overlooking the campo, on the other side of the canal, the **Galleria Cini** (*see p122*) has a collection of Ferrarese and Tuscan art.

It is a district of quiet canals and cosy *campielli*, perhaps the most picturesque being campiello Barbaro, behind pretty, lopsided **Ca' Dario** (rumoured, after the sudden deaths of owners over the centuries, to be cursed). But all that money has certainly driven out the locals: nowhere in Venice are you further from a simple *alimentari*.

The colossal magnificence of Longhena's church of **Santa Maria della Salute** (*see p123*) brings the residential area to an end. You can stroll on past the church to the old **Dogana di mare** (Customs House) on the wedge-shaped tip of Dorsoduro. Crowning the corner tower, a 17th-century weathercock figure of Fortune perches daintily on a golden ball, 'characteristic,' according to Ruskin, 'of the conceits of the time, and of the hopes and

Sightseeing

principles of the last days of Venice'. A grand view can be enjoyed here of St Mark's, the lagoon and the islands.

Galleria Cini

Dorsoduro 864, piscina del Forner (041 521 0755). Vaporetto Accademia. **Open** *Sept-Nov* 10am-1pm, 2-6pm Tue-Sun. **Admission** L7,000; L5,000 concessions. **No credit cards. Map** II 3B.

This collection of Ferrarese and Tuscan art was put together by industrialist Vittorio Cini, who founded the Fondazione Cini on the island of San Giorgio Maggiore. It's small but there are one or two gems, such as the unfinished Pontormo *Double Portrait of Two Friends* on the first floor, and Dosso Dossi's *Allegorical Scene* on the second, a vivacious character study from the D'Este palace in Ferrara. There are also some delicate late-medieval ivories and a rare 14th-century wedding chest decorated with chivalric scenes.

Peggy Guggenheim Collection

Dorsoduro 701, fondamenta Venier dei Leoni (041 520 6288). Vaporetto Accademia or Salute. **Open** *Apr-Oct* 11am-6pm Mon, Wed-Fri, Sun; 11am-10pm Sat. *Nov-Mar* 11am-6pm Mon, Wed-Sun. **Admission** L12,000; L8,000 concessions. **Credit** AmEx, DC, MC, V. **Map** II 3B.

Venice may have been bemused by the eccentric Peggy G when she bought the most outlandish palazzo on the Grand Canal in 1949, but it has had reason to be thankful since. The Palazzo Venier dei Leoni looks as if it's had its upper floors removed by Marcel Duchamp. In reality the building locals call the *Palazzo Non-finito* was left like this when the Venier family ran out of funds shortly after construction began in 1759. For Guggenheim it was love at first sight. An American heiress famous for her extravagant eyewear and retinue of poodles, she arrived in Venice with crate upon crate containing works by Max Ernst (a former husband), Picasso, Chagall, Duchamp, De Chirico, Brancusi and Giacometti – a whole generation of Paris-based artists of the 1920s and '30s, plus a few Americans such as Calder and Pollock. During the 1940s she had tried to interest art historian Herbert Read in finding a home for her collection in London, and made overtures again to museum officials in New York and Nice; but in the end it was Venice that received the honour. The museum – which also hosts exhibitions of contemporary art – acts as a cure for the post-1797 amnesia from which the lagoon city sometimes appears to suffer. It must rank as one of Venice's most pleasant art spaces: airy, luminous, with a charming garden that is best surveyed from the terrace of the café-restaurant. Everyone has a personal favourite, but among the highlights of the permanent collection are Brancusi's sublime *Bird in Space* – the very same sculpture that US customs officials insisted on classifying as a 'stair-rail' in 1929, sparking off one of the world's more absurd legal wrangles – Max Ernst's grotesque *Attirement of the Bride* – which turns up

Accademia

The Accademia is to Venetian painting what the Uffizi is to the art of the Florentine Renaissance: the essential one-stop shop. It's housed in three former religious buildings: the Scuola Grande di Santa Maria della Carità (the oldest of the Venetian *scuole*, founded in the 13th century), the adjacent church of the Carità, and the Monastery of the Lateran Canons, a 12th-century structure radically remodelled by Palladio. It was Napoleon who made the collection possible, first by suppressing hundreds of churches, convents and religious guilds, and second by moving the city's Accademia di Belle Arti art school here, with the mandate both to train students and to act as a gallery and storeroom for all the evicted art treasures, which were originally displayed as models for the academy's pupils to aspire to.

The collection is arranged chronologically, with the exception of the 15th- and 16th-century works in rooms 19-24 at the end. It opens with a group of 14th- and 15th-century devotional works by Paolo Veneziano and others, still firmly in the Byzantine tradition. This room was the main hall of the Scuola Grande: note the original ceiling of gilded cherubim, whose faces are all subtly different. Rooms 2 and 3 have devotional paintings and altarpieces by Carpaccio, Cima da Conegliano and Giovanni Bellini (a fine *Enthroned Madonna with Six Saints*). Rooms 4 and 5 bring us to the Renaissance heart of the collection: here are Mantegna's *St George* and Giorgione's mysterious *Tempest*, which has had art historians reaching for symbolic interpretations for centuries.

In Room 6 the three greats of 16th-century Venetian painting, Titian, Tintoretto and Veronese, are first encountered. But the battle of the giants gets underway in earnest in Room 10, where Tintoretto's ghostly chiaroscuro *Transport of the Body of St Mark* vies for attention with Titian's moving *Pietà* – his last painting – and Veronese's huge *Christ in the House of Levi*. Originally commissioned as a Last Supper, this painting emerged so full of anachronistic and irreverent detail that regularly at Carnevale time in costume form – and the enigmatic *The Surrealist* by émigré Romanian artist Victor Brauner. Perhaps the most startling exhibit is the rider of Marino Marini's *Angel of the City* out on the Grand Canal terrace, who thrusts his manhood at passing *vaporetti*. Never the shrinking wallflower, Peggy G took delight in unscrewing the member and pressing it on young men she fancied.

Santa Maria della Salute
Campo della Salute (041 522 5558). Vaporetto Salute. **Open** *Oct-Mar* 9am-noon, 3-5.30pm daily. *Apr-Sept* 9am-noon, 3-6.30pm daily. **Map** II 3B.

This magnificent baroque church, queening it over the entrance of the Grand Canal, is probably as recognisable an image of Venice as St Mark's or the Rialto bridge. It was built from 1631 to 1681 in thanksgiving for the end of Venice's last bout of plague, which had wiped out at least a third of the population in 1630. The church is dedicated to the Madonna, as protector of the city. The terms of the competition won by 26-year-old architect Baldassare Longhena represented a serious challenge, which beat some of the best archictects of the day. The church was to be colossal but inexpensive; the whole structure was to be visually clear on entrance, with the high altar as focal point and the ambulatory and side-altars coming into sight only as one approached the chancel; the light was to be evenly distributed; and the whole building should *creare una bella figura* – show itself off to good effect.

La Salute: as recognisable as St Mark's.

the artist was accused of heresy and ordered to alter the painting; instead, he simply changed its name. Room 11 covers two centuries, with canvases by Tintoretto (the exquisite *Madonna dei Camerlenghi*), Bernardo Strozzi and Tiepolo.

The series of rooms beyond brings the plot up to the 18th century, with all the old favourites: Canaletto, Guardi, Longhi and the soft-focus bewigged portraits by Rosalba Carriera. Rooms 19 and 20 take us back to the 15th century; the latter has the rich *Miracle of the Relic of the Cross* story cycle, a collaborative effort by Gentile Bellini, Carpaccio and others, which is packed with telling social details (check out the black gondolier in Carpaccio's *Miracle of the Cross at the Rialto*).

An even more satisfying cycle has Room 21 to itself. Carpaccio's *Life of St Ursula* (1490-5) tells the story of the legendary Breton princess who embarked on a pilgrimage to Rome with her betrothed so that he could be baptised into the true faith. It all went swimmingly until Ursula and all the 11,000 virgins accompanying her were massacred by the Huns in Cologne. More than the ropy

legend, it's the architecture, the ships and the pageantry in these meticulous paintings that grab the attention. Room 23 is the former church of Santa Maria della Carità: here are devotional works by Vivarini, the Bellinis and others. Room 24 – the Albergo Room (or secretariat) of the former *scuola* – contains the only work in the whole gallery that is in its original site: Titian's magnificent *Presentation of the Virgin*.

On Saturdays (3.30-5pm) and Sundays (10am-noon, 3.30-5pm) it is possible to visit the Quadreria (no extra ticket required), which is essentially the museum's storeroom, containing paintings - including some very major works - otherwise not on show. A guided tour of the Quadreria can be taken on Tuesday afternoon (3pm); pre-booking is essential (041 522 2247).

Galleria dell'Accademia
Dorsoduro 1050, campo Carità (041 522 2247/accademia.artive@arti.beniculturali.it). Vaporetto Accademia. **Open** 8.15am-2pm Mon; 8.15am-7pm Tue-Sun. **Admission** L12,000 (*see also p63* **Accademia**). **No credit cards. Map** II 2B.

Marino Marini's horserider extends a thrusting welcome at the **Peggy Guggenheim Collection**. See p122.

Longhena succeeded brilliantly in satisfying all these requisites – particularly the last and most Venetian one. The church takes superb advantage of its dominant position pays homage to both the Byzantine form of San Marco, across the Grand Canal, and the classical form of Palladio's Redentore, across the Giudecca Canal. Longhena said he chose the circular shape with the reverent aim of offering a crown to the Madonna. She stands on the lantern above the cupola as described in the Book of Revelations: 'Clothed in the sun, and the moon under her feet, and upon her head a crown of twelve stars.' Beneath her, on the great scroll-brackets around the

cupola, stand statues of the apostles – the 12 stars in her crown. This Marian symbolism continues inside the church, where in the centre of the mosaic floor, amid a circle of roses, is an inscription, *Unde origo inde salus* (from the origin comes salvation) – a reference to the legendary birth of Venice under the Virgin's protection.

Longhena's intention was for the visitor to approach the high altar ceremoniously through the main door. In this fashion, the six side-altars are only revealed from the very centre of the church, where they appear framed theatrically in their separate archways. However, the main door is rarely open and often the central area of the church is roped off, so you have no choice but to walk round the ambulatory and visit the chapels separately.

The three on the right have paintings by Luca Giordano, a prolific Neapolitan painter who brought a little southern *brio* into the art of the city at a time (the mid-17th century) when most painting had become limply derivative. On the opposite side is a clumsily restored *Pentecost*, by Titian, from the island monastery of Santo Spirito (demolished in 1656). The high altar has a splendidly dynamic sculptural group by Giusto Le Corte, the artist responsible (with assistants) for most of the statues inside and outside the church. This group represents Venice kneeling before the Virgin and Child, while the plague, in the shape of a hideous old hag, scurries off to the right, prodded by a tough-looking *putto* with a flaming torch. In the midst of all this marble hubbub is a serene Byzantine icon of the *Madonna and Child*, brought from Crete in 1669 by Francesco Morosini, otherwise known for blowing up the Parthenon.

The best paintings are in the sacristy (open 10-11.30am, 3-5.30pm Mon-Sat, 3-5.30pm Sun; admission L2,000). Tintoretto's *Marriage at Cana* (1551) was described by Ruskin as 'perhaps the most perfect example which human art has produced of the utmost possible force and sharpness of shadow united with richness of local colour'. He also points out how curiously difficult it is to spot the bride and groom in the painting.

On the altar is a very early Titian with *Sts Mark, Sebastian, Roch, Cosmas and Damian*, saints who were all invoked for protection against the plague; the painting was done during the outbreak of 1509-14. Three later works by Titian (c1540-49) hang on the ceiling, violent Old Testament scenes brought here from the church of Santo Spirito: the *Sacrifice of Abraham*; *David Killing Goliath*; and *Cain and Abel*. These works established the conventions for all subsequent ceiling paintings in Venice; Titian decided not to go for the worm's eye view adopted by Mantegna and Correggio, which sacrificed clarity for surprise, and instead chose an oblique viewpoint, as if observing the action from the bottom of a hill. More Old Testament rowdiness can be seen in works by Salviati (*Saul Hurling a Spear at David*) and Palma il Giovane (*Samson and Jonah* – in which the whale is represented mainly by a lolling rubbery tongue).

Le Zattere

Having rounded the **Punta della Dogana**, the mile-long stretch of Le Zattere, Venice's finest promenade after the riva degli Schiavoni, will take you all the way back past the churches of **I Gesuati** (*see p126*) and **Santa Maria della Visitazione** (*see p126*) to the city's origins in the San Nicolò zone.

This long promenade bordering the Giudecca Canal is named after the *zattere* (rafts) that used

to moor here, bringing wood and other materials from the mainland. The paved quayside was created by decree in 1519. It now provides a favourite promenade, punctuated by some spectacularly-situated benches for a picnic, and several bars and *gelaterie*. The eastern end is quiet, with the occasional flurry

Don't miss **Titian's best**

Assumption
Frari *see p112*
Titian's exercise in triumphant geometry (1516-8) announced the arrival of the High Renaissance in Venice and still dominates the enormous Franciscan church: the view from the nave through the choir screen arch is unforgettable.

St Mark (and others)
Santa Maria della Salute *see p123*
The opulent Salute contains several Titians, the best of which are in the sacristy: an early St Mark altarpiece (c.1509),and three much later ceiling paintings – the Sacrifice of Isaac, Cain Killing Abel, and David and Goliath (1542-4).

The Presentation of the Virgin in the Temple
Accademia *see p122*
Still on the wall for which it was painted, this painting incorporates many Academy members as bystanders to the ancient event.

The Transfiguration
San Salvador *see p84*
Dramatic poses and feathery brushwork indicate a majestic late Titian (c.1560); on important feast days, Titian's painting slides down to reveal the medieval altarpiece behind.

St Christopher
Palazzo Ducale *see p79*
One of Titian's few remaining frescoes, this shows a powerful St Christopher carrying the Christ Child across a river that resembles the Venetian lagoon; Titian executed the fresco (1523) in only three days.

Pietà
Accademia *see p122*
Left incomplete at Titian's death in 1576, the heavily-worked surface embodies the pre-eminence of process over finish in Venetian 16th-century painting.

Tiepolo's optical effects at **I Gesuati**.

of activity around the vast 14th-century salt warehouses, now used by rowing clubs.

Westward from these is the church of **Spirito Santo** and then the long 16th-century façade of the grimly named **Ospedale degli Incurabili**, now used as a juvenile court. Volpone's property is confiscated and sent to this hospital at the end of Ben Jonson's play of the same name; the main incurable disease of the time was syphilis.

The liveliest part of the Zattere is around the church of **I Gesuati** and the boat-stops to the Giudecca. Venetians flock here at weekends to eat good ice-cream (*see p169* **Da Nico**). The final and widest stretch of the Zattere takes you past several notable *palazzi*, including the 16th-century **Palazzo Clary**, until recently the French consulate, and the Gothic **Palazzo Molin**, used by the Società Adriatica di Navigazione.

Towards the end is the 17th-century façade of the **Scuola dei Luganegheri** (sausage-makers), with a statue of their protector, St Anthony the Abbot, whose symbol was a hog.

I Gesuati

Fondamenta Zattere ai Gesuati (041 523 0625). Vaporetto Zattere. **Open** 9am-6pm Mon-Sat; 1-6pm Sun. **Map** II 2B.

The official name of this church is Santa Maria del Rosario, but it is always known after the Gesuati,

the minor religious order that owned the previous church on the site and that merged with the Dominicans – the church's present owners – in 1668. I Gesuati is a great piece of teamwork by a trio of remarkable rococo artists: architect Giorgio Massari (he of the boring but effective Palazzo Grassi on the Grand Canal), painter Giambattista Tiepolo and sculptor Giovanni Morlaiter. The façade deliberately reflects the Palladian church of the Redentore opposite, but the splendidly posturing statues give it that typically 18th-century touch of histrionic flamboyance. Plenty more theatrical sculpture is to be found inside the church, all by Morlaiter. Above is a magnificent ceiling by Tiepolo, with three frescos on obscure Dominican themes (a mirror is provided for the relief of stiff necks). These works reintroduced frescos to Venetian art after two centuries of canvas ceiling paintings. The central panel shows St Dominic passing on to a crowd of supplicants the rosary he has just received from the cloud-enthroned Madonna. Tiepolo also painted the surrounding grisailles, which, at first sight, look like stucco reliefs. There is another brightly coloured Tiepolo on the first altar on the right, *The Virgin and Child With St Rosa, Catherine and Agnes*; Tiepolo here plays with optical effects, allowing St Rosa's habit to tumble out of the frame. In his painting of three Dominican saints on the third altar on the right, Giovanni Battista Piazzetta makes use of a narrower and more sober range of colours, going for a more sculptural effect.

Santa Maria della Visitazione

Fondamenta Zattere ai Gesuati (041 522 4077). Vaporetto Zattere. **Open** 9am-noon, 3-6pm Mon-Sat; 8am-noon, 3-6pm Sun. **Map** II 2B.

Confusingly, this has the same name as the Vivaldi church on the riva degli Schiavoni (*see p94*) – though the latter is usually known as La Pietà. Santa Maria della Visitazione stands on the Zattere just a few yards from the larger church of I Gesuati (*see p126*); it is now the chapel of the Istituto Don Orione, which has taken over the vast complex of the Monastery of the Gesuati next door (entrance by appointment via the door marked 'Istituto Artigianelli').

Built by Tullio Lombardo or Mauro Codussi in 1423, the church has an attractive early Renaissance façade. It was suppressed (that rascal Napoleon again) at the beginning of the 19th century and stripped of all its works of art with the exception of the original coffered ceiling, an unexpected delight that contains 58 compartments with portraits of saints and prophets by an Umbrian painter of the Signorelli school (mirrors are provided). This is one of the few examples of central Italian art in Venice; the others are Andrea del Castagno's frescos in San Zaccaria, the Martini chapel in San Giobbe and the Florentine Chapel in the Frari.

To the right of the façade is a lion's mouth for secret denunciations: the ones posted here went to the *Magistrati della Sanità*, who concerned themselves with matters of public health.

La Giudecca
& San Giorgio

Dominated by the church of San Giorgio Maggiore and the Molino Stucky, these islands also offer fresh views and different perspectives.

La Giudecca

The eight interconnected islands forming the Giudecca were originally known as Spinalonga, from an imagined resemblance to a fish skeleton. The origin of the present name is disputed, some attributing it to an early community of Jews, others to the fact that troublesome nobles (who had been *giudicati*, or judged) were banished there.

However, there were plenty of noblemen who came to the islands of their own free will, building villas as rural retreats. They were not alone: Michelangelo, exiled from Florence in 1529, came to the Giudecca, and three centuries later Alfred de Musset, during his torrid affair with George Sand (who had a fling with the doctor summoned to visit the poet), praised the cool Arcadian charms of 'la Zuecca'.

During the 19th century the city authorities began to make use of the numerous abandoned convents and monasteries, converting them into factories and prisons, and building over their gardens and orchards. The factories have all closed down – the last, Junghans, only recently – while the prisons (one for drug offenders and one for women) remain in use. A great deal of low-rent housing has been created over the past century, much of it on the modern island of Sacca Fisola at the western end.

Many of the factories remain abandoned, contributing to the run-down appearance of the south side of the Giudecca; however, work is under way on the transformation of the most conspicuous one, the colossal **Molino Stucky** at the west end. This former flour mill (the largest building on the lagoon) was built in 1895 in Hanseatic Gothic style; it was closed in 1954 and has since stood in rat-ridden Teutonic desolation. It is being restored to more than its former glory in an ambitious project that envisages a conference centre, a 250-room hotel, 138 apartments and a shopping centre. Venetians, used to reading about the latest extravagant plan to revitalise the city, will believe it when they see it.

The main sights of the Giudecca are all along the northern fondamenta, including **Santa Eufemia** (*see p128*), the Palladian churches of **Le Zitelle** (literally 'the spinsters'; the convent ran a hospice for girls from poor families, who were trained as lacemakers) and **Il Redentore** (*see p128*), as well as several fine *palazzi*.

Near Le Zitelle is the neo-Gothic **Casa Di Maria**, with its three large inverted-shield windows; the Bolognese painter Mario De Maria built it for himself from 1910 to 1913. It is the only private palazzo to have the same patterned brickwork as the Palazzo Ducale.

Towards the end of fondamenta Rio della Croce (no.149, close to the Redentore) stands **Palazzo Munster**, a former infirmary for English sailors. The vitriolic Anglo-Catholic writer Frederick Rolfe received the last sacraments here in 1910, after slagging the hospital off in his libelous novel, *The Desire and Pursuit of the Whole*. (He then proceeded to live for two more vituperative years.) Opposite is another ex-pat landmark – the huge '**Garden of Eden**'. The name was purely descriptive: it belonged to Frederick Eden, a disabled Englishman who, like Byron, discovered that Venice was the perfect city for those with disabilities – particularly if they could afford a private gondola and private steam-launch.

Sightseeing

Palladio's **Il Redentore**. *See p128*.

It is oddly difficult to get through to the southern side of the island, but worth the effort. Take calle San Giacomo, west of the Redentore; at the end turn left along calle degli Orti, and then right. At the end is a small public garden with benches looking out over the quiet southern lagoon and its lonely islands.

Il Redentore

Campo del Redentore (041 523 1415). Vaporetto Redentore. **Open** 10am-5pm Mon-Sat; 1-5pm Sun. **Admission** L3,000 (*see also p63* **Chorus**). **No credit cards. Map II** 3C.

Venice's first great plague church was built to celebrate the deliverance from the bout of 1575-7. An especially conspicuous site was chosen, one that could be approached in grand ceremonial fashion. The ceremony continues today, on every third Sunday of July, when a bridge of boats is built across the Giudecca Canal. Palladio (*see chapter* **Palladian Villas**), who always paid great attention to the settings of his buildings, was a natural choice as architect. He designed an eye-catching building whose prominent dome appears to rise directly behind the Greek-temple façade, giving the illusion that the church is centrally planned, as was traditional with sanctuaries and votive temples outside Venice. A broad flight of steps sweeps up to the great entrance door, an effect Palladio had often used in his mainland villas. The solemn and harmonious interior, with its single nave lit by large 'thermal' windows, testifies to Palladio's study of Roman baths. However, the Capuchin monks, the austere order to whom the building had been entrusted, were not pleased by its grandeur; Palladio attempted to mollify them by designing their choir stalls in a plain style. The best paintings are in the Sacristy, including a *Virgin and Child* by Alvise Vivarini and a *Baptism* by Veronese.

Santa Eufemia

Fondamenta Santa Eufemia (041 522 5848). Vaporetto Santa Eufemia. **Open** 9-11am Mon-Sat. **Map** II 2C.

This church has a 16th-century Doric portico along its flank. The interior owes its charm to its mix of styles. The nave and aisles are essentially 11th-

The neo-Gothic **Casa di Maria**. *See p127.*

century, with Veneto-Byzantine columns and capitals, while the decoration consists mainly of fussy 18th-century stucco and paintings. Over the first altar on the right is *St Roch and an Angel* by Bartolomeo Vivarini (1480).

Isola di San Giorgio

The island of San Giorgio, which sits in such a temptingly strategic position opposite the piazzetta di San Marco, realised its true potential under set-designer extraordinaire Andrea Palladio, whose church of **San Giorgio Maggiore** (*see p129*) is one of Venice's most recognisable landmarks. Known in the early days of the city as the *Isola dei Cipressi* (cypress island), it soon became an important Benedictine monastery and centre of learning – a tradition that is carried on today by the Fondazione Giorgio Cini (*see below*), which runs a research centre and craft school on the island.

Fondazione Giorgio Cini & Benedictine Monastery

(041 528 9900). Vaporetto San Giorgio. **Open** *Monastery* Mon-Fri by appointment only. *Library: art history* 9am-12.30pm Mon-Fri. *Library: music & Oriental studies* 9am-12.30pm, 3-4.30pm Mon-Fri. **Admission** free. **Map** III 1C.

There has been a Benedictine monastery on the island since AD 982, when Doge Tribuno Memmo donated the island to the order. The monastery continued to benefit from ducal donations, acquiring large tracts of land both in and around Venice and abroad. After the church acquired the remains of St Stephen (1109), it was visited yearly by the Doge on 26 December, the feast day of the saint. The city authorities often used the island as a luxury hotel for particularly prestigious visitors, such as Cosimo de' Medici in 1433. Cosimo had a magnificent library built here; it was destroyed in 1614, to make way for a more elaborate affair by Longhena (now open only to bona fide scholars with references to prove it).

In 1800, in a final bid for glory, the island hosted the conclave of cardinals that elected Pope Pius VII, after they had been expelled from Rome by Napoleon. In 1806 the monastery was suppressed by the French, who sent its chief artistic treasure – Veronese's *Marriage Feast at Cana* – off to the Louvre, where it still hangs. For the rest of the century the monastery did ignominious service as a barracks and ammunition store. In 1951 industrialist Count Vittorio Cini acquired the island to set up a foundation in memory of his son, Giorgio, killed in a plane crash in 1949. Restoration work was carried out and the Fondazione Giorgio Cini now uses the monastery buildings for its activities, including artistic and musical research (it holds a collection of Vivaldi manuscripts and recordings, plus illuminated manuscripts), a naval college and a craft school. A portion of the complex was given back to the Benedictines; there are currently six monks in

View inaccessible cloisters from the campanile of **San Giorgio Maggiore**.

the monastery. The foundation is not open to the public, but those with a special interest in Palladian or baroque architecture could try ringing for an appointment. There are two beautiful cloisters – one by Giovanni Buora (1516-40), the other by Palladio (1579) – an elegant library and staircase by Longhena (1641-53), and a magnificent refectory (where Veronese's painting hung) by Palladio (1561).

San Giorgio Maggiore

(041 522 7827). Vaporetto San Giorgio. **Open** *Oct-Mar* 9.30am-12.30pm, 2.30-5pm daily. *Apr-Sept* 9am-12.30pm, 2.30-6.30pm Mon-Sat; 9.30-10.30am, 2.30-6.30pm Sun. **Admission** *church* free; *campanile* L5,000. **No credit cards. Map III 1C.**
This unique spot gazing across the lagoon to the Piazzetta cried out for an architectural masterpiece. Palladio provided it. This was his first complete solo church; it demonstrates how confident he was of his techniques and objectives. Unlike earlier Renaissance architects in Venice, he drew no lessons from the city's Byzantine tradition. Palladio here develops the system of superimposed temple fronts with which he had experimented in the façade of San Francesco della Vigna *(see p90)*. The interior maintains the same relations between the orders as the outside, with composite half-columns supporting the gallery and lower Corinthian pilasters supporting the arches. The effect is of impressive luminosity and harmony, decoration being confined to the altars. Palladio believed that white was the colour most pleasing to God, a credo that happily matched the demand from the Council of Trent for greater lucidity in church services.

There are several good works of art. Over the first altar is an *Adoration of the Shepherds* by Jacopo Bassano, with startling lighting effects. The altar to the right of the High Altar has a *Madonna and Child and Nine Saints* by Sebastiano Ricci. On the side-walls of the Chancel hang two vast compositions by Tintoretto, *The Last Supper* and the *Gathering of Manna*, painted in the last years of his life. Both works emphasise the importance of the Eucharist, as laid down by the Council of Trent, and the perspective of each work makes it clear that they were intended to be viewed from the altar rails. Tintoretto combines almost surreal visionary effects (angels swirling out from the lamp's eddying smoke) with touches of superb domestic realism (a cat prying into a basket, a woman stooping over her laundry). Tintoretto's last painting, a moving *Entombment*, hangs in the Cappella dei Morti. It is possible that, as in Titian's *La Pietà*, Tintoretto included himself among the mourners: he has been identified as the bearded man gazing intensely at Christ's face. In the left transept is a painting by Jacopo and Domenico Tintoretto of the *Martyrdom of St Stephen*, placed above the altar containing the saint's remains (brought from Constantinople in 1109).

On the way to the monk-operated lift to the top of the campanile stands the huge statue of an angel that crowned the belltower until it was struck by lightning in 1993. The view from the top is extraordinary. Besides giving the best possible panorama across Venice itself and the lagoon, it also allows glimpses into the two inaccessible cloisters and gardens of the monastery on the island.

The Lido to Chioggia

Do a Dirk Bogarde or head south for a seafood lunch.

The southern part of the Venetian lagoon is protected from the open sea by two long, thin sandbanks with an average width of only a few hundred metres. To the north is the **Lido**, Venice's seaside resort and dormitory suburb. A *fin-de-siècle* backwater for most of the year, it livens up each September when it hosts the Venice Film Festival. To the south, on the other side of the **Porto di Malamocco** (one of the three *bocche di porto* that are Venice's gates to the Adriatic), is **Pellestrina**, an even narrower strip of fishing villages, kitchen gardens and boatyards. At the far end of Pellestrina, another short ferry hop across the southernmost *bocca di porto* brings you to **Chioggia**, a working fishing port that is the rough-and-ready antithesis of elegant Venice, but which has enough sights to fill a morning's sightseeing, rounded off by one of the freshest and cheapest fish lunches you'll find on the lagoon.

Getting there & getting around

The main Santa Maria Elisabetta stop on the Lido is served by frequent *vaporetti* and *motonavi* from Venice and the mainland. For details of routes, *see p275*. San Nicolò to the north is served by the 14 to Punta Sabbioni, and the car ferry from Tronchetto. To the south, the Casinò stop is active only on summer afternoons and evenings, when the 51/52 extends its service to keep the gamblers happy.

The bus routes are confusing, and you need to look carefully at the destination board on stops and buses. The A has two routes: the one marked 'San Nicolò' heads north along the lagoon road towards the church of San Nicolò, while the one marked 'Colombo' goes down to the beach, past the big hotels and the Palazzo del Cinema, and ends up in via Colombo. The B also has two routes: 'Ospedale' goes as far as the Ospedale al Mare (on the way to the northern beaches) and 'Alberoni' goes right down to Alberoni at the southern tip of the island, via Malamocco. The B/ does the same route but only goes as far as Ca' Bianca or Malamocco. Finally, the 11, which departs around the corner from the main vaporetto stop, in the Gran Viale, also heads down to Alberoni but then continues on to the car ferry, across to Pellestrina island, and down as far as the village of Pellestrina.

At least one in two of the 11 runs (check the timetable) is timed to coincide with the departure of the passenger ferry to Chioggia, from the far end of Pellestrina island (the ferry waits if the bus is late). The entire journey from the Lido to Chioggia – including the two crossings – takes just over an hour and costs L8,000 one-way. There is also a coach to Chioggia from piazzale Roma, but the scenery is depressing and the time saved minimal.

Bicycles are a great way to get around the Lido, and those with a good pair of legs might consider doing the whole 20-kilometre (12-mile) haul down to Chioggia by bike – you can put it on the passenger ferry for L7,000 as long as too many others haven't had the same idea. For bike hire outlets on the Lido, *see p276*.

Tourist information

In the summer (June-Sept) a tourist information office is open at Gran Viale 6A, Lido (041 529 8720/041 529 8711/fax 041 526 5721), 9am-12.30pm, 4-7pm daily.

The Lido

If – fired by the example of Dirk Bogarde in *Death in Venice* – you have come to the Lido looking for pale young aesthetes in sailor suits, forget it. These days, Venice-by-the-sea is more of a dormitory suburb than a playground for the idle rich – though there are still a few of the latter in the two big hotels, the **Des Bains** and the **Excelsior** (*see p47*), who keep the legend going down on the promenade. The Lido is the place to come to escape from the strangeness of Venice to a normality of supermarkets, cars and mothers pushing prams.

Things perk up in summer when the buses are full of city sunbathers with rolled-up towels, and the Casinò (which moves here from Ca' Vendramin between mid June and mid September) provides some evening glamour. But the Lido's slumber is only seriously disturbed for two weeks at the beginning of September, when the annual Film Festival rolls into town, together with its bandwagon of stars, directors, PR people and sleep-deprived, caffeine-driven journalists (*see also p204*).

The Lido has few tourist sights as such. Only the church of **San Nicolò** – founded in 1044 –

Sightseeing

Head out to the **Lido's beaches** and you'll find the Adriatic cleaner than the lagoon.

can claim any great antiquity. It was here that the doge would come on Ascension Day after marrying Venice to the sea in the ceremony known as *lo sposalizio del mare* (*see p195* **Festa e Regatta della Sensa**). Inside is the tomb of Nicola Giustiniani, a Benedictine monk who was forced to leave holy orders in 1172 in order to assure the future of his illustrious family, of which he was the sole heir. He married the doge's daughter, had plenty of kids, and once the job was done became a monk once more. Soon after his death he was beatified for his fine spirit of self-sacrifice.

Fans of art nouveau have plenty to look at on the Lido. In the Gran Viale – the shop-lined main street that runs between the vaporetto stop and the beach – there are two gems: the tiled façade of the Hungaria Hotel – formerly the Ausonia Palace – with its Beardsley-esque nymphs (No.28); and Villa Monplaisir at No.14, an art deco design from 1906. Many other smaller-scale examples can be found in and around via Lepanto. For full-blown turn-of-the-century exotica, though, it's hard to beat the Hotel Excelsior on lungomare Marconi, a neo-Moorish party piece, complete with minaret.

Malamocco & Pellestrina

The bus ride south along the lagoonside promenade of the Lido is uneventful but full of submerged history. Literally so in one case: the old town of Malamocco, near the southern end

of the island, was engulfed by a tidal wave following a seaquake in the Adriatic in 1107; until then it had been a flourishing port under the dominion of Padua. The new town, built further inland, never really amounted to much; today its sights consist of a few picturesque streets and a pretty bridge.

Just offshore from Malamocco is the tiny island of **Poveglia**, which once supported 200 families, descendants of the servants of Pietro Tradonico, a ninth-century doge who was murdered by aristocratic rivals. Fearing for their lives, his servants barricaded themselves inside the Palazzo Ducale, and only agreed to leave when safe-conduct to this new island home was promised.

The Lido ends at Alberoni, with its golf course, Fascist-era bathing establishments, lighthouse and maritime control tower. The channel between the Lido and Pellestrina is the busiest of the three *bocche di porto* between lagoon and sea, and the one used by petrol tankers on their way to and from the refineries at Porto Marghera.

The number 11 bus motors right on to the waiting car ferry for the short hop across to the island of Pellestrina – a glorified sandbar so narrow that it has more than once risked being swept away by the sea. The answer to the problem can be seen on the left as the bus continues its journey south. The *Murazzi*, solid sea walls of wooden piles and landfill clad in Istrian stone, are at their most impressive at

The tiny island of **Poveglia**, once home to 200 families. *See p131.*

the southern end of Pellestrina, where the width
of the island dwindles to almost nothing – but
the *Murazzi*, 14 metres (46 feet) wide at the
base, continue to march out towards Chioggia
for a distance of four kilometres (two and a half
miles). They were built between 1744 and 1782
to replace earlier makeshift wooden defences.
Within the last three years sloping sandy
beaches have been created to lessen the impact
of waves against them. On the lagoon side,
Pellestrina is a straggle of smallholdings,
hastily built holiday homes and boatyards, with
only two settlements to speak of: **San Pietro
in Volta** and **Pellestrina** itself, a fishing
village with a pretty centre of pastel houses
clustered around the 18th-century church of
Santa Maria di San Vito. Pellestrina once
rivalled Burano as a lace-making island, but
those days are long past.

Chioggia

The sea approach, via the Pellestrina motonave,
is the best introduction to Chioggia, a port
whose wedding to the sea has had more of the
daily grind to it than Venice's leisurely

marriage of convenience. The *chiozzotti* have
always been hardy fishermen and good sailors.

If Carlo Goldoni is to be believed, the women
were hardly less formidable; the 18th-century
playwright lived in Chioggia for five years in
his youth, and he used his memories of the town
to write *Le Baruffe Chiozzotte*, a comedy that
revolves around a huge quarrel between a
group of fishwives.

Of Roman origin, Chioggia was important
enough to have its own grand chancellor and
bishop in the early Middle Ages; but its 15
minutes of fame came between 1378 and 1380,
with the so-called War of Chioggia. This long
trial of strength between Venice and its arch-
rival Genoa (*see p14*) was only ostensibly to
do with the control of a small fishing port;
the real prize was control over the eastern
Mediterranean shipping routes. The Genoese
capture of Chioggia in 1378 was a slap in the
face for Venice, but the naval blockade mounted
by generals Vettor Pisani and Carlo Zeno
starved the Genoese into surrender by June
1380. Chioggia was almost entirely destroyed
in the process, and never fully recovered its
former prosperity. Today fishing is still a major

employer, though the fleet has to go further and further afield to bring home the catch. You'll see plenty of *chiozzotti* in Venice, too: many put their maritime skills to use crewing *vaporetti*.

Chioggia's old town spreads over a rectangular island split down the middle by the Canal Vena; it is sheltered from the sea by the long arm of **Sottomarina** to the east. Sottomarina has the big beachfront hotels, the leafy residential streets and the supermarkets; **Chioggia** itself has all the historical sights, the fishing port and the low, cramped houses. The topography of this older section of town is linear: from piazzetta Vigo, where the ferry docks, the long, wide corso del Popolo extends the whole length of the island, parallel to the Canal Vena. On either side, narrow lanes lead off towards the lagoon.

The only sight not on the Corso is the church of **San Domenico** (open 8am-noon, 2.30-5.30pm daily), on its very own island at the end of the street that begins across a ballustraded bridge from piazzetta Vigo. A barn-like 18th-century reconstruction, it contains Vittore Carpaccio's last painting, a graceful, poised Saint Paul, signed and dated 1520. There is also a huge wooden crucifix – possibly a German work of the 14th century – and a Rubens-like Tintoretto. More charming is the collection of naïve *ex voto* paintings placed by grateful fishermen in a side chapel; one shows a sea rescue by helicopter. Back on the Corso, **Sant'Andrea** (open 8am-noon, 4-6pm daily) is a mainly baroque church with little to see inside; its sturdy 12th-century campanile once doubled as a lookout tower.

A little further on is the **Granaio**, one of the few buildings in town that predates the War of Chioggia. Built in 1322, it was used as the municipal granary; today it hosts the fish market (open 8am-noon Tue-Sun), a photo-op riot of glistening colour that is the heart and soul of Chioggia. The small church of **Santissima Trinità**, just off the Corso on piazza XX Settembre, has long been *in restauro*; if you can get inside there are some good Mannerist panels by Palma il Giovane and other painters on the ceiling of the Oratory.

Midway down the Corso, the church of **San Giacomo** (open 7am-noon, 3.30-6.30pm daily), with its unfinished façade, looks like a Palladian cowshed. On the high altar is the *Madonna della Navicella*, a miraculous image of the Virgin as she appeared to a Sottomarina peasant in 1508, before making her getaway on an unmanned boat. Near the end of the Corso, two churches stand side by side on the right. The smaller one is **San Martino** (open only for special exhibitions), a Venetian Gothic jewel built in 1393 by the inhabitants of Sottomarina, who had taken refuge in Chioggia after the destruction

of their part of town by the Genoese. The church once contained a fine polyptych attributed to Paolo Veneziano, but this is currently being restored in Venice, and when returned will be housed in a new Museo Diocesano. Next door, the huge 17th-century **Duomo** was built to a project by Baldassare Longhena after a fire destroyed the original tenth-century church; there is little here to suggest that he would go on to design the Salute in Venice.

Only the 14th-century campanile – across the road – remains from the earlier structure. The high altar has some good marble relief work by Alessandro Tremignon; in a chapel off the apse is a series of grisly 18th-century paintings of martyrdoms.

The **Torre di Santa Maria** marks the end of the old town; just beyond, in campo Marconi, is the deconsecrated church of San Francesco, which has been turned into the **Museo Civico della Laguna Sud**. This brand-new collection struggles to fill a huge space. Though patchy, the museum does provide a good introduction to aspects of life on the lagoon, with displays showing how land has traditionally been reclaimed and shored up for building and,

The best Beaches

Lido di Jesolo
Discos, mega-campsites and acres of sand on the coast north of Venice.

Spiaggia comunale (Lido)
At the end of the Gran Viale and just to the left; easily reached and usually packed.

Alberoni (Lido)
At the southern end of the island, where the beach widens out into some scraggy dunes (*see also chapter* **Gay & Lesbian**).

Northern beaches (Lido)
The wide, flat, grey-sand beaches in front of the Nicelli airport are in the grin-and-bear-it category as far as cleanliness goes.

The *Murazzi* (Lido)
Plunge from huge concrete blocks used as breakwaters halfway between the Excelsior hotel and Malamocco.

Sant'Erasmo
In the lagoon, rather than the relatively cleaner Adriatic, the little stretch of sand straight across the island (*see p140*) from the main ferry port is less crowded than Lido beaches.

The folk of **Chioggia** have, by necessity, been hardy fishermen and good sailors.

on the top floor, an exhaustive collection of model fishing boats. When the museum is open, the front desk also functions as a tourist information office.

Duomo

Calle Duomo 77 (041 400 496). **Open** *Apr-Oct* 7am-noon, 2.30-6pm daily. *Nov-Mar* 10am-noon, 3.30-6pm daily.

Museo Civico della Laguna Sud

Campo Marconi 1 (041 550 0911/ lagunasud@libero.it). **Open** *Oct-May* 9am-1pm, 3.30-7.30pm Tue, Sat; 9am-1pm Mon, Wed-Fri. *June-Sept* 9am-1pm, 3.30-7.30pm Tue; 9am-1pm Mon, Wed; 9am-1pm, 7.30-11.30pm Thur, Fri; 9am-1pm, 3.30-11.30 pm Sat; 7.30-11.30pm Sun. **Admission** L4,000.

Where to stay & eat

There are 73 hotels in Sottomarina – most of them seasonal – and only four in Chioggia itself. Of the latter, the recently renovated **Grande Italia** (Rione Sant'Andrea 597, 041 400 515, rates L145,000-L300,000) by the ferry berth in piazzetta Vigo provides all the usual four-star comforts, and offers the use of a fitness centre. The tiny **Locanda Val D'Ostreghe** (rione Sant'Andrea 763, 041 400 527/fax 041 403 252, L70,000-L80,000, breakfast not included), in a narrow calle behind the church of Sant'Andrea, has 12 basic but cheap rooms above a restaurant.

Of a weekend, Venetians are apt to take a jaunt down to Chioggia for a cheap seafood lunch. The lack of tourists and the fact that fish is central to the worldview of the *chiozzotti* mean that it is difficult to go wrong, but one reliable address is **Al Bersagliere** (via Battisti 293, 041 401 044, closed Mar-Oct Tue, Nov-Feb Mon eve and Tue, ten days Nov, average L70,000), a family-run *trattoria* just off the Corso, where seafood risottos and grilled fish are cooked to perfection. *See also p156* **Ostaria al Penzo**.

Tourist information

APT

Lungomare Adriatico 101, Sottomarina (041 401 068/ fax 041 554 0855/apt_info@clodienet.it/ www.chioggia-apt.net). **Open** *Oct-Mar* 8.30am-1pm Mon-Sat. *Apr-Sept* 8.30am-1pm, 2-7pm Mon-Sat; 9am-noon, 3-6pm Sun.

The Lagoon

Glass, lace, cypresses and *i matti* are just some of the attractions of the watery expanse between the *murazzi* and the mainland.

Many visitors to Venice are so overcome by the city itself that they don't even realise that Venice has another side to it – an endless watery landscape dotted with islands, some inhabited, some home only to abandoned convents and colonies of samphire. There are 34 islands on the salt-water lagoon, which covers more than 518 square kilometres (200 square miles). Painters and photographers are just as well served out here as in the city itself, especially on clear autumn and winter days, when the horizon clears to reveal the towering, snow-capped peaks of the Dolomites beyond.

The wetlands of the lagoon are a wild, fragile environment for flora and fauna. For Venetians the lagoon is their refuge from the daily invasion of tourists. This is where they escape by boat for picnics on deserted islands, or where they go fishing for bass and bream. Others set off to dig up clams at low tide (most without the requisite communal licence), or organise hunting expeditions for duck, using the makeshift hides known as *botte* (originally wooden barrels sunk into the floor of the lagoon). Many just head out after work, at sunset, to row, in training for Venice's numerous regattas (see *p194* and *p224*).

From the lagoon, the precarious natural position of Venice and the uniqueness of its urban development come sharply into focus. Exploring some of the quieter corners of this waterscape is like going back to the sixth-century origins of the city. The classic tourist trip is usually limited to the three major islands of **Murano**, **Burano** and **Torcello**, but there are plenty of other possibilities.

EXPLORING THE LAGOON

Trips are organised by Marina Fiorita Viaggi (041 530 1865/fax 041 530 9567/ marinafioritaviaggi@tin.it) exploring parts of the lagoon untouched by the public vaporetto service. The excursions are mostly day-trips with guides (English spoken), costing L50,000-L60,000, lunch included; they run throughout the year, starting from Treporti (vaporetto 12 or 13 from Fondamente Nove). Booking is essential. Alternatively, to learn more about the ecostructure and bird life of the lagoon, catch the blue bus marked 'Chioggia' or 'Sottomarina' from piazzale Roma, ask to get off at the WWF's 'Oasi Valle Averto' (041 518 5068; open 9am-4pm Mon-Fri, Sun; admission L10,000, L5,000 children under six; guided visits at 10am, 2pm Fri, Sun; weekdays by appointment). The adventurous can rent a boat for the day. Craft with small motors don't need a permit, and can be hired from Sport e Lavoro, Cannaregio 2508, fondamenta della Misericordia (041 522 9535; L200,000 per day; if you want to take a guide along with you it is an extra L35,000 an hour; maximum six people per boat. No credit cards are accepted). (*See also p209* **Venice à la carte**.)

San Michele

Just opposite the Fondamenta Nuove, halfway between Venice and Murano, this is the island where any tour of the lagoon begins. But for many Venetians it is their last stop, as San Michele is the city's cemetery. Early in the morning, the vaporetto (41 or 42) is packed

An endless watery landscape.

with Venetians coming over to lay flowers. This is not a morbid spot, though: like Père Lachaise in Paris, it is an elegant city of the dead, with more than one famous resident.

An orderly redbrick wall runs round the whole of the island, with a line of tall cypress trees rising high behind it – the inspiration for Böcklin's famously lugubrious painting *Island of the Dead*. The vaporetto stops at the elegant **Convento di San Michele in Isola** (open 7.30am-12.15pm, 3-4pm daily). Designed by Mauro Codussi in the 1460s, this striking white building of Istrian stone is Venice's first Renaissance church, with a tripartite façade inspired by Leon Battista Alberti's Tempio Malatestiana in Rimini. The grounds of the Franciscan monastery that used to extend behind the church were seconded for burials when the city was under Napoleonic rule, in an effort to stop Venetians digging graves in the *campi* around the parish churches. Soon it was the only place to be seen dead in. Most Venetians still want to make that last journey to San Michele, even though these days it's more a temporary parking-lot than a final resting place. The island reached saturation point long ago, and even after paying through the nose for a plot, families know that after a suitable period – generally around ten years – the bones of their loved ones will be dug up and transferred to an ossuary on another island.

Visitors enter the **cemetery** (open Apr-Sept 7.30am-6pm daily; Oct-Mar 7.30am-4pm daily) through a dignified arch, marked by a 15th-century bas-relief of St Michael slaying a dragon with one hand and holding a pair of scales in the other. Beyond are the cool cloisters of the restored monastery where monks hand out rough maps of the cemetery, which are indispensable for celebrity hunts. In the Greek and Russian Orthodox section is the elaborate tomb of Sergei Pavlovich Diaghilev, who introduced the Ballets Russes to Europe, and a simpler monument to the composer Igor Stravinsky and his wife. The Protestant section has a selection of ships' captains and passengers who ended their days in La Serenissima, plus the simple graves of Ezra Pound and Joseph Brodsky. There's a rather sad children's section, and a corner dedicated to the city's gondoliers, their tombs decorated with carvings and statues of gondolas. Visit the cemetery on the *Festa dei morti* – All Souls' Day, 2 November – and the vaporetto is free.

Murano

After San Michele, the number 42 or 41 vaporetto continues to Murano, one of the larger and more populous islands of the lagoon (vaporettos 12

and 13 also put in there, but only at the Faro stop). In the 16th and 17th centuries, when it was a world centre of glass production and a decadent resort for wealthy Venetians, Murano had a population of more than 30,000. Now fewer than 5,000 people live here and most of the glass workers commute from the mainland. Murano owes its fame to the decision taken in 1291 to transfer all of Venice's glass furnaces to the island because of a fear of fire in the main city. Their products were soon sold all over Europe. The secrets of glass were jealously guarded within the island: any glass-maker leaving Murano was proclaimed a traitor. Even today, there is no official glass school, and the delicate skills of blowing and flamework are only learned by apprenticeship to one of the glass masters. In 2000 many of the smaller glass workshops were threatened with closure for failure to comply with new anti-pollution legislation.

At first sight Murano looks close to being ruined by glass tourism. Dozens of 'guides' swoop down on visitors as they pile off the vaporetto, to whisk them off on tours of glass furnaces. Even if you head off on your own, you'll find yourself immediately in the tourist trap that is **fondamenta dei Vetrai**, a snipers' alley of shops selling glass knick-knacks, most of which are made far from Murano. But there are some serious glassmakers on the island, and even the tackiest of the showrooms usually have one or two gems (*see chapter* **Glass**).

There's more to Murano, however, than glass. At the far end of fondamenta dei Vetrai, the nondescript façade of the 14th-century parish church of **San Pietro Martire** (open 9am-noon, 3-6pm Mon-Sat; 3-6pm Sun) conceals two important works by Giovanni Bellini, both backed by marvellous landscapes: an *Assumption* and a *Virgin and Child Enthroned With St Mark, St Augustine and Doge Agostino Barbarigo*. There are also two works by Veronese and assistants (mainly the latter), and an ornate altarpiece by Salviati that is lit up by the early morning sun.

Beyond the church, the wide Ponte Vivarini spans Murano's Canal Grande. To the left of the bridge stands the splendid 15th-century Gothic **Palazzo Da Mula**. Once across the bridge a very different community emerges.

In the morning, fishermen and farmers arrive in their boats and set up a small floating market, where *muranesi* bargain loudly in their brusque dialect (subtly different from Venetian) for the freshest – never the cheapest – choice. Head into the backstreets and you'll see retired glass-blowers rowing tiny boats on their way back from a morning spent fishing for squid or collecting clams at low tide.

More to **Murano** than glass. *See p136.*

Housed in the beautiful Palazzo Giustinian, built in the late 17th century for the bishops of Torcello, the museum has a huge collection of Murano glass. As well as the famed chandeliers, which only made their appearance in the 18th century, there are ruby-red beakers, opaque lamps and delicate Venetian *perle* – glass beads that were used in trade and commerce all over the world from the time of Marco Polo. One of the earliest pieces is the 15th-century Barovier marriage cup, decorated with portraits of the bride and groom. One room is devoted to blown-glass mirrors, a Muranese monopoly for centuries. On the ground floor there is a good collection of Roman glassware from near Zara on the Istrian peninsula.

Burano & Mazzorbo

A right turn at the foot of Ponte Vivarini brings you on to fondamenta Cavour and, beyond, fondamenta Giustinian. The 17th-century **Palazzo Giustinian**, situated reassuringly far from tacky chandeliers and fluorescent clowns, is the **Museo dell'Arte Vetrario**, the best place to learn about the history of glass. Around the corner, the 12th-century basilica of **Santi Maria e Donato** (open 8.30am-noon, 4-6pm Mon-Sat; 4-6pm Sun) is Murano's greatest architectural treasure. Though altered by over-enthusiastic 19th-century restorers, the exterior is a classic of the Veneto-Byzantine style, with an ornate blind portico on the rear of the apse. Inside is a richly coloured mosaic floor, laid down in 1140 at the same time as the floor of the Basilica di San Marco, with floral and animal motifs. Above, a Byzantine apse mosaic of the Virgin looms out of the darkness in a field of gold.

Venice's greatest love machine Giacomo Casanova (*see p16* **The Great Escape**), was a Murano habitué. To retrace his footsteps, turn left at the foot of Ponte Vivarini and follow the quiet fondamenta Sebastiano Venier to its end. Here, the church of **Santa Maria degli Angeli** (open Sun for 11am mass) backs on to the convent where Casanova conducted one of his most torrid affairs, with a libertine nun named Maria Morosoni. She was egged on by the convent's Mother Superior, who was herself the lover of Monsieur De Bernis, the French ambassador. De Bernis liked to watch, and Casanova was perfectly happy to give him something worth seeing.

Museo dell'Arte Vetrario
Fondamenta Giustinian 8 (041 739 586). Vaporetto 41 or 42 to Museo. **Open** *Apr-Oct* 10am-5pm Mon, Tue, Thur-Sun. *Nov-Mar* 10am-4pm Mon, Tue, Thur-Sun. **Admission** L8,000; L5,000 concessions (*see also p63* **Musei Civici Veneziani**). **No credit cards**.

Mazzorbo, the long island before Burano, is a haven of peace, rarely visited by tourists. The ferry generally stops here, then heads off to Torcello before tacking back to Burano, so it is often quicker to get off at Mazzorbo and walk to Burano across the long wooden bridge that connects the two islands and offers the bonus of a great view across the lagoon to Venice.

Mazzorbo was settled around the tenth century; when it became clear that Venice itself had got the upper hand, most of the large population simply dismantled their houses brick by brick, transported them by boat to Venice, and rebuilt them there. Today Mazzorbo is a lazy place of small farms, with a pleasant walk to the 14th-century Gothic church of Santa Caterina, whose wobbly-looking tower still has its original bell, dating from 1318 – one of the oldest in Europe. Winston Churchill, a keen amateur painter, set up his easel here more than once after World War II. Opposite Burano is an area of attractive new low-cost housing, in shades of lilac, grey and green, designed by Giancarlo De Carlo.

Don't come to **Burano** with a black and white film in your camera. Together with the manufacture of lace, its picture-postcard houses make it a magnet for tourists.

The locals are traditionally either fishermen or lacemakers, though there are increasingly few of the latter, despite efforts by the island's **Scuola di Merletti** (lace school; *see p139*) to pass on the skills to younger generations. The street leading from the main quay throbs with souvenir shops selling lace, lace and more lace – most of it machine-made in Taiwan. But Burano is big enough for the visitor to get lost in its narrow backstreets, where life goes on at a lazy pace. It was in Burano that the Venice *carnevale* was revived back in the 1970s, and the modest celebrations here are still far more authentic than anything witnessed by the masses of masked tourists cramming piazza San Marco.

Sightseeing

Fishermen have lived on Burano since the seventh century; they are said to have painted their houses different colours so that they could recognise them when fishing out on the lagoon (no matter that only a tiny proportion of the island's houses can actually be seen from the lagoon). Whatever the reason, the *buranelli* still go to great efforts to decorate their houses, and

social life centres on the *fondamente* where the men repair nets or tend to their boats moored in the canal below, while their wives – at least in theory – make lace.

Lace began to be produced in Burano in the 15th century, originally by nuns, but was quickly picked up by fishermen's wives and daughters. So skilful were the local lacemakers

Mestre

Mestre – on the mainland facing Venice across the water – is not the kind of place that people visit. If you arrive by rail, it's an unattractive rash of high-rise flats and office-blocks glimpsed before the train shoots out into the glittering expanse of the lagoon. If you arrive by road it's a tangle of murky fly-overs and underpasses. From a plane, the view is not much better.

Compared with its more glamorous neighbour, Mestre has little to offer. It is, however, trying hard to remedy this.

A small walled town from the tenth century (the only notable remnant of these medieval fortifications is the tower in its main piazza), Mestre grew no larger under Venetian control. It wasn't until the 20th century, in fact, that it expanded exponentially with the creation of the industrial port of Marghera (*see chapter* **Venice Today**), where the lure of jobs attracted thousands of workers from all over Italy. Venetians, too, moved there from the 1950s, fleeing high house prices in Venice itself, or simply seeking the convenience of mainland life, with luxurious trappings such as cars and supermarkets.

As the population of Venice dwindled, Mestre continued to expand, sprawling outwards and upwards in grim concrete but never achieving a genuine sense of identity.

This it is now striving to do. Administratively the mainland sprawl is part of Venice. But at the time of going to press, a petition was in preparation for a referendum on the separation of Mestre from Venice. It's not the first time: four such referendums have been held since 1979. The persistence of the promoters after three failures may seem perverse; however, support for the break from Venice has grown noticeably on each vote. With their parents' nostalgic connections with island Venice appearing increasingly irrelevant, young *mestrini* will, sooner or later, give a definitive snip to the umbilical cord.

And the young in Mestre are a far more significant sector of the population than they

are across the water. One evening visit to **piazza Ferretto**, the attractive (and recently refurbished) square that is the heart of Mestre, will suffice to get a sense of the city's youth-orientation. Indeed, any tourist looking for some active nightlife should consider a trip to Mestre, once the possibilities of campo Santa Margherita have been explored and exhausted. The city has more cinemas than Venice, and good discotheques are to be found both in the centre and the environs (*see chapter* **Nightlife**).

Many young *mestrini*, apart from a dutiful visit to aged relatives, see little point in going to Venice at all. Even if they feel like a spot of Sunday afternoon tourism, they are more likely to drive to Padua or Verona, where parking is so much easier.

Mestre cannot compete architecturally or artistically with Venice, although the churches of **San Rocco** (open 10.30am-noon Wed, Fri; 6-7.30pm Thur), with its 18th-century frescos, and **San Girolamo** (open 9am-noon, 4-6.30pm Mon-Sat) are worth a look, and there are a number of fine classical villas, particularly in the greener areas northwards on the way towards Carpenedo (which an imaginative Mestre legend says is where Icarus fell to earth). However, Mestre has done a good deal over recent years to establish its cultural independence. Its theatres (*see chapter* **Performing Arts**) provide musical and theatrical seasons that rival anything Venice has to offer (with the exception of opera, for Mestre has no venue to rival the Fenice or even the Palafenice). There are lively historical societies and creative-writing workshops. In 2001 a long-promised new cultural centre is due to open at last in piazzale Candiani: a five-storey building with spaces for exhibitions, workshops and multi-media events. Mestre is never likely to set any hearts a-flutter with its radiant beauty, but it is doing its best to shake off its image as a drab dormitory suburb.

that in the 17th century many were paid handsomely to work in the Alençon lace ateliers in Normandy. Today most work is done on commission, though interested parties will have to get to know one of the lacemakers in person, as the co-operative that used to represent the old ladies closed down in 1995.

The busy main square of Burano is named after the island's most famous son, Baldassare Galuppi, a 17th-century composer who set many of Carlo Goldoni's plays to music and who was the subject of a poem by Robert Browning. The square is a good place for sipping a glass of *prosecco*. The most famous *trattoria* – though not the cheapest – is Da Romano, where the walls are covered with paintings accepted by the owner in payment for meals. If your artistic talents don't stretch this far, a better-value meal can be had at Il Gatto Nero (*see p157*) by the lively morning fish market (Tue-Sat) on the fondamenta della Pescheria. Across the main square from the lace museum is the church of San Martino, which has an early Tiepolo Crucifixion.

Scuola di Merletti

Piazza Galuppi 187 (041 730 034). Vaporetto 12 to Burano. **Open** *Apr-Oct* 10am-5pm Mon, Wed-Sun. *Oct-Mar* 10am-4pm Mon, Wed-Sun. **Admission** L8,000; L5,000 concessions (*see also p63* **Musei Civici Veneziani**). **No credit cards**.

In a series of rooms with painted wooden beams are cases full of elaborate examples of lacework from the 17th century onwards; *aficionados* will have fun spotting the various stitches, such as the famous *punto burano*. Many of the older exhibits change every few months for conservation reasons, but if it's on display look out for the devout intricacy of the 17th-century altar-cloth decorated with the Mysteries of the Rosary. There are fans, collars and parasols, and some of the paper pattern-sheets that lacemakers use. Unfortunately the school that gives the Museum its name is now virtually defunct, although occasional courses are offered by some of the older generation of Burano lacemakers, who can sometimes be seen on weekday mornings at work in a corner of the museum.

San Francesco del Deserto

From behind the church of San Martino on Burano there is a view across the lagoon to the idyllic monastery island of San Franceso del Deserto. The island, with its 4,000 cypress trees, is inhabited by a small community of Franciscan monks. Getting there can be quite a challenge. Burano's one water taxi sits by the main boat quay, but the driver tends to disappear for long periods. Burano's postman will take you across on his motorboat. Either way, expect to pay at least L50,000 for the

return ride. A better, and cheaper, option is to ask one of the local fishermen to give you a lift. They are usually willing to do so for a small fee – perhaps L20,000 for the return trip.

The otherworldly monk who shepherds visitors around with agonising slowness will tell the story of how the island was St Francis's first stop in Europe on his journey back from the Holy Land in 1220. He planted his stick – they say – it grew into a pine, and birds flew in to sing for him (there are certainly plenty of them in evidence in the cypress-packed gardens). The medieval monastery – all warm stone and cloistered calm – is about as far as you can get from the worldly bustle of the Rialto.

Convento di San Francesco del Deserto

(041 528 6863). **Open** 9am-12.30pm, 3-6.30pm Mon-Sat; 3-6.30pm Sun. **Admission** by voluntary donation.

Torcello

The boat only takes a few minutes to steam over from Burano to Torcello, the sprawling, marshy island where the history of Venice began. At low tide, you could well imagine yourself in the Fens or the Camargue, and there are certainly as many mosquitoes.

Torcello today is a rural backwater with a resident population of 20; each time an inhabitant moves away for the bright lights of Burano or Mazzorbo, it is headline news in the *Gazzettino* (*see p284*). It is difficult to believe that in the 14th century more than 20,000 people lived here. This was the first settlement in the lagoon, founded in the fifth century by the citizens of the mainland Roman town of Altino. Successive waves of emigration from Altino were sparked off by Barbarian invasions, first by Attila and his Huns, and later, in the seventh century, by the Lombards. But Torcello's dominance of the lagoon did not last: Venice itself was found to be more salubrious (malaria was rife on Torcello) and more easily defendable. Even the bishop of Torcello chose to live on Murano, in the palace that now houses the glass museum (*see p137*). But past decline is present charm, and rural Torcello is a great antidote to the pedestrian traffic jams around San Marco.

From the ferry jetty the campanile of the cathedral can already be made out; to get there, simply follow the canal down Torcello's only street (recently repaved in dubious taste). To the right there's an opulent private *palazzo* that still hosts extravagant parties, and just by the **Ponte del Diavolo** (one of only two bridges in

Venice without a parapet) there is a simple *osteria*, Al Ponte del Diavolo (041 730 401; lunch only except Sat; closed Wed) with reliable cooking and prices that are almost reasonable. Torcello's main square has some desultory souvenir stalls, a small but interesting **Museo dell'Estuario** (*see below*) with archaeological finds from around the lagoon, a battered stone seat known somewhat arbitrarily as Attila's throne and two extraordinary churches.

The 11th-century church of **Santa Fosca** (open Apr-Oct 10.30am-5.30pm daily; Nov-Mar 10am-5pm daily; free) looks like a miniature version of Istanbul's Santa Sophia, more Byzantine than European with its Greek Cross plan and external colonnade; its bare interior allows the perfect geometry of the space to come to the fore. Next door is the imposing cathedral of **Santa Maria Assunta** (*see below*).

By the churches, the Locanda Cipriani (*see p157*) is rated as one of Venice's top restaurants, with prices to match. The three big Cipriani concerns in Venice – the Hotel Cipriani, Harry's Bar (run by Arrigo Cipriani, son of the founder) and the Locanda Cipriani (run by Arrigo's sister Carla, who is married to Italian soft-porn director Tinto Brass) have no business links; all have been involved in a long-running legal battle for the right to use the name 'Cipriani'.

A **cumulative ticket** for the Basilica, Campanile and Museo dell'Estuario is available at the sights themselves and costs L10,000 (L7,000 groups). No credit cards are accepted.

Museo dell'Estuario

Palazzo del Consiglio (041 730 761). Vaporetto 12 to Torcello. **Open** *Apr-Oct* 10.30am-5.30pm Tue-Sun. *Nov-Mar* 10am-5pm Tue-Sun. **Admission** L4,000.
A small but worthwhile collection of sculptures and archaeological finds from the cathedral and elsewhere in Torcello. Among the exhibits on the ground floor are late 12th-century fragments of mosaic from the apse of Santa Maria dell'Assunta, and two of the *bocche di leone* (lions' mouths) where citizens with grudges could post their denunciations. Upstairs are Greco-Byzantine icons, painted panels, bronze seals and pottery fragments, and an exquisite carved ivory statuette of an embracing couple from the beginning of the 15th century.

Santa Maria Assunta

(041 270 2464/fax 041 270 2458/ catalogo@patriarcatovenezia.it). **Open** *Apr-Oct* 10.30am-5.30pm daily. *Nov-Mar* 10.30am-5pm daily. **Admission** L5,000; L3,000 groups.
Dating from AD 638, the basilica is the oldest building on the lagoon. The interior has an elaborate 11th-century mosaic floor that rivals that of San Marco. But the main draws of this church are the vivid mosaics on the vault and walls, which range in date from the ninth to the end of the 12th century. The

apse has a simple but stunning mosaic of a Madonna and Child on a plain gold background, while the other end of the cathedral is dominated by a huge mosaic of the Last Judgment (an audioguide in English provided free at the door gives a detailed explanation). The theological rigour and narrative complexity of this huge composition suggest comparisons with the *Divine Comedy*, which Dante was writing at about the same time, but the anonymous mosaicists of Torcello were more concerned with striking fear into the hearts of their audience – hence the wicked devils pushing the damned into hell.

Campanile di Torcello

(041 270 2464/fax 041 270 2458/ catalogo@patriarcatovenezia.it). **Open** *Apr-Oct* 10.30am-5.30pm daily. *Nov-Mar* 10.30am-5pm daily. **Admission** L4,000.
The view of the lagoon from the top of the Campanile was memorably described by Ruskin: 'Far as the eye can reach, a waste of wild sea moor, of a lurid ashen grey,' concluding with the elegaic words: 'Mother and daughter, you behold them both in their widowhood, – TORCELLO, AND VENICE.' There is no lift, just a stiff walk up steep ramps.

Sant'Erasmo & Vignole

Sant'Erasmo (served by vaporetto 13) is the best-kept secret of the lagoon: larger than Venice itself, but with a tiny population that contents itself with growing most of the vegetables eaten in La Serenissima (on Rialto market stalls the sign *San Rasmo* is a mark of quality). Venetians refer to the islanders of Sant'Erasmo as *i matti* – the crazies – because of their legendarily shallow gene pool (everybody seems to be called Vignotto or Zanella); the islanders don't think much of Venetians either. There are cars on this island, but as they are only used to drive the few miles from house to boat and back, few are in top-notch condition – a state of affairs favoured by the fact that the island does not have a single policeman. It also lacks a doctor, pharmacy and school, but there is a supermarket, one fishermen's bar/*trattoria* – Ai Tedeschi (lunch only except Apr-Oct; closed Tue) – hidden away on a small sandy beach by the **Forte Massimiliano**, a crumbling Austrian fort; and a restaurant, Ca' Vignotto (via Forti 71, 041 528 5329, average L45,000; closed Tue) where bookings are essential.

The main attraction of the island consists of the beautiful country landscapes and lovely walks past traditional Veneto farmhouses, through vineyards and fields of artichokes and asparagus – a breath of fresh air after all the urban crowding of Venice.

By the main vaporetto stop (Chiesa) is the 20th-century church (on the site of an earlier one founded before the year 1000) containing, over the entrance-door, a particularly gruesome 17th-century depiction of the martyrdom of St Erasmus, who had his intestines wound out of his body on a windlass. The resemblance of a windlass to a capstan resulted in St Erasmus becoming the patron saint of sailors.

If you're around on the first Sunday in October, don't miss the **Festa del Mosto** (*see p196*), held to inaugurate the first pressing of new wine. This is perhaps the only chance you'll ever get to witness – or even participate in – the **gara del bisato**: a game in which an eel is dropped into a tub of water blackened by squid ink. Contestants have to plunge their heads into the tub and attempt to catch the eel with their teeth.

The number 13 vaporetto also stops at the smaller island of **Vignole**, where there is a medieval chapel dedicated to St Erosia.

Opposite the Capannone vaporetto stop on Sant'Erasmo is the tiny island of **Lazzaretto Nuovo**. Get off here at the weekend, shout across, and with luck a boat might row over to get you. In the 15th century the island was fortified as a customs deposit and military prison; during the 1576 plague outbreak it became a quarantine centre. At the peak of the epidemic more than 10,000 people were cooped up here. More recently it has become a research centre for the archaeologists of the Archeo Club di Venezia, who are excavating its ancient remains, including a church that may date back to the sixth century. Visitors are welcome to look round and may even get an impromptu guided tour of the site.

The southern lagoon

The southern part of the lagoon between Venice, the Lido and the mainland has 14 small islands, a few of which are still inhabited, though most are out of bounds for tourists.

San Lazzaro degli Armeni.

San Servolo is home to a private university (*see p287*). The huge **San Clemente**, once a lunatic asylum, is now a home for abandoned cats and **La Grazia** is an isolation hospital.

But pick up vaporetto number 20 from San Zaccaria (note that only a few each day stop at San Lazzaro), and you will be one of the select few who can say that they made it to the island of **San Lazzaro degli Armeni**, just opposite the Lido. A black-cloaked Armenian priest meets the boat and takes visitors on a detailed tour of the Monastero Mechitarista. This tiny island is a global point of reference for Armenia's Catholic minority, visited and supported by Armenians from Italy and abroad. Near the entrance stand the printing presses that helped to distribute Armenian literature all over the world for 200 years. Sadly, they are now silent, with the monastery's charmingly retro line in dictionaries, school and liturgical texts farmed out to a modern press.

Originally a leper colony, in 1717 the island was presented by the Doge to an Armenian abbot called Mekhitar, who was on the run from the Turkish invasion of the Peloponnese. There had been an Armenian community in Venice since the 11th century, centring on the tiny Santa Croce degli Armeni church, just round the corner from the piazza San Marco, but the construction of this church and monastery on the former leper colony made Venice a world centre of Armenian culture. The monastery was the only one in the whole of Venice to be spared the Napoleonic axe, because the emperor had a soft spot for Armenians and argued that this was an academic rather than a religious institute.

The tour takes in the cloisters and the church, rebuilt after a fire in 1883. The museum and the modern library contain 40,000 priceless books and manuscripts, and a bizarre collection of gifts from visiting Armenians, ranging from Burmese prayer books to an Egyptian mummy. The island's most famous student was Lord Byron, who used to take a break from his more earthly pleasures in Venice and row three times a week to learn Armenian (as he found that his 'mind wanted something craggy to break upon') with the monks. He helped the monks to publish an Armenian-English grammar, although by his own confession he never got beyond the basics of the language. You can buy a completed version of this, plus a number of period maps and an illustrated children's Armenian grammar, in the shop just inside the monastery gate.

San Lazzaro degli Armeni

(041 526 0104). **Open** 3.20-5pm daily for guided visits. **Admission** L10,000. **No credit cards**.

Eat, Drink, Shop

Restaurants

You won't eat cheaply but you can eat well: Venice's restaurants are getting better all the time.

Eating in Venice is getting better all the time. For most visitors, food is fairly low down on the list of reasons to be here; and there are still plenty of over-priced, under-inspiring restaurants vying with each other to keep it that way. But if you know where to go – and this proviso applies here more than in any other Italian city – you can eat well on the lagoon. Not necessarily cheaply, but well.

CUTTLEFISH OF THE WORLD, UNITE

At the top end, among luxury establishments such as **Do' Forni**, the **Locanda Cipriani** or **Harry's Bar**, the only movement is the inexorable upward march of the prices. The cuisine in these restaurants is generally good, in a high-class-comfort-food sort of way; and knowing that you'll be able to come back in three years' time and have the same meal, served, likely as not, by the same waiters, is all part of their charm. But if it's adventure you're after – the thrill of discovery, the frisson of value for money – steer clear.

The slow revolution in Venetian dining has come mainly from below. It has come from the creative relaunch of the traditional hostelry, or bacaro (see p159), and from the attempt of a handful of highly motivated local chefs to strip away the *cordon bleu* subterfuge and go back to first principles.

Yesterday's revolutionaries, of course, are today's establishment. The **Corte Sconta** (see p149) is a case in point: when Claudio Proietto opened this *trattoria* in the backwoods of Castello in 1980, his formula – based on the freshest seafood, cooked and marinated in the same way Venetian families do it (or rather, used to do it) at home – was a revelation. But now everyone has jumped on the bandwagon, and though Corte Sconta is still as good as ever, the prices are now in the upper range. To sample Corte Sconta cooking at knockdown prices, you have to head over to Mestre for the *Festa di Rifondazione*, the summer fair of the far-left *Rifondazione comunista* party, where Proietto, a diehard activist, runs the buffet.

There are still budget meals to be had on the lagoon, in *bacari* and *trattorie* that are often found in the less touristy reaches of the city – northern Cannaregio, eastern Castello and Sant'Elena, western Dorsoduro, the Giudecca,

and the outlying islands. Venetians themselves eat out, after all – and they are famous for not allowing anybody to pull a fast one on them. Of course, it sometimes happens that tourists are charged more than the Venetians on the next table for exactly the same meal; there's little you can do about this, except not go back, or accept the extra expense as a save-Venice surcharge. By and large, though, Venetian hosts are upfront, honest, and – if you can cross the language barrier – keen to share their knowledge of local delicacies and local wine.

There are one or two other rules worth bearing in mind. Menus are often recited out loud; an annoying habit, but unavoidable in some more rustic (or would-be-rustic) eateries. If this happens, and you are unsure of the price of something you have ordered, always ask. Beware of fish quoted by weight – you should ask to see the fish and ask how much it costs before you confirm. Steer well clear of those restaurants – mainly around the San Marco district – that employ sharply dressed waiters to stand outside and persuade passing tourists to come in for a meal – an immediate recipe for rip-off prices. Always ask for a written *conto* (bill) at the end of the meal, as it is illegal to leave the restaurant without one.

And finally, bear in mind that Venetians often lunch at noon, dine at seven, and hit the sack by ten. The more upmarket restaurants follow standard Italian practice, rarely serving dinner before 7.30pm and keeping the kitchen open until 10pm; but *bacari* and neighbourhood *trattorie* tend to open and close earlier. In other words, if you want to eat cheaply, eat early.

WHAT'S ON THE PLATE

Going to Venice and not eating fish is like visiting McDonald's for the salad. A writhing, glistening variety of seafood swims from the morning stalls of Rialto and Chioggia markets into restaurant kitchens; it's not always cheap, but for dedicated pescivores, there are few better stamping grounds in the whole of Italy. To make sense of the bewildering variety of sea creatures on offer, see p148 **The menu**.

There are alternatives to seafood, but you need to make an extra effort to seek them out. The once-strong local tradition of creative ways with slaughterhouse offcuts is kept alive in a

The sumptuous **Caffè Quadri**: for
splashing out in style. *See p147*.

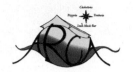

Ristorante Pizzeria "Arca"
Venezia

Ideal meeting place, the cosy and country room disposition offers,
together with the home delicious dishes, also very good pizzas.
Not to miss the genuine venetian "cicchetti".

Venezia - San Pantalon, Dorsoduro 3757
tel. (+39) 041.5242236 - fax (+39) 041.2448581
Air-conditioned dining rooms, banquets, buffet, take away. Closed on sunday
Credit cards: Visa, Master Card, Euro Card, Bancomat

couple of restaurants and one marvelous trattoria, **Dalla Marisa** (*see p153*); it can also be found in bar-counter *cicheti* (tapas-style snacks) like *nervetti* (veal cartilage) and *musetto* (headcheese) – or at least it could before the *mucca pazza* (mad cow) scare broke in Italy.

Vegetarians may at first be horrified to realise that there is not a single vegetarian restaurant in the whole of the city. But Venetian cuisine relies heavily on seasonal vegetables, so it is quite easy to eat a vegetarian meal. *Secondi* are often accompanied by a wide selection of grilled vegetables: aubergine, courgette, tomato or radicchio. Many *cicheti* are vegetables: artichoke hearts, deep-fried pumpkin flowers, *polpetti* made with ricotta cheese. And several pasta dishes are vegetable-based, using *funghi porcini*, or broccoli, or oil, garlic and chili. The sauce rarely has meat in unless it says so on the menu; but it always pays to ask.

There is something of the Spanish *tapas* mentality about the Venetian approach to meals, which rarely follow the normal *primo*, *secondo* and *dolce* pattern. If you take the risk of nodding vigorously when the waiter suggests bringing some seafood *antipasti*, you may start to regret it when the fifth plate arrives – but it is perfectly okay to just eat a plate of pasta afterwards, or to skip to the *secondo* (which might be a grilled fish such as *coda di rospo* (angler fish), a *fritto misto* (seafood fry-up) or *fegato alla veneziana* (liver lightly fried in onions). Or you could even go straight to the *dolce* – flexibility is the keyword.

The house wine – generally a fresh white Tocai or an honest red Raboso or Cabernet Franc (*see p152* **Veneto wines**), served from huge demijohns – is usually quaffable, and often surprisingly refined.

Average prices are per person for three courses, with service and cover charge, but without drinks.

The number after the name of each restaurant refers to the symbol on the maps at the back of the guide, where restaurants are marked in red.

San Marco

Al Bacareto 1
San Marco 3447, calle delle Botteghe (041 528 9336). Vaporetto Sant'Angelo or San Samuele. **Meals served** noon-3pm, 7-10.30pm Mon-Fri; noon-3pm Sat. Closed Aug. **Average** L65,000. **Credit** AmEx, MC, V. **Map** II 3A.
Friendly, family-run *trattoria* near the Palazzo Grassi museum, with a small terrace in summer, and a lively bar packed with locals downing an *ombra* and sampling the *cicheti*. The *spaghetti con le seppie* (cooked in squid ink) is excellent.

Gran Caffè Ristorante Quadri 2
San Marco 120, piazza San Marco (041 528 9299/ quadri@quadrivenice.com/www.quadrivenice.com). *Vaporetto Vallaresso or San Zaccaria.* **Meals served** *Apr-Oct* 12.15-2pm, 7.15-9.15pm daily. *Nov-Mar* 12.15-2pm, 7.15-9.15pm Tue-Sun. **Average** L150,000. **Credit** AmEx, DC, MC, V. **Map** II 4A.
If you want to splash out on a really special meal, book for lunch or dinner at the restaurant above Caffè Quadri (*see p166*). The setting is truly sumptuous: two neo-Classical salons adorned with huge mirrors, damask wall coverings and imposing Murano chandeliers. It's even better if you can secure one of the four window tables that look out over the piazza. It would be easy to soft-pedal the food in such surroundings, but the chef manages a surprisingly creative take on the Venetian tradition; there are even one or two clearly marked vegetarian options. Service is as impeccable as you would expect. The final price – all things considered – is not excessive.

Spicy seafood at **Alle Testiere**. *See p148.*

Eat, Drink, Shop

Le Bistrot de Venise 3

San Marco 4685, calle dei Fabbri (041 523 6651/ bistrot@tin.it/www.bistrotdevenise.com). Vaporetto Rialto. **Meals served** noon-0.45am daily. **Average** L65,000. **Credit** MC, V. **Map** II 4A.
A young and energetic team set up this alternative eaterie a few years back. It's aimed at tourists, but intelligently so; the menu offers revivals of near-forgotten Veneto peasant dishes such as *cisame di pesse quale tu voy* (sweet and sour sardines) or recipes gleaned from ancient manuscripts. As if this were not enough, the Bistrot also has a busy programme of concerts, poetry readings and art exhibitions (*see p210*). Open for late dining (a rarity in Venice).

Vini da Arturo 4

San Marco 3656, calle degli Assassini (041 528 6974). Vaporetto Rialto or Sant'Angelo. **Meals served** 12.30-2.30pm, 7.30-11pm Mon-Sat. **Closed** 2wks after *carnevale*, Aug. **Average** L100,000. **No credit cards**. **Map** II 3A.
This tiny place just north of La Fenice is a well-kept secret among Venetian gastronomes. There's not a whiff of fish on the menu, which features the best fillet steak on the lagoon, as well as a few less carnivorous options – including some creative salad tasters, served as an *antipasto*. For dessert, try the creamy *tiramisù*.

Castello

All'Aciugheta

See p160.

Alla Rivetta 5

Castello 4625, ponte San Provolo (041 528 7302). Vaporetto San Zaccaria. **Meals served** 11am-11pm Tue-Sun. **Closed** mid July-mid Aug. **Average** L50,000. **Credit** AmEx, MC, V. **Map** III 1B.
On an ancient bridge right behind the Hotel Danieli, the Rivetta has managed to preserve its neighbourhood *trattoria* credentials – and prices – despite the scores of tourists who troop in and out each day. At the bar, owner Stefano serves creamy *polenta con baccalà* for little old ladies to take home for lunch. Gondoliers pile in for a noisy, boozy midday meal, which is likely to feature an unbeatable *fritto misto*.

Alle Testiere 6

Castello 5801, calle del Mondo Novo (041 522 7220). Vaporetto Rialto. **Meals served** noon-2pm, 7-10.30pm Mon-Sat. **Closed** 2wks Jan, last week July, 3wks Aug. **Average** L75,000. **Credit** AmEx, DC, MC, V. **Map** III 1A.
This tiny restaurant is moving into the major league (so, unfortunately, are the prices). There are so few seats that they do two sittings each evening; booking for the later one (at 9pm) will ensure a more relaxed meal. Bruno, the cook, does creative variations on Venetian seafood, many involving spices such as ginger or coriander; sommelier Luca guides diners around a small but well-chosen wine list.

Al Mascaron 7

Castello 5225, calle Lunga Santa Maria Formosa (041 522 5995). Vaporetto Rialto. **Meals served** noon-3pm, 7-11pm Mon-Sat. **Closed** mid Dec-mid Jan. **Average** L70,000. **No credit cards**. **Map** III 1A.

The menu

ANTIPASTI

This is where Venetian cuisine really excels. *Antipasti* are so central to the local tradition, and served in such abundant quantities, that there is often no need to eat anything else. The dozens of *cicheti* – tapas-style snacks – served from the counters of the traditional *bacaro* (*see p159*) are essentially *antipasti*; in more upmarket restaurants, these will be joined – or replaced – by an even larger and more refined selection.

baccalà mantecato creamy stockfish, often served on grilled polenta

baccalà alla vicentina stockfish poached in milk

folpi/folpeti baby octopuses – the former have a double row of suckers

carciofi artichokes, even better if they are *castrauri* – raw baby artichokes served with parmesan cheese and olive oil

bovoleti tiny snails cooked in olive oil, parsley and an awful lot of garlic

canoce (or **cicale di mare**) delicate, transparent mantice shrimps

garusoli sea snails, to be winkled out with a toothpick

moleche deep-fried soft-shelled crabs

museto a boiled headcheese sausage served on a slice of bread with mustard

nerveti very strange-looking – and tasting – dish of boiled veal cartilage

polpeta a deep-fried spicy meatball

polenta this yellow or white cornmeal mush is the traditional staple of Venetian cuisine, so much so that inhabitants of the Veneto are known as *polentoni*

sarde in saor sardines marinated in a pungent mixture of onion, vinegar, pine-nuts and raisins

schie e polenta tiny grey shrimps served on a bed of soft polenta

Lively and funky, the Mascaron is still a worthwhile experience if you've never been there before; but for old Venice hands, the no-frills seafood cooking and all-crowd-in-together ambience is beginning to feel a little tired, and the prices a little steep. The counter still groans with seafood *antipasti*, *primi* such as *spaghetti con nero di seppie* (with squid ink) are still simple and filling, and the service is still of the matey, hit-and-miss school. Booking is a must unless you come very early or very late.

Antica Trattoria Bandierette 8

Castello 6671, barbaria de le Tole (041 522 0619/ www.elmoro.com/bandierette.htm). Vaporetto Ospedale. **Meals served** noon-2pm, 7-10pm Mon, Tue, Thur-Sat; noon-2pm Wed. **Closed** 2wks Aug. **Average** L50,000. **Credit** DC, MC, V. **Map** III 2A.
The decor leaves a little to be desired, but the locals who cram into this busy *trattoria* between Santi Giovanni e Paolo and San Francesco don't come for decor: they come for the great, reasonably priced seafood cooking and the friendly service. Among the *primi*, the *tagliatelle* with scampi and spinach, or with baby squid and asparagus, are especially good.

Corte Sconta 9

Castello 3886, calle del Pestrin (041 522 7024). Vaporetto San Zaccaria or Arsenale. **Meals served** noon-3.30pm, 6-10pm Tue-Sat. **Closed** Jan, mid July-mid Aug. **Average** L80,000. **Credit** AmEx, DC, MC, V. **Map** III 2B.
Claudio Proietto's trailblazing seafood restaurant in the eastern reaches of Castello is now such a firm favourite on the well-informed tourist circuit that it

is usually a good idea to book several days in advance. The main act is an endless procession of seafood *antipasti*; the day's catch might include *canoce* (mantis shrimps), *garusoli* (sea-snails), or *canestrelli* (baby scallop shells). The pasta is home-made, and the warm *zabaione* dessert is a delight. Decor is of the rustic trat variety, the ambience loud and friendly. In summer, try to secure one of the tables in the pretty vine-covered courtyard.

Dal Pampo (Osteria Sant'Elena) 10

Sant'Elena, calle Generale Chinotto 24 (041 520 8419/os.pampo@libero.it). Vaporetto Sant'Elena. **Meals served** noon-2.30pm, 7.30-9pm Mon-Wed, Fri-Sun. **Closed** Christmas, 1wk May, 1wk Aug. **Average** L40,000. **Credit** AmEx, MC, V. **Map** III 4C.
Right at the end of Venice – the last vaporetto stop before the Lido – in the working-class neighbourhood of Sant'Elena, this is home cooking at its best. Officially called the 'Osteria Sant'Elena' but known to everyone as Dal Pampo – 'Pampo's Place' – after the jolly owner, it is right by the football stadium – so it can be difficult to get a table on the Sundays when Venice are playing at home. A good place to escape for lunch when visiting the Art Biennale in the nearby Giardini.

Da Remigio 11

Castello 3416, ponte dei Greci (041 523 0089). Vaporetto San Zaccaria. **Meals served** 12.30-2.30pm Mon;12.30-2.30pm, 7.30-10pm Wed-Sun. **Closed** Christmas to late-Jan, 2wks July-Aug. **Average** L70,000. **Credit** AmEx, DC, MC, V. **Map** III 2B.

spienza veal spleen – usually served on a skewer
trippa e rissa tripe cooked in broth

PRIMI

bigoli in salsa fat spaghetti served with an anchovy and onion sauce
pasta e fagioli pasta and borlotti bean soup
gnocchi con granseola potato gnocchi in a spider-crab sauce
spaghetti al nero di seppia in thick squid ink sauce
spaghetti con astice with lobster sauce
spaghetti con caparosoli or **vongole veraci** with two different types of clam
risotto di zucca pumpkin risotto
risotto di radicchio risotto made with bitter red radicchio from nearby Treviso

SECONDI

This is a city for fish-lovers, rather than meat eaters, who will probably be confined to:
fegato alla veneziana veal liver cooked in a slightly sweet sauce of onions
castradina a lamb and cabbage broth

The choice of fish and seafood is almost endless – in addition to the *antipasti* mentioned above you are likely to find **rombo** (turbot), **branzino** (sea bass), **orata** (gilt-headed bream), **pesce spada** (swordfish), **tonno** (tuna), **anguilla** (eel), **cernia** (grouper), **sogliola** (sole), **coda di rospo** (angler-fish), **pesce San Pietro** (John Dory), **aragosta/astice** (spiny lobster/lobster), **granseola** (spider-crab), **cannocchia** (mantis shrimp), **cappe sante** (scallops), **granchio** (crab), **cozze** (mussels), **vongole** or **caparosoli** (clams) and the delicious **cape longhe** (razor clams).

DOLCI

Venice's restaurants are not the best place to feed a sweet habit – there are far more tempting pastries on the shelves of the city's *pasticcerie* (*see p170* **Cake**). The classic end to a meal here is a plate of *buranei* – sweet egg biscuits – served with a *vino dolce* such as Fragolino. Then it's quickly on to the more important matter of which *grappa* to order.

Eat, Drink, Shop

RISTORANTE
Al Giardinetto
da Severino

Le specialità della cucina tipica Veneziana servite in una
caratteristica sala del '400 e in un ampio giardino del Palazzo Zorzi.

The Specialies of Venetian typical Cusine served in a
characteristic 15th century hall and in the garden of Palazzo Zorzi.

Ruga Giuffa, Castello 4928
Tel. (+39) 041.5285332 - Fax (+39) 041.5238778
30122 Venezia

Chiuso il giovedì - *Closed thursday*

Remigio is held in high esteem by local gourmets, who are pretty much unanimous that there are few better addresses for fresh fish. This means, though, that it can be extremely difficult to get a table, despite the out-of-the-way location between San Marco and the Arsenale. The décor is glaringly orange and the acoustics are pretty awful, but any lack of ambience is easily compensated for by delicious *antipasti* such as grilled *cape longhe* (razor shells), followed by filling pasta dishes and a range of squeaky-fresh, grilled-fish *secondi*.

Trattoria dai Tosi 12

Castello 738, secco Marina (041 523 7102).
Vaporetto Giardini. **Meals served** noon-2pm, 7-9.30pm Mon, Tue, Thur-Sun. **Closed** 2wks Aug.
Average L45,000. **Credit** MC, V. **Map** III 4C.
In one of Venice's most working-class areas, in a street festooned with washing and punctuated by children's bicycles, this restaurant-pizzeria is a big hit with local families, and a welcome retreat to normality for visitors to the nearby Biennale dell'Arte. The cuisine is humble but filling, the pizzas are tasty (try the Gregory Speck – *speck* is Tyrolean ham), and you can round the meal off nicely with a killer *sgropin* (a post-prandial refresher made with lemon sorbet, vodka and *prosecco*).

Cannaregio

Al Bacco 13

Cannaregio 3054, fondamenta Capuzine
(041 721 415). Vaporetto San Marcuola or
Guglie. **Meals served** noon-2pm, 7-10pm Tue-Sun.

Closed 2wks Jan, 2wks Aug. **Average** L65,000.
Credit AmEx, DC, MC, V. **Map** I 2A.
Not many tourists make it this deep into Cannaregio, but those that do will discover an ancient and beautifully preserved *osteria*, locatred right on the Cannareggio canal , serving classic Venetian *primi* such as *bigoli in salsa* and monsters of the deep such as *pesce San Pietro* (John Dory) and *coda di rospo* (angler fish). Don't expect a cheap meal, but at least you won't feel crowded out by loads of tourists. In summer angle for a table in the charming small garden out the back.

Alla Fontana

See 161.

Alla Frasca 14

Cannaregio 5176, corte della Carità (041 528
5433). Vaporetto Fondamente Nove. Meals
served noon-2.30pm, 7-10pm, Mon-Wed, Fri-Sun.
Closed 2 wks Jan. **Average** L55,000.
Credit MC, V. **Map** I 4B.
This picturesque *bacaro*, in a tiny square near fondamenta Nuove, was once the storeroom where Titian kept his canvases and paints. New owners have transformed it from an *ombra* pitstop into a bona fide restaurant. It's a charming place to eat – especially in summer when tables are arranged under a vine-covered pergola; in winter the pergola is canvas-covered. The only drawback is the cuisine, which is variable. Stick with simple dishes such as the *spaghetti with vongole veraci* (large clams) and avoid the more ambitious spiced-fish *secondi*, which don't really cut the mustard. Monday is non-fish night, with a selection of *bolliti* (boiled meats).

The **Anice Stellato** is one of the best bargains in town. *See p152.*

Eat, Drink, Shop

Veneto wines

The Veneto produces an excellent selection of DOC red and white wines. Among the whites, one of the most common is **Prosecco**, a delicious sparkling wine from vineyards around Valdobbiadene and Conegliano in the rolling hills north of Treviso (*see p268* **Prosecco**). A good *prosecco* will be light, dry, inexpensive and guaranteed not to give you a headache the next day (unlike its sweeter cousin Asti Spumante). The most highly prized (and expensive) version of *prosecco* is known as **Cartizze**. A more rustic, unfizzy version – known as *prosecco spento* – is served by the glass in *bacari*. Bittersweet **Soave** is the best Veneto still white; reliable producers include Pieropan and Inama.

For a dessert wine, ask for a rich, alcoholic **Verduzzo Dorato** – often served in restaurants with a plate of biscuits – or, for a real treat, a **Reciotto di Soave** produced by Anselmi or Pieropan. **Fragolino** is another sweet, sparkling dessert wine which smells and tastes of strawberries (it is made from the tiny fragrant *uva fragola* – strawberry grape) and is usually a honey-pink colour. Finally, you may just come across the oddly named **Clinton**, a strange sweet-and-sour, fizzy red wine that has nothing to do with American politics.

Red wines from the Veneto are unpretentious and best drunk young; they rarely compare with the more serious reds of Tuscany and Piedmont. Several producers are trying to make more full-bodied vintages by ageing the wine in oak barrels. This can have good results with grapes such as **Cabernet, Cabernet Sauvignon, Merlot** and **Pinot Nero**, but the true Venetian taste is for a young fruity red such as **Raboso** or **Refosco**, consumed as soon as it is bottled. An exception to the disappointing showing of the region's reds is **Amarone** – a bitter-sweet wine made from partially dried Valpolicella grapes. Masi, Quintarelli, Zenato and Allegrini are producers to watch out for.

See p268 **Prosecco**.

Anice Stellato   15
Cannaregio 3272, fondamenta della Sensa (041 720 744). Vaporetto Guglie or Sant'Alvise. **Meals served** 12.30-2pm, 7.30-10pm Tue-Sun. **Closed** 1wk Jan, 3wks Aug. **Average** L40,000. **Credit** MC, V. **Map** I 2A.

It only opened at the end of 1999, but this *nouveau-bacaro* began to fill up almost from day one. The reason is simple: the ambience is friendly, the food good; but above all, this is one of the best bargains in town (pasta dishes at L10,000 or less are almost unheard-of on the lagoon these days). A walk-around bar at the entrance is always full of *cichetari* (locals doing some serious snacking); tables take up two oak-beamed rooms around and behind, and spill out onto the canalside walk in summer. The name means 'star anise', one of the spices Rialto traders imported from the East; but spices have little place in the kitchen, which turns out textbook renditions of Venetian classics such as *bigoli in salsa* and *seppie in nero con polenta*. If you want to eat here, book.

Antiche Cantine Ardenghi   16
Cannaregio 6369, calle della Testa (041 523 7691). Vaporetto Fondamente Nove. **Meals served** 8pm (single sitting) Mon-Sat. **Fixed price** L80,000. **No credit cards. Map** I 4C.

You don't just come here to eat; you come for the experience. An anonymous doorway in a calle just west of Santi Giovanni e Paolo gives on to a long bar and rustic dining room, decorated with vintage photographs of Venice. Guests – who must book in advance – are plied with a succession of delicious, utterly authentic seafood dishes, and as much (humble but drinkable) house wine as they can take, followed by biscuits, *grappa* and coffee – all for a fixed price of L80,000. The soundtrack ranges from opera to Sinatra, and Michele, the garrulous owner, is liable to break into song at the slightest excuse.

Da Alberto   17
Cannaregio 5401, calle Giacinto Gallina (041 523 8153). Vaporetto Fondamente Nove. **Meals served** noon-3pm, 7-10pm Mon-Sat. **Closed** 1wk Jan, mid July-mid Aug. **Average** L50,000. **Credit** MC, V. **Map** I 4C.

This *bacaro* with charming trad décor built its reputation in the days of Alberto himself, who has since moved on to the Innishark pub (*see p167*). The trio of young guys that took over are running more of a restaurant with bar counter than a bona fide *bacaro*. The wide menu ranges from Venetian specialities such as *granseola* (spider crab) to more creative offerings – *gnocchi* with baby squid in cinammon, or turbot with radicchio. A favourite with young Venetians, Alberto's is always buzzing and packed – so book ahead if you want to sit down and eat rather than just snacking at the bar.

Dalla Marisa   18
Cannaregio 652/B, fondamenta San Giobbe (041 720 211). Vaporetto Tre Archi. **Meals served** noon-3pm, 8-9pm Mon, Tue, Thur-Sat; 8-9pm Sun. **Closed** Aug. **Average** L60,000. **No credit cards. Map** I 1A.

Signora Marisa, the proud descendant of a dynasty of butchers, is a culinary legend in Venice, with locals calling up days in advance to ask her to prepare ancient recipes such as *risotto con le secoe* (risotto made with a special cut of beef from around the spine). Given that this may not appeal to BSE-worriers, the menu also features more standard meaty dishes. In summer, tables spill out from the tiny interior on to the *fondamenta* overlooking the busy Cannaregio canal. Book well ahead.

Fiaschetteria Toscana   19

Cannaregio 5719, salizzada San Giovanni Grisostomo (041 528 5281/fax 041 528 5521). *Vaporetto Rialto.* **Meals served** 7.30-10.30pm Mon; 12.30-2.30pm, 7.30-10.30pm Wed-Sun. **Closed** mid July-mid Aug. **Average** L90,000. **Credit** AmEx, DC, MC, V. **Map** I 4C.

Don't be fooled by the name: though this was once a depot for wine and olive oil from Tuscany, today only a good selection of Chianina steak cuts and big Tuscan red wines betray its origins. Otherwise, the cuisine, which covers all bases from fish and meat to game, is true to the Venetian tradition, with favourites such as *schie* (grey shrimps) *con polenta* and *fegato alla veneziana*. For Venice, this is a good-value gourmet experience – if you overlook the slightly tacky decor and the sometimes peremptory service. Mamma Mariuccia still makes most of the fabulous desserts, and the wine list is one of the most impressive in town.

La Colombina   20

Cannaregio 1828, campiello del Pegolotto (041 275 0622/fax 041 275 6794/www.lacolombina.it). *Vaporetto San Marcuola.* **Meals served** 12.30-2.30pm, 8.30pm-midnight Mon-Sat. *Wine bar* 12.30-3.30pm, 6.30pm-2am Mon-Sat. **Closed** 2wks Jan, 2wks Aug. **Average** L45,000. **Credit** AmEx, DC, MC, V. **Map** I 3B.

Venice is a small pond, and new arrivals are rare events. But it's not just novelty that this sit-down wine bar ten minutes' walk from the station has going for it; value for money and dedication to the cause of good food and wine are the main attractions. The decor is upbeat *osteria*, the ambience young and friendly. Alongside Venetian stalwarts such as *spaghetti ai caporossoli* (with clams), chef Biba Candiani offers a range of succulent dishes with a southern Italian slant. At the end of the single dining room is a long wooden table groaning with bottles, which you choose from a reasonably priced list. In summer tables fill the *campiello* outside.

La Colonna   21

Cannaregio 5329, campiello del Pestrin (041 522 9641). Vaporetto Fondamente Nove. **Meals served** 12.30-2.30pm, 7.30-10pm Tue-Sun. **Closed** Jan, 3 wks Aug. **Average** L70,000. **Credit** AmEx, DC, MC, V. **Map** I 4B.

On the main route between Rialto and fondamenta Nuove, this restaurant deserves a mention as one of the few proper restaurants in Venice offering high-grade cuisine at no more than average prices.

The waiters are a multicultural bunch, but the cooking is solidly (though creatively) Venetian, with one or two meaty excursions. There are some light touches – a salad of *funghi porcini*, tiny prawns and wild salad greens, for example – alongside old favourites such as *seppie alla veneziana* (cuttlefish cooked in onion and wine). The ambience is softly lit and romantic; a line of backlit Murano glass fragments just below the ceiling beams gives the traditional decor an exotic twist.

Vini da Gigio   22

Cannaregio 3628A, fondamenta San Felice (041 528 5140/fax 041 522 8597). Vaporetto Ca' d'Oro. **Meals served** noon-2.30pm, 7.30-10.30pm Tue-Sun. **Closed** 3wks Jan-Feb, 3wks Aug-Sept. **Average** L60,000. **Credit** AmEx, DC, MC, V. **Map** I 3B.

It's no longer any secret that this is one of the best-value restaurants in Venice, so make sure you book. Gigio is strong on Venetian *antipasti* such as *baccalà mantecato* (creamed stockfish) or *sarde in saor* (marinated sardines), and difficult-to-find *secondi* such as *anguilla alla griglia* (grilled eel); there are also a number of good meat and game options. As the name suggests, wine is another forte – the *cantina* even runs to bottles from Australia and South Africa, and there is always a good by-the-glass selection. The only drawback is the excruciatingly slow service; allow at least two hours for a complete meal.

Succulent dishes at **La Colombina**.

Ganesh Ji

INDIAN TRADITIONAL OWEN

S.Polo 2426 Rio Marin
30125 Venezia tel. 041719804

CLOSED ON WEDNESDAY – AIR CONDITIONED
2 MINUTES FROM RAILWAY AND P.LE ROMA

San Polo & Santa Croce

Alla Madonna 23
*San Polo 594, calle della Madonna
(041 522 3824). Vaporetto Rialto or San
Silvestro.* **Meals served** noon-3pm, 7-10.30pm
Mon, Tue, Thur-Sun. **Closed** Jan, 2wks Aug.
Average L60,000. **Credit** AmEx, MC, V. **Map** I 3C.
This big, bustling fish *trattoria* with its friendly
service and fair prices has been piling in loyal locals
and clued-up tourists for generations. It's a minute's
walk from the Rialto bridge, and while the cooking
will win no prizes, it offers competent versions of old
Venetian favourites such as *anguilla fritta* (fried eel).
Bookings are not taken; you simply join the queue
outside, which moves pretty fast.

Antiche Carampane 24
*San Polo 1911, rio terà delle Carampane
(041 524 0165). Vaporetto San Silvestro.*
Meals served 12.30-2.30pm, 7.30-10pm Tue-Sat.
Closed 1wk Jan, Aug. **Average** L70,000.
Credit AmEx, DC, MC, V. **Map** I 3C.
This compact *trattoria* between campo San Polo and
San Cassiano could win the prize for the hardest-
to-find restaurant in Venice. The militantly local
approach is reinforced by a sign on the door reading 'tourist information – L5,000' – but it's a joke,
honest, and any guest who shows the slightest interest in traditional Venetian cuisine immediately
becomes one of the family. There are a few tables
outside, but the cosy atmosphere inside is even better. They are very strong on Adriatic fish dishes; the
fritto misto (mixed seafood fry-up) is unbeatable.

Alla Zucca 25
*Santa Croce 1762, ponte del Megio (041 524 1570).
Vaporetto San Stae.* **Meals served** 12.30-2.30pm,
7-10.30pm Mon-Sat. **Closed** 1wk Aug, 1 wk Dec.
Average L45,000. **Credit** AmEx, DC, MC, V.
Map I 2B.
This cheap and friendly *osteria* in the peaceful San
Giacomo del'Orio area tries hard to break away from
traditional Venetian cuisine. There is some meat
on the menu, but a strong emphasis on vegetables
(which feature in a few *secondi* as well as the more
obvious pasta dishes) will make Alla Zucca (at the
sign of the pumpkin) especially appealing to vegetarians. Women dining alone will also feel at home;
if any men work here, they're hidden in the kitchen.
The clientele is right on, the wine list is small but
perfectly formed. In summer, book ahead for one of
the three tables outside by a pretty canal bridge.

Da Fiore 26
*San Polo 2202, calle del Scaleter (041 721 308).
Vaporetto San Stae.* **Meals served** 12.30-2.30pm,
7.30-10.30pm Tue-Sat. **Closed** Christmas to mid-Jan,
Aug. **Average** L150,000. **Credit** AmEx, DC, MC, V.
Map I 2C.
Most local (and visiting) gourmets consider this
Michelin-star to be Venice's best restaurant. The
façade and the bar at the entrance hark back to

Fiore's *bacaro* origins; but the elegant, barge-like
dining room inside is in quite a different class.
Owner Maurizio Martin treats his guests – many of
whom are visiting celebrities or local bigshots – with
egalitarian courtesy. There's only a single window,
and the space can seem rather claustrophobic, but
focus on what's on the plate and it will pass. Raw
fish and seafood – a sort of Venetian sashimi – is
a key feature of the excellent *antipasti*; the pasta
dishes and *secondi* work creative variations on the
local tradition. There is also an exceptional selection
of regional cheeses – rare in Venice – and desserts.
You pays your money, certainly; but compared to
the hugely overrated Harry's Bar, this is a bargain.

Da Ignazio 27
*San Polo 2749, calle dei Saoneri (041 523 4852/
fax 041 244 8546). Vaporetto San Tomà.*
Meals served noon-3pm, 7-10pm Mon-Fri, Sun.
Closed 2wks Dec-Jan, 3wks July-Aug. **Average**
L60,000. **Credit** AmEx, DC, MC, V. **Map** I 2C.
Venetian families come to eat in this cosy *trattoria*
between campo San Polo and the Frari, attracted
by an excellent quality/price ratio. The cooking is
traditional Venetian: mixed seafood *antipasti* might
be followed by a good rendition of *risi e bisi* (risotto
with peas), bream with potatoes, and a decent
tiramisù. There is also the possible bonus of a table
in the pretty inner courtyard.

Dorsoduro

Ai Quatro Feri 28
*Dorsoduro 2754, calle lunga San Barnaba
(041 520 6978). Vaporetto Ca' Rezzonico.*
Meals served noon-2.30pm, 7.30-10.30pm,
Mon-Sat. **Closed** 1wk Jan, June. **Average** L50,000.
No credit cards. Map II 2B.
Although the Quatro Feri only opened in 1998, the
keen young owners have already carved out a niche
for themselves on the local dining scene. Classic
antipasti such as *sarde in saor* and *insalata di polpo*
(octopus salad) are followed by a range of creative
pasta dishes (try the *gnocchi di zucca con gamberoni
e amorini* – pumpkin gnocchi with king prawns and
turnip heads). The excellent desserts are all home-
made, and a good selection of local wines includes a
few more challenging vintages.

Da Sandro
See p164.

L'Incontro 29
*Dorsoduro 3062, rio terà Canal (041 522 2404).
Vaporetto Ca' Rezzonico.* **Meals served** 7.30-
10.30pm Tue; 12.30-2.30pm, 7.30-10.30pm Wed-Sun.
Closed Jan, 2wks Aug. **Average** L60,000.
Credit AmEx, DC, MC, V. **Map** II 2A.
Meaty restaurants are rare enough in Venice, but
L'Incontro is unique: it's run by a great Sardinian
chef who specialises in meat dishes from his
Mediterranean island such as *porceddu arrosto*
(roast suckling pig). Pasta provides relief from the

Eat, Drink, Shop

beast in creations such as gnocchi with pecorino cheese and *tagliolini* in a creamy rucola sauce. The steaks – especially the *tagliata di manzo* – are out of this world, and the cellar has some interesting Sardinian vintages. Grab a table on the sunny terrace in summer, or enjoy the cosy rustic interior in winter.

La Giudecca & San Giorgio

Ai Tre Scaini   30
Giudecca 53C, calle Michelangelo (041 522 4790/fax 041 277 5176). Vaporetto Zitelle.
Meals served 1-2.30pm, 6-9.30pm Mon-Wed, Fri-Sun; 1-2.30pm Thur. **Closed** 2wks Aug.
Average L45,000. **Credit** MC, V. **Map** II 4C.
Most cheaper restaurants on the Giudecca are pizzerias, but this friendly *trattoria* tucked down an alleyway just past the Redentore church does a good line in calorific working lunches. If you arrive after the noon-time rush, its a good place to relax over some no-frills home cooking. On Sundays they often take a culinary theme – such as goose – and build a whole menu around it.

Altanella   31
Giudecca 268, calle delle Erbe (041 522 7780). Vaporetto Sant'Eufemia or Redentore.
Meals served 12.30-2pm, 7.30-9pm Wed-Sun.
Closed 6 Jan-*carnevale*, 1wk Aug.
Average L70,000. **No credit cards. Map** II 2C.
The canalside terrace of this family-run *trattoria* on the Giudecca is one of the best places for an *al fresco* meal in Venice, and the service is both friendly and professional. The cuisine is typically Venetian; the *risotto di gò* (goby – a fish prized only around Venice and in the Black Sea) is good, as is the surprisingly light *frittura di pesce*. Go for the house white, which is as quaffable as any of the bottles on offer. It's cash only, but the prices are reasonable by Venetian standards. Altanella is a good place to bring that special person – but book ahead.

Harry's Dolci   32
Giudecca 773, fondamenta San Biagio (041 522 4844/fax 041 522 2322). Vaporetto Sant'Eufemia.
Meals served noon-3pm, 7-11pm Mon, Wed-Sun.
Closed Nov-Mar. **Average** L110,000.
Credit AmEx, DC, MC, V. **Map** II 1C.
Arrigo Cipriani's second Venetian stronghold, (his first is Harry's Bar, *see p166*) towards the western end of the Giudecca, is only open from April to October, when the weather allows diners to enjoy the huge terrace with stupendous views across the Giudecca Canal. The cuisine is supposedly lighter and more summery that on offer at Harry's Bar, but in practice many dishes are identical, and just as competently prepared. What changes is the price: the *cannelloni alla piemontese*, for example, cost L30,000 here, L69,000 at the mothership. A selection of seasonally changing fixed-price menus offers an even greater saving. Come prepared for mosquitoes on summer evenings.

Hotel Cipriani   33
Giudecca 10, off fondamenta San Giovanni (041 520 7744/fax 041 520 3930/info@hotelcipriani.it/ www.hotelcipriani.it). Vaporetto Zitelle.
Meals served noon-2.30pm, 8-10.30pm daily. **Closed** Nov-Mar. **Average** L160,000.
Credit AmEx, DC, MC, V. **Map** II 4C.
Sitting out on the Hotel Cipriani's terrace, overlooking the blue swimming pool (the only hotel pool in island Venice), with the campanile of San Marco in the distance, is an unforgettable experience. A private launch (complimentary for those who have booked a table) whisks clients over from San Marco. Chef Renato Picciolotto keeps the hotel's jet-set clientele happy with a range of dishes that are more generic Mediterranean than Venetian: green *tagliolini* with ham au gratin; broiled sea bass with olives, cherry tomatoes and oregano. A serious wine list carries a serious mark-up. To soften the final blow, come for the lunch buffet. The hotel has opened another restaurant, **Cip's Club**, on the Venice-facing *fondamenta*; but while the view across to San Marco is certainly impressive, the high-class-comfort-food cuisine is neither as impressive, nor much cheaper, than that on offer inside the hotel.

Mistrà   34
Giudecca 212A (041 522 0743). Vaporetto Redentore. **Meals served** noon-3.30pm Mon, noon-3.30pm, 7.30-10.30pm Wed-Sun. **Closed** Jan.
Average L50,000. **Credit** AmEx, DC, MC, V.
Map II 3C.
The unvisited southern side of the Giudecca is about as far as you can get from tourist Venice. Amidst a sprawl of boatyards stands a plain white building; an outside staircase leads up to this first-floor trattoria with spectacular views over the lagoon. Once patronised exclusively by local shipwrights and gondola makers, Mistrà has become a word-of-mouth success among local gourmets for its excellent fish menu and range of Ligurian specialities; game-based *secondi* can be sampled too, if ordered in advance.

Lido to Chioggia

Ostaria al Penzo
Chioggia, calle larga Bersaglio 526 (041 400 992). **Meals served** *Sept-May* 12.15-2.15pm Mon; 12.15-2.15pm, 7.15-10.15pm Wed-Sun. *June-Aug* 12.15-2.15pm, 7.15-10.15pm Mon, Wed-Sun. **Closed** 2wks Dec-Jan. **Average** L50,000.
No credit cards.
Chioggia is all about fish and there is no shortage of restaurants offering marine fare, generally at prices well below anything you'll find across the water in Venice. In this small and friendly family-run restaurant, Fabrizio, the cook, is from the Marche and has an original approach to otherwise traditional lagoon dishes. The *tagliolini al Fabrizio*, sepia-black egg-pasta with mussels and scampi in a fresh tomato sauce, are definitely worth trying. He also does a good *fritto misto*.

The Lagoon

Al Gatto Nero   35

*Burano, fondamenta della Giudecca 88 (041
730 120/fax 041 735 570/www.gattonero.com).
Vaporetto 12 to Burano.* **Meals served** noon-3pm,
7-9pm Tue-Sun. **Closed** 1wk Jan, Nov.
Average L65,000. **Credit** AmEx, DC, MC, V.
Map Burano.

Most guidebooks point visitors to the lace-making
island of Burano towards the more famous Da
Romano or Il Pescatore-Da Paolo, both in the
brightly painted main square. But a better-value
meal is to be had by wandering past the souvenir
stalls, through the backstreets, to this friendly
trattoria across a canal from the fish market. It's a
charming, photogenic place for an *al fresco* lunch;
the service is attentive, and there's a wonderfully
creamy *risotto di pesce*.

Busa alla Torre   36

*Murano, campo Santo Stefano 3 (041 739 662).
Vaporetto Faro.* **Meals served** noon-3.30pm daily.
Average L65,000. **Credit** AmEx, DC, MC, V.
Map Murano.

This is Murano's ultimate gastronomic stop-off, and
a perfect place for regaining your strength after a
bout of resisting the hard sell at the island's many
glass workshops. In summer – which, when the elements oblige, can stretch from March to November
– tables spill out into a pretty square opposite the
church of San Pietro Martire. The service is deft and
professional; the cuisine is reliable, no-frills seafood
cooking; the excellent *primi* go from the classic
spaghetti alla busara (with anchovies and onions) to
homemade *ravioli di pesce*. The jovial owner, Lele,
is a giant of a man, and a real character. Note the
lunch-only opening.

Locanda Cipriani

*Torcello, piazza Santa Fosca 29 (041 730 150/
fax 041 735 433/booking@locandacipriani.com/
www.locandacipriani.com). Vaporetto 12 to Torcello.*
Closed Jan. **Average** L110,000. **Credit** AmEx,
DC, MC, V.

There is a lot to like about the high-class Locanda
Cipriani (only distantly – and acrimoniously – related to Arrigo Cipriani of Harry's Bar fame, *see p166*),
which was a favourite haunt of Ernest Hemingway.
The setting, just off Torcello's pretty main square, is
idyllic; tables spread over a large vine-shaded terrace
in summer. And although there is nothing remotely
adventurous about the cuisine, it's good in a professional, old-fashioned way; and so are the waiters.
Specialities such as *risotto alla Torcellana* (with seasonal vegetables) or *filetti di Sanpietro alla Carlina*
(John Dory fillets with capers and tomatoes) are done
with reliable competence, and the desserts – including a calorific giant meringue – are tasty treats for
rich kids. If you want to arrive in style, the Locanda
provides a boat service from San Marco to Torcello
for L30,000 per person return (ring to book). This is
a great place to come if someone else is paying.

What, more Murano glass? Recoup with Lele at the **Busa alla Torre**.

Eat, Drink, Shop

Pizzerie

Like all major Italian cities, Venice has its fair share of pizza joints. But frankly, the standard here is not desperately high. That said, prices in *pizzerie* remain low – around L20,000 a head, including wine – which make them a good standby for a carbohydrate-and-protein injection between more expensive restaurant meals. In the rest of Italy, *pizzerie* are generally open only in the evening; tourist demand, though, means that almost all Venetian pizza emporia serve the doughy discs at lunch too. Average prices cover one pizza, a beer, service and cover charge.

Al Nono Risorto   37
Santa Croce 2337, calle della Regina (041 524 1169). Vaporetto San Stae. **Meals served** noon-2.30pm, 7-11pm Mon, Tue, Fri-Sun; 7-11pm Thur. **Closed** 2 wks Jan. **Average** L25,000. **No credit cards. Map** I 3C.
There's plenty of attitude in this lively spot. If you want to hang out over a *pizza margherita* in a shady garden with Venice's bright young 30-somethings, this is the place to come. There's traditional *trattoria* fare as well as pizzas.

Da Crecola   38
Santa Croce 1459, campo del Piovan (041 524 1496). Vaporetto Riva di Biasio. **Meals served** *Apr-Nov* noon-3pm, 6-10pm Mon, Wed-Sun. *Dec-Mar* noon-3pm, 6-10pm Mon, Wed-Sun. **Average** L20,000. **Credit** MC, V. **Map** I 2B.
Da Crecola is best in summer, when there are seats outside in the pretty canalside *campiello*. There are some creative toppings, especially vegetarian, but expect slow service.

La Perla   39
Cannaregio 4615, rio terà dei Franceschi (041 528 5175). Vaporetto Ca' d'Oro. **Meals served** noon-2pm, 7-9.45pm Tue-Sun. **Closed** Aug. **Average** L25,000. **Credit** AmEx, MC, V. **Map** I 4B.
Many locals reckon that La Perla makes the best pizza in town; the doughy base comes garnished with a variety of mix-and-match toppings. The ambience is of the all-packed-in-together variety, with tablefuls of students sawing away at the pizzas and knocking back some good draught beer.

Trattoria dai Tosi
See *p151*.

International

The locals are decidedly conservative when it comes to exploring foreign food; and few tourists come to Venice to eat Chinese. Until a few years ago, there were virtually no international restaurants in the city; the situation is a little better now, though we're barely into double figures.

Frary's   40
San Polo 2559, fondamenta dei Frari (041 720 050/www.ristorantearabofrarys.it). Vaporetto San Tomà. **Meals served** noon-3.30pm, 6.30-11.30pm Mon, Wed-Sun; noon-3pm Tue. **Average** L30,000. **Credit** AmEx, DC, MC, V. **Map** II 2A.
A reasonably priced, friendly restaurant specialising in Arab cuisine, though there are some Greek dishes as well. Couscous comes in two versions – with mutton or vegetarian; the *mansaf* (rice with chicken and yoghurt) is good, as are the tzaziki and taramasalata.

Gam-Gam   41
Cannaregio 1122, sottoportego del Ghetto Vechio (041 715 284/gamgam@jewishvenice.org/ www.jewishvenice.org). Vaporetto Guglie. **Meals served** noon-10pm Mon-Thur, Sun; noon-sunset Fri. **Closed** Passover. **Average** L40,000. **No credit cards. Map** I 2B.
The only kosher restaurant in Venice, Gam-Gam is right at the entrance of the ancient Ghetto, with a terrace overlooking the Cannaregio canal. The food mixes influences from the Israeli, Italian-Jewish and Ashkenazi traditions, with dishes such as *latkes* and *gefillte fisch* alongside a few pan-Italian classics. It's not particularly cheap.

Sahara   42
Cannaregio 2519, fondamenta della Misericordia (041 721 077/fax 041 715 977). Vaporetto San Marcuola or Orto. **Meals served** *Apr-Oct* 7pm-2am daily. *Dec-Mar* noon-3pm, 7pm-2am daily. *Nov* 7pm-2am Mon, Fri-Sun. **Average** L45,000. **Credit** MC, V. **Map** I 3B.
If you want to be really different, head for this Syrian-Egyptian restaurant on Cannaregio's trendiest *fondamenta*, where clients cluster around outside tables on fine summer evenings. The friendly owner, Mouaffak, conjures up a range of unrefined but tasty couscous-and-vegetable dishes, shawarma kebabs and the usual sticky desserts. Late opening and decent prices make this one of Venice's best exotic options, though the service can be a little on the slow side. On Friday and Saturday evenings there is a belly dancer.

Shri Ganesh   43
San Polo 2426, ponte del Cristo (041 719 804). Vaporetto Riva di Biasio. **Meals served** *May-Oct* 12.30-2pm, 7-11pm daily. *Nov-Mar* 12.30-2pm, 7-11pm Mon, Tue, Thur-Sun. **Average** L45,000. **Credit** MC, V. **Map** I 2C.
The only Indian restaurant in Venice, with real Indian chefs in the kitchen. For old Bombay hands – or even visiting Londoners – the food will seem far from exciting, but on a good night it's not at all bad. And Shri Ganesh has one thing your local Indian is certain to lack: a romantic, candle-lit terrace overlooking a Venetian canal.

Bacari & Snacks

Like wine bars only different, *bacari* are a way of life in Venice.

The *bacaro* is Venice's wine-only equivalent of the British pub. With their blackened beams and rickety wooden tables, *bacari* (accent on the first syllable) are usually hidden down back streets or in quiet *campielli*. Here locals crowd the bar, swiftly downing a glass of wine (*un'ombra*) between work and home, and taking the edge off their appetite with one of the *cicheti* (*tapas*-like snacks) that line the counter.

In some *bacari*, long wooden tables at the back of the shop or in a side room are laid on for those looking for something more substantial: a pasta dish or a risotto, a plate of *sopressa* (rustic salami) and polenta, or in those that have a full kitchen, a wide selection of *secondi*. Such places are the saving grace of the city's tourist-oriented eating-out scene and the guardians of the endangered species that is traditional Venetian cuisine.

Bacari themselves, though, are by no means endangered. In a city not known for its good-value eats, the *bacaro* formula appeals to locals,

students and budget-conscious tourists alike, and in recent years a spate of new ones have opened, most with decor so traditional they look as if they've been around for centuries.

Once you've taken up your position at the bar and ordered drinks, you can do the *cicheti* thing yourself. You'll be expected to keep tabs on how many you've consumed – though you can expect the barman to have kept a fairly accurate count. Pay for drinks and snacks together at the end. It is very rare for such salt-of-the-earth *osterie* to accept credit cards, and many close early in the evening.

Sometimes the line between *bacaro* and restaurant is difficult to draw. In the *bacari* listed, bar counter snacks and drinks play a predominent role; for places where sit-down meals are the main thing, *see chapter* **Restaurants**. Borderline cases are cross-referenced.

Most *bacari* have a limited selection of local wines from the Veneto and Friuli regions. A few – such as **Do Mori** (*see p164*), **All'Aciugheta** (*see p160*) and **Bancogiro** (*see 163*) – have an above-average selection of fine wines, but only **Vino Vino** (*see p160*) and **La Mascareta** (*see p160*) have the range and depth of choice that allows them to call themselves 'wine bars' (an English term that has a faintly pretentious ring to it in Italian).

The numbers after names refer to green dots on the maps at the back of this guide.

Chips are down at **Alla Patatina**. See p162.

San Marco

Al Bacareto
See p147.

Osteria alla Botte   **1**
San Marco 5482, campo San Bartolomeo (041 520 9775). Vaporetto Rialto. **Open** 10am-3pm, 5-11pm Mon, Tue, Fri, Sat; 10am-3pm Wed, Sun. **Closed** July. **No credit cards. Map** I 4C.
Campo San Bartolomeo is Venice's liveliest evening meeting place; after seeing and being seen, many young Venetians then head off to the nearby Botte for a quick *ombra*. At the tiny, barrel-like bar (*una botte* is a barrel) clients jostle for a glass of wine, a seafood *cicheto* or a sandwich made with a slice from the immense mortadella on the counter. There's a back room where simple meals (*lasagna al forno, fegato all veneziana*) are served. It can get extremely packed late at night.

Vino Vino 2

San Marco 2007A, calle del Cafetier (041 523 7027).
Vaporetto Vallaresso or Santa Maria del Giglio.
Open 10.30am-midnight Mon, Wed-Fri, Sun; 10.30am-
1am Sat. **Credit** AmEx, DC, MC, V. **Map** II 3A.
Overlooking a canal near poor old La Fenice, Vino
Vino was the city's first authentic wine bar. You can
sample vintages from as far afield as Australia,
California and Spain, as well as local crus from the
Veneto and Friuli regions. Best to stick to the wines
(including a good selection *a mescita* – by the glass)
and the bar snacks, rather than the food served in
the adjoining dining room, where the culinary quality does not match the establishment's oenological
standards. But the atmosphere is always lively and
the barmen are fun and friendly.

Castello

All'Aciugheta 3

*Castello 4357, campo Santi Filippo e Giacomo (041
522 4292). Vaporetto San Zaccaria.* **Open** noon-
10.30pm daily. **No credit cards. Map** III 1B.
It looks like a real tourist-trap pizzeria from the
outside – we're only two minutes from piazza San
Marco, after all – but muscle your way through to
the bar and you'll see the other face of the 'little
anchovy': a bar packed with locals sampling some
excellent wines, and fuelling up on a selection of
cicheti. These include *polpete* (meatballs), filled
peppers, *crostini* (open sandwiches) with *lardo*
(fatty ham) or gorgonzola, and the trademark
pizzette (mini-pizzas) with anchovies. Just remember: don't sit down.

Alle Alpi (Da Dante) 4

Castello 2877, corte Nova (041 528 5163).
Vaporetto Celestia or San Zaccaria. **Open** 8am-9pm
Mon-Sat. **Closed** 1wk Aug. **No credit cards.**
Map III 2A.

Tourists? Here? If you want to slum it with the locals
in a place that is as Venetian as they come, head for
this out-of-the-way *bacaro* in the depths of Castello,
on the way to San Francesco della Vigna. Dante's
wife serves up specialities such as *bovoleti* – tiny
snails in garlic – and delicious baby octopus.

Al Mascaron

See p149.

Al Portego 5

Castello 6015, calle Malvasia (041 522 9038).
Vaporetto Rialto. **Open** 10am-3pm, 5-9.30pm
Mon-Fri; 10am-3pm Sat. **Closed** 2wks Feb; Aug.
No credit cards. Map I 4C.
Ask most Venetians where the Portego is and they'll
say they've never heard of it, as this rustic *osteria* is
better known by its two former names, Ciro's and
Da Alberto. The ambience smacks of mountain
chalet, with a big barrel of wine resting on the bar.
The simple but honest cuisine includes a good range
of *cicheti* and different pasta dishes and risottos
served up each day. Eat at the bar, or queue for one
of the tiny tables, as no reservations are taken.

Mascareta 6

*Castello 5183, calle lunga Santa Maria Formosa
5183 (041 523 0744). Vaporetto Rialto.* **Open** 6pm-
1am Mon-Sat. **Closed** Dec-mid Jan. **No credit
cards. Map** III 1A.
Originally set up by the Mascaron guys (*see p149*),
the Mascareta is now under new and, it has to be
said, rather frostier management. Still, the ambience
continues to be refined and pleasurable: this is a
serious wine bar lined with wooden shelves, with
platters of cheese, or salami, or salad, plus a dessert
or two, to soak up the alcohol. Wines by the glass
are more expensive than at your average *bacaro*, but
with star crus like Ascewi sauvignon from Friuli,
the extra expense is more than justified.

Un giro di ombre

The Venetian dialect word for a glass of wine
is *un'ombra* (literally, a shade) – perhaps
because wine was originally stored in any
shady patch in a city where digging a cellar is
out of the question. Whatever the etymology,
if a local says *andemo par ombra* or, better
still, invites you to *fare un giro di ombre*, gird
up your liver: you're in for the Venetian
version of a pub crawl, and it could be heavy
going. Venetians are among the few serious
drinkers left in Italy, and with *un'ombra*
costing around L1,000 a glass, they can
afford to indulge their oenological passions.
  The barman will immediately ask if you want
an *ombra di rosso* (red) or an *ombra di bianco*
(white); locals often use the diminutive term

ombreta. The wine will be served either from
a two-litre bottle or straight from a huge
demijohn on the counter. It will inevitably
come from a local producer in the Veneto
region, and will probably be a **Tocai**, a
Verduzzo or a **Sauvignon**, if white, and a
Cabernet Franc, **Raboso** or **Cabernet
Sauvignon** if red.
  In October and November most bars have a
jug of a cloudy-looking brew called **Torbolino**
on the counter. This is the new wine, straight
from the grape harvest, which is still in the
process of fermenting. It has a delicious,
sweetish flavour, is great with chestnuts
and changes flavour each day as it becomes
more alcoholic.

Eat, Drink, Shop

Cow teat and
oesophagus at
All'Arco. *See p162.*

Cannaregio

Al Bacco
See p151.

Alla Fontana 7
Cannaregio 1102, fondamenta Cannaregio (041 715 077). Vaporetto Ponte delle Guglie. **Open** 8.30am-2.30pm, 6-10pm Tue-Sat; 6-10pm Sun. **Closed** Aug. **No credit cards. Map** I 2B.
It's only two minutes from the station, but walking into this *bacaro* is like stepping back in time. Wine is stored in ancient two-litre bottles, and Bruno, the owner, offers some rustic wines from the Piave (Hemingway country) that you won't find anywhere else in Venice. After years of offering little more than cheese, salami and bread, the Fountain has begun to offer some filling, cheap trattoria dishes: tagliatelle with eel, *spezzatino* (braised strips of veal) with polenta, vegetable gratin. In summer, tables line the busy canal pavement outside.

Alla Frasca
See p151.

Anice Stellato
See p152.

Bentigodi 8
Cannaregio 1423, Calesele (041 716 269). Vaporetto San Marcuola. **Open** 11am-3pm, 6pm-midnight Mon-Sat. **Closed** Jan. **No credit cards. Map** I 2B.
With its blackened beams and heavy wooden tables, Bentigodi is always full of locals, crowding around the long marble bar, engaged in passionate discus-

sions on food, sport or politics. In the kitchen they begin with the basic traditions of Venetian cuisine, then add surprising innovations: beef *in saor* rather than the statutory sardines, *penne* with swordfish and aubergines, or an irresistible chocolate cake.

Ca D'Oro – Alla Vedova 9
Cannaregio 3912, ramo Ca' d'Oro (041 528 5324). Vaporetto Ca' d'Oro. **Open** 11.30am-2.30pm, 6.30-11pm Mon-Wed, Fri, Sat; 6.30-11pm Sun. **Closed** Aug. **No credit cards. Map** I 3B.
The official name of this hostelry, which has been in the same family for over 120 years, alludes to its proximity to the Ca' d'Oro; but most Venetians know it as *Alla Vedova* – the Widow's Place. The widow has now, alas, joined her *marito*, but her spirit marches on in the traditional decor and intimate, romantic atmosphere of what is probably the most perfectly preserved *bacaro* in the city. Tourists head for the tables (which can and should be booked), where the food is excellent, though not cheap – while locals stay at the bar eating fried artichokes, or the best *polpete* (spicy meatballs) in Venice.

Cantina Vecia Carbonera 10
Cannaregio 2329, rio terà Maddalena, ponte Sant'Antonio (041 710 376). Vaporetto San Marcuola. **Open** *Oct-May* 4pm-midnight Thur, Fri; 11.30am-midnight Sat, Sun. *June-Sept* 11am-9pm daily. **No credit cards. Map** I 3B.
It is difficult to imagine that this incredibly authentic looking *bacaro* was, until a few years ago, a shop selling fuel and household items. It has been painstakingly renovated, and the young owners are now running a fun bar with good local wine and basic snacks (*crostini* with gorgonzola and radicchio,

Lagoon picnics

Venice is not the greatest city for takeaways or picnics, simply because there is almost nowhere to sit down and consume those *tramezzini*. There are virtually no parks or bench-filled squares, and visitors sitting down on narrow bridges to eat lunch risk getting trampled by speeding locals. If the weather's really too nice, or funds are too low, to make a meal of it, opt for one of the following carefully selected spots. Some even have Grand Canal views.

Campo San Simeon Profeta
Map I 1-2B.
Right on the Grand Canal and handy for the station; there are even a few benches.

Campo San Giacomo dell'Orio
Map I 2C.
Great neigbourhood square with benches under the plane trees.

Parco Savorgnan
Map I 1-2B.

Few people know about this unassuming little park around the corner from the souvenir hell of Lista di Spagna.

Fondamenta Nuove, near the Gesuiti church
Map I 4B.
There are a few benches at the western end of Venice's northern promenade, with views across to San Michele and Murano.

Campo San Vio
Map II 3B.
The best of all the Grand Canal picnic spots, near the Peggy Guggenheim Collection, with one or two highly sought-after benches from which to contemplate the bobbing traffic.

Punta della Dogana
Map II 4B.
For panoramic value, it's difficult to beat the steps of the Dogana (customs house); the view stretches from the Giudecca via San Giorgio to piazza San Marco.

---

ham rolls) that is fast establishing a reputation as a hot nightspot. On Sunday evenings between October and May there is often a free concert of anything from jazz to flamenco. (*See also p210.*)

Da Alberto
See p152.

Dalla Marisa
See p153.

La Colombina
See p153.

San Polo & Santa Croce

Ai Postali   11
Santa Croce 821, fondamenta Rio Marin (041 715 156). Vaporetto Riva di Biasio or San Tomà. **Open** 11am-3pm, 7pm-2am Mon-Sat. **No credit cards**. **Map** I 2C.
Just across the bridge and down a narrow canal from the train station, Ai Postali is a funky, modern *bacaro*, with a right-on clientele. In summer there are tables outside along the bank of the canal. You may want to explore their good selection of whiskies and grappas. (*See also p213.*)

Al Diavolo e l'Acqua Santa   12
San Polo 561B, calle della Madonna (041 277 0307). Vaporetto Rialto. **Open** 10am-3pm, 6-10pm Mon, Wed-Sun. **Credit** AmEx, DC, MC, V. **Map** I 3C.

The 'devil and the holy water' is spanking new, but it pulls off the usual Venetian trick of looking time-worn. There's range of seafood and meat *cicheti* at the bar, with more substantial pasta-and-*secondo* meals served at the cramped tables. Service can be offhand, but for a quick, competent Venetian meal at a reasonable (though not rock-bottom) price, this is a good Rialto standby. For solitary drinkers, there is a good selection of wines by the glass.

Alla Patatina (Al Ponte)   13
San Polo 2741, ponte San Polo (041 523 7238). Vaporetto San Tomà. **Open** 9.30am-2.30pm, 4.30-9pm Mon-Fri; 9.30am-2.30pm Sat. **Closed** 2wks Aug. **Credit** AmEx, DC, MC, V. **Map** I 2C.
A favourite student haunt, primarily because of the cheap bar-counter eats. Though officially called Al Ponte, this pine-tabled hostelry is known to all and sundry as *Alla Patatina*, a moniker that will become instantly clear when you see the huge tray of chunky potato chips, fried with rosemary, on the bar. If you perch and snack, the prices are rock-bottom (those potatoes have seen more than one student through a financial crisis); but the sit-down fare – *spaghetti con le vongole*, fried cuttlefish, etc – is reasonably priced, too. Proper meals are served only at lunch; in the true *bacaro* tradition, they shut up shop by nine.

All'Arco   14
San Polo 436, calle dell'Ochialer (041 520 5666). Vaporetto San Silvestro or Rialto. **Open** 8am-3pm, Mon-Sat. **Closed** 2wks Aug. **No credit cards**. **Map** I 3C.

Campo Bandiera e Moro

Map III 2B.

One of the nearest feasible picnic spots to San Marco; very local, with kids playing football and crumbling Gothic *palazzi*.

Giardini Pubblici

Map III 3-4C.

Only a ten-minute vaporetto-hop from San Marco, Venice's only proper park has swings and benches and real live *bambini*. There's more green – and an even more local feel – further along in Sant'Elena.

Stocking up

For wine, either pop into one of the *bacari* that also sell bottles, or search out one of the *Vinaria Nave de Oro* shops, which sell excellent quality wine from demijohns and will usually provide a plastic bottle for free (*see p180*). *Alimentari* (grocers) and *salumerie* (delicatessens) sell prosciutto (ham), salami, cheese and olives, and most will be prepared to put them inside a *panino* (bread roll) for

you. Alternatively, the following outlets are good places to pick up ready-made supplies for your lagoon-side picnic.

Cip Ciap

Castello 5799, calle del Mondo Novo (041 523 6621). Vaporetto Rialto. **Open** 9am-9pm Mon, Wed-Sun. **No credit cards. Map** III 1A.

The one exception to the Venetian rule of execrable takeaway pizza, this excellent outlet is situated just before the bridge over to campo Santa Maria Formosa.

Rosticceria San Bartolomeo

San Marco 5424, calle della Bissa (041 277 0043). Vaporetto Rialto. **Open** Apr-Oct 9.30am-9.30pm daily. *Nov-Mar* 9.30am-9.30pm Tue-Sun. **Credit** AmEx, DC, MC, V. **Map** II 4A.

Has a mouth-watering display of everything from roast beef to *fritto misto* (seafood fry-up), *baccalà* and a magnificent *mozzarella in carrozza* (mozzarella cheese and an anchovy between two slices of fried bread).

If you're anywhere near the Rialto markets, don't miss this tiny *bacaro* in a narrow lane off ruga Vecchia, which is one of Venice's most authentic. There are a few tables outside in summer, but do the local thing: perch at the bar, and sample owner Francesco's great *cicheti*, which include (mad cows permitting) difficult-to-find traditional meaty titbits like *tetina* (cow teat) and *rumegal* (oesophagus, if you must know). Fried fish, mozzarella or vegetables are a recent innovation. For the time being, it's open only at lunch; Francesco got bored with working all day.

Bancogiro   15

San Polo 122, campo San Giacomo di Rialto (041 523 2061). Vaporetto Rialto. **Open** 10.30am-3pm, 6.30pm-midnight Tue-Sat; 10.30am-3pm Sun. **No credit cards. Map** I 3C.

Three cheers for Andrea. The bearded giant who was formerly half of Bentigodi (*see p161*) has gone it alone in this groundbreaking modern *osteria*, which opened in August 2000. The location is splendid: the main entrance gives on to the Rialto square of San Giacometto, while the back door gives access to a prime bit of Grand Canal frontage that until two years ago was open only to market traders. Downstairs, Andrea dispenses excellent wines to an appreciative crowd of locals; above, at a few well-spaced tables under the brick ceiling vaults, a decidedly creative menu is served. Grilled radicchio with gorgonzola, spicy raw diced meat, bean soups and vaguely oriental desserts; not every dish lives up to

its ambition, but it's certainly a change from *bacalà mantecato* – and it's cheap, too, at around L40,000 a head for a full meal.

Da Lele   16

Santa Croce 183, campo dei Tolentini (no phone). Vaporetto Piazzale Roma. **Open** 6am-2pm, 4.30-8pm Mon-Fri; 6am-2pm Sat. **No credit cards. Map** I 1C.

There are plenty of bars around the bus station at piazzale Roma, but most of them are either sleazy or overpriced. Gabriele's (Lele's) place is the first authentic *osteria* for those arriving in Venice – or the last for those leaving. It's so small in here there isn't even room for a phone – but there are always freshly made, fat *panini* and *tramezzini*, and a fine selection of local wines from Piave, Lison and Valdobbiadene, which those who suffer from claustrophobia should consume outside by the canal.

Da Pinto   17

San Polo 367, campo delle Becarie (041 522 4599). Vaporetto Rialto. **Open** 7.30am-7pm Tue-Sun. **Closed** 1wk July. **Credit** AmEx, DC, MC, V. **Map** I 3C.

Open from the early hours of the morning, this market *bacaro* doubles as a tourist trat; but it's still good (market traders wouldn't pile in there if it wasn't), busy and local. Don't be shy about pushing to the bar: it's Who Dares Wins in here. The owner, Gianni, has a fine selection of local wines (check out the Verduzzo and prosecco), and the proximity of the fish market ensures that the seafood *cicheti* are unbeatable, especially the grilled baby squid.

Eat, Drink, Shop

Bancogiro's location is splendid. See p163.

Ai Quatro Feri
See p155.

Ai Vini Padovani　　　　　20
Dorsoduro 1280, calle dei Cerchieri (041 523 6370).
Vaporetto Ca' Rezzonico. **Open** 10am-8pm Mon-Fri.
Closed Aug. **No credit cards. Map** II 2B.
A difficult place to find, in a quiet calle between the
Accademia and San Barnaba. This used to be run
by a formidable ancient lady, before being closed for
a long period. But it escaped the dreaded kiss of fast
food, and has been restored to its former glory by
two young guys who have given it a second name:
Dai Fioi – the lads' place. They close early in the
evening, but this is a good place for a quick lunch of
cotechino salami and polenta.

Al Bottegon　　　　　21
Dorsoduro 992, fondamenta Nani (041 523 0034).
Vaporetto Zattere. **Open** 8am-2.30pm, 3.30-9.30pm
Mon-Sat; 8am-2.30pm Sun. **Closed** 2wks Aug.
No credit cards. Map II 2B.
Set on the pretty San Trovaso canal, the Bottegon is
an institution among Venetian bohemians and
tuned-in expatriates. It boasts one of the city's best-
stocked wine cellars, and doubles as a takeaway
enoteca. Three generations of the Gastaldi family
work here, filling glasses, carting cases of wine, and
preparing huge *panini* with mortadella or more delicate *crostini* with, for example, egg, cress and sun-
dried tomato paste. Great for lunch, and great, too,
in the early evening, when the action spills out on to
the canalside *fondamenta*.

Al Pantalon　　　　　22
Dorsoduro 3958, calle del Scaleter (041 710 849).
Vaporetto San Tomà. **Open** 10am-3pm, 5-11pm
Mon-Sat. **Closed** 3wks Aug. **Credit** AmEx, DC, MC,
V. **Map** II 2A.
Students pile into this lively *bacaro* near the university, which lays on a good range of *cicheti*, including *olive ascolane* (like Scotch eggs except with
olives inside) and *crostini* with *bacalà mantecato*.
More substantial meals, firmly in the local tradition,
can be ordered from a sitting position. Graduation
parties – which tend to get pretty wild in Venice –
are a regular feature.

Da Sandro　　　　　23
*Dorsoduro 2753A, calle lunga San Barnaba (041
523 0531). Vaporetto Ca' Rezzonico.* **Open** 9am-
3pm, 6-11pm Tue-Sat. **Closed** Aug. **Credit** AmEx,
DC, MC, V. **Map** II 2B.
Once one of the fishy herd, Sandro has gone out on
a limb in his new, cramped but friendly *bacaro*. It's
meat or nothing here – well, nothing apart from *baccalà* (cod), which the locals don't classify as fish. At
the counter, grab a *polpeta* (meatball) or a *crostino
di baccalà*; for something more substantial, sit down
at a table and order from a range of pasta dishes –
many with vegetables – followed by braised meat
or rabbit casserole.

Do Mori　　　　　18
San Polo 429, calle dei Do Mori (041 522 5401).
Vaporetto Rialto. **Open** 8.30am-9pm Mon-Sat.
Closed 1wk July, 2wks Aug. **No credit cards.**
Map I 3C.
The Do Mori – in a narrow lane in Rialto market
territory – claims to be the oldest *bacaro* in Venice,
and it certainly looks it. The management changed
recently, but little else has: batteries of copper pans
still hang from the ceiling, and at peak times the
narrow bar is a heaving mass of bodies, all lunging
for the excellent *tramezzini* and the tremendous
selection of fine wines. But don't point to a label at
random, as prices can sometimes be in the
connoisseur bracket. You won't go far wrong if you
stick to a glass of their classic *spento – prosecco*
minus the bubbles.

Ruga Rialto　　　　　19
San Polo 692, calle del Sturion (041 521 1243).
Vaporetto San Silvestro. **Open** 10am-3.30pm, 6pm-
midnight Tue-Sun. **Credit** DC, MC, V.
Map I 3C.
Just off the busy Rialto drag of Ruga Vecchia, in
calle Sturion, an unassuming door gives on to a
long bar lined with tempting *cicheti*. Go along to
the end and a second room opens up, all wood and
mirrors; beyond this is a third even larger space,
bedecked with Venezia Calcio football team flags.
Good value pasta (especially the *bigoli in salsa*) and
risotto dishes change each day, making this an
excellent option for a quick, cheap lunch. The
waiters are young and friendly.

Eat, Drink, Shop

Cafés & Bars

Venetian café culture is nothing if not catholic, embracing the gamut from Guinness and darts to *frittelle* and *cappuccino*.

Venice's relationship with coffee is a long and serious one. The city's first *bottega del caffè* opened in 1683. By the late 18th century as many as 24 coffee shops graced piazza San Marco alone. San Marco continues to function as the city's coffee-sipping drawing room, with two landmark cafés staring each other out across the square: the **Caffè Florian** and the **Gran Caffè Quadri**, both finely preserved examples of 19th-century café culture.

But there's a cosier side to Venetian bar-going too, in the friendly, pastry-perfumed local *caffè-pasticcerie* that abound in each neighbourhood: hard to beat for breakfast.

Or, for a complete change in tone, there's the original **Harry's Bar**, a temple to the American cocktail culture of the 1930s and '40s.

San Marco

(*See also* **Marchini** *p171*, **Rosa Salva** *p171*, **Le Café** *p169*.)

Bar all'Angolo
San Marco 3464, campo Santo Stefano (041 522 0710). Vaporetto Sant'Angelo. **Open** *June-Oct* 6.30am-midnight Mon-Fri, Sun. *Nov-May* 6.30am-9.30pm Mon-Fri, Sun. **No credit cards.** **Map** II 3B.
If you are lucky enough to grab a table outside, this is a great place to enjoy a *caffè* or spritz and watch the Venetians saunter through campo Santo Stefano. Staff are friendly and eager to please; the *tramezzini* (sandwiches) and *panini* (rolls) are tasty.

Bar al Teatro
San Marco 1916, campo San Fantin (041 522 1052). Vaporetto Sant'Angelo. **Open** *Mar-Oct* 7.30am-midnight daily. *Nov-Feb* 7.30am-midnight Tue-Sun. **Credit** MC, V. **Map** II 3A.
Before La Fenice opera house burned down, this was filled with opera-goers every night, but the Teatro remains a Venice institution. As well as serving up drinks and fat *tramezzini* at the bar, it doubles as a newsagent's and tobacco shop – and is one of the few places where desperate smokers can find cigarettes late in the evening and on Sundays.

Caffè Florian
San Marco 56/59, piazza San Marco (041 520 6541/ www.caffeflorian.com). Vaporetto Vallaresso. **Open** *May-Oct* 10am-midnight daily. *Nov-Apr* 10am-midnight Mon, Tue, Thur-Sun. **Credit** AmEx, DC, MC, V. **Map** II 4A.

Caffè Florian: mirrored and stuccoed.

This mirrored, stuccoed and frescoed jewel of a café was founded by a certain Floriano Francesconi in 1720 as 'Venezia Trionfante'. Its present appearance – with dozens of intimate wooden séparés dates from a 1859 rehaul. Rousseau, Goethe and Byron hung out here – the last in sympathy, no doubt, with those loyal Venetians who boycotted the Quadri across the square, as that was where the Austrian officers used to meet. These days, having a drink at Florian is not so much a political statement as a bank statement – especially if you sit at one of the outside tables when the resident orchestra is playing, when nothing – not even a humble *caffè* – comes in at less than L10,000.

Caffè Lavena

San Marco 133, piazza San Marco (041 522 4070/ www.venetia.it/lavena). Vaporetto Vallaresso. **Open** *Apr-Oct* 9.30am-12.30am daily. *Nov-Mar* 9.30am-10.30pm Mon, Wed-Sun. **Credit** AmEx, DC, MC, V. **Map** II 4A.

Though less well-known than Florian and Quadri, the Lavena has equally good historical credentials: it was founded in 1750 as the 'Ungheria'. It is the favourite piazza bar of many Venetians, partly because there are fewer tourists and prices are slightly lower, but mainly for the coffee, which they rate as the best in the city.

Devil's Forest

San Marco 5185, calle degli Stagneri (041 520 0623/www.devilsforest.com). Vaporetto Rialto. **Open** 8am-12.30am daily. **No credit cards**. **Map** II 4A.

Just by the Rialto bridge, this pub draws a lively, young crowd attracted by the cheap drinks, snacks and pizzas – as well as those two quintessentially Venetian institutions, draught Guinness and a dartboard.

Gran Caffè Quadri

San Marco 120, piazza San Marco (041 522 2105/www.venetia.it/quadri). Vaporetto Vallaresso. **Open** 9am-midnight daily. **Closed** Mon in Oct-Mar. **Credit** AmEx, DC, MC, V. **Map** II 4A.

Though it opened more than half a century after its rival on the other side of the piazza, the Quadri was the first café in Venice to serve dark, concentrated *caffè alla turca* – the precursor of today's *espresso*. It has given Florian a run for its money in the famous-client race – Stendhal and Balzac were Quadri-philes, and Proust used to sit inside in winter, changing tables frequently in order to escape those horrid draughts. But Quadri became unfashionable when the Austrians chose it as their favourite hangout during their 50-year occupation of the city, and despite its similar orchestra and prices, it has never really caught up with Florian as the place to be seen. The luxury restaurant upstairs (*see p147*) is a good place in which to celebrate that lottery win/bank robbery.

Harry's Bar

San Marco 1323, calle Vallaresso (041 528 5777). Vaporetto Vallaresso. **Open** 9.30am-11pm daily. **Credit** AmEx, DC, MC, V. **Map** II 4B.

This historic watering-hole, founded by Giuseppe Cipriani in 1931, has changed little since the days when Ernest Hemingway came here to work on his next hangover, except for the prices and the numbers of Japanese tourists. But despite the pre-dinner crush and some offhand service, a Bellini (fresh peach juice and sparkling wine) at the bar is as much a part of the Venetian experience as a gondola ride, and, at L23,000, far cheaper. At mealtimes, the tables upstairs and down are reserved for diners who enjoy

Caffè Lavena: arguably the best coffee in town.

Harry's Bar: historic watering hole. *See p166.*

the Venetian-themed international comfort food served here and are prepared to pay outrageous prices (L200,000-plus for three courses) for the privilege of being seen *chez* Harry. Stick with a Bellini, and don't even think of coming in here in shorts.

Osteria ai Rusteghi

San Marco 5529, calle della Bissa (041 523 2205). Vaporetto Rialto. **Open** 9am-3pm, 5-8.30pm Mon-Sat. **No credit cards. Map** II 4A.
This *osteria* serves some excellent wines by the bottle or glass to wash down its delicious little sandwich triangles in 30 or more varieties, including bacon and rosemary, eggs and asparagus, and prawns and boletus mushroom.

Vitae

San Marco 4118, calle Sant'Antonio (041 520 5205). Vaporetto Rialto. **Open** 9am-1am Mon-Fri; 3pm-1am Sat. **No credit cards. Map** II 3A.
Few tourists discover this smart designer bar in a side street between campo Manin and campo San Luca, a firm favourite with Venice's yuppie crowd. It gets packed around early evening cocktail time and again after midnight. There are a few pavement tables, at which to munch Vitae's tasty *panini*.

Castello

(See also **Da Bonifacio** *p171,* **Chiusso** *p171,* **Marchini** *p171,* **Rosa Salva** *p171,* **Boutique del Gelato** *p169.)*

Al Vecio Penasa

Castello 4585, calle delle Rasse (041 523 7202). Vaporetto San Zaccaria. **Open** 6.30am-11.30pm daily. **No credit cards. Map** III 1A.
Al Vecio Penasa offers coffee and pastries at breakfast and *panini* and delicious *tramezzini* any time of day. Friendly service on an otherwise heavily touristed street where taking a seat at one of the tables inside will more than double your bill.

Bar Orologio

Castello 6130, campo Santa Maria Formosa (041 523 0515). Vaporetto Rialto. **Open** 7am-11pm Mon-Sat. **No credit cards. Map** III 1A.
This is a good meeting-point with plenty of tables outside, on one of Venice's most beautiful *campi*, Santa Maria Formosa; but prices are a bit steep, a waiter-service *cappuccino* costing L5,000. On Sundays, when the bar's closed, join Venetians at the outdoor tables reading their papers in the sun.

L'Olandese Volante

Castello 5658, campo San Lio (041 528 9349). Vaporetto Rialto. **Open** 10am-midnight Mon-Sat; 5pm-midnight Sun. **Credit** DC, MC, V. **Map** II 4A.
The 'Flying Dutchman' pub is a big hit with the local student population. Beer is the drink of choice; there is also a big selection of salads and one or two hot dishes. Lively in summer, when the tables that spill out onto the *campiello* stay crowded until late.

Inishark Irish Pub

Castello 5787, calle Mondo Novo (041 523 5300). Vaporetto Rialto. **Open** 6pm-1.30am Tue-Sun. **No credit cards. Map** III 1A.
Tucked away in a small calle between San Lio and Santa Maria Formosa, the Inishark is one of Venice's newest and most popular pubs, serving Guinness, spritz and a variety of sandwiches and snacks. Satellite TV keeps soccer fans happy.

Aperitivi

For Venetians, the *ora dell'aperitivo* is sacred. Indulged in at any point beween 6pm and 8.30pm, it's the time to meet friends/business associates/lovers, take stock of the day's events and plan the evening ahead.

In a city where wine is cheaper than beer – sometimes even than water – it's no surprise that many locals opt for an *ombra* (*see p160*), a small shot of wine. Other favourites include: **spritz** – an aperitif that dates back to the end of the 19th century when Venice was under Austrian rule. Half a glass of white wine, a twist of lemon peel (never a whole slice) and a strong measure of some bitter aperitif, topped up with a shot of seltzer (though this is sometimes substituted by unsatisfactory mineral water). It only costs around L2,000 and it's deadly. There are several variations on the theme: spritz al bitter with Campari; spritz al aperol with the bitter non-alcoholic drink of the same name; and spritz al select mixed with a sweeter aperitif. Ask for the fat, green olives which go so well with spritz.
americano – made with vermouth, bitter campari and soda.
negroni – perfect when a stronger drink is needed to pick you up after a long day getting lost among the *calli*; made from gin, bitter campari and vermouth.To participate in the ritual while avoiding the alcohol, go for the non- or low-alcoholic gingerino, Sanbitter or Crodino.

Eat, Drink, Shop

QUADRI

Gran Caffè Ristorante,
since 1683,
in St. Mark's square, n° 121

Restaurant

**Light - Lunch,
A' la Carte Restaurant,
Gala Dinner**

**Onto "the finest drawing-room in the world"
with supreme quality gastronomy**

**Welcome Coffee,
Cocktail Reception,
Caffè Concerto
After Dinner Drinks**

Café

Piazza San Marco, Venezia, Ph. 041 5222105 - 5289299 - Fax 041 5208041
http://www.quadrivenice.com   e-mail: quadri@quadrivenice.com
Closed on Monday in the winter season

Cannaregio

(*See also* **Boscolo** *p171*, **Puppa** *p171*, **Isola del Gelato** *p169*, **Fiddler's Elbow Irish Pub** *p211*.)

Da Aldo

Cannaregio 2710, fondamenta degli Ormesini (041 715 834). Vaporetto San Marcuola. **Open** 10.30am-3pm, 8.30pm-2am Mon-Sat. **No credit cards.** **Map** I 2A.

You can't miss the huge shape of Aldo sitting behind his narrow bar. Serving more than 100 different beers, this place is popular with Venice's student population. After midnight, the crowds outside often spread right down the fondamenta, the social heart of northern Cannaregio.

Algiubagiò

Cannaregio 5039, fondamenta Nuove (041 523 6084/www.albiubagio.com). Vaporetto Fondamente Nove. **Open** 6.30am-8.30pm daily. **Credit** V, MC. **Map** I 4B.

Situated right by the vaporetto stop, this is a great place to stop off for a *cappuccino* on the way to or from the northern islands. There's a terrace overlooking the lagoon, from where you can watch the boats come and go over a beer and a *panino*. The bar has branched out into neighbouring ice-cream and take-away pizza extensions.

La Cantina

Cannaregio 3689, campo San Felice (041 522 8258/ www.lacantina.com). Vaporetto Ca' d'Oro. **Open** 8.30am-8.30pm Mon-Sat. **No credit cards.** **Map** I 3B.

Serving draught beer, a selection of good wines and some excellent *bruschette* with toppings ranging from suckling pig to olive paste, this is an excellent place to take the edge off your hunger as you watch the world rush by on the nearby Strada Nova.

San Polo & Santa Croce

(*See also* **Rizzardini** *p171*, **Ai Postali** *p 213*.)

Ciak 1

San Polo 2807, campo San Tomà (041 528 5150). Vaporetto San Tomà. **Open** 7am-9pm daily. **Credit** AmEx, MC, V. **Map** II 2A.

This bright, modern bar aims to be a fun, funky venue. It is busy for early evening aperitifs, as locals heading for the San Tomà gondola-traghetto call in on their way home from work.

Bar Ai Nomboli

San Polo 2717C, rio terà dei Nomboli (041 523 0995). Vaporetto San Tomà. **Open** June-Sept 7am-8pm Mon-Fri. Oct-May 7am-8pm Mon-Fri; 7am-1.30pm Sat. **No credit cards.** **Map** I 2A.

You'll need to summon all your decision-making skills when entering this bar with over 85 sandwich combinations to choose from: try the Serenissima with tuna, peppers, peas and onions. The few tables outside are great for people-watching while enjoying a midday snack.

Caffè dei Frari

San Polo 2564, fondamenta dei Frari (041 524 1877). Vaporetto San Tomà. **Open** 7.30am-9pm Mon-Sat; 9.30am-3pm Sun. **No credit cards.** **Map** I 2C.

Gelaterie

Gelateria Nico

Dorsoduro 922, Zattere (041 522 5293). Vaporetto Zattere. **Open** June-Sept 7.30am-11.30pm daily. Oct-May 7.30am-9.30pm daily. **No credit cards.** **Map** II 2B.

Nico's serves a lot more than just ice-creams, including spritz, prosecco, pizzas and the usual range of bar food. Dedicated bar-loungers are attracted by the splendid view from its terrace. If you dare, try the *gianduiotto*, a slab of hazelnut-and-chocolate ice-cream immersed in thick whipped cream.

Boutique del Gelato

Castello 5727, salizzada San Lio (041 522 3283).Vaporetto Rialto. **Open** 10am-8.30pm daily. **No credit cards.** **Map** III 1A.

Most Venetians agree that the city's best ice-cream is served in this tiny booth on the busy salizzada San Lio. Be patient, though: there is always a huge crowd waiting to be served.

Il Doge

Dorsoduro 3058, rio terà Canal (041 523 4607). Vaporetto Ca' Rezzonico. **Open** 10.30am-midnight daily. **No credit cards.** **Map** II 2A.

Open late, this is an immensely popular gelateria looking out over the lively campo Santa Margherita, scene of Venice's liveliest nightlife activities (*see p210*).

Le Café

San Marco 2797, campo Santo Stefano (041 523 7201) Vaporetto Accademia. **Open** May-Oct 8.30am-9.30pm daily. Nov-Jan 8.30am-8.30pm Mon, Tue, Thur-Sun. Feb-Apr 8.30am-8.30pm daily. **Credit** MC, V. **Map** II 3A-B.

When you're sick of true Italian ice cream, this is the place to come for a fix of Häagen Dazs. Prices are steep, but they have see-and-be-seen tables on the campo.

Eat, Drink, Shop

Cosy bar with an even cosier mezzanine, popular with students skipping lectures at the nearby university. The walls feature art nouveau interpretations of 18th-century Venice.

Bar Ai Tribunali
San Polo 101, campo San Giacomo di Rialto (041 522 7581). Vaporetto Rialto. **Open** 4am-9pm Mon-Sat. **No credit cards. Map** I 3C.
Everyone knows this near-legendary Rialto dive as *Il Peoco* (the mussel) – an oblique reference to the bald head of its owner, Alberto. He opens the Ai Tribunali at four in the morning, when clients range from market tradesmen setting up stalls for the day, to those returning from mainland discos. Beware of his lethal cocktail, *La Bomba*, the ingredients of which are kept secret.

Dorsoduro

(See also **Gobbetti** *p171,* **Tonolo** *p171,* **Gelateria Nico** *p169,* **Il Doge** *p169,* **Margaret Duchamp** *p215,* **Café Blu** *p213,* **Café Noir** *p213.)*

Il Caffè
Dorsoduro 2963, campo Santa Margherita (041 528 7998). Vaporetto Ca' Rezzonico. **Open** 7.40am-2am Mon-Sat. **No credit cards. Map** II 2A.
Known as the Caffè Rosso, on account of its bright red exterior, this lively bar, beloved of the city's bohemian and 30-something population, is great for people-watching. The bar is dominated by a shining art deco coffee machine, which makes a great *cappuccino*, rivalled only by the bar's other speciality, a killer spritz al bitter.

Osteria ai Carmini
Dorsoduro 2894A, rio terà della Scoazzera (041 523 1115/www.alexia.it). Vaporetto Ca' Rezzonico. **Open** 9am-midnight daily. **No credit cards. Map** II 1-2A.
Only open in the evening, this attracts a young crowd. For late eaters there is an eclectic range of snacks or full meals in which Greek and Middle Eastern dishes are to be found alongside standard Italian fare.

Corner Pub
Dorsoduro 684, calle de la Chiesa (0340 258 1448). Vaporetto Accademia. **Open** 11am-1am Tue-Sun. **No credit cards. Map** II 3B.
In one of the quieter residential corners of Venice, this is a haven for under-30s looking for a raucous night out in what tends otherwise to be a very sedate neck of the woods.

Bar da Gino
Dorsoduro 853A, piscina Venier (041 528 5276). Vaporetto Accademia. **Open** 6am-8pm Mon-Sat. **No credit cards. Map** II 2B.
You'll always be greeted with a smile by the Scarpa family, whether it's your first or your 100th visit. During the warmer months tables outside along the calle are excellent for watching the constant flow of gallery-goers. Some of the best *tramezzini* around.

It's never dull at **Rizzardini**. *See p171.*

Giudecca

Cantina Veneta
Giudecca 93, fondamenta della Croce (041 522 2195). Vaporetto Zitelle. **Open** 8am-midnight Mon-Wed, Fri-Sun. **No credit cards. Map** II 4C.
This is undoubtedly the friendliest bar on the Giudecca, right next to the Venice youth hostel, with a perfectly situated terrace looking out over the Zattere and San Marco.

Cake

Every Italian town has its cake- and pastry-eating rituals, and Venice is no exception. Here as elsewhere, the day begins with a *cappuccino* and *brioche* (pronounced the French way), preferably a hot one baked on the premises; any important lunch invitation – and that includes Sunday at family or friends' – involves investing in a big tray of dainties. But in the lagoon city, cakes – be they the dry, biscuity Venetian variety or lush cream-filled pan-Italian ones – are also a fixture at *aperitivo* time: some of the best spritz *(see p167* **Aperitivi***)* in town is served at the *pasticcerie* listed below.

Venetian specialities include: **baicoli**, a light, dry biscuit named after a small lagoon fish that it is supposed to resemble; **busolai**, a sweet S-shaped biscuit with a slight aftertaste of aniseed made on the island of Burano; and **zaleti**, a lemony-vanilla-flavoured cornmeal biscuit packed with raisins.

At *carnevale* time (*see p194*), the range is extended to include **frittelle**, fried lumps of dough containing raisins and/or with zabaglione or thick cream filling; and **crostoli**, light thin flakes of pastry that are fried and then dusted with icing sugar.

Da Bonifacio

Castello 4237, calle degli Albanesi (041 522 7507). Vaporetto San Zaccaria. **Open** 7.30am-8.30pm Mon-Wed, Fri-Sun. **No credit cards. Map** III 1B.
Hidden away in a narrow calle at the back of the Danieli Hotel, this is a firm favourite with Venetians. As well as a tempting array of traditional cakes such as *mammalucchi* (deep-fried batter cakes with candied fruit), it serves what is generally considered the finest *americano* aperitif in town.

Boscolo

Cannaregio 1818, campiello de l'Anconeta (041 720 731). Vaporetto San Marcuola. **Open** 6.45am-8.40pm Tue-Sun. **No credit cards. Map** I 2B.
Maria Boscolo runs a busy *pasticceria* with a packed bar. Locals come for the extra-strong spritz al bitter; there is also an excellent assortment of Venetian sweets – *frittelle* during *carnevale*, *zaleti* and *pincia* (a sweet bread made with cornflour).

Chiusso

Castello 3306, salizzada dei Greci (041 523 1611). Vaporetto San Zaccaria or Arsenale. **Open** 8am-1.30pm, 4-9pm Mon, Thur, Fri-Sun; 8am-1.30pm Tue. **No credit cards. Map** III 2B.
Throughout the morning, steaming trays of excellent pastries – try the one with apples and almond paste – roll out of the kitchen behind this diminutive bar-*pasticceria*. Take whatever's hottest and freshest and savour it with Chiusso's excellent *cappuccino*.

Gobbetti

Dorsoduro 3108B, rio terà Canal (041 528 9014). Vaporetto Ca' Rezzonico. **Open** 7.45am-1pm, 4pm-8pm daily. **No credit cards. Map** II 2A.
This small *pasticceria* makes some of the most delicious cakes in Venice. Popular with locals stocking up with cakes for lunch on Sunday mornings.

Marchini

San Marco 2769, ponte San Maurizio (041 522 9109/www.golosessi.com). Vaporetto Santa Maria del Giglio. **Open** 8.30am-8.30pm Mon, Wed-Sun. **Credit** AmEx, DC, MC, V. **Map** II 3B.
Marchini is probably Venice's most famous cake shop, and probably also the most expensive. The tempting window display of the main outlet creates traffic jams of tourists making their way to San Marco. Come for exquisite pastries and chocolate,

including **Le Baute Veneziane** – small chocolates in the forms of *carnevale* masks. The branch listed below is quieter, overlooking a canal on the aptly named Cake Bridge.
Branch: Castello 5991, ponte de le Paste (041 522 2889).

Puppa

Cannaregio 4800, calle del Spezier (041 523 7947). Vaporetto Ca' d'Oro. **Open** 7am-1.30pm, 3.30-8.30pm Tue-Sun. **No credit cards. Map** I 4B.
Roberto Puppa and his wife run this tiny *pasticceria*, which is a local favourite. It's strictly a stand-up or take-away point of place, with the interior frozen in time circa 1970. Not only do they provide some of the city's most delicious cakes – try the *meringa* (meringue and cream) or their famous *crostella* – they also serve as good a spritz as you'll find anywhere.

Rizzardini

San Polo 1415, campiello dei Meloni (041 522 3835). Vaporetto San Silvestro. **Open** 7am-9.30pm Mon, Wed-Sun. **No credit cards. Map** II 3A.
One of the most beautiful of the shops belonging to the Antiche Pasticcerie Veneziane association. When owner Paolo is behind the bar, there's never a dull moment. Especially good for traditional Venetian pastries, and *frittelle* during *carnevale*.

Rosa Salva

Castello 6779, campo Santi Giovanni e Paolo (041 522 7949). Vaporetto Fondamente Nove. **Open** 7.30am-8.30pm Mon-Tue, Thur-Sat; 8.30am-8.30pm Sun. **No credit cards. Map** III 1A.
Rosa Salva rivals Marchini as Venice's most famous cake dynasty, though not in attitude. The main branch is the one listed below, but for all-out charm come to this lovingly restored outlet in campo Santi Giovanni e Paolo. Great home-made gelato.
Branch: San Marco 4589, campo San Luca (041 522 5385).

Tonolo

Dorsoduro 3764, calle San Pantalon (041 523 7209). Vaporetto San Tomà. **Open** 8am-8.45pm Tue-Sun. **No credit cards. Map** II 2A.
On a busy street that runs into campo Santa Margherita, this is a favourite with students. The coffee is excellent, and on Sundays the place fills up with locals buying sweet offerings to take to lunch.

Rosa Salva: a famous cake dynasty.

BRASSERIE
Vecchia Bruxelles

Locale tipico con snacks creativi
Ogni giovedì musica dal vivo
Banchetti cerimoniali su prenotazione
Tv Stream e D+ / Sala non fumatori

Country Brasserie serving creative snacks
Live music on thursday
All parties catering upon booking
Tv Stream e D+ / Non smoking room

BRASSERIE "VECCHIA BRUXELLES"
Santa Croce, 81 - Calle Vinante
Tel. (+39) 041.710636
Venezia - Italy

Shops & Services

Discerning shoppers have just as much cause to celebrate as dedicated souvenir hunters.

For centuries, Venice has been a busy commercial centre, with luxury goods heading the traditional shopping list. With the steady demographic drop and the resulting demise of 'useful' shops – bread, fruit and veg, milk, and meat are increasingly difficult to get hold of – this holds truer today than ever. The main retail areas are the **Mercerie** – the maze of crowded, narrow alleyways leading from piazza San Marco to the Rialto – and the streets known collectively as the **Frezzeria**, which wind between La Fenice and piazza San Marco. The densest concentration of big-name fashion outlets can be found around the calle larga XXII Marzo, just west of the piazza, where top names such as Prada, Valentino, Fendi, Versace and Gucci have all staked their boutiques.

Despite some off-putting sales techniques that veer between the hard-sell and the snooty look-what-the-cat-brought-in approach, shopping in Venice can be fun, especially for those who venture away from the busiest and most obvious thoroughfares. Reasonably priced gifts and souvenirs produced by local crafts-people can be found all over the city – often clustered in trade enclaves, another medieval legacy. Calle della Mandola is the street for paper products and glass beads, while antique shops are thick on the ground around campo Santo Stefano. The Dorsoduro side of the Ponte dell'Accademia is one of the best places to go for hand-crafted masks.

Devotees of kitsch should not miss the stalls and shops near the train station, where plastic gondolas, illuminated gondolas, flashing gondolas, musical gondolas and even gondola cigarette lighters reign supreme.

For more tasteful souvenirs, Venice's glass, lace, fabrics and handmade paper are legendary – as are the made-in-Taiwan substitutes that are passed off as the genuine article by unscrupulous traders. Sticking to the outlets listed below will help you to avoid unpleasant surprises.

OPENING HOURS

Most food shops are closed on Wednesday afternoons, while most non-food shops stay shut on Monday mornings. During high season (which in Venice includes *carnevale* in February/March, Easter, the four weeks leading up to Christmas and the summer season from June to October) many shops abandon their lunchtime closing, and

Don't be a dummy – visit **Godi Fiorenza** for exquisite designs. *See p179.*

stay open all day, even opening on Sundays, too.

It pays to be sceptical about the hours posted on the doors of smaller shops: opening times are often determined by volume of trade or personal whim. If you want to be sure of not finding the shutters drawn, call before you set out.

Incomprehensibly – given that summer is Venice's busiest season – some shops do close for holidays in August, but the majority of these are smaller ones that cater more for residents than tourists, such as *tabacchi*, photocopying centres and dry-cleaners.

If you are not an EU citizen, remember to keep your official receipt (*scontrino*) as you are entitled to a rebate on IVA (sales tax) paid on purchases of personal goods costing more than L300,000 as long as they leave the country unused and are bought from a shop that provides this service. Look for a sign in the window and ask for the form to show at customs upon departure.

timeout.com

The World's Living Guide

One-stop shopping

Shopping centres and department stores are few and far between in Venice proper. If you're suffering from mall withdrawal, head for Mestre. Be warned: although prices there may be competitive, the selection is unimaginative and the trip to Mestre can be physically, emotionally and aesthetically draining.

Auchan Centro Commerciale

Via Don Tosatto 22, Mestre (041 507 4300). Free bus service to and from piazzale Roma. **Open** 1.30pm-10pm Mon, 9am-10pm Tue-Sat. **Credit** varies.
One of the largest shopping malls on the Venetian mainland with 70 shops including restaurants, a supermarket and sporting goods shops.

Centro Le Barche

Piazza XXVII Ottobre 1, Mestre (041 977 882). Bus 4 or 4/ from piazzale Roma. **Open** 9am-8pm Mon-Sat. **Credit** varies.
In addition to trendy city-centre stores, you'll find the Feltrinelli bookshop with some titles in English, a theatre box office and a well-stocked record shop – and there's a food-court on the top floor.

Coin

Cannaregio 5787, fontego salizzada San Grisostomo (041 520 3581). Vaporetto Rialto. **Open** 9.30am-7.30pm Mon-Sat; 11am-7.30pm Sun. **Credit** AmEx, DC, MC, V. **Map** I 4C.
Stylish, above-average department store chain that started life in the Veneto. The prices aren't exactly rock-bottom, but there are bargains to be had during sales. The houseware department is good for unpretentious sheets and linens.

Standa

Cannaregio 3659, strada Nuova (041 523 8046). Vaporetto Ca' D'Oro. **Open** 8.30am-7.20pm daily. **Credit** AmEx, MC, V. **Map** I 3B.
Italy's Woolworth's. Cheap clothes (not all of them awful), toiletries, and a modest selection of articles for the home. There's also a well-stocked supermarket.

Antiques

Antique shops can be found throughout the city, though the concentration is greatest around campo San Maurizio and calle delle Botteghe (near campo Santo Stefano). There is also a Mercatino dell'Antiquariato (Antiques Fair) twice a year, in the week before Easter and Christmas, in campo San Maurizio.

Antiquus

San Marco 3131, calle delle Botteghe (041 520 6395). Vaporetto Sant'Angelo. **Open** 10am-12.30pm, 3-7.30pm Mon-Sat. **Credit** AmEx, DC, MC, V. **Map** II 3A.
This charming shop has a beautiful collection of Old Master paintings, furniture, silver and antique jewellery, including Moors' heads brooches and earrings.

Guarinoni

San Polo 2862, calle del Mandorlin (041 522 4286). Vaporetto San Tomà. **Open** 8am-noon, 3-7pm Mon-Sat. **Credit** AmEx, MC, V. **Map** II 2A.
An assortment of antique furnishings from as early as the 16th century are sold here. The shop also has a workshop that restores gilded ceilings and the like.

Kleine Galerie

San Marco 2972, calle delle Botteghe (041 522 2177). Vaporetto Sant'Angelo. **Open** 10am-12.45pm Mon; 10am-12.45pm, 4-7.30pm Tue-Sat. **No credit cards.** **Map** II 3A.
The Kleine Galerie specialises in antique books and prints as well as majolica and porcelain.

Art supplies

Angeloni

Galleria Matteotti 2, Mestre (041 974 166/fax 041 974 236) Bus 4 from piazzale Roma to piazza Ferretto. **Open** 9am-12.30pm, 3.30pm-7.30pm Mon-Sat. **Credit** AmEx, MC, V.
Nice service and wide range of supplies, where real artists go. The prices are much better than anything you'll find in island Venice.

Cartoleria Accademia

Dorsoduro 1044, rio terà della Carità (041 520 7086). Vaporetto Accademia. **Open** 8am-12.30pm, 4-7pm Mon-Fri; 8am-12.30pm Sat. **No credit cards.** **Map** II 2B.
This small but well-stocked store carries a wide range of artists' supplies and is conveniently located just behind the Accademia. It has been in the business since 1810, so it must be doing something right. **Branch**: Dorsoduro 2928, campo Santa Margherita (041 528 5283).

Cartoleria Arte e Design

Santa Croce 53, campiello Mosca (041 710 269). Vaporetto Piazzale Roma. **Open** 8am-1pm, 3-7.30pm Mon-Sat. **Credit** AmEx, DC, MC, V. **Map** I 1C.
Art supplies of all kinds, including paper of every imaginable shape, colour and size. Mont Blanc, Waterman and Filofax, as well as an impressive range of computer supplies.

Testolini

San Marco 1756/58, fondamenta Orseolo (041 522 9265). Vaporetto Vallaresso/ or Rialto. **Open** 9am-7pm Mon-Sat. **Credit** AmEx, MC, V. **Map** II 4A.
The place to go for Post-its and paintbrushes. Testolini carries stationery, backpacks, briefcases, calendars and art/office supplies. It also has an annexe filled with computers and accessories. The service tends towards the unfriendly but the choice is huge.

Bookshops

Ca' Foscarina 2

Dorsoduro 3259, campiello degli Squellini (041 522 9602). Vaporetto Ca' Rezzonico. **Open** 9am-7pm Mon-Fri; 9am-12.30pm Sat. **Credit** MC, V. **Map** II 2A.

The official bookstore of the Università Ca' Foscari, with the city's largest selection of books in English, covering literature, poetry, history and travel.

Fantoni Libri Arte

San Marco 4119, salizzada San Luca (041 522 0700). Vaporetto Rialto. **Open** 9am-7.45pm Mon-Sat. **Credit** AmEx, DC, MC, V. **Map** II 4A.
Beautifully illustrated art, architecture, design, photography and textile books, mostly in Italian. There's also a small selection of cookbooks and works on Venice in English.

Filippi Editore Venezia

Castello 5763, calle del Paradiso (041 523 6916/041 523 5635/filippi@doge.it). Vaporetto Rialto. **Open** 9am-12.30pm, 3-7.30pm Mon-Sat. **Credit** AmEx, DC, MC, V. **Map** III 1A.
The oldest publishing house in Venice. This father-and-son operation has more than 400 titles on Venetian history and folklore – all limited editions in Italian. A favourite stop for scholars.

Laboratorio Blu

Cannaregio 1224, campo del Ghetto Vecchio (041 715 819). Vaporetto Guglie. **Open** 3.45-7.30pm Mon, 9.30am-12.30pm, 3.45-7.30pm Tue-Sat. **No credit cards**. **Map** I 2A.
The only children's bookshop in Venice. It carries a good selection of books in English and offers courses for kids – drawing, painting, weaving and storytelling.

Libreria San Pantalon

Dorsoduro 3950, salizzada San Pantalon (041 522 4436). Vaporetto San Tomà. **Open** 9am-7.30pm Mon-Sat. **Credit** AmEx, DC, MC, V. **Map** II 2A.
Known to Venetians as the bookshop with the cat in the window, it's a place you can spend hours in. As well as a good selection of books on music – especially opera – it carries beautiful arts and craft books, gifts, games, children's books and greetings cards. Rosa the cat keeps watch at the window or roams around the store.

Libreria Toletta & Toletta Studio

Dorsoduro 1214, calle Toletta (041 523 2034). Vaporetto Accademia. **Open** 9am-7.30pm Mon-Sat. **Credit** AmEx, DC, MC, V. **Map** II 2B.
A good source of cheap books, the Toletta offers 20-40% off its stock, depending on the publisher. Italian classics, art, cookery, children's books, history (mostly in Italian) and a vast assortment of dictionaries. Next door is the Toletta Studio, which specialises in architecture books as well as selling T-shirts and small gifts.

Patagonia

Dorsoduro 3490B, calle Contarini (041 528 5333). Vaporetto Piazzale Roma. **Open** 9am-12.30pm, 3.30-7.30pm Tue-Sat. **Credit** AmEx, DC, MC, V. **Map** II 1A.
For books on contemporary art and cinema (mostly in Italian), this is the place to come first. Patagonia also often organises presentations of new books by local authors.

Studium

San Marco 337C, calle Canonica (041 522 2382). Vaporetto Vallaresso. **Open** 9am-7.30pm Mon-Sat. **Credit** AmEx, DC, MC, V. **Map** II 4A.
Located behind Saint Mark's basilica, this two-room shop has a wide selection of works on Venice, travel books and novels in English. Its speciality is revealed in the back room, which is filled with theology studies, icons and prayer books.

Cosmetics & perfumes

Cosmetics and toiletries can be found in the one-stop stores listed above or in *farmacie*, but you may find prices are lower in smaller, more specialised *profumerie*. For herbal products of any description, including aromatherapy oils, head for an *erboristeria*.

The Body Shop

Cannaregio 3844, strada Nuova (041 277 0333). Vaporetto Ca' D'Oro. **Open** 10am-1pm, 3-7.30pm Mon; 9.30am-1pm, 3-7.30pm Tue-Thur; 9.30am-7.30pm Fri, Sat; 3-7.30pm Sun. **Credit** AmEx, MC, DC, V. **Map** I 3B.
Italian Body Shops carry all the usual products at prices that are higher than in the UK.

Erboristeria Mediterranea

San Polo 1735, calle dei Botteri (041 723 215). Vaporetto San Silvestro. **Open** 9.15am-1pm, 4-7.30pm Tue-Sat. **No credit cards**. **Map** I 3C.
A quaint shop near the Rialto where a herbalist will mix up concoctions for you. Alternatively, choose from a variety of prepared creams and perfumes.

Ceramics

Camilla

Dorsoduro 2609, campo dei Carmini (041 523 5277). Vaporetto Ca' Rezzonico or San Basilio. **Open** 10am-6pm Tue-Sat. **No credit cards**. **Map** II 1A.
This shop stocks pottery worked and decorated by Camilla herself. The imaginative motifs are inspired by the Venetian landscape.

Ceramiche

Santa Croce 2345, sottoportico della Siora Bettina (041 723 120). Vaporetto San Stae. **Open** 9.30am-1pm, 3.30-7pm Mon-Sat. **Credit** AmEx, MC, V. **Map** I 2B.
A wonderful collection of hand-painted terracotta designed by the English-speaking owner. Plates, bowls and teapots all at reasonable prices.

Materia Prima

San Marco 3436, piscina San Samuele (041 523 3585/041 523 3282). Vaporetto Sant'Angelo. **Open** 11am-1pm, 4-7.30pm Tue-Sat. **Credit** AmEx, DC, MC, V. **Map** II 3A.
Interesting and affordable objects from around the world as well as ceramic, glass and textile works by local artisans. Materia Prima also co-ordinates Pandora, a Venetian arts and crafts workshop.

Eat, Drink, Shop

Sabbie e Nebbie

San Polo 2768A, calle dei Nomboli (041 719 073). Vaporetto San Tomà. **Open** 10am-12.30pm, 4-7.30pm Mon-Sat. **Credit** MC, V. **Map** I 2C.
A beautiful selection of contemporary Italian ceramic pieces as well as highly refined Japanese works. Also handmade objects by Italian designers such as lamps, candleholders and notebooks.

Design & household

Domus

San Marco 4746, calle dei Fabbri (041 522 6259). Vaporetto Rialto. **Open** 9.30am-7.30pm Mon-Sat; 11am-7.30 Sun. **Credit** AmEx, DC, MC, V. **Map** II 4A.
Domus is good for all sorts of houseware from rustic Italian ceramic pieces to fine bone china. Murano vases and stemware by names such as Nason-Moretti can also be found. Check in the windows for discounts on plate sets, bowls and gifts.

Fabrics & accessories

Arras

Dorsoduro 3234, campiello Squellini (041 522 6460). Vaporetto Ca' Rezzonico. **Open** 9am-1pm, 3.30-7.30pm Mon-Sat. **Credit** AmEx, DC, MC, V. **Map** II 2A.
Hand-woven fabrics are created here in a vast range of colours and textures using silk, wool and cotton. The shop is run by a co-operative that organises weaving courses for the handicapped, whose work is also on sale alongside other items.

Bevilacqua

San Marco 337B, ponte della Canonica (041 528 7581). Vaporetto San Zaccaria. **Open** 10am-7.30pm Mon-Sat. **Credit** AmEx, DC, MC, V. **Map** II 4A.
This small shop behind St Mark's basilica offers exquisite examples of both hand- and machine-woven silk brocades, damasks and velvets. The Venetian textile tradition is kept alive by three weavers who use original 17th-century looms.

Gaggio

San Marco 3451-3441, calle delle Botteghe (041 522 8574). Vaporetto Rialto. **Open** 9.30am-1pm, 3.30-7.30pm Mon-Sat. **Credit** AmEx, DC, MC, V. **Map** II 3A.
A legend among dressmakers and designers, Emma Gaggio's sumptuous handprinted silk velvets (from £120 a metre) are used to make cushions and wall hangings as well as bags, hats, scarves and jackets.

M Antichità e Oggetti d'Arte

San Marco 1691, Frezzeria (041 523 5666). Vaporetto Vallaresso. **Open** 4-7.30pm Mon; 10am-12.30pm, 4-7.30pm Tue-Sat. **Credit** AmEx, DC, MC, V. **Map** II 4A.
A tasteful selection of antique baubles can be found in this jewel of a shop; its speciality, however, are the richly painted velvets created by the owner in her workshop. A favourite among interior designers.

Fabulous fabrics at **Venetia Studium**.

Il Milione

Castello 6025, campo Santa Marina (041 241 0722). Vaporetto Rialto. **Open** 10am-12.30pm, 5pm-7.30pm Mon-Sat. **Credit** MC, V. **Map** II 1A.
Handmade lamps which look like Fortuny knock-offs and are a little more affordable. Il Milione's craftman worked for the renowned Venetia Studium *(see below)* before setting out on his own.

Trois

San Marco 2666, campo San Maurizio (041 522 2905). Vaporetto Santa Maria del Giglio. **Open** 4-7.30pm Mon; 10am-1pm, 4-7.30pm Tue-Sat. **No credit cards. Map** II 3B.
The only place in Venice where you can buy original Fortuny fabrics – and at considerable savings on UK/US prices (though this still doesn't make them particularly cheap). Trois also does made-to-order beadwork masks and accessories.

Venetia Studium

San Marco 2403, calle larga XXII Marzo (041 522 9281). Vaporetto Santa Maria del Giglio. **Open** 9.30am-8pm Mon-Sat; 10.30am-7.30pm Sun. **Credit** AmEx, DC, MC, V. **Map** II 3B.
Venetia Studium stocks beautiful pleated Fortuny-style silk fabrics, used for elegant pillows, lamps, scarves, handbags and other accessories in a marvellous range of colours. They are certainly not cheap, but they do make perfect gifts for those who have it all.

Fashion

All the big-name boutiques (**Armani**, **Prada**, **Gucci** and so on) are clustered around four streets in the vicinity of San Marco: calle Vallaresso; salizzada San Moisè and its continuation, calle larga XXII Marzo; calle Goldoni; and the Mercerie.
    The outlets listed below offer something a little different.

Accessories

Balocoloc

Santa Croce 2134, calle Longa (041 524 0551/info@balocoloc.com/www.balocoloc.com). Vaporetto San Silvestro. **Open** 2-7pm Mon-Sat. **Credit** MC, V. **Map** I 2C.
This out-of-the-way shop offers a nice selection of stylish and reasonably priced handmade hats. It also stocks a line of *carnevale* wear, too.

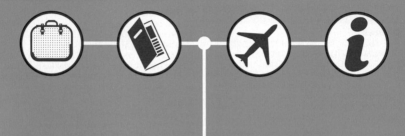

Bampa

San Marco 787, Merceria San Zulian (041 522 3310).
Vaporetto Rialto or Vallaresso. **Open** 9.30am-1pm, 3-
7.30pm Mon-Sat. **Credit** AmEx, DC, MC, V. **Map** II 4A.
If you really can't resist the call of the kitsch souvenir, this is the place to buy the official gondolier's
striped shirt, plus pins, patches and T-shirts.

Gualti

Dorsoduro 3111, rio terà Canal (041 520 1731/
gualti@go.to/www.gualti.go.to) *Vaporetto Cà*
Rezzonico. **Open** 10am-1pm, 3-7.30pm daily.
Credit MC, V. **Map** II 2A.
One-of-a-kind jewellery creations using glass and a
resin mixture. Every piece by Gualti makes a statement – dramatic but wearable.

Hibiscus

San Polo 1060, ruga Rialto/calle dell'Olio (041 520
8989) *Vaporetto San Silvestro.* **Open** 9.30am-7.30pm
Mon-Sat; 11am-7pm Sun. **Credit** MC, V. **Map** I C3.
Viaggio nei colori – a voyage into the world of colours
– is the Hibicus motto. Jewellery, handmade scarves,
bags and ceramics with an ethnic flare. Not cheap,
but a refreshing change from glass and mask shops.

Designers

Araba Fenice

San Marco 1822, calle dei Barcaroli (041 522
0664). *Vaporetto Santa Maria del Giglio.*
Open 9.30am-7.30pm Mon-Sat. **Credit** AmEx,
DC, MC, V. **Map** II 4A.
A classic yet original line of women's clothing by
Loris, who works exclusively for this boutique. Plus
jewellery in ebony and mother of pearl.

Godi Fiorenza

San Marco 4261, rio terà San Paternian
(041 241 0866). *Vaporetto Sant'Angelo.*
Open 10am-12.30pm, 3.30-7.30pm Mon-Sat.
Credit AmEx, MC, V. **Map** II 3A.
The London-trained Godi designer-sisters sell
exquisite knitwear, stylish coats and chiffon evening
tops that will reconcile you to sequins. All made on
the premises, and complemented with jewellery.

Pinco Pallino

Castello 5641, campo San Lio (041 523 5500)
Vaporetto Rialto. **Open** 9am-1pm, 2.30pm-7pm
Mon-Sat. **Credit** AmEx, MC, V. **Map** II 4A.
The entire collection of clothes and accessories by
the Venetian designer Giovanna Zanella offers an
alternative to the Italian standards. Beautiful colours
and interesting fabrics make each design unique.

Trend-setters

BA BA

Dorsoduro 3929, calle della Donna Onesta (041 520
8115/infobaba@katabusiness.com/www.katabusiness.
com/ve/baba). *Vaporetto San Tomà.* **Open** 9.30am-
8pm Mon-Sat. **Credit** AmEx, MC,V. **Map** II 2A.

Giovanna's fancy footwear at **Pinco Pallino**.

All the latest from young Italian designers – Zinco
and Aspesi Blu – to name but a few. Not everyone
can wear it, nor should they.

Diesel Jeans

San Marco 4663, calle dei Fabbri (041 522 5260).
Vaporetto Rialto. **Open** 10am-7.30pm Mon-Sat.
Credit AmEx, DC, MC, V. **Map** II 4A.
'Only the Brave' is the motto of this Veneto-based
company, whose kooky, club-wise styles and ad
campaigns have invaded Europe. Whether the motto
refers to those who wear their clothes or those who
dare to disturb the occasionally unhelpful staff is
difficult to say.

Prima Visione

Cannaregio 2340, rio terà Maddalena (041 524
2356). *Vaporetto Ca' D'Oro.* **Open** 9am-7.30pm
Mon-Sat. **Credit** AmEx, DC, MC, V. **Map** I 3B.
Stocks smaller Italian trend-setters such as Gas,
Caterpillar, Fornarina and Onyx. You'll also find
discounted Levi's.

Shoes, bags & leather goods

Bruno Magli

San Marco 1302, calle dell'Ascensione (041 522
7210). *Vaporetto Vallaresso.* **Open** 10am-7.30pm
Mon-Sat; 11.30am-6.30pm Sun. **Credit** AmEx, DC,
MC, V. **Map** II 4A.
Classic line of designer shoes, bags and jackets, more
conservative than trendy, and by now indelibly
linked with the OJ Simpson case after footprints
from a pair of Bruno Magli shoes were found at the
scene of his wife's murder. Look out for sales in
January and July.
Branches: San Marco 1583-85, Frezzerie (041 522
3472); San Marco 2288, calle Larga XXII Marzo (041
520 8280).

Francis Model

San Polo 773A, ruga Rialto/ruga del Ravano (041
521 2889). *Vaporetto San Silvestro.* **Open** *Apr-Dec*
9.30am-7.30pm Mon-Sat. *Jan-Mar* 9.30am-1pm, 3-
7.30pm Mon-Sat. **Credit** AmEx, DC, MC, V. **Map** I 3C.

Handbags and briefcases are produced in this tiny *bottega* by a father-and-son team that has been in the business for more than 40 years.

Italo Mariani

San Marco 4775, calle del Teatro (041 523 5580). Vaporetto Rialto. **Open** 9.30am-1pm, 3-7.30pm Mon-Sat; 10.30am-6.30pm Sun. **Credit** AmEx, DC, MC, V. **Map** II 4A.

Stylish Italian shoes for men and women at affordable prices. Bargains abound at the sale in January.
Branch: Castello 4313, ponte della Canonica (041 522 5614).

Mori & Bozzi

Cannaregio 2367, rio terà Maddalena (041 715 261). Vaporetto San Marcuola. **Open** 9.30am-12.30pm, 3.30-7.30pm Mon-Sat. **Credit** AmEx, DC, MC, V. **Map** I 3B.

Shoes for the coolest of the cool – square-toes, platforms and thick-soled men's shoes. Trendy names and designer copies.

Rolando Segalin

San Marco 4365, calle dei Fuseri (041 522 2115). Vaporetto Rialto. **Open** 9am-12.30pm, 3.30-7.30pm Mon-Sat. **Credit** AmEx, DC, MC, V. **Map** II 4A.

'The Cobbler of Venice' has been creating made-to-order shoes for more than 50 years. Some of the most interesting are on display in the window, including a pair of gondola-shoes… there's no accounting for taste. Repairs done as well.

Second-hand clothes

Laboratorio Arte & Costume

San Polo 2199, calle Scaleter (041 524 6242). Vaporetto San Silvestro. **Open** 10am-12.30pm, 3.30-7pm Mon-Sat. **Credit** MC, V. **Map** I 2C.

Hidden away behind campo San Polo, this shop is jam-packed with used clothing, hats, toys and God-knows-what in disorganised heaps. Some of the most impressive pieces can be rented as *carnevale* attire.

Laura Crovato

San Marco 2995, calle delle Botteghe (041 520 4170). Vaporetto Sant'Angelo. **Open** 4-7.30pm Mon; 10am-12.30pm, 4-7.30pm Tue-Sat. **Credit** MC, V. **Map** II 3A.

Nestling between expensive galleries and antique shops, Laura Crovato offers a selection of used clothes and a sprinkling of new items, including raw-silk shirts and scarves, costume jewellery and sunglasses. This being Venice, they're not giving the stuff away – even though it's second-hand.

Food & drink

For the freshest fruit, vegetables, meat and fish at the most competitive prices – plus a slice of everyday Venetian life that should not be missed – the market held every morning except Sunday at the foot of the **Rialto** bridge (San Polo side) is difficult to beat.

Francis Model for bags. See p179.

If markets are your thing but crowds aren't, go for the quieter, more local market that springs up halfway along **via Garibaldi** in eastern Castello every morning but Sunday: at the far end, purchase your fruit and veg from one of Venice's few remaining boat-emporia.

Grocery shops (*alimentari*) offer all the usual staples from around Italy, as well as the odd Venetian speciality such as *baccalà mantecato* (a delectable spread made with dried cod) and *mostarda veneziana* (a sweet and sour sauce made with dried fruit). Other regional favourites include olive oil from Lake Garda, flavoured vinegars, mountain honey from Belluno, fruit liqueurs and grappa, a fiery brandy distilled from the lees after the grapes are pressed (*see p264*). Butchers and bakers, though, are becoming thin on the ground as the mushrooming malls across on the mainland steal their trade.

Venetians are famous for their sweet tooth, and there is, therefore, an extraordinary variety of calorific delights to devour while strolling through the *calli: see p170*.

Alimentari

Aliani

San Polo 654-55, ruga Rialto/ruga vecchia San Giovanni (041 522 4913). Vaporetto San Silvestro. **Open** 8am-1pm Mon, Wed; 8am-1pm, 5-7.30pm Tue, Fri, Sat. **No credit cards. Map** I 3C.

A traditional grocery with a selection of cold meats and cheeses from every part of Italy. Also on offer is an assortment of prepared dishes and roast meats.

Drogheria Mascari

San Polo 381, ruga Speziati (041 522 9762). Vaporetto San Silvestro. **Open** 8am-1pm, 4-7.30pm Mon-Sat. **No credit cards. Map** I 3C.

Shops like this were quite common in Venice before the onslaught of commercial shopping centres on the mainland; this is the only one left. The best place to find exotic spices, nuts, dried fruit and mushrooms, as well as oils and wines from different regions in Italy. It has more than 3,000 items to choose from.

Giacomo Rizzo

Cannaregio 5778, calle San Giovanni Crisostomo (041 522 2824). Vaporetto Rialto. **Open** 8.30am-1pm, 3-7.30pm Mon, Tue, Thur-Sat; 8.30am-1pm Wed. **No credit cards. Map** I 4C.

Offers a wide variety of traditional products, many produced especially for the shop – pasta includes phallic noodles and gondola-shaped macaroni. The homesick traveller should head here for imported orange marmalade and Betty Crocker cake mixes; it also stocks ethnic food ingredients.

Drink

See also p159 **Bacari & Snacks**.

Bottiglieria Colonna

Castello 5595, calle della Fava (041 528 5137).
Vaporetto Rialto. **Open** 9am-1pm, 4-8pm Mon-Sat.
No credit cards. Map I 4C.
Extensive selection of local and regional wines. Helpful assistants will gladly give advice on which wines to try, and prepare travel boxes or arrange for shipping.

Vinaria Nave de Oro

Dorsoduro 3664, campo Santa Margherita
(041 522 2693) Vaporetto Ca' Rezzonico.
Open 5-8pm Mon; 9am-1pm, 5-8pm Tue-Sat.
No credit cards. Map II 2A.
Bring your own bottles and staff will fill them with anything from Tocai and Pinot Grigio to Merlot. The latest craze is for Torbolino, a sweet and cloudy first-pressing white wine.
Branches: Castello 5786B, calle del Mondo Nuovo (041 523 3056); Cannaregio 1370, salizzada San Leonardo (041 719 695); via Lepanto 24D, Lido (041 276 0055).

Vino e... Vini

Castello 3301, fondamenta dei Furlani
(041 521 0184). Vaporetto San Zaccaria.
Open 9am-1pm, 5-8pm Mon-Sat. **Credit** AmEx, DC, MC, V. **Map** III 2A.
A vast selection of major Italian wines from every region. It's one of the few places that carries an assortment of French, Spanish, Californian and even Lebanese wines.

Health foods

Cibele

Cannaregio 1823, campiello Anconetta
(041 524 2113). Vaporetto San Marcuola.
Open 9am-12.45pm, 3.30-7.45pm Mon-Sat.
Credit MC, V. **Map** I 2B.
A full range of natural health foods, cosmetics and medicines. Staff will also prepare blends of herbal teas and remedies.

Rialto Bio Center

San Polo 366, campo Beccaria (041 523
9515). Vaporetto San Silvestro. **Open** 8.30am-1pm, 4.30-8pm Mon-Sat. **Credit** AmEx, DC, MC, V.
Map I 3C.
A little bit of everything can be found here in this shop, located behind the Rialto fish market, from wholewheat pasta, grains, honey and freshly baked breads to natural cosmetics and incense.

Supermarkets

Billa

Dorsoduro 1491, Zattere (041 522 6187).
Vaporetto San Basilio. **Open** 8.30am-8pm daily.
No credit cards. Map II 1B.
The only real supermarket in Venice that is open seven days a week. Fruit and veg and other staples can be found at lower prices than in the *alimentari*.

Hardware & kitchenware

Ratti

Castello 5825, calle delle Bande (041 240 4600).
Vaporetto San Zaccaria. **Open** 9am-12.30pm, 3.30-7.15pm Mon-Fri; 9am-12.30pm Sat.
Credit AmEx, MC, V. **Map** III 1A.
If Ratti doesn't have what you're looking for, it's time to worry. There are kitchen utensils, locks and other security items, household goods, appliances, adapters, televisions, radios and all kinds of electronic gadgets. Knowledgeable staff are on hand with useful advice, and you can even have a spare set of keys for your Venetian palazzo cut here.

Fratelli Regini

Castello 5615, calle al Ponte di Sant'Antonio
(041 520 4347). Vaporetto Rialto. **Open** 8.40am-noon, 3-7.30pm Mon-Fri; 8.40am-noon Sat.
No credit cards. Map III 1A.

Good food from all over Italy comes to **Aliani**.

FASHION MAGAZINE №200

twenty

subscribe

subscribe and get i-D Magazine monthly. 11 issues per year uk £30.00 europe £45.00 world £60.00

For further information go to: www.i-dmagazine.com

A rubber fetishist's dream, and the best place in town for *acqua alta* boots; it supplies all the leading hotels when the going gets splashy.

Jewellery & watches

Shops such as Nardi and Missiaglia in piazza San Marco have the most impressive and expensive jewellery. The smaller shops on the Rialto bridge offer more affordable silver and gold chains and bracelets sold by weight. Though Cartier (Mercerie San Zulian) and Bulgari (calle larga XXII Marzo) have their outlets here, you will find handmade items in workshops far from the chi-chi areas of town.

Laberintho

San Polo 2236, calle del Scaleter (041 710 017). Vaporetto San Tomà. **Open** 9.30am-1pm, 3.30-7pm Tue-Sat. **Credit** AmEx, DC, MC, V. **Map** I 2C.
A group of young goldsmiths runs this tiny *bottega* hidden away behind campo San Polo. They specialise in inlaid stones. In addition to the one-of-a-kind rings, earrings and necklaces on display, they will produce made-to-order pieces.

Sigifredo Cipolato

Castello 5336, Casselleria (041 522 8437). Vaporetto Rialto. **Open** 11am-7.30pm Tue-Sat. **Credit** MC, V. **Map** III 1A.
This jeweller painstakingly carves ebony to recreate the famous Moors' heads brooches and earrings.

Swatch

San Marco 4947, Mercerie del Capitello (041 522 8532). Vaporetto Rialto. **Open** 10am-8pm Mon-Sat, 11am-8pm Sun. **Credit** AmEx, DC, MC, V. **Map** II 4A.
The Swatch store has special preview launches of new models and carries a selection of spare parts.

Beads

See also p189 **Glass**.

Antichità

Dorsoduro 1195, calle Toletta (041 522 3159). Vaporetto Accademia. **Open** 9am-1pm, 3.30-7.30pm Mon-Sat. **No credit cards. Map** II 2B.
Beautiful, hand-painted antique glass beads that can be purchased individually or made into jewellery. There's also a nice selection of antiques and lace.

Anticlea Antiquariato

Castello 4719A, calle San Provolo (041 528 6946). Vaporetto San Zaccaria. **Open** 10am-1.30pm, 2-7.30pm Mon-Sat. **Credit** AmEx, DC, MC, V. **Map** III 1B.
Packed with curious antique treasures, as well as an outstanding selection of Venetian glass beads.

Costantini

San Marco 2627, calle Zaguri (041 521 0789). Vaporetto Santa Maria del Giglio. **Open** 9.30am-1.30pm, 3.30-7.30pm Mon-Sat. **Credit** MC, V. **Map** II 3B.

Constantini has a fantastic collection of Venetian glass beads sold by weight or already made up into necklaces, bracelets and brooches.

Perle e Dintorni

San Marco 3740, calle della Mandola (041 520 5068). Vaporetto Sant'Angelo. **Open** 10.30am-7.30pm daily. **Credit** AmEx, DC, MC, V. **Map** II 3A.
Buy bead jewellery or assemble your own, choosing from a vast assortment of glass beads, the majority of which are new versions based on antique designs.

Lace & linens

Lace is cheaper on the island of Burano than in the centre of Venice. Bear in mind in both places, however, that if it's cheap, it's machine made, and if it's very cheap it almost certainly hails from Taiwan rather than from some dark Venetian back room where ancient crones sit hunched over their age-old craft. If you want reliable, top-quality (and exorbitant) lace without taking the trip across to Burano, stick to big names such as Jesurum and Martinuzzi.

Annelie

Dorsoduro 2748, calle lunga San Barnaba (041 520 3277). Vaporetto Ca' Rezzonico. **Open** 9.30am-12.30pm, 4-7.30pm Mon-Fri; 9.30am-12.30pm Sat. **Credit** AmEx, MC, V. **Map** II 2B.
A delightful shop run by a delightful lady who has a beautiful selection of sheets, tablecloths, curtains, shirts and baby clothes, either fully embroidered or with lace detailing. Antique lace can also be had at reasonable prices.

Jesurum

San Marco 60-1, piazza San Marco (041 522 9864). Vaporetto Vallaresso. **Open** 9.30am-7.30pm Mon-Sat; 10am-1pm, 2-7pm Sun. **Credit** AmEx, DC, MC, V. **Map** II 4A.
Extremely elegant embroidered linens, towels and fabrics, from a lace company that has been going for more than 100 years. In the 19th century it was considered the only place to come for really good lace; it is still renowned for its sophisticated, traditional lacework. Be warned – quality costs.

La Fenice Atelier

San Marco 3537, campo Sant'Angelo (041 523 0578). Vaporetto Sant'Angelo. **Open** 10am-1.30pm, 3.30-7.30pm Mon-Sat. **Credit** AmEx, DC, MC, V. **Map** II 3A.
Slightly more affordable than Jesurum (*see above*), this tiny boutique has its workshop on the opposite side of town. Delicately hand-embroidered nightgowns, towels and sheets, as well as a catalogue full of designs for made-to-order items.

Martinuzzi

San Marco 67A, piazza San Marco (041 522 5068). Vaporetto Vallaresso. **Open** *Apr-Dec* 9am-7.30pm daily. *Jan-Mar* 9am-7.30pm Tue-Sat; 9am-12.30pm, 3-7pm Sun. **Credit** AmEx, DC, MC, V. **Map** II 4A.

The oldest lace shop in Venice, it has exclusive designs for bobbin lace items such as placemats, tablecloths and linens. If you have an odd-sized bed, not to worry – Martinuzzi will create a sheet set especially for you.

Masks

The carnival mask craze in Venice is a relatively recent phenomenon. In the early 1980s you could count the number of mask-making workshops on the fingers of one hand. With the local tourist board flogging its revamped *carnevale* for all it's worth, however, these characteristic collectibles became more of a money-spinner, and Venice is now suffering from a plague of uninspired, tourist-oriented mask shops, the worst of which feature some truly nauseating designs. Don't be fooled by cheaper imported versions, or those with local decorations painted on to ready-made surfaces.

Ca' Macana
Dorsoduro 3172, calle delle Botteghe (041 520 3229). Vaporetto Ca' Rezzonico. **Open** 10am-7.30pm daily. **Credit** AmEx, DC, MC, V. **Map** II 2A.
Easy to spot because of the eerie masked mannequin standing at the entrance, this workshop is packed with traditional *papier-maché* masks from the *commedia dell'arte*. A careful explanation of the mask-making process – from the clay model to moulds – is enthusiastically given by the artist-in-residence, who also organises courses.

MondoNovo
Dorsoduro 3063, rio terà Canal (041 528 7344). Vaporetto Ca' Rezzonico. **Open** 10am-7pm Mon-Sat. **Credit** AmEx, DC, MC, V. **Map** II 2A.
Venice's best-known *mascheraio* offers an enormous variety of masks both traditional and modern.

Papier Maché
Castello 5175, calle lunga Santa Maria Formosa (041 522 9995). Vaporetto Rialto. **Open** 9am-7.30pm daily. **Credit** AmEx, DC, MC, V. **Map** III 1A.
With more than 20 years' experience, this workshop uses traditional techniques to create contemporary masks. The artists draw inspiration from the works of Klimt, Kandinsky, Tiepolo and Carpaccio. The decoration determines the price, with simple designs starting at L50,000.

Tragicomica
San Polo 2800, calle dei Nomboli (041 721 102). Vaporetto San Tomà. **Open** 10am-7pm daily. **Credit** AmEx, DC, MC, V. **Map** I 2C.
A spellbinding collection of mythological masks, Harlequins, Columbines and Pantaloons, as well as 18th-century dandies and ladies. All are handmade and painted by an artist trained at Venice's Accademia di Belle Arti.

Paper products

Ebrû
San Marco 3471, campo Santo Stefano (041 523 8830). Vaporetto Accademia. **Open** 10am-7pm Mon-Sat; 11am-6pm Sun. **Credit** AmEx, DC, MC, V. **Map** II 3A-B.
Beautiful marbled hand-crafted paper, scarves, ties and other collectibles. These are Venetian originals, whose imitators can be found in a host of other shops around town.

Il Pavone
Dorsoduro 721, fondamenta Venier (041 523 4517). Vaporetto Accademia. **Open** 9.30am-1.30pm, 2.30-6.30pm Mon-Sat. **Credit** AmEx, DC, MC, V. **Map** II 3B.
Handmade paper with floral motifs in a variety of colours. Il Pavone also stocks boxes, picture frames, key chains and other objects, all decorated in the same style. Quality products at decent prices. **Branch**: San Marco 3287, salizzada San Samuele (041 523 8216).

Legatoria Piazzesi
San Marco 2511, campiello Feltrina (041 522 1202). Vaporetto Santa Maria del Giglio. **Open** 10am-1pm, 4-7pm Mon-Sat. **Credit** AmEx, DC, MC, V. **Map** II 3B.
The last remaining paper-maker in Venice to use the traditional wooden-block method of printing. Legatoria Piazzesi has an amazing selection of stunningly printed paper and cards.

Legatoria Polliero
San Polo 2995, campo dei Frari (041 528 5130). Vaporetto San Tomà. **Open** 10.30am-1pm, 3.30-7.30pm Mon-Sat. **Credit** AmEx, DC, MC, V. **Map** II 2A.
This bookbinding workshop, near the Frari church, sells leather-bound diaries, frames and photograph albums. But it's not cheap.

Records & music

Il Tempio della Musica
San Marco 5368, ramo dei Tedeschi (041 523 4552). Vaporetto Rialto. **Open** 9am-12.30pm, 3.30-7.30pm Mon-Sat. **Credit** AmEx, DC, MC, V. **Map** I 4C.
A large selection of all musical genres, though classical, jazz and opera are its forte.

Nalesso
San Marco 2765, calle Spezier (041 520 3329). Vaporetto Accademia or Sant'Angelo. **Open** 9.30am-12.30pm, 3.30-7.30pm Mon-Sat. **Credit** AmEx, DC, MC, V. **Map** II 3A.
In a music-filled courtyard just around the corner from the Conservatory, Nalesso sells musical instruments, books, magazines and sheet music. Nalesso also produces its own CDs and has the largest selection of classical music in Venice; it specialises, naturally, in Venetian music and composers.

Il Pavone for handmade paper. *See p184.*

Toys & curiosities

Agile
Castello 4895, campo San Lio (041 528 3426/
0339 1691 223/agile@virtualvenice.net/
www.virtualvenice.net/agile). Vaporetto Rialto.
Open 10am-7.30pm Mon-Sat (weather permitting).
No credit cards. Map II 4A.
An outdoor stand run by a group of professional
jugglers. In addition to equipment such as hi-tech
yo-yos and frisbees, you'll find a fantastic selection
of all sorts of odd toys, games, puppets and hats for
kids of all ages.

Bambolandia
San Polo 1462, calle Madonnetta (041 520
7502/beatrice@rialto.com/www.rialto.com/beatrice).
Vaporetto San Silvestro. **Open** 10am-12.30pm,
2-6pm Tue-Sat. **Credit** AmEx, DC, MC, V.
Map II 3A.
Entering into this Land of Dolls can be a bit unsettling – glass eyes, wigs and limbs of all kinds are
assembled here into perfect porcelain people. You'll
find Tom the Gondolier, Pinocchio and many other
finely dressed dolls.

Emporio Pettenello
Dorsoduro 2978, campo Santa Margherita (041 523
1167). Vaporetto Ca' Rezzonico. **Open** 9am-1pm,
3.30-8pm Mon-Sat. **No credit cards. Map** II 2A.
Run by the same family for more than 100 years,
this toy store still has its original furnishings.
Choose from marionettes, puppets, wooden toys,
dolls and incredible kaleidoscopes.

Wood, sculpture & frames

Cornici Trevisanello
Dorsoduro 662, campo San Vio (041 520 7779).
Vaporetto Accademia. **Open** 9am-7pm Mon-Fri;
9am-1pm Sat. **Credit** AmEx, DC, MC, V. **Map** II 3B.
Strategically located between the Accademia and
the Guggenheim, this father-son-and-daughter team
makes beautiful gilded frames, many with pearl,
mirror and glass inlay. Custom orders and shipping
are not a problem.

Dalla Venezia
Santa Croce 2074, calle Pesaro (041 721 276).
Vaporetto San Stae. **Open** 8am-noon, 2.30-7pm
Mon-Sat. **Credit** AmEx, DC, MC, V. **Map** I 3B.
Using the traditional technique of Venetian *tira-oro*
(gold leaf decoration), Dalla Venezia creates exquisite
gilded frames in his enchanting studio near Ca' Pesaro.

Gilberto Penzo
San Polo 2702, calle II dei Saoneri (041 719 372).
Vaporetto San Tomà. **Open** 9am-12.30pm, 3-6pm
Mon-Sat. **Credit** MC, V. **Map** II 2A.
A fascinating workshop for those interested in
Venetian boats of all kinds. Gilberto Penzo creates
detailed models of gondolas, sandolos and toppos
and remarkable reproductions of vaporettos. Inex-
pensive kits are also on sale if you would like to
practise the fine art of shipbuilding.

Livio De Marchi
San Marco 3157, salizzada San Samuele
(041 528 5694). Vaporetto San Samuele.
Open 9.30am-12.30pm, 1.30-6.30pm Mon-Fri;
Sat by appointment. **Credit** AmEx, DC, MC, V.
Map II 3A.
Livio de Marchi has remarkably lifelike wooden
sculptures of anything from paintbrushes and
books to hanging underwear and crumpled jeans.
Definitely something to see.

Spazio Legno
Giudecca 213B, fondamenta San Giacomo
(041 2777 5505). Vaporetto Redentore.
Open 9am-7pm Mon-Sat. **No credit cards.**
Map II C3.
The place to come when you need a new *forcola*
for your gondola, or a pair of oars. Saverio Pastor
is one of only three recognised *marangon* (oar-
makers) in Venice; he specialises in making the
elaborate walnut-wood rests (*forcole*) that are the
symbols of the gondolier's trade; each gondolier
has his own customised *forcola*, which he guards
with his life. Bookmarks, postcards and some
books on Venetian boat-works in English are also
available here.

Services

Finding conveniences in an inconvenient city
such as Venice can be frustrating, but if you're
determined, you can track down one-hour dry-
cleaning or a swift film developing service.

Servizio Città
San Polo 1886, calle dei Botteri (041 524 2606).
Vaporetto San Silvestro. **Open** 9am-12.30pm,
4-7.30pm Mon, Tue, Thur, Fri; 9am-12.30pm Wed,
Sat. **No credit cards. Map** I 3C.
Try Servizio Città for a wide range of services
including domestic help, translation, plumbers,
electricians and painters. With luck you might even
find you can get sitters for your baby, your house
or your pet.

Clothing & shoe repairs

Tolin Roberto
Dorsoduro 3769A, calle Crosera (041 524 4090)
Vaporetto San Tomà. **Open** 3pm-7pm Mon;
8.30am-1pm, 3-7.30pm Tue-Fri; 8.30am-noon Sat.
No credit cards. Map II 2A.

Eat, Drink, Shop

Shopping by area

San Marco

Antiquus (antiques, p175); **Araba Fenice** (fashion: designers, p179); **Bampa** (fashion: accessories, p179); **Bevilacqua** (fabrics & accessories, p177); **Bruno Magli** (fashion: shoes, p179); **Cassa di Risparmio** (ticket agency, p188); **Costantini** (jewellery: beads, p183); **Danilo Carraro Ottica** (optician, p188); **Diesel Jeans** (fashion: trendsetters, p179); **Domus** (design & household, p177); **Ebrû** (paper, p184); **Fantoni Libri Arte** (bookshops, p176); **Gaggio** (fabrics & accessories, p177); **Godi Fiorenza** (fashion: designers, p179); **Il Tempio della Musica** (records & music, p184); **Italo Mariani** (fashion: shoes, p180); **Jesurum** (lace & linens, p183); **Kleine Galerie** (antiques, p175); **La Fenice Atelier** (lace & linens, p183); **Laura Crovato** (fashion: second-hand, p180); **Legatoria Piazzesi** (paper, p184); **Livio De Marchi** (sculpture, p185); **M Antichità e Oggetti d'Arte** (fabrics & accessories, p177); **Martinuzzi** (lace & linens, p183); **Materia Prima** (ceramics, p176); **Nalesso** (records & music, p184); **Perle e Dintorni** (jewellery: beads, p183);

Rolando Segalin (fashion: shoes, p180); **Studium** (bookshops, p176); **Swatch** (jewellery & watches, p183); **Testolini** (art supplies, p175); **Trois** (fabrics & accessories, p177); **VeLa** (ticket agencies, p188); **Venetia Studium** (fabrics & accessories, p177).

Castello

Agile (toys, p185); **Anticlea Antiquariato** (jewellery: beads, p183); **Bottiglieria Colonna** (drink, p181); **Contatto Video** (video rental, p188); **Filippi Editore Venezia** (bookshops, p176); **Fratelli Regini** (hardware & kitchenware, p181); **Il Milione** (fabrics & accessories, p177); **Papier Maché** (masks, p184); **Pinco Pallino** (fashion: designers, p179); **Ratti** (hardware & kitchenware, p181); **Sigifredo Cipolato** (jewellery, p183); **Vidal e Fantini** (clothing repairs, p186); **Vino e... Vini** (drink, p181).

Cannaregio

Body Shop (cosmetics & perfumes, p176); **Centro Pulisecco** (dry-cleaner's, p186); **Cibele** (health foods, p181); **Coin** (one-stop, p175); **Giacomo Rizzo** (food: alimentari,

This genuine Venetian shoemaker will make your shoes new again for a reasonable price – he usually asks all foreign clients to send him a postcard. It's a small shop and sometimes the fumes are over-whelming, but he'll get the job done.

Vidal e Fantini

Castello 5754, calle del Paradiso (no phone).
Vaporetto Rialto. **Open** 10am-5.30pm Tue-Sat.
No credit cards. Map II 4A.
Two ladies carry out minor repairs and alterations. A hem job costs between L12,000-L18,000 and takes about a week. If it is urgent, the price goes up.

Carnevale costume rentals

Atelier Pietro Longhi

San Polo 2604B, rio terà Frari (041 714 478/
pietrolonghi@rialto.com) Vaporetto San Tomà.
Open 9am-1pm, 2-7.30pm Tue-Sun. **Credit** AmEx, DC, MC, V. **Map** I 2C.
Rents cost L200,000 for the first day and each additional day at half price.

Nicolao Atelier

Cannaregio 5590A, calle del Magazen
(041 520 7051). Vaporetto Rialto.
Open 9am-1pm, 2-6pm Mon-Fri, by appointment only. **No credit cards. Map** I 4C.

Costume rentals for television, films and theatre, as well as for individuals. Costumes cost from L120,000 up to L400,000 per day, with a reduction for each additional day thereafter.

Dry-cleaners & launderettes

In Venice there is only one self-service laundrette, and only a small number of laundries that will do your wash, charging by the kilo. Small, family-run dry-cleaners are more expensive than the chains that have opened up in recent years.

Bea Vita Lavanderia

Santa Croce 665A-B, calle delle Chioverette
(0348 301 7457). Vaporetto Ferrovia.
Open 8am-10pm daily. **Map** I 1B.
The first of its kind in Venice, this coin-operated launderette is a five-minute walk from the station. Be sure to bring lots of change because the machines only operate with small bills and coins. L6,000 for 8kg, L10,000 for 10kg and L1,000 for the dryer.

Centro Pulisecco

Cannaregio 6262D, calle della Testa
(041 522 5011). Vaporetto Ca' d'Oro.
Open 8.30am-12.30pm, 3-7pm Mon-Fri.
No credit cards. Map I 4C.

p180); **Laboratorio Blu** (bookshops, p176); **Mori & Bozzi** (fashion: shoes, p180); **Nicolao Atelier** (costume rentals, p186); **Punto Vista** (opticians, p188); **Standa** (one-stop, p175); **Surya Viaggi** (travel agencies, p188).

San Polo & Santa Croce

Aliani (food: alimentari, p180); **Atelier Pietro Longhi** (costume rentals, p186); **Balocoloc** (fashion: accessories, p177); **Bambolandia** (toys, p185); **Bea Vita Lavanderia** (launderette, p186); **Cartoleria Arte e Design** (art supplies, p175); **Ceramiche** (ceramics, p176); **Dalla Venezia** (frames, p185); **Drogheria Mascari** (food: alimentari, p180); **Erboristeria Mediterranea** (cosmetics & perfumes, p176); **Francis Model** (fashion: bags, p179); **Gilberto Penzo** (wood, p185); **Graphoprint** (photocopies, p188); **Guarinoni** (antiques, p175); **Hibiscus** (fashion: accessories, p179); **Interpress Photo** (film & development, p187); **Laberintho** (jewellery, p183); **Laboratorio Arte & Costume** (fashion: second hand, p180); **Legatoria Polliero** (paper, p184); **Prima Visione** (fashion: trendsetters, p179); **Rialto Bio Center** (health foods, p181); **Sabbie e Nebbie** (ceramics, p177); **Salone Mary** (hairdressers, p187); **Servizio Città** (services, p185); **Tragicomica** (masks, p184).

Dorsoduro

Annelie (lace & linens, p183); **Antichità** (jewellery: beads, p183); **Arras** (fabrics & accessories, p177); **BA BA** (fashion: trendsetters, p179); **Billa** (supermarkets, p181); **Ca' Foscarina 2** (bookshops, p175); **Ca' Foscarina Puntocopie** (photocopies, p188) **Ca' Macana** (masks, p184); **Camilla** (ceramics, p176); **Cartoleria Accademia** (art supplies, p175); **Cesana Photo** (film & development, p187); **Cornici Trevisanello** (frames, p185); **CTS** (travel agencies, p188); **Emporio Pettenello** (toys, p185); **Gualti** (fashion: accessories, p179); **Il Pavone** (paper, p184); **Libreria San Pantalon** (bookshops, p176); **Libreria Toletta & Toletta Studio** (bookshops, p176); **MondoNovo** (masks, p184); **Patagonia** (bookshops, p176); **Pulilavanderia** (dry cleaners, p187); **Studio Parrucchieri 90** (hairdressers, p187); **Stik Travel** (travel agencies, p188); **Tolin Roberto** (shoe repairs, p185); **Vinaria Nave de Oro** (drink, p181).

La Giudecca & San Giorgio

Spazio Legno (wood, p185).

Mestre

Angeloni (art supplies, p175); **Auchan Centro Commerciale** (one-stop, p175); **Centro Le Barche** (one-stop, p175).

Centro Pulisecco offers dry-cleaning only. Trousers cost L4,000, jackets L5,000 and sweaters L3,000. A one-hour service is available.
Branch: Cannaregio 1749, rio terà del Cristo (041 718 020).

Pulilavanderia

Dorsoduro 3411, campo Santa Margherita (041 521 2609). Vaporetto Ca' Rezzonico. **Open** 8.45am-1pm, 3-6.30pm Mon-Fri. **No credit cards. Map** II 2A.
Express dry-cleaning for shirts; ironing service; clothes washed for L8,000 per kilo (minimum 5kg).

Film & development

Cesana Photo

Dorsoduro 879, rio terà Antonio Foscarini (041 522 2020/041 522 7888). Vaporetto Accademia. **Open** 9am-1pm, 2.20-7pm Mon-Fri. **Credit** AmEx, MC, V **Map** II 2B.
You won't find low prices but you will find fast service at this shop near the Ponte dell'Accademia: colour developing in 25 minutes and slides in an hour.

Interpress Photo

San Polo 365, campo delle Beccarie (041 528 6978). Vaporetto San Silvestro. **Open** 3.30-7.30pm Mon; 9am-12.30pm, 3.30pm-7.30pm Tue-Sat. **Credit** MC, V. **Map** I 3C.

This is definitely one of the cheapest places in Venice for film development, and probably one of the best: 24 exposures will set you back L15,000. This small photographic agency also provides a one-hour service and passport photographs.

Hairdressers

Prices are *à la carte*: each dab of styling foam or puff of hair spray pushes up the bill. Appointments are recommended and most salons are closed on Mondays.

Studio Parrucchieri 90

Dorsoduro 2855, calle lunga San Barnaba (041 523 7922). Vaporetto Ca' Rezzonico. **Open** 9am-5pm Tue-Sat. **No credit cards. Map** II 2B.
Where chic young Venetians (male and female) go for a trim or a full makeover.

Salone Mary

Santa Croce 2176, campo Santa Maria Mater Domini (041 524 1372). Vaporetto San Stae. **Open** 9am-12.30pm, 3-7pm Tue-Thur; 9am-5pm Fri, Sat. **No credit cards. Map** I 3C.
A no-frills women's salon with reasonable prices. Try with or without an appointment. Cuts cost from L15,000 to L30,000. You can also get manicures, hair colouring and highlighting.

Photocopies & faxes

Thanks to the Università Ca' Foscari and the University Institute of Architecture (both in Dorsoduro), finding a place to make a photocopy or two is not overly difficult or expensive. The many *tabacchi* that send faxes usually announce the fact in their front windows, as do other service centres (for Internet points, *see p282*).

Ca' Foscarina Puntocopie
Dorsoduro 3224, calle Foscari (041 523 1814). Vaporetto Ca' Rezzonico. **Open** 9am-1.30pm, 2.30-6pm Mon-Fri. **No credit cards. Map** II 2A.
Get photocopies, binding and laser printing here. Serves stressed-out students with a thesis deadline; L100 per photocopy.

Graphoprint
Santa Croce 180, fondamenta dei Tolentini (041 528 7035). Vaporetto Piazzale Roma. **Open** 9am-7pm Mon-Fri. **No credit cards. Map** I 1C.
Photocopies can be had at L100 per copy. It's located just a couple of steps from the University Institute of Architecture and is therefore used to outsize and delicate documents.

Opticians

Most opticians will do minor running repairs on the spot and (usually) free of charge.

Danilo Carraro Ottica
San Marco 3706, calle della Mandola (041 520 4258/www.otticacarraro.it). Vaporetto Sant'Angelo. **Open** 9am-1pm, 3-7.30pm Mon-Sat. **Credit** AmEx, DC, MC, V. **Map** II 3A.
Get yourself some unique and funky eyewear – the frames are exclusively produced and guaranteed for life. Extraordinary quality at reasonable prices.

Punto Vista (Elvio Carraro)
Cannaregio 1982, campiello Anconetta (041 720 453). Vaporetto San Marcuola. **Open** 3.30-7.30pm Mon; 9am-12.30pm, 3.30-7.30pm Tue-Sat. **Credit** AmEx, MC, DC, V. **Map** I 2B.
Eyeglasses, sunglasses, saline solution; sells cameras too. Walk-in eye examinations, contact lenses and repairs.

Ticket agencies

Cassa di Risparmio
San Marco 4216, campo San Luca (041 521 0161). Vaporetto Rialto. **Open** 8.30am-1.30pm Mon-Fri. **Credit** AmEx, DC, MC, V **Map** II 3A.
At this branch of the Cassa di Risparmio bank you will find tickets to most of the theatrical events and concerts taking place in Venice, including those at La Fenice (or the temporary PalaFenice). Next to going directly to the theatre, this is your best bet for getting seats.

VeLa
San Marco 1018, calle dei Fuseri (041 972 073/041 240 9150/fax 041 240 9127/vela@velaspa.com/ www.velaspa.com). Vaporetto Rialto. **Open** 7.30am-7pm Mon-Sat. **No credit cards. Map** II 4A.
Through its new merchandising operation VeLa, the Venetian public transport company ACTV sells tickets to museums, concerts and exhibitions in both Venice and Mestre. Tickets can also be purchased from the following ACTV vaporetto stops as well: Tronchetto, Piazzale Roma, Ferrovie, Rialto, San Zaccaria and Zattere.

Travel Agencies

CTS (Centro Turistico Studentesco)
Dorsoduro 3225, calle Foscari (041 520 5660/ info@cts.it/www.cts.it/). Vaporetto Ca' Rezzonico or San Tomà. **Open** 9.30am-1.30pm, 3-7pm Mon-Fri. **No credit cards. Map** II 2A.
This agency caters to its own members as well as to students in general. Discount airfares, international train tickets and lots of information for student travellers. ISICs cost L15,000: bring a passport-sized photo with you and a document proving you are a student. It also has tickets to concerts, exhibitions and the theatre at discounted prices for members.

Stik Travel
Dorsoduro 3944, calle San Pantalon (041 520 0988/ stiktrv@interbusiness.it). Vaporetto San Tomà. **Open** 9am-1pm, 2-7pm Mon-Fri. **Credit** AmEx, MC, DC, V. **Map** II 2A.
The Stik Travel staff are not only friendly but extraordinarily efficient – a winning combination. Stik offers specials to Paris and has a money-changing service as well.

Surya Viaggi
Cannaregio 2530, fondamenta della Misericordia (041 275 0131/fax 041 275 8287/ suryaviaggi@libero.it). Vaporetto San Marcuola. **Open** 10am-6pm Mon-Fri. **Credit** AmEx, DC, MC, V. **Map** I 3B.
Plane and train tickets, and tickets for cruise ships departing from Venice. You are assured of extremely professional, courteous service.

Video rental

Contatto Video
Castello 6153, calle lunga Santa Maria Formosa (041 522 8962). Vaporetto Rialto. **Open** 10am-2.30pm, 3.30-8pm daily. **Credit** AmEx, DC, MC, V. **Map** III 1A.
Video sales and one-day rentals; stocks about 150 films in English. Non-members pay L7,000 for new releases and L5,000 for old releases; members pay L5,000 and L3,000 respectively. To join, you should take along L30,000 and photo ID.

Glass

Some of the lagoon city's charms are quite transparent – this one especially so.

Glass has been made in and around Venice for over 1,000 years. The industry shifted to Murano in 1291, when all glass furnaces, except those engaged in faking gem stones, were ordered there to limit the fire hazard in Venice, and to confine the glass-works to an area more easily serviced. The glass-workers enjoyed a privileged position in Venetian society that reflected the economic importance of the goods they created for an international market.

Glass manufacture – a romance of sand and fire, liquid and air – enthralled visitors to Venice in the 15th century for the same reasons that a visit to a factory fascinates today's tourist. Murano has a profusion of small- and medium-sized factories, each with its own speciality. Many of these are still in the hands of an elite group of glass families, who have been involved in glass production since the 13th century. A 'large' factory seldom has more than five or six *piazze* (workplaces), each occupied by a *maestro*.

Most serious production houses are not open to the public (for exceptions, *see p190* **The real**

Murano thing). But opportunities to see glass being blown are not lacking. It's almost impossible to come here and not be accosted by hucksters offering free trips to 'the' glass factory in Murano. These offers are usually sponsored by and paid for by one of the large showrooms, which will expect to recoup its investment. If you accept the 'free' trip, you'll be met by a salesperson. There's no obligation to buy, but the pressure is difficult to resist.

Many outlets in Venice offer prices that are as low or lower than on Murano. Glass gallery owners are a charming breed, who warm to serious collectors. Should your favourite glass artist not be showing when you visit, a gallerist may try to arrange a private viewing.

Showrooms & blowing

CAM Vetri D'Arte
Murano, piazzale Colonna 1B (041 739 944). Vaporetto Colonna. **Open** *Apr-Oct* 9-6pm (demonstrations till 4.30pm) daily. *Nov-Mar* 9am-4.30pm daily. **Credit** AmEx, DC, MC, V. **Map** Murano.

Eat, Drink, Shop

Glassware from **Antiquaria Micheluzzi**. *See p191*.

CAM specialises in mirrors, goblets, and objets d'art. Their adjoining factory offers demonstrations of traditional Venetian chandelier manufacture.

Mazzega
Murano, fondamenta da Mula 147 (041 736 888/ www.mazzega.it/info@mazzega.it). Vaporetto Museo or Venier. **Open** 9am-5pm daily. **Credit** AmEx, DC, MC, V. **Map** Murano.
Excellent Venetian glass of all types; demonstrations of chandelier production and glass sculpture.

The real Murano thing

Gaining access to factories, rather than showroom outlets, is difficult. The following are among the best, and will allow limited numbers of visitors who may buy at factory prices.

Elite Murano
Murano, calle del Cimitero 6 (041 736 168). Vaporetto Venier. **Open** 8.15am-5pm Mon-Fri. **Credit** MC,V. **Map** Murano.
Elite produces the highest-quality Venetian goblets and reproductions of Venetian antique glassware.

Fornasier Luigi
Murano, calle del Paradiso 70 (041 736 176). Vaporetto Navagero. **Open** 8am-1pm, 2.30-5.30pm Mon-Fri. **Credit** MC, V. **Map** Murano.
Not easy to find, the factory of the Fornasier family – Fabio, Roberto and Lucia – makes traditional Venetian chandeliers to order.

Fratelli Barbini
Murano, calle Bertolini 36 (041 739 777). Vaporetto Colonna. **Open** 7am-6pm Mon-Fri. **Credit** MC, V. **Map** Murano.
Some of the best, and most original, Venetian mirrors are to be had here. The Barbini brothers have been innovative leaders on Murano for decades.

Galleries

These galleries are dedicated to work in glass by fine contemporary artists.

Berengo Fine Arts
Murano, fondamenta Vetrai 109A (041 739 453). Vaporetto Colonna. **Open** 10am-6pm daily. **Credit** AmEx, DC, MC, V. **Map** Murano.
Adriano Berengo is establishing a fiefdom producing works in glass designed by international artists.
Branches: Murano, fondamenta Manin 68 (041 527 4198); calle larga San Marco (041 241 0763); San Marco 3337, salizzada San Samuele (041 522 1028).

Galleria Daniele Luchetta
San Marco 2513A, campiello de la Feltrina (041 528 5092). Vaporetto Santa Maria del Giglio. **Open** 10am-1pm, 3.30-7.30pm Mon-Sat. **Credit** AmEx, DC, MC, V. **Map** II 3B.
One-offs and limited-editions from designs by international artists, produced by Murano craftsmen.

Galleria D'Arte & Divetro
San Marco 2671, campo San Maurizio (041 520 7859). Vaporetto Santa Mario di Giglio. **Open** 10am-1pm, 2.30-7.30pm Wed-Sat; 11am-7pm Sun. **Credit** AmEx, MC, V. **Map** II 3B.
This branch of Caterina Tognon's larger gallery in Bergamo features Italian and international artists.

Galleria Marina Barovier
San Marco 3216, salizzada San Samuele (041 522 6102/www.barovier.it/barovier@gpnet.it). Vaporetto San Samuele. **Open** 9.30am-12.30pm, 3.30-7pm Tue-Sat. **Credit** AmEx, MC, V. **Map** II 3A.
Renowned for its collections of classic 20th-century Venetian glass, Marina Barovier's gallery is the sole Venetian source for contemporary glass by Lino Tagliapietra and other contemporary artists.

Galleria Regina, Arte in Vetro
Murano, riva Longa 25A (tel/fax 041 739 202). Vaporetto Museo. **Open** 10am-4pm Mon-Sat. **Credit** AmEx, MC, V. **Map** Murano.
Unique and limited-edition works by Muranese and Italian artists principally.

Galleria Rosella Junck
San Marco 2360, calle delle Ostreghe (041 520 7747). Vaporetto Santa Maria del Giglio. **Open** 10am-12.30pm, 4-7.30pm Mon-Sat. **Credit** AmEx MC, V. **Map** II 3B.
Rosella Junck shows Murano glass from the 1920s-80s, and rare works from the 16th-19th centuries and contemporary glass in her other branches.
Branches: San Marco 3463, calle delle Botteghe (041 528 6537); San Marco 1997, campo San Fantin (041 521 0759).

Galleria San Nicolò
Dorsoduro 2793, fondamenta Traghetto (041 522 1535). Vaporetto Ca' Rezzonico. **Open** 10.30am-1pm, 3.30-7pm Tue-Sat. **Credit** AmEx, MC, V. **Map** II 2A.
In her space on the Grand Canal, Louise Berndt specialises in established and emerging artists.

Contemporary design

L'Isola
San Marco 1469, campo San Moisè (041 523 1973). Vaporetto Vallaresso. **Open** 9am-7.30pm Mon-Sat; 10am-7pm Sun. **Credit** AmEx, DC, MC, V. **Map** II 4B.
Original glass pieces designed by Carlo Moretti.

La Murrina
Murano, piazzale Colonna 1 (041 527 4605). Vaporetto Colonna. **Open** 9.30am-5pm daily. **Credit** AmEx, DC, MC, V. **Map** Murano.
Modern glass produced to its own designs.
Branch: Murano, riva Longa 17 (041 739 255).

Murano Collezioni
Murano, fondamenta Manin 1C (041 736 272). Vaporetto Colonna. **Open** Apr-Oct 10am-6pm Mon-Sat. Nov-Dec 10am-5pm Mon-Sat. **Credit** AmEx, DC, MC, V. **Map** Murano.

Eat, Drink, Shop

This innovative retail venture provides access to the entire collections of three glass-houses: Barovier & Toso, Carlo Moretti and Venini.

Pauly

San Marco 4391A, calle larga San Marco (041 520 9899). Vaporetto Vallaresso. **Open** *Nov-Mar* 10am-1pm, 3-7pm Mon-Sat. *Apr-Oct* 10am-7pm daily. **Credit** AmEx, DC, MC, V. **Map** II 4A.
Though just off piazza San Marco, Pauly often has a more reasonable mark-up on its range of Murano glass than many of the outlets on Murano itself.

Venini

San Marco 314, piazza San Marco (041 522 4045/www.venini.it/venini@venini.it). Vaporetto Vallaresso. **Open** 9am-12.30pm, 3.30-7.30pm Tue-Sat. **Credit** AmEx, EC, MC, V. **Map** II 4A.
Top-of-the-line contemporary hand-blown glass. Now owned by Royal Copenhagen of Denmark, Venini is no longer the essential point of reference it once was, but is still a must for glass fans.

Individual outlets

Some glass artists prefer to retail their own work in modest shops. Don't let the simple surroundings fool you: many of these glass-makers are noted international artists.

Antiquaria Micheluzzi

Dorsoduro 1071, calle della Toletta (041 528 2190). Vaporetto Accademia. **Open** 10am-1pm, 4-7pm Tue-Sat. **Credit** AmEx, MC, V. **Map** II 2B.
Great deals on classic glass. Recently the owner, Massimo Micheluzzi, has begun to design some stunningly original pieces in glass.

Cesare Toffolo

Murano, Bressagio, viale Garibaldi 8A (041 736 460). Vaporetto Faro or Colonna. **Open** *Feb-Oct* 10am-6pm daily. *Nov-Jan* 10am-6pm Mon-Sat. **Credit** AmEx, DC, MC, V. **Map** Murano.
Cesare Toffolo specialises in own-design unique and limited-series pieces, flame-worked in Pyrex.

Costantini

Cannaregio 5311, calle del Fumo (041 522 2265). Vaporetto Fondamenta Nove. **Open** 9am-1pm, 2-6pm Mon-Sat. **Credit** AmEx, MC, V. **Map** I 4B.
Vittorio Costantini is recognised as one of the most original Venetian lamp work specialists. His animals, insects, fish and birds are stunningly realistic.

Galleria Bellus

Dorsoduro 369, campo Barbaro (041 523 4881). Vaporetto Salute. **Open** 11am-6pm Wed-Sun. **Credit** AmEx, MC, V. **Map** II 3B.
Studio-gallery with works by Orlando Zennaro, son Stefano Zennaro, and Stefano's wife Daniela Zentilin.

Genninger Studio

Dorsoduro 2793A, calle del Traghetto (041 522 5565). Vaporetto Ca' Rezzonico. **Open** 10.30am-1.30pm, 2.30-6pm Mon-Sat. **Credit** AmEx, MC, V. **Map** II 2B.

Leslie Ann Genninger exhibits her glass jewellery and her lamps, goblets and drinking glasses in her studio-home on the Grand Canal.

Sent Gugliemo

Murano, fondamenta Vetrai 8A (041 739 100). Vaporetto Colonna. **Open** *Apr-Oct* 8am-6pm daily. *Nov-Mar* 8am-6pm Mon-Fri. **Credit** AmEx, DC, MC, V. **Map** Murano.
The Sent family are a reliable source of beautifully displayed craft and good design. They specialise in vases, paper weights and drinking glasses.

Susanna & Marina Sent

Dorsoduro 669, campo San Vio (041 520 8136). Vaporetto Accademia. **Open** 11am-6pm Mon, Wed-Sat. **Credit** AmEx, DC, MC, V. **Map** II 3B.
Among Venice's best contemporary glass jewellery.

Tiozzo Sergio di Claudio Tiozzo

Murano, fondamenta Manin 45 (041 527 4155/ www.tiozzosergio.com/info@tiozzosergio.com). Vaporetto Colonna or Faro. **Open** *Apr-Oct* 10.30am-6pm daily. *Nov-Mar* 11am-5pm Mon-Sat. **Credit** AmEx, DC, MC, V. **Map** Murano.
Jewellery and objects in the Murano tradition of *murrine* (mosaic glass). The activity has recently passed from father to son; some of the latter's designs are well on the way to becoming classics.

For something different

FGB

San Marco 2514, campo Santa Maria del Giglio (041 523 6556). Vaporetto Santa Maria del Giglio. **Open** 10am-7pm daily. **Credit** AmEx, DC, MC, V. **Map** II 3B.
Handmade objects including insects, animals, plates and jewellery. Christmas tree ornaments a speciality.

Ivano Soffiato

Dorsoduro 1188, calle della Toletta (041 521 0480) Vaporetto Accademia. **Open** 9.30am-6.30pm daily. **Credit** AmEx, MC, V. **Map** II 2B.
One of the best places to pick up souvenirs in Venice. Ivano makes about half of the tourist goodies sold in the city: here you can watch him do it.

L'Angolo di Passato

Dorsoduro 3276A, campiello degli Squellini (041 528 7896). Vaporetto Ca' Rezzonico or San Tomà. **Open** 4-7pm Mon; 10am-noon, 4-7pm Tue-Sat. **Credit** MC, V. **Map** II 2A.
Giordana Naccari's small shop is where Venetian antique glass dealers go to find great buys. She specialises in Murano glass from the end of the 1800s to the present, and unique contemporary glassware.

Totem Gallery – Il Canale

Dorsoduro 878, campo Carità (041 522 3641/fax 041 943 158). Vaporetto Accademia. **Open** 10am-1pm, 3-7pm Mon-Sat. **Credit** AmEx, V. **Map** II 2B.
Totem Gallery is full of *gioielli poveri,* jewellery made from non-precious materials, including some beautifully strung trade beads.

Eat, Drink, Shop

VETRERIA ARTISTICA COLLEONI

DOVE OSANO... I MAESTRI MURANESI

di Luigi Moro & C.
30141 Murano (Venezia)
Fond.ta dei battuti 12
Tel. +39 041 5274872
fax +39 041 736329
E-mail: colleoni@colleoni.com
http://www.colleoni.com

Arts & Entertainment

By Season

Tourism-boosting masked pageantry and regattas galore.

Since the earliest days of the Republic, festivals, processions and popular celebrations have been an intricate part of Venice's social fabric. The government of La Serenissima used pageantry both to assert the rigidly hierarchical nature of Venetian society, and to give the lower orders the chance to let off steam.

Just as the middle classes had the *Scuole* – which worked like gentlemen's clubs – so the working classes had crude entertainments such as the *corsa al toro* (bullfight) in campo Santo Stefano, or bloody pitched battles organised between rival sections of the populace. The government set an example by parading whenever the occasion arose; the church, too, was a strong force, and each of the 100-plus saints that the city's churches and convents were dedicated to had feast days to celebrate.

Some of Venice's annual festivities are modern revivals – **Carnevale** (*see below*) being the most successful in PR terms. But one should not underestimate Venetians' attachment to their own traditions – especially boat-related ones. The **Festa del Redentore** (*see p195*) is a huge excuse for a party, while the **Regata Storica** (*see p196*) may look like it's funded by the tourist board, but Venetians do get seriously involved in the boat races that lurk beneath the pageantry.

See also p289 **When to go: Holidays**.

Spring

Carnevale

Date ten days ending on Shrove Tuesday.
Though it had existed since the Middle Ages, Carnevale came into its own in Venice in the 18th century. Until then, religious processions had dominated the city's ceremonies; but as the Venetian Republic went into terminal decline, the city's pagan side began to emerge. Carnevale became an outlet for all that had been prohibited and controlled for centuries by the strong arm of the Doge. During the carnival, elaborate, fanciful structures would be set up in piazza San Marco as stages for acrobats, tumblers, wrestlers and other performers. Masks served not only as an escape from the drabness of everyday life but to conceal the wearer's identity – a useful ploy for nuns on the lam or slumming patricians.

The Napoleonic invasion in 1797 brought an end to the fun and games, and Carnevale was only resuscitated in 1980. The city authorities

and hoteliers' association saw the tourist potential of all those long-nosed masks and frilly dresses, and today the heavily subsidised celebrations draw revellers from all over the world. The party starts ten days before *martedì grasso* (Shrove Tuesday). On the first Saturday of Carnevale there is usually a masked procession and party in piazza San Marco. The highlight of the first Sunday is the *Volo della Colombina*, when a mechanical dove slides along a rope strung between the campanile and the basilica, scattering confetti on the crowds below. On *giovedì grasso* (the Thursday before Shrove Tuesday) – generally around 4pm – the competition for best costume takes place. On Friday evening there is usually a masked ball in piazza San Marco, which is open to all appropriately dressed revellers who can dance a minuet. The final Saturday sees yet another masked procession, this time by gondola along the Grand Canal. The whole thing culminates on Shrove Tuesday with clowns, acrobats and fireworks in piazza San Marco, and a concert in the church of the Pietà.

Su e Zo Per I Ponti

Date 4th Sun of Lent. **Information** 041 590 4717. **Enrolment** L5,000; for individuals this can be done in piazza San Marco on morning of event; groups should phone ahead.
Literally 'up and down bridges', this privately organised excursion through island Venice offers a great opportunity to get to grips with the city. Inspired by the traditional *bacarada* (bar crawl), it is an orienteering event in which you are given a map and a list of checkpoints to tick off. Old hands take their time checking out the *bacari* (*see chapter* **Bacari & Snacks**) along the way.

Benedizione del Fuoco

Basilica di San Marco. Vaporetto Vallaresso or San Zaccaria. **Date** Thur before Easter Sun. **Map** II 4B.
Just after dusk, all the lights are turned off inside St Mark's basilica and a fire is lit in the narthex (entrance porch). Bearing the holy fire, a procession winds its way around the church, lighting all the candles one by one.

Festa di San Marco

Bacino di San Marco. Vaporetto Vallaresso or San Zaccaria. **Date** 25 Apr.
The traditional feast day of Venice's patron saint is a low-key affair. In the morning there is a solemn mass in the Basilica, followed by a gondola regatta between the island of Sant'Elena and the Punta della

The revived **Carnevale** draws tourists in their many thousands. *See p194.*

Dogana at the entrance to the Grand Canal. The day is also known as *La Festa del boccolo* ('bud'): red rose buds are given to wives and lovers.

Festa e Regata della Sensa

San Nicolò del Lido & Bacino di San Marco.
Date May. **Information** 041 274 7762.
Back in the days of the Venetian Republic, the Doge would board the glorious state barge, the *Bucintoro*, and be rowed out to the island of Sant'Andrea, facing the lagoon's main outlet to the Adriatic, followed by a fleet of small boats. Here he would throw a gold ring overboard, to symbolise *lo sposalizio del mare* – Venice's marriage with the sea. Today the mayor takes the place of the Doge, the Bucintoro looks like a glorified fruit boat and the ring has become a laurel wreath. The ceremony is now performed at San Nicolò, on the northernmost point of the Lido, and is followed by a regatta. Venetians pray it doesn't rain; if it does, local lore says, it'll tip down for the next 40 days (*'Se piove il giorno della Sensa per quaranta giorni non semo sensa'*).

Vogalonga

Date May, first Sun after Ascension.
Information 041 529 8711/041 274 7739.
This relatively new regatta is open to anyone in any type of rowing boat who has enough strength to complete the 33km (20.5 miles) route through the lagoon and the city's two main canals – the Canale di Cannaregio and the Grand Canal. Boats set off from San Marco at 8.30am.

Summer

Biennale D'Arte Contemporanea

Giardini di Castello. Vaporetto Giardini.
Date mid June-Nov every odd-numbered year.
Information 041 521 8711. **Map** III 4B.
Established in 1895, this biennial bunfight is the *Jeux Sans Frontières* of the contemporary art world (*see p203* **The Biennale**).

Festa di San Pietro

San Pietro in Castello. Vaporetto Giardini.
Date week around 29 June. **Map** III 4B.
The most lively and villagey of Venice's many local festivals. A week of events centres on the church green of San Pietro in the furthest-flung eastern part of Castello: there are concerts, competitions, food stands and a puppet theatre.

Cinema all'aperto

Campo San Polo. Vaporetto San Silvestro.
Date mid July-early Sept. **Map** I 2C.
In a city of small spaces, this is a unique opportunity to see movies on a big screen. *See chapter* **Film**.

Festa del Redentore

Bacino di San Marco, Canale della Giudecca.
Date 3rd weekend of July. **Map** II 4B.
The Redentore is the oldest continuously celebrated date on the Venetian calendar. At the end of a plague epidemic in 1576, the city celebrated her deliverance by commissioning Andrea Palladio to build a church

on the Giudecca, to be known as 'Il Redentore' – the Redeemer. Every July a pontoon bridge is built across the canal that separates the Giudecca from Venice proper, so people can make the pilgrimage to the church on foot. But what makes this weekend so special are the festivities on Saturday night. During the afternoon, boats of every shape and size gather in the lagoon between St Mark's, San Giorgio, the Punta della Dogana and the Giudecca, each holding local families supplied with food and drink. This party carries on through the evening, culminating in an amazing fireworks display.

Ferragosto – la Festa dell'Assunta
Date 15 Aug.
If you want Venice without Venetians, this is the time to come, as everyone who can leaves the city. Practically everything in the city shuts down. There is usually a free concert in the cathedral of Torcello (*see p140*) on the evening of the 15th.

Mostra Internazionale D'Arte Cinematografica (Film Festival)
Palazzo del Cinema, Lido di Venezia. Vaporetto Lido. **Date** 12 days, starting on Tue between 29 Aug and 5 Sept. **Information** 041 521 8711.
A highlight of the social calendar as well as the international film year, this two-week bonanza gives locals the chance to see stars and directors shooting past in their water taxis. *See also chapter* **Film.**

Regata Storica
Grand Canal. **Date** 1st Sun in Sept.
Recalling the extravagant waterborne processions of the past, this annual event begins with a procession of ornate boats down the Grand Canal, rowed by locals in 16th-century costume. Once the tourist prelude is over, the races start – which is what most locals have come to see. There are four: one reserved for young rowers, one for women, one for rowers of *caorline* – long canoe-like boats in which the prow and the stern are identical – and the last and most eagerly awaited, featuring two-man sporting *gondolini*, each painted a different colour. The finishing line is at the sharp curve of the Grand Canal between Palazzo Barbi and Ca' Foscari: here the judges sit in an ornate raft known as the *machina*, where the prize-giving ceremony takes place.

Autumn

Sagra del Pesce
Island of Burano. Vaporetto 12 to Burano. **Date** 3rd Sun in Sept.
Fried fish and copious quantities of white wine are consumed in this feast in the *calli* between Burano's brightly painted houses. Rowers not left legless by the festivities take part in the last regatta of the season.

Sagra del Mosto
Island of Sant'Erasmo. Vaporetto 13 to Chiesa. **Date** 1st weekend in Oct.

Sant'Erasmo is the garden island of Venice (*see chapter* **Sightseeing: The Lagoon**), and this annual festival is a great excuse for Venetians to spend a day 'in the country', getting light-headed on the first pressing of new wine. The salty soil of the island does not lend itself to superior wine – which is why it's best to down a glass before the stuff has had much chance to ferment. Sideshows, grilled sausage aromas and red-faced locals.

Venice Marathon
Date last Sun in Oct. **Information** 041 940 644.
This marathon starts out on *terra firma*, following the Riviera del Brenta, and finishes up in piazza San Marco. It's small-scale and informal; anyone interested in taking part should just give the organisers a call. One of the best places to see the runners is on the Zattere.

Winter

Festa di San Martino
Date 11 Nov.
Kids armed with *mamma*'s pots and wooden spoons raise a ruckus around the city centre, chanting the saint's praises and demanding trick-or-treat style tokens in return for taking their noise elsewhere. Horse-and-rider-shaped San Martino cakes, with coloured icing dotted with silver balls. proliferate in cakeshops.

Festa della Madonna della Salute
Church of Madonna della Salute. Vaporetto Salute. **Date** 21 Nov. **Map** II 3B.
In 1631 Venice was delivered 'miraculously' from its last major bout of plague, which had claimed almost 100,000 lives – one in every three Venetians. The Republic had already commissioned a plague-deliverance church from Baldassare Longhena some months before, though La Madonna della Salute was not completed until 1687. On this feast day, a pontoon bridge is strung across the Grand Canal from campo Santa Maria del Giglio to La Salute so that a procession led by the Patriarch of Venice can make its way on foot from San Marco. Along the way, stalls sell cakes and candy floss, and candles that pilgrims light once they are inside the church. Then they go home for a lunch of *castradina* – a sort of cabbage and mutton stew that tastes nicer than it sounds.

Christmas, New Year & Epiphany (La Befana)
Venice's Yuletide festivities are all pretty low-key affairs. There are two minor events: the New Year's Day swim off the Lido, when a few hardy swimmers brave the icy deep, and the *Regata delle Befane* on 6 January, a rowing race along the Grand Canal in which the competitors, all of whom are aged over 50, are dressed up as *La Befana* – the ugly old witch who gives sweets to good children and pieces of coal to bad ones.

Children

For out-and-out weirdness, Venice beats even Harry Potter.

While the clichéd comparison of Venice with Disneyland is mercifully an exaggeration still, the city has enough of the adventure playground about it to make it a truly magical place for kids. If they have even the tiniest jot of imagination, the water-surrounded, lion-defended city with its crooked *campanili*, twisting alleys and weird transport can rival anything out of Harry Potter.

However, in your exploration of the city's marvels, don't expect any help from the tourist office. 'Special events? For children? But signora, why?' an amazed voice is likely to say.

It is the usual Italian contradiction: children are petted, over-dressed and placed proudly on public display but little is laid on specifically for them. It is also, in miniature, the contradiction inherent in the whole Venetian tourist experience. Visitors are Venice's biggest industry by far, but they are expected to take it, gratefully, as they find it, lack of services and all.

Getting around

The proximity of so much water, and the frequent absence of any barrier between pavement and canal, presents a problem for parents travelling with mobile toddlers. It may be time to break out those psychologically incorrect safety reins you were once given.

Toddlers and pre-walkers present another dilemma. Remember, the only ways of getting around Venice are by boat or on foot, and there are a daunting number of bridges. Pushchairs mean a lot of picking up and putting down. After your umpteenth canal crossing in a day, a comfortable baby backpack may begin to look like a gift from heaven.

Vaporetto travel will be high on your older children's list of Venetian priorities, but it is horribly expensive. In theory, kids more than one metre tall pay adult fares; children under that height go free. But inspectors don't carry measuring tapes; the general feeling is that you should start paying when they're about six.

Still, look on the means of transport as a Venetian experience in itself, and the cost will not seem so outrageous. A complete circle on line 82 (red) from the riva degli Schiavoni will take your fascinated offspring across to the Giudecca, then up to the station and port areas,

Ciao bella!

giving them a glimpse of Venice's industrial underbelly as well as a triumphal march down the Grand Canal.

Small kids will enjoy a ride on the majestic Motonave to the Lido from San Zaccaria: in the 15-minute journey they can explore all the decks and stairways and savour the illusion of embarking on a major cruise.

Most children will clamour for the ultimate Venetian transport treat – a gondola trip, with or without the accompaniment of a would-be Pavarotti – but remember that this expensive experience (*see p26* **Messing about in *gondole***) can be substituted by or supplemented with rides on the humbler but much more useful traghetto gondolas that ply across the Grand Canal at points distant from bridges (*see p276* **Traghetti**).

Arts & Entertainment

Local festivities provide endless free entertainment for your children.

Make the crossing more authentic by explaining that only tourists sit down: real Venetians always stand up.

Sightseeing

Venice will knock all but the most cynical youngsters sideways, so keeping them amused should not take too much effort. Of course, you may be able to bore them to death with church after church and museum after museum, but you'll have to work hard at it. By taking things easy, and allowing time for Venice's peculiarities to soak in, you and your kids should have a great time.

Under-tens, especially, are a pushover. For a start, the city's 416-odd bridges are a joy. Allow the kids to watch boats slipping under one side and emerging from the other: sounds stupid, but it's infinitely more captivating than watching cars passing under motorway flyovers. Don't forget to take them to the junction between Ponte del Paradiso and Ponte dei Preti near **campo Santa Maria Formosa**, where you can jump from one bridge to the

other without touching the pavement in between. And if you're feeling really mean, keep them busy for the rest of your stay by issuing a challenge to find another example (there isn't one).

Then there are the boats themselves. Like all other cities in the modern world, Venice has to have its supplies, the only difference being that they arrive by water. So watch out for the Coca-Cola boat, the Findus fish finger boat, the consumer durables boat, the builder's boat, the undertaker's boat, the fire boats and ambulances and myriad others. Deliveries have never been so exciting.

For a glimpse of the more illustrious craft of the past, head for the **Museo Navale** (*see p94*), where Venice's maritime history is charted in beautiful scale models of ships built in the Arsenale through the centuries. Everything from galleons to modern naval cruisers is displayed here, giving you some idea of the grandeur that reigned until not so long ago in what is today the sadly abandoned Arsenale. Don't miss the model of the Bucintoro, the gold-leaf-clad vessel used by the Doge in official celebrations.

When not busy building up their vast naval and commercial empire, the Venetians devoted large amounts of time to games and sport, a fact you and your kids can verify with a visit to the **Museo Querini Stampalia** (*see p90*), where a huge collection of 18th-century scenes of Venetian life includes some very unlikely amusements. Aside from the obligatory hunting parties and antics on the frozen lagoon, there's the mass boxing match (*La Guerra dei Pugni* by Antonio Strom), which occurred frequently between families with bones to pick. These took place on bridges with no railings, with the initial four competitors – before the fight degenerated into a free-for-all – starting out with one foot on the white inlaid footprint on the corners of the top step: try it out for yourselves on Ponte dei Pugni near **campo San Barnaba**, Ponte della Guerra near **campo San Zulian** and Ponte di Santa Fosca.

But the prize for the weirdest (and most alarming) collection of games goes to another painting, *La Festa del due febbraio a Santa Maria Formosa* by Gabriel Bella, which should have a Parental Guidance certificate. It includes such light-hearted pastimes as head-butting cats to death, trying to break the neck of a suspended goose while leaping off a bridge and shinning up a greasy pole to wring the necks of two ducks hanging from the top. The bear- and bull-baiting also taking place in this painting look quite tame in comparison.

A reminder that bull-baiting used to be popular can still be spotted on fondamenta dei Cerari at Dorsoduro 2448A, where a plaque dated 16 February 1709 bans *le cacce de tori* (bull hunts). Given this devotion to the weird and the grisly, the edict of 1668 in ramo Cimesin, near campo San Rocco, banning games of *carte balla balon* – cards, balls and large balls – seems a trifle small-minded.

While on the subject, don't forget to introduce your kids to the most famous Venetian game of all. With the lagoon behind you, and the lagoon-facing façade of the Doge's palace in front of you, go to the third column from the left. Place your back firmly against it, then walk round it, all the way. Can you circumnavigate it without slipping off the shiny, shoe-worn marble pavement?

Most of Venice's other museums are singularly hands-off, but some may still appeal to kids. If the vast Tintorettos and echoing halls of the **Palazzo Ducale** (*see p80*) inspire only yawns, combine your visit there with a tour of the palace's secret corridors (*see p82*), which will take you into dungeons and torture rooms. The small collection of 18th-century costumes at **Palazzo Mocenigo** (*see p110*) brings paintings of the period to life.

In the **Scuola-Museo del Merletto** (Lace Museum, *see p139*) on the island of Burano you might, if you're lucky, find some local ladies still demonstrating this traditional craft (mornings during the week are the best time to try). On nearby Murano, the **Museo dell'Arte Vetrario** (*see p137*) contains many examples of the island's 800-year-old glass-making tradition but does not, unfortunately, include displays of glass-making. For this you will have to visit the shop-workshops, where the demonstration tends to be desultory and the hard sell suffocating (*see p189*).

As far as art goes, try breaking your children in with visits to some of Venice's less demanding exhibits, such as the **Scuola di San Giorgio degli Schiavoni** (*see p96*), where Vittorio Carpaccio's St George cycle is packed with the kind of detail that invites a game of I-spy. And don't be scared off from really big galleries such as the **Accademia** (*see p122*): if you're lucky, you might well link up with one of the gallery's child-friendlier guides, who will bend over backwards to interest your offspring in the collection.

In early 2001, the *Musei Civici* announced plans for 'family days' on alternate Sundays at the **Palazzo Ducale**, **Museo Correr**, **Palazzo Mocenigo**, **Lace Museum** and **Glass Museum**. These will offer kids' activities and tours for adults. Special I-spy cards for children were being prepared at various museums, though only in Italian to start. For information, call the museums' 'didactic section' on 041 522 4951.

When the culture all gets too much, take Junior up a campanile for a bird's-eye view of the city. The one in piazza San Marco is the highest; the one attached to San Giorgio Maggiore affords a more detached vantage point. Time your ascent to coincide with the striking of an hour (midday is particularly deafening) and have a close encounter with the clappers.

Parks & entertainment

Hmmm. Well, it's not what you come to Venice for, is it? The **Giardini pubblici** (*see p93*) at the Giardini vaporetto stop have been spruced up in recent years but still remain rather threadbare; however, they have good swings and slides for smaller children. Further away from the city centre, at **Sant'Elena** (*see p94*), things improve with a grassy play area along the lagoon, a roller skating/cycling rink and plenty of long, smooth walkways ideal for in-line skaters.

Sant'Elena is also where Venice's football team has its home ground, if your teenagers fancy catching a match (*see p225*).

In summer, break up the culture monotony with a trip across to the **Lido**, where there are some halfway-acceptable beaches. Most of the main ones are sewn up by the big hotels, which will charge you for a small stretch of sand, sometimes with deck chair and umbrella and always with huge numbers of neighbours within close range. (*See p133* for details of where to find the best beaches.)

Sant'Erasmo, Venice's greenhouse island, also provides a pleasant break. Green and rural, with Venice's *campanili* fading into the hazy horizon, Sant'Erasmo can be cycled around in an hour or so (*see p140*). There is a small beach (though this one's in the lagoon, rather than the somewhat cleaner open Adriatic) straight across the island from the ferry landing stage.

Local feast days may also provide entertainment for your children, usually in the shape of puppet theatres. Watch walls around the city for posters announcing *feste*. Particularly picturesque is the feast of Saints Peter and Paul in the parish of San Pietro in Castello, culminating on 29 June (*see p195*).

Babysitting

Larger hotels should have childminders on hand; smaller ones can probably arrange them for you.

Città e Ambiente

San Polo 2680A, calle Doanetta (041 277 0646). **Rates** from L24,000 per hour during the day, L35,000 in the evening. **No credit cards.** Provides English-, French- and Spanish-speaking childminders for children up to 12 years old; 48 hours' notice required.

Books

There is an excellent children's guide to Venice – *Viva Venezia* by Paolo Zoffoli and Paola Scibilia (Elzeviro, 1998) – complete with games, informative illustrations and interesting facts. A translation into English is due out soon.

Venice for Kids by Elisabetta Pasqualin (Fratelli Palombi, 2000) belongs to an attractive series of books on the principal cities of Italy. (For bookshops, *see chapter* **Shopping**.)

Contemporary Art

After slowly sinking into lagoon gloom, the contemporary art scene is making a welcome return in Venice – and not just at the Biennale.

Anyone witnessing the designer-clad, air-kissing ('*ciao* darling, haven't seen you since Kassel!') press-fuelled frenzy of Biennale vernissages (*see p203* **The Biennale**) might think they had stumbled across the heart of the contemporary art world. They haven't. In recent years, however, a number of small galleries with a wide-ranging, alternative slant have appeared on a languishing scene. Finally, it would seem, Venice is taking its first, shaky steps towards a return to the contemporary art world. (For glass – contemporary and otherwise – *see chapter* **Glass**.)

Don't, however, approach Venice's art galleries expecting to find an equivalent to London or New York. Galleries truly dedicated to fostering growth and understanding of contemporary art are few: most eschew the cutting edge for more established artists, staging exhibitions that tend to be repetitively mainstream; some suspend their regular activities over the summer to give space to individuals or nations without exhibition space in the Biennale.

The situation isn't helped much by a decidedly inactive Galleria dell'Accademia (*see p122*). All of which doesn't mean that there isn't good-quality art out there. Do beware, though: some of the places calling themselves galleries are little more than outlets for arty knick-knacks.

A&A
San Marco 3073, calle Malipiero (tel/fax 041 277 0466/2775519@iol.it). Vaporetto San Samuele. **Open** 11am-1pm, 2-6pm Tue-Sat. **No credit cards.** **Map** II 2A.
A non-profit exhibition space sponsored by the Slovenian ministry of culture. It hosts several shows each year, mainly dedicated to Slovenian artists or related projects.

Bugno Art Gallery
San Marco 1996A, campo San Fantin (041 523 1305/fax 041 523 0360/mabugno@tin.it). Vaporetto Vallaresso. **Open** 4-7.30pm Mon, Sun; 10.30am-12.30pm, 4-7.30pm Tue-Sat. **Credit** AmEx, DC, MC, V. **Map** II 3A.
This large gallery – a long room downstairs and an upstairs space – shows a variety of works in various media especially by younger artists, including students from the local Accademia (*see p122*). Opening times tend to be fluid.

Il Capricorno
San Marco 1994, campo San Fantin (tel/fax 041 520 6920). Vaporetto Santa Maria del Giglio. **Open** 11am-1pm, 5pm-8pm daily. **Credit** AmEx, DC, MC, V. **Map** II 3A.
This active, well-established gallery stages various shows each year mostly dedicated to younger international artists working in a variety of media.

Contini Galleria d'Arte
San Marco 2765, campo Santo Stefano (041 520 4942/fax 041 520 8381/www.continiarte.com/ contiinigallery@continiarte.com). Vaporetto Santa Maria del Giglio/Accademia. **Open** 10am-1pm, 3.30-7.30pm daily. **Credit** AmEx, MC, V. **Map** II 3A.
Like its sister gallery in Cortina d'Ampezzo, the Contini stages exhibitions mainly of well-known 20th-century artists. It also has an impressive permanent collection of works by renowned international artists including Picasso, Chagall and Jorn.

Two works by **Fabio Aguzzi** – *Venezia...*

... and *Black Bic* at **Contini Galleria d'Arte**.

Bevilacqua

At the end of the 19th century, the Duchess Felicità Bevilacqua La Masa left her palace of Ca' Pesaro (*see p109*) to the city, to give younger local artists a space in which to explore new trends. In the early years of the 20th century, the foundation that bears her name rivalled the then-young Biennale (*see p203* **The Biennale**) in providing a forum for contemporary artistic debate. But the city-administered foundation floundered – like the rest of Venice's modern art scene – during the middle of the last century, only to be revamped during the 1990s by two successive energetic directors.

Revived and now fulfilling its artistic mission, the Fondazione Bevilacqua has two large gallery spaces that are playing an increasingly active role. Recent important shows dedicated to modern and contemporary art have ranged from Louise Bourgeois and Joseph Beuys to film-maker Abbas Kiarostami. The annual *esposizione collettiva*, dedicated to Veneto-based artists under 30, helps inject life into local artistic production. The output of the foundation's artist-in-residence programme at Palazzo Carminati (Santa Croce 1882A, salizzada San Stae; 041 523 7819; open by appointment only) provides an interesting window on to what's being produced in the city.

Fondazione Bevilacqua La Masa

Exhibition space: *San Marco 71C, piazza San Marco (041 523 7819/info@bevilacqualamasa.it /www.bevilacqualamasa.it).* Vaporetto Vallaresso. **Open** 10am-1pm, 4pm-7pm Mon, Wed-Sun. **Map** II 4A.
Offices and exhibition space: *Dorsoduro 2826, fondamenta Gerardini (041 520 7797/041 520 8879/fax 041 520 8955).* Vaporetto Ca' Rezzonico.
Open *offices* 8am-1.30pm Mon, Thur, Fri; 8am–5.30pm Tue, Wed; *exhibition space* varies. **Map** II 2B.

Galleria Traghetto

San Marco 2456, calle delle Ostreghe (041 522 1188/fax 041 528 7984/www.galleriatraghetto.it/ galleriatraghetto@tin.it). Vaporetto Santa Maria del Giglio. **Open** 10.30am-12.30pm, 3.30-7.30pm Mon-Sat; Sun by appointment. **Credit** AmEx, DC, MC, V. **Map** II 3B.
This renowned gallery in the history of abstract Venetian art shows mainly abstract painting, with the occasional show of contemporary jewellery, in a small, low-ceilinged space. The new branch is dedicated to emerging artists..
Branch: Traghetto Immagine, San Marco 2545, campo Santa Maria del Giglio (041 522 1188).

Galleria d'Arte L'Occhio

Dorsoduro 181, calle San Gregorio (tel/fax 041 522 6550). Vaporetto Salute. **Open** 10.30am-12.30pm, 3-6pm Mon, Wed-Sat; Sun by appointment. **Credit** AmEx, DC, MC, V. **Map** II 3B.
A tiny, friendly gallery with four short individual shows a year, as well as its permanent collective show. It represents young local and international artists in various media, mostly figurative.

Galleria Multigraphic

Dorsoduro 728, calle della Chiesa (tel/fax 041 528 5159/multigraphicve@infinito.it). Vaporetto Accademia. **Open** 8.30am-6.30pm Mon-Sat. **Credit** AmEx, DC, MC, V. **Map** II 2B.
Multigraphic has its own printing room at the back, where the graphics and etchings of the gallery's artists are produced. It deals mainly in modern abstract art.

Imagina

Dorsoduro 3126, rio terà Canal (041 241 0625/imagina.venezia@tin.it). Vaporetto Ca' Rezzonico. **Open** 3.30-7.30pm Tue-Sat. **No credit cards**. **Map** II 2A.
This gallery is quite unique in Venice, being the only one solely dedicated to photography; as well as prints, it has a good collection of photography books. It has been known to lend its space to national organisations staging non-photography-related exhibitions during the Biennale (*see p203*).

San Gregorio Art Gallery

Dorsoduro 164, calle San Gregorio (tel/fax 041 522 9296). Vaporetto Salute. **Open** 10.30am-12.30pm, 3-6pm Mon, Wed-Sun. **Credit** AmEx, DC, MC, V. **Map** II 3B.
Set on a quiet calle near the Peggy Guggenheim Collection, this gallery has about three exhibitions a year, focusing on abstract and contemporary Italian art in all media.

Galleria Venice Design

San Marco 3146, salizzada San Samuele (041 520 7915/fax 041 520 5276/artgallery1@tin.it). Vaporetto San Samuele. **Open** 10am-1pm, 3-7pm daily. **Credit** AmEx, DC, MC, V. **Map** II 3A.
This ambitious gallery deals in all art forms, with a preference for sculpture as the form that is 'nearest to the art of living'. It has hosted good

The Biennale

When Venice's bi-annual exhibition of visual arts – officially known as the Esposizione Internazionale d'Arte della Biennale di Venezia – got off the ground in 1895 it was the world's first showcase for international contemporary art. Over the years, the organisation spawned the Venice Film Festival (see p204 **The Film Festival**), and created architecture and performing arts sections beneath its unique umbrella, as well as setting up a unique arts archive.

While the film festival went from strength to strength, under-funding and political interference hampered the original visual arts Biennale section, which grew old and rather predictable with contemporary art itself. Since its 100th birthday in 1995, the whole Biennale has been subjected to a major shake-up: there's been a structural overhaul and a push towards more ambitious, year-round scheduling, especially for theatre, music and dance. Opening the state-funded Biennale up to injections of private cash has helped move things along, too. Though there's still a long way to go, there are unmistakable steps in the right direction... especially for the languishing visual arts section.

Since its inception, the visual arts Biennale has been held in the Giardini, a series of nationally owned pavilions scattered around a leafy park at the far eastern end of the *sestiere* of Castello. The first pavilion was built by Belgium in 1907; many other countries followed suit, commissioning architects to design fitting containers for the artists chosen to carry their flag every two years.

Some of these buildings are works of art in their own right, such as Alvar Aalto's 1956 design for Finland, or Sverre Fehn's 1961 Scandinavian pavilion. Quaintly fascinating as the Giardini may be, they have only ever opened for those few weeks every second (odd) summer when the Biennale is in full swing. Plans are now afoot, however, to put the Giardini to other, more regular, uses.

The sheer size of recent art Biennali – and the development of its architecture companion, held in alternate (even) years – have forced organisers to turn elsewhere for exhibition space. Large swathes of the abandoned Arsenale (see p95) are being renovated to take the overflow: exhibits have spread into the Corderie (rope factory), Artiglierie (gun foundry), and Gaggiandre (dry docks).

Moreover, the growing importance of merely being there for this artistic bean-feast has forced 'have-not' countries (not to mention self-promoting artists keen to exploit the press barrage that the Biennale generates) to rent exhibition spaces elsewhere in the city, prompting a welcome influx of funds and attention for Venice's private galleries.

Note that anyone who's anyone turns up only during the three-day vernissage in mid-June, open to press and invitees, which is an endless round of *spumante*-oiled openings.

La Biennale di Venezia

Ca' Giustinian, San Marco 1364 (041 521 8711/fax 5210038/www.labiennale.org). Vaporetto Vallaresso. **Open** 9am-6pm Mon-Fri. **Dates** art & architecture mid June-early Nov in alternate years (odd for art 2001, 2003, even for architecture 2002, 2004). **Venues** Giardini di Castello, vaporetto Giardini; Arsenale, vaporetto Arsenale. **Open** 10am-6pm Tue-Sun. **Admission** (allowing access to all official shows) L25,000; L15,000 concessions. **No credit cards**.

The Biennale's massive art archive, the **Archivio Storico delle Arti Contemporanee** (Ca' Corner della Regina, Santa Croce 2214, calle Corner, 041 521 8711) has been in restauro for many years, with no reopening date yet set (see also p283).

shows featuring artists ranging from Richard Hamilton to Henry Moore and Anthony Caro. **Branch**: San Marco 1310, calle Vallaresso (041 523 9082/fax 041 523 8530/artgallery2@tin.it).

Nuova Ikona

Giudecca 454, calle del Forno (tel/fax 041 521 0101/ nuovaikona@iol.it). Vaporetto Palanca. **Open** by appointment only. **No credit cards**. Map II 2C

Nuova Ikona is a non-profit association dedicated to contemporary art: the only thing in Venice that approaches the London art scene. The association collaborates with a variety of institutions and independent curators and artists, both international and local. It organises shows or commissions projects that are presented in the gallery space or at other venues around the city. The calendar of events is packed though irregular.

Film

Don't look now – unless it's the first week of September.

The watery city has long been a seedbed for those who use words, images or music to create things of beauty. Cinema, which combines all three, was born only after Venice had become an emasculated appendage of the Italian state. But it was not long before celluloid took over from those other, dustier muses as the art that most directly mediates our experience of the city.

The mystery and menace of the fogbound canal and the dark calle is bound up with memories of Nicolas Roeg's *Don't Look Now* (*see p206* **'I know this place'**); the *belle époque* languors of the Lido are viewed through the sepia-tinted spectacles of Luchino Visconti's *Death in Venice*. Walking through Venice, it sometimes feels as if you have a steadycam in your head; little dramas are framed, and soundtracks well out of open windows.

But although Venice is a great place to make films, it leaves a lot to be desired as a place in which to view them. As with theatre

and nightlife, the problem is simple: this is a small town, with a small and ageing population, rather than a great cinema-going metropolis. Island Venice has only four cinemas, and though local film buffs are always complaining about this fact, it is a pretty accurate reflection of the local demand for celluloid.

There are two exceptions to this uninspiring scenario. The first is the annual **Venice Film Festival** (*see below* **The Film Festival**) at the beginning of September, when the Lido shakes off its sleepy, *fin-de-siècle* deck-chair and beach-umbrella image and, for 12 days, becomes the world capital of cinema.

The second is **Circuito Cinema** (*see p206*), a recently created film promotion initiative run by Venice council's highly active film department. Circuito Cinema is a centre of cinema-related research and activity, but it also runs and programmes a group of local arthouse cinemas.

The Film Festival

Venice has at least as many supporters as Cannes. Everybody agrees it's a more laid-back festival; and more about cinema. Cannes has the semi-nude starlets; Venice still has earnest cineastes who still use words like – well, 'cineaste' for one. In the domestic setting of the Lido – Venice's dormitory suburb – festival-goers pedal to screenings on hired bicycles, past mothers pushing prams and old ladies out doing the shopping. Parties are rarer, and the ones there tend to be smaller and more exclusive. If the producers of a film really want to impress, they will host their post-screening do in a palazzo over the water in Venice itself, with private launches on hand to ferry guests to and from the event.

For the past decade, though, the festival has been angling for some of that Cannes glam, making the most of its traditional early September date to tempt studios and stars keen to promote their autumn slew of big-budget movies. The result is that the festival now runs on two parallel tracks: the out-of-competition blockbusters, with their media-

friendly entourage of big names; and the films in competition, which, with a couple of exceptions each year, tend to be solidly uncommercial arthouse fare. Even more unrepentantly experimental are the films in the off-off Critics' Week (*Settimana della critica*) section.

The 12-day festival pans out along the main, sea-facing Lido esplanade, between the Hotel des Bains – where most of the really big stars stay – and the Excelsior, the neo-Moorish pile where the press conferences take place, and whose beachside terrace is the place to make contacts, arrange interviews, be photographed and generally not relax over a martini.

Between the two hotels is the marble-and-glass Palazzo del Cinema, where official competition screenings take place in the Sala Grande; other festival screens can be found in the nearby PalaGalileo and inside the Casinò, around which a forest of promotional and media tents spring up for the duration of the festival. The best way to ensure a cinema overdose, entirely free of

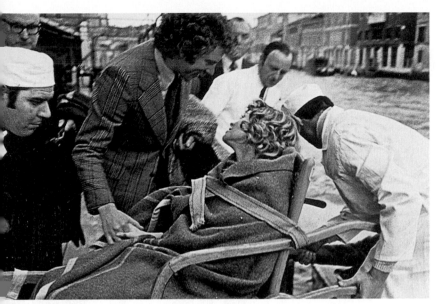

'I know this place.' An appointment with destiny in *Don't Look Now. See p206.*

charge, is to get press accreditation; the press pass ensures priority access to a number of special screenings, mostly in the morning and early evening. For those who feel qualified to try, this needs to be arranged at least two months in advance via the Biennale press office (041 521 8857/fax 041 520 0569).

'Cultural' accreditation – given for a small fee to experimental directors, those who run student film clubs and so on – is another option; it allows free access to a narrower range of screenings. Again, this should be arranged well in advance, and is not quite the cinch it used to be; as with the press pass, documents and letters will need to be produced to back up your claim.

Failing this, the only thing for it is to stand in line and buy tickets for single showings. This is best done the day before for competition films and anything that is being talked about: for details see the listings below. If you have left it until the same day, get there at least an hour before the film you want to see.

There is one advantage to paying for your ticket: the big competition and official screenings in the Palazzo del Cinema are open only to holders of bona fide tickets, not freebie press and cultural tickets; and these are the screenings that count in terms of flash-gun atmosphere and star-power.

Venice Film Festival

Palazzo del Cinema, lungomare Marconi 90, Lido (information 041 521 8711/ www.labiennale.org). Vaporetto Lido. **Date** 12 days end Aug/beginning Sept. **Tickets** season tickets (L100,000-L300,000) on sale in two complete weeks prior to festival from ACTV-VeLa outlets (*see p188*) or online. Tickets for individual screenings (L10,000-L30,000) available previous day from ACTV-Vela outlets or ticket office at the Casinò on Lido (8.30am-11pm); same-day tickets may also be available. Special offer for under-26s, *Una settimana da leoni*, with festival pass and accommodation; for details, consult www.venicesystem.com/ita/biennale.htm. **Credit** AmEx, DC, MC, V.

'I know this place'

While it may be true that Venice is a gift to filmmakers, with its eerie perspectives and sudden descents into water, not all attempts to adapt works of fiction set in the lagoon city have succeeded. Large numbers of filmgoers have swooned over Luchino Visconti's *Death in Venice* (1971), going back to see it time and time again, but, equally, many have resisted its charms. Geoff Andrew in the *Time Out Film Guide* considers it a 'dire adaptation of Thomas Mann's novella' and goes on to describe the film's content as 'camped-up', Dirk Bogarde's performance as 'mannered' and the film itself as 'overblown' and 'entirely risible'.

Andrew mourns the loss of Mann's 'metaphysical musings on art and beauty', but anyone who has struggled through the turgid text, whether for misguided pleasure or educational duty, will be glad to wave bye-bye to the most soporific passages of this acclaimed masterpiece of German literature, especially the seemingly interminable maunderings that fill the first 20 pages or so. If you think the film is slow, wait till you wade into Mann's prose, which doesn't come with study-aid extracts from Mahler's Fifth.

A book of similar length also set in Venice, although the city is never named, is Ian McEwan's 1981 novel *The Comfort of Strangers*. It's early McEwan, vintage stuff: curiously unsettling, needling, atmospheric. His characters come to life the moment you open the book. The strangeness of the situation in which they find themselves never seems arbitrary, foisted upon them by the author.

On paper the 1990 film version was a dream: directed by Paul Schrader, scripted by Harold Pinter, music by Angelo Badalamenti,

The newest and most interesting of these is the **Giorgione Movie d'Essai** (*see p207*), a former porn palace in Cannaregio. Two of the other screens in the Circuito Cinema group – the **Mignon Arthouse** in Mestre and the **Aurora Movie d'Essai** in Marghera – are on the mainland; the fourth is the **Sala Perla** on the Lido, previously open only during the Festival, but now the venue for a Friday evening series of first-run films. Local papers carry details of times and programmes.

In Italy the dubber is king, and the scarcity of original-language films even in big cities such as Rome or Milan becomes a full-scale drought in quiet little Venice. Outside of the festival (where everything is rigorously *versione originale* with subtitles) it is better to give up the uneven struggle and take in an Italian classic, if you can find one.

SCREENINGS & TICKETS

Screening times in Venice are a rule unto themselves: check local press for details. Tickets cost between L8,000 and L13,000 depending on screen and time of day.

Associations

Circuito Cinema

Santa Croce 1882, Palazzo Carminati, salizzada Carminati (041 524 1320/fax 041 524 1342/ www.comune.venezia.it/cinema/circuitocinema@ comune.venezia.it). Vaporetto San Stae. **Map** I 2C.
The Circuito Cinema operates on various fronts: as a publisher; as a cine-club, organising a series of themed seasons; and as a promoter, via its Cinemacard, an annual (July-June) card that gives variable entry discounts to all of Venice's cinemas as well as a number of theatres, restaurants, shops, and museums. It costs L25,000 and can be bought from the Giorgione cinema (*see p207*).

Cinemas

Cinema Accademia d'Essai

Dorsoduro 1018, calle Gambara (041 528 7706). Vaporetto Accademia. **No credit cards. Map** II 2B.
A Venetian institution, the Accademia changes programmes almost every day, with a good range of European arthouse films, American independents and the occasional blockbuster.

starring Christopher Walken (*see picture p206*), Natasha Richardson, Helen Mirren. And Rupert Everett. But it would be unfair to lay the blame for the film's artistic failure entirely at his door. Everett's no more guilty than Walken, who for once doesn't play himself (which he usually does to brilliant effect), but some more wooden version thereof. Neither Mirren nor Richardson can resurrect the film, which is under the tight control of Schrader, who cannot make it work. Pinter's script may be the root of the problem. Or possibly McEwan's novels carry a hidden virus that resists adaptation. Opinion is divided over *The Cement Garden* (1992), but pretty much unanimous regarding *The Innocent* (1993).

An author whose work translates much less problematically to celluloid is Daphne Du Maurier. Think of *Rebecca* (1940), *The Birds* (1963) – and *Don't Look Now* (1973). The ease of transfer may have a lot to do with the fact there's less cargo to get damaged in transit; Du Maurier is neither weighed down with intellectual baggage like Mann, nor does she write in a highly individualistic style like McEwan. But her stories make damn good films. In Nicolas Roeg's superb adaptation of *Don't Look Now*, John (Donald Sutherland) and Laura Baxter (Julie Christie; *see picture above*) are not merely tourists in Venice – John is restoring mosaics in the church of San Nicolò dei Mendicoli (*see p116*) – yet they soon lose themselves, and each other, in the city's hallucinatory labyrinth. 'I know this place,' John mutters, shortly before his appointment with destiny. Do we not all know this place, when the time comes?

Giorgione Movie D'Essai

Cannaregio 4612, rio Terà dei Franceschi (041 522 6298). Vaporetto Ca' d'Oro. **No credit cards.** **Map** I 4B.

This ex-porn cinema is now a comfortable arthouse two-screener run by Circuito Cinema (*see p206*); it alternates first-run fare with themed seasons, kids' films (in Italian, on Sat and Sun at 3pm) and original language (usually English) offerings on Tuesdays – though this may be subject to change.

Open-air

Arena di Campo San Polo

San Polo, campo San Polo (041 524 1320). Vaporetto San Silvestro. **Season** six weeks from late July to early Sept. **No credit cards. Map** I 2C.

This open-air arena in one of Venice's liveliest squares has become a fixture, attracting Venetians and tourists alike. With an average of 1,000 spectators a night, the arena packs in more people in six weeks than any other Venetian cinema in the whole year – proof that the atmosphere of this great night out are as important as the films themselves, which are generally repeats of first-run favourites from the previous season, and always dubbed. The exception is at festival time (early Sept), when a selection of original-language sneak-preview films are shown here a day or two after their Lido screening.

Videotheques

Videoteca Pasinetti

Santa Croce 1882, Palazzo Carminati, salizzada Carminati (041 524 1320/fax 041 524 1342). Vaporetto San Stae. **Open** *Video archive* 8am-2pm, 2.30-5.30pm Mon, Fri; 8am-2pm Tue-Thur. *Video-projected cinema classics Oct-May* 4pm, 9pm Mon-Wed, Fri. **Entrance** by membership card (L25,000), valid for four months (Oct-Jan/Feb-May). **No credit cards. Map** I 2C.

Another emanation of the city council's energetic *Ufficio attività cinematografiche*, this video archive was set up in 1991 with the aim of collecting, conserving and allowing access to the huge wealth of audiovisual material that deals with Venice, in whatever format: feature film, TV documentary, newsreel, amateur video. More than 2,000 videos are kept here – around half of them feature films – and there is also a screening room where brief, ultra-cineaste film seasons are organised.

Gay & Lesbian

Tit bridges and Byron's 'sea sodom' may have vanished, but there's a welcome tolerance in Venice, and a scene to be found if you look.

There are few cities in the world that can compete with Venice in the romantic stakes: it's a place made for lovers of all persuasions, as the countless gays and lesbians who flock here each year testify.

Its romantic nature, along with its unique artistic and cultural offerings, are, however, its biggest draw: if it's bars, clubs or a frenzied scene you're after, you'll have to be prepared to board a train or bus for Mestre or Padua (*see below, and chapter* **The Veneto: Padua**).

Built on a very human scale, and thronged by crowds, Venice is the perfect place to exercise your 'gaydar'. Young Venetians tend to be very exhibitionist; even if they aren't looking for a same-gender pick-up, they are more than willing to be admired by all and sundry. Which is, admittedly, a far cry from Byron's 'sea-sodom', or from 16th-century Venice in which authorities bent on stamping out rampant same-sex antics allowed female prostitutes to display their wares on specially-designated *ponti delle tette* (tit bridges, *see p106* **Quivers open to every arrow**). But centuries of licentiousness has bred the kind of tolerance that makes Venice the safest, most relaxed of Italian cities for homosexual travellers (give or take the occasional gay-bating pronouncement by the anti-gay, anti-black, anti-southern – in fact anti-just about everything – Northern League party, *see chapter* **Venice Today**).

For something less laid-back in the nightlife line, Padua (25mins by train) is one of the hottest cities in Italy for sex clubs and gay discos. A quick hop across the lagoon from island Venice, Mestre has a livelier scene, too, and boasts the Venice area's first sauna, the Metro (*see p209*), which at the time of going to press was still under-subscribed but unlikely to remain so for long.

The national **ArciGay** association has local chapters that sponsor activities, festivals, counselling and AIDS awareness. ArciGay membership is needed for entry to several of the venues listed below. A one-month *tessera* (membership card) for visitors costs L10,000 and can be purchased at ArciGay Dedalo (c/o Scuola Pellico, via Costa 38A, Mestre; 041 538 4151; open 9-11pm Tue; phone enquiries answered 7-9pm Mon, 9-11pm Thur) or at the door of venues that require it.

Venice

Open-air

Il Muro (The Wall)

Behind the **Procuratie Nuove**, by the **Giardinetti Reali** (at the lagoon end of the **piazzetta di San Marco**, turn right and keep on walking), *Il Muro* has long been Venice's favourite after-dark cruising area, especially in the warmer months. As temperatures drop, the scene quietens down, and locals call it *Il Muro del Pianto* (the Wailing Wall): on the right night, you'll have a fine moonlit view of the church of San Giorgio Maggiore across the water.

Alberoni Beach, Lido

Bus B/(Alberoni) from Santa Maria Elisabetta to the last stop, then turn right and walk ten minutes towards the dunes.

The quaint situation of gay life in Venice is well illustrated by the 'unofficially' gay beach at Alberoni on the Lido. Nuns from the nearby rest-homes come here for their morning constitutional, and later, families enjoy picnics under the shade of *ombrelloni* set up along the shoreline. The dunes and pine forest are peaceful, very gay and mostly nudist. Cruising and action in the woods.

Accommodation

Il Lato Azzurro

Via Forte 13, Sant'Erasmo (041 523 0642/ other.venice@flashnet.it). Vaporetto 13 to Sant'Erasmo-Punta Vela. **Rates** L70,000 single; L90,000 double; L120,000 triple (breakfast L5,000; dinner L25,000). **No credit cards.**

This gay-owned and -operated guest house is on Venice's vegetable-garden island (*see p140* **Sant'Erasmo**). Excellent for a very quiet retreat, the island is a 45 minute ferry trip across the northern lagoon from the centre.

Art

BAC Art Studio

Dorsoduro 862, campo San Vio (041 522 8171/fax 041 241 9201/info@bacart.com/www.bacart.com). Vaporetto Accademia. **Open** 10.30am-6.30pm daily. **Credit** MC, V. **Map** I 3B.

A great gallery both for important pieces or less ambitious gift buying. Sensual works by Baruffaldi, and more scenic Venetian pieces by Cadore.

A relaxed city for homosexual travellers.

Tailor-made, personalised holidays, catering for a wide variety of cultural interests and credit limits, organised by American gondola-builder Thom Price and his partner Alvise Zanchi, a native Venetian and expert tour guide. Member of IGLTA.

Padua

For whatever reasons – a larger young population and the second-oldest university in Europe or, perhaps, the anonymity guaranteed by a relatively large industrialised city – Padua has by far the most thriving gay scene in the Veneto. The following list contains only those gay places that are most easily accessible by public transport or taxi (*see chapters* **Directory: Getting Around** *and* **The Veneto: Padua**). Note that open-air cruising here has become very risky, and is to be avoided if you don't have a car.

Eating & drinking

Antico Panificio
San Polo 945, campiello del Sole (041 277 0967).
Vaporetto San Silvestro. **Open** noon-3pm, 7-11pm Mon, Wed-Sun. **Credit** AmEx, MC, V. **Map** I 2C.
Good pizza and fantastic service by Tiziano. Two minutes on foot from the Rialto.

Marguerite Duchamps
Dorsoduro 3019, campo Santa Margherita (041 528 6255). *Vaporetto Ca' Rezzonico.* **Open** 9am-2am Mon-Sat. **No credit cards. Map** II 2A.
A hyper-trendy bar of wood and steel – but who goes inside? Outside is the place to be, watching the world go by. Young, mixed clientele. *See also p215.*

Alla Zucca
Santa Croce 1762, ponte del Megio (041 524 1570). *Vaporetto San Stae.* **Open** 12.30-2.30pm, 7-10.30pm Mon-Sat. **Credit** AmEx, MC, DC, V. **Map** I 2B.
Venice's lesbian scene is almost non-existent; but in this comfortable, women-run restaurant in the peaceful San Giacomo dall'Orio district, no one will stare if you feel like holding hands (*see p155*).

Sauna

Metro Venezia
Via Cappuccina 82B, Mestre (041 538 4299/ www.metroclub.it). Bus 2 or 7 from piazzale Roma/train to Mestre. **Open** 2pm-2am daily.
Admission L25,000 (L30,000 Sun) with ArciGay membership (*see p208*). **Credit** MC, V.
Opened in November 2000, the Metro is the Venice area's first gay club. The facility hosts a bar, dry sauna, steam sauna, hydro massage, private rooms, dark room, and massage.

Tours

Venice à la Carte
Dorsoduro 3167, campo San Barnaba (041 277 0564/thom@tourvenice.org/www.tourvenice.org).
Rates vary according to tour. **Credit** AmEx, MC, V.
Map II 2B.

Bars & entertainment

Flexo Videobar
Via Nicolò Tommaseo 96B (049 807 4707).
Open 9.30pm-3am Wed, Thur, Sun; 9.30pm-5am Fri, Sat. **Admission** L12,000-L20,000 (depending on events) plus ArciGay membership (*see p208*).
Credit MC, V.
A friendly private club arranged over three levels, with bars, and labyrinthine darkrooms downstairs. About ten minutes' walk from the station; the front door (ring the bell) is at the back of a courtyard on the right side of the road as you approach from the station. If you find yourself walking past a 'sexy shop' with the tackiest of display pouches, you have gone just a little too far. Your membership card is also valid for the Metro sauna listed below.

Black & White
Via Navigazione Interna 38A (Zona industriale Nord) (049 776 414/www.whydisco.com). **Open** 11pm-5am Fri, Sat. **Admission** L30,000 Fri; L35,000 Sat. **No credit cards**.
This gay and lesbian club has a small dance floor and darkroom, and is frequented by a slightly younger crowd than Flexo Videobar (*see above*). A taxi from the station is advisable: this bar is not easy to find.

Sauna

Metro Sauna
Via Turazza 19 (049 807 5828/www.metroclub.it).
Open 2pm-2am daily. **Admission** L25,000 Mon-Sat; L30,00 Sun with ArciGay membership (*see p208*).
Credit MC, V.
Large, modern and well-equipped, this place has a proper work-those-pores Finnish sauna rather than just the usual warm cabin that smells of pine. It also has the usual well-earned rest facilities.

Arts & Entertainment

Music & Nightlife

There is a scene, but you may have to cross the water to find it.

A slow, night-time walk down the main streets of this most serene town would probably have you believing that once the pigeons have gone to bed, so have the rest of the city's inhabitants. Not true: the locals are living it up in their own style. It all starts by having a glass of wine or two and *cicheti* in a cosy little *bacaro* (*see p159*), before moving on to their favourite haunts – **Iguana** (*see p211*), perhaps, or **Paradiso Perduto** (*see p211*) – for a bit of jazz and another couple of drinks until the early hours: the empty bar you saw in the afternoon when you were lost may be transformed at night into the centre of the Venetian nightlife. Venice has strict noise pollution regulations, which creates this night-owl society around the outskirts and quieter areas of the city. The Venetians are just as partial to a good time as any other citizen of the world, it's just that they've learned to be flexible and creative in their search for late-opening and/or musical fun and games.

MUSIC

The local rock, jazz and ethnic scene is small but not entirely dormant. There is a shortage of good venues, and the prohibitive cost of building work means that the acoustics are generally bad.

But despite this, Venice (and the surrounding mainland area) has carved itself out a small music scene that revolves around reggae and jazz. Why Jamaican vibes should be so popular on the misty lagoon is anybody's guess – but local rude boys **Pittura Freska** (the best known), **Radio Rebelde** and **So Vibes** have taken to it like a Rasta to ganja. The jazz scene is small, but has produced some fine local musicians such as brothers **Pietro** and **Marcello Tonolo** (sax and keyboards). In the city, opportunities for playing (and hearing) music tend to be pegged to particular festivities or festivals. At *carnevale* time (*see p194*), stages are set up in many *campi*, especially in the more out-of-the way residential districts.

Then there are the big summer festivals (*see p195*) plus the occasional mini-event financed by the city council. If anything at all is happening, the chances are it will be in **campo Santa Margherita**, the city's most turned-on square, though the **fondamenta della Misericordia** in Venice's northern reaches is running it a close race for the title of trendiest area. But don't turn up late: stringent noise

regulations mean that the volume is kept low and the plug is pulled at 11pm on the dot.

Mestre offers more in terms of venues and late opening, but for the real quality acts local groovers are often forced to go as far afield as Padua, Bologna, or Pordenone, where the **Rototom club** (*see p217*) is a music mecca for the whole north-east.

DANCE ACTION

If it's techno you're after, it can always be found in summer a mere vaporetto and bus ride away, across the lagoon in the beach resort of **Jesolo**; or in the cold winter months, a train hop away in the industrial sprawl of Mestre and Marghera. There's no shortage of early-morning boats, buses and trains for getting home.

INFORMATION AND TICKETS

Day-to-day listings are carried by the two local papers, *Il Gazzettino* and *La Nuova Venezia* (*see p284*). For a more complete overview of concerts and festivals, with features in both Italian and English, the monthly listings magazine *Venezia News* is indispensable. Also keep your eyes peeled around town for notices of upcoming concerts, film nights and the like. These events are often organised by the University and other community organisations. Tickets are available for most concerts, theatre, dance and Biennale performances at the main VeLa office (*see p275*). Otherwise tickets will be available at the venue.

Bars with music

See also *217* **Rototom**, *p217* **Magic Bus**, and *p217* **Other Live Venues**.

Le Bistrot de Venise

San Marco 4685, calle dei Fabbri (041 523 6651/ www.bistrotdevenise.com/bistrot@tin.it). Vaporetto Rialto. **Open** 9am-1am daily. **Credit** DC, MC, V. **Map** II 4A.
The Bistrot (for information on eating, *see p148*) has a busy, eclectic programme of concerts, poetry readings, plays and art exhibitions in old-fashioned, cosy surroundings.

Cantina Vecia Carbonera

Cannaregio 2329, rio terà Maddalena (041 710 376). Vaporetto San Marcuola. **Open** *Oct-May* 4pm-midnight Tue-Fri; 11am-midnight Sat, Sun. *June-Sept* 4pm-midnight Tue-Fri; 11am-9pm Sat, Sun. **No credit cards.** **Map** I 3B.

Arts & Entertainment

Bacaro Jazz attracts a young, international crowd. *See p213.*

A quiet *bacaro* by day, the Cantina becomes one of Venice's coolest spots after dark. Sunday nights mean music, with some of the best soul, jazz and bossanova musicians in town. *See also p161.*

Fiddler's Elbow Irish Pub
*Cannaregio 3847, campiello Testori
(041 523 9930). Vaporetto Ca' d'Oro.*
Open 5pm-1am daily. **No credit cards. Map** I 3B.
Guinness and British beers are served in this lively pub. The *campiello* outside is the site of summer concerts of Irish music, usually on Saturdays. Also hosts Hallowe'en and St Patrick's Day parties.

Iguana
*Cannaregio 2515, fondamenta della Misericordia
(041 713 561). Vaporetto San Marcuola.*
Open 6pm-2am Tue-Sat; noon-3pm, 6pm-2am Sun.
Credit AmEx, DC, MC, V. **Map** I 3B.
Iguana serves up colossal plates of Mexican food to the beat of Brazilian blues. The music comes live on Tuesdays, while happy hour (7-9pm daily) with 'Cubinos' (rum and cola) and an extensive cocktail menu packs in the crowds.

OK Pizza
*Cannaregio 2578, fondamenta della Misericordia
(041 717 315). Vaporetto San Marcuola.*
Open 11am-3pm, 6.30pm-midnight Mon, Wed-Sun.
Credit MC, V. **Map** I 3B.
This Jordanian-owned restaurant has live Latin, salsa and blues on Sunday evenings and occasional belly dancing to help the pizza (or Middle Eastern fare, if you put in an order before you show up) go down.

Osteria da Codroma
*Dorsoduro 2540, ponte del Soccorso (041 524 6789).
Vaporetto San Basilio.* **Open** 8am-midnight Mon-Fri,
Sun. **Closed** 2wks Aug. **No credit cards.**
Map II 1A.
This homely *bacaro* has been hosting graduation celebrations since the 17th century. There's jazz, rock or blues on Tuesday nights, as young, laid-back locals kick back and unwind after a hard day's work.

Paradiso Perduto
*Cannaregio 2540, fondamenta della Misericordia
(041 720 581). Vaporetto San Marcuola.*
Open 7pm-2am Mon, Thur-Sat; noon-2am Sun.
Closed 2wks Aug. **No credit cards. Map** I 3B.
A 'lost paradise' well worth finding. The refectory tables of this crowded *osteria* have occupied the former stables since 1979. The colourful and chaotic mix of seafood, Sambuca and succulent sounds (mainly jazz and blues, often somewhat impromptu) comes together under the watchful eye of Maurizio, owner, chef and proud possessor of the bushiest beard in town. Restaurant serves until 11pm.

Pizzeria 900 Jazz Club
*San Polo 900, campiello del Sansoni (041 522 6565).
Vaporetto Rialto.* **Open** noon-3pm, 7pm-midnight
Tue-Sun. **No credit cards. Map** I 3C.
Well off the beaten track, this family-run pizzeria and jazz club has hosted local and international musicians since 1985. Booking is recommended for the Wednesday night concerts, a mellow mix of *peperoni* and percussion.

CASANOVA DISCO®
MUSIC CLUB

The only one real disco in Venice

www.casanova.it

open from 6.00 p.m. to 4.00 a.m.
100 metres from the railway station you can reach it by
boat from s.marco or rialto line n. 1 - 82 stop FERROVIA

Lista di Spagna Cannaregio 158/a 30121 VENEZIA

0339 4171727
041 2750199
041 5347479

Further afield

Al Vapore

Via Fratelli Bandiera 8, Marghera (041 930 796).
Train to Mestre, or bus 6 or 6/from piazzale Roma.
Open noon-3pm, 6pm-2am Tue-Sun. **Admission**
L15,000 including first drink. **No credit cards.**
This smallish live music bar just behind Mestre
station has been putting on very good jazz, blues and
soul concerts for years. At weekends well-known
Italian and international musicions perform on
its tiny stage.

T.A.G. Club

Via Giustizia 19, Mestre (041 921 970/
tagclub@tin.it/www.v4u.it/tag). Train to Mestre.
Open 10pm-5am Wed-Sat. **Admission** L10,000
including first drink. **No credit cards.**
Small but lively club just behind the train station,
which vies with Al Vapore (*see above*) for the title of
best live venue in Mestre. There are rock, blues, soul
and jazz concerts by Italian and international musicians (Fri, Sat), followed by a techno/rock disco.

Teranga

Via della Crusca 34, Mestre (041 531 7787).
Bus 82 from piazzale Roma. **Open** 9pm-4am Fri, Sat.
Membership L20,000. **Admission** L10,000-
L20,000, depending on event. **No credit cards.**
Just about the only place around Venice to specialise
in African music, with mixed Venetian/African
clientele. At weekends the joint – run by the Arci
leisure association, hence the membership fee –
really hops, and concerts are frequent.

Late-opening bars

There is no admission charge for the following
late-opening bars.

Ai Postali

Santa Croce 821, fondamenta Rio Marin
(041 715 156). Vaporetto Riva di Biasio or San
Tomà. **Open** 11am-3pm, 7pm-2am Mon-Sat.
No credit cards. Map I 2C.
Across the bridge and down a narrow canal from
the train station, Ai Postali is a favourite with students, who let the background jazz and the late
hours distract them from the prospect of eternally
postponed exams. In summer there's a terrace on the
bank of the canal.

Bacaro Jazz

San Marco 5546, salizzada del Fontego dei Tedeschi
(041 528 5249/bacarojazz@iol.it). Vaporetto Rialto.
Open 11am-2am Mon, Tue, Thur-Sun.
Credit AmEx, DC, MC, V. **Map** I 4C.
Right opposite the main post office, the flashing
lights of the Bacaro Jazz attract a young, international crowd for food, drinks and occasional live
music till the early hours. Don't leave without trying the 'FraBellini' cocktail, a modern take on a
traditional favourite.

Café Blue

Dorsoduro 3778, salizzada San Pantalon (041 710
227). Vaporetto San Tomà. **Open** 8am-2am Mon-
Fri; 5pm-2am Sat. **No credit cards. Map** II 2A.
What do hip young Venetians do of an evening?
Play Scrabble, of course, or one of the other board
games on offer at this pub-style late bar near campo
Santa Margherita. A delicious afternoon tea is
served daily, and homesick Scots can enjoy a wee
dram in the Whiskeria. Happy hour is 8.30-9.30pm.

Café Noir

Dorsoduro 3805, salizzada San Pantalon (041 710
925/cafenoir@hotmail.com) Vaporetto San Tomà.
Open 7am-2am daily. **No credit cards. Map** II 2A.
A young bar with new owners, Café Noir is a winter favourite among the university and 20-some-
thing crowd. Internet access, tasty *panini* (filled
rolls) and the thickest of hot chocolate mean there is
something to warm the cockles of the coldest heart.

Haig's Grill

San Marco 2477, campo Santa Maria del Giglio
(041 528 9456). Vaporetto Santa Maria del Giglio.
Open 9.30am-midnight daily. **Credit** AmEx, DC,
MC, V. **Map** II 3B.
A loucher version of Harry's Bar (*see p166*), Haig's
is a cocktail bar and restaurant. The prices are on
the high side, the clientele well-heeled; but in the
small hours the mix becomes more interesting.

Café Noir: e-mail, *panini* and the
thickest of hot chocolate.

Arts & Entertainment

La Colombina

Cannaregio 1828, campiello Pegolotto (041 275 0622/www.lacolombina.it). Vaporetto San Marcuola. **Open** 6.30pm-2am Mon; noon-3pm, 6.30pm-2am Tue-Sat. **Closed** 2wks Jan, Aug. **Credit** AmEx, DC, MC, V. **Map** I 2B.
Count down to the early hours with the Colombina cheese clock and some of the best wines to be found in Venice. Functions as a serious restaurant at mealtimes (*see also p153*).

Margaret Duchamp

Dorsoduro 3019, campo Santa Margherita (041 528 6255) Vaporetto Ca' Rezzonico. **Open** *Apr-Oct* 9am-2am daily. *Nov, Dec, Feb, Mar* 9am-2am Mon, Wed-Sun. **Closed** Jan. **No credit cards.** **Map** II 2A.
The largest and most upmarket of this popular campo's nightspots, Duchamp serves a range of international beers and bulging *panini* to a hip young crowd of Venetian revellers into the early hours. The party moves outside in summer for live music in the campo.

Discos & clubs

Casanova Music Café

Cannaregio 158A, lista di Spagna (041 534 7479). Vaporetto Ferrovia. **Open** 6pm-4am Tue,Thur-Sat. **Closed** Aug. **Admission** free Tue, Thur, Sat; L12,000 Fri including first drink. **Credit** AmEx, MC, V. **Map** I 1B.
The largest and newest disco in Venice, a stone's throw from the railway station, caters mainly to local smoothies (of all ages) and passing tourists. Tuesday is pop and rock, Thursday student night with the best and worst of the European charts,

Friday brings Latino salsa, while on Saturdays the music is commercial house. Being female – or having female company – ensures swift passage past the bouncers.

Piccolo Mondo

Dorsoduro 1056A, calle Contarini-Corfù (041 520 0371). Vaporetto Accademia. **Open** 10pm-4am Tue-Sun. **Admission** L15,000. **Credit** MC, V. **Map** I 2B.
Piccolo (small) is the word in this tiny bar where elderly *flaneurs*, bouncing students, lost tourists and passing sailors jostle for position. Formerly known as El Souk, the club's trophy cabinet of celebrity snapshots testifies to the better days gone by.

Further afield

From May to September most of Venice's nightlife moves to **Jesolo**, the sprawling, tacky seaside resort at the north end of the lagoon that is everything the Lido never wanted to be. The Lido di Jesolo bus (information 041 520 5530) leaves from piazzale Roma, but it's more fun to get the no.12 *motonave* to Treporti, and bus it to Cavallino or Jesolo from there; at least two boats make the return journey from Treporti between 3am and 6am, and plenty thereafter. Most of the clubs on the seaside strip open at 11pm, but nobody who's anybody shows up until 1am.

Area Club

Via Don Tosatto 9, Mestre (0336 490 200). Bus 20 or 21 from piazzale Roma. **Open** 10.30pm-4am Fri-Sun. **Admission** L28,000 including first drink; L25,000 concessions. **No credit cards.**

Red square(s)

Stumble into the campo Santa Margherita on a late August evening and you could be forgiven for thinking you had been warped back to 1950s Havana. A hammer and sickle flies atop each market stall, and the iconic features of comrade Che stare out from the T-shirts of local children. The campo turns communist as the *Rifondazione Comunista* party turns on the charm to swell the coffers and garner support for forthcoming elections.

Bemused tourists, Milanese Marxists and intoxicated locals jostle for position at the military-style canteen, where plates of fried fish, sausages and other sustaining dishes are served up to hungry militants. A division of bronzed gondoliers, perhaps the most fanatic comrades in Venice, forms a blockade of the beer tent, forgoing a potentially remunerative evening of summer serenades

to slake their thirst and do their bit for the cause. Housewives crowd the bingo tent, the lucky ones emerging with exotic plants and shrubs to the jealous jeers of friends and foes. Perhaps the most popular of the attractions on offer are the mighty nightly concerts; each of a different flavour with salsa, blues, rock, reggae and country bands of the highest quality to keep the masses bouncing until late into the night.

Festa dell'Unità

Campo del Ghetto. **Date** mid-Sept. **Map** I 2A.
Merrymaking organised by the once-Communist *Democratici di sinistra* party.

Festa di Liberazione

Campo Santa Margherita.
Date end Aug-early Sept. **Map** II 2A.
Rifondazione's shindig.

Venice's newest, largest club:
Casanova Music Café. *See p215*.

The first place in the Venice area to specialise in hardcore techno, Area Club has recently lost its edge in a miasma of commercial house, 1970s and '80s revival and easy listening. A good place to dance.

Magic Bus
Via delle Industrie 118, Marcon (041 595 2151).
Venice-Trieste motorway, exit Quarto d'Altino, follow signs to Marcon, II zona industriale.
Open 11pm-5am Fri, Sat. **Membership** L18,000.
Admission L25,000 including first drink.
No credit cards.
A real live rock club – run by the ARCI association, hence the membership fee – in a warehouse in the industrial area of Marcon, a small town 12km (7.5 miles) north-east of Mestre (there's no public transport; Venetians share taxis to get there). There is a rock/punk/metal disco and the occasional concert, featuring both local and international talent.

Matilda
Via Bafile 342, Jesolo (information 0339 417 1727).
Open *Apr-July, Sept* 11pm-4am Wed, Fri, Sat. *Aug* 11pm-4am daily. **Admission** L30,000-L50,000.
Credit AmEx, MC, V.
Under new management, it remains to be seen whether this summer-only club will retain its reputation as the most happening club in Jesolo. House, jungle and drum 'n' bass are the resident sounds and guest DJs often drop in.

Puta's
Discoteca Empire, via Fausta, opposite Union Lido campsite, Cavallino Treporti (0336 734 477). **Open** *June-Aug* 10pm-4am Sat.
Admission L20,000. **Credit** AmEx, DC, MC, V.
The Magic Bus in Marcon (*see above*) runs this summer offshoot in Cavallino, halfway between Treporti and Jesolo. Strictly for rockers, it puts on the occasional live gig.

Rototom
Zoppola di Pordenone (0434 977 314/ www.rototom.com). **Open** *disco* 10pm-4.30am Sat; *concerts* Thur, Fri, Sun 9.30pm-4am. **Admission** Sat (disco) free before 11pm, L10,000 after; Thur-Fri, Sun (concerts) L15,000-L35,000. **Credit** AmEx, MC, V.
It's quite a trek (100km/62 miles north-east of Venice, just off the SS13 Pordenone-Udine road), but with a car, a trip to the best club/disco in the region is feasible. Massive Attack, Primus and Senser have played here, and in the summer it organises Italy's biggest reggae festival, the Rototom Reggae Sunsplash (*phone or check website for information*). Of the three spaces within this temple of sound, the largest hosts a Saturday disco (rock, pop, hip-hop) and concerts every Friday and occasionally on Thursdays and Sundays, while the other two are given over to reggae/afro and jungle/drum 'n' bass.

Sound Code
Via delle Industrie 29A, Marghera (0339 4171727). Bus to Mestre from piazzale Roma. **Open** 10pm-4am Fri, Sat. **Admission** free Fri; L20,000 Sat. **Credit** AmEx, MC, V.

Only ten minutes by bus from piazzale Roma, this is the mainland disco nearest to Venice, and also one of the best. It features the latest techno, big beat and drum 'n' bass, with guest appearances by international DJs, plus the odd live concert.

Sound Garden
Via Aleardi 18A, Jesolo (0421 372 345/ www.soundgardencafe.com). **Open** 10pm-4am daily.
Admission L10,000. **No credit cards.**
More a disco-bar than a dance factory, the Sound Garden (formerly the trend-setting Mithos) plays commercial pop, rock and soul, as well as classic rock and new wave, and hosts concerts on Fridays. One of the few *locali* in Jesolo that is open all year round, it also has pool and internet access.

Other live venues

Aula Magna Tolentini
Istituto Universitario di Architettura, Santa Croce 191, campo dei Tolentini (041 257 1806/ sds@iuav.unive.it/www.iuav.it/sdsweb). Vaporetto *Piazzale Roma.* **No credit cards. Map** I 1C.
The Architecture Faculty students' union organises at least two music festivals a year, with high-quality experimental and avant-garde music as well as jazz. They also host the occasional contemporary music concert, organised by La Fenice (*see p220* **PalaFenice**. Entrance is either free or cheap (in the L5,000-L10,000 range). For up-to-date listings check out the local press or student notice boards.

Further afield

Centro Sociale Occupato Rivolta
Via Fratelli Bandiera 45, Marghera (041 538 7343). Bus 6 or 6/ from piazzale Roma. **Open** 9pm-4am for events usually Fri & Sat (check local press for details). **Admission** varies. **No credit cards.**
If all that art and beauty is getting you down, this is the place to come for a shot of post-industrial angst. This former factory on the Porto Marghera industrial estate hosts performances, plays, and often excellent rock, soul and hip-hop concerts by Italian and international musicians (CSI, Miriam Makeba, Casino Royale).

Teatro Toniolo
Piazzetta Battisti 1, Mestre (041 274 9070/fax 041 274 9049/cultura.spettacolo.me@comune.venezia.it/ www.comune.venezia.it/teatrotoniolo/). Bus 2, 7, 9 *from piazzale Roma.* **Box office** (041 971 666) 11am-12.30pm, 5-7.30pm Tue-Sun. **Performances** 9pm daily. **Credit** MC, V.
The Venice area's largest theatre, in the centre of Mestre, is the venue for about 40 high-calibre concerts each year. Recent pulls have included Buena Vista Social Club, Eddie Reader, Courtney Pine and Baaba Maal. It remains very much a theatre, however, and is not always the most atmospheric of music venues. Tickets are in the L25,000-L65,000 range. *See also p221.*

Arts & Entertainment

Performing Arts

Visitors may not come to Venice for its theatre, dance and classical music, but increasingly there are signs that they might start doing so.

'I was at one of their play-houses where I saw a Comedie acted. The house is very beggarly and base in comparison of our stately Play-houses in England: neyther can their actors compare with us for apparell, shewes and musick.' So wrote the indefatigable traveller Thomas Coryat in the early 17th century of Venice's performing arts scene.

A century and a half later, Venice was buzzing. Already bumbling along nicely with the Commedia dell'Arte offerings of playwrights Pietro Chiari and Carlo Gozzi, the Venetian theatre scene went hurtling into top gear in 1748 when the Teatro Sant'Angelo signed up Carlo Goldoni. In the 1750-1 season alone, he calmly rolled out 16 works.

A dramatic slump followed, out of which Venice was slow to crawl. Even today, the productions on offer in the city at any given time can be counted on the fingers of one hand. But the picture is not as bleak as it was in Coryat's day.

If the standard of performances on offer sometimes leaves much to be desired, the recent revamping of some small theatres in the centre itself, and the birth of non-mainstream facilities on the mainland, has brought about a minor dramatic upturn. And when the historic **Teatro Malibran** (inaugurated in 1678 as the Teatro San Crisostomo) finally reopens after a 15-year face-lift – an event scheduled for May 2001 – the picture will be even rosier.

THEATRE

Keeping the fire of Venice's dramatic tradition burning are the **Teatro Carlo Goldoni** (*see p220*), and the much younger **Teatro Toniolo** (*see p221*) on the mainland. Both pepper their mainly mainstream programmes with the occasional offbeat offering; this is especially true of the Toniolo, which has its own recently formed Teatro Stabile del Veneto theatre company. Things improve still further in summer, during the **Biennale del Teatro, Musica e Danza** (*see p222* **Festivals**).

But for anything approaching real avant-garde, Venetians head for the tiny theatres in Mestre, such as the **Teatrino della Murata** (*see p221*), or to the **Teatro Fondamenta Nuove** (*see p221*), where contemporary dance heads the bill and where the murky territory between technology and dramatic creation is explored. The **Teatro a L'Avogaria** (*see p220*) dedicates its energies to exploring the outer reaches of Venetian and Italian theatre, while at the **Teatro Comunale Villa dei Leoni** (*see p221*) along the Brenta canal on the mainland, ancient oral storytelling traditions have been revived and revamped.

DANCE

If the amount of drama staged in Venice is limited, dance events are even thinner on the ground, although the **PalaFenice** (*see p220*) season always includes the obligatory classical ballet features. The **Teatro Toniolo** (*see p221*) has contemporary dance offerings, but for something a little more cutting edge, the **Teatro Fondamenta Nuove** (*see p221*) specialises in interactive and multimedia productions, mixing technology with Terpsichore.

CLASSICAL MUSIC & OPERA

Venice has become a victim of its own musical tradition. With tourists far outnumbering whatever may be left of a local music-going public, more than half of all concerts offer an undiluted programme of Venetian baroque, with Vivaldi naturally taking the lion's share.

For the visitor, this is both good and bad news. The technical level of locally based groups ranges from average to good, and for many visitors the experience of Vivaldi in Venice is a must. But the same diet year in year out, and the lack of critical feedback, are clear signs that the real aim of many musical events in Venice is a quick fix for the tourist – something that has been highlighted in recent years by the proliferation of musicians playing in 18th-century costume.

An obvious exception is the orchestra of **La Fenice**, which is one of the best in the country. As well as its opera and ballet seasons, La Fenice, under resident conductor Isaac Karabtchevsky, has at least two concert seasons a year at its temporary home | at the PalaFenice. It offers the standard repertoire of any large orchestra, and in recent years has shown a penchant for 20th-century

Hear baroque music on period instruments at the **Scuola Grande di San Rocco**. *See p221*.

music. Unlike any other musical event in town, La Fenice attracts concert-goers from deep inside the mainland.

Venice has no concert hall – and, until La Fenice is rebuilt, no opera house either. The Teatro Malibran (information 041 786 520) will help breach this gap when it reopens in 2001. There are also plans to convert the **Scuola Vecchia della Misericordia**, an elegant 15th-century Gothic structure in Cannaregio, but for the moment the rebuilding of La Fenice takes precedence.

This means that most musical events take place in churches or *scuole* (*see p63*). Some of these, such as Vivaldi's church of **La Pietà** (*see p221*) or the **Scuola Grande di San Rocco** (*see p221*), have played an important part in the history of music in Venice; others, including the **Basilica dei Frari** (*see p221*) and the churches of **San Samuele**, the **Gesuati**, **Santo Stefano**, and the **Zitelle**, have fewer musical connections but bags of atmosphere. In these churches the acoustics are generally good, but it is a pity, given the setting, that the concerts feature predominantly instrumental music, most of it of a far-from-high standard. Visiting choirs sometimes make up the shortfall with free, better-quality concerts. American, British and German choirs are frequent visitors. For one-off concerts of this type, keep your eyes open for posters.

St Mark's Basilica offers fewer concerts than it used to, and they are usually of a ceremonial nature, with the Patriarch deciding who is to attend. But lovers of church music should catch one of two regular Sunday appointments: the sung mass at St Mark's (10.30am) and the Gregorian chant on the island of **San Giorgio** (11am). Venice also has a wealth of fine 18th-century organs by master organ-builder Gaetano Callido. Three of the best can be found in the churches of **San Moisè**, **San Stae** and **San Polo**; keep an eye out for recitals.

THE SEASON

Venice's theatre and dance season stretches from October to May – though La Fenice (in its temporary premises) keeps on going most of the year, closing only for August – but the entertainment does not stop there.

Tourist-oriented classical music concerts are held as long as there's a visitor to attend. And as temperatures rise, productions move outdoors, and a host of smaller groups, encouraged by an active local council, take to Venice's open spaces (*see p222* **Festivals**).

But the colder months are not without their serious music attractions either: the **Giornate Wagneriane** (*see p222* **Festivals**) concert cycle attracts top-class international musicians, while the **Premio Venezia** (*see p222* **Festivals**) international competition for solo pianists comes to a head in early December with a ceremony usually hosted by La Fenice.

INFORMATION & TICKETS

In general, tickets can by purchased at theatre box offices immediately prior to shows; the tourist information office near piazza San Marco (*see p289*) and the VeLa office (*see p275*) sell tickets for 'serious' events; many travel agents and hotel receptions will provide tickets for Vivaldi concerts. For high-profile or first-night productions at such major venues as the PalaFenice, the Teatro Carlo Goldoni or the Teatro Toniolo, or for summer festivals, some shows will sell out days or even weeks in advance: in these cases, tickets should be reserved at the theatres themselves at least ten days before performances, and picked up – in most cases – no later than one hour before the show begins.

Alternatively, book through an agency (*see p188* **Ticket agencies**).

Local newspapers *Il Gazzettino* and *La Nuova Venezia* (*see p284* **Venice dailies**) carry listings of theatrical events, as does the bi-lingual monthly *Venezia News* listings magazine.

Theatres

PalaFenice

Tronchetto island (041 786 501/fax 041 786 580/www.cosi.it/fenice/www.teatrolafenice.it/ fenice@interbusiness.it). Vaporetto Tronchetto. **Box office** *at the door* (041 520 4010) opens one hour before performances; Cassa di Risparmio di Venezia, San Marco 4216, campo San Luca (041 521 0161) 8.30am-1.30pm Mon-Fri; VeLa (see p275). **Performances** 8pm; some 5pm matinées. **Credit** AmEx, MC, V.

This huge white tent, set up on an island in Venice's ugly outskirts (yes, even Venice has ugly outskirts) soon after the La Fenice opera house was gutted by fire in 1996, hosts the occasional classical ballet, as well as the opera and classical music season. The setting is a far cry from the central location and gilded opulence of the mother opera house, but seats are always available and it's convenient for people coming from the mainland. A special vaporetto, marked 'La Fenice', leaves for the PalaFenice from the Vallaresso vaporetto stop 45 minutes before each performance, stopping to pick up at the Zattere on the way; a normal ACTV ticket is required. Capacity in the old Fenice was 870; in the PalaFenice it's 1,200.

Teatro a l'Avogaria

Dorsoduro 1617, corte Zappa (041 520 6130). Vaporetto San Basilio. **Performances** 8.30pm, days vary. **No credit cards. Map II B1.**

This experimental theatre (entry is by voluntary donation) was founded in 1969 by internationally renowned director Giovanni Poli. Here he continued the experimental approach he had first developed in the 1950s at Venice University's drama department – another of his own creations. Through the long years when the Teatro Carlo Goldoni (*see below*) was closed for restoration, Poli's theatre was the city's most important. Since his death in 1979, Poli's disciples have pressed on with the master's experiments, staging works by little-known authors from the 15th to the 19th centuries. A theatre school offers two-year courses for young actors.

Teatro Carlo Goldoni

San Marco 4650B, calle Goldoni (041 520 7853/ fax 041 520 5241/www.teatrogoldonive.it/ info@teatrogoldonive.it). Vaporetto Rialto. **Box office** 10am-1pm, 3-7pm Mon-Sat; one hour before performances. **Performances** 8.30pm Mon-Wed, Fri, Sat; 4pm Thur, Sun. **Credit** MC, V. **Map II A4.**

Based in Venice's most beautiful theatre, the Goldoni's Teatro Stabile di Venezia company serves up Venetian classics by Ruzante, Chiari, Selvatico and Gallina, as well as those by Goldoni himself. But its repertoire doesn't stop there: in the 19th century, plays by Pirandello and D'Annunzio premiered here; today, some of Italy's leading directors stage works by big contemporary names. The Goldoni – which over the years has been called the San Luca, the Vendramin di San Salvador and the Apollo – was given its current name in 1875 to mark the centenary of the famous playwright's death. The teetering structure was closed down after World War II and given a thorough overhaul before reopening in 1979. Youth theatre projects, readings, poetry afternoons and some musical performances are also organised.

Teatro Comunale Villa dei Leoni
Villa Principe Pio, via Don Minzoni 26, Mira (041 560 0212 /fax 041 560 0790/ www.teatridellariviera.it/info@teatridellariviera.it). Bus 53 from piazzale Roma. **Box office** 10.30am-1.30pm Mon, Wed, Thur; 10.30am-1.30pm, 5.30-7pm Tue, Fri; 10am-noon Sat; VeLa (*see p275*). **Performances** 9pm. **No credit cards**.
Located in Mira, a small town on the Brenta canal (*see p243*), the theatre focuses on upbeat productions for a younger audience, under the guiding hand of experimental writer-director-minstrel Marco Paolini, who has a huge following in Italy thanks to his (recently televised) one-man shows on socially committed topics. The Villa dei Leoni also plays an important role in the Festival delle Ville summer theatre festival (*see p222* **Festivals**).

Teatrino della Murata
Via Bruno 19, Mestre (041 989 879/fax 041 980 649/www.tiscalinet.it/teatromurata/ass.tmp@tin.it). Bus 2 from piazzale Roma. **Box office** half hour before performances. **Performances** 9pm Mon-Sat; 5pm, 9pm Sun. **No credit cards**.
The tiny Murata (60 seats) is situated in a former warehouse under the remains of the ancient city walls. Funded by the city and regional councils, it specialises in multicultural theatre, and provides a venue for new actors and local theatre companies.

Teatro Fondamenta Nuove
Cannaregio 5013, fondamenta Nuove (041 522 4498/fax 041 523 1988). Vaporetto Fondamente Nuove. **Box office** 10am-8pm on performance days. **Performances** 8.30pm, days vary. **No credit cards**. Map I B4.
Opened in 1993 in an old joiners' shop, the Fondamenta Nuove stages contemporary dance and avantgarde performances, and organises film festivals, symposiums, exhibitions and workshops. Experimental events exploring the relationship between artistic creativity and technology are held as part of its ongoing Art and Technology project.

Teatro Toniolo
Piazzetta Battisti 1, Mestre (041 274 9070/fax 041 274 9049/www.comune.venezia.it/teatrotoniolo/ cultura.spettacolo.me@comune.venezia.it). Bus 2, 7, 9 from piazzale Roma. **Box office** (041 971 666) 11am-12.30pm, 5-7.30pm Tue-Sun. **Performances** 9pm daily. **Credit** MC, V.
The Teatro Toniolo in Mestre was founded in 1913. Since being taken over by the local council in 1997, it has served up a varied assortment of performances, ranging from vernacular favourites to contemporary plays, new stagings of Italian and foreign classics, cabaret, contemporary music concerts, and contemporary dance and ballet.

Churches & *scuole*

For information on events in churches, check the local press.

Basilica dei Frari
San Polo, campo dei Frari (041 522 2637/041 719 308). Vaporetto San Tomà. Map I C2.
The Frari is the biggest church in Venice and one of the best venues for sacred music. It has regular seasons in the autumn and spring, organ recitals (the church boasts three organs: two single keyboard 18th-century instruments and a 1928 Mascioni hidden behind the high altar) and a number of free or low-cost afternoon concerts, especially over Christmas and the New Year, sponsored by the local paper *Il Gazzettino*. From May to July and September to October there are concerts on Fridays at 9pm. If you go to one of the winter concerts, wrap up warm, as the church is not heated.

Santa Maria della Pietà
Castello, riva degli Schiavoni (041 523 1096/ www.vivaldi.it). Vaporetto San Zaccaria. Map III B2.
Usually known as La Pietà or simply 'the Vivaldi church', it dates from the mid-18th century, and was built alongside the original charitable *ospedale* foundation where Vivaldi taught. Though proportioned with an eye and an ear for music-making, the excellent acoustics are not generally exploited to their full potential by the prettily costumed groups arranged around the high altar. In the days of the *ospedale*, it was the sound experience that counted: Vivaldi's girls could be heard but not seen as they sang from behind wrought-iron grilles in the gallery. Today, the wigs and silk gowns of ensembles Le Venexiane and Le Putte di Vivaldi are supposed to make up for the occasional dropped note.

Scuola Grande di San Giovanni Evangelista
San Polo 2469A, campiello della Scuola (041 522 8125). Vaporetto Riva di Biasio. Map I C2.
A 14th-century *scuola* with an imposing marble staircase. In recent years this has been the venue for an interesting series of chamber music concerts (*see p222* **Società Veneziana di Concerti**), as well as being home to the costumed baroque outfit, L'Orchestra di Venezia.

Scuola Grande di San Rocco
San Polo, campo San Rocco (041 962 999). Vaporetto San Tomà. Map I C2.
A few yards from the Frari, its gleaming façade recently renovated, stands the Scuola Grande di San Rocco. It has an unbroken musical tradition stretching back over half a millennium; the director of music at St Mark's was also *ex officio* director at San Rocco. The sixteenth-century composer Giovanni Gabrieli was organist here for 27 years, and Monteverdi also had a long association with the Scuola. In 1958, a choral work by Stravinsky, *Threni*, premièred here. A recently formed ensemble,

Arts & Entertainment

the Accademia di San Rocco (*see below* **Musical associations**), gives regular concerts of baroque music on period instruments, usually on Tuesday and Saturday evenings from April to October. During the interval the Upper Gallery is opened to allow concert-goers to admire the Tintorettos – just as well, as tickets are far from cheap. Expect to pay upwards of L50,000.

Other music venues

Museo Querini-Stampalia

Castello 4778, campiello Querini Stampalia (041 271 1411). Vaporetto Rialto. **Admission** *museum* L12,000; L8,000 concessions. **Concerts** of ancient music 5pm, 8.30pm Fri, Sat, included in admission price. **Credit** MC, V. **Map** III A1.

Offering more of an entertainment than a full-scale concert, the *soirées* organised by this enterprising museum and cultural foundation take the form of a half-hour recital of lesser-known (usually Renaissance or baroque) works.

Musical associations

Accademia di San Rocco

Via Ca' Venier 8, Mestre (041 962 999/ fax 041 982 037/sanrocco@musicinvenice.com/ www.musicinvenice.com).

One of the newest groups, the Accademia di San Rocco are baroque specialists who perform on authentic instruments. They organise concerts at the Scuola di San Rocco from Feb-Dec, and at the Ateneo Veneto (campo San Fantin, next to the Fenice Theatre) or the church of San Giacometo (Vaporetto Rialto) in November and December.

Centro di Co-ordinamento Culturale

Via Forte Gazzera 11, Mestre (041 917 257).

This is the oldest-established group promoting regular concerts for visitors. Based at the church of La Pietà, it is associated with two ensembles, I Virtuosi dell'Ensemble di Venezia, a 12-member string orchestra, and Le Putte di Vivaldi, an all-female quintet that performs in costume, complete with pomaded wigs. They take their name from the orphan girls (*putte*) who were brought up and trained to sing or play instruments in the *ospedali* of 17th-century Venice.

L'Offerta Musicale

San Polo 1541, calle dei Botteri (tel/fax 041 524 1143).

L'Offerta Musicale – or L'Orchestra da Camera di Venezia, as it is officially known – organises two seasons of concerts in autumn and spring, currently held at Palazzo Mocenigo (*see p110*). The ensemble frequently offers imaginatively framed programmes, and does not limit itself to the usual baroque repertoire. During the intermission, the audience may visit the palazzo's collection of fabric and clothes from the 18th and 19th centuries.

Festivals

With the advent of warm weather, various local council-sponsored summer drama events get under way, luring Venetians and visitors alike to an evening soaking in dramatically lit magic in *campi* and courtyards. The only possible disadvantage to outdoor theatre-going in Venice is that the urban backdrop tends to distract one's attention from what's going on on stage. On the other hand, given that standards vary greatly from production to production, this is not always a bad thing.

Since its foundation in 1995, the **Teatro in Campo** festival has had a stop-go career but now seems a permanent fixture during the summer months, gracing campo Pisani near the Accademia, and venues around the islands of the lagoon, with good-quality drama and some 18th-century opera. Though the festival has its own drama company, it also provides a stage for other young theatre groups from around the region.

More adventurous culture-seekers make their way along the Brenta canal (*see p243*) to enjoy music and theatre in the gardens of the spectacular Palladian villas that line that waterway. The **Festival delle Ville** takes place from June to August. Organised by the Moby Dick-Teatri della Riviera co-operative, the festival offers high-quality drama and music – both classical and contemporary – to audiences that have grown steadily since the festival was launched a decade ago. Bus 53 leaves piazzale Roma every half hour and stops off at all canalside towns along the road to Padua (check the timetable for the return trip). Some productions are accompanied by snacks or themed dinners.

Società Veneziana di Concerti

Fondazione Ugo e Olga Levi, San Marco 2893, campo San Vidal (041 786 764). **Tickets** L50,000; L15,000 concessions. **Box office** Cassa di Risparmio di Venezia, San Marco 4216, campo San Luca (041 521 0161) 8.30am-1.30pm Mon-Fri. **Credit** AmEx, MC, V. **Map** II B3.

The best of Venice's musical groups, the *società* organises a varied programme of chamber music – with mercifully little hackneyed Venetian baroque – at the Scuola Grande di San Giovanni Evangelista, with two or three concerts a month. These concerts are often heavily subscribed by season-ticket holders,

Arts & Entertainment

In a brave attempt to revive the contemporary scene and to stimulate the production of contemporary performing arts, both Italian and international, the **Biennale di Venezia** has allotted new funds to its Dance, Music & Theatre department. The programme remains limited, with performances restricted to the summer months, but what there is takes place in interesting newly restored venues: the **Teatro Tese** – an open-air space for 500 people – and the smaller **Teatro Piccolo Arsenale**, both inside the Arsenale (*see p95*) and open only for Biennale performances. Other shows (including dance performances by the Biennale's dance school, the Accademia Isola Danza, presided over by Carolyn Carson) take place in the stunning but little-used **Teatro Verde**, an amphitheatre inside the Fondazione Cini (www.cini.it; *see p128*) behind the church of San Giorgio Maggiore.

In November and December, Wagner is the star of a serious of world-class concerts organised by the Associazione R. Wagner; the **Giornate Wagneriane** also includes conferences on the great man, and visits to the house he occupied while in Venice.

In December, the **Premio Venezia** international solo pianist competition culminates – after closed-doors auditions and heats – in a final concert by prize winners, held at the PalaFenice with tickets available free through the Fondazione Teatro La Fenice.

La Biennale di Venezia, Danza-Musica-Teatro

Ca' Giustinian, San Marco 1364A, calle del Ridotto (041 521 8711/fax 041 521 0038/ www.labiennale.org/press@labiennale.org). Vaporetto Vallaresso. **Open** *9am–6pm Mon-Fri.* **Box office** *VeLa (see p275).* **Map** II B4.

Festival delle Ville

Villa Principe Pio, via Don Minzoni 26, Mira (041 560 0212/ festivalville@provincia.venezia.it/ www.provincia.venezia.it/festivalville). **Open** *11am-1.30pm, 6-7pm Mon-Fri; 10am-noon Sat, Sun.* **Box office** *VeLa (see p275).* **Performances** *times vary.*

Le Giornate Wagneriane

Associazione R Wagner, c/o Associazione Culturale Italo-Tedesca, Palazzo Albrizzi, Cannaregio 4118, fondamenta Sant'Andrea (041 523 2544/ fax 041 524 5275). Vaporetto Ca' d'Oro. **Open** *9am-6pm Mon-Fri.*

Premio Venezia

Fondazione Teatro La Fenice, Palazzo Franchetti, San Marco 2847, campo San Maurizio (041 786 562 /fax 041 786 580/ www.teatrolafenice.it). Vaporetto Accademia/ Santa Maria del Giglio. **Open** *9am-noon Mon-Fri.* **Map** II B3.
Associazione Amici della Fenice, c/o Ateneo Veneto, San Marco 1897, campo San Fantin (041 522 7737/fax 041 520 0487). Vaporetto Santa Maria del Giglio. **Open** *9am-noon Mon-Fri.* **Map** II 3A.

Teatro in Campo

Associazione Pantakin da Venezia, Giudecca 218, fondamenta San Giacomo (041 277 0407/fax 041 277 6394/ www.pantakin.it/info@pantakin). *Vaporetto Palanca.* **Open** *9.30am-12.30pm Mon-Fri.* **Map** II C3.
Venue *campo San Pisani. Vaporetto Accademia.* **Tickets** *L20,000; L15,000 concessions.* **Box office** *at the entrance of the open theatre.* **No credit cards.** **Map** II B3.

but there are occasional cut-price repeat performances at the Cinema Corso in Mestre (corso del Popolo; bus 4 from piazzale Roma).

Other musical groups

Collegium Ducale (041 523 2381) performs its Venetian baroque repertoire in various churches, including Santo Stefano (Vaporetto Accademia), San Samuele (Vaporetto San Samuele), Santa Maria Formosa (Vaporetto Rialto). **I Musici Veneziani** (c/o Associazione Culturale Musica & Musica, 041 521 0294/041 524 0153) play in costume at the Ateneo San Basso (vaporetto Vallaresso), while the **Interpreti Veneziani** (041 277 0561/041 524 2232) are Vivaldi specialists associated with the church of San Bartolomeo (vaporetto Rialto). The **Orchestra di Venezia** (041 522 8125) is another baroque chamber orchestra, which plays in costume at the Scuola Grande di San Giovanni Evangelista, and the **Venetia Antiqua Ensemble** (041 962 999) performs Venetian baroque music on period instruments at the church of San Giacometto (vaporetto Rialto).

Sport & Fitness

Rowing, running, and climbing bridges are the staples of the
Venetian exercise routine.

The average Venetian's keep-fit routine is
uniquely suited to his or her unique city. If
gyms are few and swimming pools well-nigh
non-existent, it's not because Venetians are
lazy: few cities force their inhabitants to exert
themselves – covering miles on foot each day,
climbing and descending innumerable flights of
steps – as Venice does. Moreover, any *vaporetto*
trip across the lagoon will reveal Venetians
doing what they like to do best in their leisure
hours: sweating off excess calories rowing
around their watery back yard.

Other traditional sports have fallen into
disuse… though, given the violent nature
of many of these, maybe it's no bad thing.
If the massive tugs-of-war or competitions
to build the biggest human pyramids were
comparatively harmless, not so the boxing
matches, which began with two contestants
but often ended up involving whole *sestieri*, and
massive injuries. *Massa e pindolo* was a form of
Venetian baseball, *cimbani* a local obstacle race,
and *tacco* a kind of bowls played with stray
heels purchased from cobblers' shops; but for
many, these pastimes were too tame for words,
and the *tauromachia* – bullfight – in campo
San Polo provided more gory entertainment.

Unlike land sports, traditional water-borne
competitions have stood the test of time. The
Regata Storica, the series of rowing races
that are fought out on the first Sunday in
September (*see p196*), has been going strong
since the 15th century. If you can't do without
a more prosaic sports schedule, head for the
Lido, where you'll find tennis courts and an
18-hole golf course.

Water sports

Among the reeds and mosquitoes of the
lagoon, two activities dominate: Venetian
rowing (*voga alla veneta – see p225* **Venetians
do it standing up**) and three-sail sailing (*vela
al terzo*). Courses in both are available from
some of the sports clubs listed below.

Three-sail sailing

Once used for trade and transport the length
and breadth of Venice's Adriatic dominions,
the traditional Venetian wooden flat-bottomed

sailing craft is now to be found only in the
lagoon, being used exclusively for pleasure
and sport. Depending upon their length, these
boats can hoist one or two square sails, plus the
classic triangular jib. They can also be rowed in
the traditional standing up position.

Rowing races

There are more than 120 regattas in the
lagoon each year, most of them involving
Venetian rowing. The most sumptuous is the
Regata Storica in September. The regatta
is much more than the extravagant pageant
of tourist brochures: rowers of all ages in
craft of various classes compete for glory and
prizes. Perhaps even more spectacular is the
Vogalonga, a 32-kilometre (20-mile) parade
around Venice and the northern lagoon. Held
in May (*see p195*), it is open to anyone who
can get their hands on a boat of any kind and
an oar or two. Thousands do.

Boat clubs

Canottieri Diadora

Via Sandro Gallo 136B, Lido (041 526 5742).
Vaporetto Lido, then Bus B or B/. **Open** *Oct-May*
8am-12.30pm, 2.30-6.30pm Tue-Sun; *June-Sept* 8am-
12.30pm, 3.30-7.30pm Tue-Sun. **Rates** L46,000
enrolment; L38,000 one month; L150,000 three
months. **No credit cards.**
Lessons in Venetian stand-up rowing are organised
for beginners.

Reale Società Canottieri Bucintoro

Dorsoduro 10, 15, 261, Zattere (041 522 2055/
041 520 5630/041 523 7933/fax 041 522 2055).
Vaporetto Zattere or Salute. **Open** *office* 2-4pm
Tue, Fri; *lessons* 9am-5pm Tue-Sat; 9am-1pm Sun.
Rates L80,000 enrolment; L80,000 for 8 lessons.
No credit cards. Map II 3-4C.
Founded in 1882, this is one of Italy's oldest sports
clubs, with a slew of Olympic rowing champions.
Offers canoeing, kayaking and Venetian rowing,
plus a well-equipped gym. Short *vela al terzo* cours-
es, open to non-members, are held in March/April.

Remiera Canottieri Cannaregio

Cannaregio 732, calle della Cereria (041 720
539). Vaporetto Tre Archi. **Open** 3-7pm Mon-Fri.
Rates by arrangement. **No credit cards.**
Map off I 1A.

Arts & Entertainment

Beginners' *voga alla veneta* courses by arrangement. This club around the back of the station is one of the friendliest of the lot, and in Giorgio Costantini it has one of the best instructors on the lagoon. There's a well-equipped gym too.

Società Canottiere Francesco Querini

Canareggio 6576E, Fondamente Nuove (041 522 2039). Vaporetto Ospedale. **Open** 8am-6pm Mon-Sat; 8am-1pm Sun. **Rates** L50,000 enrolment fee; L80,000 for 10 lessons. **No credit cards. Map III 2A.**
Venice's second-oldest boat club, the Querini now boasts a well-equipped gym too. The club offers rowing, canoeing and Venetian rowing.

Football

Venetians are just as *calcio*-crazed as the Milanese or the Neapolitans. Come Sunday afternoon, supporters grab their green, black and orange scarves, jump into their boats or

board a vaporetto, and sail off to the football stadium at the far eastern end of the island of Sant'Elena – the only major league ground in Europe to be entirely surrounded by water. The opposing team's supporters are met from the train, herded on to their own steamer and transported across the lagoon like a bunch of convicts heading off to Alcatraz.

For years, a seriously talent-starved 'Venezia Calcio 1907' bobbed up and down between the second and third divisions of the Italian league. Then, much to everyone's surprise, at the end of the 1997-8 season, they limped back to Serie A after an absence of 31 years; the glory lasted only two seasons. Venezia's home matches take place on alternate Sunday afternoons from September to June. Tickets cost from L30,000 and are on sale at the ground, at main ACTV and ACTV-VeLa (*see p275*) ticket offices, and at two branches of the Banca Antoniana Popolare Veneta: San Marco 5400, campo San

Venetians do it standing up

The Venetian style of rowing, in which the rower stands up, facing the direction of travel, is known as *voga alla veneta*. Venetians find it difficult to understand why anybody would row any other way: the standing position allows one to put all one's force behind the stroke; moreover, facing forwards is a major aid to navigation.

There are various types of *voga alla veneta* – team-rowing is one, and the impressive solo, cross-handed, two-oar method known as *voga alla valesana* is another.

But the most famous type is the *voga ad un solo remo*, as practised by Venetian gondoliers. It may look effortless, but the single-oar scull is one of the most difficult rowing strokes of all.

Most other forms of rowing rely on pairs of oars, whose equal and opposite forces keep the boat travelling in a straight line. The gondolier, on the other hand, only ever puts

his oar in the water on the right side of the boat – where it rests in a *forcola*, an elaborate walnut-wood rowlock. Pushing on the oar (*premer* in Venetian dialect) has the obvious effect of making the gondola – or the humbler *sandolo*, which is what most beginners train in – turn to the left. The trick consists in using the downstroke (*la stalia*) – during which the oar stays in the water – to correct the direction. Of course, if the check were equal to the push, the boat would go nowhere; it is the ability to correct the boat's course with almost minimal resistance that marks out the experienced rower from the beginner. It has been calculated that a gondolier uses up no more energy rowing a half-ton gondola with three passengers than the average person expends in walking.

Visitors to the city can enrol for beginners' rowing courses (*see p224* **Boat clubs**); these generally take at least a month, but it is often possible to arrange intensive courses direct with the instructors.

Don't alienate your trainer by clamouring to be let loose on the Grand Canal, which is strictly for experts; lessons tend to take place on calmer – if somewhat less picturesque – stretches of water, such as the channel that runs alongside the railway bridge.

And never wear gloves, not even in winter; hand on wood is the first commandment of *voga alla veneta*; you'll wear the blisters with pride for weeks afterwards.

Bartolomeo and Cannaregio 3682, strada Nova. For further information check the club's website at www.veneziacalcio.it).

Golf

Golf Club Lido
Via del Forte, Alberoni-Lido (041 731 333). Vaporetto Lido, then bus B to Alberoni. **Open** *Oct-Mar* 8.30am-6pm Tue-Sat. *Apr-Sept* 8.30am-6pm Tue-Fri; 8.30am-8pm Sat, Sun. **Rates** L90,000 Tue-Fri; L100,000 Sat, Sun. **Credit** AmEx, DC, MC, V.
Considered one of Italy's top ten courses, the Lido links have three practice courses as well as an 18-hole one. Open to non-members, though only those with proof of membership of golf clubs elsewhere.

Gyms

See also p224 RSC Bucintoro and RC Cannaregio, and *p225* SC Francesco Querini.

Palestra Delfino
Dorsoduro 788A, Zattere (041 523 2763/fax 041 241 7616). Vaporetto Zattere. **Open** 9am-10pm Mon-Fri; 9am-noon Sat. **Rates** L21,000 per day; L65,000 per week; L130,000 per month. **Credit** AmEx, DC, MC, V. **Map** II 2B.
Equipped with two fully computerised Technogym fitness rooms, a sauna, a Turkish bath, a solarium and massage services. Bring a fitness certificate signed by your doctor.

Club Venice Fitness Gymnos
Cannaregio 3475A, calle della Gradisca (041 720 100). Vaporetto Madonna dell'Orto. **Open** 8.30am-10pm Mon-Fri; 10am-6pm Sat. **Rates** L25,000 enrolment fee; L70,000 per month. **No credit cards**. **Map** I 3A.
Club Venice has bodybuilding, cardio-fitness and circuit training facilities.

Running

Most runners head for the wider stretches of pavement on the **Zattere**, on the *fondamenta* by the **Giardini** vaporetto stop, or further east under the umbrella pines of **Sant'Elena**.

The **Venice Marathon** takes place in October, usually on the fourth Sunday of the month. The starting line for this 42km (26-mile) run is at the Villa Pisani at Strà; the race passes along the banks of the Brenta canal, road bridge to Venice, then by a specially-erected pontoon over the lagoon to the finishing line on the riva degli Schiavoni. For information, call 041 940 644 or e-mail organisers at venice@gpnet.it or via the website at www.venicemarathon.it.

The less competitive **Su e Zo Per i Ponti** *(see p194)* takes place in spring in island Venice and tends to degenerate into a bar crawl.

A lagoon-side run in Sant'Elena.

Skating

Skating of any kind is strictly forbidden in central Venice, which doesn't stop hordes of kids-on-wheels whizzing through the gardens at Sant'Elena and along the relatively quiet, relatively bridge-free alleyways in the outer reaches of the Castello sestiere.

Swimming

The sea water around Venice is not immensely appetising, although – as local authorities repeat *ad nauseam* – it is getting cleaner; and indeed, locals in their thousands brave the Adriatic and come to no harm. The Lido's more accessible beaches are sewn up by umbrella-renting operations. For public beaches, *see chapter* **The Lido to Chioggia**. Unless you're splashing out at the Hotel Cipriani *(see p45)*, you can forget swimming pools.

Tennis

Tennis Club Ca' Del Moro
Via Ferruccio Parri 6, Lido (041 770 965/fax 041 770 676). Vaporetto Lido, then Bus B or B/. **Open** 9.15am-12.30pm Mon, Wed, Fri, Sun; 9.15am-12.30pm, 3.30-9.30pm Tue, Thur; 9.15am-12.30pm, 3.30pm-8.30pm Sat. **Rates** L16,000 an hour per court. **No credit cards**.
This sports centre is equipped with ten tennis courts, a swimming pool (members only), football pitches, gymnasium and pool rooms.

Green Garden Sporting Club
Via Asseggiano 65, Chirignago, Mestre (041 914 344/041 914 990/fax 041 544 0352). Bus 7 from piazzale Roma. **Open** 8am-10pm Mon-Fri; 8am-8pm Sat, Sun. **Rates** *tennis* L30,000 an hour indoor court; L22,000 an hour outdoor court; *football* L100,000 a game. **No credit cards**.
The Green Garden offers six tennis courts, four football pitches and a gym.

The Veneto

Getting Started

The region surrounding Venice may boast fewer canals, but it is packed with a variety of other delights.

Timeless (anachronistic) Venice is the capital of a region – the Veneto – which has not only kept pace with the changing times: economically speaking at least, it has led the way (*see chapter* **Venice Today**). If the region's natural beauties were never as striking as, say, Tuscany's, the environmental ravages of the economic miracle have spared some lovely, untouched and under-visited corners, particularly in the hills and mountains: the Colli Euganei beyond Padua, and the Colli Berici south of Vicenza roll pleasantly above the industrial sprawl, dotted with their share of those Palladian villas (*see chapter* **Palladian**

Villas) that pop up in the unlikeliest places around the region. Alternatively, the flat, reed-fringed waterscapes of the wildfowl-filled **Po Delta** on the southern border of the Veneto provide endless scope for messing around in boats, or on bicycles.

The Veneto's prime attractions, however, lie in the big towns on the plain: Roman, operatic **Verona**; scholarly, devout **Padua**; and self-made, Palladian **Vicenza**.

Venice has no medieval paintings to match Giotto's frescos in the Scrovegni Chapel (*see p237*) in Padua, no civic Renaissance interiors quite as perfect as Palladio's Teatro Olimpico

The **Po Delta** is a peaceful haven of flora and fauna. *See p243.*

(*see p260*) in Vicenza, and no Romanesque churches to match San Zeno (*see p250*) in Verona – to say nothing of Verona's fine bevy of Roman remains.

Heading north, the mountains loom and the scene changes. **Treviso** is still on the plain, and was once a mere satellite of La Serenissima, but its frescoed *palazzi* already give a taste of the elaborate decorations to be found in **Feltre** further north, and its economic vitality – of which the Benetton empire is the most famous flag-bearer – gives the town a lively, dynamic feel. The first, gentle foothills of the Dolomites are edged by a string of interesting towns: the wine-producing centres of **Conegliano** and **Valdobbiadene**; **Asolo** and **Possagno**, given up respectively to the leisured laziness of *il dolce far niente* and the cold neo-classical visions of Antonio Canova; **Bassano del Grappa**, home of a celebrated bridge and of a fiery spirit that keeps the *veneti* going through those foggy winter evenings (and mornings, come to that); and **Marostica**, where you may just run into a game of chess played with human pieces.

Beyond **Belluno** – Venice's pre-Alpine fiefdom – the mountains begin in earnest, bringing hordes of *beau monde* skiers to the elegant resort of Cortina d'Ampezzo and queues of summer hikers to attempt one of the seven *alte vie* (high-altitude footpaths) that traverse the Dolomites.

Heading north-east from Venice, a straggle of seaside resorts with high-density beach umbrellas, campsites and discos stretches from Lido di Jesolo to the border of the Veneto, just short of Lignano Sabbiadoro. Beyond here, in the region of Friuli-Venezia Giulia, are the twin pulls of **Aquileia** – a tiny village with a glorious Roman past – and **Grado**, one of the pleasantest of the northern Adriatic resorts, with a quiet, island-studded lagoon of its own.

Getting around

By train

(For general information on Italian trains, *see p277*.)

Padua (30 mins), Vicenza (55 mins) and Verona (85 mins) are all connected to Venice by frequent fast Intercity or Eurostar trains on the Venice-Milan-Turin line. Padua is where the line to Bologna branches off, with around one fast train an hour during the day stopping at Rovigo (55 mins) and Ferrara (75 mins) along the way; slower *interregionali* trains also stop at smaller towns such as Monselice (53 mins). From the latter, the branch line to Mantua

serves the stations of Este (12 mins from Monselice) and Montagnana (35 mins from Monselice), though study the timetable carefully as these trains are infrequent.

Heading north from Venice is less straightforward. Treviso (20-30 mins) and Conegliano (40-50 mins) are on the main line from Venice to Udine, served mainly by *interregionale* trains. To the north-west, Castelfranco Veneto (40 mins) and Bassano del Grappa (60 mins) are served by a local line with around 15 trains a day. Around seven local trains a day make the agonisingly slow but very pretty haul up the Piave valley from Padua to Feltre (90 mins) and Belluno (two hours); some proceed beyond to Calalzo-Pieve di Cadore (three hours), which is connected by bus to Cortina d'Ampezzo.

There are buses from Grado and Aquileia to the station of Cervignano (85 mins) on the main Venice-Trieste line.

By bus

Italian long-distance buses are usually neither as frequent, cheap or relaxing as the train. An exception is on mountain routes, where they are often the only mode of public transport. The ski resort of Cortina d'Ampezzo, for example, is best reached by the morning ATVO (041 520 5530) bus from piazzale Roma at 7.50am; the journey takes three and a half hours.

Many destinations can be reached by combining train and bus journeys. See individual chapters in the Veneto section for details of bus services to more out-of-the-way destinations. In almost all cases, Sunday services are very limited.

By car

The larger towns in the Veneto are all connected to Venice by fast motorway links: note that Italian motorways (*autostrade*, prefix A followed by number) are expensive, with tolls averaging out at L10,000 per 100 kilometres.

Surprisingly, A-roads (*strade nazionali* or *strade statali*, prefix N or SS followed by number) are not always as good as they are further south, and often head right through the centre of towns (with a high risk of encountering traffic confusion) rather than by-passing them.

For more out-of-the-way destinations and mountain roads, a good map is essential; those in the 1:200,000-scale series published by the Touring Club Italiano (TCI) have plenty of detail and are available in most bookshops and in motorway service stations. For car-hire information, *see p277*.

The Veneto

Palladian Villas

Country houses with a difference – they were designed by a genius.

Andrea Palladio – the man who was to become arguably the most influential architect of all time – had a lowly start in life. He was born in Padua on 30 November 1508 and baptised Andrea di Pietro della Gondola. His father, who milled grain and transported it for a living, apprenticed him at the age of 13 to a local sculptor and decorator. In 1524 Andrea moved to Vicenza and began working in the workshop of Giovanni da Porlezza, a stonecarver. The workshop, recognising his talent, put up the money for Andrea's guild entrance fee. Palladio learned to design and carve church altars, tombs and architectural elements, many of them commissioned by members of the Vicenza nobility.

Between 1530 and 1538, while working on the decorative details of a new villa on the outskirts of Vicenza, he met its owner, Count Giangiorgio Trissino, an influential and very wealthy local aristocrat who was the leader of a group of local Humanist intellectuals dedicated to reviving all aspects of classical culture. This chance meeting was to change the course of western architecture. Trissino, a poet and amateur architect, was immensely impressed with the skills and intellect of the young stonecutter and decided to take him under his wing, encouraging and funding his studies of the art and architecture of Rome.

Over the next few years, Trissino set about turning Andrea into a worthy heir to Vitruvius, the ancient architect whose treatise *De Architectura* underpinned the return to classical models in the Italian Renaissance. He began with finding a suitable name: 'Palladio' was a helpful angel in Trissino's epic poem *Italia Liberata dai Goti* (*Italy Liberated From the Goths*). In transferring it to his protégé Trissino was expressing the hope that Andrea would go on to liberate Italian architecture from the Gothic. Andrea was introduced to Humanist circles around the Veneto, given time off to study Roman antiquities in Verona and Padua, and taken to Rome on three lengthy visits between 1540 and 1550. (Palladio made two more trips to the Eternal City on his own.) There he scrutinised, measured and sketched all the major classical remains; he also studied the examples of Renaissance greats throughout Italy, including Sanmicheli, Bramante, Raphael and Giulio Romano. In 1554 he published his Roman findings in a sort of early guidebook, *Le antichità di Roma*.

The result of this research and study was a fully developed and newly confident classical style that the architect had already begun to apply in a number of commissions for wealthy clients. Palladio's early patrons were part of the Trissino circle, who made sure the architect received both work and intellectual stimulation after Trissino died in 1550. Among these enlightened Vicentine nobles were Pietro Godi – whose villa at Lonedo di Lugo (*see p231*) was Palladio's first independent commission, in 1537 – and the Barbaro brothers, a gifted pair of scholars and statesmen who dabbled in design themselves and whose collaborative encouragement of the young architect generated one of his country-house masterpieces, the **Villa Barbaro** (*see p232*) at Maser (1550-7). Girolamo Chiericati, another of Palladio's patrons, was on the board of commissioners who gave the architect his first big break in 1549, when plans he had submitted for the reconstruction of Vicenza's town hall (now known as the **Basilica Palladiana**, *see p259*) were accepted. This revolutionary design, in which the Gothic structure was wrapped in a huge, two-storey classical loggia, established Palladio as one of the leading architects of his day. His writings (published in user-friendly Italian, not Latin) and his prominent churches in Venice reinforced his fame. By the time of his death in August 1580, his influence was beginning to be felt from London to Moscow.

Palladio never simply copied ancient Roman models: he re-elaborated classical motifs, creating a style that was entirely his own. The most instantly recognisable feature of his buildings is the use of the Greco-Roman temple front as a portico; equally innovative, though, were the dramatic high-relief effects he created on façades. He frequently employed the thermal window (a semicircular opening divided by two vertical supports) to evoke the monumentality and grandeur of the ancient Roman bath complexes. Though always unmistakably his, each of Palladio's buildings is startlingly different. He was capable both of the stark simplicity to be found at the **Villa Pisani Ferri** (*see p232*) at Bagnolo di Lonigo, which is almost totally devoid of decorative elements, and of the immense complexity of the statue-

Palladio's first villa, **Villa Godi Valmarana ora Malinverni**, completed by 1542.

swamped **Palazzo Chiericati** in the centre of Vicenza (*see p259* **Museo Civico**). Much decoration was also functional: the gracious entrance ramp at the **Villa Emo** (*see p233*) also provided an ideal platform for threshing grain.

But Palladio's inventiveness and sensitivity were not limited to the buildings themselves. He was also obsessed with the smallest details of the natural environment in which his buildings were to be inserted. Building near a river or canal was highly recommended by the architect; as well as allowing easy access by boat, water guaranteed cool breezes during the hot summer months and irrigated the gardens. A villa, wrote Palladio in *I Quattro libri dell'architettura* (*The Four Books of Architecture*, 1570), should 'help conserve the health and strength of its inhabitants, and restore their spirits, worn out by the agitation of city life, to peace and tranquillity'.

What follows is a critical selection of the most important, visitable villas designed entirely or mostly by Palladio himself. For the Basilica Palladiana and the townhouses in Vicenza, *see chapter* **Vicenza**. Note that the names of villas change when they pass from one family to another, though the original owner's surname is generally retained, and occasionally some of the intermediate ones. In the listings below we refer to the villas by their most commonly accepted names. Since the following are mostly private homes, the

opening hours change frequently; telephoning in advance is always recommended. Many villas, such as the **Villa Pisani** in Montagnana (*see p243*), are not open to the public and can only be admired from the outside.

Vicenza province

All transport instructions apply from central Vicenza; unless otherwise stated, services depart from the rural FTV bus service terminal (information 0444 223 115) in front of Vicenza railway station.

Villa Godi Valmarana ora Malinverni

Via Palladio 44, Lonedo di Lugo (0445 860 561/fax 0445 860 806/info@villagodi.com/ www.villagodi.com). Bus to Thiene; change at Thiene to hourly bus for Lugo di Vicenza.
Open *June-Sept* 3-7pm Tue, Sat, Sun. *Mar-Nov* 2-6pm Tue, Sat, Sun. Mornings and other days available for groups with reservations. **Admission** L10,000. **No credit cards**.
Palladio's first villa, built before he ever set foot in Rome and already completed by 1542, is in some ways one of his most radical, pared-back designs. Its matter-of-fact solidity also reminds us that most of these villas were built as working farms. Set in a vast park, the villa has some good 16th-century frescos as well as a former owner's collection of 19th-century art, artefacts and fossils (including a palm tree 5m/16ft high).

Villa Piovene

*Via Palladio 51, Lonedo di Lugo (0445 860 613).
Bus to Thiene; change at Thiene to hourly bus for
Lugo di Vicenza.* **Open** *Gardens only Apr-Oct* 2.30-
7pm daily. *Nov-Mar* 2-5pm daily. **Admission**
L8,000; L6,000 concessions. **No credit cards.**
This may have been one of the architect's last
commissions. The formulaic Palladian style – the
portico, the colonnaded wings, the theatrical double
staircase out front – is proof for some that self-
parody was beginning to set in (or that Palladio's
followers were not quite up to the level of the
master). However, only the central block is plausi-
bly by Palladio; the rest may be by his follower
Vincenzo Scamozzi.

Villa Pisani

*Via Risaie 1, Bagnolo di Lonigo (0444 831 104/
fax 0444 835 517). Bus for Cologna Veneta.*
Open *Apr-Oct* 10am-noon, 3-6pm Wed; open all
year to groups of over 20 people by appointment.
Admission L10,000; groups L8,000; under18s
L5,000. **No credit cards.**
This early commission (begun in 1542) shows
Palladio honing his style and experimenting with
some features – such as rusticated arches – that
would later be abandoned. Looking at the building-
block simplicity of the façade, it's difficult to appreciate how revolutionary this must have seemed at
the time; the revolution continues inside, where the
division of rooms and design details such as the thermal windows are purely classical in inspiration.

Villa Pojana

*Via Castello 41, Pojana Maggiore (0444 898
554/cpojana@tin.it). Bus for Noventa Vicentina.*
Open 10am-12.30pm, 2-6pm Tue-Sun.
Admission L8,000; L5,000 groups of 15
or more, under-14s. **No credit cards.**
A Palladian bungalow or one of the architect's
most original creations, depending on your point
of view. Dating from around 1550, the villa offers
no projecting temple portico, for once, and the
façade is dominated by a serliana arch (in which a
central arched opening is flanked by two rectangular ones) topped by telephone-dial openings – giving an oddly contemporary feeling and suggesting
that Palladio was the original post-modernist. The
interior has perfectly symmetrical rooms, with
frescos by Bernardino India and Anselmo Canera.

Villa Rotonda

Via della Rotonda 45 (0444 321 793). Bus 8 or 13.
Open *Gardens all year* 10am-noon, 3-6pm Tue-Sun.
Interior mid Mar-Oct 10am-noon, 3-6pm Wed.
Admission *gardens* L5,000; *interior* L10,000.
No credit cards.
Perhaps the best-known of the Veneto villas, the
Rotonda – designed by Palladio between 1567 and
1570, but not completed until 1606 – was the first to
be given a dome, a form previously associated with
ancient temples or Renaissance churches. The suc-
cessful reconciliation of the circle and the square
resolved a problem that had baffled generations of

architects. The Rotonda (officially called the Villa
Almerico-Capra Valmarana) was planned not as a
family home but as a pleasure pavilion for a retired
cleric, Paolo Almerico, and thus although the structure has a huge footprint it actually comprises
relatively few rooms. The four temple-like façades
still face out on to lush green countryside on three
sides, despite the site's proximity to the city centre.
Scholars (or talented bluffers) keen to examine the
inside of one of the most famous buildings in
Western architecture may be granted permission
to visit the Rotonda's lavish interior outside the
limited opening times. Those left outside need not
complain: the building's exterior was far more influential and circling it offers the visitor extraordinary
aesthetic pleasure.

Villa Saraceno

*Via Finale 8, Finale di Agugliaro (0444 891 371).
Bus for Noventa Vicentina; change at Ponte Botti for
local service.* **Open** *Apr-Oct* 2-4pm Wed. *Nov-Mar* by
appointment. **Admission** by donation (usually
L5,000). For weekly rental (sleeps 12): Landmark
Trust UK (01628 825 925/www.landmark.trust.uk).
Until a few years ago this jewel of a villa was in a
state of disrepair, in use as a barn. Then, in 1988, it
was bought up by the British Landmark Trust and
beautifully restored, reopening as self-catering
accommodation in 1994 – giving one a unique
chance to stay in a Palladian villa. The designs for
the villa, published by Palladio in his *Four Books of
Architecture,* show two wings that failed to materi-
alise. Its farmyard fate was at least in keeping with
the building's original function: like many of
Palladio's villas, it was built for a gentleman farmer,
with an attic-granary lit by large grilled windows,
so that the wheat was kept well ventilated.

Villa Thiene

*Piazza IV Novembre 2, Quinto Vicentino (0444 584
224/biblioteca.quinto@keycomm.it). Bus 5 from
Vicenza (piazza Matteotti).* **Open** 9.30am-12.30pm, 3-
7pm Mon, Tue, Thur; 9.30am-12.30pm Wed, Fri, Sat;
other times/days by appointment. **Admission** free.
Now the town hall of the otherwise unremarkable
town of Quinto Vicentino, the imposing Villa Thiene
is only a fraction of what was to be an even more
immense villa designed by Palladio in 1546. The
inside was frescoed by Giovanni De Mio and
Bernardino India.

Treviso province

Villa Barbaro at Maser

*Via Barbaro 4, Maser (0423 923 004/fax 0423
923 002/www.villadimaser.it). Autoservizi La
Marca bus from Treviso bus station to Maser.*
Open *Mar-Oct* 3-6pm Tue, Sat, Sun. *Nov-Feb* 2.30-
5pm Sat, Sun; other times/days by appointment.
Admission L10,000; L8,500 groups (by
appointment). **No credit cards.**
The Villa Barbaro is deservedly the most famous of
all Palladian villas. The charm of this out-and-out

Villa Barbaro at Maser. *See p232.*

exercise in rural utopianism derives partly from Palladio's intellectual communion with the Barbaro brothers for whom it was designed and built between 1550 and 1557, and partly from the quality of the decoration: for only here did the architect find a painter, Paolo Veronese, capable of matching his genius. The natural setting is superb, with a rising, wooded hill behind tamed into classical symmetry by the semi-circular lawn with its classical statuary in front. Two traditional parts of the Veneto farmhouse have been dressed up in a new classical disguise: those two arcaded wings flanking the main porticoed building are actually two *barchesse*, or farmhouse wings; while the mirror-image sundial-adorned chapel fronts on either end are in fact dovecotes. Behind is a nymphaeum – a semi-circular pool surrounded by statues. Even this served a practical function: the water flowed from here into the kitchen, from there into the garden for irrigation, and ultimately to the orchard on the far side of the road. Veronese's *trompe l'oeil* frescos inside – including the magnificent ceiling in the central Hall of Olympus – are in the same playful classical tradition as their frame. The meeting of minds is completed by Alessandro Vittoria, a pupil of Sansovino, who designed and carved all the statues and ornamental details. By the side of the road in front of the villa is the Tempietto Barbaro, designed in the late 1570s as a memorial to Daniele Barbaro. This – Palladio's last church – is also one of his most geometrically ambitious, despite its small scale: looking back past the architect's own Redentore in Venice to the Pantheon in Rome, the design ingeniously reconciles the circle-in-a-square plan with the Greek cross layout, a satisfying resolution of paganism and Christianity.

Villa Emo
Via Stazione 5, Fanzolo di Vedelago (0423 476 414/ fax 0423 487 043/villaemo@apf.it). Autoservizi La Marca bus from Castelfranco Veneto station for Montebelluno.

Open *Apr-Oct* 3-7pm daily. *Nov-Mar* 2-6pm Sat, Sun. **Admission** L10,000; L9,000 groups; L5,000 concessions. **No credit cards**.
In the same mould as the Villa Barbaro (*see p232*) but a tad more rustic, with more recognisable dovecotes at the end of the long *barchesse*, this surprisingly intimate villa was one of the first properties built as part of a Venetian scheme to encourage landowners to develop uncultivated land and exert greater government control over the *terra ferma*. The striking beauty of the exterior resides in its austerity and proportions rather than its decoration. Still owned by the Emo family, it has joyous frescos by Giambattista Zelotti, one of the major fresco artists of the late Italian Renaissance.

Venice province

Villa Foscari 'La Malcontenta'
Via dei Turisti 10, Malcontenta (041 547 0012). Bus 53 from Venice's piazzale Roma. **Open** *Apr-Oct* 9am-noon Tue, Sat. **Admission** L15,000. **No credit cards**.
The splendid classical proportions of this villa, together with its dramatic position on a curve of the Brenta canal close to its entrance to the Venetian lagoon, have made the Malcontenta, designed in 1555, one of Palladio's most celebrated creations. The name of the village (and nickname of the villa) refers to the land disputes of discontented peasants in the 15th century, and not – as legend claims – to an unhappy wife exiled from the fun in Venice. With its double staircase and elegant Greek temple façade, the Villa Foscari has been the model and inspiration for thousands of buildings in Europe and America. Although the graceful frescos by Battista Franco and Giambattista Zelotti are damaged and faded (and despite the present proximity to Marghera's oil refineries) the villa remains one of the most attractive and pleasant country houses in the world. It can be visited as part of the Burchiello boat excursion down the Brenta (*see p243*).

Padua province

Villa Cornaro
Via Roma 92, Piombino Dese (049 936 5017). SITA bus from Padua (piazzale Boschetto) for Trebaseleghe. **Open** *May-Sept* 3-6pm Sat; other times by appointment for groups only. **Admission** L8,000. **No credit cards**.
This is one of the most satisfying and elegant of Palladio's free-standing, two-storey villas (as opposed to the elongated farmhouse-style of the Villa Barbaro or Emo). Probably completed between 1560 and 1570, it features a double-tiered Greek temple-style front porch with genetically more evolved Corinthian columns (they of the acanthus-leaf capitals) above more primitive Ionic ones, with scrolled volutes. The interior has some drab 18th-century frescos by Mattia Bortoloni and stucco statues of members of the Cornaro family by Camillo Mariani.

The Veneto

Padua

A meadow with no grass, a café with no doors and a saint with no name – just what is going on here?

Padua (Padova) began its life as a fishing village in the easily defended loop of the Bacchiglione river, some time in the ninth or tenth century BC. The Romans turned it into a thriving town; the Barbarian hordes did their best to lay it to waste.

But plucky Padua pulled itself up by its bootstraps, prospering under Byzantine and Lombard rule, and declaring itself an independent republic in 1164. It was under the Carrara family (1338-1405) that Padua reached the height of its political power. The Venetians put a stop to that in 1405, and Padua was governed by La Serenissima until its fall in 1797. After a period under Napoleon, Padua became restless in Austrian hands (1815-1866), and played an active part in the struggle to free northern Italy from foreign dominion.

Apart from the incomparable Giotto frescos in the Scrovegni Chapel, Padua's prestige rests on its University, the Basilica di Sant'Antonio, and its rags-to-riches place in the north-eastern economic miracle (*see chapter* **Venice Today**).

The society born of the boom has led some in this city in the Veneto's Catholic heartland to bemoan the loss of traditional values. But one trait remains deep-rooted: Padua's perpetual inferiority complex with regard to Venice. If La Serenissima is the locus of mystery and enigma, Padua has, since the 19th century, tried hard to compete, proudly presenting itself in a sphinx-like riddle as a city possessing 'a meadow with no grass, a café with no doors and a saint with no name'. The meadow in question is the large urban square of Prato della Valle, and the café with no doors was Pedrocchi's (which never closed).

Prato della Valle has now been turfed and, newly restored, Pedrocchi's shuts its doors at regular times (*see p237*).That leaves only the saint with no name, *il Santo*, as the Basilica of Saint Anthony is still so economically known.

Sightseeing

Three piazze stand at the heart of the city: **Della Frutta**, **Delle Erbe** and **Dei Signori**. The first two flank the **Palazzo della Ragione** (*see p239*), known to locals as the Salone; the third lies a little to the west.

Basilica di Sant'Antonio: economically known as Il Santo. *See p235.*

During the morning (Mon-Sat) **piazza delle Erbe** and **piazza della Frutta** are home to bustling and colourful fruit and vegetable markets. To the west, **Caffè Pedrocchi** (*see p237*) and the **university** stand between the squares and the old **Ghetto** (*see p237*).

Piazza dei Signori is dominated by the façade of the **Palazzo del Capitanio** (1532), by Paduan architect Giovanni Maria Falconetto's 1532. This was the residence of the official who was one of the ruling authorities in the Venetian government of the city. The clock housed in the palazzo's tower is a replica of the original created in 1344, the first of its kind in Italy.

To the left is the **Loggia del Consiglio**. This construction, again by Falconetto, housed the *Maggior consiglio*, the ruling body of the city under Venetian rule. Opposite the Palazzo del Capitanio stands the church of **San Clemente**. South along via Dante, **piazza del Duomo** is home to Padua's **cathedral**.

Still further south, the once-swampy area called **Prato della Valle** had been used as a fairground for many years before 1775, when it was turned into an elegant market-place. After years of neglect, the canal around the central island has now been dredged and cleaned, the statues lining the canal restored, the lawns replanted and the central fountain repaired. Note the statue of the notable near the southern bridge over to the island: to pre-empt future indignities, the sculptor provided his statue with its own pigeon.

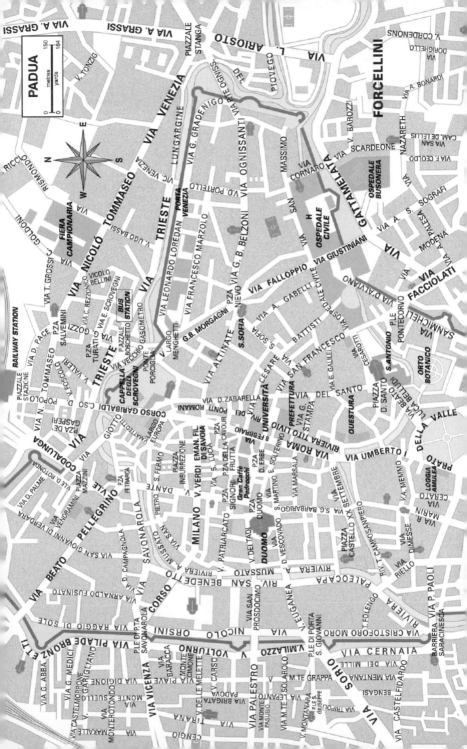

South of the Prato stands one of Christendom's biggest churches, **Santa Giustina** (*see below*). To the east, the **Orto Botanico** (*see p239*) lies between the Prato and Padua's nameless basilica: **Il Santo** (*see below*). If the treasures contained in this best-loved of Paduan churches aren't too overwhelming, the little **Scoletta del Santo** (*see p239*) and **Oratorio di San Giorgio** (*see p238*), both in piazza del Santo, have interesting frescos.

But if you only see one thing in Padua, make it the **Scrovegni Chapel** (*see p237*). North of piazza della Frutta, along via VIII Febbraio and corso Garibaldi, the chapel outshines the neighbouring **Museo Civico** (*see p237*) and **Eremiti** church.

TICKETS

Note that a cumulative ticket costing L15,000 (L10,000 concessions) and valid for two years allows access to the Museo Civico, the Palazzo della Ragione, the Baptistery, the Scoletta del Santo, the Oratorio di San Giorgio, and the Botanical Gardens. This can be purchased at the sights covered by the ticket, and at the IAT tourist office at the train station (*see p240*). The ticket does not cover the booking fee for the Scrovegni Chapel and allows one visit only to each site. No credit cards are accepted.

Basilica di Santa Giustina

Prato della Valle (049 875 1628). **Open** *Apr-Sept* 9am-noon, 3-7.15pm Mon-Sat; 7am-1pm, 3-7.45pm Sun. *Oct-Mar* 8am-noon, 3-5pm Mon-Sat; 7am-1pm, 3-5pm Sun.
Built in 1532-79, this is the 11th-largest Christian church in the world; its size is best appreciated as you look along its broad and bare transepts. The south transept leads to the altar of Prosdocimo, with a fine marble iconostasis dating from the sixth century. To the east of the transept is St Luke's Chapel, which contains the tomb of Elena Lucrezia Cornaro Piscopia (*see p241* **Better the devil than a woman**, the first woman in the world to get a university degree.

Basilica di Sant'Antonio (Il Santo)

Piazza del Santo (049 878 9722/fax 049 878 9735/ pdsanto@alata.it). **Open** *Apr-Sept* 6.15am-8pm daily. *Oct-Mar* 6.15am-7pm daily.
Popularly known as Il Santo, this is one of the most important pilgrimage churches in Italy. Saint Anthony was not a local saint but a Portuguese Franciscan, a powerful preacher against the evils of usury, who died in Padua in 1231. Work on the church dedicated to him began soon after his canonisation in 1232; the main structure remained unfinished until around 1350, when the saint's body was moved to its present tomb in the Cappella dell'Arca. Visited by a steady stream of devotees, this chapel

also contains one of the basilica's great artistic treasures: marble bas-reliefs of scenes from the life of the saint by artists such as Jacopo Sansovino, Tullio Lombardo and Giovanni Minello. The chapel's ceiling, by Giovanni Maria Falconetto, dates from 1533. The other great art treasures of the Basilica – most of them placed so as to be almost impossible to see – are Donatello's bronze panels on the high altar (1443-50). Behind the altar, his stone bas-relief of a *Deposition* is more accessible, as are two of the bronzes – a bull and a lion, representing the evangelists St Mark and St Luke.

Other works of interest in the church include Altichiero's late-14th-century frescos in the Cappella di San Felice (on the south wall), Giusto de Menabuoi's frescos in the Cappella del Beato Luca Belludi and two fine funeral monuments – to Alessandro Contarini (died 1553) and Cardinal Pietro Bembo (died 1547) – both by the sculptor and military architect Michele Sanmicheli.

At the back of the apse is the baroque Cappella del Tesoro, containing 'miraculous' relics. The Reliquary containing the Tongue of Saint Anthony was recently stolen, but then recovered, so the story goes, with the help of underworld bosses horrifiethat any of their confraternity could carry out such a heinous act.

In the piazza outside the church stands Donatello's famous monument to the *condottiere* (mercenary soldier) Erasmo da Narni, aka Gattamelata.

Duomo

Piazza del Duomo (church 049 662 814/ baptistery 049 656 914). **Open** *Church* 7.30am-noon, 3.45-7.30pm Mon-Sat; 7.45am-1pm, 3.45-8pm Sun. *Baptistery* 10am-6pm daily. **Admission** *Duomo* free. *Baptistery* L4,000; L3,000 concessions. **No credit cards**.
Paduans claim that Michelangelo designed the apse of their city's cathedral; it is obvious, however, that he didn't have much to do with its uninspiring final form. Nowadays the church is worth visiting mostly for the paintings in the Sacristy, by Bassano, Tiepolo and others, and even more so for the nearby Baptistery, containing a series of powerfully vivid frescos by the 14th-century Florentine artist Giusto de' Menabuoi.

Gli Eremitani

Piazza degli Eremitani 9 (049 875 6410). **Open** 8.15am-12.15pm, 4-6pm Mon-Sat; 9.30am-12.15pm, 4-6pm Sun.
The original building, dating from the late 13th century, was hit in an air raid on 11 March 1944: the fine trilobate wooden ceiling is a copy of the early-14th century original. The bombs almost totally destroyed the church's artistic treasure, Andrea Mantegna's frescos of the *Life and Martyrdom of St James and St Christopher* (1454-7). Fortunately, two panels of the work, together with the main altarpiece of the *Assumption*, had been removed before the raid. Two other panels – the *Martyrdom of Saint James and Saint Christopher Converts the Knights* – were partially reassembled from the rubble; even

so, the work is impressive though the gate to the chapel is always kept padlocked, making it difficult to get a good view. Also worthy of note in the church is Bartolomeo Ammanati's *Tomb of Marco Mantova Benavides* (1544-46), on the north wall near the main entrance – a fine allegorical composition with the renowned humanist flanked by statues representing Time, Fame, Immortality, Wisdom and Labour. A further curiosity is the neo-classical bronze medallion in the west wall of the south transept commemorating Protestant hero Wilhelm George Frederick of Orange… in a Catholic church.

Il Ghetto

A stone's throw from piazza delle Erbe and the University of Padua medical faculty – the first in Europe to accept Jewish students (who were, however, obliged to pay double fees) – stands what was once the Jewish Ghetto, now a beautifully preserved pedestrian zone. The area only became a Ghetto proper at the beginning of the 17th century, when it was shut off behind four gateways. A plaque commemorates the old synagogue, destroyed in 1943 by anti-Semitic *padovani*.

Gran Caffè Pedrocchi

Via VIII Febbraio 15/piazzetta Pedrocchi (049 878 1231/049 820 4506/caffe.pedrocchi@tiscali.net).
Open *Architectural rooms* 9.30am-12.30pm, 3.30-6pm Tue-Sun. **Admission** L5,000; L3,000 concessions. **No credit cards.**
Known as 'the café without doors' because it never closed, Pedrocchi's – a mixture of neo-classical and Strawberry Hill gothic – was designed by the early-19th century architect Giuseppe Japelli. It was the scene of a student uprising in 1848, and later developed a reputation as a Fascist watering hole. After years of twilight glory, the café closed down for restoration in 1995.

It reopened in 1999, with all the renovated theme rooms on show upstairs (entrance in the right-hand wing of the side colonnade). The Greek staircase leads up to a condensed tour of Western culture: the Etruscan room leads into the Roman, then into the Herculaneum room, followed by the Renaissance – with a Gothic side-branch that goes nowhere. The whole culminates in a large white and gold neo-classical room dedicated to Rossini, on the opposite side of which is the Egyptian Room, with its squatting dog-gods and starry vaults. *See also p240.*

Museo Civico & Scrovegni Chapel

Piazza Eremitani 8 (049 820 4550/fax 049 820 4585/ musei.comune@padovanet.it/www.padova.net.it).
Open *Museum Feb-Oct* 9am-7pm Tue-Sun. *Nov-Jan* 9am-6pm Tue-Sun. *Scrovegni chapel Feb-Oct* 9am-7pm daily. *Nov-Jan* 9am-6pm daily. **Admission** L10,000; L7,000 concessions. **No credit cards.** Note that visits to the Scrovegni Chapel must be booked in advance (L3,000 booking fee).
This complex contains an odd mix, consisting of a moderately interesting public collection, two private collections and one of the great art treasures of the

world. Whatever your staying power, start with the great art treasure. Due to time limits for visiting the chapel (15mins max), it's best to read up on the frescos before entering.

The Scrovegni Chapel

It is said that Giotto's frescos in the Scrovegni Chapel (painted between 1303 and 1305) were to art what Dante's *Divine Comedy* was to literature. The chapel is dedicated to the Virgin of the Annunciation, depicted on either side of the arch leading through to the altar directly opposite you as you enter. The wall frescos not only relate the story of Christ's life but also depict mainly apocryphal stories of Mary's parents Joachim and Anne.

The cycle opens (top right – alongside the Virgin of the Annunciation) with Joachim being driven from the temple because his marriage has so far proved infertile. Banished, Joachim wanders off into the wilderness to make an offering to God. An angel

Piazza delle Erbe: the morning market is a must for self-caterers. *See p234, p239.*

appears to both him and Anne telling them they will have a child, and that when Joachim returns to Jerusalem he will encounter his wife at the Golden Gate. In the meeting scene, Giotto reveals the power of his innovative narrative realism: the embracing couple are surrounded by gossiping ladies, carelessly commenting on the coincidence of this meeting between husband and wife.

The top row on the wall opposite recounts the childhood and marriage of the Virgin. The story of Christ unfolds in the middle and lower rows, with the middle of the right hand wall dominated by the scene of Judas's kiss. The traitor's yellow cloak enfolds Christ – but He is still the dominant figure. Note the fan of spears, clubs and torches around the central couple, leading the eye left down to St Peter as he severs the ear of the high priest's attendant.

The high dado at the base of the walls is decorated with fine grisaille paintings of the seven Virtues and Vices. Particularly striking are the figures of Envy blinded by her own serpentine tongue and Prudence equipped with pen and mirror.

Prato della Valle, elegantly restored. *See p234.*

The Scrovegni Chapel was saved from total ruin in the 19th century partly due to the indignant intervention of the *Times* of London. The Scrovegni Palace that stood alongside was not so fortunate and was demolished in 1827.

The Archeological Wing
Though small, this collection of Greek and Roman antiquities contains some fine pieces. In room nine there is a noble female head of the fourth century AD, while in the antechamber to room ten is a carved Greek panel, the rear of which is decorated with a stork.

Moving into room ten itself there is an impressive funeral stele of a young girl slave (only the stele of women were decorated with acanthus leaves) with an inscription informing us that she was more than happy to elude the disfigurement of age by dying at the age of 19. The room also contains some stele of married couples, as well as interesting floor mosaics.

The Egyptian collection is mainly a tribute to the Paduan GB Belzoni who succeeded in moving the massive bust of Rameses II from Thebes to Cairo.

The Picture Gallery
The gallery opens with two rooms of angels by 14th-century Guariento di Arpo, followed by a Giotto *Crucifixion* that originally hung in the Scrovegni Chapel; note the contrast between the very hieratic, stylised cross and the very unstylised Christ. What follows includes Squarcione's Lazarus Polyptych, a striking *Sailing of the Argonauts* by Lorenzo Costa and a fine *Portrait of a Young Man* by Alvise Vivarini. Don't miss some marvellous landscapes lurking behind the miserable-looking saints by the anonymous 'Pittore Veneto'. There's a very intriguing *Sacra Conversazione* by Bernardino Luini (the figures having the same blank stare as Grant Wood's American realist pitchfork-totin' farmer and wife) and two marvellous postcard-sized landscapes attributed to Giorgione.

If you haven't given up in exhaustion by this point, there are fine works to be seen by the Bassano family, Pozzoserrato, Luca Giordano (note Job's comforter literally holding his nose in disgust at the pestilential state the poor man is reduced to), some interesting 16th- and 17th-century Dutch and Flemish works (including one by Quentin Metsys), altarpieces by Romanino and Veronese (his surprisingly static *Martyrdom of Santa Giustina* is particularly impressive, with all the horror of death being portrayed through the rearing of the snorting horses), portraits by the early 17th-century Chiara Varotari and, to end on a bathetically light-hearted note, a portrait of a pudgy Venetian captain by Sebastiano Mazzoni (1611-78).

Oratorio di San Giorgio
Piazza del Santo 11 (049 875 5235). **Open** *Nov-Mar* 9am-12.30pm, 2.30-5pm daily. *Apr-Oct* 9am-12.30pm, 2.30-7pm daily. **Admission** L3,000; L2,000 concessions. Ticket includes the Scoletta del Santo (*see below*). **No credit cards.**

This Oratory, constructed in 1377 for the Lupi di Soragna family, contains a cycle of frescos by Altichiero (1379-1384) depicting scenes from the lives of saints Catherine and George. Altichiero is at his best here, and worth a visit even after the long hike around the Basilica.

Orto Botanico (Botanical Gardens)

Via Orto Botanico 15 (049 827 2119/ ortob@ux1.unipd.it). **Open** *Nov-Mar* 9am-1pm Mon-Sat. *Apr-Oct* 9am-1pm, 3-6pm daily. **Admission** L5,000. **No credit cards.**
The Orto Botanico started life in the 1540s as a Garden of Simples (medicinal herbs), providing raw materials for the University's medical faculty. It was the first of its kind in Europe. The original layout, with stone borders enclosing the different species, has been maintained in the central section of the garden (a circle within a square).

Palazzo della Ragione (Il Salone)

Via del Municipio 1 (049 820 5006). **Open** 9am-6pm Tue-Sun. **Admission** L7,000; L4,000 6-17s. **No credit cards.**
Note that parts of the Salone are closed for restoration until 2002.
The *Salone*, as locals call it, was built between 1218 and 1219 and served as the law courts. In the early 14th century the building was raised and the external loggia of the *piano nobile* was added, giving it the structure it maintains today. Inside, the *Salone* proper is frescoed with signs of the zodiac, the months and seasons; it is claimed that the original frescos, destroyed in a disastrous fire in 1420, were by Giotto but contemporary records make no reference to what would already have been seen as a terrible loss. The impressive ship's keel ceiling is a replacement of the 14th-century original, which was torn off by a whirlwind in 1759. The huge wooden horse was created for a tournament in 1466.

Scoletta del Santo

Piazza del Santo 11 (049 875 5235). **Open** *Nov-Mar* 9am-12.30pm, 2.30-5pm daily. *Apr-Oct* 9am-12.30pm, 2.30-7pm daily. **Admission** L3,000; L2,000 concessions. **No credit cards.**
Contains 16th-century frescos, some of which Titian is said to have had a hand in.

Università di Padova, Palazzo del Bò (University)

Via VIII Febbraio 2 (049 820 9773/www.unipd.it). **Open** *Guided tours Feb-Oct* 3pm, 4pm, 5pm Mon, Wed, Fri; 10am, 11am, noon Tue, Thur, Sat. *Nov-Jan* 3pm, 4pm Mon, Wed, Fri; 10am, 11am Tue, Thur, Sat. **Admission** L5,000; L2,000 concessions. **No credit cards.**
The second-oldest university in Italy after Bologna, occupies a building – Palazzo del Bò (bull) – that takes its name from the butchers' inn that used to stand on the site.
The Old Courtyard was designed by Andrea Moroni and decorated with the coats-of-arms and family crests of illustrious rectors and students. The beautiful oval wooden-benched Anatomy Theatre on the first floor, built by Girolamo Fabrizi Aquapendente in 1594, was the first of its kind in the world. Galileo Galilei worked here from 1592 to 1610. Past students include Copernicus, Sir Francis Walsingham and Oliver Goldsmith, all of whom are remembered in the *Sala dei Quaranta*, which also houses Galileo's lectern. Europe's first ever female graduate, Elena Lucrezia Cornaro Piscopia, studied here (*see p241* **Better the devil than a woman**).

Where to eat & drink

Self-caterers should head for the morning markets in piazza delle Erbe or piazza della Frutta; shops in the arcades around the markets offer a wide range of cheeses and meats.

If you'd prefer something ready-prepared, the finest *tramezzini* and *panini* in Padua are to be had just outside the station, at the small Bar Maximilian, which stands on the corner of corso del Popolo and via Nicolò Tommaseo (closed Sat, Sun).

L'Anfora

Via dei Soncin 13 (049 656 629). **Meals served** 12.30-4.30pm, 6.30-10pm Mon-Sat. **Average** L30,000. **Credit** AmEx, MC, V.
The ingredients of the traditional fare served in this bustling *osteria* are as fresh as can be. Prices are low, cooking standards high, and the wine list – which includes many fine examples served by the glass – excellent. There's live music some evenings, too.

Le Calandre

Via Liguria 1, Sarmeola di Rubano (049 630 303/ alajmo@calandre.com/www.calandre.com). **Meals served** noon-2pm, 8-10pm Tue-Sat. **Average** L180,000. **Credit** AmEx, DC, MC, V.
With two stars in the Michelin guide, this restaurant 4km west of the city should not be missed if you are in the mood for a treat. Try the *crème brulée alla lavanda* – yes, lavender.

Graziati

Piazza della Frutta 40 (tel/fax 049 875 1014). **Meals served** noon-2.30pm Tue-Sun.
Closed 2 wks Aug, 20 Dec-7 Jan. **Average** L40,000 **No credit cards.**
Graziati is essentially a *pasticceria* (open 7.30am-8.30pm Tue-Sun), specialising in a large and calorific range of tantalising puff pastries. For something less frivolous, however, the subterranean tea room serves wholesome lunchs. The decor is simple, the dining-room intimate and on display is a beautiful 14th-century wooden door rediscovered during a recent restoration.

Osteria Dal Capo

Via degli Obizzi 2 (049 663 105). **Meals served** noon-2.30pm, 7-10pm Mon-Sat. **Average** L45,000. **Credit** AmEx, MC, V.

The Veneto

There *is* nightlife in Padua. *See below.*

Small with a lot of 1930s leatherette, this place is excellent value for money – so you have to book if you want a table in the evening. The desserts are to die for – especially *latte in piedi* (a sort of junket).

Bars & nightlife

For gay & lesbian venues in Padua, *see p208.*

Bar dei Osei

Piazza della Frutta 1 (049 875 9606). **Open** 7am-9pm Mon-Sat. **No credit cards.**
A very pleasant central bar with convenient people-watching tables outside in summer in one of Padua's busiest squares. A good lunchtime stop, with a delicious range of fresh *panini* and sandwiches.

Gran Caffè Pedrocchi

Via VIII Febbraio 15/piazzetta Pedrocchi (049 878 1231). **Open** *bar* 8am-midnight daily; *restaurant* 12.30-3pm, 7-10.30pm daily. **Average** L55,000. **Credit** AmEx, DC, MC, V.
For centuries Padua's most elegant watering hole, and now restored to its former glory, Pedrocchi's is a landmark in its own right (*see p237*).

Where to stay

Majestic Toscanelli

Via dell'Arco 2 (049 663 244/fax 049 876 0025/ majestic@toscanelli.com/www.toscanelli.com). **Rates** L150,000-L195,000 single; L270,000-L320,000 double; L400,000 suite. **Credit** AmEx, DC, MC, V.

Every room in this hotel offers attractive views over the quaint streets of the Ghetto. It's one minute's walk away from the town's main squares.

Leon Bianco

Piazzetta Pedrocchi 12 (049 875 0814/fax 049 875 6184/leonbianco@toscanelli.com/www.toscanelli.com). **Rates** L120,000-L143,000 single; L175,000-L185,000 double; breakfast L16,000 extra. **Credit** AmEx, DC, MC, V.
Just behind the Gran Caffè Pedrocchi, this central hotel is small and friendly. The rooms are rather utilitarian but not cramped.

Sant'Antonio

Via San Fermo 118 (049 875 1393/fax 049 875 2508). **Rates** L65,000-L107,000 single; L94,000-L133,000 double; breakfast L13,000 extra. **Credit** DC, MC, V.
Good value for money, unless you are unlucky enough to get one of the rooms on what becomes a busy street corner very early in the morning.

Resources

Getting there

By car
Padua is on the A4 La Serenissima motorway.

By train
All trains bound south-west from Venice (on the Bologna line) stop at Padua. Journey time 25-30 mins.

By bus
From Venice's piazzale Roma bus terminus, orange ACTV buses trundle slowly to Padua, stopping off near several Palladian villas en route; blue SITA buses (049 820 6811), on the other hand, speed along the motorway. In Padua, both stop at the bus station in piazzale Boschetti.

Getting around

City buses are operated by ACAP (049 824 1111/fax 049 824 1112/acap@pd.nettuno.it/ www.acap.it); tickets, which must be bought before boarding, cost L1,600. Destinations outside the city covered in this chapter are served by blue SITA buses (*see above*).

Tourist information

IAT (Informazione ed Assistenza Turistica)
Inside Padua railway station (049 875 2077/fax 049 875 5008/www.padovanet.it). **Open** 9am-5.45pm Mon-Sat; 9am-noon Sun.
Galleria Pedrocchi by piazza del Santo (049 876 7927). **Open** 9.30am-12.30pm, 3.30-7pm Mon-Sat.
Piazza del Santo, opposite the Basilica (049 875 3087). **Open** *Apr-Oct* 9am-1pm, 2-6pm daily. *Nov-Mar* 9am-2pm daily.

The Veneto

Better the devil than a woman

Elena Lucrezia Cornaro (1646-1684), a member of the wealthy Piscopia branch of the Venetian Cornaro dynasty, blazed her name in history as the first woman ever to be awarded a university degree. Descended from a long line of intellectuals, Elena had gained a reputation throughout Europe for her scientific knowledge and mastery of foreign languages even before receiving her degree.

At the age of seven she began studying Greek and Latin, also mastering Hebrew, Spanish, French and Arabic, earning the title of *Oraculum Septilingue*, loosely translated as 'smarty-pants'. She also managed to fit in some time for maths, astronomy, philosophy and theology. Not content with being an intellectual prodigy, Elena was also a gifted musician and composer, playing the harpsichord, clavichord, harp and violin.

In 1677 she took part in a public philosophical debate in Greek and Latin. It was this event, plus a pushy dad, that brought her close to receiving a degree in theology. This was blocked, however: the Catholic church refused to grant a theology degree to a female, with one cardinal exclaiming, 'Better the Devil than a woman!'

Elena was finally awarded a degree in philosophy by Padua University on 25 June 1678, when she was 32. She went on to teach maths at her alma mater, as well as writing academic discourses, translations and devotional treatises.

The last 19 years of her life were devoted to charity and study: in 1665 she had withdrawn from society, taking the habit of the Benedictine nuns. She died, probably from TB, at the age of 38 and is buried in Santa Giustina in Padua (*see p235*).

Among other tributes, she is commemorated by a statue at the University of Padua, a stained glass window at Vassar College, and a grant in her name awarded by the Italian School of Pretoria (SA).

Around Padua

Abano Terme

To the south of Padua stand the verdant Euganean Hills. The restorative powers of the area's volcanic springs and muds were recognised in Roman times and are still exploited by the many spa-hotels offering restorative treatments in such health resorts as Abano Terme and Montegrotto.

Six kilometres (four miles) west of Abano, the **Abbazia di Praglia** was founded by Benedictine monks in the 12th century, though the abbey's present buildings date from the 15th century. The monastery itself consists of an interesting series of cloisters (one of which serves as a botanical garden).

South of Abano lies **Arquà Petrarca**: it was here that the poet Francesco Petrarch (1304-74) chose to spend the last years of his life, and was buried in the church. The town has retained much of its medieval atmosphere and it is possible to visit the 14th-century house where the poet lived.

Abbazia di Praglia
Via Abbazia 16, Bresseo di Teolo (049 990 0010). **Open** *Apr-Sept* 3.30-5.30pm Tue-Sun. *Nov-Mar* 2.30-4.30pm Tue-Sun. **Admission** free (donations welcome).

Petrarch's House
Via Valleselle 3, Arquà Petrarca (0429 718 294). **Open** *Oct-Jan* 9am-noon, 2.30-5pm Tue-Sun. *Feb-Sept* 9am-noon, 3-7pm Tue-Sun. **Admission** L6,000; L4,000 concessions. **No credit cards**.

Where to eat

Just outside the town centre is **La Cucina d'Arquà** (via Scalette 1, Arquà Petrarca, 0429 777 170, closed Tue, average L40,000), serving what seem to be endless courses of traditional dishes, with meat being the speciality. It pays to work up a healthy appetite before you go.

Getting there

By car
Take the A13 Padua-Bologna motorway, turning off at Padova Sud for Abano, and about 20km further south at the Terme Euganee exit for Arquà; Praglia is accessible by minor roads from Abano.

By train
Infrequent services to Abano on the Padua-Bologna line.

By bus
ACAP city buses and SITA buses (*see p240*) run approximately every 15mins from Padua to Abano; SITA buses serve Praglia and Arquà.

The Veneto

Tourist information

APT (Azienda di Promozione Turistica)

Terme Euganee Via P D'Abano 18, Abano Terme (049 793 3845/fax 049 866 9053/ info@termeeuganeeapt.net/www.termeeuganeeapt.net) **Open** 8.30am-1pm, 2.30-7pm Mon-Sat.

Monselice

Monselice's most impressive sight is the **Ca' Marcello**, a complex that includes the 13th-century Palazzo di Ezzelino, the Palazzo Marcello, an 18th-century chapel, and a crenellated structure built in the 15th century. But there's also the **Santuario delle Sette Chiese**, designed by Vincenzo Scamozzi, Palladio's most gifted pupil, who acted as guide to the English architect Inigo Jones. The church was completed between 1592 and 1593, the chapels coming later in 1605.

Getting there

By car
Leave the the A13 Padua-Bologna motorway at the Monselice exit.

By train
Direct services on the Padua-Bologna line.

By bus
SITA buses *(see p240)* run from Padua.

Tourist information

IAT (Informazione ed Assistenza Turistica)

Piazza Mazzini 15 (0429 783026/ www.provincia.padova.it/comuni/monselice). **Open** 10.15am-12.30pm; 2-3.45pm Mon, Tue, Fri; 10.15am-12.30pm Thur, Sat, Sun.

Este

This town spawned the Este family, a minor branch of which moved to Germany in the 12th century and established the Brunswick-Lüneburg dynasty that would culminate in the Hanoverians, ancestors of Britain's own august royals. The more illustrious branch of the Este family would become the dukes of Ferrara and rule over one of the most artistically fertile courts of the Italian Renaissance.

Nowadays, the town of Este reflects little of these past glories, though the **Museo Nazionale Atestino**'s picture gallery can boast a very pretty *Madonna and Child* by Cima da Conegliano.

The **Scrovegni Chapel** contains one of the world's art treasures. *See p237.*

Turning left from the museum, the via Principe Umberto takes you past the 13th-century façade and bell-tower of the church of San Martino. Turning the other way, you come to the **Duomo** (open 10am-noon, 4-6pm daily), which contains Giambattista Tiepolo's *Saint Thekla Interceding with God the Father to Free the City from the Plague* (1757).

Museo Nazionale Atestino
Via Guido Negri 9 (0429 2085). **Open** 9am-8pm daily. **Admission** L4,000; L2,000 concessions. **No credit cards**.

Where to eat

For a lunchtime snack, the **Tavernetta Da Piero** (via Pescheria Vecchia 16A, 0429 2855, closed Thur, Wed dinner Nov-Mar, average L45,000) is a bustling place full of local characters and colour.

Getting there

By car
Take the A13 Padua-Bologna motorway, exiting at Monselice; take the SS10 from there to Este.

By train
Direct services on the Padua-Mantua line, or change at Monselice on the Padua-Bologna line.

By bus
By SITA *(see p240)* bus from Padua.

Tourist information

IAT Pro-Loco Este
Piazza Maggiore 9A (0429 3635). **Open** *Apr-Nov*
10am-noon, 4-6pm Mon-Fri; 10am-noon Sat, Sun.
Dec-Mar 10am-noon daily.

Montagnana

Montagnana's perfectly preserved town
walls, composed of a total of 24 towers and
intervening walls, all beautifully offset by a
sweep of uncluttered grass all around, were
built between 1360 and 1362.

The town boasts two other architectural
gems. The first is Palladio's **Villa Pisani**
(*see p232*). The rear view of the villa from
the road alongside the garden is perhaps the
most impressive.

The second, inside the town walls, is the
Duomo (open 8am-12.30pm, 4-7.30pm daily), a
striking mix of Gothic and Renaissance. Begun
in 1431, it was not consecrated until 1502 and
the present main portal, attributed to Jacopo
Sansovino, was not added until around 1530.
The two pilasters alongside it are topped by
white stone spheres that, because of the
alignment of the church, are the first part of the
façade to be lit up by the sun at midday.

Above the main altar is a *Transfiguration* by
Paolo Veronese, while on the second altar along
the south wall is an altarpiece of the *Madonna
and Child Enthroned*, which is considered one
of the masterpieces of the artist Giovanni
Buonconsiglio. Buonconsiglio has also been
credited with the two damaged panels depicting
David with the Head of Goliath and *Judith with
the Head of Holofernes* on either side of the
main portal; Giorgione is another candidate.

The greatest curiosity in the church,
however, is in the Rosary Chapel, on the left
just before the crossing. During cleaning in
1959, the baroque altar was removed to reveal
the original 15th-century frescos, which form
an esoteric astrological allegory, with two bears
(orsa major and orsa minor) separated by the
curls of a dragon (the constellation draco)
alongside a representation of Pegasus and
the ship of the Argonauts. It has been argued
that all of these astrological figures represent
a particular conjunction of the heavenly bodies
relating to the Feast of the Annunciation. The
iconographical scheme is similar to one at
the Castle of Esztergom in Hungary; the 15th-
century physician and astrologer Galeotto
Marzio da Narni is known to have lived in both
places for some time.

Ruled by Venice from 1405, Montagnana was
renowned for its hemp, used to produce sails for
La Serenissima's fleet.

Getting there

By car
Leave the A13 Padua-Bologna motorway at the
Monselice exit, then take the SS10 to Montagnana.

By train
Services on the Padua-Mantua line.

By bus
SITA (*see p240*) buses run from Padua.

Tourist information

IAT Pro-Loco di Montagnana
Piazza Trieste 3 (0429 81320/proloco@netbusiness.it).
Open *Apr-Oct* 9.30am-12.30pm Mon; 9.30am-
12.30pm, 3-6pm Wed-Sun. *Nov-Mar* 9.30am-12.30pm
Mon; 9.30am-12.30pm, 3-6pm Wed-Sun.

The Brenta Canal

When Goethe glided down the Brenta Canal in
1786 'the banks [were] studded with gardens
and summer houses, small properties
stretch[ed] down to the edge of the river and
now and then the busy high road [ran] beside
it.' These days, the busy high road still makes
its presence felt, though gardens and summer
houses have been gobbled up by industrial
sprawl. A number of Palladian villas still grace
the waterway, part of which can visited in a
boat that chugs up the Brenta from Venice as
far as Strà, where you are transfered on to a bus
to Padua. The journey includes visits to the
villas of Malcontenta (*see p233*), Widmann and
Pisani. The boat trip culminates at the Villa
Pisani in Strà, a remarkable villa of the early-to-
mid 18th century. Note that you can cover the
same route at a fraction of the price by taking
the ACTV number 53 bus from piazzale Roma.

SITA – Divisione Navigazione 'il Burchiello'
*Via Orlandini 3, Padua (049 876 3035/fax 049 876
3044/siamic@tin.it/www.ilburchiello.it)*. **Services**
Apr-Oct. Venice-Padua departure from Pietà boat
stop (near San Zaccaria) at 9am Tue, Thur, Sat;
Padua-Venice departure from piazzale Boschetti at
8.15am on Wed, Fri, Sun. **Rates** L110,000 (includes
entrance to two villas but NOT Villa Pisani or return
journey); L65,000 6-17s; free under-6s; lunch L45,000
extra. **Credit** MC, V.

The Po Delta

The Po Delta is a rare haven in a country where
the line between land and sea is more often
associated with free-for-all development and
swimming bans. Here, at last, you can travel for
miles – walking or cycling along the high banks

The Veneto

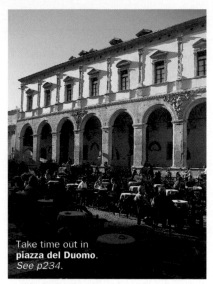

Take time out in **piazza del Duomo**. *See p234.*

of the *valli* (fishing lagoons) – without seeing another person. The only signs of life are the *casoni* – low, peach-coloured fishing lodges with green shutters.

The *valli* fill in a lot of the dead space between the delta branches, where the meandering Po splits into a confusion of channels. In the 19th century, steam-powered pumping stations allowed vast tracts of land to be reclaimed; but plenty of water has been left for the herons, eels and reed beds. Outside of the rice paddies (Italy's prized arborio rice is grown here), this can be poor agricultural terrain, because of the high salinity of the soil. By way of compensation, though, the salt pans provide much of Italy's sea salt.

As the main fluvial artery of Italy's industrial heartland, the Po is heavily polluted by toxic waste. This makes the famous, fat Po eels a hazardous delicacy. But despite the pollution, the delta is a haven for wildlife, with rare birds such as the *cavaliere d'Italia*, red herons and marsh falcons. Some species, unfortunately, are lost for ever: beavers and pelicans were wiped out by hunters in the 17th century. But there are signs of a turnabout: spoonbills returned to the delta in 1989, and there are hopes that flamingos will one day return to nest here.

The secrecy and inaccessibility of this waterscape has long made it a place of refuge. It was here that Garibaldi shook off his Austrian pursuers in the summer of 1849. During the war, this was also a centre of partisan activity, later commemorated in Roberto Rossellini's film *Paisà*.

The only town of any size is **Comacchio**, which is over the border into Emilia-Romagna. This southern area is in many ways more interesting than the smaller Veneto slice of the delta to the north. As well as Comacchio itself, with its Venetian-style canals and famous three-way bridge (the Trepponti) there is the **Abbazia di Pomposa**, a magnificent Benedictine monastic complex dating back to the eighth century. Nearby is the **Bosco di Mesola** (open 8am-dusk Sat, Sun), the only remnant of the woodland that once covered most of the delta area: here Italy's last surviving native population of red deer took refuge, protected by the malarial swamps all around.

The Po is the last of Europe's four major river deltas to have been granted protected status: an inter-regional *Parco Delta del Po* was finally instituted at the beginning of 1998.

Where to stay & eat

Total delta immersion is assured at the **Rifugio Parco Delta del Po** (0425 215 30/ fax 0425 262 70, full board L46,000) in the tiny village of Gorino Sullam. The refuge offers cycle and canoe hire, plus guided nature treks with overnight camping stops. For a more luxurious but equally natural experience, the **Cannevié Hotel** (via Per Volano, Codigoro, 0533 719 103/ www.cannevie.com, rates L100,000-L140,000; closed Jan) is a restored 16th-century fishing lodge on the Cannevié-Porticino lagoon. The hotel's restaurant (closed Mon, average L70,000) occupies the old *tabarra*, where nets and fishing utensils were stored.

Getting there

By car
Leave the A13 Padua-Bologna motorway at Ferrara Sud, then follow the *superstrada* to the Lidi.

By bus
SITA (*see p240*) runs early morning and late evening services from Padua.

Tourist information

IAT (Informazione ed Assisenza Turistica)
Piazza Folegatti 28, Comacchio (0533 310161/ fax 0533 310 269/www.comune.comacchio.fe.it). **Open** *Nov-Mar* 9.30am-1pm, 3-6.30pm Fri, Sat, Sun. *Apr-Oct* 9.30am-1pm, 3-6.30pm daily. This extremely helpful and friendly office organises boat trips around the town's canals and in the Valli di Comacchio, where a multi-sited museum of natural history and fishing techniques – accessible only by boat – has been set up.

Verona

Placid, prosperous Verona is built on ancient foundations – many of which remain on view.

From gladiatorial antics to operatic arias: the **Arena** has had a checkered career. *See p247.*

If remarkably placid, uneventful Verona had a finest hour, it probably came in the late 13th century, when the exiled poet Dante was living here at the court of the Duke Cangrande Della Scala, whose family controlled much of northern Italy.

But for most of its history Verona was dominated by other cities and powers. Amid Montagu and Capulet-style family feuding, the Della Scala family fell in 1387, only to be replaced by the Viscontis of Milan, then by the Venetian Republic, which remained in power until 1797, and finally by Austria. Only in 1866 did Verona rid itself of foreign rulers, when it joined the newly united Kingdom of Italy.

What it lacks in historical fireworks, however, Verona makes up for in art and architecture: the splendid – and splendidly preserved – **Arena** (Roman amphitheatre) testifies to the city's importance in ancient times; it has a rich heritage of medieval art and sculpture; and a Verona native, Paolo Veronese, was to leave his vibrant mark on the art of the Renaissance.

Until World War II, Verona was a sleepy provincial town with a mainly agricultural economy. This changed during the economic miracle of the 1970s, when family-run businesses mushroomed, producing everything from machine tools to ice-cream making equipment. Printing and pharmaceuticals are also big, and getting bigger.

In recent years, a growing immigrant community from Africa, Asia and Eastern Europe has beefed up the city's ethnic mix, giving it a truly metropolitan and international flavour. Oriental and Latin American restaurants – unheard of only a few years ago – have multiplied; in Veronetta – the university quarter – spices and tropical fruit abound in colourful, fragrant Afro-Caribbean shops.

Sightseeing

For more than 2,000 years, the solid burghers of Verona have lived their lives on unchanging foundations: the city centre is still contained within its massive 16th-century walls; many

The Veneto

of the thousands of brick, tufa and marble-ornamented houses stand on Roman foundations; the streets are still laid out according to the grid plan decreed by Emperor Augustus; even the more modern buildings have little bits of Roman marble-work inserted into their fabric.

In fact, the presence of Rome is inescapable: the **Arena** (Verona's Colosseum; *see p247*), the **Teatro Romano** (*see p251*) and the Roman **walls**, bridge and city gates all set the tone. These monuments owe their remarkable state of preservation to having been in constant use through the centuries. The fact that the surrounding hills are rich in stone quarries also helped: the kind of pilfering from ancient monuments that was so common in medieval and Renaissance Rome, for example, was simply unnecessary here.

Even the pavements in Verona testify to this ready availability of quality stone: look carefully and you'll see they are dotted with the fossils of prehistoric sea-creatures. Leonardo Da Vinci made a note of the fact in a codex that now belongs to Bill Gates.

Verona's medieval architecture dates mostly from after the great north Italian earthquake of 1117. In the building boom that followed this catastrophe, the city was adorned with some of its finest buildings: the basilica of **San Zeno** (*see p250*), the **Duomo** (*see p248*) and the Gothic churches of **Sant'Anastasia** (*see p250*) and **San Fermo** (*see p249*).

At the centre of Verona's everyday bustle are two squares, the **piazza delle Erbe** and the **piazza dei Signori**. The former was the site of Verona's Roman forum; today it hosts a food and souvenir market (Mon-Sat), and is surrounded by buildings dating from the medieval to the baroque.

At the northern end is the huge 14th-century **Casa Mazzanti** with its splendid late-Renaissance frescos on the outer façade, the highly ornamented baroque **Palazzo Maffei** and the medieval **Torre Gardello**, Verona's first clock tower, built in 1370. The basin of the fountain (1368) is of Roman origin, as is the body of the statue known as the 'Madonna Verona' (Lady Verona), which stands above it; the head is medieval. The tall houses at the southern end once marked the edge of the Jewish ghetto. The recently restored 19th-century **synagogue** (open 9am-1pm Mon-Fri) is in via Portici, off via Mazzini.

Piazza dei Signori, also known as piazza Dante because of the statue of the poet in the centre, contains the 15th-century **Loggia del Consiglio** with its eight elegant arches. The building, topped by statues of distinguished Veronese citizens, including the poet Catullus

Piazza delle Erbe: Verona's Roman forum.

(who was exiled from Rome to the shores of Lake Garda, thus making him an honorary citizen), marked the beginning of Renaissance architecture in Verona.

Linking the two squares is the 12th-century **Palazzo della Ragione**, which until recently housed the law courts. A gateway on the piazza dei Signori side of the palazzo leads into the Mercato Vecchio courtyard, with its huge Romanesque arches and magnificent outdoor Renaissance staircase. The palazzo is dominated by the **Torre dei Lamberti** (1462; *see p251*).

At the eastern exit from piazza dei Signori are the **Della Scala** (Scaligeri) family **tombs** (*see p251*) and, almost opposite, the so-called **casa di Romeo** (via Arche Scaligere 4, not open to the public), a fascinating medieval walled dwelling that may or may not have once belonged to the Montagu family of Shakespearian fame. To find the **casa di Giulietta** (Juliet's House, via Cappello 27, not open to the public), just follow the dreamy-eyed tourists drifting from the southern end of piazza delle Erbe. An almost total reconstruction, the house had a famous balcony tacked onto it in the 1920s to fit in with the myth.

Further down via Cappello is the **Porta Leoni**, a picturesque fragment of a Roman city gate that is now part of a medieval house. Recent excavations, visible from the street, have exposed the full extent of the towered and arched structure.

To the north of the central squares is a captivating labyrinth of narrow alleyways dotted with medieval and Renaissance *palazzi*, houses and churches. In via Pigna, take a look at the carved marble Roman pine cone (*pigna*) placed on a cylindrical Roman tombstone, before heading left down the narrow via San Giacomo alla Pigna to the **Duomo**, or right towards the imposing church of **Sant'Anastasia**.

Close by is the **Ponte Pietra**, Verona's oldest bridge and for centuries the only link between the city centre and the suburbs beyond. The two stone arches on the left bank of the river are Roman, and date back to before 50 BC. The other three brick arches are thought to date from between 1200 and 1500.

The bridge was blown up by German soldiers as they retreated at the end of World War II – as were all of Verona's bridges, including the medieval bridge of Castelvecchio – but was subsequently rebuilt with infinite care using the original stones fished from the river bed.

On the left bank of the river, towards Castel San Pietro, stand some of Verona's most beautiful churches, the **Museo Archeologico** (*see p248*), and the remains of the **Teatro Romano**.

Corso Porta Borsari, Roman Verona's busy main street, leads out of the north end of piazza delle Erbe towards the **Porta Borsari**, the best-preserved of the city's Roman gates. Built with blocks of local white marble, it probably dates from the reign of Emperor Claudius (AD 41-54).

Along corso Cavour, a continuation of corso Porta Borsari, in a garden next to the medieval fortress – now converted into a museum – of **Castelvecchio** (*see p249*) is the **Arco dei Gavi**, a triumphal arch attributed to Vitruvius, dating from about 50 BC.

TICKETS

An admission fee is charged by some churches and all museums in Verona. Cut costs by purchasing a three-day **Verona Card** (L22,000, free for under-11s), valid for all the sights that charge. It can be bought at the ticket office of any of the churches or museums participating in the scheme and it includes all bus fares around the city. No credit cards are accepted.

Arena

Piazza Brà (045 800 3204). **Open** 9am-6.30pm Tue-Sun; *during opera season* 9am-3pm. **Admission** L6,000; L4,000 students. **No credit cards**.

The third-largest Roman amphitheatre in Italy (beaten only by Rome's Colosseum and the one in Capua near Naples), Verona's Arena was large enough to seat the city's whole population of 20,000 when it was constructed in about AD 30. The huge and remarkably well-preserved structure in pink marble quarried from nearby hills was the site of gladiatorial games and – when filled with water for the occasion – naval battles.

During the Barbarian invasions in the fifth and sixth centuries, the city's terrified population took refuge inside. Later its darker corners became the haunt of prostitutes and cut-throats, and medieval *veronesi* were firmly convinced that it had been built by the devil. Perhaps as an exercise in exorcism, the construction was used as a law court in the Middle Ages, and a few unlucky heretics met their fate there. The earthquake of 1117 destroyed most of the Arena's outer ring, though much damage was restored immediately. By the 16th century, Verona's Venetian overlords had realised the historic value of the building and took steps to preserve it by making it illegal to pilfer the ancient stone. Regular maintenance work was carried out, and sports events – including jousting and bullfighting – were staged. It was already functioning as an open-air theatre in the 17th and 18th centuries. The first

Dante graces **piazza dei Signori**. *See p246.*

'Get me ink and paper'

An estimated 500,000 visitors stream annually into the courtyard of a house (*see p246*) that at the time of Juliet's turbulent adolescence was almost certainly an inn of very ill repute, to coo and sigh beneath a balcony thoughtfully added by the tourist board in 1928.

But Verona's Montagu & Capulet fun doesn't stop there: the city and its citizens keep the star-crossed lover flame alight each summer in a Shakespeare-inspired theatre festival in the Teatro Romano (*see below*), and – more bizarrely – in an international letter-writing competition.

Exploiting the sentimental pull of the Romeo and Juliet myth, a jury appointed by the *Club di Giulietta* sifts through letters (*see below* for address) from all over the world in scores of languages. Anything goes: happy love, sad love, young love, old love, virtual love, even lack of love... as long as it throbs with emotions and passion. The most heart-wrenching are published in the club's bulletin; the very best receive a prize, awarded in 'Juliet's' house sometime around Valentine's Day each year.

Club di Giulietta

Via Galilei 3, 37133 Verona (045 533 115/ club.giulietta@libero.it/ www.digilander.iol.it/clubgiulietta). Membership of the club costs L50,000 per year, for which members receive – by post or e-mail – a quarterly Romeo and Juliet-related bulletin.

Estate Teatrale Veronese

Palazzo Barbieri, via degli Alpini 2 (information 045 806 6485/ estateteatrale@comune.verona.it/ www.comune.verona.it). **Box office** (during season only) 10.30am-1pm, 4-7pm Mon-Sat. **Tickets** L15,000-L40,000. **No credit cards**. Tickets are also available at the Teatro Romano (*see p251*) immediately before performances.

---

opera performances came in the mid 19th century, though these nobler pursuits were interrupted during the first half of the 20th century when the Arena was used as a football stadium.

A celebrated outdoor opera season (for booking details, *see p255*) takes place in the Arena between the end of June and the end of August each year. The 44 tiers of stone seats inside the 139 x 110m (456 x 361ft) amphitheatre are virtually intact, as is the columned foyer where an international crowd of opera-goers swill champagne each summer.

Duomo

Piazza Duomo (045 595 627). **Open** *Mar-Oct* 10am-6pm Mon-Sat; 1.30-6pm Sun. *Nov-Feb* 10am-1pm, 1.30pm-4pm Mon-Sat; 1.30-5pm Sun. **Admission** L3,000. **No credit cards**.

Verona's cathedral, begun in 1139, is Romanesque downstairs, Gothic upstairs and Renaissance at the top half of the bell-tower. The elegant front portico is decorated with Romanesque carvings of the finest quality, showing Charlemagne's paladins Oliver and Roland (who feature in the *Chanson de Roland*, the medieval literary equivalent of *Saving Private Ryan*) wielding their swords while a fan club of saints looks on.

Inside, the first chapel on the left has a magnificent *Assumption* by Titian. To the left of the façade is a gateway leading to a tranquil Romanesque cloister where Roman remains and mosaics are on show. In the same complex is the ancient church of Sant'Elena with the remains of an earlier Christian basilica and Roman baths.

At the back of the cathedral, to the right of its graceful apse, is the chapel of San Giovanni in Fonte, with a large carved octagonal Romanesque baptismal font.

Giardino Giusti

Via Giardino Giusti 2 (045 803 4029). **Open** *Apr-Sept* 9am-8pm daily. *Oct-Mar* 9am-7pm daily. **Admission** L8,000; L3,000 under-14s; L5,000 students over 14; L6,000 groups. **No credit cards**.

The dusty façades of one of Verona's most traffic-clogged streets hide one of the finest Renaissance gardens in Italy. Tucked in behind the great Renaissance townhouse of the Giusti family – the Palazzo Giusti del Giardino – the statue-packed gardens with their tall cypresses were laid out in 1580. The lower level is typically formal in the Italian style. The wild upper level climbs the steep slopes of the hill behind, which offers superb views over the city. Under every shady tree lurks a potential picnic spot.

Museo Archeologico

Rigaste Redentore 2 (045 800 0360). **Open** 9am-7pm Tue-Sun. **Admission** L5,000; L3,000 students. **No credit cards**.

This small museum, containing a fine, though patchily labelled, collection of Roman remains, is situated in a former monastery high above the Teatro Romano. Even visitors with the strongest aversion to yet more ancient bits and pieces are advised to take the lift from the theatre through the cliffs and up to the museum: the views over Verona and the river Adige are incomparable.

Museo Castelvecchio

Corso Castelvecchio 2 (045 801 5435/045 592
985/fax 045 801 0729). **Open** 9am-7pm
Tue-Sun. **Admission** L6,000; L3,000 students.
No credit cards.

This castle was built by Duke Cangrande II between
1355 and 1375 as an unbreachable refuge from the
potential fury of Veronese citizens upset by his
famously hefty tax bills. Strong though his bolt-hole
was, Cangrande was taking no chances: the magnificent fortified medieval bridge (destroyed by the
Germans in 1945, but lovingly reconstructed) was
intended as an emergency escape route.

The castle is now a museum and exhibition venue,
with interiors beautifully redesigned in the 1960s by
the Venetian architect Carlo Scarpa (*see p267*). The
various parts of the castle are linked by overhead
walkways and passages offering superb views of
the city and surrounding hills.

The museum itself contains important works by
Mantegna, Crivelli, Pisanello, Giovanni Bellini,
Veronese, Tintoretto, Gianbattista Tiepolo, Canaletto and Guardi, besides a vast collection of local
artists. On the first floor is a magnificent collection
of 13th- and 14th-century Veronese religious
statuary. Note the life-sized *Crucifixion with Saints*,
a clear indication that Veronese artists were influenced as much by the grittier art from north of
the Alps as the softer, dreamier stuff on offer in
Tuscany. An armoury contains swords, shields and
some local jewellery.

Museo Lapidario

Piazza Brà 28 (045 590 087). **Open** 9am-2.30pm
Tue-Sun. **Admission** L4,000; L3,000 concessions.
No credit cards.

This collection of chiefly Greek and Roman architectural stone fragments and inscriptions was put
together mainly by Scipione Maffei, a rich and
learned local 18th-century aristocrat.

San Fermo Maggiore

Stradone San Fermo (045 592 813/045 800 7287).
Open *Mar-Oct* 9.30am-6pm Mon-Sat; 1.30-6pm Sun.
Nov-Feb 10am-1pm, 1.30-4pm Tue-Sat; 1-5pm Sun.
Admission L3,000. **No credit cards**.

At San Fermo you get two churches for the price of
one, although the bottom one tends to be a little
damp: the lower church is Romanesque and the
upper church, built in the 14th century, is Gothic.
While the lower church is intimate and solemn, the
upper part is towering and full of light. Its wooden
ceiling, resembling an upturned Venetian galleon,
is similar to that of San Zeno (*see p250*). The
church contains important frescos, including an
Annunciation by Antonio Pisanello to the left of the
main entrance.

San Giorgio in Braida

Piazzetta San Giorgio 1 (045 834 0232).
Open 9-11am, 5-6.30pm Mon-Sat; 5-6.30pm Sun.

This great domed Renaissance church, said to have
been designed by the Veronese military architect
Michele Sanmicheli between 1536 and 1543, contains
some of the city's greatest treasures. Shining in
this light-filled Renaissance masterpiece are a
Baptism of Christ by Tintoretto, above the entrance
door, and a moving *Martyrdom of Saint George*
by Paolo Veronese. But even these greats are put
in the shade by a serene *Madonna and Child
With St Zeno and St Lawrence* by local dark horse
Girolamo dai Libri.

Blown up and rebuilt with infinite care:
the **Ponte Pietra**. *See p247*.

The Veneto

San Giovanni in Valle

Via San Giovanni in Valle 36 (045 803 0119).
Open *Oct-May* 9-11am, 5-6pm Mon-Sat; 10-11am
Sun. *Jun-Sept* 9-11am Mon-Sat; 10-11am Sun.
Built in the Romanesque style, San Giovanni is part
of a much older complex with parish buildings
dating back to the eighth century. The church's
beautiful crypt (open 10-11am Sun) contains fine
examples of early Christian sculpture.

Santa Maria Antica

Via Arche Scaligere 3 (045 595 508). **Open** 7.30am-
noon, 3.30-7pm daily.
This tiny Romanesque church was the family chapel
of the powerful Della Scala family. Intimate and lit
by hundreds of candles, this exquisite building is
much loved by the *veronesi*, especially stallholders
from the market in nearby piazza delle Erbe. The
church as such is overshadowed, however, by the
extravagant Scaligeri tombs tacked on to its side
wall (*see p251*).

Santa Maria in Organo

Piazzetta Santa Maria in Organo (045 591 440).
Open 7.30am-noon, 12.30-6pm daily.
The Renaissance church of Santa Maria in Organo
has a host of frescos by the Veronese painters
Caroto, Giolfino and Farinato, but you might want
to pass them by and make your way straight to the
apse and Sacristy to see what Giorgio Vasari once
described as the most beautiful choir stalls in Italy.
A humble monk, Fra Giovanni da Verona (died
1520), worked for a quarter of a century cutting and
assembling these infinitely complex, coloured wood-
en images of animals, birds, landscapes, cityscapes,
religious scenes and musical and scientific instruments in dozens of intricate intarsia panels.

Sant'Anastasia

*Piazza Sant'Anastasia (045 592 813/045 800
4325).* **Open** *Mar-Oct* 9.30am-6pm Mon-Sat; 1.30-
6pm Sun. *Nov-Feb* 10am-1pm, 1.30-4pm Mon-Sat;
1-5pm Sun. **Admission** L3,000. **No credit cards.**
This imposing brick Gothic church is best visited
early in the morning, when sunlight streams in to
illuminate Antonio Pisanello's glorious fresco of St
George girding himself to set off in pursuit of the
dragon that has been pestering the lovely princess
of Trebizond (1433-8), in the sacristy to the right of
the apse. Carved scenes from the life of St Peter
Martyr adorn the unfinished façade, while inside
two delightful *gobbi* (hunchbacks) crouch down to
support the holy water font; the one on the left was
carved by Paolo Veronese's father in 1495.

Santo Stefano

Vicolo Scaletta Santo Stefano 1 (045 834 8529).
Open 8.30am-noon, 4.30-7.30pm daily.
A church has stood on this site since the sixth
century, and parts of that original church can still
be seen in the apse of the current building. But even
the existing Romanesque church ranks as one of the
oldest in Verona, and served as the city's cathedral

until the 12th century. Santo Stefano boasts an
unusual octagonal brick tower, a complicated two-
storey apse and a stunning 14th-century marble
statue of St Peter.

San Zeno Maggiore

Piazza San Zeno 2 (045 592 813/045 800 6120).
Open *Mar-Oct* 8.30am-6pm Mon-Sat; 1.30-6pm
Sun. *Nov-Feb* 3-4pm Mon; 10am-1pm, 1.30-4pm
Tue-Sat; 1.30-5pm Sun. **Admission** L3,000.
No credit cards.
One of the most spectacularly ornate Romanesque
churches in northern Italy, San Zeno was built
between 1123 and 1138 to house the tomb and shrine
of San Zeno, an African who became Verona's first
bishop in 362 and is now the city's much-loved
patron saint. The façade, with its great rose window
and porch, is covered with some of Italy's finest
examples of Romanesque marble sculpture. Scenes
from the Old Testament and the life of Christ min-
gle with hunting and jousting scenes, attributed to
the 12th-century sculptors Nicolò and Guglielmo.

With the graceful porch supported by columns
resting on two carved marble lions, the sculptures
serve as a frame for the great bronze doors of the
Basilica; the 48 panels have scenes from the Bible
and from the life of San Zeno, and a few that experts
have been hard-pressed to pin down, including a
woman suckling two crocodiles. The panels on the
left-hand door date from about 1030 and came from
an earlier church. Those on the right were produced

Museo Castelvecchio. *See p249.*

a century later. Inside the lofty church (note the magnificent ceiling built in 1386), the main altar is placed on a raised platform reached by twin staircases. A third staircase descends into the crypt, which contains the tomb of San Zeno.

Dominating the altar is a stunning triptych depicting a *Madonna and Child* with a bevy of saints, an early work by Andrea Mantegna painted between 1457 and 1459. The lower panel, showing Christ on the cross, is a copy: the original was looted by Napoleon, and is now in the Louvre in Paris.

The enduring love affair between San Zeno and the city that adopted him may have something to do with the huge – and hugely appealing – early 12th-century marble statue of the African bishop having a grand old chuckle, which is to be found in a niche to the left of the apse. His black face, with its distinctly African features, is unique in Italian religious statuary, as is his singularly jovial and not-particularly-saintly aspect.

Covering the inside walls of the basilica are frescos dating from the 12th to the 14th centuries, but perhaps more interesting than the paintings themselves is the 15th- to 17th-century graffito scratched into them by the faithful invoking Zeno's protection from earthquakes and pestilence.

To the right of the church is a massive bell-tower, 72m (236ft) high, begun in 1045. To the left is a lower tower, which is all that remains of the Benedictine monastery that stood on the site before the basilica was built, and that, according to local lore, stands over the grave of King Pepin, son of Charlemagne. Behind is an open, light-filled Romanesque cloister.

Scaligeri Tombs

Via Santa Maria in Chiavica. Visible from outside.
The Gothic tombs of the Della Scala family, which ruled Verona and vast parts of northern Italy in the 13th and 14th centuries, date from 1277 to the final years of the 14th century and give a good idea of the family's sense of its own importance. Carved by the most sought-after stonemasons of the era – in particular those from the small town of Campione, now an Italian enclave in Switzerland – the more lavish tombs are topped with spires. Note the family's odd taste in first names. The monument to Cangrande (Big Dog, died 1329) above the doorway to the church of Santa Maria Antica with its equestrian statue shows the valiant duke smiling in the face of death. (This is a copy: the original is in the Museo Castelvecchio, *see p249.*) Poking out from above the intricate wrought-iron fence surrounding the tombs are the spire-topped final resting places of Cansignorio (Lord Dog, died 1375) and Mastino II (Mastiff the second, died 1351). Among the less flamboyant tombs is that of Mastino I (died 1277), founder of the doggy dynasty.

Teatro Romano

Regaste Redentore 2 (045 800 0360/fax 045 801 0587). **Open** 9am-6.30pm Tue-Sun. **Admission** L5,000; L2,000-L3,000 concessions. **No credit cards.**

The Roman theatre, dating from around the first century BC, was buried under medieval houses until the late 19th century, when the semi-circular seating was brought to light. Built into the side of the hill where Verona's earliest pre-Roman and Roman settlements were located, the theatre offers beautiful views over the city, and is an evocative venue for an annual festival of theatre, ballet and jazz. Nowadays Shakespeare's a firm favourite (*see p248* **'Get me ink and paper'**).

Torre dei Lamberti

Piazza dei Signori (045 803 2726).
Open 9.30am-6.30pm Tue-Sun. **Admission** *lift* L4,000; *stairs* L3,000; L3,000 concessions. **No credit cards.**
This massive medieval tower, 83m (273 feet) high, offers superb views of the city and, on clear days, a spectacular panorama of the local mountains and Italian Alps. The climb is only for the fittest.

Where to eat

Cooking in Verona is very meat-oriented: Veronese restaurateurs will roll out great trolleys loaded with boiled and roasted meats, and serve it all up with *cren*, the local take on horseradish sauce, or a delicacy called *peará*, made of bone marrow (BSE scares permitting), bread and pepper. *Pastissada de caval* – stewed sliced horsemeat – is also to be found in abundance. Before vegetarians take the next train out, meat-free pumpkin-stuffed ravioli are also a speciality, as are *bigoli*, a local version of spaghetti that can be served with meat-free sauces.

Bottega del Vino

Vicolo Scudo di Francia 3 (045 800 4535/ bottega.vino@ifinet.it/www.ifinet.it/bottega). **Meals served** noon-3pm, 7pm-midnight Mon, Wed-Sun. **Average** L80,000. **Credit** AmEx, DC, MC, V.
Once a typical smoke-filled late-night *osteria*, the Bottega has recently gone upmarket. Serves excellent local dishes, including horse meat and a delicious pasta e *fagioli* (bean) soup. A huge and very fine wine list. Booking advisable.

Capitan Trinchetto

Lungadige Porta Vittoria 35 (045 800 9140/ capitan.trinchetto@supernet.it). **Meals served** 8pm-midnight Tue-Sun. **Closed** 1wk Aug. **Average** L30,000. **No credit cards.**
This tiny restaurant serves generous portions of Mexican, Greek, Tunisian, Cajun or Sri Lankan food. Walter, the owner, will talk you through his medley of international tastes. Booking is advisable.

Ciccarelli

Via Mantovana 171, località Madonna di Dossobuono (045 953 986/www.ristorante ciccarelli.com). **Meals served** noon-2.30pm, 7.30-10pm Mon-Fri, Sun. **Closed** mid July-mid Aug. **Average** L55,000. **Credit** AmEx, DC, MC, V.

The Veneto

Situated on the state highway to Mantua, 6km from the city centre, this country trat is frequented by truckers and business-people, who flock here for one of the great eating experiences of northern Italy. The menu never varies: home-made *tagliatelle* with a choice of four sauces, including chicken livers. This is followed by a massive serving of fresh veg and the obligatory meat trolley. Booking advisable.

Il Desco
Via Dietro San Sebastiano 7 (045 595 358/fax 045 590 236). **Meals served** *Sept-Nov, Jan-June* 12.40-2pm, 7.40-10.15pm Tue-Sat. *July-Aug, Dec* 7.40-10.15pm Mon; 12.40-2pm, 7.40-10.15pm Tue-Sat. **Closed** Christmas, 2wks June. **Average** L180,000. **Credit** AmEx, DC, MC, V.
Refined and beautifully furnished, every detail of the service and, above all, of the food in this widely lauded restaurant is studied to perfection. Among the inventions of its creator, Elia Rizzo, are potato ravioli with rosemary and crackling lard, and guinea fowl with its own liver, garnished with truffles. His fish dishes are rightly celebrated.

Al Duomo
Via Duomo 7 (045 800 4505). **Meals served** noon-2pm, 8-10pm Mon-Sat; bar 11am-3pm, 6pm-midnight Mon-Sat. **Average** L30,000. **Credit** MC, V.
Elderly mandolin players congregate here of a Tuesday and/or Wednesday evening to strum traditional music. Near the Duomo, this *osteria* is much-frequented by the people of the quarter who know a well-priced meal when they see one.

Ostaria La Stueta
Via Redentore 4 (045 803 2462). **Meals served** *Oct-June* noon-2pm, 7-10pm Tue-Sun. *Aug-Sept* noon-2pm, 5-10pm Tue-Sun. **Closed** July. **Average** L50,000. **Credit** AmEx, MC, V.
The menu in this tiny restaurant is limited and traditional, but unfailingly delicious. In autumn, their mushrooms are a treat; try the polenta with *moscardini* (baby octopus) in summer. Helpful, discreet staff and a good wine list. Booking is advisable.

La Torretta
Piazza Broilo 1 (045 801 0099/latorretta@ifinet.it/ www.ifinet.it/latorretta). **Meals served** noon-3pm, 7-11pm Mon-Sat. **Closed** Mon, Sun in July & Aug. **Average** L80,000. **Credit** AmEx, DC, MC, V.
There's loads of atmosphere in this excellent restaurant, opposite the Ponte Pietra, which serves traditional fare revisited with imagination and flair. High-beamed ceiling and, in summer, the possibility of eating in the cobbled square outside.

Tre Marchetti
Vicolo Tre Marchetti 19B (045 803 0463). **Meals served** 7-10pm Mon; 12.15-2.30pm, 7-10pm Tue-Sat. **Closed** 2wks June, 1wk Sept, 2wks Dec. **Average** L70,000. **Credit** AmEx, DC, MC, V.
Meals have been served on these premises just round the corner from the Roman Arena since 1291, making it one of the most ancient eating houses in

Europe. It has lost none of its allure over the centuries: informal and crowded, it specialises in *bigoli* (home-made spaghetti) with duck, *pastissada de caval* (a horsemeat dish) and *baccalà alla vicentina*, a delicious dish of stewed cod. Booking advisable, especially during the opera season.

Bars & nightlife

Ai Preti
Interrato dell'Acqua Morta 27 (045 597 675). **Open** 9am-2am Mon-Sat. **No credit cards**.
Much favoured by ageing left-wing radical types, who join the heterogeneous mix of young single women, English-speaking foreigners and university teachers. Hots up – in a lukewarm kind of way – towards midnight.

Alter Ego Disco Club
Via Torricelle 9 (045 834 3016/ info@alteregoclub.it/www.alteregoclub.it). **Open** 11pm-5am Fri, Sat. **Closed** Aug. **Credit** AmEx, DC, MC, V.
In the hills immediately behind Castel San Pietro, this commercial disco is much favoured by Verona's glittering youth.

Bar Leon d'Oro
Via Pallone 10A (045 595 076). **Open** 6pm-4am Tue-Sun. **No credit cards**.
Late-night hangout for the city's *glitterati*, with a strong gay element. The bar is situated in a late-18th century townhouse with a large front garden where drinks can be sipped under the stars on balmy summer nights.

Caffè Al Duomo
Piazza Duomo 4A (045 800 7119). **Open** 8am-7.30pm Tue-Sun. **No credit cards**.
You'll need to look hard to find this lovely *pasticceria-caffetteria* opposite the Duomo. The entrance hall of an old palazzo has been converted into the main seating area; there's a secluded walled garden out the back.

Caffè Il Piccolo Principe
Via Carlo Cattaneo 24A (045 800 8585). **Open** 7.30am-8pm Mon-Sat. **Closed** 2wks Aug. **No credit cards**.
A pleasant, relaxing little bar just behind piazza Brà and the Arena. Has a good wine list and serves organic snacks and delicacies.

Gelateria Pampanin
Via Garibaldi 24 (045 803 0064). **Open** 7.30am-midnight Mon, Wed-Sun. **Closed** Aug. **No credit cards**.
Pampanin's ice-creams are Verona's finest. Such is the popularity of Pampanin *gelato* with the well-heeled Veronese that it shuts down in the hottest month of the year, just when its trade should be briskest. The reason is simple: its clientele has fled en masse to plush summer retreats.

'We mean well in going to this mask'

Venice's *carnevale* (*see p194*) may be glam and world-famous but it's nothing – the Veronese will tell you – but an upstart. For Europe's oldest *carnevale* festival takes place in Verona and has done since the Middle Ages... with no tourist-board PR job or subsidies needed to get a flagging event back off the ground.

Presiding over the festivities is the 'Re del Gnoco', a chubby, red-cheeked monarch who makes his regal way though the city on a donkey, wielding a giant potato dumpling (*gnocco*) on his golden trident. The *gnocco* theme continues on '*venerdì gnocolar*' – the

Friday before Shrove Tuesday – when there's a communal *gnocco* binge in piazza San Zeno. The weekend is a noisy, multi-coloured jamboree with the masked *veronesi* and their fancy-dressed children out in force, jugglers and street entertainers from around Europe who perform in piazza Brà, and a procession of floats, plus a boat race on the River Adige.

The misty, mysterious backdrop of winter Venice may be missing, but for sheer civic jollity, Verona's *carnevale* wins hands down.

For dates of events, contact the **Azienda di Promozione Turistica** (*see p254*).

Pizzeria Bar San Mattia

Viale Colli 43 (045 834 8246/www.barpizzeria sanmattia.it). **Open** 10am-1am Tue-Sun. **No credit cards.**
The Bar San Mattia has a pleasant terrace overlooking the city. Serves light snacks all day and pizza in the evenings.

The Stonehenge

Via Ponte Florio 70 (045 886 8122/ www.stonehenge-vr.com). **Open** 7pm-2am Tue-Sun. **No credit cards.**
Past the Ponte Florio and about half a mile up a narrow lane between two ancient stone walls, the Stonehenge is well sign-posted. This is where Verona's youth comes to while away summer evenings, with music and ever-changing offerings on a giant screen in the spacious garden. There's an international choice of beers on tap, snacks at lunchtime and pizza in the evening.

Where to stay

Campeggio Castel San Pietro

Via Castel San Pietro 2 (045 592 037). **Closed** Oct-mid June. **Rates** L7,000-L10,000 plot; L8,500 per person; L6,000 under-8s. **No credit cards.**
In a spectacular position above the city centre, within the old city walls, and 15 minutes' walk from the centre. Good bathroom facilities. Hires out caravans.

Due Torri Hotel Baglioni

Piazza Sant'Anastasia 4 (045 595 0444/fax 045 800 4130/duetorri.verona@bagliohotels.com/ www.baglionihotels.com). **Rates** L380,000-L540,000 single; L570,000-L750,000 double. **Credit** AmEx, DC, MC, V.
This celebrated hotel (Beethoven and Goethe were on its illustrious guest list) is widely considered the city's finest. Each room is tastefully furnished in a different style with antique furniture, and the service is immaculate.

Hotel Antica Porta Leona

Corticella Leoni 3 (045 595 499/fax 045 595 214/ htlanticaportaleona@tiscalinet.it). **Rates** L120,000-L180,000 single; L150,000-L250,000 double. **Credit** AmEx, DC, MC, V.
This pretty little hotel is in the pedestrian heart of the old city.

Hotel Aurora

Piazzetta XIV Novembre 2 (045 594 717/045 597 834/fax 045 801 0860). **Rates** L120,000-L190,000 single; L160,000-L210,000 double. **Credit** AmEx, DC, MC, V.
Facing piazza delle Erbe, this simple hotel is friendly and efficiently run.

Hotel Bologna

Piazzetta Scalette Rubiani 3 (045 800 6830/ fax 045 801 0602/hotelbologna@tin.it/ www.italiaabc.it/az/bologna). **Rates** L170,000-L200,000 single; L210,000-L280,000 double. **Credit** AmEx, DC, MC, V.
Situated just off piazza Brà, this comfortable, unpretentious hotel is in a perfect position from which to explore the city.

Hotel Mazzanti

Via Mazzanti 6 (045 800 6813/fax 045 801 1262). **Rates** L95,000-L125,000 single; L140,000-L185,000 double. **Credit** AmEx, DC, MC, V.
Very central, this simple but clean little hotel is one of Verona's oldest, dating back to the 13th century.

Locanda Armando

Via Dietro Pallone 1 (045 800 0206/fax 045 803 6015). **Rates** L70,000 single; L130,000-L160,000 double; breakfast L15,000 extra. **Credit** MC, V.
Spartan but cheap, and reasonably central.

Ostello della Gioventù (Youth Hostel)

Salita Fontana di Ferro 15 (045 590 360/fax 045 800 9127). **Rates** L23,000 per person; family rooms L26,000 per adult, L13,000 per child. **No credit cards.**

Verona's traditional emporia are supplemented by colourful, fragrant Afro-Caribbean shops.

This friendly and efficient youth hostel is situated in a 17th-century villa with a small park, in one of Verona's oldest quarters. In summer, when the hostel is booked out, camping is sometimes permitted in the park. Family groups can book special group rooms in advance.

Resources

Getting there

By air
Verona's Valerio Catullo Airport (045 809 5666) is a 20min bus ride from the train station. The shuttle bus between the airport and the train station leaves every 20mins; tickets cost L7,000 on the bus.

By train
Regular train services from Milan and Venice (75-90mins) to Verona Porta Nuova railway station (045 800 0861).

By car
Take the A4 La Serenissima motorway from either Venice or Milan.

Getting around

By bus
The APT Verona bus company (045 800 4129) runs services (blue coaches) to towns and villages in the area around Verona, including Lake Garda and the Monti Lessini. Buses depart from the bus station, in front of Porta Nuova train station. The AMT (045

887 1111) runs the city bus service (orange buses) most of which start and terminate at the train station. Bus tickets can be purchased at the station or any tobacconist's. A L1,600 ticket is valid for one hour and should be punched on each bus boarded during that time.

By bicycle
Noleggio Biciclette on the corner of via Roma and piazza Brà (0338 955 0056, open Apr-Sept 9am-6pm daily) rents cycles at L7,000 per hour or L20,000 for a whole day. No credit cards.

Tourist information

APT (Azienda di promozione turistica)
Via degli Alpini 9 (045 806 8680/fax 045 800 3638/ info@tourism.verona.it/www.tourism.verona.it). **Open** 1-7pm Mon; 9am-7pm Tue-Sat; 9am-3pm Sun.
Inside the train station, piazza XXV Aprile (tel/fax 045 800 0861). **Open** 9am-6pm Mon-Sat.
Verona airport (tel/fax 045 861 9163). **Open** 11am-5pm Mon-Sat.

Hotel reservations

CAV
Via Patuzzi 5 (045 800 9844). **Open** *Oct-May* 9am-6.30pm Mon-Fri. *June-Sept* 9am-7.30pm Mon-Sat; 2-7pm Sun.
The Verona hoteliers' association CAV runs a free hotel-booking bureau.

Opera festival tickets

Fondazione Arena di Verona
Via Dietro Anfiteatro 6B, 37121 Verona (information/bookings 045 800 5151/fax 045 801 3287/ticket@arena.it/www.arena.it). **Season** end June to early Sept approx. **Performances** June, July 9.15pm Thur-Sun; Aug, Sept 9pm Tue-Sun. **Box office** (in front of the Arena) 29 June-2 Sept 9am-noon, 3.15-5.45pm Mon-Fri; 9am-noon Sat; during the season on performance days 10am-9pm; on non performance days 10am-5.45pm. **Tickets** L38,000-L270,000 Tue-Thur, Sun; L42,000-L300,000 Fri, Sat. **Credit** AmEx, DC, MC, V.
Reservations can be made by post, enclosing a bank draft with the corresponding amount, indicating the date of the performance, seat sector and number of tickets desired. Credit card phone bookings are accepted at the number given above. The cheapest seats are not numbered: get there two hours before the performance to grab a decent spot. Seats are sometimes available on the same day, especially Tue-Thur. Remember, you'll be spending three hours on a cold stone step: bring a cushion.

Internet

Locanda del Fiume
Via Santa Maria Rocca Maggiore 15A (045 800 7751). **Open** 11am-2.30pm, 4.30pm-12.30am Tue-Fri, Sun; 6.30pm-12.30am Sat. **Rates** L5,000 per hour. **Credit** AmEx, MC, V.
Check your email while munching on the Locanda's good *bruschetta.*

Internet b@r
Via Redentore 9 (045 801 4188/ info@internetbarverona.it/www.internetbarverona.it). **Open** *Nov-May* 7.15am-midnight Mon-Sat. *June-Sept* 8.30am 2am Mon-Sat. **Rates** L8,000 per hour. **No credit cards.**
A pleasant bar, not far from Teatro Romano.

Around Verona

Verona is 250 kilometres (155 miles) from the dramatic ravine known as Chiusa, which is the entrance to the Adige Valley and the gateway to Germany and central Europe. Little more than an hour's drive to the north are the wild, rugged Dolomites, with marvellous skiing and trekking. To the west is Lake Garda, the largest of Italy's northern lakes. The area to the south of Verona, on the other hand, is a culinary paradise with scores of rural *trattorie.*

Caldiero

Verona's ancient Roman inhabitants flocked to Caldiero's hot springs – the Terme di Giunone – to splash about in the same stone pool used by today's wallowers. Other more modern pools have been added to accommodate the crowds in this spa 18 kilometres (11 miles) east of Verona, where water bubbles up at a temperature of 28 degrees centigrade.

Terme di Giunone
Via delle Terme 2 (045 765 0191/045 765 0933). **Open** *June-Aug* 7.30am-10pm daily. *15-30 May, Sept* 11am-5pm daily. **Closed** Oct-Apr. **Admission** *June-Aug* L10,000 Mon-Sat, L16,000 Sun; *15-30 May, Sept* L6,000 daily. **No credit cards.**

Getting there

By bus
Regular APT service from Verona bus station for Caldiero.

Valeggio sul Mincio

At the centre of the carriage-building industry, Valeggio went into a severe economic slump as the combustion engine edged out the horse-drawn vehicle. Salvation came at the hands of the area's canny womenfolk who, superb cooks all, opened scores of tiny restaurants serving some of the best food around. The excellent local *tortelli di zucca* (pumpkin-stuffed pasta) and the grilled fish, fresh from the nearby Lake Garda, are part of this tradition.

Where to eat

Alla Borsa
Via Goito 2, Valeggio (045 795 0093/ www.valeggio.com/borsa). **Meals served** 12.15-2pm, 7.15-10pm Mon, Thur-Sun. **Closed** mid-July to mid-Aug. **Average** L50,000. **Credit** AmEx, MC, V.
This family-run *trattoria* serves perhaps the most delicious pumpkin *tortelli* in existence. Informal and noisy, Alla Borsa also specialises in trout and other fish from nearby Lake Garda, plus stuffed guinea fowl, roast pork shanks and duck. Delicious home-made desserts.

Antica Locanda Mincio
Via Michelangelo 12, Località Borghetto (045 795 0059/www.valeggio.com/anticalocanda). **Meals served** 12.30-2.30pm, 7-9.30pm Mon, Tue, Thur-Sun. **Closed** 2wks Feb, 2wks Nov. **Average** L70,000. **Credit** AmEx, DC, MC, V.
The Antica Locanda is located in a beautiful ancient milling village just a stone's throw from Valeggio. In summer you can eat out under the trees by the rushing river Mincio. The home-made pumpkin *tortelli* and the trout and other river fish are all excellent.

Getting there

By bus
Regular APT bus service from Verona.

The Veneto

Vicenza

Visit a city where the ancient Roman layout remains virtually intact, and where modernisation, by Palladio and others, adds rather than takes away.

As a city of patrician *palazzi*, Vicenza is second only to Venice – a phenomenon explained not so much by the wealth of medieval and Renaissance Vicenza as by the local dynasties' particular sense of their own aristocratic worth. Unlike the recent upstarts across the lagoon, most of the city's leading families had been ennobled in the early Middle Ages by various Holy Roman emperors. The fact that since 1404 Venetian parvenus had ruled their city irritated the *vicentini* intensely. They consoled themselves – and cocked a snook at their so-called masters – by commissioning sumptuous townhouses and country villas. In Vicenza, the nobleman's house was the outward sign of his family's worth, taste and good breeding. Thus it was a little more than coincidence that Andrea Palladio should have been born here in 1508, just as the building frenzy was reaching its peak. The architect who did more than any other to apply classical models, and humanist values, to the villas and *palazzi* he designed for a circle of wealthy, cultivated local nobles, was a product of this time and this place (*see chapter* **Palladian Villas**).

After a short-lived flirtation with Austria at the beginning of the 16th century, Vicenza was forced back into the Venetian fold, and the city settled down to accepting the dominance of La Serenissima, enjoying – albeit resentfully – the prosperity and peace that such an arrangement offered. Austria returned in 1797, this time uninvited; and Vicenza showed its spirit of wilful independence by becoming a hot-bed of revolt against foreign domination. After 1866, when the Austrians were finally forced to leave, the city joined united Italy and began to prosper again.

The business acumen that made Vicenza such a flourishing place in the Middle Ages is still there today, and this city of 111,000 inhabitants is now one of Italy's wealthiest. Its thousands of goldsmiths produce some of Europe's finest jewellery; in and around Vicenza, there is one factory or business for every 14 inhabitants. Vicenza's per capita GDP tops Italian league tables, and unemployment is almost non-existent.

This vast wealth and activity has a distinctly negative side. Vicenza's countryside was once considered as beautiful as Tuscany's. Now much of it has disappeared under industrial sprawl that often reaches out to blight the Palladian villas and other monuments which were designed to blend harmoniously into a rural landscape. On the upside, part of the city's wealth has been channelled into restoring its scores of palaces and churches.

Sightseeing

The ancient Roman layout of Vicenza is still virtually intact. The main street, **corso Palladio**, was the *decumanus maximus*, the central axis of the Roman street grid. The Retrone and the Bacchigione rivers – the moats in the city's medieval defence system – are now sluggish streams running round the north and east of the city centre. On the western side, the defensive walls built by the Della Scala family – the dukes from Verona who dominated the city before the Venetians arrived – can still be seen.

Walking north up viale Roma from the station, the first sight of interest is the **Giardino Salvi**, just outside Porta Castello. Inside this public park is Palladio's charming **Loggia Valmarana**, a Doric-style temple spanning the waters of a wide canal. Nearby, over another branch of the canal, is a baroque loggia by Baldassare Longhena.

Inside the town's western gate, **Porta Castello**, is piazza del Castello, at the southern end of which stands **Palazzo Porto Breganze**, designed by Palladio but never finished. This tall, awkward fragment, with its grandiose columns and two elaborately carved windows and decorative balconies, should have extended to occupy the entire southern end of the piazza.

At the far end of piazza del Castello, Vicenza's straight-as-a-die main street begins. Corso Palladio is lined with numerous grandiose *palazzi*, five of which Andrea Palladio had a hand in. The first of note, on the lefthand side, is the magnificent **Palazzo Thiene Bonin Longare**, begun in 1562; note the impressive double loggia at the back of the building. At no.45 is **Palazzo Capra**, almost certainly designed by the young Palladio between 1540 and 1545. Though alterations have been made since, Palladio's original façade and doorway remain. At no.92 is **Palazzo**

Loggia del Capitaniato, piazza dei Signori, once home to the Venetian governor of Vicenza.

Pojana (1564-6), which consists of two separate buildings cunningly joined together by Palladio; where the front door would normally be, the architect left room for a street to run through. A detour to the right leads to the Gothic brick church of **San Lorenzo** (*see p260*); off to the left, on the other hand, stands the **Duomo** (*see p259*).

Back on the corso at no.98 is **Palazzo Trissino** (*see p260*), designed in 1592 by Palladio's student Vicenzo Scamozzi; it is now the city council headquarters.

The overwhelming presence of Palladio is to be felt once more in the vast and elegant **piazza dei Signori**, slightly south of the corso. Apart from the slender, spectacular 82m-high (269ft) 12th-century **Torre di Piazza** clock tower, the prevailing spirit of the square is definitely late Renaissance. Tacked gracefully on to the square side of the Gothic **Palazzo della Ragione** (*see p259*) assembly hall (better known as the Basilica, in the ancient Roman sense of the word – as a public place where justice is dispensed) is Palladio's marvellous loggia. Opposite is the same architect's **Loggia del Capitaniato**, a fragment of a building that was intended to continue along most of the northern side of the square. This highly decorated brick arcade was built to celebrate Venice's victory over the Turks in the Battle of Lepanto in 1571; it was the official residence of the all-powerful Venetian governor of Vicenza. On the same side is the vast complex of the **Monte di Pietà**, the city's elegant 16th-century pawn shop, which extends on either side of the baroquified church of **San Vincenzo**.

There is a morning clothes and food market in piazza dei Signori (Tue & Thur). Food stalls spill over into **piazza delle Erbe**, around the other side of the Basilica, a square dominated by a medieval tower where Vicenza's recalcitrant wrong-doers were taken for a little tongue-loosening torture.

In the labyrinth of streets to the south of piazza delle Erbe is the **Casa Pigafetta** (contrà Pigafetta 9, closed to the public). Dating from 1444 and built in late Spanish Gothic style, this strange, highly decorated townhouse was the birthplace of Antonio Pigafetta, the adventurous nobleman who was one of only 21 survivors of Magellan's epoch-making circumnavigation of the globe from 1519 to 1522.

Off corso Palladio north of piazza Signori is contrà Porti, which offers a real palazzo feast. The Porto family was very rich, very influential and very clannish; all its members chose to build their townhouses in the same short street. At no.11 is the **Palazzo Barbaran Da Porto**, designed and built by Palladio between 1569 and 1571, with an interior elaborately decorated with stuccoes by Lorenzo Rubini. Currently used to house temporary exhibitions, the palazzo has long been earmarked as the site of a new museum dedicated to the life and works of Palladio – but progress is slow.

Casa Porto (no.15) is an undistinguished 15th-century building that was badly restored in the 18th century but is of interest as the

Palazzo della Ragione, also known as the **Basilica Palladiana**. *See p259.*

home of Luigi Da Porto (died 1529), who wrote the first known account of the Romeo and Juliet story. At no.19 the exquisite, late-Gothic **Palazzo Porto Colleoni** is a typical 15th-century attempt to beat the Venetians at their own game. Be sure to take a quick peek through the open gateway into the secluded back garden. **Palazzo Iseppo Da Porto**, at no.21, is one of Palladio's earliest creations.

At the far end of this street, across a bridge over the river Bacchiglione, contrà San Marco is a wide street lined with fine 16th- and 17th-century *palazzi*, including **Palazzo Da Schio**, an elegant townhouse designed by Palladio in the 1560s.

Back on corso Palladio, the huge palazzo that stands on the corner with contrà Porti is the **Palazzo Dal Toso**, a flamboyant Gothic jewel, which once boasted gilded capitals – hence its other name, the Ca' d'Oro. The Gothic theme continues in the church of **Santa Corona** (*see p260*), further down the corso; past the church, the **Gallerie del Palazzo Leoni Montanari** (*see below*) contains charming 18th-century genre paintings by Pietro Longhi. Almost at the end of corso Palladio, tiny, elegant **Casa Cogollo**, at no.167, is thought to have been Palladio's home in later life; according to some acounts, he may even have designed it.

The main street ends in piazza Matteotti, where two of Vicenza's real artistic treats await: **Palazzo Chiericati** (1550), one of Palladio's finest townhouses, now the city's art gallery (*see below* **Museo Civico**); and the architect's final masterpiece, the **Teatro Olimpico** (*see p260*).

Towering above town to the south, the **Santuario di Monte Berico** can be reached on foot in the shade of an 18th-century loggia joining it to the centre.

TICKETS

Vicenza's tourist board offers three cumulative tickets.

Biglietto unico: L13,000 (free under-14s; L6,000 groups), gives access to Teatro Olimpico, Museo Civico, Museo Naturalistico Archeologico in contrà Santa Corona, Basilica Palladiana.

Vicenza Musei e Palazzi: L20,000, gives access to the sites above, plus the Villa Guccioli museum of the Risorgimento and the Resistance, Palazzo Barbaran da Porto, and Palazzo Leoni Montanari.

Vicenza e le Ville: L40,000, gives access to all of the above, plus the two country villas of Villa Rotonda (*see p232*) and Villa Valmarana ai Nani (*see page 263*).

All three can be bought at the Teatro Olimpico ticket office; the *Biglietto unico* is also on sale at the other museums on the circuit. No credit cards are accepted.

Basilica Palladiana (Palazzo della Ragione)

Piazza dei Signori (0444 323 681). **Open** *Sept-June* 9am-5pm Tue-Sun. *July, Aug* 10am-7pm Tue-Sun. **Admission** by Biglietto unico (*see above*); *loggia only* L2,000. **No credit cards**.

Palladio's most famous piece of urban restyling is a neat alternative to scaffolding. The original Palazzo della Regione, seat of the city government, was built in the 1450s; but the loggia that once surrounded it – and helped to support it – collapsed in 1496, making it necessary to find an elegant way of shoring up the building. The city fathers canvassed most of the leading architects of the day from 1525 onwards; luckily for Palladio – who was only 17 at this time – they dithered for 20 years before accepting the audacious solution proposed by the home contender in 1546. Palladio's double-tiered loggia, Doric below and Ionic above, encases the original Gothic palazzo in a Renaissance shell. The main *salone* is a barn-like space, with impressive ornate arches holding up the wooden ship's keel roof.

Duomo

Piazza Duomo (0444 325 007). **Open** 10.30am-noon, 3.30-5.30pm Mon-Fri; 10.30am-noon Sat; Sun for mass only.

Founded in the ninth century, the Duomo suffered extensive damage in World War II. The Palladian dome, finished in 1574, has been painstakingly restored to its former splendour, as has the elegant Gothic pink marble façade, attributed to Domenico da Venezia (1467). The brick interior contains an important polyptych by Lorenzo Veneziano, signed and dated 1366.

Gallerie del Palazzo Leoni Montanari

Contrà Santa Corona 25 (tollfree 800 578 875). **Open** 10am-6pm Fri-Sun. **Admission** L6,000; L4,000 concessions. **No credit cards**.

Situated in the recently restored baroque Palazzo Leoni Montanari, this remarkable collection of 14 masterpieces by the 18th-century Venetian genre painter Pietro Longhi, together with other important examples of Venetian art, should not be missed. Also on display is a collection of Russian icons.

Museo Civico

Palazzo Chiericati, piazza Matteotti 37/39 (0444 325 071). **Open** *Sept-June* 9am-5pm Tue-Sun. *July-Aug* 9am-7pm Tue-Sun. **Admission** by Biglietto unico (*see above*). **No credit cards**.

The art gallery on the second floor of this Palladian palazzo contains a fascinating collection of works by local painters, Bartolomeo Montagna (1450-1523) in particular. It also houses excellent work by Van Dyck, Tintoretto, Veronese, Tiepolo and Giovanni

Bellini. Outshining them all is a crucifixion by the Flemish master Hans Memling, the central part of a triptych the side panels of which are in New York. In the ticket office is a 16th-century portrait of the Valmarana family that allows an intimate peek at some of Palladio's keenest fans and employers.

Palazzo Trissino

Corso Garibaldi 98 (0444 221 229). **Open** 9am-1.30pm Mon-Sat. **Admission** free, interior by appointment only.

Now Vicenza's town hall, this design by Palladio's student Vincenzo Scamozzi was begun in 1592 but was not completed until 1667. On the corso, a portico with Ionic columns is surmounted by a Corinthian-inspired *piano nobile*. Nobody minds if you stroll into the courtyard.

San Lorenzo

Piazza San Lorenzo (0444 321 960). **Open** 10.30am-noon, 3.30-6pm Mon-Sat; 3.30-6pm Sun.

None of the city's neo-classical or baroque places of worship can hold a candle to San Lorenzo's Gothic glory. The magnificent marble portal encases an exquisite 14th-century lunette depicting the *Madonna and Child*. Inside, three grandiose naves are lit by high monoforate windows. The Poiana altar in the right transept is a fine late-Gothic assemblage of paintings and frescos by various artists, while the peaceful 16th-century cloister contains a pretty medieval well-head.

Santa Corona

Contrà Santa Corona (0444 323 644). **Open** 8.30am-noon, 2.30-6.30pm daily.

This Gothic brick church was built between 1260 and 1270, to house a much-travelled stray thorn from Christ's crown. Its interior, consisting of three unequally sized naves, contains an *Adoration of the Magi* (1573) by Paolo Veronese in the third chapel on the right. In the crypt is the Valmarana chapel, designed by Palladio. The church's other artistic treasure, in the fifth chapel on the left of the nave, is a *Baptism of Christ* by Giovanni Bellini (1502).

Santuario di Monte Berico

Viale X Giugno 87 (0444 320 998). **Open** *Oct-Mar* 8am-12.30pm, 2.30-6pm Mon-Sat; 8am-7pm Sun. *Apr-Sept* 8am-12.30pm, 3.30-7.30pm Mon-Sat; 8am-8pm Sun.

Monte Berico was where hot and bothered *vicentini* used to come for a bit of greenery and a breath of fresh air in summer. The exhaust fumes of countless pilgrim coaches grinding up to the spot where the Virgin is said to have appeared in 1426 and 1428 spoil the effect these days, though some pedestrian protection is afforded by a shady 18th-century arcade that flanks the road up to the basilica for over half a kilometre. The church itself was largely rebuilt in the 18th century. It contains Veronese's *Supper of St Gregory the Great* (1572) in the refectory (ask to see it) as well as a moving *Pietà* by local boy Bartolomeo Montagna, and a fine collection of fossils in the cloister.

Teatro Olimpico

Piazza Matteotti 11 (0444 222 800). **Open** *June, July* 9am-7pm Tue-Sun; *Oct-Mar* 9am-5pm Tue-Sun. **Admission** by Biglietto unico (*see p259*).

Palladio's last masterpiece, the Teatro Olimpico was the first permanent indoor theatre built in Europe after the fall of the Roman Empire. Palladio got to work on designing the theatre in 1579 but died just before construction began the following year. His son Silla and star pupil Vincenzo Scamozzi completed the project, taking considerable liberties with the original blueprint. The decorative flamboyance of the wood-and-stucco theatre itself contrasts notably with its modest entrance and severe external walls. Built on the model of Greek and Roman theatres, it has 13 semi-circular wooden steps rising in front of the stage, crowned by Corinthian columns holding up an elaborate balustrade topped with elegant 'antique' sculpted figures. The permanent stage set, with its five elaborate *trompe l'oeil* street scenes, represents the city of Thebes in Sophocles' *Oedipus Rex*, which was the theatre's first performance, in 1585.

The elaborately frescoed antichambers to the theatre were also designed by Scamozzi and were used for meetings and smaller concerts of the Accademia Olimpica, the learned society of humanists that commissioned the place. Don't miss the *chiaroscuro* fresco in the entrance hall depicting a delegation of Japanese noblemen who visited Vicenza in 1585; their presence in Vicenza gives some idea of the city's enduring economic clout.

The theatre has only recently begun to realise its potential as a venue for plays and concerts. A season of classical dramas in September and October usually includes a staging of *Oedipus Rex* (in Italian), and may take in other Greek and Shakespearian tragedies. Concerts tend to be concentrated in May and June. For information, contact the tourist office (*see p262*). Tickets for shows can be bought in advance from Viarte, contrà San Marco 33 (0444 540 072), open 9.30am-12.30pm, 3-6.30pm Mon-Fri. Any tickets left on the night are sold directly at the theatre.

Where to eat & drink

The staple of the local cuisine is *baccalà alla vicentina* – stewed stockfish (dried cod), eaten with cornflour polenta. Game and poultry are firm favourites, especially grilled, and bean soups keep the cold and mist out of your marrow on raw winter evenings. Many of the best restaurants are to be found in the countryside around Vicenza.

Cinzia e Valerio

Piazzetta Porta Padova 65 (0444 505 213). **Meals served** 12.30-2.30pm, 8-10pm Tue-Sat; 12.30-2.30pm Sun. **Closed** Aug. **Average** L75,000. **Credit** AmEx, DC, MC, V.

Try to find the time to dine at Vicenza's best fish

restaurant: try their speciality fish risottos, spaghetti with shrimps, and *tagliolini* with various shellfish. The mixed fish grill is outstanding, and there is an excellent wine list.

Da Zamboni
Via Santa Croce 14, Arcugnano (0444 273 079).
Meals served 12.30-2pm, 7.30-9.30pm Wed-Sun.
Closed 2wks July, Aug. **Average** L50,000.
Credit DC, MC, V.
The ultimate *vicentino* Sunday lunch stop, in the Colli Berici hills, is a half-hour drive – or taxi ride – from the town centre. Chef Severino Trentin alternates local classics like *tagliatelle* in liver sauce with more creative offerings based on local meat, game, freshwater fish, mushrooms, truffles and garden produce. There is an excellent cheese board, and the desserts are calorific treats.

Ostaria Grottino
Piazza delle Erbe 2 (0444 320 138). **Open** 8.30am-2.30pm, 5pm-2am Tue-Sun. **Average** L30,000.
No credit cards.
This wine bar, which occupies part of the cellars of the Basilica Palladiana, could hardly be more central. The selection of wines by the glass stretches to more than 50 whites and as many reds; there is also a range of tasty cheeses and cured meats for lunch and dinner snacking.

Osteria Il Cursore
Stradella Pozzetto 10 (0444 323 504).
Meals served 10.30am-3pm, 6pm-1am Mon, Wed-Sun. **Closed** 1wk Feb, 3wks July, Aug.
Average L35,000. **Credit** MC, V.
This old-fashioned *vicentino* drinking den – a veritable hotbed of support for the local football team, Vicenza Calcio – is a great place to tune into the city's more working-class side over a glass of Valpolicella. For a quick snack there are various bar nibbles, otherwise, the kitchen turns out excellent versions of local specialities such as *bigoli con sugo di anatra* (fat spaghetti with duck sauce) or *baccalà alla vicentina*.

Pasticceria Sorarù
Piazzetta Palladio 17 (0444 320 915). **Open** 8.30am-1pm, 3.30-8pm Tue, Thur-Sun. **No credit cards.**
One of Italy's most charming *pasticcerie*, Sorarù is worth a look even if you don't have a sweet tooth. The columns, marble counters and ornate wooden shelves backed with mirrors are all 19th-century originals; the cakes, firmly in the Austro-Hungarian tradition, are a tad fresher. Sit at outside tables in summer drinking coffee as you gaze across to the basilica.

Remo
Via Ca' Impenta 14 (0444 911 007).
Meals served noon-2.30pm, 8-10.30pm Tue-Sat.
Closed Aug, 23 Dec-6 Jan. **Average** L65,000.
Credit AmEx, DC, MC, V.
Situated in an old farmhouse a little to the east of Vicenza, this country restaurant offers some of the best cooking anywhere in the Vicenza area. The trolley of boiled and roasted meats is a fixture, and Remo's *baccalà alla vicentina* is spectacular. Excellent sweets and house wine.

Where to stay

Hotels are not Vicenza's strong point: the bleak anonymous suburbs offer bleak, anonymous, business-oriented accommodation, and in the centre there are slim pickings. Better to stay in the surrounding countryside, where there are some charming country-house hotels.

Camping Vicenza
Strada Pelosa 239 (0444 582 311/fax 0444 582 434). **Rates** L18,000-24,000 camper; L9,000-13,000 tent; L8,000-11,000 per person. **Credit** AmEx, DC, MC, V.
Situated near the Vicenza Est exit of the Milan-Venice motorway, this upmarket campsite is well-equipped; but it's a serious hike from the city centre.

Hotel Castello
Contrà piazza Castello 24 (0444 323 585/fax 0444 323 583). **Rates** L190,000 single; L250,000 double.
Credit DC, MC, V.
Comfortable, unpretentious hotel with 1980s-style interiors, in the city centre close to corso Palladio and all the main sights.

Hotel Giardini
Viale Giuriolo 10 (tel/fax 0444 326 458).
Rates L160,000 single; L220,000 double.
Credit AmEx, DC, MC, V.
Small, comfortable, modern hotel, located across piazza Matteotti from Palladio's Teatro Olimpico (*see p260*).

Hotel Palladio
Via Oratorio Dei Servi 25 (0444 321 072/fax 0444 547 328). **Rates** L110,000 single; L130,000 double.
Credit AmEx, DC, MC, V.
Close to piazza Dei Signori and the Teatro Olimpico (*see p260*), this unassuming but friendly little hotel occupies a 16th-century palazzo.

Ostello della gioventù (Youth Hostel)
Via Giuriolo 7/9 (0444 540 222/fax 0444 547 762).
Rates L27,000. **No credit cards.**
This central youth hostel, just across from the Teatro Olimpico (*see p260*), has 86 beds, which can be booked in advance by phone. Bicycles are available for hire.

Resources

Getting there & getting around

By train
There are regular trains to and from Venice (55 mins) and Verona (30 mins).

Palladio's **Villa Rotonda**, officially the Villa Almerico-Capra Valmarana. *See p232.*

See p232.

By bus
FTV (0444 223 115) buses run from Padua
to Vicenza, and serve most towns and villages
in Vicenza province. The terminus is by the
railway station.

By car
Take the A4 La Serenissima motorway from Venice
or Padua towards Milan.

Tourist information

Azienda Provinciale di Turismo
*Piazza Matteotti 12 (tel/fax 0444 320 854/
www.ascom.vi.it/aptvicenza).* **Open** 9am-1pm,
2.30-6pm Mon-Sat; 9am-1pm Sun.

Around Vicenza

Although architect Andrea Palladio and
his stunning creations are undoubtedly the
biggest single draw for visitors to the area
surrounding Vicenza (*see chapter* **Palladian
Villas**), don't let his overwhelming presence
blind you to the pretty towns, restored villas
by other architects and all the beautiful
countryside nearby.

Marostica

The little walled town of Marostica is
famous for its human chess game, featuring
real-live pieces: horses and kings, queens,
bishops, knights and soldiers in medieval
garb. Competitions take place on the vast
red and white marble chess board in piazza
Castello, Marostica's main square, every
even-numbered year, usually in September
(see tourist information below for information
and bookings). The pageant was invented in
1923 as a ploy to bring in more tourists; it
commemorates the chess match played by two
15th-century noblemen over who should win the
hand of Leonora, the castle guardian's beautiful
daughter. Chess aside, Marostica is one of the
most perfectly preserved medieval towns in
the Veneto, with a fine (and walkable) stretch
of rampart between the Castello Superiore and
the Castello Inferiore.

Villas around Vicenza

Below is a selection of the most important
country villas in Vicenza province, all of
which testify to the lasting influence of

Andrea Palladio. For villas in which the local architect actually had a hand, *see* *chapter* **Palladian Villas**.

Unless otherwise indicated, buses leave from the FTV terminal in front of Vicenza railway station.

Villa Cordellina Lombardi
Via Lovara 36, Montecchio Maggiore (0444 696 085). Bus to Recoaro. **Open** *Apr-mid Oct* 9am-1pm Tue-Fri; 9am-noon, 3-6pm Sat, Sun. **Closed** mid Oct-Mar. **Admission** L5,000. **No credit cards**.
This beautifully restored villa, built between 1735 and 1760 in the grand Palladian style, contains some flamboyant frescos by Giambattista Tiepolo. Painted in 1743, they include one of the painter's favourite Enlightenment allegories, *The Light of Reason Driving out the Fog of Ignorance*. There is also a charming French-style park and garden.

Villa Pisani Ferri 'Rocca Pisana'
Via Rocca 1, Lonigo (0444 831 104). Bus to Lonigo. **Open** *Apr-Nov* 10am-noon, 3-6pm Wed, Fri, Sun. **Admission** L10,000. **No credit cards**.
This magnificent villa perched on a high hill was designed in 1576 on the ruins of a medieval castle by the architect Vincenzo Scamozzi, Palladio's star pupil. Like La Rotonda (*see p232*), La Rocca has four main windows facing the four points of the compass, and a dome with a hole at the top. But whereas the Rotonda hole is covered with glass, and was conceived to allow light into the building, the hole at the Rocca is open, like the Pantheon in Rome, allowing air to circulate on hot summer days.

Villa Trissino Marzotto
Piazza GG Trissino 2, Trissino (0445 962 029/fax 0445 962 090). Bus to Recoaro. **Open** *by appointment* 9am-noon, 2.30-5pm Mon-Fri. **Admission** *garden* L10,000; *villa* L10,000. **No credit cards**.
This elaborate complex, consisting of two villas (the lower one a romantic ruin), is set in one of the most charming of Italy's private parks. The upper villa and the park were designed by Francesco Muttoni between 1718 and 1722. The garden is a typically 18th-century mixture of art and nature, in which allegorical statues frame tree-lined walks; the lower villa – destroyed by lightning in 1841 – acts as a theatrical focal point.

Villa Valmarana ai Nani
Via dei Nani 2-8, Vicenza (0444 543 976/0444 544 546). Bus 8 from viale Roma. **Open** *Mar, Apr* 10am-noon Thur, Sat, Sun; 2.30-5.30pm Tue-Sun. *May-Sept* 10am-noon Thur, Sat, Sun; 3-6pm Tue-Sun. *Oct, Nov* 10am-noon Thur, Sat, Sun; 2-5pm Tue-Sun. **Admission** L10,000. **No credit cards**.
This delightful villa, exuding elegance and urbanity, was designed by Antonio Muttoni in 1688; it still belongs to the Valmarana family. For once it's the interior that is the main attraction, thanks to a remarkable series of frescos painted by Giambattista Tiepolo and his son Giandomenico in 1757.

The father's airy flights of fancy in the main block, known as La Palazzina, are as transcendental as ever. Giandomenico's *chinoiserie* decoration of the *Foresteria* offer a melancholy take on Arcadian pleasures. The statues of dwarfs (*nani*) lining the wall to the right of the main villa are not a sign of the family's lack of taste; they bear witness instead to the sensitivity of a Valmarana father who wished to comfort his own dwarf child by giving him friendly familiars to gaze on.

Where to eat & sleep

In Marostica, stay with the chess theme at the **Dama Bianca**, or 'white queen' (via Montello 16/C, 0424 470 239; closed Wed & Aug; average L40,000), which offers excellent, reasonably priced country cooking.

Serious hikers should ring ahead to book a bunk at the **Rifugio General Papa** (0445 630 233; open 20 June-20 Sept daily; 30 May-20 June, 20 Sept-15 Nov Sat, Sun; rates L60,000 half board), a refuge on nearby Monte Pasubio which also provides filling meals.

To turn a visit to the Villa Trissino Marzotto into an indulgence, dine at **Ca' Masieri** (località Masieri, restaurant 0445 962 100, hotel 0445 490 122, closed Sun, Mon lunch, average L90,000), 2 kilometres (1.25 miles) west of Trissino town. This charming 18th-century stone relais offers serious meat, game and fish cooking at fairly serious prices; it also has 12 rooms and suites (L160,000 single; L220,000 double), and a swimming pool.

For the ultimate gastro-treat, head for the village of Montecchio Precalcino, 15 kilometres (9.5 miles) north of Vicenza, where the Michelin-starred Locanda da Piero (via Roma 32/33; 0445 864 827; closed Sun, Mon lunch, Sat lunch, 2 wks in Jan, Aug; average L80,000) does a cordon bleu take on the local tradition; as splash-outs go, it's good value for money.

Resources

Getting there

By bus
All destinations are served by FTV buses which leave from the main terminal outside Vicenza train station; ring 0444 223 115 for timetable information. For Monte Pasubio and the Rifugio General Papa, take the bus to Pian di Fugazze.

Tourist information

Associazione Pro Marostica
Piazza Castello 1, Marostica (0424 72127/fax 0424 72800/www.telemar.it/marostica.htm). **Open** 9am-noon, 3-6pm daily.

North from Venice

Head north for *grappa*, Benetton HQ, *prosecco* and triumph over the Dolomites.

North from Venice lies a world of extremes: there are elbow-to-elbow-deckchair seaside resorts; ugly, industry-plagued plains; and the soaring fastnesses of the snow-capped Dolomites, which hold an irresistible attraction for earnest trekkers and mink-swathed society skiers alike. Least known – and least visited – of all, perhaps, is the landscape of rolling hills, olive groves, vineyards, orchards and ancient walled towns in the unspoilt foothills of the Dolomites.

North-west from Venice

The pleasant medieval town of **Castelfranco Veneto**, surrounded by moats and a 13th-century fortified red-brick wall, is famous as the birthplace of the painter, Giorgione (*see p35*).

The **cathedral** (open 9am-noon, 3-6pm daily) is home to one of his few surviving masterpieces, a *Madonna and Child With Saints*. That's about it for the sights of Castelfranco; on piazza Duomo, the **Casa Giorgione** (open 9am-12.30pm, 3-6pm Tue-Sun, admission L2,500) – the artist's birthplace – will only be of interest to committed fans.

Dominated by the broad outline of Monte Grappa, picturesque **Bassano del Grappa** sits astride the Brenta river. The scene of fierce fighting between Italian and Austrian troops at the end of World War I, it has an austere war memorial and **museum** at the top of the mountain.

But the austerity stops there, for Bassano is one of the wealthiest towns in Italy, famous for its ceramics and fiery spirit, *grappa*. Now extremely fashionable, *grappa* was born out of hardship as the simplest, cheapest form of alcohol. After the grapes have been pressed, the material left over is known as *vinaccia*, or pommace. While the wine is fermenting, the pommace is left in silos to mature for one to two months. Then begins the process of distillation, the pommace is heated until an alcoholic vapour is given off, which, when cooled, produces the clear liquid *grappa*. The oldest and most famous name in *grappa* is Nardini , a company that has been in operation since 1779.

Bassano is built around two main squares, **piazza Garibaldi** and **piazza Libertà**, both of which fill up with stalls each Thursday and Saturday morning for a lively fruit and vegetable market.

On piazza Garibaldi is the **Museo Civico** (*see below*), housed in the beautiful convent and cloistered gardens of the 14th-century church of San Francesco. The museum contains a fine collection of Bassano ceramics and an archaeological section devoted to the city's Roman origins. It also has a selection of works by the local-born 16th-century artist Jacopo da Ponte – known as Jacopo Bassano (1510-92) – and by sculptor Antonio Canova.

Piazza Libertà is dominated by the medieval **Palazzo Municipale**, covered with faded frescos. A short walk up the hill is Bassano's showpiece, the **Ponte degli Alpini**. Though the original bridge was probably constructed in the 1150s, what we see now is a faithful copy of Palladio's magnificent covered wooden bridge built in 1586. The copy dates back no further than 1948, Palladio's having been blown up by retreating German troops at the end of World War II. At one end of the bridge stands the **Museo degli Alpini** (*see below*), with its collection of World War I memorabilia. Perched on the bridge is the family-run **Bottega Nardini** (*see below*), where the local *grappa* can be consumed on the premises or taken away.

Bottega Nardini
Ponte Vecchio 2, Bassano (0424 227 741). **Open** *Oct-May* 8am-8pm Tue-Sun. *June-Sept* 8am-8pm daily. **Credit** AmEx, MC, V.

Museo Civico
Piazza Garibaldi, Bassano (0424 522 235). **Open** 10am-6.30pm Tue-Sat; 3.30-6.30pm Sun. **Admission** L7,000; L4,000 concessions. **No credit cards**.

Museo degli Alpini
Via Angarano 2, Bassano (0424 503 662). **Open** 8.30am-8pm Tue-Sun. **Admission** free.

Where to stay & eat

In Bassano, **Birraria Ottone** (via Matteotti 50, 0424 522 206, closed Mon pm & Tue, average L45,000) is an excellent restaurant serving mainly regional and Austrian dishes. **Trattoria del Borgo** (via Margnan 7, 0424 522 2155, closed Wed, average L35,000) is good value. The town's top hotel is **Il Belvedere** (piazzale Giardino 14, 0424 529 845, L130,000-L255,000), while **Al Castello** (piazza Terraglio 20, 0424 228 665, L80,000-L140,000) is a reasonably priced three-star.

The Veneto

The centre of **Treviso** is laced with tranquil canals.

Getting there

By car
The SS245 from Venice-Mestre passes through Castelfranco to Bassano.

By train
Frequent Venice-Bassano trains also stop at Castelfranco.

By bus
La Marca (0422 577 311) run services from Treviso to Castelfranco and Bassano.

Tourist information

APT
Largo Corona d'Italia 35, Bassano (0424 524 351/fax 0424 525 301/infotour.bassano@ tiscalinet.it). **Open** 9am-12.30pm, 2-5pm Mon-Fri; 9am-12.30pm Sat.

Pro Loco
Via Francesco Maria Preti 39, Castelfranco (0423 495 000/fax 0423 720 760/cfrproloco@tiscalinet.it). **Open** 8.30am-12.30pm, 3-7pm Mon-Fri; 8.30am-12.30pm, 3.30-6.30pm Sat; 9am-12.30pm, 3-6pm Sun.

Treviso

Treviso is a city of meandering waterways, frescoed mansions and Renaissance churches, large sections of which were painstakingly rebuilt after devastating bombing at the end of World War II. It's also the heart of north-east Italy's booming economy. And at the forefront of Treviso's economic miracle is the Benetton clothing empire, which is based here.

It is a vibrant, wealthy place, with plenty of shopping and nightlife to supplement its historic attractions. The lion of Venice is very much in evidence around the city, but Treviso was already well established in Roman times, long before it came under the control of the

Venetian Republic in 1389. The city's early Gothic buildings testify to its vibrant pre-Venetian history, as do the wonderful frescos of Tommaso da Modena, considered by some to be the greatest 14th-century artist after Giotto.

Treviso is surrounded by walls built by the Venetians and has three 16th-century gates, the **porta San Tomaso** being the most impressive. It's bordered on one side by the river Sile; the town is a maze of tiny willow-fringed canals. At the centre lies piazza dei Signori, which is dominated by the **Palazzo dei Trecento**, the ancient town hall, dating back to 1217 but heavily restored. In piazza San Vito are two medieval churches, **San Vito** and **Santa Lucia** (both open 9-11.45am, 4-6pm daily), with splendid frescos by Da Modena. More works by this artist, including his masterpiece *The Life of Saint Ursula*, are tucked away in the deconsecrated church of **Santa Caterina** in piazza Giacomo Matteotti (closed to the public). However, for a fresco fest, head to the church of **San Francesco** (open 9am-noon, 4-6pm daily) with beautiful works by Da Modena and colleagues. Work on the main chapel's ceiling, including the wonderful *Saint Francis with Stigmata* and the four Evangelists in studious mode, is by an anonymous 14th-century painter, though some argue that this, too, should be attributed to Da Modena.

The **Duomo** (open 9am-noon, 3-6pm daily) contains an *Annunciation* by Titian (1570) and a beautiful *Adoration of the Magi* by Pordenone (1520). The Romanesque-Gothic church of **San Nicolò** (open 9am-noon, 3-6pm daily) has interesting tombs, including one framed by pageboys frescoed by Lorenzo Lotto. Da Modena pops up yet again in the chapter house of the adjoining Dominican **monastery** (open 8am-6pm daily) with a remarkable series of frescos; one of the 40 *studiosi* represented is wearing the first pair of glasses depicted in art.

Works attributed to Titian and Lorenzo Lotto grace the **Museo Civico** (*see below*), while one-off exhibitions are held in the privately run Casa dei Carraresi in via Palestra.

Museo Civico

Borgo Cavour 24 (0422 591 337). **Open** 9am-12.30pm, 2.30-5pm Tue-Sat; 9am-noon Sun. **Admission** L3,000; L1,000-L2,000 concessions.

Where to stay & eat

Toni del Spin (via Inferiore 7, 0422 543829, closed Mon lunch, Sun, average L35,000) is a pretty, intimate *osteria* serving local specialities at reasonable prices. **Alfredo el Toula** (via Collalto 26, 0422 540 275, closed Mon, Sun dinner, average L100,000) is Treviso's gastronomic shrine. **Osteria Trevisi** (vicolo Trevisi 6, 0422 545308, closed Sun) serves great wines and bar snacks. Hotels are scarce in the town centre. One of the best bets is the **Campeol** (piazza Ancilotto 4, 0422 56601, rates L90,000-L135,000).

Getting there

By car

Take the Treviso Sud exit from the A27 motorway; alternatively, take the SS13 from Venice-Mestre.

By train

Regular Venice-Treviso services (25mins).

By bus

ACTV and ATVO buses run regularly from Venice's bus terminus in piazzale Roma.

Tourist information

APT

Piazza Monte di Pietà 8 (0422 547 632/fax 0422 419 092/www.sevenonline.it/tvapt/tvapt@ sevenonline.it). **Open** 9am-noon, 3-6pm Mon-Sat.

The Veneto

North from Treviso

Surrounded by hills and valleys rich with vineyards, **Conegliano** is the perfect place to base yourself for a few days of serious wine tasting, standing as it does at the junction of two *strade del vino*. The **Strada del Vino Rosso** ventures into the flat Piave valley to the south-east, home of reds such as Cabernet Franc, Cabernet Sauvignon and the indigenous Raboso, while the **Strada del Prosecco** – Italy's first oenological route, founded in 1966 – wends its fizzy way westwards towards Valdobbiadene (*see p268* **Prosecco**). Conegliano is also the site of Italy's first wine school, founded in 1876.

Since 1969, this has been an area of DOC Prosecco and Cartizze production, with over 3,000 producers. The breathtaking combination of natural beauty and medieval architecture scattered across this zone make it a worthwhile visit even for non-imbibers of the local bubbly. The Strada del Prosecco is best visited by car, but a regular bus service plies the route between Conegliano and Valdobbiadene (*see p269*).

Conegliano's 14th-century **duomo** is home to a painting of the *Virgin and Child With Saints and Angels* by the town's most famous son, Giambattista Cima, known as Cima da Conegliano.

Conegliano's cultural treasures end there, but visit the **Sala dei Battuti** (open Apr-Sept 3.30-7pm Sun, Oct-Mar 3-6.30pm Sun) next to the duomo: dedicated to a brotherhood of flagellants, it's decorated with some truly odd 15th- and 16th-century biblical frescos.

Copies of Cima's paintings can be surveyed in the **Casa-Museo del Cima** (*see p268*). A rebuilt tenth-century castle contains the **Museo Civico** (*see p268*), which allows beautiful views from the roof.

To the west of Conegliano, the stunning **Abbazia di Santa Maria** at Follina (0438 970 231, open 9am-12.30pm, 2.30-6pm daily) is part-Romanesque, part-Gothic. Six kilometres (3.5 miles) south-west of Conegliano, **Susegana** is dominated by the 14th-century **Castello di San Salvatore**, a perfect example of a walled fortress-village.

The town of **Vittorio Veneto** sprang to life in 1866 when the smaller towns of Ceneda and Serravalle were united and renamed to mark the unification of Italy under King

Beautiful, medieval **Belluno**. *See p267.*

Carlo Scarpa

When Palladianism palls and you're craving modernity, seek out the quintessentially Venetian architect Carlo Scarpa.

Born in the lagoon city in 1906 (he died in Japan in 1978 after falling down a flight of temple steps), Scarpa was imbued with his city's traditional fascination with the East, and with a desire to fuse ancient and modern in functional but striking spaces.

After completing his architectural studies at Venice's Academy of Fine Arts in the early 1920s, Scarpa began lecturing at the Istituto Universitario di Architettura di Venezia, luring students back to what had been a flagging faculty with his gift for informal, intimate communication. He would continue to lecture there until 1976, becoming the institute's director in 1972-4.

But Scarpa's interests ranged far beyond architecture. He was also artistic director of Venini glass producers (1933-47), his many stunning creations demonstrating his interest in Eastern culture and design. From 1948, he collaborated with the Venice Biennale, revolutionising the art of exhibiting with his extraordinary use of colours, textures and light.

Scarpa's pet hate was what he termed 'architectural habit'. His projects were all experimental; he delighted in using new materials, and discovering their creative limitations. This desire to question

constraints and be timeless is evident in the fragmentary nature of his work: distortions and contradictions abound. His use of natural elements as raw material and his eye for combining inner and outer space are a Scarpa trademark.

Examples of this abound in the Veneto. His designs can be seen in the following places:

Venice
Museo della Fondazione Scientifica Querini Stampalia (*see p90*).
Olivetti showroom, piazza San Marco (041 523 5955).
Entrance to the Architecture Institute (IUAV), Santa Croce 191, campo dei Tolentini (041 529 7711).

Verona
Museo Castelvecchio (*see p249*).
Banca Popolare di Verona, piazza Nogara 2 (045 8675 111).

Near Belluno
Chiesa Villaggio ENI, Borca di Cadore (*see p268*).

Possagno
Gipsoteca Canoviana (*see p270*).

Near Possagno
Tomba Monumentale Brion, San Vito di Altivole Cemetery (*see p269*). Scarpa is buried here.

Vittorio Emanuele II. An Italian victory here over the Austrians in World War I is celebrated at the **Museo della Battaglia** (*see p268*), located inside the 16th-century Loggia Cenedese in the Ceneda part of town. Old Serravalle, with its frescoed *palazzi*, is the town's prettiest area.

The town boasts a minor work by Titian over the altar in the **Duomo** (open 8am-noon, 4.30-6.30pm daily), but there's little else to detain the tourist. It is, however, a good jumping-off point for the **Bosco di Cansiglio**, a beautiful area of thickly forested lakes and hills little frequented by tourists and perfect for trekking. There are plenty of reasonable hotels and some wonderful restaurants, serving wild venison and boar, home-cured sausages and mushrooms fresh from the forest.

Belluno, a medieval town perched high in the mountains, overlooks the swirling confluence of two rivers, the Piave and the Ardo. Beyond loom giant, jagged Dolomite

peaks. Many people head straight to the ski slopes or trek off in summer to high mountain refuges, but Belluno itself has enough sights to merit a stopover.

Although it spent a long period under the influence of Venice, and later Austria, the town dates back to Roman times, when it was an important centre along the route to the limestone quarries in the mountains.

Some well-preserved arcaded Renaissance houses and the 15th-century **Palazzo dei Rettori**, where Belluno's Venetian rulers lived, border the piazza Mercato, where the 12th-century **Torre Civica** is all that remains of the town's medieval castle. The 16th-century **Duomo** (open 7am-noon, 3-7pm daily) offers panoramic views over the dramatic surrounding countryside from its baroque bell-tower. The **Baptistery** (open 8am-noon, 3-7pm daily) by the Duomo contains a carving of John the Baptist by Andrea Brustolon.

If you're heading into the mountains from here, go west for the jet-set capital of the Dolomites, **Cortina d'Ampezzo** – beautiful, but expensive – stopping off on your way at **Borca di Cadore** to check out Carlo Scarpa's amazing church (open 9am-noon, 4-6pm daily; *see also p267* **Carlo Scarpa**) built in 1959.

Borca itself is a time-warp experience. Constructed by the state-owned ENI fuel company as a holiday camp for its sickly workers, this village has remained virtually unchanged since the 1950s. If you're looking for a mountain retreat that doesn't resemble Heidi's homestead, check in to one of the village apartments or main hotel. To book, contact the Centro Vacanze at Borca di Cadore (Gestione Gestitur, on the Strada Statale 51, 0435 487 500, www.gestitur.it, open 8.30am-12.30pm, 2-6pm Mon-Fri). They can also put you in touch with the priest with the keys to the Scarpa church. North of Belluno is the spectacular **Cadore valley**, birthplace of Titian and favourite vacation destination of Pope John Paul II.

Casa-Museo del Cima

Via Cima 24, Conegliano (0438 21660). **Open** *Apr-Sept* 3.30-7pm Sat, Sun. *Oct-Mar* 3-6.30pm Sat, Sun. **Admission** L3,000; L1,000 concessions. **No credit cards**.

Museo Civico

Piazzale Castelvecchio 8, Conegliano (0438 22871). **Open** *Apr-Sept* 10am-noon, 3.30-7pm Tue-Sun. *Oct-Mar* 10am-12.30pm, 3-6.30pm Tue-Sun. **Closed** Nov. **Admission** L3,000; L2,000 concessions. **No credit cards**.

Museo della Battaglia

Piazza Giovanni Paolo I, Vittorio Veneto (0438 57695). **Open** *May-Sept* 10am-noon, 4-6.30pm Tue-Sun. *Oct-Apr* 10am-noon, 2-5pm Tue-Sun. **Admission** L5,000. **No credit cards**.

Where to stay & eat

Conegliano

For good value local cuisine, try the **Trattoria Stella** (via Accademia 3, 0438 22178, closed Sun, average L40,000). Alternatively, for something more upmarket, head for **Ristorante Salisà** (via XX Settembre 2, 0438 0438 24288, closed Tue pm & Wed, average L70,000) and indulge in a bottle from their excellent wine list. On the same street, lined with bars and restaurants, is the **Hotel Canon d'Oro** (via XX Settembre 129, 0438 34246, L85,000-L150,000).

Vittorio Veneto

The **Leon d'Oro** hotel (via Cavour 8, 0438 940 740, L80,000-L100,000) is a short walk from the Duomo.

Prosecco

Sheltered from cold northerlies by the Dolomites, and enjoying warmer air sweeping up the Adriatic, the *prosecco* grape – a native Veneto variety – grown between Conegliano and Valdobbiadene is used to fill some 28 million bottles annually. Great soil and easily drained hills exposed to the summer sun after the spring rains all contribute to the *prosecco* magic. If the fizzy version of the popular dry *aperitivo* wine with a slightly bitter aftertaste is best known, the bubble-free *spento* is just as delicious, and an ideal accompaniment to Venetian *cicheti* (*see p159*).

From the cooler Cartizze subzone comes another bubbly: slightly sweeter than its more famous cousin, Cartizze has a more concentrated flavour and aroma.

WHERE TO BUY AND TASTE

Luigi Gregoletto produces a good *prosecco* in Premaor di Miane (via San Martino 1, 0438 970 463). For something more sophisticated try the special-cru Cartizze prosecco produced by the Azienda Bisol (via Fol 33, 0423 900 138) in the village of Santo Stefano. Call to make an appointment before visiting.

Belluno

The rustic **Al Borgo** restaurant (via Anconetta 8, 0437 926 755, closed Mon pm & Tue, average L35,000) offers smoked ham and sausages, and unusual pasta dishes that are so filling you're unlikely to make it to the main course. For accommodation try the friendly, centrally located **Hotel alle Dolomiti** (via Carrera 46, 0437 941 660, L85,000-L130,000).

Getting there

By car

From Treviso take the SS13 to Conegliano, then the SS51 to Vittorio Veneto and Belluno. The three towns can also be reached by the A27 motorway.

By train

Fast Venice-Udine trains stop at Conegliano; local Venice-Belluno trains call at all three towns.

By bus

Services from Venice's piazzale Roma to Belluno run during the summer season, stopping at Conegliano and Vittorio Veneto. La Marca (0422 577 311) runs services from Treviso's bus station to the three towns.

Tourist information

For information on ski resorts in the region, consult www.dolomitisuperski.it.

APT

Via XX Settembre 61, Conegliano (0438 21230/fax 0438 428 777). **Open** *May-Oct* 3.30-6.30pm Tue; 9am-1pm, 3.30-6.30pm Wed-Sat. *Nov-Apr* 9am-1pm, 3-6pm Tue-Fri; 9am-1pm Sat.
Provides brochures on the Strada del Vino and will organise visits to the surrounding vineyards.

APT

Piazza del Popolo 18, Vittorio Veneto (0438 57243/ fax 0438 53629). **Open** 9am-1pm, 3-6pm Mon-Sat.

APT

Piazza dei Martiri 7, Belluno (0437 940 083/fax 0437 940 073/www.dolomiti.it/apt). **Open** *Sept-June* 9am-12.30pm, 3-6pm Mon-Sat; 10am-12.30pm Sun. *July, Aug* 9am-12.30pm, 3-6pm Mon-Sat; 10am-12.30pm, 3.30-6.30pm Sun.

North-west from Treviso

If you are seduced by the medieval town of **Asolo**, surrounded by a picture-postcard landscape of rolling hills covered with cypress trees, olive groves and vineyards, you're not the first. Robert Browning fell so deeply in love with Asolo that he named a collection of his poems, *Asolando* (1889), after the town. In 1489 the exiled Venetian-born Queen of Cyprus, Caterina Cornaro, established her illustrious court here. In the 19th century, it was the famed actress, Eleonora Duse, who set up a more decadent circle, gathering intellectuals, musicians and artists around her.

Asolo has steep, narrow cobbled lanes lined with Renaissance *palazzi* – some with frescoed façades – and Gothic arcades. This is not a place for serious sightseeing; settle instead for a lazy day of window-shopping at chic boutiques, glasses of wine in a cool *osteria*, and a long post-prandial walk in the countryside.

Every second weekend of the month, the 15th-century piazza Maggiore is turned into a giant open-air antiques market, but unless you're on a big-budget holiday you may have to settle for just rummaging.

The tiny village of **Possagno** was the birthplace of Antonio Canova, whose marble statues were imbued with the spirit of neo-classicism. His busts have been slammed as precursors of Totalitarian Art. Fans hail him as the greatest sculptor since Michelangelo.

Canova certainly left his mark here: on a rise above his native town sits an imposing Doric temple known simply as **Il Tempio di Canova** – an unwieldy neo-classical version of Rome's Pantheon.

Window-shop at chic boutiques in **Asolo**.

The sculptor also left a more welcome gift: the contents of the fascinating **Gipsoteca** (*see p270*), a museum housed in Canova's family home. Evidence of the man's obsession with accuracy can be seen in the *remore*, tiny nails with concave heads that were used to plot the proportions of the model, so that the same cast could be used to produce various marble copies.

A more modern gem is Carlo Scarpa's (*see p267*) extension to the Gipsoteca, built between 1955 and 1957. Scarpa's dramatic use of natural light brings Canova's statues to life. For further Scarpa treats, head out of Possagno by car or bus towards Castelfranco. At **San Vito d'Altivole**'s cemetery (open 9am-7pm daily) is a huge monument, the Tomba Brion: it's 2,200 square metres of pure Scarpa, who spent over nine years (1969-78) constructing this monster.

The 40 kilometres (25 miles) of spectacular valleys from **Valdobbiadene** to Conegliano (*see 266*) contain vineyards growing not only Prosecco (*see p268*), but also Merlot, Chardonnay, and many more varieties. They also contain a host of producers keen to let you taste and buy.

The last major settlement on the Piave River before reaching the Dolomites, **Feltre** was a Roman fortress. The perfectly preserved 16th-century town owes its splendours to the munificence of Venice, which financed a sumptuous rebuilding programme after its stout ally was razed to the ground in 1510 by the troops of the Holy Roman Emperor Maximilian I.

Paintings and statues of the lion of St Mark, symbol of the Most Serene Republic of Venice, are just about everywhere. The **piazza Maggiore** is the ancient centre of the city. Many of the *palazzi* along Feltre's high street, via Mezzaterra, are frescoed by local artist Lorenzo Luzzo (1467-1512). Frescos on simple merchants' houses down the town's narrow alleyways are often just as striking. More works by Luzzo – known as the 'dead man of Feltre' because of his waxy complexion – can be admired in the **Museo Civico** (*see p270*). This also houses a small collection of artefacts charting Feltre's Roman and Etruscan roots.

Gipsoteca Canoviana

Piazza Canova 84, Possagno (0423 544 323). **Open** *May-Sept* 9am-noon, 3-6pm Tue-Sun. *Oct-Apr* 9am-noon, 2-5pm Tue-Sun. **Admission** L6,000; L4,000 concessions. **No credit cards**.

Museo Civico

Via Lorenzo Luzzo 23, Feltre (0439 885 241). **Open** *Nov-Mar* 10am-1pm, 3-6pm Tue-Sun. *Apr-Oct* 4-7pm Tue-Sun. **Admission** L8,000; L3,000 concessions; free under-6s. **No credit cards**.

Where to eat & drink

Asolo

Try a Tintoretto – the local brew, sparkling prosecco wine (*see p268*) and pomegranate juice – or a delicious ice-cream on the terrace of the venerable **Caffè Centrale** (via Roma 72, 0423 952 141, www.caffecentrale.com, closed Tue). The **Enoteca alle Ore** (via Browning 185, 0423 952 070, closed Mon & 3wks Jan) has an extensive selection of regional wines, while for more elaborate local dishes, try **Ca' Derton** (piazza D'Annunzio 11, 0423 529 648, closed Mon, Sun dinner & 2wks Aug, average L60,000).

The elegant **Villa Cipriani** (via Canova 298, 0423 523 411, L360,000-L760,000) is the perfect place for a romantic stopover, while the **Hotel Duse** (via Browning 190, 0423 55 241, L85,000-L250,000) is a perfectly clean, comfortable three-star alternative.

Possagno

Forget restaurants and hotels in tourist-oriented Possagno itself, and head two kilometres (1.25 miles) east to Cavaso del Tomba, where there is an excellent hotel, **Locanda Alla Posta** (piazza XIII Martiri 13, 0423 543 112, L55,000-L90,000). It has a lively bar and good restaurant (closed Wed pm & Thur, average L45,000).

Valdobbiadene

Valdobbiadene itself has little to grab your attention, but if you haven't already imbibed enough, make up for it at the friendly **Bar**

Alpino (via Piva 25, 0423 972 122, closed Fri), which stocks over 30 different makes of the local laughing juice, plus a great selection of snacks.

Feltre

The venerable **Osteria da Piero Ostia** (via Tofana 4, 0439 2478, closed Sun, 2wks Sept) is a good spot for a glass of wine, while **Osteria Mezzaterra** (via Mezzaterra 5, 0439 89020) is a funkier late-night venue. The **Trattoria al Cappello** (via Monte Tomatico 4, 0439 2350, closed Sat, average L30,000) is a down-to-earth and friendly spot, with great home-made *gnocchi* and puds.

Getting there

By car

The SS348 goes from Treviso to Feltre; Asolo, Possagno and Valdobbiadene are short distances off the SS348 on marked minor roads.

By train

Local services from Treviso to Fener-Valdobbiadene, Pederobba-Possagno and Feltre.

By bus

La Marca (0422 577 311) runs services from Treviso to Asolo, Castelfranco, Possagno, Feltre and Valdobbiadene.

Tourist information

APT

Piazza G D'Annunzio 3, Asolo (0423 529 046/fax 0423 524 137). **Open** 10am-noon, 4-7pm Mon-Sat.

APT

Piazzetta Trento e Trieste 9, Feltre (0439 2540/ fax 0439 2839). **Open** 9am-12.30pm, 3-6pm Mon-Sat; 9am-12.30pm Sun.

Pro Loco

Viale Canova 11, Possagno (tel/fax 0423 544 423). **Open** 9am-noon, 3-6pm Tue-Sun.

East towards Trieste

A quiet backwater today, **Aquileia** was once one of the most important cities in the Roman Empire, with a population of more than 100,000. Legend has it that an eagle (*aquila*) soared overhead as the outline of the new town was being ploughed up in 181 BC, giving it its name. Emperor Augustus met Herod the Great here in 10 BC. In the fourth century Aquileia became one of Italy's most important patriarchates, but constant harrying by Barbarian tribes forced the bishop to shift his residence to nearby Grado. The town passed into Venetian control in 1420, then Austrian in 1509.

The 11th-century **Basilica Teodoriana** (open 7am-7pm daily) contains 700 square metres of mosaic paving dating back to the fourth century, with a mishmash of imagery both Christian (Jonah and the whale, the Good Shepherd) and pagan (tortoises and cockerels). In the apse, frescos dated 1031 show the patriarch Poppo, who founded the basilica in the 11th century, with Emperor Conrad II and his wife and son before the Virgin Mary. Twelfth-century frescos depicting the lives of Christ and Mary are to be found in the **Crypt** beneath the presbytery (entrance by **Museo Archeologico** ticket, *see below*). The Roman **ruins** nearby – and the **Museo Paleocristiano** – give some idea of Aquileia's past.

For a few days of sea and sun, **Grado** is a far better bet than either Venice's cramped Lido or the tacky, downmarket Lido di Jesolo. It's an hour and a half east of Venice on the Venice-Trieste motorway; there are also occasional steamers to and from Trieste between March and September. As at any Italian beach resort, the serried ranks of umbrellas and matching deck chairs set up – and charged for – by local bathing clubs are unavoidable. But to compensate, Grado has a superb location – at the tip of a curving spit of land, between a dreamy lagoon and the Adriatic sea – and its old town centre and fishing port haven't yet been swallowed up by ghastly modern hotels.

Grado was founded by inhabitants of Aquileia fleeing the Barbarian invasions; others kept on going until they reached the Venetian lagoon, where they became the settlers of Venice's first urban centre on Torcello (*see p139*).

Aquileia, quieter now than 2,000 years ago.

The town's **Duomo** (open 8am-7.30pm daily), which dates back to the sixth century, has a fine collection of columns with Byzantine capitals and a beautiful sixth-century mosaic floor. Mosaics of the same period are to be found in the church of Santa Maria delle Grazie and in the Baptistery between Duomo and church.

Museo Archeologico

Via Roma 1, Aquileia (0431 91016/ www.museoarcheo-aquileia.it/ archeologico@museoarcheo-aquileia.it). **Open** 8.30am-2pm Mon; 8.30am-7.30pm Tue-Sun. **Admission** L8,000; L4,000 concessions. **No credit cards**.

Museo Paleocristiano

Via Monastero, Aquileia (0431 91131/ www.museoarcheo-aquileia.it/ paleocristiano@museoarcheo-aquileia.it). **Open** 8.30am-1.45pm Mon; 8.30am-7.30pm Tue-Sun. **Admission** free.

Where to stay & eat

Of **Grado**'s hotels, the **Antares** (via delle Scuole 4, 0431 84961, L85,000-L220,000), pleasantly situated along the seafront, is one of very few open all year round. In season, a cheaper option is **Serena,** on the quiet residential island of La Schiusa (riva Sant'Andrea 31, 0431 80697, L130,000-L140,000). The **Tavernetta all'Androna** (calle Porta Piccola 4, 0431 80950, closed Tue, Dec-Jan, average L60,000) has the best seafood in town; more rustic – but better value – is the friendly **Trattoria de Toni** (piazza Duca d'Aosta 37, 0431 80104, closed Wed, Jan-Feb, average L40,000).

Getting there

By car

Take the Palmanova exit from the A4 Venice-Trieste motorway, then head south on the SS352.

By train

Venice-Trieste trains stop at Cervignano, then hop on a bus (Autoservizi SAF, 0431 80055/0432 608 111) at the station.

Tourist information

APT

Piazza Capitolo 4, Aquileia (0431 919 491). **Open** *Apr-Oct* 8.30am-12.30pm, 3.30-6pm daily. *Nov-Mar* 2.30-5pm Mon, Tue, Fri-Sun.

APT

Viale Dante Alighieri 72, Grado (0431 899 111/fax 0431 899 278/www.aptgrado.com/ info@aptgrado.com). **Open** *mid Nov-Feb* 8am-1pm, 2-6pm Mon-Fri; *Mar-mid Nov* 8am-7pm daily.

The Veneto

Directory

Directory

Getting Around

Arriving & leaving

By air

Venice Marco Polo Airport

Viale Galilei 30, Tessera (041 260 6111/fax 041 260 6260/www.veniceairport.it). **Open** ticket counters open 5.30am-9pm daily.

Venice's airport is at Tessera on the northern edge of the lagoon; it is connected to the city by regular bus and boat services (*see below*). Marco Polo has exchange and car hire facilities, as well as cash dispensers and an office of the APT tourist information bureau. For information on flights and services, contact the following telephone numbers:
Arrivals 041 260 9240
Departures 041 260 9250
General information 041 260 9260.

Treviso Sant'Angelo Airport

Via Noalese 63E, Treviso (handling 0422 315 131/bookings 0422 315 331).

Treviso's tiny airport is used by Ryanair (toll free 199 114 114) and a few other charter services to and from London.

To & from Venice airport

BY BOAT

Cooperativa San Marco

(San Marco office 041 240 6711/fax 041 240 6700/airport office 041 541 5084).

The Cooperativa runs its Alilaguna (041 523 5775/fax 041 522 1939/www.alilaguna.com) motorlaunch service hourly between 6.15am and five minutes past midnight from the airport to San Marco and vice versa. Tickets (L17,000) can be purchased at the Cooperativa's counter in the arrivals hall or on board. You should allow 70 minutes from or to San Marco; the launch also stops at Murano and the Lido.

Water taxis

A ride from the airport right to your hotel in Venice will cost upwards of L150,000 (no credit cards). There is a taxi jetty at the main dock to the left of the arrivals hall; make sure the taxi is licensed.

BY BUS

ATVO

Marco Polo Airport, arrivals hall (041 541 5180/fax 041 261 1242/ www.atvo.it). **Open** 8am-0.20am daily. **Tickets** L5,000 from ticket-office in arrivals hall.

ATVO runs fast coach services to and from piazzale Roma to coincide with most incoming and outgoing planes. The trip takes approximately 25 minutes; buses leave hourly or more frequently between 8.35am and 0.20am (from airport) and 5.20am and 8.30pm (from piazzale Roma).

ACTV

(041 528 7886/fax 041 522 2633/ direzione@actv.it/www.actv.it).

Bus 5 plies between the airport and piazzale Roma, leaving from both ends every half hour from 4.40am to 12.40am, journey time 35-40 mins. Tickets (L1,500) can be bought at the ACTV counter inside the arrivals hall and at the *tabacchi*/newsstand inside the departure hall or from the ACTV office in piazzale Roma.

To & from Treviso airport

ATVO buses run from Venice's piazzale Roma and back to coincide with flights. Telephone 041 541 5180 for timetable information. Bus 6 does the 20-minute trip from in front of Treviso train station to the airport twice an hour.

Airlines

Alitalia

Via Sansovino 7, Mestre (information 041 258 1111/domestic bookings 848 865 641/international bookings 848 865 642). **Open** 9am-4.30pm Mon-Fri. **Credit** AmEx, DC, MC, V.

British Airways

Marco Polo Airport (information 041 541 5629/bookings 848 812 266/www.britishairways.com/Italy). **Open** 8am-8pm Mon-Fri; 9am-5pm Sat. **Credit** AmEx, DC, MC, V.

Ryanair

Treviso Sant'Angelo Airport (information/bookings 0422 315 331). **Open** *June-Sept* 8.30-10.30am, 2-4pm, 7-9pm daily. *Oct-May* 8.30-10.30am, 7-9pm daily. **Credit** MC, V.

By bus

Bus services to Venice all terminate at piazzale Roma, which is connected by vaporetto (*see also p275* **Getting around: By boat**) to the rest of the city centre. For bus services in mainland Venice and the Lido, *see also p275* **Getting around: by bus**.

For bus services from Venice to other destinations in the Veneto, *see section* **The Veneto**.

By rail

Most trains arrive at Santa Lucia station in the north-west corner of island Venice, though a few will only take you as far as Mestre on the mainland, where you will need to change to a local train (every ten minutes or less during the day) for the ten-minute hop across the lagoon. *See also p277* **Getting around: By train.**

By road

Venice is connected to other large Italian and European cities by fast motorway links, but prohibitive parking fees make this one of the least practical modes of arrival, especially for stays of more than 24 hours. Note, though, that many Venetian hotels offer their guests discounts at car parks. The main car parks are listed below.

Autorimessa Tronchetto
Isola del Tronchetto (041 520 7555/fax 041 528 5750). Vaporetto Tronchetto. **Open** 24 hours daily. **Rates** L30,000 a day. **Credit** MC, V (for sums over L50,000). **Map** off I 1C.

Autorimessa Comunale
Santa Croce, piazzale Roma (041 272 7301/fax 041 272 7313). Vaporetto Piazzale Roma. **Open** 24 hours daily. **Rates** L36,000 a day. **Credit** AmEx, DC, MC, V. **Map** I 1C.

Parcheggio Sant'Andrea
Santa Croce, piazzale Roma (041 272 7304/fax 041 723 131). Vaporetto Piazzale Roma. **Open** 24 hours daily. **Rates** L8,000 per two hours. **No credit cards.** **Map** I 1C.

Park Serenissima
Viale Stazione 10, Mestre (041 938 021). Bus 2/train to Mestre station. **Open** 24 hours daily. **Rates** L9,000 a day. **No credit cards.**

Park Terminal Fusina
Via Moranzani 79, Fusina (tel/fax 041 547 0160/ www.terminalfusina.it). Vaporetto 16 to Fusina. **Open** 24 hours daily. **Rates** L15,000 for up to 12 hours; L24,000 for up to 24 hours. **No credit cards.**

Getting around

Public transport – including *vaporetti* and buses – in Venice itself and in some mainland areas is run by

ACTV (Azienda Comunale per il Trasporto di Venezia); ACTV's new marketing wing is called **VeLa**. Another company, **ATVO**, runs more extensive bus services to mainland destinations (*see also section* **The Veneto**).

ACTV
Santa Croce, piazzale Roma (041 528 7886/fax 041 522 2633/ www.actv.it). **Open** 7.30am-8pm daily. **No credit cards.** **Map** I 1C.

VeLa
San Marco 1810, calle dei Fuseri (041 241 8029/fax 041 241 8028/www.velaspa.com). Vaporetto Vallaresso or Rialto. **Open** 7.30am-7pm Mon-Sat. **No credit cards.** **Map** II 4A.

ATVO
Santa Croce 497, piazzale Roma (041 520 5530/www.atvo.it). Vaporetto Piazzale Roma. **Open** 6.40am-7.30pm daily. **Map** I 1C.

By bus

Orange ACTV buses serve both Mestre and Marghera on the mainland, as well as the Lido, Pellestrina and Chioggia (*see chapter* **The Lido to Chioggia**). Services for the mainland depart from piazzale Roma.

Bus tickets, costing L1,500, are valid on any number of buses for 60 minutes, though you are not permitted to make a return journey on the same ticket. They can be purchased from ACTV ticket booths at piazzale Roma, the Lido and elsewhere, or from *tabacchi* anywhere in the city. They should be bought before boarding the bus and stamped on board.

From midnight until 5am, buses N1 (every 30 minutes) and N2 (every hour) depart from Mestre for piazzale Roma and vice-versa. There are also regular Lido night buses (departing at least hourly) to Malamocco, Alberoni and Pellestrina.

By boat

Vaporetti

Strictly speaking, it is wrong to refer to all Venetian passenger ferries as *vaporetti*; only the larger, slower, more rounded boat with more room for luggage and those much sought-after outside seats at the front is a genuine vaporetto, while the sleeker, smaller and faster boat with outside seats only at the back is a *motoscafo*. As for the charming double-decker steamer that crosses the lagoon to Burano and Torcello, that's a *motonave*. Even Venetians tend to lump them all together as *vaporetti* when talking in general about the service. But disabled travellers should learn to spot the different boats, as wheelchairs can be accommodated on *vaporetti* and *motonavi* but not on *motoscafi* (*see p279* **Disabled travellers**).

Vaporetti run to a tight schedule, with sailing times marked clearly at stops for each line that ties up there. Regular services run from about 5am to shortly after midnight, after which a frequent night service (N) follows the route taken by Line 82 during the day.

The main lines ply the Grand Canal, or circle the island. Without a clear idea of Venetian topography, taking the wrong boat in the wrong direction is alarmingly easy. It is worth picking up a free timetable and route map from the central ACTV/VeLa office, tourist offices (*see p188*) or any large ACTV booth. This is advisable since the ACTV offices are notorious for making frequent changes in the timetables as well as adding or eliminating lines.

As a rule of thumb, remember that if you're standing with your back to the station and want to make your way down the Grand Canal, take Line 1 (slow) or Line 82 (faster) heading left.

The stop called San Zaccaria is the closest to piazza San Marco. Minimally further away, the stop now called Vallaresso used to be called San Marco; you may still find it labelled thus on old maps or timetables.

Services to islands in the northern lagoon depart from Fondamenta Nove (the alternative route from San Zaccaria via the Lido is very roundabout). For the rarely visited southern islands (San Servolo, San Lazzaro degli Armeni) and the Lido, the starting point is San Zaccaria.

Line 12 leaves about every 30mins from Fondamenta Nove for Cimitero (San Michele), Faro (Murano), Mazzorbo, Torcello, Burano, Treporti and Punta Sabbioni. Certain boats call at Torcello after Burano; others skip Torcello altogether. Check before boarding.

Line 13 hourly from Fondamenta Nove to Cimitero (San Michele), Faro (Murano), Vignole, Capannone (Sant'Erasmo), Chiesa (Sant'Erasmo) and Vela (Sant'Erasmo). Some boats continue for Treporti.

Line 20 from San Zaccaria to San Servolo and San Lazzaro.

TICKETS

Individual and fixed-period tickets can be purchased at most stops, at *tabacchi*, at the main ACTV office in piazzale Roma or the VeLa office (*see p188*). When other sales points are closed, they can be obtained from machines at the train station and some larger stops. They can also be bought on board with a L800 surcharge. Tickets must be stamped in the yellow machines at the entrance to the jetty before boarding a vaporetto.

The privilege of seeing Venice from the water does not come cheap: a single ticket for one ride will set you back L6,000 – unless you're just using the boat to cross the Grand Canal, or hopping from the Lido to Sant'Elena or from San Giorgio to San Zaccaria, in which case it's L3,000. If you are staying for longer than a few hours, and planning to make good use of *vaporetti*, *motonavi* and ACTV buses, cut costs by investing in a 24-hour ticket (L18,000), a three-day ticket (L35,000) or a seven-day ticket (L60,000).

Alternatively, three people can invest in joint one-ride (L15,000) or 24-hour (L45,000) tickets; groups of four pay L20,000 for one ride and L60,000 for 24 hours; groups of five pay L25,000 for one ride and L75,000 for 24 hours.

If you are staying a week or more, an *abbonamento* is a sound investment. Available from main ACTV and VeLa offices, this three-year pass allows you to pay the same much lower rates as Venetian residents (who hold Cartavenezia passes). A one-off charge of L10,000 is made for the *abbonamento* card, for which you will need one passport photo. You must buy a monthly season ticket (L45,000; L30,000 students) when applying for the *abbonamento*; after the month is up, you can buy single tickets for L1,500.

Traghetti

Traghetti are the very best way of crossing from one side of the Grand Canal to the other when you're far from any of the three bridges that span it. They are also the best way to get a ride in a gondola without the kitsch trappings, and for a mere L800. These large, unadorned *gondole* are rowed back and forth across the canal in a service laid on by the

gondoliers' cooperative, in collaboration with the city council. The jostling, chatting Venetian habitués of this unique ferry service brave the rocky wakes of passing motor boats and always ride *traghetti* standing up.

Traghetti ply between the following points:
San Marcuola-Fontego dei Turchi (*June-Sept* 9am-12.30am Mon-Sat. *Oct-May* 7.45am-1pm Mon-Sat). **Map I** 2B.
Santa Sofia-Pescheria (7.30am-8.30pm Mon-Sat; 8am-7pm Sun). **Map I** 3C.
Riva del Carbon-riva del Vin (8am-2pm Mon-Sat). **Map I** 3C.
Ca' Garzoni-San Tomà (7.30am-8pm Mon-Sat; 8am-7.20pm Sun). **Map II** 2A.
San Samuele-Ca' Rezzonico (7.30am-1.30pm Mon-Sat). **Map II** 2A.
Santa Maria del Giglio-Santa Maria della Salute (8am-6pm daily). **Map II** 3B.
San Marco-Dogana (9am-noon, 2-6pm daily). **Map II** 2B.

Water taxis

Venetian water taxis are breathtakingly expensive: expect to pay L150,000 from the airport to San Marco and only slightly less from San Marco to the railway station or piazzale Roma. A quick trip along the Grand Canal will cost upwards of L140,000. Between the hours of 10pm and 7am there is a surcharge of L15,000.

Beware of unlicensed taxis, which will charge you even more than the authorised ones. The latter have a black registration number on a yellow background.
Cooperativa San Marco
(041 522 2303/fax 240 6747/ www.veneziamotoscafi.com). **Open** 24 hours daily. **No credit cards**.

Gondole

For gondola hire, *see p26*.

By bicycle

Be prepared to fight off hordes of wired-up, sleep-deprived journalists and film critics to get your hands on a bike on the Lido during the Film Festival in early

September (*see p204* **The Film Festival**). At other times, try the following.

Giorgio Barbieri

Via Zara 5, Lido (041 526 1490). **Open** *Mar-Oct* 8.30am-7.30pm daily. **Rates** L15,000 a day. **No credit cards. Map** Lido.

Bruno Lazzari

Gran viale Santa Maria Elisabetta 21/B, Lido (041 526 8019/fax 041 276 9406). **Open** 8am-7pm daily. **Rates** L15,000 a day. **Credit** MC, V. **Map** Lido.

By car

(For car parks, *see p275.*) Car-hire firms are listed below.

Avis

Santa Croce, piazzale Roma 496G (041 523 7377/fax 041 522 5825/ www.avisautonoleggio.it). **Open** *Apr-Oct* 8am-6.30pm Mon-Fri; 8am-12.30pm Sat, Sun. *Nov-Mar* 8.30am-12.30pm, 2.30-6pm Mon-Fri; 8am-12.30pm Sat, Sun. **Credit** AmEx, DC, MC, V. **Map** I 1C. **Branch**: Arrivals hall, Marco Polo Airport (041 541 5030).

Europcar

Santa Croce, piazzale Roma 496H (041 523 8616/fax 041 523 7357/ www.europcar.it). **Open** *Apr-Oct* 8.30am-1pm, 2-6.30pm Mon-Fri; 8.30am-12.30pm Sat, Sun. *Nov-Mar* 8.30am-12.30pm, 2.30-6pm Mon-Fri; 8.30am-noon Sat. **Credit** AmEx, DC, MC, V. **Map** I 1C. **Branch**: Arrivals hall, Marco Polo Airport (041 541 5654).

Hertz

Santa Croce, piazzale Roma 496E (041 528 3524/fax 041 528 7). **Open** *Apr-Oct* 8am-6pm Mon-Fri; 8am-1pm Sat, Sun. *Nov-Mar* 8am-12.30pm, 3-5.30pm Mon-Fri; 8am-1pm Sat. **Credit** AmEx, DC, MC, V. **Map** I 1C. **Branch**: Arrivals hall, Marco Polo Airport (041 541 6075).

Maggiore National

Mestre railway station (041 935 300/ fax 041 932 224/www.maggiore.it). **Open** 8.30am-12.30pm, 2.30-6.30pm Mon-Fri; 8.30am-12.30pm Sat. **Credit** AmEx, DC, MC, V. **Branch**: Arrivals hall, Marco Polo Airport (041 541 5040).

Mattiazzo

Santa Croce, piazzale Roma 496E (041 522 0884/fax 041 520 0936). **Open** 8.30am-7.30pm daily. **Credit** AmEx, DC, MC, V. **Map** I 1C. Chauffeur-driven limousine hire.

By train

Venice is connected to the rest of Italy via two rail lines: the first heads south via Padua, Ferrara, Bologna and Florence to Rome and points south; the second heads west through the Po Valley via Padua to Verona, Brescia, Milan and Turin. This is the main line for international services to France; other international routes from Venice head north-west via Verona to Innsbruck and Munich over the Brenner pass, and north-east via Udine to Vienna over the Tarvisio pass.

The rail information office (*timetable information* 848 888 088) in the main hall of Santa Lucia station is open 8.30am-1.30pm and 3.30-5.30pm daily.

Train tickets can be purchased from windows or cash-only vending machines in the station itself, or from travel agents around the city displaying the FS (*Ferrovie dello Stato* – state railways) logo.

Alternatively, they can be ordered by phone between two months and the day of the departure by ringing 041 275 0492, 9am-1pm, 3-6pm daily and collected from the station (home delivery L4,800 extra).

In Venice station check that the ticket window you are queueing for is the right one: the first four windows are for domestic travel while windows 6-11 are for reservations and international tickets.

At the time of writing, ticket prices were tied to kilometres travelled, on top of which supplements were charged for high-speed trains – marked either ES (Eurostar), IC (Intercity) or EC (Eurocity, the same as Intercity except that it goes across a national border).

Seat bookings are obligatory (and free) on ES trains on Fridays and Sundays and all week at certain peak times of year. An R inside a square on train timetables indicates this;

it is a good idea to check when purchasing your ticket. Booking a seat on IC and internal EC routes costs only L5,000 and is well worth it to avoid standing in a packed corridor at peak travel times, especially on Friday and Sunday evenings. If your ES or IC train arrives more than 30 minutes late and you have a seat booking, you can ask the ticket office at your destination (at the booth marked *Rimborsi*) to reimburse the cost of the supplement.

The Santa Lucia ticket office accepts all major credit cards.

Those under 26 can purchase cut-rate tickets at the Transalpino office in the main hall (041 524 1334/fax 041 716 600; open 8.30am-12.30pm, 3-7pm Mon-Fri; 8.30am-12.30pm Sat).

Remember that **you must stamp your ticket – and any supplement – in the yellow machines at the head of each platform before boarding the train**. Failure to do so can result in a fine, though looking foreign and contrite usually works. If you are running for your train and forget to stamp your ticket, locate the inspector as soon as possible after boarding and s/he will waive the fine.

On foot

Much of your getting around Venice will inevitably be done on foot. Walking is the main means of locomotion for Venetians, too, which explains why they are perhaps the only Italians who stride purposefully, rather than dawdling; understandably, then, the locals take a dim view of tourists who obstruct narrow thoroughfares as they stand to gawp, or – worse still – spread out their picnics on busy bridges. For a list of less inconvenient picnic spots, *see p162*; for high-water etiquette, *see p28* **Acqua alta**.

Directory

Resources A-Z

Accommodation

For on-the-spot hotel reservations, make your way to booths run by the **Associazione Veneziana Albergatori** (Venice Hoteliers' Association, 041 523 8032) in the train station (041 715 288), the arrivals hall in Marco Polo airport (041 541 5133) or the Comunale car park in piazzale Roma (041 522 8640/041 523 1397).

Banks & money

The Italian currency is the *lira* (plural *lire*). Italian banknotes come in denominations of L1,000, L2,000, L5,000, L10,000, L50,000, L100,000 and L500,000, though this last is rarely seen. There are coins for L50, L100, L200, L500 and L1,000 (*see also p286* **The Euro cometh**).

ATMs

Most banks have 24-hour cashpoint (Bancomat) machines, and the vast majority of these accept cards with the Maestro and Cirrus symbols. Most cashpoint machines will dispense the daily limit of L500,000; older ones may only let you have L300,000.

Banking hours

Most banks are open from 8.20am-1.20pm and from 2.45-3.45pm Mon-Fri. All banks are closed on public holidays and work reduced hours the day before a holiday, usually closing at 11am. Banks are listed under *Banche ed Istituti di Credito* in the Yellow Pages.

Foreign exchange

Banks usually offer better exchange rates than bureaux de change (*cambio*).

Commission rates in banks vary considerably. Don't be fooled by 'no commission' signs in exchange offices: these usually mean that the exchange rate is dire.

It's a good idea to take your passport with you, especially if you want to change travellers' cheques or draw money on your credit card.

American Express

San Marco 1471, salizzada San Moisè (041 520 0844/ amexvenezia@tin.it). Vaporetto Vallaresso. **Open** *May-Oct* 9am-8pm Mon-Sat; 9am-6pm Sun. *Nov-Mar* 9am-5.30pm Mon-Fri; 9am-12.30pm Sat. **Map** II 4B.
Exchange with no commission, travellers' cheque refund, card replacements, 24-hour money transfers, plus a variety of extra services such as hotel reservations, car rentals, train and plane tickets and the organisation of tours. There is also an ATM.

Thomas Cook

San Marco 5126, riva del Ferro (041 528 7358/fax 041 328 9228). Vaporetto Rialto. **Open** 9.30am-7pm Mon-Sat; 9.30am-5pm Sun. **Credit** MC, V. **Map** I 3C.
These are among the few change bureaux open on Sundays; cash and travellers' cheques exchanged with no commission. Mastercard cardholders can also withdraw cash. **Branch**: San Marco 142, piazza San Marco (041 277 5057).

Credit cards

Plastic has made great inroads into what was until very recently a cash-only country, but you still can't rely on every shop, hotel and restaurant to accept them happily. However, most hotels of two stars and over will take most major cards.

Report lost credit or charge cards to the appropriate emergency number listed below. All lines are toll-free, operate 24 hours a day, and have English-speaking operators.

American Express 800 864 046
American Express (cheques) 800 872 000
Diners' Club 800 864 064
Eurocard/CartaSi 800 868 086
Mastercard 800 874 299
Visa 800 877 232.

Business

If you are planning to do business in Venice, a call to your embassy's commercial sector in Rome (*see p280* **Embassies & consulates**) is always a good idea. Note that few countries have consulates in Venice, and those that exist are often short on useful data. **Comitato Venezia Vuole Vivere** (via Brunacci 28, Marghera, 041 549 9111/fax 041 935 952), an umbrella group of local industrial and retail associations, provides useful insights into setting up and doing business in Venice.

Conferences

Venice has extensive facilities for business conferences and congresses. The same goes for the rest of the Veneto, where functions can be held in Palladian villas and other historic landmarks.

For information on trade fairs in Venice, contact **Venezia Fiere** (San Polo 2120, campo San Polo, 041 714 066/fax 041 713 151, www.veneziafiere.it).

Most of the organisers listed below will provide hotel and boat booking services as well as the usual facilities.

Codess Settore Cultura

San Polo 2120, campo San Polo (041 710 200/fax 041 717 771/ venezia@codesscultura.it/ www.codesscultura.it). **Map** I 2C.

Endar

Castello 4966, fondamenta de l'Osmarin (041 523 8440/fax 041 528 6846/congress@endar.it/ www.endar.it). **Map** III 1B.

Nexa

*San Marco 3870, campo de l'Alboro
(041 521 0255/fax 041 528
5041/nexa@doge.it).* **Map** II 3A.

Studio Systema

*San Polo 135, campo San Giacomo
di Rialto (041 520 1959/fax
041 520 1960/studiosy@tin.it/
www.studiosistema.iti.it).* **Map** I 3C.

Venezia Congressi

*Dorsoduro 1056, calle Gambara (041
522 8400/fax 041 523 8995).* **Map**
II 2B.

Couriers

Local

Bartolini 041 531 8944/fax 041 531
8943/www.bartolini.it
Executive 041 994 085/fax 041 990
879/www.executivegroup.com
Pony Express 041 957 500/
bbr@pn.itnet.it/www.pony.it
Venice Express 041 523 1626
Nuova Serenissima 041 523 5415/
fax 041 531 6586/
www.paginegialle.it/nuovaser
SDA Express 041 595 1717/fax 041
595 1697/www.sda.it
TNT Traco 041 250 0111/fax 041
531 9787/www.tntitaly.it

International

DHL (toll free) 800 345 345/
www.dhl.it
Federal Express (toll free) 800 123
800
MBE 041 985 868/fax 041 974 289/
mbe160@libero.it
UPS (toll free) 800 877 877

Interpreters

Most of the conference
organisers listed above will
also provide interpreters.

Lexicon

*Viale Garibaldi 7, Mestre (041 534
8005/fax 041 534 9720/
www.traduttori.com).*

TER Centro Traduzioni

*Cannaregio 1076C, ramo San
Giovanni (041 717 923/fax 041 524
4021).* **Map** I 1A.

Crime & safety

Venice is, on the whole, an
exceptionally safe place at any
time of day or night, and
violent crime is almost
unknown. Lone women would
be advised to steer clear of
dark alleyways late at night,

though even there they are
more likely to be harassed than
attacked (*see p290* **Women**).
Bag-snatchers are a rarity,
mostly because of the logistical
difficulties Venice presents for
making quick getaways.
However, pickpockets operate
in crowded thoroughfares,
especially around San Marco
and the Rialto, and on public
transport, so make sure you
leave passports, plane/train
tickets and at least one means
of getting hold of money in
your hotel room or safe.

If you are the victim of theft
or serious crime, call one of the
emergency numbers listed
under **Emergencies** *p280*.
The following rules will help
avoid unfortunate incidents:
● Don't carry wallets in back
pockets, particularly on buses
or boats. If you have a bag or
camera with a long strap, wear
it across your chest and not
dangling from one shoulder.
● Keep bags closed, with your
hand on them. If you stop at a
pavement café or restaurant,
do not leave bags or coats on
the ground or the back of a
chair where you cannot keep
an eye on them.
● Avoid attracting unwanted
attention by pulling out large
wads of *lire* to pay for things
at street stalls or in busy bars.
Keep some small bills and
change easily accessible.
● Crowds in general offer
easy camouflage for
pickpockets. Be especially
careful when boarding buses,
boats, and entering museums.

If you have your bag or
wallet snatched, or are
otherwise a victim of crime, go
immediately to the nearest
police station to report a *scippo*
(*see p280* **Emergencies**). A
denuncia (written statement) of
the incident will be made by or
for you. Give police as much
information as possible,
including passport number,
holiday address, and flight
numbers. The *denuncia* will be
signed, dated, and stamped

with an official police seal. It is
unlikely that your things will
be found, but you will need the
denuncia for making an
insurance claim.

Customs

Anyone arriving from another
EU country does not have to
declare goods imported into or
exported from Italy for their
personal use.

For people arriving from
non-EU countries the following
limits apply: 400 cigarettes or
200 cigarillos or 100 cigars or
500 grams (17.64 oz) of
tobacco; 1 litre of spirits or two
litres of wine; 1 bottle of
perfume (50 gr/1.76 oz).
Anything above will be subject
to taxation at the port of entry.
There are no restrictions on
imports of cameras, watches or
electrical goods.

Disabled travellers

The very things that make
Venice unique make it extra-
difficult for disabled travellers:
no barriers between pavements
and canals; 400 picturesque
but wheelchair-unfriendly
bridges; museums that are
either unrepentantly
inaccessible or that proudly
boast that they have state-of-
the-art disabled facilities –
once you've made it up the
stairs. The city should not,
however, be automatically
crossed off the holiday
destination list, as there has in
recent years been an effort to
provide facilities and make at
least some areas of the city
viable for disabled travellers.

There is now a handy one-
stop source of information,
Informahandicap, which has
collaborated with the local
tourist board to mark in yellow
on the standard free tourist
map of Venice the areas of the
city that are easily accessible
to wheelchair-bound travellers.

The bridges that have
wheelchair ramps (five in the

Directory

sestiere of San Marco, one on the island of Burano and one on Murano) are marked, as well as the public toilets which are accessible to wheelchair-users. The map is available in APT offices (*see p288* **Tourist information**), as are the keys for operating the automated ramps (you can keep the keys: they work for ramps all over Italy).

Public transport is one area where Venice scores higher than many other destinations, as standard *vaporetti* and *motonavi* (but not *motoscafi – see p275* **Getting around: By boat**) have a reasonably large, flat deck area, and there are no steps or steep inclines on the route between quayside and boat. The vaporetto lines that currently guarantee disabled access (though peak times should be avoided) are 1, 4, N, 6, 12, 14 and 82. Some of the buses that run between Mestre and Venice also have wheelchair access: ring ACTV for information (041 528 7886), or go to the Informahandicap website (www.comune.venezia.it/handicap), which is in any case worth a look before you set out.

A bronze relief near the entrance to the Museo Correr (*see p77*) on piazza San Marco depicts the square in all its glory, with braille explanations.

Informahandicap
Viale Garibaldi 155, Mestre (041 534 1700/fax 041 534 2257/ informahandicap@comune.venezia.it/ www.comune.venezia.it/handicap). **Open** 3.30-6.30pm Tue, Thur, Fri; 9am-1pm Wed, Sat.
A city council service that provides information – in English, if necessary – on disabled travel in Venice and the Veneto, and on hotels, restaurants and museums with facilities for the disabled. All the information is contained in a free guide, which can be sent on request.

COINtel
(06 712 9011/fax 06 712 90125/ turismo@coinsociale.it/ www.coinsociale.it).

This Rome-based organisation provides nationwide information on the wheelchair-friendliness of hotels, museums and other disabled facilities.

Transport

Contact the following numbers for further information on services for the disabled.
ACTV (buses and vaporetti) 041 528 7886/fax 041 272 2588
FS (state railways) 041 785 570/fax 041 275 0744
Marco Polo Airport tel/fax 041 260 9260.

Drugs

If caught in possession of drugs of any type you will be taken before a magistrate. If you can convince him or her that the tiny quantity you were carrying was for purely personal use then you will be let off with a fine or be ordered to leave the country. (Habitual offenders will be offered rehab. Holders of Italian driving licences may have them temporarily suspended.) Anything more than a tiny amount will push you into the criminal category: couriering or dealing can land you in prison for up to 20 years.

It is an offence to buy drugs, or even to give them away. Sniffer dogs are a fixture at most ports of entry into Italy; customs police will take a dim view of visitors entering with even the tiniest quantities of narcotics, and are likely to allow them to stay no longer than it takes a magistrate to expel them from the country.

Electricity

Italy's electricity system runs on 220/230v. To use British or US appliances, you will need two-pin adaptor plugs: these are best bought before leaving home, as they tend to be expensive in Italy and are not always easy to find. If you do

need to buy one here, try any electrical retailer (*casalinghi* or *elettrodomestici*).

Embassies & consulates

There are few diplomatic missions in Venice: for most information, and in case of emergencies, you will probably have to contact offices in Rome or Milan.

Consulates in Venice

British
Dorsoduro 1051, campo della Carità (041 522 7207). Vaporetto Accademia. **Open** 10am-1pm Mon-Fri. **Map** I 1A.
In emergencies phone 0337 367 487 on Mon-Fri, from 9 to 10am and 2 to 4pm; outside of these hours refer to the duty officer at the consulate in Milan on 0335 810 6857.

South African
Santa Croce 466G, fondamenta *Sant'Andrea (041 524 1599/fax 524 2698). Vaporetto Piazzale Roma.* **Open** 9.30am-12.30pm Mon-Thur. **Map** II 1A.
In emergencies contact the Milan consulate on 02 809 036.

Embassies in Rome

Australian 06 852 721
British 06 482 5551
Canadian 06 445 981
Irish 06 697 9121
New Zealand 06 441 7171
South African 06 852 541
US 06 46 741.

Consulates in Milan

Australian 02 777 041
British 02 723 001
Canadian 02 675 81
New Zealand 02 4801 3164
US 02 290 351.

Emergencies

(*See also p279* **Crime & safety**.)
Thefts or losses should be reported immediately at the nearest police station (either of the Polizia di Stato or the nominally military Carabinieri). Report the

loss of your passport to the nearest consulate or embassy (*see p280* **Embassies**). Report the loss of a credit card or travellers' cheques to your credit-card company (*see p278* **Banks & money**).

National emergency numbers

Polizia di Stato 113
Carabinieri 112
Fire brigade 115
Ambulance 118
Car breakdowns (Automobile Club d'Italia) 116
Guardia forestale (forest rangers and mountain rescue) 1515
Coast guard 1530.

Local emergency numbers

Polizia di Stato

Santa Croce 500, piazzale Roma (041 271 5511/fax 041 271 5824). Vaporetto Piazzale Roma. **Map** I 1C. *Via Nicolodi 22, Marghera (041 271 5511). Bus 6/.*

Carabinieri

Castello 4693A, campo San Zaccaria (041 520 4777). Vaporetto San Zaccaria. **Map** III 1B.

Fire brigade

041 520 0222

Ambulance

041 523 0000

Coast guard (Capitaneria di Porto)

041 520 3044

Domestic emergencies

If you need to report a malfunction in any of the main public services, call one of the following:
Electricity (ENEL) 800 846 006
Gas (Italgas) 800 900 777
Telephone (Telecom Italia) 182
Water (ASPIV) 800 212 742/041 521 2952.

Health & hospitals

The **pronto soccorso** (casualty department) of all public hospitals provides free emergency treatment for travellers, but it is also worth taking out private health insurance (*see p282* **Insurance**).

If you are an EU citizen and need minor treatment, take your E111 form with you to any doctor for a free consultation. Drugs he or she prescribes can be bought at chemists at prices set by the health ministry.

Tests, or specialist examinations carried out in the public system (*sistema sanità nazionale*, SSN), will be charged at fixed rates (*il ticket*) and a receipt issued.

For urgent medical advice from local health authority doctors during the night call 041 529 4060 in Venice, 041 526 7743 on the Lido and 041 534 4411 in Mestre (8pm-8am Mon-Fri; 10am Sat-8am Mon). Non-residents will be charged L50,000.

Contraception

Condoms are on sale near the checkout in supermarkets, or over the counter at chemists. The contraceptive pill is freely available on prescription at any pharmacy.

Dentists

Dental treatment in Italy is on the expensive side and may not be covered by your health insurance.

For urgent dental treatment at weekends, go to the Ambulatorio Odontostomatologico at the Ospedale Civile (*see below*).

Hospitals

The public relations department of Venice's Ospedale Civile (041 529 4588) provides general information on being hospitalised in Venice.

The hospitals listed below all have 24-hour *pronto soccorso* (casualty) facilities. For an ambulance-boat, call 041 523 0000.

Ospedale Civile

Castello 6777, campo Santi Giovanni e Paolo (041 529 4111/casualty 041 529 4516). Vaporetto Ospedale. **Map** II 1A.
Housed in the 15th-century Scuola di San Marco, Venice's main hospital has helpful staff and doctors who are quite likely to speak English.

Ospedale al Mare

Lungomare D'Annunzio 1, Lido (041 529 4111/casualty 041 529 5234). Vaporetto Lido. **Map** Lido.
Smaller than the Ospedale Civile, and offering a smaller range of services, the hospital on the Lido does, however, have fine sea views.

Ospedale Umberto I

Via Circonvallazione 50, Mestre (041 260 7111).
A modern hospital on the mainland.

Ospedale di Padova

Via Giustiniani 2, Padova (049 821 1111).

Ospedale di Verona

Piazzale Stefani 1, Verona (045 807 1111).

Pharmacies

Pharmacies (*farmacie*), identified by a red or green cross above the door, are run by qualified chemists who will dispense informal advice on and assistance for minor ailments, as well as filling doctors' prescriptions. Over-the-counter drugs such as aspirin are considerably more expensive in Italy than in the UK or US.

Most chemists are open 9am-12.30pm, 3.45-7.30pm Mon-Fri; 9am-12.45pm Sat. A small number of pharmacies remain open on Saturday afternoon, Sunday and at night on a duty rota system, details of which are posted outside every pharmacy and published in the local press.

Alternatively call the city council's information service on 041 531 1592 (7.30pm-8am Mon-Fri; 24-hour Sat, Sun). There is a fixed surcharge (L7,000 at night

Directory

and L3,000 during the day) per transaction at pharmacies on after-hours duty.

Most pharmacies carry homeopathic medicines. All will check your blood pressure. If you require regular medication, bring adequate supplies of your drugs with you. Ask your GP for the chemical rather than the brand name of your medicine: it may only be available in Italy under a different name.

Veterinary care

Servizio Veterinario
Dorsoduro 3494, rio Nuovo (041 529 5938/after-hours emergencies 041 529 4111). **Open** 9am-noon Mon-Fri. **Map** II 1A.
This service run by the city council looks after strays and dispenses emergency information to pet-owners, as well as recommending vets for further treatment.

Insurance

EU citizens are entitled to reciprocal medical care in Italy provided they leave their own country with a E111 form, available from local health authorities. If used for anything but emergencies (which are treated free anyway in casualty departments, *see p281*), it will entail dealing with the intricacies of the Italian state health system. For short-term visits, it may be advisable to take out private health insurance.

Non-EU citizens should review their private health insurance plans to see if they cover expenses incurred while travelling. If not, travel insurance should be obtained before setting out from home. If you are a student, you may want to check with your student travel organisation: some offer basic health cover with the purchase of their IDs.

If you rent a car, motorcycle or moped while in Italy, make sure you pay the extra charge for full insurance cover.

Internet & email

Cyber-cafés have mushroomed all over the city, as everywhere else; if you plan to surf or check your email from a hotel or private house, check that the phone jack on the end of the cable works in an Italian phone socket; generally, US jacks (RJ11) are fine, British ones not. If you need an adaptor for a British jack, buy it before you leave home.

Some places still have old three-pin phone sockets; adaptors for these can be found in large supermarkets and most phone and electrical shops.

Le Café Noir
Dorsoduro 3805, crosera San Pantalon (041 710 925/ cafenoir1@hotmail.com). Vaporetto San Tomà. **Open** 7am-2am daily. **Internet access** L6,000 per hour; L4,000 per 30 mins. **No credit cards. Map** II 2A.
Five computer terminals, each with ISDN modems (*see also p213*).

Net House
San Marco 2967-2958, campo Santo Stefano (041 277 1190/ info@venicepages.com/ www.venicepages.com). Vaporetto San Samuele. **Open** 24 hours daily. **Internet access** L250 per minute; L15,000 per hour (minimum charge L3,750 for 15 mins). **Credit** AmEx, DC, MC, V. **Map** II 3A-B.
With 38 computers, this is the biggest internet café in the city. They also offer web page design, laser printing, fax services and computer courses. Discounted calls to the US and Britain.

The Netgate
Dorsoduro 3812A, calle Crosera (041 244 0213/ venezia.foscari@thenetgate.it/ www.thenetgate.it). Vaporetto San Tomà. **Open** 11am-8pm Mon-Sat; 2-8pm Sun. **Internet access** L10,000 per hour; L8,000 students. **Credit** AmEx, DC, MC, V. **Map** II 2A.
Located near the university, the Netgate attracts mostly students. Twenty computers and multilingual staff in a pleasant atmosphere.

Horus Explorer
Santa Croce 220, fondamenta Tolentini (041 710 470/fax 041 275 8399/horusexplorer@katamail.com). Vaporetto Piazzale Roma. **Open** 8.30am-12.30pm, 3-7.30pm Mon-Fri.

Internet access L10,000 per hour; L5,000 per 30mins. **No credit cards. Map** I 1C.
Small but well-equipped and friendly. Fax service, photocopies, computer scanning and binding.

Service providers

A number of Italian providers offer free Internet access, including **Caltanet** (www.caltanet.it), **Libero** (www.libero.it), **Tiscali** (www.tiscalinet.it) and **Kataweb** (www.kataweb.com).

Left luggage

Most hotels will look after your luggage even after you have checked out.

Venice-Santa Lucia railway station
(041 785 531). **Open** 4am-midnight daily. **Rates** L5,000 per item per 12 hours. **No credit cards. Map** I 1B.

Marco Polo airport
(0349 528 3126). **Open** 6am-9pm daily. **Rates** L4,500 per item per day. **No credit cards.**

Piazzale Roma bus terminus
(041 523 1107). **Open** 6am-9pm daily. **Rates** L5,000 per item per day. **No credit cards. Map** I 1C.

Legal advice

If you are in need of legal advice, your first stop should always be your consulate or embassy (*see p280*).

Libraries

You will need some form of photo-ID to get into all the libraries listed below.

Biblioteca Nazionale Marciana
San Marco 7, piazzetta San Marco (041 520 8788/fax 041 523 8803/biblioteca@marciana.sbn.it/ www.marciana.venezia.sbn.it). Vaporetto Vallaresso. **Open** 9am-6.45pm Mon-Fri; 9am-1.30pm Sat. **Map** II 4B.
The city's main public library, the Marciana has medieval manuscripts and editions of the classics dating back to the 15th century.

Biblioteca Fondazione Scientifica Querini Stampalia

Castello 5252, campo Santa Maria Formosa (041 271 1411/fax 041 271 1445/ querini@provincia.venezia.it/www.pro vincia.venezia.it/querini). Vaporetto Rialto or San Zaccaria. **Open** *Reading room & catalogues* 4pm-midnight Mon-Fri; 2.30pm-midnight Sat; 3-7pm Sun. *Catalogues only* 8.30am-4pm Mon-Fri (or online 24hrs daily).* **Map** II 1A.

Housed in a 16th-century palazzo, the Querini Stampalia library is attached to the museum of the same name (*see p90*) and has a fine collection of works on Venice and all things Venetian. Post-graduate students and professors may ask to use the library's quiet study rooms.

Biblioteca Generale dell'Università di Ca' Foscari

Dorsoduro 3199, calle Bernardo (041 257 7062/www.cesbi.unive.it). Vaporetto Ca' Rezzonico. **Open** 8.30am-10.45pm Mon-Fri; 8.30am-1pm Sat. **Map** II 2A.

The university library is strong on the humanities and economics.

Biblioteca Centrale Istituto Universitario di Architettura di Venezia

Santa Croce 191, fondamenta Tolentini (041 257 1106/fax 041 523 8291/bc@marcie.iuav.it/ http://iuavbc.iuav.it). Vaporetto Piazzale Roma. **Open** 9am-midnight Mon-Fri; 2pm-midnight first Mon of the month. **Map** I 1C.

The library of one of Italy's top architecture faculties has a vast collection of works on the history of architecture, town planning, art, engineering and social sciences.

Biblioteca Fondazione Giorgio Cini

Isola di San Giorgio Maggiore (041 528 9900/fax 041 523 8540/fondacini@cini.it/http://opac. sbn.it). Vaporetto San Giorgio. **Open** *Art history & music* 9am-12.30pm Mon-Fri. *Oriental studies* 9am-noon, 2.30-4.45pm Mon-Fri. **Map** III 1C.

The Fondazione Cini specialises in art history, with sections dedicated to the history of Venice and the Venetian state and society, literature, theatre, music, and a large archive of microfilms and photographs. Apply for permission to use the library prior to your visit.

Biblioteca Museo Correr

San Marco 52, piazza San Marco (041 522 5625/fax 041 520 0935/http://huavbc.iuav.unive.it/ easyweb/correr). Vaporetto Vallaresso. **Open** 8.30am-1.30pm Mon, Wed, Fri; 8.30am-5pm Tue, Thur. **Map** II 4A.

Part of the Museo Correr (*see p77*), this small library contains books on Venetian history and art history. Scholars may request permission to view the library's collection of prints and drawings.

Archivio Storico delle Arti Contemporanee

Santa Croce 2214, calle della Regina (041 521 8711/fax 041 524 0817). Vaporetto San Stae. **Map** I 3C.

The library, in the 18th-century Ca' Corner della Regina, is the archive of the Venice Biennale contemporary art festival. At the time of writing, the building was closed for long-term restoration, and accessible only by written request to the curator.

Archivio di Stato

San Polo 3002, campo dei Frari (041 522 2281/fax 041 522 9220/ www.tin.it/venva/avv/archivio/isp/ven iva.htm). Vaporetto San Tomà. **Open** 8.30am-2pm Mon, Fri, Sat; 8.30am-6pm Tue-Thur. **Map** I 2C.

Houses all official documents relating to the administration of the Venetian Republic, as well as a host of other historic manuscripts (*see also p12* **Modern history starts here**). Material must be requested between 8.30am and 1pm.

Your mislaid belongings may end up at one of the *uffici oggetti smarriti* listed below. You could also try the police (*see p280* **Emergencies**), or ring AMAV, the city's rubbish collection department, on 041 521 7011.

ACTV

Santa Croce, piazzale Roma (041 272 2179). Vaporetto Piazzale Roma. **Open** 8am-7.30pm daily. **Map** I 1C. For items found on *vaporetti* or buses.

FS/Stazione Santa Lucia

Santa Lucia railway station (041 785 238). Vaporetto Ferrovia. **Open** 8am-4pm Mon-Fri. **Map** I 1B. All items found on trains in the Venice area and in the station itself are brought to this deposit.

Marco Polo Airport

Via Galilei 30, Tessera (041 260 9222). Bus 5 to Aeroporto. **Open** 9am-8pm daily.

Comune (City Council)

San Marco 4136, riva del Carbon (041 274 8225). Vaporetto Rialto. **Open** 8.30am-12.30pm, 2.30-4.30pm Mon, Wed; 8am-12.30pm Tue, Thur, Fri.

National dailies

Italian newspapers can be a frustrating read. Long, indigestible political stories with very little background explanation predominate. On the plus side, Italian papers are delightfully unsnobbish and happily blend serious news, leaders by internationally known commentators, and well-written, often surreal, crime and human-interest stories.

Sports coverage in the dailies is extensive and thorough, but if you're not sated there are the mass-circulation sports papers *Corriere dello Sport, La Gazzetta dello Sport* and *Tuttosport*.

Corriere della Sera

www.rcs.it
To the centre of centre-left, the solid, serious but often dull Milan-based *Corriere della Sera* is good on crime and foreign news.

Il Manifesto

www.ilmanifesto.it
A reminder that, though the Berlin Wall is a distant memory, there is still some corner of central Rome where hearts beat Red.

La Repubblica

www.repubblica.it
The centre-ish, left-ish *La Repubblica* is good on the Mafia and the Vatican, and comes up with the occasional major scoop on its business pages.

La Stampa

www.lastampa.it
Part of the massive empire of Turin's Agnelli family – for which read Fiat – *La Stampa* has good (though inevitably pro-Agnelli) business reporting.

Venice dailies

Il Gazzettino

www.gazzettino.it
Il Gazzettino is one of Italy's
most successful local papers. A
conservative broadsheet, it provides
national and international news on
the front and local news inside, with
different editions for towns around
the region.

La Nuova Venezia

www.nuovavenezia.it
Local coverage dominates in
this small-circulation daily, which
emerged in 1984. Young, lively
and strong on crime stories, *La
Nuova* (as locals call it) carries up-to-
date Venetian news and listings.

Foreign press

The *Financial Times*,
Wall Street Journal, *USA
Today*, *International Herald
Tribune* (with its *Italy Daily*
supplement) and most
British and European
dailies can be found on the
day of issue at newsstands all
around town – especially those
at the station, within striking
distance of St Mark's and the
Rialto, and at the large *edicola*
at the Accademia *vaporetto*
stop. US dailies take a day or
two to appear.

Magazines

With the naked, glistening
female form emblazoned
across their covers most
weeks, Italy's serious news
magazines are not always
immediately distinguishable
from the large selection of
soft porn on newsstands. But
Panorama and *L'Espresso*
provide a generally high-
standard round-up of the
week's news, while *Sette* and
Venerdì – respectively the
colour supplements of
Corriere della Sera
(Thursday) and *La Repubblica*
(Friday) – have nice photos,
though the text often leaves
much to be desired.

For tabloid-style scandal,
try *Gente* and *Oggi* with their
weird mix of sex, glamour

and religion, or the execrable
Eva 3000, *Novella 2000* and
Cronaca Vera.

Internazionale
(www.internazionale.it)
provides an excellent digest
of interesting bits and pieces
gleaned from the world's press
the previous week. *Diario della
Settimana* (www.diario.it), is
informed, urbane and has a
real flair for investigative
journalism.

But the biggest-selling
magazine of them all is
Famiglia Cristiana – available
from newsstands or in most
churches – which alternates
Vatican line-toeing with
Vatican-baiting, depending
on the state of relations
between the Holy See and
the idiosyncratic Paoline
monks who produce it.

Listings & classified ads

Venezia News

A bilingual listings magazine, out
on the first of each month; includes
music, film, theatre, art and sports
listings, plus interviews and features.

Gente Veneta

This weekly broadsheet, produced by
the local branch of the Catholic
Church, blends cultural and religious
listings with reports on Venetian
social problems.

Boom

A small-ads paper thrust free
through every letterbox each week.
The place to look for flats, jobs and
lonelyhearts.

Aladino

Issued every Thursday, has
classified ads for everything from
flats for rent to *gondole* for sale.

Television

Italy has six major
networks (three owned
by state broadcaster RAI,
three belonging to Silvio
Berlusconi's Mediaset group),
together with two channels
operated across most of the
country by third-ranking
Telemontecarlo. When these

have bored you, there are local
stations to provide hours of
channel-zapping, compulsively
awful fun.

The standard of TV
news and current affairs
programmes varies; most,
however, offer a breadth of
international coverage that
makes British TV news look
like a parish magazine. RAI-3
supplements its 7pm and
10.30pm news programmes
with regional round-ups.

Local radio

Radio Venezia

FM 101.1 & 92.4
News and pop music with the
Venetian housewife in mind.

Radio Venezia Sound

FM 98.5
Heavy on advertising, but generous
with information on events in the
city, especially cinema. Does regular
chart countdowns.

Post & fax

Besides its main post office
(*see below*), Venice has
smaller branches in each
district that are open 8.10am-
1.30pm Mon-Fri; 8.10am-
12.30pm Sat and 8.10am-noon
on the last working day of the
month. The railway station
branch is open from 8.15am-
6pm Mon-Sat.

Posta Centrale (Central Post Office)

*San Marco 5554, salizzada del
Fontego dei Tedeschi (041 271
7111)*. *Vaporetto Rialto*. **Open**
8.15am-7pm Mon-Sat. **Map 1 4C**.
The main post office is housed in the
16th-century Fontego dei Tedeschi,
once a base for German merchants in
the city, and formerly frescoed by
Giorgione. Provides letter boxes and
a *fermo posta* (poste restante) service.
Packages and Posta Celere (swift
post, *see below*) letters can only be
sent between 8.15am and 1.30pm,
Mon-Fri, and 8.15am to noon Sat.

Stamps & charges

Big improvements have been
made recently in Italy's
notoriously unreliable postal

service (www.poste.it) and you can now be more or less sure that your letters will arrive in reasonable time.

Italy's new equivalent to first-class post, *posta prioritaria*, generally works very well: it promises delivery within 24 hours in Italy, three days for EU countries and four or five for the rest of the world; more often than not, it delivers. A letter of 20g or less to Italy or any EU country costs L1,200 by *posta prioritaria*; outside the EU the cost is L1,500; special stamps can be bought at post offices and *tabacchi* and posted in any box.

Stamps for slower regular mail are also sold at post offices and *tabacchi* shops only. A 20g letter costs L800 to EU countries, L900 to non-EU European countries, L1,000 to the US and Canada, and L1,400 to Australia and New Zealand.

The **CAI Post-Posta Celere** service (available only in main post offices) guarantees 24-hour delivery to major cities in Italy and two- to three-day delivery to major cities abroad; you can track the progress of your letter or parcel on the service's website (www.postacelere.com) or by calling (800 222 666).

Registered mail (*raccomandata*, only at post offices) costs L5,000 extra.

Letter boxes are red and spread throughout the city. They have two slots: *Per la città* (Venezia, Mestre and Marghera), and *Tutte le altre destinazioni* (everywhere else).

Telegrams & telexes

The main post office provides these services 24 hours a day, seven days a week (use the door at number 5552 when the main office is shut). Telegrams to any destination can be sent and dictated over the phone by

dialling 186 from a private phone, which will be billed automatically for the service.

Faxes

The main post office will send faxes 24 hours a day, seven days a week. The service is costly, however: there is a fixed charge of L2,500 per page to fax within Italy; faxing the UK costs L4,760 for the first page and L4,160 for subsequent pages; for the US, the first page costs L5,370 and each subsequent page L4,760. Most photocopy and tabacchi shops offer fax services, too; ask for prices before you send your fax, as they vary significantly.

Religion

Mass times vary from church to church, and are posted by front doors. The church of San Zulian (041 523 5383; map II 4A) has mass in English from May to September. Listed below are the non-Catholic denominations in the city:

Jewish Synagogue
Cannaregio 1149, campo del Ghetto Vecchio (041 715 012/fax 041 524 1862/com.ebra.ve@libero.it). Vaporetto San Marcuola. **Services** before sunset Fri; 9.30am Sat. **Map** I 2A.

Greek Orthodox Church – San Giorgio dei Greci
Castello 3412, fondamenta dei Greci (041 522 7016/fax 041 523 9569). Vaporetto San Zaccaria. **Services** 10am Sun; Vespers 6pm Sat. **Map** III 1B.

St George's Anglican Church
Dorsoduro 870, campo San Vio (041 520 0571). Vaporetto Accademia. **Services** Sung Mass 10.30am Sun; Vespers 6pm daily. **Map** II 3B.

Lutheran Church
Cannaregio 4448, campo Santi Apostoli (041 522 7149). Vaporetto Ca' D'Oro. **Services** 10.30am second & fourth Sun of month. **Map** I 4C.

Methodist (Valdese) Church
Castello 5170, fondamenta Cavagnis (041 522 7549). Vaporetto Rialto. **Services** 11am Sun. **Map** III 1A.

Relocation

Bureaucracy

You may need any or all of the following documents if you plan to work or study in Venice.

Permesso di soggiorno (permit to stay)
The key document for anyone staying in Italy for more than a short period, the *permesso di soggiorno* can be obtained from the *Questura* (police HQ). Take your passport and a photocopy of it; three passport photos; (students) proof that you are enrolled in a course or that you are in Italy on a scholarship; (employees) a statement from your employer; (freelancers) a bank or tax statement showing you have means of support; a L20,000 *marca da bollo* (official stamp) available from *tabacchi* shops. **Questura** *via Nicolodi 22, Marghera (041 271 5701/041 271 5744). Bus 6/ from piazzale Roma.* **Open** 8.30am-1.30pm Mon-Fri.

Carta d'Identità (identity card)
This official Italian ID card is not strictly necessary for foreigners, who can use their own national IDs and passports as a means of identification. Obtainable from the *Ufficio anagrafe* of the town hall. Take your ID, your *permesso di soggiorno*, and three photographs. **Ufficio anagrafe** *San Marco 4142, calle Loredan (041 274 8221/fax 041 274 8184). Vaporetto Rialto.* **Open** 8.45am-1pm Mon-Sat. **Map** II 3A.

Codice Fiscale (tax code)
A *codice fiscale* is required to work legally in Italy, or to open your own business. You will need one to open a bank

Directory

account or get a phone line, and for some kinds of treatment under the national health. Take your passport and *permesso di soggiorno*.
Ufficio Imposte Dirette *San Marco 3538, campo Sant'Angelo (041 271 8111/fax 041 271 8293)*. *Vaporetto Sant'Angelo*. **Open** 8.45am-12.45pm Mon, Wed, Fri, Sat; 8.45am-12.45pm, 2.45-4.45pm Tue, Thur. **Map** II 3A.

Partita IVA (VAT number)

Freelancers or company owners may need a VAT number for invoicing. There is a form to be filled in, but no charge.
Ufficio IVA *San Marco 3538, campo Sant'Angelo (041 271 8111)*. *Vaporetto Sant'Angelo*. **Open** 8.45am-12.45pm Mon, Wed, Fri, Sat; 8.45am-12.45pm, 2.45-4.45pm Tue, Thur. **Map** II 3A.

Permesso di lavoro (work permit)

Non-EU citizens must have a work permit to be employed in Italy. Employers will usually arrange this; if not, pick up an application form at the address given below, get it signed by your employer and return it with a photocopy of your *permesso di soggiorno*.
Ufficio provinciale e regionale del lavoro *via Ca' Marcello 9, Mestre (041 531 8880)*. *Train to Mestre*. **Open** 9am-noon Mon-Fri.

Certificato di residenza (residence permit)

Necessary if you want to buy a car or import your belongings without paying customs duties, the *certificato di residenza* can cause diplomatic rows with your landlord: to obtain it, the tax on rubbish collection (*nettezza urbana*) must have been paid for the property you reside in – which means that either you have to volunteer to pay it (and landlords renting out property but not paying taxes on the income run the risk of being discovered), or you have to persuade the owner to. In either case, you'll need to

present your passport and *permesso di soggiorno*.
Ufficio anagrafe *San Marco 4142, calle Loredan (041 274 8221)*. *Vaporetto Rialto*. **Open** 8.45am-1pm Mon-Sat. **Map** II 3A.

Work

Openings for picking up casual employment in Venice are few, though language schools (*scuole di lingua* in the Yellow Pages) are sometimes on the lookout for native English speakers, especially with TEFL experience. Women *di bella apparenza* (as the advertisements put it) might try conference organisers, or the smart boutiques in the Frezzerie area around San Marco, which sometimes advertise for *commesse* (sales assistants). The more exclusive hotels may have openings for experienced babysitters. The main Ca' Foscari University building at Dorsoduro 3246, calle Foscari (vaporetto San Tomà) often has employment opportunities posted on the noticeboards. Alternatively, try the following agencies:

Manpower

Via Piave 120, Mestre (041 935 900/ fax 041 936 666/www.manpower.it). *Bus 2 from piazzale Roma*. **Open** 9am-6pm Mon-Fri.

Temporary

Via Manin 38A, Mestre (041 979 048/fax 041 962 033/tempve@uol.it). *Bus 7 from piazzale Roma*. **Open** 9am-noon, 2-6pm Mon-Fri.

Accommodation

Expect to pay upwards of a million lire a week for a very basic apartment in Venice. Cheaper student-type shares can be found through the noticeboards at Ca' Foscari University (*see above*) and local listings magazines (*see p283* **Media**).

Otherwise, an agency is your best bet; agencies will take the equivalent of one month's rent as a commission, while landlords will demand at least one month's (and sometimes as much as three months') rent as a deposit.

Immobiliare Veneta

San Polo 3132, campiello San Rocco (041 524 0088/fax 041 524 0025/immobilvenetasnc@libero.it). *Vaporetto San Tomà*. **Open** 9am-1pm, 3.30-7pm Mon-Fri. **Map** I 2C. A reliable agency with apartments at reasonable prices.

Giaretta

San Marco 514, campo della Guerra (041 528 6191/fax 041 520 0786/info@giaretta.com). *Vaporetto Rialto*. **Open** 9am-1pm, 2-7pm Mon-Fri. **Map** II 4A. Pleasant if pricey apartments to let.

The Euro cometh

Like its Euro-zone cronies, Italy will abandon its currency – long Europe's biggest brain-teaser with its serried ranks of zeros – in favour of the Euro in 2002.

If all goes to plan, the new notes (worth five, ten, 20, 50, 100, 200 and 500 Euros) and coins (worth one and two Euros, and one, two, five, ten, 20 and 50 cents) will come into circulation on 1 January 2002, and will circulate alongside *lire* until 28 February 2002, after which the old Italian currency will cease to be legal tender. The pictures on each country's Euros will differ, but all will be valid in any of the 12 Euro-zone member countries.

One Euro is equivalent to L1,936.27. To prepare for the monetary upheaval, Italian bank accounts, utilities bills, and receipts of all kinds have shown both lira and Euro totals since 1999. For a conversion chart, *see p3*.

Smoking

Smoking is not permitted in public offices (including post offices, police stations) or on public transport. For where to buy cigarettes, *see below* **Tabacchi**.

Study & students

All lectures and examinations – the majority of which are oral in the Italian system – at Venice's two main universities are in Italian, making a thorough knowledge of the language essential if you wish to get the full benefit of studying here.

To find out about entrance requirements and contact telephone numbers, consult the faculty websites at www.iuav.unive.it (**Istituto Universitario di Architettura di Venezia**) and www.unive.it (**Università degli Studi di Venezia Ca' Foscari**). Both universities run exchange programmes with foreign institutions and participate in the EU Erasmus scheme.

A third university – the **Venice International University** (041 271 9511/fax 041 271 9510/viu@unive.it/ www.viu.unive.it) – was created recently on the island of San Servolo.

Students currently registered at one of the VIU member universities are eligible to apply for VIU undergraduate activities; the VIU member Universities are Duke University, Università Ca' Foscari di Venezia, Istituto Universitario di Architettura di Venezia, Universitat Autònoma de Barcelona, Ludwig Maximilians Universität and Tel Aviv University.

Several foreign universities (including the University of California, Warwick University, Wake Forest University, Colgate University and New York University) run their own programmes in Venice.

All non-EU citizens studying in Italy for more than three months should apply for a student visa. All students must register as such upon arrival with the local Questura (*see p285* **Relocation**).

Language courses

The Venice Institute

Dorsoduro 3116A, campo Santa Margherita (041 522 4331/fax 041 528 5628). Vaporetto Ca' Rezzonico. **Open** 9am-1pm, 3-5pm Mon-Thur; 9am-3pm Fri. **Credit** MC, V. **Map** II 2A.
Courses in Italian for foreigners; group and individual sessions.

ASCI – Associazione Socio-Culturale Internazionale

Dorsoduro 3861, calle larga Foscari (041 504 0433/fax 041 506 8777/ascionlus@libero.it/ www.ascionlus.com). Vaporetto San Tomà. **Open** 6-8pm Mon, Wed. **No credit cards. Map** II 2A.
Courses in Italian, French, German, Spanish, Greek, Arabic, Hindi and Chinese. If languages aren't your thing, try computing, tango or belly-dancing.
Branch: Corso del Popolo 81, Mestre (041 504 0433).

Tabacchi

Tabacchi or *tabaccherie* (identified by signs with a white T on a black or blue background) are the only places where you can legally buy tobacco products. They also sell stamps, telephone cards, individual or season tickets for public transport, lottery tickets and the stationery required when dealing with Italian bureaucracy.

Most of Venice's *tabacchi* pull their shutters down by 7.30pm. If you're gasping for nicotine late in the evening or on Sunday, you'll have to go to the one in the main hall of the railway station, or try the following:

Bar Al Teatro

San Marco 1916, Campo San Fantin (041 522 1052). Vaporetto Sant'Angelo or Santa Maria del Giglio. **Open** 7.30am-midnight Tue-Sun. **Map** II 3A.

Telephones

Phone numbers

All Italian phone numbers must be dialled with their prefixes, even if you are phoning within the local area. All numbers in Venice and its province begin 041; numbers in Padua province begin 049; in Vicenza 0444; in Verona 045. Phone numbers generally have seven or eight digits after the prefix; some older ones still have six, and some switchboards five. If you try a number and cannot get through, it may have been changed to an eight-digit number. Check the directory (*elenco telefonico*) or ring directory enquiries (12).

Numbers beginning with 800 are freephone lines (until recently these began 176; if you find an old-style number listed, replace the prefix with 800). Numbers beginning 840 and 848 (formerly 147) are charged at a nominal rate. These numbers can be called from within Italy only; some are only available regionally.

Rates

The pressure of competition has led to continual price cuts, and Italy's once-exorbitant telephone company (Telecom Italia) is edging its rates down.

The minimum charge for a local call from a private phone is about L150 (L200 from a public phone); the normal rate for a minute to the UK is L1,070; to the rest of northern Europe L1,245; to the US L1,237, and to Australia and New Zealand L2,421. In all cases, it's more if you're using a public phone. One way to keep costs down is to phone off-peak (10pm-8am Mon-Sat, all day Sun). Another is to avoid using phones in hotels, which usually carry extortionate surcharges.

Public phones

There is no shortage of public phones in Venice, especially along tourist routes. Some bars also have payphones.

Most public telephones operate only with phonecards (*schede telefoniche*). Some newer models take major credit cards, while the few remaining old-style ones take L100, L200 and L500 coins. Phonecards costing L5,000, L10,000, and L15,000 can be purchased at post offices, *tabacchi* and some newsstands, or from the occasional vending machine near banks of public phones; to use your card, tear off one corner as marked, insert it into the appropriate slot and dial. Your credit balance will be displayed on the phone. Check the expiry date on your phonecard: no matter how much credit remains, you can't use it after that date.

Telecom Italia also supplies international phone credit cards (*schede telefoniche internazionali*) costing L12,500, L25,000, L50,000 and L100,000, also available from *tabacchi*. They work by dialling 1740#* (or 1740 from a private phone), then the PIN number on the card. Similar cards for the rival phone company Infostrada (155) can be found at some *tabacchi* shops. While you can't use the Infostrada cards from Telecom public phones, it is worth looking into because the rates are often cheaper.

International calls

To make an international call from Venice dial 00, then the country code (Australia 61, Canada and USA 1, Eire 353, New Zealand 64, UK 44, South Africa 27), then the area code (usually without the initial 0) and the number. International directory enquiries is on 176.

When calling an Italian land line from abroad, the whole prefix, including the 0, must be dialled, so dial 00 39 041... for Venice from the UK. From June 2001, the initial zero was due disappear from cell phone number prefixes, so the zero you had to drop if you were calling from abroad will no longer be present at all.

For operator-assisted calls abroad, dial 170. To make a collect (reverse-charge) call abroad through an operator in the country you are calling, dial 172 plus the appropriate four-digit country code listed in the 'Country Direct' service instructions in the phone directory (0044 for BT in the UK; 1011 for AT&T in the US; 1161 for Optus in Australia).

Operator services

Other services provided by Telecom Italia include:
182 problems with national calls (24-hour)
172 3535 problems with international calls (7am-9pm Mon-Fri; 8am-3pm Sat)
114 alarm call
186 telegrams
161 speaking clock
197 interrupts a conversation on an engaged line.

Mobile phones

Owners of GSM phones can use them in Italy on both 900 and 1800 bands, though reception in Venice can be patchy.

Time

Italy is one hour ahead of London, six ahead of New York, eight behind Sydney, and 12 behind Wellington.

Tipping

There are no hard and fast rules on tipping in Italy, though Venetians know that foreigners tip generously back home and therefore expect them to be liberal. Some upmarket restaurants (and a growing number of cheaper ones) will add a service charge to your bill: feel free to ask *il servizio è incluso?* If it isn't, leave whatever you think the service merited (and remember that Italians rarely leave more than five to ten per cent).

Bear in mind that all restaurants charge a cover fee (*coperto*), which is a quasi-tip in itself. In bars, a L100 or L200 coin placed on the counter with your receipt may speed up service.

Tourist information

Getting hold of comprehensive tourist information in Venice has become easier of late.

Most hotels will provide you with a copy of *Un Ospite di Venezia/A Guest in Venice*, a bilingual booklet compiled by hoteliers, which contains useful addresses and timetables. It is published every fortnight in high season and monthly in winter.

The official tourist board, along with the *Promove* association, produces a free quarterly magazine in English and Italian called *Pocket Venice*, available at APT offices (*see below*). The local press – and the bilingual monthly *Venezia News* in particular – is another source of useful information on events (*see p283* **Media**), as are the posters plastered on walls all over the city.

Visitors between the ages of 14 and 29 can sign up for the Rolling Venice programme, organised by the town council and youth organisations. Holders of a Rolling Venice card are eligible for discounts at selected hotels, museums (up to 50 per cent), restaurants and shops (10-15 per cent) around the city, as well as cut-price (L25,000) three-day vaporetto passes and 50 per cent off tickets for classical concerts (not operas) at La Fenice.

The card costs L5,000; get it by taking two passport-sized photos to the Rolling Venice booth at the Santa Lucia railway station (041 524 2852/041 524 2904, open *July-Sept* 8am-8pm daily). They can also be picked up at the Transalpino ticket office (main hall of the train station, 041 524 1334/fax 041 716 600, open 8.30am-12.30pm, 3-7pm Mon-Fri; 8.30am-12.30pm Sat), the AIG office (San Polo 3101, calle Castelfiore, 041 520 4414, open 8am-2pm Mon-Sat), Agenzia Arte e Storia (Santa Croce 659, corte Canal, 041 524 0232, open 9.30am-1pm, 3.30-7pm Mon-Fri) or the CTS – Centro Turistico Studentesco e Giovanile (Dorsoduro 3252, ponte Ca' Foscari, 041 520 5660, open 9.30am-1.30pm, 3-7pm Mon-Fri).

Tourist information offices

See **Tourist information** in individual chapters in section **The Veneto** for information offices outside Venice.

Azienda di Promozione Turistica (APT)

San Marco 71F, piazza San Marco (041 529 8711/fax 041 529 8734/ apt-06@mail.regione.veneto.it/ www.turismovenezia.it). Vaporetto Vallaresso. **Open** 9.45am-3.30pm Mon-Sat. **Map II 4A.**
APT provides maps of the city and surrounding areas, as well as info on sights and events, and a list of hotels. They will also put you in touch with registered guides, and give details of official fees for guided tours (*see below*). The Palazzetto Selva office (*see below*, map II 4B), has a selection of books, sells concert tickets, and provides Internet access, too. Main offices tend to become very crowded in the high season, when supplementary kiosks are set up around the city. Offices are also open on Sundays in peak periods.

Branches: San Marco 2, Palazzetto Selva, Giardinetti Reali (041 522 5150); Venice-Santa Lucia railway station. Vaporetto Ferrovia; Marco Polo Airport arrivals hall (tel/fax 041 541 5887); Santa Croce, piazzale Roma, ASM Garage (041 241 1499); Viale Santa Maria Elisabetta 6/A, Lido (041 526 5721/fax 041 529 8720)

Tours

See also p209 **Venice à la Carte.**

Associazione guide turistiche

San Marco 750, calle Morosini de la Regina (041 520 9038/fax 041 521 0762/guideve@tin.it). Vaporetto San Zaccaria. **Open** 9am-5pm Mon-Fri; 9am-1pm Sat. **Rates** L212,000 for two-hour tour for groups of up to 30 people; L6,500 for every extra person. **No credit cards. Map II 4A.**
Venice's only official tour guide co-operative has around 40 guides on its books offering made-to-measure tours in Italian, English, French, German, Spanish, Portuguese and various other languages. The only drawback is the L212,000 minimum charge, which makes this pricey for small groups. In high season, ring or fax at least a week in advance to book tours.

Water & drinking

Forget *Death in Venice*-style cholera scares: Venice's water is safe to drink. ASPIV – the Venetian water company – has operated the city's aqueduct since 1978, supplying the city and surrounding territories on the mainland with water that is checked regularly. For further information visit www.aspiv.ve.it.

When to go

Holidays

(*See also chapter* **By Season**.) On public holidays (*giorni festivi*) public offices, banks and post offices are closed. So, in theory, are shops – but in tourism-oriented Venice, this rule is often waived, especially in high season. Some bars and restaurants may choose to observe holidays: if in doubt,

call ahead to check. You'll be hard pushed to find much open on Christmas Day and New Year's Day.

Public transport is reduced to a skeleton service on 1 May, Christmas Day and New Year's Day, and may be re-routed or curtailed for local festivities such as the Vogalonga, Festa del Redentore and the Regata Storica (*see chapter* **By Season**); details are posted at vaporetto stops and at the bus terminus in piazzale Roma.

The public holidays are:
1 January New Year's Day (*Capodanno*)
6 January Epiphany (*Befana*)
Easter Monday (*Pasquetta*)
25 April Liberation Day (*Festa della Liberazione*) and patron saint's day (*San Marco*)
1 May Labour Day (*Festa del Lavoro*)
15 August Assumption (*Ferragosto*)
1 November All Saints' Day (*Ognissanti*)
21 November Festa della Salute
8 December Immaculate Conception (*L'Immacolata*)
25 December Christmas Day (*Natale*)
26 December Boxing Day (*Santo Stefano*)

Holidays falling on a Saturday or Sunday are not celebrated on the following Monday. By popular tradition, if a public holiday falls on a Thursday or Tuesday, many people will also take the Friday or Monday off as well, a practice known as *fare il ponte* (doing a bridge).

Weather

Venice's unique position does nothing at all for its weather: high levels of humidity often make winter days seem colder than their average of a few degrees above zero, and summer days become breathless as soon as the thermometer rises above

25°C. Strong north-easterlies in winter, coming off snow in the mountains (snow in the city is rare), may drive temperatures finger-freezingly low, but they turn the sky a glorious shade of turquoise and make Venice's colours zing. Autumn and spring are generally mild, though November and March are also the rainiest months.

Women

Venice is an exceptionally safe place for women travellers, both by day and by night. A solitary female may attract the usual gaggle of local male pursuers, but however dogged they seem, remember, the vast majority of them are all bark and no bite.

If you want to play extra safe at night, keep away from quieter, more outlying islands, and from the Tronchetto car park. Stick to main through-routes to avoid getting lost in dark alleyways; if in doubt, cut walking to a minimum by taking the vaporetto to as near to your destination as possible. Vaporetto stops

provide well-lit, highly visible refuges in the unlikely event that you are seriously hassled.

Tampons (*assorbenti interni*) and sanitary towels (*assorbenti esterni*) are cheaper in supermarkets, but can also be found in pharmacies and in some *tabacchi* shops.

Women suffering gynaecological emergencies should make for the Pronto Soccorso (emergency ward) at the Ospedale Civile (*see p281* **Health & hospitals**).

Family planning

Consultori familiari are run by the local health authority, and EU citizens with a E111 form are entitled to use them, paying the same low charges for services and prescriptions as locals. Non-EU citizens may use the service and, depending on their insurance plan, claim refunds. The *consultori* are staffed by good gynaecologists (book ahead for a visit).

The pill is available on prescription. Abortions are legal when performed in public hospitals.

Dorsoduro 1454, Campo della Lana (041 529 4004). Vaporetto Piazzale Roma or Ferrovia. **Map** I 1C.
Giudecca 936, Campo Marte (041 528 9258). Vaporetto Zitelle. **Map** II 4C.
Ospedale al Mare, Lungomare D'Annunzio 1, **Lido** (041 529 5325/6/7). Vaporetto Santa Maria Elisabetta. **Map** Lido.

Visas

For EU citizens, a passport or a national identity card valid for travel abroad is sufficient. Non-EU citizens must have full passports. Unrestricted entry is granted to all EU citizens. Citizens of the US, Canada, Australia and New Zealand do not need visas for stays of up to three months. In theory, visitors are required to declare their presence to the local police within a few days of arrival, unless they are staying in a hotel, where this will be done for them. In practice, you will not need to report to the police station unless you decide to extend your stay, and you apply for a *permesso di soggiorno* (permit to stay – *see p285* **Relocation**).

Vocabulary

In tourist offices, upmarket hotels and restaurants you'll have no problem finding someone who speaks English; further off the tourist track, however, a basic grasp of Italian is useful.

Italian is spelt as it is pronounced. Stresses usually fall on the penultimate syllable; a stress on the final syllable is indicated by an accent. There are two 'you' forms: the formal third-person *lei*, to be used with strangers, and the informal second-person *tu*. Masculine nouns and their accompanying adjectives generally end in 'o' (plural 'i'), female nouns and their adjectives in 'a' (plural 'e').

Venetian
The distinctive nasal Venetian drawl is more than just a simple accent: locals have their own vocabulary, too, some of it derived from Byzantine roots. For example, 'shop' (*negozio* in Italian) is '*botega*'; 'boy/girl' (*ragazzo/a*) is '*fio/fia*'; 'fish' (*pesce*) is '*pesse*'; 'money' (*soldi*) is '*schei*'; 'table' (*tavola*) is '*tola*'; 'old' (*vecchio*) is '*vecio*'.

PRONUNCIATION

Vowels
a – as in ask
e – like a in age (closed e) or e in sell (open e)
i – like ea in east
o – as in hotel (closed o) or in hot (open o)
u – as in boot

Consonants
c before a, o or u is like the c in cat
c before an e or an i is like the ch in check (sh as in ship in Venetian)
ch is like the c in cat
g before a, o or u is like the g in get
g before an e or an i is like the j in jig
gh is like the g in get
gl followed by an i is like lli in million
gn is like ny in canyon
qu is as in quick
r is always rolled
s has two sounds, as in soap or rose
sc before an e or an i is like the sh in shame
sch is like the sc in scout
z has two different sounds, like ts and dz

Double consonants are meant to be sounded more emphatically, a rule Venetians tend to ignore: in fact, they sometimes omit consonants altogether, running vowels together in long dipthongs (explaining, maybe, how *'vostro schiavo'* – your servant – became *'ciao'*.)

USEFUL PHRASES

hello and **goodbye** – *ciao*; used informally in other parts of Italy, *ciao* is used in any and all social situations in Venice
good morning, good day – *buon giorno*
good afternoon, good evening – *buona sera*
I don't understand – *non capisco/non ho capito*
do you speak English? – *parla inglese?*
please – *per favore, per piacere*
thank you – *grazie*
when does it open? – *quando apre?*
where is... ? – *dov'è…?*
excuse me – *scusi* (polite), *scusa* (informal)
open – *aperto*; **closed** – *chiuso*
exit – *uscita*
left – *sinistra*; **right** – *destra*
ticket/s – *biglietto/i*
I would like a ticket to... – *Vorrei un biglietto per…*

postcard – *cartolina*; **stamp** – *francobollo*
coffee – *caffè*; **tea** – *tè*
water – *acqua*; **wine** – *vino*; **beer** – *birra*
bedroom – *camera*
booking – *prenotazione*
Monday – *lunedì*; **Tuesday** – *martedì*; **Wednesday** – *mercoledì*; **Thursday** – *giovedì*; **Friday** – *venerdì*; **Saturday** – *sabato*; **Sunday** – *domenica*
yesterday – *ieri*; **today** – *oggi*; **tomorrow** – *domani*
morning – *mattina*; **afternoon** – *pomeriggio*; **evening** – *sera*; **this evening** – *stasera*; **night** – *notte*; **tonight** – *stanotte*

The come-on

Do you have a light? – *hai da accendere?*
What's your name? – *come ti chiami?*
Would you like a drink? – *vuoi bere qualcosa?*
Where are you from? – *di dove sei?*
What are you doing here? – *che fai qui?*
Do you have a boy/girlfriend? – *hai un ragazzo/una ragazza?*

The brush-off

I don't smoke – *non fumo*
I'm married – *sono sposato/a*

I'm tired – *sono stanco/a*
I'm going home – *vado a casa*
I have to meet a friend – *ho un appuntamento con un amico/una amica*

Offensive brush-offs

shit – *merda*
idiot – *stronzo*
fuck off – *vaffanculo*
dickhead – *testa di cazzo*
what the hell are you doing? – *che cazzo stai facendo?*

Numbers & money

0 *zero*; 1 *uno*; 2 *due*; 3 *tre*; 4 *quattro*; 5 *cinque*; 6 *sei*; 7 *sette*; 8 *otto*; 9 *nove*; 10 *dieci*; 11 *undici*; 12 *dodici*; 13 *tredici*; 14 *quattordici*; 15 *quindici*; 16 *sedici*; 17 *diciassette*; 18 *diciotto*; 19 *diciannove*; 20 *venti*; 21 *ventuno*; 22 *ventidue*; 30 *trenta*; 40 *quaranta*; 50 *cinquanta*; 60 *sessanta*; 70 *settanta*; 80 *ottanta*; 90 *novanta*; 100 *cento*; 1,000 *mille*; 2,000 *duemila*; 100,000 *centomila*; 1,000,000 *un milione*; 1,000,000,000 *un miliardo*
How much does it cost/is it? – *quanto costa?/quant'è?*
Do you accept credit cards? – *si accettano le carte di credito?*
Can I pay in pounds/dollars? – *posso pagare in sterline/dollari?*

Further Reference

Books

Non-fiction

Svetlana Alpers, Michael Baxandall *Tiepolo and the Pictorial Intelligence*
An essay in the history of ideas, which stoutly defends Tiepolo against the charge of frivolity.

Regis Debray *Contre Venise*
Love of Venice is the ruling creed – so Debray philosophically sets himself up (in French only) as leader of the opposition.

Deborah Howard *The Architecture of Venice*
The definitive account; shockingly out of print.

WD Howells *Venetian Life*
During his four years as US consul (1861-5), Howells penned this fascinating account of the lives of ordinary Venetians before the advent of mass tourism.

Frederick C Lane
Venice: A Maritime Republic

The best single-volume scholarly history of Venice.

Ian Littlewood *A Literary Companion to Venice*
Interesting compendium of accounts by literary visitors from Coryat on.

Giulio Lorenzetti *Venice and Its Lagoon*
The definitive guide to just who painted that Madonna and Child in the third altar on the left, in a patchy English translation.

Mary McCarthy *Venice Observed*
Brief, witty, intelligent account of Venetian art; usually published with the equally seminal *Stones of Florence*.

Michael Marquese *Venice, an Illustrated Anthology*
Trawl second-hand bookshops for this excellent selection of words and images, with an introduction by Anthony Burgess.

Wortley Montagu *The Letters of Lady Wortley Montagu*
The 18th-century traveller and proto-feminist lived in Venice for the last five years of her life.

Jan Morris *Venice*
Impressionistic history. The same author's The Venetian Empire extends the lyrical approach to the republic's overseas dominions.

John Julius Norwich *A History of Venice*
More readable but more rambling than Lane.

John Pemble *Venice Rediscovered*
Stimulating set of essays centring on the 19th-century English obsession with things Venetian.

Ruth Redford *Venice and the Grand Tour*
The origins of tourism as character-formation (currently out of print).

John Ruskin *The Stones of Venice*
Ruskin's prose hymn to Venetian Gothic architecture is an essential point of departure for those interested in the subject – however much you disagree with his dogmas.

Tony Tanner *Venice Desired*
Tanner traces the myth of Venice as a slippery, ambivalently romantic place through studies of Byron, Ruskin, Pound et al.

Directory

Fiction & literature

Lord Byron *Childe Harold's Pilgrimage* and *Beppo*
In *Childe Harold*, Byron draws Venice as a dream; in *Beppo* the poet views the city at carnival time.

Giacomo Casanova *Story of My Life*
The early sections of this 12-volume account of the great seducer's conquests and other escapades paint a vivid picture of life in mid-18th century Venice.

Michael Dibdin *Dead Lagoon*
Venetian-born police chief Aurelio Zen returns to his native city to solve another mystery in the unchallenging tourist-oriented crime series.

Steve Erickson *Days Between Stations*
Apocalyptic transatlantic romance (set mainly in the US and Paris) culminating in a bicycle race through the dried-up canals of Venice.

Anthony Hecht *Venetian Vespers*
A moving modern *Childe Harold* by this American poet.

Ernest Hemingway *Across the River and into the Trees*
The fall-out from war and love in Venice. Also known as Across the Canal and into the Bar.

Henry James *The Wings of the Dove*
A Venetian melodrama concealed behind a wall of elegant prose.

Donna Leon *Acqua Alta*
One of a series featuring detective commissario Guido Brunetti, set in a modern, unromanticised Venice.

Ian McEwan *The Comfort of Strangers*
A rich, menacing stranger disturbs a couple's reassuringly rocky marriage. Curiously, in this early, excellent novel by McEwan, the city itself is never named.

Thomas Mann *Death in Venice*
A male writer obsesses over a young boy in Venice. Disease, decadence, indecision, voyeurism – they don't write 'em like this any more.

Ezra Pound *The Cantos*
Still fresh, if you can wade through them, Pound's poetic diaries are full of abstruse Venetian details.

William Rivière *A Venetian Theory of Heaven*
An atmospheric novel set among the 1980s English ex-pat community in Venice. Rivière manages to go beyond the usual clichés, and is especially good on local boat lore.

Frederick Rolfe (Baron Corvo) *The Desire and Pursuit of the Whole*
Camp, vitriolic account of the late-19th-century expatriate community in Venice – veers between hilariously funny and just plain weird.

William Shakespeare *The Merchant of Venice*
Shylock fails to get his pound of flesh in one of the bard's least politically correct comedies.

Barry Unsworth *The Stone Virgin*
A statue links three stories – the US restorer who is working on it, the 15th-century sculptor who crafted it in the likeness of his mistress, and the noble Venetian family that owned it in the 18th century.

Film

The Comfort of Strangers
(Paul Schrader, 1990)
Disfunctional couple Miranda Richardson and Rupert Everett have salt rubbed in the emotional wounds of their relationship in a chance encounter with Christopher Walken and Helen Mirren against an unsettling Venetian backdrop, in Harold Pinter's halting, disorienting screen adaptation of Ian McEwan's novel.

Death in Venice
(Luchino Visconti, 1971)
Ageing aesthete Dirk Bogarde chases sailor-suited Björn Andresen around soft-focus, cholera-plagued Venice in this slow-moving adaptation of Thomas Mann's novella. The Bogarde character is a composer, changed from Mann's writer, but it's a good excuse to fill the soundtrack with the heart-rending strains of Mahler's Fifth.

Don't Look Now
(Nicolas Roeg, 1973)
Hypnotically chilling tale of a couple (Donald Sutherland and Julie Christie) who go to Venice to get over the death of their daughter, only to be drawn into greater horror in the suffocating, menacing *calli* of the city (*see also p206* 'I know this place').

Eve
(Joseph Losey, 1962)
In stark, wintry Venice, budding novelist Stanley Baker is ensnared by ferocious temptress Jeanne Moreau whose driving forces are money and power.

Senso
(Luchino Visconti, 1954)
Venetian countess Alida Valli falls violently in love with egotistic, sadistic Austrian soldier Farley Granger, betraying her husband and her country in her blinding passion for the younger man.

Vampires in Venice
(Augusto Caminito, 1988)
Nosferatu (Klaus Kinski) is summoned to present-day Venice by a Transylvanian princess, and proceeds to wreak the usual kind of vampire-havoc until a young virgin volunteers to let him have his blood-sucking way.

Music

Lorenzo Da Ponte (1749-1838)
Expelled from Venice for his fast and loose behaviour, Father Lorenzo Da Ponte fled to Vienna where he penned the libretti for Mozart's Marriage of Figaro, Don Giovanni and Così fan tutte. (He later taught Italian for many years at Columbia College in New York.)

Andrea Gabrieli (c1510-1586)
Organist of St Mark's basilica, Gabrieli senior's madrigals were favourites in all the best Venetian drawing rooms.

Giovanni Gabrieli (c1556-1612)
Nephew and student of Andrea, Gabrieli junior composed sacred and choral music, particularly motets for a number of choirs stationed at different points around churches to create a stereophonic effect; In ecclesiis is perhaps his masterpiece.

Antonio Vivaldi (1678-1741)
There's no escaping his *Four Seasons* in Venice, where costumed orchestras perform it ad nauseam. But there are nearly 500 more concertos and 16 surviving operas to choose from, too.

Websites

The first port of call for information on museums and exhibitions in Venice is the cultural heritage ministry's informative (but Italian-only) site at www.beniculturali.it.

Other useful sites include:

www.virtualvenice.net
Historical, cultural, and events information (Italian).

www.venezia.net
Everything from apartment rents to online booking for concerts (English).

www.venetia.it
History, useful phone numbers and good links (English).

www.doge.it
Cultural information, courses, and online hotel booking (English).

www.osterie.it
Reliable restaurant recommendations (Italian).

www.comune.venezia.it
City council's site with useful practical information (Italian).

www.regione.veneto.it/cultura
Cultural offerings and happenings around the Veneto region. Parts (including museum info) in English.

www.iuav.unive.it/~juli/venindx.html
Excellent links to information, much of it in English, on all conceivable topics relating to Venice.

Index

Index

Index

Maps

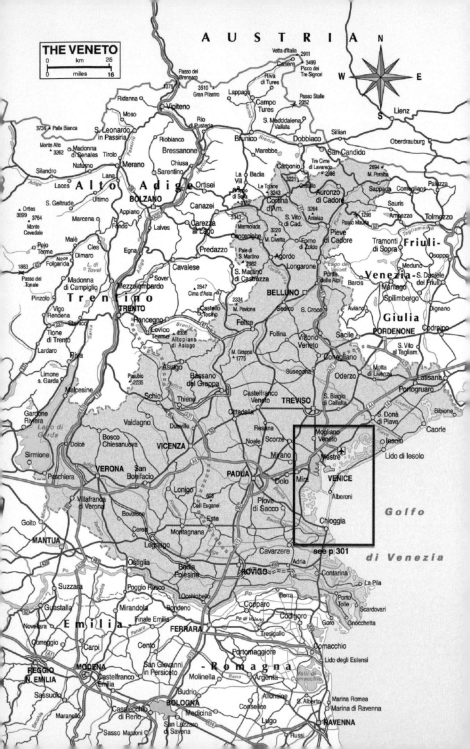

THE VENETIAN
LAGOON

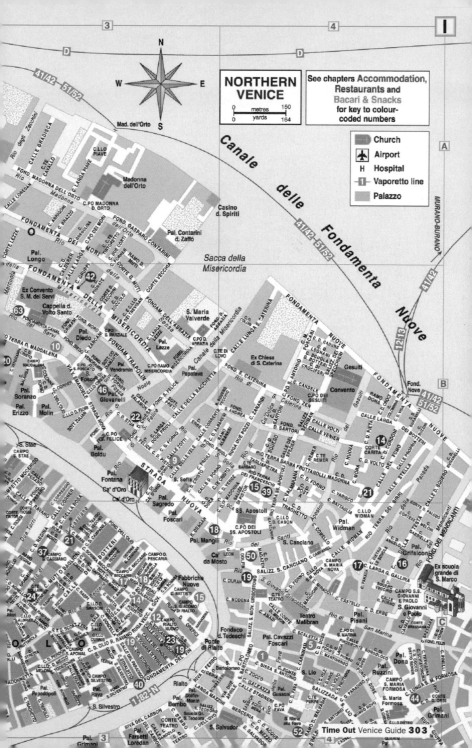

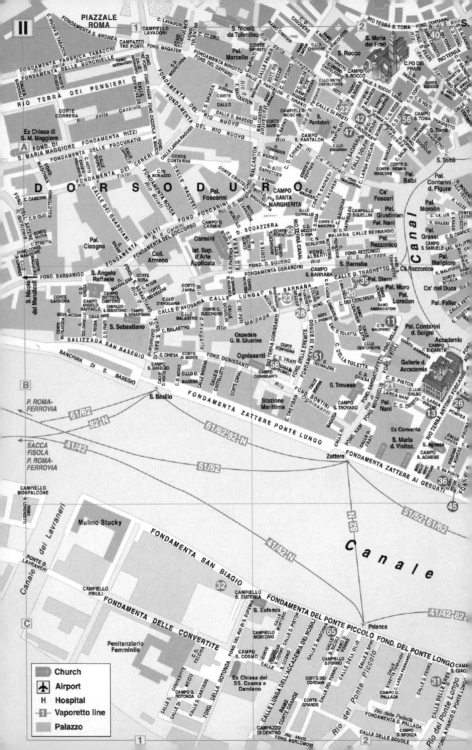

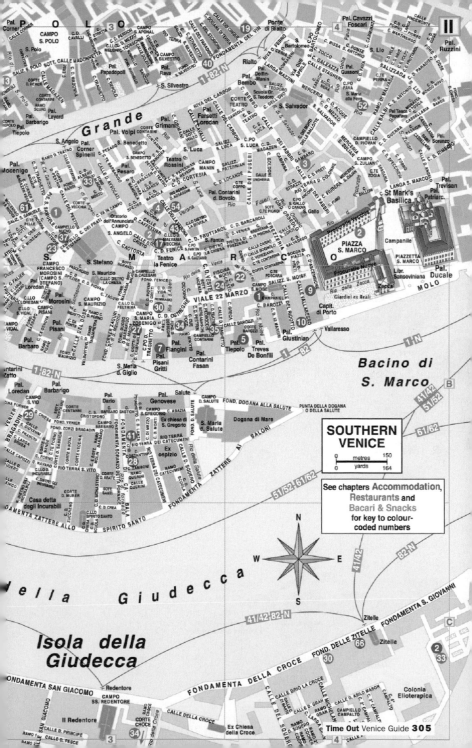

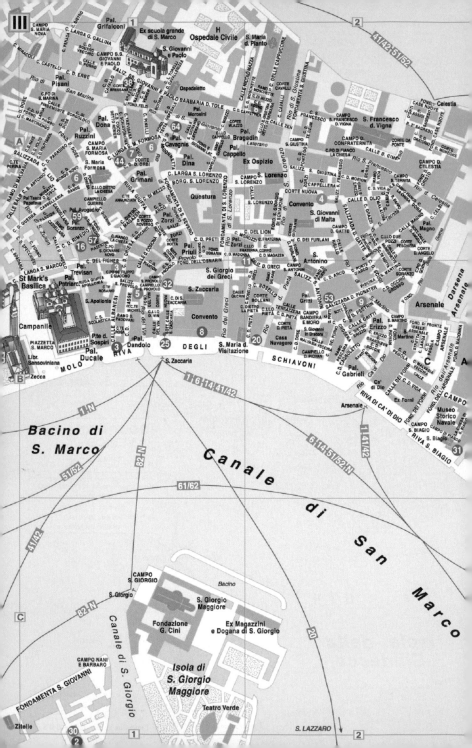

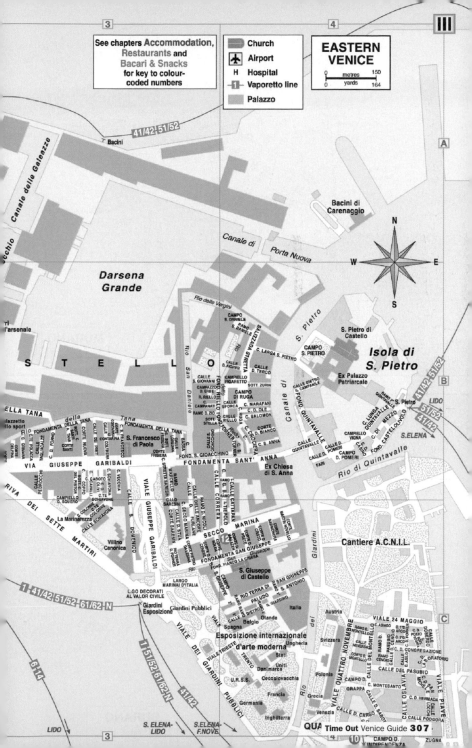

See chapters Accommodation,
Restaurants and
Bacari & Snacks
for key to colour-
coded numbers

Church
Airport
H Hospital
Vaporetto line
Palazzo

EASTERN
VENICE

metres 150
yards 164

41/42·51/52
Bacini

N
W E
S

Bacini di
Carenaggio

Canale delle Galeazze
Vecchio
l'arsenale

Canale di Porta Nuova

Darsena
Grande

S. Pietro

S. Pietro di
Castello

Isola di
S. Pietro

Rio delle Vergini

CAMPO S. DANIELE
RAMO S. DANIELE

CAMPO S. PIETRO
C. LARGA S. PIETRO

Ex Palazzo
Patriarcale

41/42·51/52

LIDO

S T E L L O

Rio San Daniele

CALLE D. FIGHER
CALLE S. GIOVANNI
CAMPAZZO D. ERBE
IL RIELLO
CAMPANATI
RAMO C. ZID
SOTT STELLA
FOND. RIELLO

SALIZZADA STRETTA
CALLE D. TERGO

SOTT. ZURLIN

CAMPIELLO FIGARETTO
CAMPO DI RUGA
C. MARAFANI
CALLE SFORCA
C. D. OLE
C. RIGA
C. D. SALOMON
CORTE D. BIANCO
CALLE
RIGA
C. S. ANNA
C. CROGERA

CALLE DIETRO IL CAMPANILE
CALLE D. FOND QUINTAVALLE

RAMO C. S. Pietro
C. LUNGA QUINTAVALLE

FOND CASTELLOLIOLO
S.ELENA

51/52
41/42

ELLA TANA
Palazzetto Rio sport

Tana
FONDAMENTA DELLA TANA
della TANA
C. D. FORNO
CORTE GIOVANA
CORTE DELFINA
CT. POLACCA
CORTE SANTI
CORTE NUOVA
C. CONTARINA
C. DEI PRETI

S. Francesco
di Paola

FOND. S. GIOACCHINO

FONDAMENTA SANT' ANNA

Ex Chiesa
di S. Anna

CALLE QUINTAVALLE
C. D. POMERI
FARI
CAMPIELLO VIGNA
CAMPO D. POMERI

RIVA DEI SETTE MARTIRI

VIA GIUSEPPE GARIBALDI

CAMPIELLO PEDROCCHI
C. SQUERO
C. R. FORNO
C. CABOTO
C. VECCHIA
RAMO MARCELLO
CALLE STRETTA SARESIN
CALLE CORRERA
C. TIEPOLO
C. CATTAPAN
RAMO C. NICOLO
CALLE SECCO MARINA
CORTE SOLCONIN
C. COLONNE
CALLE SCHIAVONA
CALLE D. FORNER
RIO TERA
CALLE FICAI

VIALE GIUSEPPE GARIBALDI

Villino
Canonica
Villino
S. DOMENICO

SECCO
MARINA

FONDAMENTA SAN GIUSEPPE
FOND. FIANCO LA CHIESA
FOND. PIANCO LA CHIESA

S. Giuseppe
di Castello

Rio di Quintavalle

Cantiere A.C.N.I.L.

1 41/42·51/52·61/62·N

LARGO MARINAI D'ITALIA
L.GO DECORATI AL VALOR CIVILE

Giardini
Esposizione
Giardini Pubblici

1 51/52·61/62·N

Esposizione internazionale
d'arte moderna

Giardini Pubblici

VIALE DEI GIARDINI PUBBLICI

41/42

6·14

Austria

VIALE 24 MAGGIO
C. ASIAGO
RAMO D. ARCO
C. D. ARCO
C. D. POZZO
C. D. CONGREGAZIONE
CORTE MONTELLO
CALLE NEVERSA
C. D. ORATORIO
CALLE DEL PASUBIO
C. MONTESANTO
C. D. HERNADA
CALLE OSLAVIA
CALLE PIAVE
CALLE PODGORA

VIALE QUATTRO NOVEMBRE

Svizzera
Ungheria
Stati
Uniti
Danimarca
U.R.S.S.
Cecoslovacchia
Germania
Francia
Inghilterra

Belgio
Spagna
Olanda
Italia
S. ANTONIO

RIO TERRA CH.
RAMO SAN GIUSEPPE
CALLE SAN PIETRO
IL GIARDINO
PALUDO

Rio dei Giardini

Polonia
Grappa
Grecia
Venezia

CALLE D. CARGO SABOTI

VIALE 24 MAGGIO
VIALE TRIESTE
VIALE TRENTO

LIDO

QUA...
CAMPO D.
INDIPENDENZA
ZUGNA

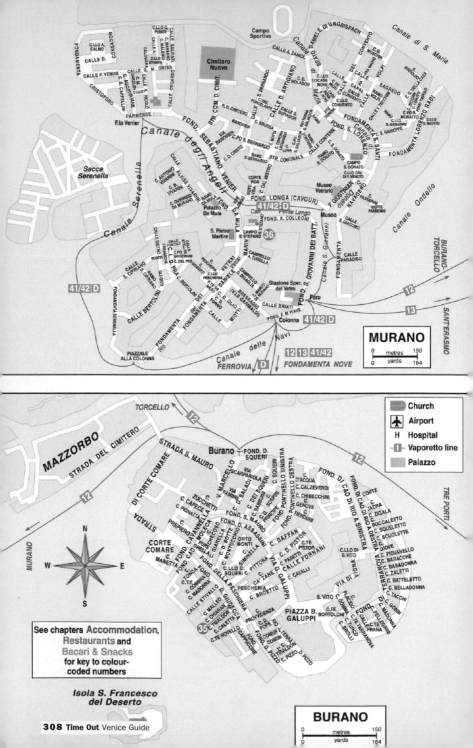

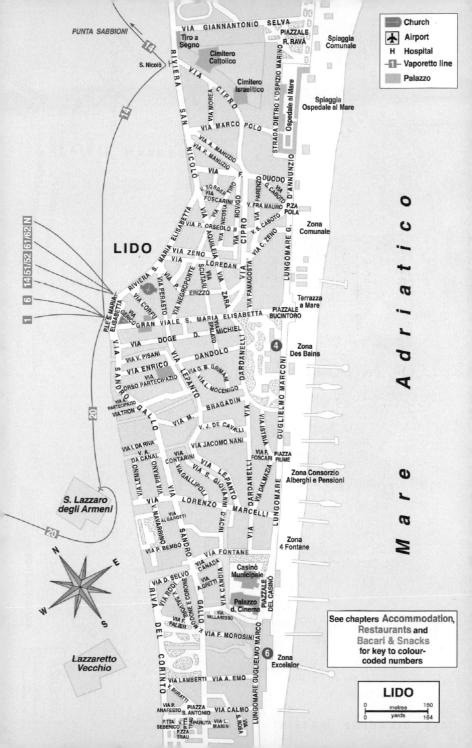

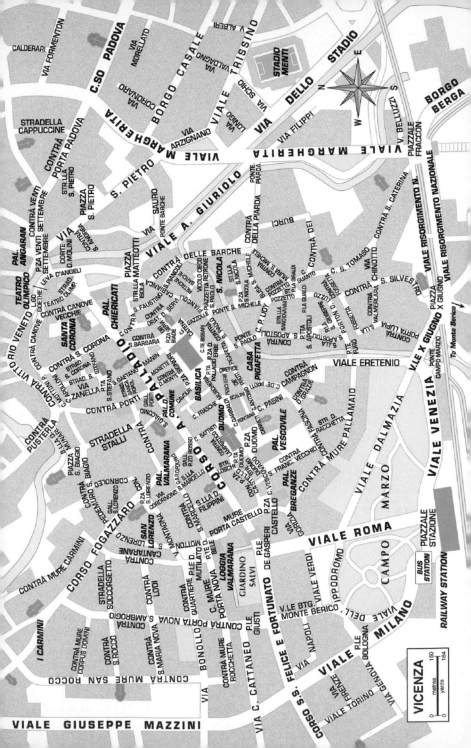

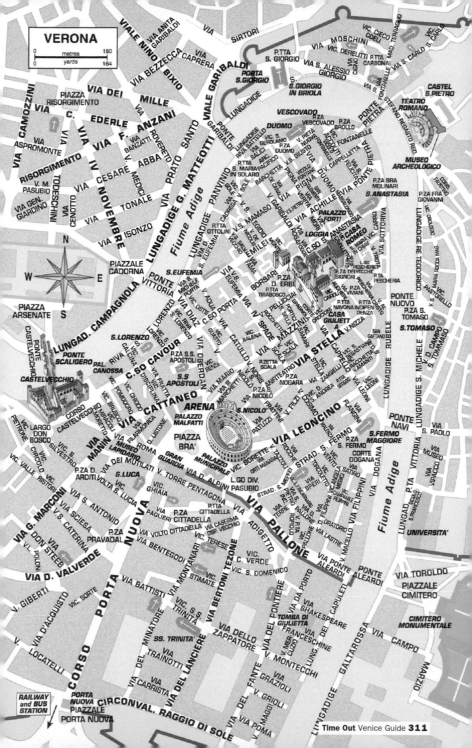

Street Index

GABRIELLA CALLE	C 4 I	PORTON CALLE DEL	A 2 I	VARISCO CALLE	B 4 I	FORNO CALLE DEL	C 2 I
GALLINA C. LARGA	C 4 I	POSTA CALLE D.	B 4 I	VECCHIA C.TE	B 3 I	FRARI CAMPO DEI	C 2 I
GARNACE FONDAMENTA	A 2 I	POZZO C.LLO	B 2 I	VELE CALLE D.	B 3 I	FRARI FOND. DEI	C 2 I
GESUITI C.PO DEI	B 4 I	POZZO SOTT. DEL	B 2 I	VENDRAMIN CALLE	B 3 I	FRUTTAROLA CALLE D.	C 3 I
GHELTOF (LOREDAN)CALLE	A 2 I	PRETI CALLE DEI	B 2 I	VENDRAMIN FOND.	B 3 I	FRUTTAROLA FOND.	C 3 I
GHETTO NUOVISSIMO C.	A 2 I	PRETI SOTT. DEI	B 3 I	VENDRAMIN C. LARGA	B 3 I	GALEAZZA CALLE	C 3 I
GHETTO NUOVO CAMPO DI	A 2 I	PRIMA - CALLE	A 1 I	VENIER CALLE	B 4 I	GALIZZI CALLE	C 3 I
GHETTO NUOVO FOND.	B 2 I	PRIULI CALLE	B 4 I	VENIER FOND.	B 2 I	GALLIPOLI CALLE STRETTA	C 2 I
GHETTO VECCHIO	A 2 I	PRIULI FOND.	B 4 I	VERDE CALLE DEL	A 1 I	GAMBERO CALLE DEL	C 3 I
GHETTO VECCHIO SOTT. D	B 2 I	PROCURATIE CALLE D.	B 2 I	VERGOLA CALLE	B 2 I	GOZZI CALLE	C 2 I
GIOACCHINA CALLE	B 1 I	PROPRIA CALLE	B 4 I	VIDA CALLE D.	B 4 I	LACA CALLE DELLA	C 2 I
GIURATI FOND.	A 2 I	QUERINI CALLE	B 2 I	VITELLI CORTE DEI	A 1 I	LARGA CALLE	C 2 I
GIUSTINIANA CORTE	A 1 I	RABBIA CALLE DELLA	B 2 I	VITTORIO EMANUELE VIA	B 2 I	LATE FOND.	C 2 I
GONELLA CORTE	A 1 I	RACCHETTA C. D.	B 3 I	VOLTI CALLE DEI	B 4 I	LUGANEGHER CALLE	C 3 I
GRADISCA CALLE	A 3 I	REMER CALLE DEL	B 4 I	VOLTO CALLE DEL	B 4 I	MADONNA CALLE DELLA	C 3 I
GREGOLINA CALLE	A 3 I	REMER C.TE DEL	B 4 I	WIDMAN CALLE	C 4 I	MADONNETTA CALLE	C 3 I
GRIMANI FOND.	B 3 I	REMIER C.LLO	B 2 I	WIDMAN C.LLO	C 4 I	MADONNETTA SOTT.	C 3 I
GRUPPI CALLE	B 3 I	RIELLO CALLE	B 1 I	ZANARDI CALLE	B 4 I	MAGAZEN CALLE DEL	C 2 I
GUGLIE PONTE	B 2 I	RIFORMATI CALLE DEI	A 2 I	ZAPPA CORTE	A 2 I	MALVASIA CALLE DELLA	C 2 I
LABIA FOND.	A 2 I	RIFORMATI FONDAMENTA D.	A 2 I	ZEN FOND.	B 4 I	MELONI C.LLO D.	C 3 I
LARGA CALLE	A 3 I	RIZZO CALLE	A 2 I	ZOCCOLO CALLE DEL	B 3 I	MEZZO CALLE DI	C 1 I
LEGNAME CALLE LARGA D.	A 2 I	ROTONDA CALLE DELLA	A 2 I	ZOLFO CALLE DEL	B 2 I	MIANI CALLE	C 3 I
LEGNAMI CALLE D.	B 4 I	RUZZINI CALLE	B 4 I	ZOLFO RAMO DEL	B 2 I	MICHIEL CORTE	C 3 I
LEON CALLE	C 4 I	RUBINI CALLE	A 2 I	ZOTTI CALLE	B 3 I	MORO CALLE	C 2 I
LEZZE CALLE LARGA	B 3 I	SACCA S. GIROLAMO FOND.	A 1 I	ZUDIO CALLE	A 2 I	MUTI CALLE DEI	C 3 I
LEZZE CORTE	A 3 I	SACCHERE CORTE	A 2 I	ZULIAN SOTT.	B 3 I	NARANZERIA	C 3 I
LISTA DI SPAGNA RIO TERRA	B 1 I	SALAMON CALLE	B 3 I			NOMBOLI CALLE DEI	C 2 I
LOMBARDO CALLE	B 2 I	SAN CANCIANO SALIZZADA	C 4 I	**SESTIERE DI SAN POLO**		NOMBOLI RIO TERRA DEI	C 2 I
LOREDAN CALLE	A 3 I	SAN FELICE CALLE	B 3 I	ALBANESI CALLE DEGLI	C 2 I	NUOVA C.TE	C 2 I
MADDALENA C.PO D.	B 3 I	SAN FELICE CAMPO	B 3 I	ALBRIZZI CALLE	C 3 I	OLIO FONDAMENTA DELL'	C 3 I
MADDALENA RIO TERRA' D.	B 3 I	SAN FELICE FOND. DI	B 3 I	ALBRIZZI C.LLO	C 3 I	OLIO CALLE	C 2 I
MADONNA CALLE DELLA	A 1 I	SAN GEREMIA CAMPO	B 2 I	AMOR DEGLI AMICI CALLE	C 2 I	OREFICI RUGA DEGLI	C 3 I
MADONNA CALLE DELLA	B 4 I	SAN GEREMIA SALIZZADA	B 2 I	ANGELO CALLE DELL'	C 3 I	OSTERIA CAMPANA C. D.	C 3 I
MADONNA D. ORTO C.PO	A 3 I	SAN GIOBBE CAMPO	A 1 I	ARCHIVIO CALLE DIETRO L'	C 2 I	PARADISO CALLE DEL	C 2 I
MADONNA D. ORTO FOND.	A 3 I	SAN GIOBBE FOND. DI	A 1 I	ARCO CALLE DELL'	C 3 I	PARRUCCHETTA RIO TERRA'	C 2 I
MAGAZEN CALLE DEL	A 1 I	SAN GIOVANNI CALLE DI	A 2 I	BADOER CORTE	C 2 I	PASSION CALLE D.	C 2 I
MAGAZEN CALLE DEL	A 2 I	SAN GIOV. GRISOSTOMO S.C	4 I	BANCO SALVIATI CALLE	C 3 I	PERDON CALLE DEL	C 3 I
MAGAZEN RAMO	B 2 I	SAN GIROLAMO CALLE	A 2 I	BARZIZZA CALLE	C 3 I	PESCARIA CAMPO D.	C 3 I
MAGGIONI CALLE DEI	C 4 I	SAN GIROLAMO FOND.	A 2 I	BATTISTI CAMPO	C 3 I	PEZZANA O TASSO CALLE	C 2 I
MAGGIORE CALLE	B 2 I	SAN LEONARDO CAMPO	B 2 I	BECCARIE CALLE DELLE	C 3 I	PINO CALLE	C 3 I
MALVASIA CALLE	B 3 I	SAN LEONARDO RIO TERRA'	B 2 I	BECCARIE CAMPO	C 3 I	PISANI RAMO	C 3 I
MALVASIA CALLE DELLA	A 2 I	SAN MARCUOLA CAMPO	B 2 I	BERNARDO CALLE	C 2 I	PISTOR CALLE DEL	C 2 I
MASENA CALLE DELLA	B 2 I	SANT'ANDREA FOND.	B 4 I	BERNARDO RAMO	C 2 I	PISTOR C.TE DEL	C 2 I
MASENA RAMO DELLA	B 2 I	SANT'ANTONIO CALLE	B 4 I	BIANCA CAPPELLO CALLE	C 3 I	POSTE VECCHIE CALLE D.	C 3 I
MELONI CALLE DEI	C 4 I	SANT'ANTONIO C.PO	B 4 I	BO CALLE DEL	C 3 I	POZZETTO CALLE DEL	C 3 I
MILION CALLE DEI	C 4 I	S.TA CATERINA C. LUNGA	B 4 I	BOLLANI CORTE	C 3 I	POZZETTO SOTT.	C 3 I
MILION C.TE DEI	C 4 I	S.TA CATERINA FOND.	B 4 I	BOTTA CALLE DELLA	C 3 I	POZZOLONGO C.LLO	C 2 I
MIRACOLI CALLE DEI	C 4 I	S.TA FOSCA C.PO	B 3 I	BOTTERI CALLE DEI	C 3 I	RAFFINERIA CALLE	C 3 I
MISERICORDIA CALLE D.	B 1 I	S.TA LUCIA FONDAMENTA	B 1 I	BUSINELLO CALLE	C 3 I	RAMPANI CALLE	C 3 I
MISERICORDIA C.PO	B 3 I	S.TA MARIA NOVA C.LLO	C 4 I	BUSINELLO FONDAMENTA	C 3 I	RAMPANI RIO TERRA'	C 3 I
MISERICORDIA FOND. DELLA	B 3 I	S.TA MARIA NOVA C.PO	C 4 I	CAFFETTIER CALLE	C 2 I	RASPI CALLE DEI	C 3 I
MISERICORDIA RAMO DELLA	B 1 I	SS. APOSTOLI C.PO DEI	C 4 I	CALDERER C.TE	C 2 I	RAVANO RUGA	C 3 I
MISERICORDIA RAMO DELLA	B 3 I	SS. APOSTOLI RIO TERRA	B 4 I	CALICE CALLE DEL	C 2 I	REMER CORTE DEL	C 2 I
MORA CALLE	B 4 I	SARTORI CALLE D.	B 4 I	CAMPANILE CALLE DEL	C 3 I	RIALTO NUOVO CAMPO	C 3 I
MORI CAMPO DEI	A 3 I	SARTORI FOND.	B 4 I	CAMPAZZO CALLE DEL	C 1 I	RIO TERRA'	C 2 I
MORI FONDAMENTA DEI	A 3 I	SAVORGNAN FOND.	B 1 I	CAMPAZZO RAMO DEL	C 1 I	RIO TERRA' CALLE	C 2 I
MORO FOND.	B 3 I	SCALA MATTA CORTE	A 2 I	CAPPELLER CALLE DEL	C 3 I	RIVETTA CALLE	C 3 I
MOSTO CA' DA	B 2 I	SCALZI FOND. DEGLI	B 1 I	CAPPELLER SOTT. DEL	C 3 I	RIZZO CALLE	C 3 I
MOSTO CORTE	B 2 I	SCALZI PONTE	B 1 I	CASSETTI RAMO	C 2 I	RIZZO RAMO	C 3 I
MUNEGHE CALLE DELLE	A 2 I	SCARLATTO CALLE D.	A 1 I	CASTELFORTE C. DIETRO	C 2 I	SACCHERE CALLE D.	C 1 I
MUTI CORTE DEI	B 3 I	SCUOLA DEI BOTTERI C.	B 4 I	CASTELFORTE C.LLO D.	C 2 I	SACCHERE FOND.	C 1 I
MUTI RAMO DEI	A 3 I	SCUOLE C. DIETRO LE	C 4 I	CAVALLI CALLE DEI	C 3 I	SALE CALLE DEL	C 3 I
NUOVA STRADA	B 3 I	SCUOLE C.LLO D.	B 2 I	CENTANNI CALLE	A 2 II	SALE C.LLO DEL	C 3 I
NUOVA CALLE	A 1 I	SCURO CALLE D. SOTTO	A 1 I	CHIESA CALLE DELLA	C 2 I	S. APONAL CAMPO	C 3 I
NUOVA CALLE	B 2 I	SELLE CALLE	B 2 I	CHIESA C.PO DELLA	C 2 I	S. BOLDO CAMPO	C 2 I
NUOVE FOND.	B 4 I	SENSA FONDAMENTA DELLA	A 2 I	CHIOVERE CALLE DELLE	C 1 I	S. CASSIANO CAMPO	C 2 I
OCA CALLE DELL'	B 4 I	SERIMAN SALIZZADA	B 4 I	CHIOVERE C.LLO DELLE	C 1 I	S. GIACOMO DI RIALTO C.PO	C 3 I
OLIO CALLE DELL'	B 2 I	SORANZO CALLE	B 2 I	CIMESIN RAMO	C 1 I	S. GIOVANNI RUGA VECCHIA	C 3 I
ORMESINI CALLE D.	B 2 I	SPECCHIERI SALIZZADA D.	B 4 I	CINQUE CALLE DEI	C 3 I	S. MATTIO CALLE	C 3 I
ORTO CALLE DELL'	A 2 I	SPEZIER CALLE DEL	B 4 I	COLLALTO CALLE	C 2 I	S. NICOLETTO CALLE	C 2 I
PAGLIA CALLE DELLA	B 2 I	SQUERO CALLE DEL	B 4 I	CONTARINI FOND.	C 2 I	S. NICOLETTO RAMO	C 2 I
PALUDO CORTE D.	C 4 I	SQUERO VECCHIO C. DEL	C 4 I	CONTARINI C.TE	C 2 I	S. POLO CAMPO	C 2 I
PAZIENZA C.LLO DELLA	A 1 I	SQUERO VECCHIO RAMO D.	B 4 I	CORNER CALLE	C 2 I	S. POLO SALIZZADA	C 2 I
PEGOLOTTO CORTE DEL	B 2 I	STAZIONE S. LUCIA	B 1 I	CORTI CALLE	C 2 I	S. ROCCO C.PO	C 2 I
PEGOLOTTO SOTT. DEL	B 2 I	STELLA CALLE	B 4 I	CRISTI CALLE DEI	C 3 I	S. ROCCO SALIZZADA	C 2 I
PENITENTI CALLE LARGA D.	A 1 I	STUA CALLE DELLA	B 3 I	CRISTO CALLE DEL	C 2 I	S. SILVESTRO CAMPO	C 3 I
PERLERI CALLE DEI	B 2 I	TAGLIAPIETRA CALLE	B 4 I	CURNIS C.LLO	C 3 I	S. SILVESTRO FOND.	C 3 I
PESARO CALLE	B 1 I	TAGLIAPIETRA RAMO DELLA	B 1 I	DANDOLO CALLE	A 2 II	S. SILVESTRO RIO TERRA'	C 3 I
PESARO C.LLO	B 1 I	TEATRO MALIBRAN C.TE D.	C 4 I	DOANETTA CALLE	C 2 I	S. STIN CAMPO	C 2 I
PESCARIA FOND.	B 2 I	TESTA CALLE DELLA	C 4 I	DOGANA DI TERRA CALLE	C 3 I	S. TOMA' CAMPO	A 2 II
PIAVE CALLE LARGA	A 3 I	TINTOR - CALLE DEL	A 3 I	DOLERA CALLE	C 2 I	S. TOMA RIO TERRA	C 2 I
PIAVE CAMPIELLO	A 3 I	TINTORETTO CALLE DEL	A 3 I	DONA' O SPEZIER CALLE	C 2 I	SANSONI C.LLO DEI	C 2 I
PIETA' CALLE DELLA	A 3 I	TINTORETTO CORTE	A 3 I	DONNA ONESTA FOND.	A 2 II	SANT'AGOSTIN CAMPO DI	C 2 I
PIGNATER O D. TABACCO C.	B 2 I	TINTORIA CALLE	A 1 I	DONZELLA CALLE	C 3 I	SANUDO CALLE	C 2 I
PIGNATE CALLE D.	B 2 I	TIRACANNA CALLE DEL	B 2 I	DONZELLA CALLE 1 DELLA	C 3 I	SAONERI CALLE DEI	C 2 I
PISANI CORTE	A 2 I	TRAGHETTO CALLE DEL	C 4 I	ERBE CALLE	C 3 I	SAONERI CALLE 2	C 2 I
PISCIUTTA CALLE	B 3 I	TRAPOLIN FOND.	B 3 I	FIGHER CALLE	C 3 I	SBIANCHESINI CALLE	C 3 I
PISTOR CALLE DEL	B 3 I	TREVISAN CALLE	B 3 I	FONDERIA CALLE DELLA	C 2 I	SCALETER CALLE DEL	C 3 I
PISTOR SALIZZADA DEL	B 4 I	TREVISAN C.LLO	B 3 I	FORNER C.LLO D	C 2 I	SCIMMIA CALLE DIETRO LA	C 3 I
PONTE STORTO C.LLO	B 2 I	TURLONA CALLE	A 2 I	FORNER FOND. D.	A 2 II	SCIMMIA CALLE DELLA	C 3 I
PORPORA CALLE DELLA	A 1 I	VALMARANA CALLE	B 4 I	FORNER RAMO DEL	C 2 I	SCOAZZERA RIO TERRA' D.	C 3 I

Advertisers' Index

Please refer to the relevant sections for addresses/telephone numbers

Venice Please let us know what you think

About this guide...

1. How useful did you find the following sections?

	Very	Fairly	Not very
In Context	☐	☐	☐
Accommodation	☐	☐	☐
Sightseeing	☐	☐	☐
Eat, Drink, Shop	☐	☐	☐
Arts & Entertainment	☐	☐	☐
The Veneto	☐	☐	☐
Directory	☐	☐	☐
Maps	☐	☐	☐

2. Did you travel to Venice...?

Alone ☐ With children ☐
As part of a group ☐ On vacation ☐
On business ☐ To study ☐
With a partner ☐ I live here ☐

3. How long was your trip to Venice? (write in)

_____ days

4. Where did you book your trip?

Time Out Classifieds ☐
On the Internet ☐
With a travel agent ☐
Other (write in) ☐

5. Where did you first hear about this guide?

Advertising in *Time Out* magazine ☐
On the Internet ☐
From a travel agent ☐
Other (write in) ☐

6. Is there anything you'd like us to cover in greater depth?

_____
_____

7. Are there any places that should/ should not* be included in the guide?
(*delete as necessary)

_____
_____
_____
_____
_____
_____

8. How many other people have used this guide?

none ☐ 1 ☐ 2 ☐ 3 ☐ 4 ☐ 5+ ☐

9. What city or country would you like to visit next? (write in)

_____

About other Time Out publications...

10. Have you ever bought/used any other *Time Out* magazine?

Yes ☐   No ☐

11. Have you ever bought/used any other Time Out City Guides?

Yes ☐   No ☐

If yes, which ones? _____

12. Have you ever bought/used other Time Out publications?

Yes ☐   No ☐

If yes, which ones? _____
_____

About you...

13. Title (Mr, Ms etc):

First name: _____
Surname: _____
Address: _____
_____ P/code: _____
Email: _____
Nationality: _____

14. Date of birth: ☐☐/☐☐/☐☐

15. Sex: male ☐   female ☐

16. Are you...?

Single ☐
Married/Living with partner ☐

17. What is your occupation?

_____

18. At the moment do you earn...?

under £15,000 ☐
over £15,000 and up to £19,999 ☐
over £20,000 and up to £24,999 ☐
over £25,000 and up to £39,999 ☐
over £40,000 and up to £49,999 ☐
over £50,000 ☐

☐ Please tick here if you do not wish to receive information about other Time Out products.
☐ Please tick here if you do not wish to receive mailings from third parties.

Time Out Guides

FREEPOST 20 (WC3187)
LONDON
W1E 0DQ